BLACKNESS AND MODERNITY

# Blackness and Modernity

## The Colour of Humanity and the Quest for Freedom

### CECIL FOSTER

McGill-Queen's University Press
Montreal & Kingston • London • Ithaca

© McGill-Queen's University Press 2007

ISBN 978-0-7735-3105-5

Legal deposit third quarter 2007
Bibliothèque nationale du Québec

Printed in Canada on acid-free paper

McGill-Queen's University Press acknowledges the support of the
Canada Council for the Arts for our publishing program. We also
acknowledge the financial support of the Government of Canada
through the Book Publishing Industry Development Program (BPIDP)
for our publishing activities.

---

**Library and Archives Canada Cataloguing in Publication**

Foster, Cecil, 1954–
  Blackness and modernity: the colour of humanity and the quest for
freedom / Cecil Foster.

Includes bibliographical references and index.
ISBN 978-0-7735-3105-5

1. Black Canadians.  2. Black Canadians – Ethnic identity.
3. Multiculturalism – Canada.  I. Title.

FC106.B6F667 2007    305.896'071    C2006-905094-5

---

Typeset by Jay Tee Graphics Ltd. in Sabon 10/12

*For my mother and father*
*Doris Goddard*
*Cleophus (Freddy) Goddard*

*Dedicated to*
*Angela Drayton*
*Mervin Drayton*
*and*
*Jasmine (Princess) Pinder*

# Contents

# Acknowledgments

This book would not have been possible without the help, encouragement, sacrifices, and directions of many people. First and foremost among them is Howard Adelman, who guided me as my dissertation supervisor in the department of Social and Political Thought at York University. Howard not only encouraged and supported me in this exercise, but he was always pushing me to rethink many things that I thought I had already sorted out. Even when my studies were over, Howard continued to have faith in this work and was always generous with his advice and time.

Similarly, I want to thank Alan Simmons of York University for his encouragement and patience and for helping me on issues of immigration and citizenship. Alan took on the role of making sure that I was mindful of the sociological and anthropological disciplines, while encouraging me to see how links can be drawn with a wider political economy. Les Jacobs at York University was indispensable in helping me to think through such matters as human rights, citizenship, liberalism, and many of those issues that we may try to neatly place under a heading of moral and political philosophy. And speaking of moral and political philosophy, there are few practitioners as able as Queen's University professor Will Kymlicka, who, in many respects, is the one person that I always seem to find myself in conversation with on these issue. This book benefited significantly from comments by Kymlicka on the earliest draft.

Also special thanks go to Nigel Thomas, professor of English at Laval University, John Burbidge, professor emeritus of philosophy at Trent University, and Ivan Macfarlane, at the University of Toronto. They read and commented on drafts of the manuscript. I extend gratitude to the anonymous readers who offered suggestions that helped me to better say what I intended. Special thanks to Philip Cercone, executive editor at McGill-Queen's University Press, and to Stephanie Fysh for indexing and proofreading. I just want to "give a shout out" to David Schwinghamer, one of the most patient, tireless, and competent editors I have known. This book was blessed to have David as an editor. Thank you, David. While all of the above contributed significantly, I am solely responsible for any errors or misstatement, or for not having the wisdom to incorporate, or leave out, much more of what they suggested.

Finally, I want to thank all members of my family wherever they are in the Black/African diaspora. I hope this book reminds my children of some watershed years, and of our surviving them. In this long journey I was fortunate to have the most wonderful person at my side – my love, partner, and best friend, Dr Sharon Morgan Beckford.

# Prologue

One cannot express oneself too strongly ... regarding the conceptual barbarism which applies the category of *composition* ... even to light, and makes brightness consist of seven *darknesses:* one might as well say that clear water consists of seven sorts of earth.[1]

## UNDERSTANDING BLACKNESS

What do I mean when *I* say *I* am Black? Does that meaning change when I am *called* Black or if, tomorrow, I should call *you* Black? What about Black *and* Canadian, Black Canadian, and Canadian Blacks – do any of these terms mean a specific and distinct species of humanity within Canada itself, a meaning that is also different in the wider world? And does it matter to this meaning whether I am male or female, straight or gay, if I am being stopped by a police officer or if I am the police officer stopping someone? Does it matter if I am a borrower or just a lender, if I am overseas in a Canadian peacekeeping uniform or if I was/am talking and thinking in the past or in the present? And does the colour of my skin matter or is it the only thing that matters? In other words, do the terms "Black" and "Blackness" come to us with given meaning that is specific and non-changing, exacting a knowledge and understanding of the terms that is not based on experience alone? Indeed, do the experiences of being Black have any bearing on what might be construed a posteriori as universal meanings and the knowledge embodied in these concepts and signifiers? Thus, for example, with so much of the international and national discussion these days about terrorism, or its Blackness and of the Black characters of those who would inflict torture or mass death, does the meaning of Black and Blackness change? And if, alternatively, this meaning is not purely experiential or *empirical*, is it the work of perceptions and feelings that are based on the idea of a transcendent morality and even ethical order that supersedes any given context?

If I am a Black Canadian, does that mean that, in all good faith, I am automatically a *good* Canadian with all the rights, privileges, and entitlements of citizenship and belonging? Does the meaning change whether I am a student, a worker, a father, a mother, of swarthy complexion or jet black countenance, a just-off-the-boat immigrant, a sixth-generation immigrant or a so-called indigenous Canadian Black, a musician or basketball player, if I am just the stranger you so happen to meet in a deserted alley – does my Blackness ever have a non-changing and unequivocal meaning? Indeed, is there a unique and distinctive *being* and/or universal *consciousness* that is Black, and that, as a means of existence, is *being* Black or Blackness? Can the effects of my Blackness be cancelled out, enhanced, or even sublimated by my Canadianness, or vice versa? And, idealistically, are these consciousnesses different in Canada from anywhere else in the world? *Why* – and this is the key word that should engage us in this book – do concepts or identities like Black, White, Asian, multicultural, and Canada have meaning, and is this meaning always stable, wholesome, and unchangeable?

In trying to answer these question, we might be reminded of a similar series of questions asked by the man who at the beginning of the last century worried about a racial colour line and how it would affect the lives of those who were identified then as Black, or negro, not only in the United States, but throughout the western hemisphere. "Here then, is the dilemma, and it is a puzzling one, I admit," writes W.E.B. Du Bois about a choice that was facing him and others socially constructed like him: a choice of assimilation into a wider American nation-state or of remaining as a group separate and apart, as a member of an assimilated worldwide Black/African race. Dilemma or not, the choice was limited to assimilation – either into a particular or into a universal – such was the extent of the day's freedom. As Du Bois states:

No Negro who has given earnest thought to the situation of his people in America has failed, at some time in life, to find himself at these cross-roads; has failed to ask himself at some time: What, after all am I? Am I an American or am I a Negro? Can I be both? Or is it my duty to cease to be a Negro as soon as possible and be an American. If I strive as a Negro, am I not perpetuating the very cleft that threatens and separates Black and White America? Is not my only possible practical aim the subduction of all that is Negro in me to the American? Does my black blood place upon me any more obligation to assert my nationality than German, or Irish or Italian blood would?[2]

A century later and with much debate over what has become of the colour line – has it faded, or has it become more resolute, maybe not as apparent but just as rigid – the questions raised by Du Bois are still relevant for much of the discussion on race, ethnicity, citizenship, and overall identities. For sure, these are still profound questions. But do we need to provide clear and unambiguous answers to any of his questions and can we not question some of the very concepts and identities he has thrown out, and which seem to make sense in a given context but to be meaningless and even racist in another? Indeed, a century later, Canadians in particular might not have to answer any of these questions directly if Du Bois were to present them now. The same might not be true of different groups of people living according to different understandings of what it means to be part of a specific nation-state. Canadians may simply say – to avoid having to answer them, or even to deal with these questions – that we have become officially multicultural. Multiculturalism allows us not to worry too much about assimilation, unless we so desire it, or, on the other hand, not to fret too much about los-ing an ethnic or any other identity than Canadian – unless, that is, we choose to so fret. Multiculturalism offers freedom, just to be in any form and identity – as long as it is within a Canadian universe. By not calling themselves officially multicultural, members of other nation-states, even in acknowledging the necessity of their own diversity, differences, and plural-ism, might not have given themselves the same options as Canadians.

## MULTICULTURALISM: A STRUGGLE FOR MEANING

But what exactly do we mean by multiculturalism? Is it a form of assimila-tion or just another determination of pluralism where difference must equate an inequality bounded by tolerance and benevolence? For example, it may be asked, is multiculturalism another form of social and political integration and how much does it gesture towards genuine power sharing? Some may argue, as do critics Himani Banerji and Neil Bissoondath, that multiculturalism in Canada is a kind of ethical fraud, one where the entrenched keep power and offer a few crumbs to the powerless. Some argue that multiculturalism is simply an illusion, intended to place immi-grants and visible minorities in ethnic ghettoes. Others argue that multicul-turalism is a debasement of the purity of the country, in terms historically of either the racial or ethnic stock of its people. Others, still, see it as a way of integrating those – such as immigrants and visible minorities – who have historically been outside of the mainstream of most Western states by decentring the state or breaking down its proposed homogeneity. Some critics see such deconstruction as an attack on national unity and as a major digression from and betrayal of the modernist aim of producing a unified and single state, with specific and valid norms of living. Theorists like Will Kymlicka, undoubtedly one of the foremost voices on this issue, argue that multiculturalism is a natural outgrowth of liberalism[3] – rising out of an eternal quest for freedom that makes us all human. Multicultural-ism is about split identities that should not produce split personalities or ethical values.

Can we examine the body and the consciousnesses separately, looking for the splits within the same system or social order and determining which part is truly the genuine, essential, authentic, and even dominant one, and would we find values that make us better and more knowledgeable if we did? What, then, do we make of these two phenomena: the Black body and citizen in the modern nation-state and, second, the existence of this nation-state in a form that is now described as multicultural? Do these two phenomena have anything in common, so that an understanding of one would help us understand the other, or are they simply separate and distinct orders and universes, having nothing vital in common?

These are ethical questions that go beyond what we may simply know through experience, scientifically or otherwise, and which end up in the realms of beliefs, dreams, wishes, and expectations. Knowing this, we can better understand the resilience of such things as racialization and racism and why an appeal to meaning and knowledge solely based on experience, or attempts at a re-education, seldom work with any satisfaction. These are questions that test the limits of reason and reasonableness within the given system. At the same time, they can help explain why, in the face of such resilience, there can still be so much hope, as a social and ethical order, in as idealistic and transcendent a proposed way of living as is multiculturalism.

The explanation is that in any discussion of these major concepts – Black, Blackness, White, Whiteness, and multiculturalism – we are often trying to conflate two distinctive and often opposing ways of knowing the same things. And as the German idealist Kant has shown us, when we are dealing with two different ways of knowing, we often end up with contradictions or antinomies – or we defy what are usually called common sense ways of knowing for a better world that is grounded in the transcendent, but which offers us the myths, dreams, wishes, concepts, and even beliefs – our ideologies – out of which we try to shape our daily lives.

This book is an enquiry into Black, Blackness, and multiculturalism, and into a specific site or location that is physically and imaginatively Canada. It starts from the position that Black and Blackness are two different consciousnesses, even though in a common sense way they are often conflated into one. The same is true of the consciousnesses that are White and Whiteness. However, these consciousnesses share the social order and exist together in a lordship and bondage relationship that is characterized by a struggle for dominance of the entire order. This book suggests that multiculturalism is part of the consciousness of Blackness and that, at least ontologically, epistemologically, and ethically, multiculturalism is Black and an exercise in Blackness. It is always in a struggle with Whiteness that is marked by ethnic purity, or even a form of pluralism based on one or more ethnic groups as authentic to the social order, and that all others are to be tolerated as they do not have the same sense or history of belonging. The Blackness of multiculturalism says that every and any group that qualifies socially belongs – that no group has a higher ranking or sense of belonging than any other, and that in terms of citizenship all individuals and groups belong and are equal. In this indeterminacy, history does not matter as much as the intent of all the individuals and groups to work and survive together, and to make tomorrow better than today or even yesterday. So how do we prove this, and are there any nuances in differences of meaning when I say that citizens of a country like Canada who are commonly called Black because of the colour of their skin and that multiculturalism as a practical and idealistic form of state formation are both exercises in Blackness? The specific exercise we are following is akin to a journey of exploration to find and explain meaning and knowing with certainty, but one which will almost assuredly never arrive at such an ideal terminus or destiny. Indeed, it is a journey that will likely produce the several and equivocal levels of meaning of the consciousnesses that are Black, Blackness, and Canada or Canadian, with each meaning having a specific importance to its time and place.[4]

Instead of producing a unity of meaning, it will gesture to the fractured, fragmentation, and alienation of this supposedly single body and self – whether referring to the individual or a collective – that are now intrinsic to any discussion on these modernist concepts. And it will produce a higher level of understanding of that consciousness that emerges idealistically when all the different forms of meaning are reconciled transcendentally into a unique and distinct unity called *Multicultural Canada*: a unity that is fractured, fragmented, and often alienating because it is assembled out of the plenitude of many ethnic and racialized groups held together only by a universalizing intent to do what is both good and right. This is multiculturalism that, as I shall show, is idealized Blackness that aspires to be idealized Whiteness.

This exercise will produce an answer similar to the one Hegel offered for reason in his *Phenomenology of Spirit*: namely that meanings for Black and Blackness always have to be placed in a context and within a specific social system; they must be contained within their own individual boundaries and limits; they must, as this book will argue, be always placed within a time and space, and, importantly, within a dominant ideology or mythology that determines the very meaning that as reasonable people we seek. I argue that the overarching social order is what we call Western civilization, and that Canada is a separate entity and social order within that greater universe. Therefore, we will have to keep asking always on what level, experiential or mythical, we are thinking. I will argue that existentially, as a development grounded in the Americas, Canadian multiculturalism is specifically a form of creolization – a cultural and idealized form of Blackness as, Édouard Glissant and others show, that is so endemic to the Americas and the Pacific islands.[5]

Tending towards this end, this exercise is an enquiry to explain contradictions of meaning that surround these concepts of interest, some of which

we will be conscious of, but with many others remaining quite unconscious. The latter are like the archetypes that are constantly appearing in
our dreams, thoughts, images, and hopes. They are also present in the use
of language when we self-reflexively live out a concept that is holistically
given to us, such as Multicultural Canada. The contradictions we will find
are in what we think we know with certainty, the categories of thought that
explain the real world as given to us by common sense, or what Hegel calls
phenomenologically sense-certainty. This is an unreflective, unsophistica-
ted, and even naïve way of knowing. As we shall find out, these categories
are not as clear, precise, and certain as we – who are equally members of the
same social order – may think.

Their givenness is always in doubt, and will change depending on the position and attitude of the person making the assessment, and the position and
placement of the concept as it is given to us at any moment. Indeed, it is not
the given meaning per se that is in doubt; rather it is our understanding of
what is given that is always subject to greater clarification, learning, and
knowledge. The object or the carrier of the given identity might appear
unchangeable, such as the way it is structured and its appearance; what is
changeable is our knowledge, until we can declare with absolute certainty
that we really know all there is to be known about the identity and its bearer.
This is especially the case when we say, in our social dealings, that there is a
category of Canadian in this multicultural country that is *Black* either ethnically and culturally or by historical positioning. And it is for this reason that
a second major aim of this book is to examine and to try to pin down what is
*change* or *changeable* in these concepts, especially when within them subjects
become others or vice versa; when how within them it is a matter of, in an
ethical sense, one asserting an identity as a citizen. Is citizenship always a
state of being, or is it one of becoming? Is it changeable or unchangeable, idealistically perfectly White or simply a state of Blackness?

## REASONS FOR KNOWING BLACKNESS

Indeed, it is important socially and ethically that we should know the categories of Black and Blackness if we are to know how to position them in
our society and if we are to know if there should be any use for them. Apart
from giving us a common sense of meaning and knowing, these categories
do a wider job epistemically and phenomenologically. They help establish a
sense of ontology in so far as they help identify the real and genuine. In the
case in which we explain them in this book, the categories help us to position and place Black and Blackness as concepts in a culture and give them a
cultural embeddedness and liveliness. In this sense, the categories imbed
Black and Blackness within a natural environment and culture of what we

shall call Western thought and in a moment or consciousness within that thought that we call late modernity.

This is a period that in Canada is now authoritatively marked by official multiculturalism. Multiculturalism in Canada is itself publicly marked by inclusivity of citizenship where anyone that qualifies can be changed into a full citizen; where citizenship itself is constantly changing as new rights are extended to all those claiming full citizenship. Multiculturalism is always ill-defined, always resisting an exact a priori meaning, and is always dynamic, slippery, and creative – as I shall argue, it is always culturally and idealistically Black, and that imprecision or ambiguity is the beauty and challenge of living and life itself. With this embedding for Black and Blackness in Western thought come discursive positions that shape and determine what we think and what we think we know about who and what Black and Blackness are at this specific moment. This embeddedness determines how the concepts are given to us and how, in turn, we receive them and project meaning onto them.

By knowing and understanding these categories, we are helping, in a sense, rewrite the consciousness of modernity, in the general, and Canadian nation-state building, in the specific, as this is to treat Black and Blackness as living cultures and as changeable consciousnesses. This re-examination allows us, from standing at this present moment in time, to do what Martin Heidegger and Stuart Hall talk about: to try to know ourselves as a single being over time.[6] This consciousness includes even those who might not identify themselves as Black or see themselves as embedded in Blackness. At the latest moment in time, by discovering the cultural representations and categories of knowing that are contained in our current knowledge of ourselves, we can better understand who we are and why we may claim a unified multicultural identity that, contradictorily, is often shot through with ethnic and racialized identities that are separate and different.

This knowing comes about, as Heidegger says, in a discovery that is really an "uncovering" of the past. It is a reaching back into the historical narrative and, as Hegel would have added, an act of raising up and carrying forward meaning that had been buried, overlooked, and even discarded. It is finding those aspects of the self, individually or collectively, which are covered and in need of a new clearing and even a moral and ethical cleansing. It is finding how the old that we now call history once changed into the present that is today, and it also involves speculating on how the present that is now may change into a new consciousness that is in the future. As Hall says in tandem with Hegel, because the knowing must always be representational and relational, the meaning itself comes to us highly mediated, and is changeable and pliable based on the prevailing dominant conditions and norms of behaviour in the consciousness.

In this regard, I am thinking of what Philip Fisher says in his book *Hard Facts* is the task of these rewritten narratives. He states that active and living cultures are always re-evaluating their pasts, in effect reconsidering what is taken as the given on which perception is based, and rewriting them from a more recent moral and political standpoint. It is as if they are always trying to answer a profound question: Where did the split in our humanity occur? And there are two related questions: When, then, did we become so conflicted? And what must we do for healing? This is what makes cultures ethical phenomena. This is what, I would argue in a Hegelian sense, makes epistemology ultimately a question of the ethical. As Fisher says in a statement worth quoting at length:

There is ... meaning to the work of culture when we consider what the present does in the face of itself, for itself, and not for any possible future. Culture, in this sense, does work that, once done, becomes obvious and unrecoverable because it has become part of the habit structures of everyday perception. Within the present, culture stabilizes and incorporates nearly ungraspable or widely various states of moral or representational or perceptual experience. It changes again and again what the census of the human world looks like – what it includes or excludes – and it often does so in tandem with changes in social facts or legal categories that make, from the standpoint of a later perspective, the facts seem obvious.[7]

In effect, this uncovering rearranges all that was previously accepted without challenge or critique as the given on which we base meaning and knowledge. Here, we are reminded of the suggestion by philosophers like Levinas and others, who, in encouraging us to re-examine what we mean by our categories of knowing, ask us to consider a return to the very beginning of our culture and consciousness, to a time even before we had received our concepts and categories of knowing, and to restate them with the knowledge that we now have.[8] The return is to a moment before the proverbial fall: before the conflicts within the system announced themselves. This is a return to what Hegel calls a moment of sense certainty, a moment with its own limits and boundaries on not only what we know, but on how we may know, and one which, because of these limitations and boundaries, we may construe as the point at which we genuinely become social beings.

## REGISTERS OF KNOWING

This new position is where we come to rely on what I shall be calling in this book the neo-mythic register, a primarily discursive way of attaining meaning that is effectively received knowledge, but is knowledge based on our beliefs, wishes, historical conditioning, memories, and ideals for the future.

This is a register that suggests the world is made up of many different objects, some of which are good and some evil. The register suggests there are ways of knowing the good from the evil whereby the measurement has little to do with the differences in the way the diverse objects appear, but instead with knowing what they genuinely are like – with knowing, as it were, metaphorically what is the colour of their heart or core and their intentions. On this register, we, like any newborn baby, believe perceptually that the I that is We is good. Perceptually, and originally, there is no evil in this self. Once this knowledge is known, it can be used as the basis for an ethical relation – one that is ultimately based on whether specific people or individuals intend to be good or evil towards others. This register leaves the door open to the likelihood of diversity in society, allowing for a community to be made up in a post-creation moment of individuals with different mixtures of good and evil, but who might come together around a common intent, while maintaining their diversity and uniqueness. This meaning comes to us via such things as myths and proverbs that, like an ideology, we live and perform daily without questioning the sources of our behaviour. This is a way of having meaning that flows from the group or collective consciousness to the individual, rather than, as modernity would suggest, the individual in all her or his selfhood imposing a rational meaning and acting out of this self-legislated morality. This is a meaning that is usually given to us with such subtlety that we are often unconscious of how uncritically we have accepted it.

Yet this meaning shapes the very lenses through which we view the world and positions us in a way that we can only privilege one understanding or meaning, the one based on our placement. A key question for us is whether neo-mythic knowledge is unchangeable, or whether it can adjust to circumstances, whether, in our bid to make sense, we make all our experience and knowledge conform to what has been given to us as unchangeable truth. This is a question that holds great importance for our understanding the "rationality" of race and racism, and for understanding what is genuine and real about citizenship and multiculturalism. In effect, this will help us understand if there is any way in which Black and Blackness, in all but the somatic forms, can become White and Whiteness, or what would make possible the magical transfiguration that would be needed for such a transformation – a change that would produce a state where change is possible from a state that is now viewed as unchangeable.

Another form of knowledge that is an ideal of our culture is the knowing that provides semiotic meaning from dialoguing with an object – in that we assume that there is something called objective truth that is not based on a specific subject position or the prevailing context. This is where we believe we can take any object or body and read it for the truth that it is willing to give up, so that the object or body shapes the truth that is known about it.

The latter meaning is very much at the heart of what I will call the ethno-racial understanding of Black and Blackness, where the semiotic meaning of the semantic or skin colour supposedly contains all the truth about Black and Blackness and gives them a specific meaning and ethical hue.

Particularly with the advent of modernity, the ethno-racial register has been presented as an assimilationist tool, as a way of homogenizing all the differences and diversities among specific groups of people so that they can be known as a specific and objective entity. This way of knowing is based on outer attributes which can be used analogously to determine the good or evil that is hidden within an individual or group of people. The outer characteristics are supposedly an irrefutable estimation of the internal good or evil. In this way, all who had these particular externalities – the colour of skin, type of hair, facial features, voices, place of birth, and so on – were deemed under this register to be of the same type and to be interchangeable: they were assimilated into the same group, and on this basis it was presumed to be ethical for subjects to treat members of this group as if they were, indeed, all the same rather than differentiated in individuality, cultures, or aspirations.

This register is where knowing is based, as far as possible, on what we encounter in the so-called real world – or on how the real world encounters and has positioned us – where meaning does not necessarily spring forward from the autonomous consciousness within each of us. It is sensory, and it aims to place objects that we encounter in the world in clear categories – into classifications that do not bleed into one another, where all categories are finite, systematic, and self-containing. Given their characteristics, these categories are also supposedly unchangeable, distinctive, and authentic.

In a sense, too, this way of knowing flows from the group of Black bodies and Blackness rather than from the individual, per se. This semiotic way of knowing, I contend, is always dependent on, and is even reducible, to the neo-mythic or discursive in shaping our knowledge of Black and Blackness. In this regard, one way of knowing is imposed on another; it is considered to be true, genuine, and the unchangeable, is considered to be dominant in a lordship and bondage relationship, where one must serve the other. In this regard, the neo-mythic is the unchangeable, if only because in a modern state citizenship with its constructed equality is always our primary and universal identity, and the ethno-racial the changeable. This is the method that underpins what we may call common sense, the daily practical and pragmatic way of knowing the world.

However, in our practical life, under closer examination, this relationship is not so easily apparent. We might not even notice when we are deferring to the neo-mythical and we might not be aware when we choose to be stuck on the ethno-racial register. This is so because much of what we do, or act as if we know, is based on a subconscious way of knowing. By necessity, multiculturalism is always questioning this very behaviour; it is always calling on us to choose and to be conscious of our actions; and it is always challenging what we would readily accept as given to our common sense way of knowing the world. Multiculturalism is always asking us to account in our knowledge for what is the changeable, for what does not fit nicely into one or any other of our presumed categories of knowing. When this happens, it also even asks us to question the validity of the very categories into which we automatically try to place things, to check for our ideological biases and prejudices, to ask if the categories themselves are really natural, pure, and unchangeable, or whether they are determined in time based on human imaginings.

This urge to take things as simple and given acts very much as Marx sees the role of ideology in giving the world meaning. And this thinking is what multiculturalism, ethically, challenges. As Marx says, to be critical we often have to take the information we receive and turn it on its head – to correct for the filter of the photographic lens that is ideology and which distorts actuality and meaning in our minds. Indeed, the semiotic meaning can only be received knowledge or perception – what is taken as the given from the neo-mythic and discursive way of knowing. It is what is projected onto the Black body discursively or what is read into the body, rather that what meaning the body or consciousness offers up on its own. The ethno-racial register is given to us out of a perception determined by the neo-mythic. It is what in a Hegelian sense we may call the "supersensible," which is the essence, force, kernel, or sprit of the thing or object we are examining. It is the "reality," the unchangeable, or the irreducible that we hope to eventually achieve when we have exhausted all questions that begin with why.

## BLACKNESS AND WHITENESS: CIVIL SOCIETY AND THE POLITICAL STATE

Indeed, in looking at what we now call political life in a multicultural Canada and by examining the two different registers of meaning, we may be attempting to understand what Marx had explained in *On the Jewish Question*, where he argued that what is now presented as the modern unified nation-state is a composite of what we call civil society and the political state – each with its own distinctive attributes and apparent ways of socially producing meaning.

Civil society comes with its individual determinations, with its egotistical rights-of-man attitude to an identity based on sovereign individuality, where the idea is to separate individuals and classes of specific types of humans out of the totality and indeterminacy of a universal group of humans. The political state is a later development on the civil state; it is a second form of negation, having as its intention to produce citizens as abstract but moral beings – to give them back, ironically, an indeterminacy from which they had apparently fled in the first case. Except that the return would be to a higher level of determinacy in a severely restricted universe of equals – and to one exercised as a choice or freedom of identity. Citizens would lose their individual determination so that they can be part of a collective. Their interests would be in having an ethical relation that is based on the improvement of all individuals in the group rather than one or two individuals at the expense of the wider collective. Marx says these two different strains, goals, and intentions of state formation are at the heart of the modern experience in nation-state formation.

The first state – that of aiming for a civil society into which a self-reliant individual or group emerges – received meaning and can be accounted for through the ethno-racial register. Indeed, it is worth emphasizing that Marx saw this state appearing directly out of European feudalism, when he said the basic resulting element was conceptually *Man* – as he posited in a patriarchal way in keeping with his times – and out of the egoist seeing itself as distinct among all categories of beings, including those that were already acknowledged as human. We can see the direct relationship here between somatic and cultural Blackness in such historic events as the rise and decline of Trans-Atlantic Slavery in the Americas. It can also be seen in European feudalism and in the rise of liberalism, where identities were no longer ascribed as under feudalism but were freely attained and asserted individually and in groups. The new recognitions reached their highest expressions in the forms of abstract and universal identities. The reformulation from an ascribed identity to one of choice occurred within the state as a second form of negation that resulted in the citizen being identified as having rights and entitlements based on specific individual and group attributes. This differentiation of those that belong – those who were effectively recognized as the *Man* – and others who did not was to become the hallmark of the bourgeois society and its privileging of liberal rights and identities. The second negation was into what I call idealistic Whiteness, and it is on this Whiteness that issues of citizenship and belonging were determined. However, the classes or categories of human considered to be Black were not viewed by the dominant powers as having the same liberal rights and aspirations. They were not the liberal or bourgeoisie *Man*; they did not belong in a state where membership was based on Whiteness. They were viewed not as full citizens in the early stages of modernity. From a Eurocentric perspective, they did not have the identity of those that belonged within the modern state. This was especially the case for those who were somatically and culturally Black. Supposedly, the dialectics of history that produced the modern state had left them behind at the end of slavery – at the point where they were stuck on the ethno-racial register, in a civil society with no momentum for positive change, and without the transfiguration from group attributes to individual identities and full freedom.

The second state, that of humanising and producing citizens in a political state, received its meaning from what I am calling the neo-mythic register. This is a register for evaluating good and evil, for teaching and recognizing morals in higher human beings whose humanity was no longer in doubt. This was so because they had been brought into the political nation-state, and as a privilege to which they were entitled from belonging in this state, had received its humanistic polishing and refinement. Marx suggests that it is in a political community that humans attain their highest recognition. Until then, they are merely individuals looking after their own affairs. They would operate as if they have a true and indeterminate nature based on self-interest and self-preservation. But in the political society, they become fully human: they were able to make moral determinations between good and evil. Such moral agents were recognized universally as social beings, but importantly as human beings of a specific type or citizenship – one in which they had a special ethical relationship with like-minded agents who shared the same history, culture, and morality. Therefore, in political society, they are constructed as if they naturally have rights, as if figuratively speaking they have already attained the ethno-racial status of the *Man*, even if these rights are only truly useful in a specific society. As Marx stated, and in a quote we should note at length:

The *formation of the political state*, and the dissolution of civil society into independent *individuals* whose relations are regulated by *law*, as the relations between men in the corporations and guilds were regulated by *privilege*, are accomplished by *one and the same act*. Man as a member of civil society – *non-political* man – necessarily appears as the *natural* man. The rights of man appear as natural rights because *conscious* activity is concentrated upon political *action*. *Egoistic* man is the *passive*, *given* result of the dissolution of society, an object of *direct apprehension* and consequently a *natural* object. The *political revolution* dissolves civil society into its elements without *revolutionizing* these elements themselves or subjecting them to criticism. This revolution regards civil society, the sphere of human needs, labour, private interest and civil law, as the *basis of its own existence*, as a self-subsistent *precondition*, and thus as its *natural basis*. Finally, man as a member of civil society is identified with *authentic man*, man distinct from citizen, because he is man in his sensuous, individual and *immediate* existence, whereas *political* man is only abstract, artificial man, man as an *allegorical, moral* person. Thus man as he really is, is seen only in the form of *egoistic* man, and man in his *true* nature only in the form of the *abstract citizen*. [9]

This tells the story of Blackness ethically and existentially, of how modernity with its goal of the unified and assimilated political nation-state, as a refinement or Whitening of the Black civil society, was not intended for somatic and cultural Blacks. They were considered to be stuck in their humanitarian evolution in the civil state, as natural or authentic beings, and incapable of going on to a higher attainment of development or idealized Whiteness. They were incapable of becoming the liberal and bourgeoisie *Man*, a being that received the highest recognition on both the ethno-racial and neo-mythic registers. Thus, even when they appeared within the political state, somatic and cultural Blacks were deemed to be stuck solely on the ethno-racial register, with its rational explanation of racism and ethnocentrism, and its group classifications that positioned them as less than fully human and as products of modernity's finest achievement, the nation-state. Because somatic Blacks were considered not equal beings to the (White) *Man*, the being around whom the ethno-racial and neo-mythic registers converged to give one meaning, they were considered different in character and values. If the *Man* was good, as lesser beings they could not be the same. They were, therefore, evil, and worthy of a lesser positioning on both registers in the modern state than the superior being. Within the political state so constructed, the more rational, higher meaning of judging based on morality or according to the neo-mythic register was reserved for those who were considered to be genuine citizens – for those deserving of freedom.

Therefore, we see the contradictions in multiculturalism when people who were deemed historically to be suited for a civil society that is just one refinement above a state of nature were brought, nay, fought their way into the political state and sought the same recognition as moral abstract citizens, and to claim this as their human nature or essence. We see these contradictions displayed via the two registers of meaning, and in many cases the contradictions and apparent solution in the political state appear to be just as suggested by the Hegelian student, Marx:

Political emancipation is a reduction of man, on the one hand to a member of civil society, an *independent* and *egotistic* individual, and on the other hand, to a *citizen*, to a moral person. Human emancipation will only be completed when the real, individual man has absorbed into himself the abstract citizen; when as an individual man, in his everyday life, in his work, and in his relationships, he has become a *species-being*; and when he has recognized and organized his own powers (*forces propres*) as *social* powers so that he no longer separates this social power from himself as *political* power.[10]

## BLACKNESS: OVERCOMING THE MAN AND THE SELF

In other words, for our purposes, genuine meaning about Blackness and about Blacks will only come to us when we ideologically and unconsciously see them semiotically as explainable by the two registers, but even more importantly, when they are seen as having attained the universal status of species-being that is recognized as the species itself (instead of as beings that are part of a class within the species, as the ethno-racial register would suggest), when somatic and cultural Blacks are viewed as full citizens in all the abstractions and Whiteness this implies. Idealistically, put another way, this would be when the state considers all its citizens to be equally placed and positioned in their equality on both the neo-mythic and ethno-racial registers, and when it ceases to view any of them as fully determined on one or the other register – when they are no longer inflicted with a dualism of meaning. This is the task that Canada has set for itself idealistically by deeming itself to be officially a multicultural nation-state.

Thus, the result and explanations that were hinted at by Marx are likely to emerge from subjecting both the neo-mythic and semiotic-based registers to a phenomenology. This is where we try to establish the fundamentals of knowing, and, in effect, to tell if within any culture or ideology these two ways of knowing are mutually exclusive of each other. A phenomenological study, especially one aimed at discerning clear categories of knowing, helps us to uncover what has been covered up and disguised. It takes us to the ground or the very basic concepts ontologically. This allows us to then test if our meaning is grounded in what is actual and real, ontologically, or is largely received knowledge, and is, therefore, socially constructed out of choices. The latter is where epistemology is always trumping ontology. It is also where our ethical relations are based on epistemological categories of knowing and not so much on the ontics or the different forms of beings that the epistemology represents.

The basis, then, for our acting and performing, for our making concrete and actual, is epistemic, and, as Kant explains, is based ultimately on our ways of determining what is good and evil: "The sole objects of a practical reason are thus those of good and evil. By the former, one understands a necessary object of the faculty of desire, and by the latter, a necessary object of aversion, both according to a principle of reason."[11]

Again we are reminded by Fisher of one of the current features in modernity, the symbiosis between group knowing and individual action. Fisher says this symbiosis is noticeable particularly if there is a "redesign of categories within culture [that] takes place primarily in a liberal direction, [so that the] work of culture includes equally powerful value-free changes and, at the other extreme, the installation of such categories as 'the Barbarian,' 'the Pagan,' or 'the Jew' within cultures where the categories exist only to isolate our targets."[12] Indeed, at the heart of multiculturalism in Canada is the idea that it is a liberal democracy, an approach that privileges the neo-mythic way of knowing and its idealism. Fisher's example of how the categories of knowing had moral and political consequences for the First

Nations people of North America holds much poignancy for the categorical homogenization and totalization that are also found in Black and Blackness as concepts within modernity, in general, and within Canada
specifically. As Fisher says:

Within 19th-century America the policy of removing the Indians and, later, confin-
ing them to reservations, had in the background the collapse of differences, in the
white mind, so that Apache and Creeks, farming and hunting nations, Christianized
and savage, no matter what their differences or dangers, were simply designated
"Indians" and subjected to a common fate. The very choice within a culture to
attend to increasingly refined differences or to more and more inclusive categories is
a political act for which the inner practice and the memorization takes place infor-
mally and continuously.[13]

We shall take most of what Fisher has just said about a dominant ethical
order and place it in categories of knowing for Black, Blackness, and multiculturalism, and we shall describe these categories as (1) the idealistic, (2)
the somatic, (3) status, and (4) the cultural. Indeed, this is just as the venerable Black and Caribbean critic C.L.R. James tells us we should expect if
we accept Hegel's insistence "that the importance of dialectics is the capacity to speculate into the future."[14] For as James goes on to say in *Notes on
Dialectics,* "the end, as Hegel insists, is the beginning, although you can
understand that beginning only when you approach the end."[15] And James
notes that we depend on the recognition of contradictions as a way of making sense of the world, by analysing opposites that are reflections of each
other. These are opposites, such as the subject and other, mind and material, any of the ones given to us by Fisher above, that coming together
express, as James reminds us, the unity of the concept or identity: "This
entails a recognition that the two parts of the unity are in violent opposition, contradiction, to each other. It is when Subject realizes that 'Contradiction' is a fundamental principle of all life, that it jams the opposites
together and so unlooses (in speculative thought) inherent movement. The
idea thus logically divined, is the Ideality of the next stage of reality."[16] And
so the journey to deeper knowledge continues, on to the next stage, built-in
contradictions and all.

### TRAVELLING THE ROADS AND TIMES OF BLACKNESS

So, our journey will begin with what we think we know, or what we may
accept as uncontested givens in a common sense way, and then run on parallel tracks: one to explain the conscious and what we think is known, and
the other to excavate and then explain the unconscious; one proceeds
semiotically and the other mythologically, or with what we shall call the

neo-mythic; one existentially and ontologically and the other ethically. Ultimately, both tracks will lead us epistemologically, ontologically, and ethically back into the heart of our darkness – back into indeterminacy, if even at new levels of understanding. By proceeding this way, we will appear to be escaping from one level of consciousness of knowing that is riddled with contradictions only to arrive at a higher one that is beset by its own contradictions and, indeed, givenness. This is what we shall achieve by using a Hegelian method of dialectics to examine the categories of Black and Blackness, and ultimately multiculturalism and citizenship, that we think we know with certainty and precision.

We will be applying a system to acquire greater knowledge where, as David Kolb says in *The Critique of Pure Modernity*, "the early categories [of knowing] are abstract versions of the fuller thought structures of the later categories, which include the earlier ones properly unified and put in their mutual relationships."[17] This means that we will never be totally in the clear, if by that we mean that we transcend contradictions and have absolute certainty, and arrive at where meaning is never given to us, but is absolute, discrete, and autonomous. There will always be contradictions, even when we end up dialectically at higher and deeper levels of understanding. The difference will be that they would be *new* contradictions and that most of the old ones will have been clarified in the process, whether through negation or refutation, and they may very well be included in some of the newer contradictions, and challenges, and in the new meanings.

And there will always be confusion over exact meanings and truth of knowledge if we either consciously or unconsciously switch tracks, by for example conflating different ideas and meaning that were derived in different contexts into seemingly simple words, such as Black, Blackness, and multiculturalism. Again, as Kolb explains of our journey: "in general the chain of categories [of knowing] moves from less to more differentiated, but there are doublings and twists; there is no simple advance." This Hegelian method or system of logic that we will be applying will consist "of a series of narrated transitions, but the movement is not a linear sum of a series of microtransitions. It is better to think of the movement as one large gesture consisting of itself repeated in ever smaller units until it is made full at the end, which encompasses the beginning. The large motion consists of workings out of itself in the small, but it is not built up from little independent transitions."[18]

However, in return for these new contradictions we shall have what James first called insights, a point that John Russon also makes when he refers to insights as the key characteristics of understanding – higher knowledge and understanding that come through examination of the "given" perceptions. Although more than mere received knowledge, these insights are also of greater familiarity, something akin to a kind of art, to the point where we seem to be moving way from a reliance on "rules" to give us an understanding, and towards the expertise of just knowing, a consciousness, even if we cannot explain away all contradictions – especially the new ones that are always arising.[19] However, these insights of understanding are not the same as absolute knowledge or total truth. These insights are always conditional, primarily from the perspective of the viewing subject. As James says: "Understanding is the same as intelligent reflection. Understanding cannot, does not express the concept of things and their relations. Its determinations are what is familiar to it, not what is familiar in general but what is familiar to it, what once it worked out ... But Understanding relates these determinations (of things familiar to it) – it thinks, it has perspective. It says, 'this is what it is, and this is what it ought to be.' You are able to glimpse the genuine concept. It shows through the contradiction."[20] In the end such thoughts are mere subjective perception, and not truth.

Therefore, to avoid confusion we have to keep our thinking straight by always keeping before us the genealogy and lineage of a specific meaning, and why we think that we have meaning with certainty. Again, this is why we have to return to the basic concepts, the fundamentals, and the supposed essences of what we are investigating. This takes us back to our categories of knowing. Indeed, this is a journey that never ends, so that in the absence of essences, we will never have that full and complete knowledge to which Kolb just alluded.

In this regard, and borrowing from our mythology, we would be very much always in the position of the Greek hero Theseus after he has killed the Minotaur. What to do next? Which way is forward? How will what we have done in the past and know with some supposed certainty affect the future? And why, instead of being in a land of absolute certainty and praises, do we appear to be in a cursed land of exile and epistemic Blackness, a labyrinth? In that moment of pure negativity and indeterminacy, of absolute power, potential, and possibilities, we are in a place that Jean-Luc Nancy equates with the pre-political and the restlessness of the negative – a place that I call epistemic Blackness.[21]

This is the site of negative freedom: the right to resist all forms of determination, and it is also the positive side of nihilism, when we realize that we live in a world marked by the constancy of change and where there are no essences or unchangeables, where we are, indeed, free to become whatever we wish. This could also be the land of existential dread, of feeling absolute nihilism, where there is no genuine authority, and God, if ever there was one, is dead or at least far away and preoccupied with other matters. As Robert C. Solomon says in his book *In the Spirit of Hegel,* this preoccupation with both the negative freedoms from and the positive freedoms to become are at the heart of Hegel's concern with "freedom of self-expression or self-realization ... Freedom, in other words, means the realization of self-identity, for Hegel." As Solomon says, the realization of an identity as a citizen of a state or as part of a political group is only an aspect of this overall Hegelian quest for freedom.[22] This, too, is the tragedy of self and its subjective quest for absolute freedom – a pure, singular, and never-changing identity, and even existence – at the heart of modernity, and why the modern individual will always be fragmented, fractured, alienated, and idealistically Black, a divided and unhappy consciousness through no fault of her or his own. But, as I said, this is also the point of the positivity in nihilism – in recognizing the radical freedom that exists in a world devoid of fixity, of one where social and cultural values and qualities are privileged over essences. If there is not a real god, the individual is free to act as if he or she were more than the *Man*. She or he can make a way out of the darkness or labyrinth by seeking perfection – by becoming other than what she or he is – and calling the result progress.

All our modern-day Theseus has is the thread – or in our case the threads – that lead us only *backwards*. We can only with certainty return, even if in greater knowledge and with a clearer history, to where we started. And the return ethically is back into the Weberian iron cage that is the meaninglessness and sheer formalism of a society in which we found ourselves in a state of *thrownness* and from which we initially sought flight and escape. For the way forward is still an epistemological leap in the dark. This, too, is all that multiculturalism promises, and why the driving force behind it has to be an idealistic leap – a transcendental faith and hopefulness.

Such uncertainty is also what we should know and expect, as a long list of thinkers on identity – including Plato, Aristotle, Kant, Hegel, Nietzsche, Heidegger, and our modern-day Stuart Hall – tells us that this uncertainty is the intriguing thing about identity: we are better at explaining what we were in the past than at capturing what we are in the present and what we will be in the future. Indeed, our identity at any given moment is a thread linking all our actions and intentions, but only from the present to the past.

It is always historical and can be known only after the fact, after the uncovering of what was given. This, too, is why, in the Hegelian sense, the wise owl of knowledge flies only at dusk and why the Benjamin-like angel of progress is always being blown backwards out of paradise. As Hall says, "one soon discovers that meaning is not straightforward or transparent, and does not survive intact the passage through representation [or categories of knowing]. It is a slippery customer, changing and shifting with context, usage and historical circumstances. It is always putting off or 'deferring' its rendezvous with Absolute Truth."[23]

Indeed, we are reminded of a similar image invoked by Kant in the *Critique of Pure Reason* where he suggests that an application of dialectics and phenomenology can help us to arrive at reason that is both pure and practical – one that is free of dogma, that is absolute, cognitive, and free of internal contradictions. By testing and examining what may very well be an illusion, reason would arrive at the truth. "This can be done only through a complete critical examination of the entire pure faculty of reason; the antinomy of pure reason, which becomes obvious in its dialectics, is, in fact, the most fortunate perplexity in which human reason could ever have become involved, since it finally compels us to seek the key to escape from this labyrinth."

As Kant suggests, idealistically, the desired key would unlock the path to "a view into a higher immutable order of things in which we already are, and in which to continue our existence in accordance with the supreme decree of reason we may now, after this discovery, be directed by definite precepts."[24] What might very well be decreed to us by reason, that is, our culture, is not the essence of who we are or what we have become, but the values by which we may live our lives and conduct ethical relations in a world marked by our indeterminate becoming rather than our specificity of being. These values have a history, they are socially constructed and negotiated, and by this very definition they must be changeable. This, too, is the *reality* or the *genuineness* of multicultural values: they are never unchangeable. They are always given to us by some culture or the other – or the hope in a universal sense is that the giver will be the Canadian culture of our own making.

### BLACKNESS: NEVER LEAVING, NEVER ARRIVING

On this journey, we will be better at explaining the contradictions that we have passed through than the ones into which we have emerged. If there is an essence of Blackness, this process of succeeding levels of uncertainty and contradictions is it. This is why Whiteness has always been posited against it as certainty, cognizance, and wholesomeness, and as an end to history when we will be without contradictions, when our world will have transformed into an unchangeable one. It is the will to power that, as Parvis Emad states, is a Nietzschean goal "capable of conjoining durability and transience because it has access to the conditions of its own enhancement i.e., value."[25] This is why this book argues that, phenomenologically, none of us is ever fully White, not even somatically. This is why, no sooner than we have explained one level of contradictions, we find ourselves facing another, if higher, level of contradictions that is blocking our way forward into this Eden of certainty, everlasting life, and unchangeableness.

The ending of one journey is merely the beginning of another. A single meaning as a destination is always another journey away. So that at any moment, as long as there is life, we are never home; in the labyrinth that is life all roads definitely do not lead to home; we are never at the end of history. Yet, we still yearn to be home. We yearn for when we will no longer have to pass through the veil of tears of changeableness, instability, uncertainty, and arbitrariness; for when we can stop being in a state of always becoming something else; when we can idealistically know ourselves in the mythical purity of a single concept or identity. As Hegel suggests, dialectically contradictions seem never to be resolved for any length of time, and appear only to produce more and deeper contradictions. But then, instead of viewing this uncertainty with dread, we may mine it for all that is good, in particular for its creativity and freedoms, thereby realizing that each moment can find and leave us free or enslaved. Yet we try to end each moment as free beings.

That supposedly is life: epistemic, ethical, and existential Blackness. Life is not lived in the idealistic transcendent, for that too would only produce a one-sided view of what it takes to be happy and to enjoy life; that would be an ideal when humans would be robbed of their creativity, their indeterminacy, and their humanity or Blackness. That is why we are always fighting against this conceptual barbarism, as Hegel calls it in the quote above, and why we are always reaching for some light that appears to be only in the transcendent, never in the spot where we are but always at the end of the journey. Idealistically, then, Whiteness is death: the end, or transcendence, as Heidegger says, that towards which being exists.[26] It is the home that is the grave. And that is why, as this book suggests, in every new moment the need arises for yet another phenomenology of Blackness and life and, by extension, their opposite and other, Whiteness.

## BLACKNESS: WRITING A BLACK PERSPECTIVE ON WHITENESS

It is necessary to give a brief explanation for the perspective that I bring to this exercise, especially as this is a study that goes against the grain of much that has been advanced as a structural and nationalistic explanation of race, citizenship, identity, and belonging in Canada. Significantly, even though my analysis is attempted and intended as that of a rational self-consciousness that can be objective, it occurs from the perspective of an embodied ego, one that is already in the world and having to deal with specific material limitations and boundaries that are of this world. Along with a culture-derived knowledge of good and evil, my position and place in society have already been given to me. They come from the ethno-racial register. My desires and dreams, and the value and appropriateness of my positions come from the neo-mythic register.

Therefore, in the end, just as a search for essences usually ends in a failure to find essences phenomenologically, this supposed exercise in objectivity invariably ends in a subjective approach – the paradoxical and ironic opposite to what is intended. This does not mean that, idealistically, such approaches should not be attempted or that they are useless endeavours. This does not mean that we even have to buy into the notion of resolving contradictions in the transcendent, especially one that is outside or beyond us. As Hegel would say, even with these known failures we would still end up with greater knowledge. As Glissant argues, much of what we take for certainty of knowledge is really errantry at work – especially a wandering kind of journey instead of a straight progressive path towards an always higher and more certain "truth." And, for those transcendentalists, what about the notions of trying to overcome the human condition, or even gesturing towards a Nietzsche *overman,* if that is still a goal for some? In all cases, we are talking about ethical relations. Issues of Blackness and Whiteness are first and foremost ethical. More than that, every human, by definition, must live in an ethical relation.

Much of this study is informed by a lived experience as an immigrant from the Caribbean and as a Black person somatically and culturally and who is socially Black in terms of his placement in the society. This means that objectively and subjectively I have been positioned in the prevailing ideology as a Black person. However, this immigrant eventually became a Canadian citizen and has had opportunities to observe Canada from journalistic, literary, teaching, and academic vantage points.[27] In this regard, I am admonished by cultural theorist Stuart Hall that "We all write and speak from a particular place and time, from a history and a culture which is specific. What we say is always 'in context', *positioned.*"[28] At the same time, I take the position that I am also a Canadian, possessing that abstract universal identity and culture as much as any of my fellow citizens, such that I can also abstractly attempt to measure what are the characteristics and values of my Canadian society, a society where I at times sit in the abyss of its conflicts about itself and must make meaning out of how it acts out a split personality that often includes self-hatred. I can reflect on how close Canadians in general come to keeping their ethical words to *all* Canadians in their abstractness.

Indeed, I am also reminded of the statement by Edward Said that "each humanistic investigation must formulate the nature of that connection in the specific context of the study, the subject matter, and its historical circumstances."[29] Therefore, in trying to bring these approaches and concerns to the study of Blackness and multiculturalism, I recognize that my subject position is influenced by the study itself and this in turn determines, again as Said suggests, such things as where I begin the study, what I think to be so important that it leads me to the point of seeming overemphasis and repetition, and the politics of my positioning.

My position has always been that of an outsider, in a cultural and status sense as another form of being Black, for it was very soon after my arrival in Canada that I became aware of the type of structural functionalism that places and keeps racialized and ethnicized Black bodies on the periphery of Canadian society. Blackness for this group is more than somatic; it is a cultural and status determinant too in a Canada that is historically positioned as idealistically White.[30] Somatically Black bodies acquire a new hue of Blackness that is based on their inferior status in society. I soon realized that many of the Black people I knew and admired felt that Canada did not offer them social mobility. Idealistically, it did not allow them to escape into the rarefied enlightened Whiteness reserved for certain Canadians of a given somatic and cultural recognition. This was not simply an issue of class but one of an unchangeable caste system, based on notions of race and ethnicity as unchangeable social constructs.

This was primarily true of the many professionals or aspirants to elitism who like me had emigrated from the Caribbean in the post-1960s. Many of them felt that they would have fared better, at least economically, if they had gone to the United States instead of coming to Canada. While some native-born Blacks might have the same feeling about Canada, and some might have even emigrated from Canada in search of self-actualization, and primarily to the United States, this feeling is based on the notion that there is an ethical problem resulting from differing expectations and which resulted in systemic hurdles.

Many of us who emigrated from the Caribbean had left at a heady time in the region. As we shall see, this was the culmination of a dialectical process that came with one of the goods chosen by humanity at the beginning of modernity. This was a good based on the ideal of freedom and liberalism, and was best captured in the Haitian Revolution with its uplifting of somatic, cultural, and idealistic Blackness. In opposition was another dialectical strain that positioned modernity as a quest for the freedom inherent in a Whiteness that accentuated European somatic and cultural characteristics.

These immigrants were leaving the Caribbean in the first years of political independence for new Black nations or nation-states. For us, in that time, this was the fullest expression of freedom, the end of a colonial period, even if we did not readily accept it as a beginning of neo-imperialist and neo-colonial times. Indeed, we were the poster children for the postmodernity, for as phenomena we and our nation-states were the very opposite of what modernity, colonialism, and imperialism intended. Either as Black individuals or collectively as Black states, we were, in many respects, particularly somatic and cultural, Subjective Blackness. We were not what modernity intended, or what Western civilization had always presented mythically as the end of history – the attainment of full subjectivity. In many respects, we were the Others of modern thought, claiming the lineage and full freedoms that were supposedly identified as intended only for those recognized as having liberal subjectivity – in effect those who were by lineage pure European in a general sense and, more specifically, Western European.

We were the products of a new Black idealism, one that spoke to the creativity that resulted from our creolization and hybridization and of an acceptance that there was, at least, an African presence in all us.[31] Indeed, there were also traces of Asia, the aboriginal and indigenous Americas – indeed of the entire world, including a dominant European ethos, in all of us. We were the first official attempts at recognized national pluralism and what would become recognized officially as multiculturalism. This was a Blackness that positioned us at the centre of humanity, as equal to and no better than any other group of humans.[32] We considered ourselves prototypical of what was to become the new *Man* of late modernity. In this case, many of us felt that we were better prepared to be Canadian elites: we spoke the languages and were highly educated, we were products of modernity's rationalist ideology, and we had an acute notion of social justice that was a somewhat misplaced idealism based on rational transcendentalism in general. As Hegel, Fanon, Aimé Césaire, and others would argue, this was a Blackness that was idealistically White in our mythologies, philosophies, and religions.

This idealism produced a false consciousness that we could quickly and easily transform or recreate ourselves into full-fledged Canadians and claim full status, belonging, and entitlement. We assumed there would be an easy and instant transformation of us from the inside. This would be a transfiguration within our subjectivity, a change that would perfect us as Canadians while rewiring us to reveal itself somatically. The external, we had believed, did not so much count in such matters as citizenship and belonging, as did the internal – that which was not objectively visible or available to the senses.

As the product of such a history, this perspective is shared by those who, like me, are watching a new generation of Blacks seek entry into the Canadian mainstream, while all the early signals indicate that entry is still highly restricted, even if a few more Blacks are making it in. What could account for this false consciousness and the resulting alienation that seem entrenched now in a second and, even third, generation? The answer could be that the Blacks of this new generation are really idealistically White, but this time they are fully Canadian creations. There is no primordialism for them that is outside of Canada and outside of memory. Yet, despite this difference, they seem to have to struggle just as hard as did their parents and earlier generations of Blacks for recognition in avenues that are reserved for idealistically White Canadians of any colour, culture, or social standing.

They are fixated on a universal racelessness that is an idealistic transcendentalism. They believe cognitively, that even though somatically Black, they are White culturally and in status, and that they are products of a fully formed culture and civilization. They arrived in Canada expecting to be treated ethically as idealistically White. Instead, they were homogenized into a Blackness that turned them psychologically into the Other that they had rejected. In Canada, theirs is a struggle for recognition, for the attainment of full self-knowledge and for moral democratic citizenship on a par with all other idealized Whites.

As Paget Henry argues in *Caliban's Reason*, Caribbean peoples share an idealistic, transcendentalist view of the world that results from a mixing of philosophies from mainly Africa, Europe, India, and China.[33] This is an ideology that translates into a way of living, of making meaning out of the world, of having a particular perspective and point of view. Building on Henry's point, such a view is contingent on almost 3,000 years of memory for a people who in their state formations and ideals of themselves draw on a history that extends back to antiquity.

Indeed, the English-speaking Caribbean has produced two Nobel laureates in literature in Derek Walcott and V.S. Naipaul who have always returned to their claim for an explanation of modern events.[34] This is a knowledge based on the mythologies that explain their present condition, their past, and which encode their future. Every thought, decision, and action happens in this framework. Nothing can happen outside of it unless there is a rupture in the thinking.

The tear or irruption in the narrative can still be part of the old mythology, but there would be new meaning to what has happened, what is happening, and the ideas and thoughts of what should happen. Such changes can result in new frameworks, resulting in a different way of life, and bringing new meaning to the world. There would be new priorities, new expectations, and possibly new outcomes.

Caribbean people in the main, especially those who migrated to Canada, had seen how under this rationalist, transcendental ideology people who were constructed as Black could escape the most obvious limitations of status imposed by race. As Henry argues, because of the way the Caribbean was inserted in a colonial hegemonic world, a hierarchy developed there. Such ranking decided status and positioning for individuals within this world: "In the Caribbean, this process of racialization turned Africans into Black, Indians into brown, and Europeans into white. The process was most extreme between Blacks and whites. In the origin narratives, stories of conquest, civilizing missions, and other legitimate discourses of European imperialism, the Blackness of Africans became their primary defining feature. In these narratives, color eclipsed culture. The latter became more visible as Africans were transformed into negroes and niggers in the minds of Europeans."[35]

But there were changes in this world view, and by the 1960s Caribbean peoples constructed as Black not only felt themselves to be fully part of their society, but produced their own worlds. "The formation as a whole has been the works of ministers, doctors, lawyers, historians, economists, political activists, creative writers all working together" to produce a Caribbean philosophy.[36] This was a philosophy with specific roles for individuals for whom Blackness, based on the colour of their skin, was only one aspect of an identity. This was an identity that neither fixed nor permanently determined roles for individuals.

Coming to Canada, many of the Caribbean immigrants found that they were taking a step backwards in time in terms of their ontological development, back to a period before they became full, self-conscious subjects. They had escaped the freedom of the Caribbean for the race-engendered limits, boundaries, and determinations of Canada. In the modernist sense, in coming to Canada they had exchanged freedom as lord for the slavery of a bondsman. Just as importantly, they had entered into a lordship and bondage ethical relation freely – unlike their ancestors, who were largely dragged across great waters, either of the Transatlantic Middle Passage or the Kali Pani out of Asia, into bondage in the Caribbean.

In a wider geopolitical sense, Caribbean immigrants to Canada felt that they had exchanged one form of societal marginalization for another: from being on the periphery of British colonialism to being on the periphery in "an American-dominated world economy."[37] On the surface this was something that they shared with Canadians, who were just as conscious of "critiques of doctrines of manifest destiny ... of being in America's backyard, and of equally, if not virulent, anti-Black practices."[38] Immigration to Canada provided a different experience than their perception had led them to expect: the Caribbean expatriates found themselves quickly determined in a functionalist structure as Black, which is to say significantly lower in status.

They were incorporated into the Canadian society in positions that offered limited scope of their becoming the professionals they were when contributing to a Caribbean philosophy. They also found that anti-Black practices were just as virulent in Canada. Part of the reason, undoubtedly, is that although Canada was separated from England, it never fully considered itself as marginalized as the Caribbean; its dominant people saw themselves as somatically and culturally no different from the dominant groups in British society. Idealistically, they even believed in the same good for their societies. And while Canadians might initially have viewed incorporation into the United States with alarm, such anxieties have been receding over the generations. Indeed, they had not become the same as the *Man*, even if they never gave up hope, or ceased struggling for this recognition.

The result is that although Caribbean immigrants shared a transcendentalist idealism similar to that of most peoples in Canada, they found that it produced different senses and levels of justice, and of hope for the future.

The key determinant in their positioning in Canada was their supposed Blackness – one that Canada was forced to construct as an ethnicity as justification for its positioning of such individuals from around the world, and one that is based strictly on the external and objective notions of knowing, and hence citizenship and belonging. So what then, we may ask, are Black and Blackness as consciousnesses? And is it possible to study these consciousnesses apart from the bodies that carry them and are deemed to be internally analogous of Black and Blackness? These are questions we aim to answer.

## WHITENESS: AIMING TO SHAPE A BLACK DISCOURSE ON CANADA

Finally, this study challenges other analyses and epistemologies on Blackness in Canada. Indeed, there is not nearly enough academic scholarship about somatic Blacks in Canada, perhaps a most potent sign of the group's marginalization,[39] and even less about the phenomenology that is Black and/or Blackness. The empirical studies that have been published look at the distribution of somatic Blacks, at how they are positioned and in what numbers in specific areas of society. There is very little theoretical discussion about what this placement and positioning mean. Indeed, there is very little philosophical debate on what it means to be Black in Canada, and none so far that looks at this issue as part of the neo-mythic understanding of identity.

In putting together this study, I am reminded of the excellent work by somatically Black theorists like Orlando Patterson, C.L.R. James, Frantz Fanon, Stuart Hall, Paul Gilroy, Cornell West, Lewis Gordon, and bell hooks in the Caribbean, Britain, and the United States, especially in the latter where there is a well-developed attempt by somatic and cultural Blacks to have a say in the defining of Blackness and Whiteness as separate, and even intertwining, discourses.[40] As Yancy states, to have such a say is an empowering act; it is a statement about one's subjectivity and agency, about choosing one's determination and labels, and participating in a wider discourse on Whiteness and Blackness without letting only non-White determine the limits, boundaries, and concepts of the debate.[41] In Canada, we do not have such names or levels of scholarship on Blackness. Indeed, in much of academia, Canada is still somatically and culturally a White man's country. The study of even somatic and cultural Blacks and Blackness is still largely restricted to externalities of being and less to the authenticity of being and belonging.

Yet, Canada is part of the somatic Black diaspora in the Americas. There is need, therefore for a philosophical, sociological, anthropological, and cultural studies, among other disciplines, of Blackness and the privilege of

Whiteness in Canada by those who are not only constructed as Black but live normatively a Canadian Black experience. This study is intended as an overture to the understanding and recognition of Blackness in Canada. Again to quote Stuart Hall, in his examination of a similar concern among Caribbean people living in Britain, we who live in Canada must "theorise identity as constituted, not outside but within representation ... not as a second-order mirror held up to reflect what already exists, but as the form of representation which is able to constitute us as new kinds of subjects, and thereby enable us to discover places from which to speak."[42] We must fully explain the ethical implications of our creation as Canadians, and, we must fully explain our attempts to create a new Canada in our image, too.

In doing this, I am also reminded of another admonition, this time by Kant in his *Critique of Pure Reason* as he tried to reconcile the arguments that life can be explained either exclusively as a theoretical exercise or, alternatively, as one based only on the sensation of empirical data.[43] The first was the rationalist argument of Leibniz and the second of Hume and other sceptics. These appear to be genealogical forerunners of what I call the neo-mythic and ethno-racial registers. Either approach on its own, Kant suggests, is too limited: rationalism provides form without content, and empiricism provides content without form.

The solution, according to Kant, is a synthesis – and dare I say methodological Blackness – of the two positions, and that is an aim of this study. It is why we are undertaking an exercise in what idealistic thinkers call transcendental understanding. But first let us begin our journey by specifying the main goals of the exercise and by explaining the methods we propose to invoke.

# PART ONE

# Blackness and the Quest for Freedom

# I

# Introduction

This book travels along four main paths to tell its story. The first is to explain how a specific group of people in Canada came to be identified in a positive way, ethno-racially and by assimilation, as Black. The goal is to explain some of the social and political implications of such labelling, as, for these people, their identity of Black and their culture of Blackness place limits around them and take place within a specific ethical relationship and ethos that is multicultural Canada. This labelling is sociological and anthropological in its emphasis on relations and cultures, and is based on ontological determinations.

This classification is different from the erstwhile notion in our mythology, and even in our philosophical and theological approaches, that all humanity is Black because humans are mortal and immoral, never in full knowledge, existentially prone to despair and angst of living, and are not as pure and White as gods. Because humans are by this nature Black, this understanding points towards epistemological and ethical undertakings. It is the basis for what I call the neo-mythic register for understanding differences, especially differences of identity in such areas as citizenship and belonging. In a multicultural setting, however, Black and Blackness is expected to have a single, clear meaning as an identity for a specific group and its culture. Is this meaning at any given time supposedly ethno-racial, neo-mythic, or a combination of both? The answer is important, for it speaks to the consistency of ethical relations, especially in a multiethnic state where power is usually held by those described as non-Black, and towards those described as Black.

Immediately, we see that, even when assuming a common sense meaning in conceptualizing Black and Blackness, we have lapsed cognitively into the two different registers: the ethno-racial, which is an appeal to semiotics as a way of knowing, especially through the symbol of the Black skin; and the neo-mythic, based on the mythological positing of ideals and distinct categorical forms in the Platonic sense. The second register informs the very way we think and is at the heart of our discursive practices when talking about being and becoming. A phenomenological study would tell us if it is possible to find a commonality, or an essence, between the two registers so that we can have a single meaning no matter which form of thinking we are using at a given moment. Such a finding would have important ethical implications for what we mean by Black and Blackness in *all* situations and contexts.

Importantly, and, indeed, ironically, the recognition of a finite assimilated group of humanity as being Black ethno-racially is occurring in a moment when, supposedly, race and ethnicity no longer have any significance in terms of nation-state formation, the self-actualization of citizens, and for personal and collective freedoms. Yet, is it possible within this single social system for Black and Blackness not to be reduced, ultimately and mainly, to race and inferior status? Can the differences and diversity of Black be assimilated always into indeterminacy, or even into a particular and never-changing determinacy that can be judged ethically as either good or evil? Or can there be positive meaning within the term as well? Indeed, in a mythological sense, it can be argued that by being recognized as racially and ethically Black, this finite group is being acclaimed as the Blackest group of the mythologically Black human family.

In a phenomenological sense, Black used in a common sense way is simply a symbol for racial inferiority based on the outer appearance of the body. In this regard, we ask the question, Can there be anything good and positive in the racialized or ethnicized labels Black and Blackness? In this situation, do intentions matter? Do ethical values matter? And in terms of our Blackness, when is it appropriate to have hope in human experiences and such ethical relations as citizenry and communal, national, and even supranational belonging? Indeed, in a neo-mythic sense, is it possible for someone to be Black in an ethno-racial determination but not be part of the Blackness consciousness, and in fact be idealistically White? Of course, the argument goes the other way for those who claim somatically and even culturally to be White ethno-racially, but ethically, as has been claimed by writers as old as the author of the original western slave narrative, Equiano, to be steeped in Blackness?[1]

Conceptually, race, racism, and to a lesser extent ethnicity have been explicitly removed in this social order as primary determinants of ethical relations in multicultural Canada, yet Canada's multiculturalism depends on group affiliations, even if such affiliations are voluntary. I am thus trying to explain why Canada, as a single consciousness and with every concept supposedly having a single and specific meaning, generalizes some of its citizens as Black, especially at a time when it is generally accepted that there are no group essences and that, ethically, membership in any ethno-racial group is a matter of choice. There is a contradiction in this, one that multiculturalism, as an ideology, should explain. Particularly, it should answer the questions, What has multiculturalism done to race in a national discourse? and What has race done to multiculturalism in making it the dominant discourse in a place like Canada that was previously heralded as a White man's country? In this book, I will try to account for this generalization over identity, belonging, and acceptance within Blackness.

However, identity is at least a dualism in a pragmatic sense: it is partly a result of how an individual sees her- or himself and what she or he wishes for, and just as importantly, how others see and determine the individual. In terms of the latter, the members of this group called Black are constructed out of the same determinants of, and according to, a historical legacy of exclusions and perceived inferiority – a point that is still material enough to give this group's existence and the citizenship of its individual members a peculiar epistemic tone and colour, even in what are seen as being more enlightened and tolerant times.[2] This is where the so-called essences of Blackness and being Black, and the lived experiences of the two, supposedly add up to a specific existence or consciousness. Therefore, Black and Blackness have a history of different meaning from what is now proclaimed. But which meaning is authentic to the Canadian social order?

Particularly, these individuals described as Black come out of a consciousness in the Americas that is based on members having what Du Bois calls a double consciousness.[3] This is an attempted assimilation that smothers all differences of any major kind between people with Black skins or who have an ancestry that can be traced, no matter how marginally, to the African continent. While assimilation in Canada might not be based on assimilation in the wider sense of the universal melting pot of Americanism, it was an assimilation nonetheless into an ontological Black and cultural Blackness that were melting pots themselves in their particularist sense. Once so recognized, the assimilating Black and Blackness were to be universals for all Blacks. They were to be totalized as a consciousness that, ethno-racially, supposedly has an existence that is peculiar to those with neo-mythic double consciousnesses. This existence, again as Du Bois showed, has been developed ethically under specific conditions and in many different landscapes, whether in segregated areas like the old Philadelphia and many parts of the southern United States,[4] places like Halifax and parts of southern Ontario in Canada,[5] in the islands of the Caribbean[6] and on the African continent, or in other parts of the world where African slaves were taken.[7]

What is considered Black and Blackness cannot be easily separated from received conceptions of the group members – with such conceptions implied as already having authoritative perceptions and accepted meanings.[8] Black and Blackness as bodies or consciousnesses have their own characteristics. Therefore, a *Black* body confirmed in its own *Blackness* of culture and behaviour has specific demands and challenges.

To this end, we will try to understand the contradiction in multicultural-ism around the issue of Blackness: is being Black a group and generalized identity or one that individuals can accept or reject as they please? If there is a choice, multiculturalism will be performing in keeping with the ideals of a liberal democracy: specifically, a democracy where individuals can choose their own identities and determine themselves how they want to be seen and situated in the prevailing ethical relations. In our analysis, we will search for the perception or understanding of what Black is as a generaliza-tion in multiculturalism, such as when Black is presented as an ethnicity or a racial category applicable to each member of a finite group in society. Ultimately, this exercise is about finding out what good there is for Black-ness and Blacks, and, in searching for this goodness, this book will gesture to the primacy of the neo-mythic register to that of the ethno-racial, and thereby give a more consistent understanding of these concepts under query.

## INTERDISCIPLINARY KNOWLEDGE AS BLACKNESS

This book, therefore, is an interdisciplinary examination of an idea and ideal: of how neo-mythically over time a specific group of people came to be associated with evil and were initially excluded from the modern state that is the idealized neo-mythic social order. Indeed, here we are reminded of the statement by Susan Neiman in her widely respected book *Evil in Modern Thought* that "the history of philosophy is so steeped in the prob-lem of evil that the question is not where to begin but where to stop."[9] And it goes without saying that in defining evil we are also determining and defining what is good.

As an idealistic exercise, this book will also show how, ultimately, mem-bers of this group came to be involved in moral and ethical relations across history with other groups whose behaviour towards them was determined solely by the colour of their Black skin and by the perception of the good or evil denoted by this skin colour. In doing this, I will be following the exam-ple set by Charles Taylor, one of the foremost scholars on both identity for-mation in the modern state and on multiculturalism. Taylor's explanation will help us understand how these two concepts came together as the par-ticular ethical relationship that is Canadian multiculturalism. At the outset of his enquiry, Taylor states: "I want to explore the various facets of what I will call the 'modern identity'. To give a good first approximation of what this means would be to say that it involves tracing various strands of our modern notion of what it is to be a human agent, a person, or a self. But pursuing this investigation soon shows that you can't get very clear about this without some further understanding of how our pictures of the good have evolved. Selfhood and the good, or in another way selfhood and morality, turn out to be inextricably intertwined themes."[10]

Further, modernity itself has always purported that its goal is the idealistic White citadel that is the individual self – whether this self is the atomic individual that is essentially only a pure ego in the midst of the world, or it is the singular unity of a collective or of a pure and distinct people that comprise a nation. The modern, unitary state is the highest achievement for the human project and is the promise of modernity. According to Taylor, knowing who is good and evil and how this knowledge positioned different people within and without the state is important to understanding modernity. Good and evil are thus viewed as important determinants of who is human and who can be fully humanized in the nation-state – which is modernity's highest ideal.

Working from Taylor's perspective, we will come to see how multiculturalism is a post-modern moment, one of idealized or cosmopolitan Blackness because the singular and pure nation-state cannot be attained. This will also be the case because the individual that is an ego is unsustainable unless she or he is embedded in a culture. He or she must have ethical relations with fellow individuals, who themselves rely on mutual recognition and the formalism of cultural institutions for their recognition as liberal individuals. Blackness comes in with the realization that the individual must be a compromise between the embodied ego and the culture it is embedded in. As Hegel argues, identities are never immediate; they are always mediated, impure, and contextualized. Likewise, Fredric Jameson, this book will show, also described post-modernity as idealized Blackness, especially when he equated post-modernity with "the 'death of the subject' or, to say it in a more conventional language, the end of individualism as such."[11] Jameson first describes modernity and its goals: "The great modernisms were, as we have said, predicated on the invention of a personal, private style, as unmistakable, as your fingerprint, as incomparable as your body. But this means that the modernist aesthetic is in some way organically linked to the conception of a unique self and private identity, a unique personality and individuality, which can be expected to forge its own unique, unmistakable style."[12] However, for various reasons, Jameson suggests that the notion of having such an individual identity is a thing of the past: "The old individual and individualist subject is 'dead'; and ... one might even describe the concept of the unique individual and the theoretical basis of individualism as ideological."[13]

Much of the determination traditionally associated with Black and Blackness, this book argues, inscribes in a finite way only the negatives of human nature on Black bodies. Significantly, the argument is that such inscriptions rob a group of humanity of hope, that quality so germane to freedom and the innate belief in the ability to successfully transform oneself in the ideals and infinity of one's dreams. This is a hope, the White light in rational transcendentalism. As Joseph Godfrey says in *A Philosophy of Human Hope,* this is a projection of the past and the present into the future, into a time, and sometimes even a place, that is not yet discovered and is currently marked by *incognition.* It is a hope that is critical, for as psychoanalyst Julia Kristeva suggests, the depressed and without hope become children of a Black sun, ruled by the Blackness of depression and melancholia that is so natural to them and that was, for so long, mythologically associated with the Black planet, Saturn.[14] Left without this hope, humans, in general, have to deal with the existential Blackness of despair and angst. This is partly the dread that confronts them in the present and which could affect how they position themselves to face a future that is unknown. It also could leave them, at the personal level, with a fear for themselves in daily living – a fear or even melancholia that is the opposite of hope.[15]

For a specific group of humans, however, the black colour of their skin is rationally and objectively associated almost exclusively with the undesirable and inferior, with what at best might be merely contingent. The skin colour is recognized as a visible approximation of inner qualities and virtues, or it is coupled with specific stereotypes and virtues that are uniformly common and basic to all members of this specific and inferior group in Western civilization and is used as a means or rationale for exclusion.[16] Indeed, the term "Western civilization" has been creeping back into our discussion at a time when the West is dealing with terrorism, an evil whose supposed goal is to bring Western civilization to its doom.[17] In considering this evil, we are reminded of the quote by Edward Said: "Therefore as much as the West itself, the Orient is an idea that has a history and a tradition of thought, imagery, and vocabulary that has given it reality and presence in and for the West. The two geographical entities thus support and to an extent reflect each other."[18] In the popular imagery of Western thought or mind, the West is White by assimilation, and the Orient Black. In this regard, recent events in the "war on terrorism" have been depicted as a contest between mythological Black foes in an evil empire of sorts, now called an axis of evil, and a Western civilization characterized by purity of thought and intentions for good only.[19] In this case, we are again dealing with identities that are both general and specific—those that neo-mythically we take to be good or evil in a general sense, and those that ethno-racially in an us-and-them relationship we use as specific examples of good and evil. It is necessary to know when one or the other identity, the universal or particular, is being used, and why.

Indeed, central to the ideology that produces Western civilization as a dominant narrative is the concept of eschatology, the physical death of an ethno-racial being, as an evil, as a physical ending of a time and being.[20] However, eschatology also contains the ideals of freedom and liberation, of where an ethno-racial body can be transformed into a good through a death that is the overcoming of finite human limits and boundaries. This transformation takes place in two ways: either as a rebirth as a new ethno-racial being, or in the neo-mythic sense where what is evil is transfigured into a good. This book asserts that an important understanding of what Black and Blackness is can be had by examining the dialectics of what is commonly accepted as Western thought. Here one finds such oppositional and binary concepts as good versus evil, White versus Black, death versus life, and hope versus despair.

In this thinking only one end of the binary is unchangeable and "natural" and this is usually established on the neo-mythic register as the good. The other is deemed a degeneration or departure from the real, authentic, and genuine and by determination is evil. By implication, this means that, whereas good can take only one form, evil can take a multiplicity of determinations, as many as there are points on the supposed sliding scale between the binaries of good and evil. In this regard, good is always unchanged. It is pure, stable, and whole. Evil, on the other hand, is mythologically diverse, the site of difference. It is impure, dynamic, and fragmented. It is changeable, too, as through miracles of a sort it can be converted into the unchanging good. However, under the ethno-racial register it is taken for granted as an act of common sense that all points on the sliding scale that are not White, and that is all but one, can be assimilated into one identity. This is the identity Black, having not-good or evil as its value positions – so that within the non-White positions of the sliding scale everything has lost its determinacy, and has been reduced to an indeterminacy that is a totalizing Black, cosmopolitan Blackness, or evil.

Just as important is understanding how, in our conception, we believe and expect one end of the binary to change into the other: how evil is to become good, and in the case of multicultural Canada how those who are idealistically Black are to become genuinely White – to attain the Whiteness of full citizenship and belonging. For an explanation of such a transformation, we much look to our myths, to the neo-mythic register, for in a common sense way such changes do not occur based on practical phenomena changing externally, as would be necessary for a change on the ethno-racial register. This change must be internal and largely hidden – but accepted nonetheless as if the change has been external and visible. To this end, we may note that the ethno-racial register is usually a recognition of externalities and of objects in space, whereas the neo-mythic speaks to internalities and changes that over time convert evil to good on the inside.

## BLACKNESS AT HOME IN THE AMERICAS

But our study is also an examination of how the people constructed historically and racially as Black have fought for inclusion in the states of the Americas. It is a look at how they have achieved individual freedom by struggling to negate what is commonly, though erroneously, perceived as being complete knowledge of them. In effect, it is about how they fought individually and collectively, and even prevailed against the dominant thought and core beliefs of what people as varied as Charles Taylor and American president George W. Bush call Western civilization. What they are generalizing about is a way of life or universal culture, as it were, that traditionally positioned specific types or norms of people traditionally as outsiders in the real human family. In this case, their positioning is based on a perceived generalization. It suggests there are common group traits, characteristics, or even essences that allow for the separation of specific people into idealized groupings. The groups ultimately become rarefied expressions of good or evil. They become norms of deviance according to an archetypal construction of specific groups that contained universal notions about them.

At this moment, official multiculturalism as pioneered in Canada since 1971 offers members of the group called Black a dual promise: entry into a land and time where they are full members of humanity and full citizens in the state, and one where the colour of their skin would mean only the good that they intend it to signify. Put another way, the promise is that Blacks and Blackness would be cut loose from the pejorative and perceptual association with evil and exclusion, and be realigned instead to a new way of knowing. The promise is that they will enter as equals into the state and take up this equality of citizenship based on an identity called Black. As Blacks they would be fully and genuinely part of the universal that is Canadian. In this Canadian nation-state, and as full members, they would supposedly live in hope, where the nation-state is the site of hope as a form of idealistic Whiteness for the future. This is opposed to those who, in this particular case, are not Canadian and do not share the social insurances that engender hope. Instead, the others-than-fully Canadian are among the hopeless, or those subject to fear and despair about the future. But what does it mean to be Black either in the specific that is Canada itself, or more generally in the wider world?

By seeking to understand if there is a specific meaning for Black and Blackness, we are trying to overcome the concern for good and evil, as isolated by Taylor, as an important issue going back to the beginning of modern thought. This would allow us to move away from group analysis and expectations to the ideal of treating individuals as persons who may choose to associate with a group and take a fluid identity from it, rather than see the individual ascribed a group identity, and one which it can never shake off.

The problem of multiculturalism is whether this movement away from generality to specific identities is cognitively possible, and if in an ethical relationship this re-creation is possible as a lived reality. However, one glaring contradiction of claiming to fully know is that, because identity is at least a dualism between subjects and objects, this shift from the general to the specific might not be as easy as the individual may want, with the result that he or she remains trapped in a group identity and culture, what Canada calls an individual's ethnicity. To understand this contradiction, we must examine the basis for the dialectical identities that are general and specific and the legacy they hold from an earlier time when the identities were associated with good and evil and with inclusion or exclusion from the nation-state. This examination is provided through a phenomenological dissection of Black and Blackness as idealized bodies themselves, rather than as mere descriptions of other bodies. The meaning of Black and Blackness is therefore central to knowing what is genuinely and truly Black in the specific in a universal multicultural setting and what currency Black and Blackness have in the ensuing ethical relations. This is where we also need to pursue a phenomenology of multiculturalism to get a clear picture of these identities.

This book, therefore, analyses circumstances peculiar to a place called Canada and to an identity called Canadian. Its intent is to show how these identities were devolved and evolved within a wider context that is, first, Western civilization, and then the construction of the Americas. These are meant as physical places and identities in a part of the world that from the outset were considered to be what Europe and Whiteness were not. This book argues that the significant promise of multiculturalism is the hope and idealism that it offers: a promise that individuals can overcome the social death of finite limits and boundaries for the infinity of dreams, authenticity, and justice.

The hope is that individuals would first be recognized as infinities, and so be always in the position of having to choose from an endless array or plenitude of possibilities and options for themselves. These choices also include how they should interact with others who likewise have infinite possibilities and choices. Idealistically, then, the hope is that individuals thus shorn of what others think of them will be free in any contingent moment to become whatever form, manifestation, or identity they freely choose. In this way, individuals would be free of the generalities that modernity had previously deemed necessary for knowing some perceived nature that makes them either good or evil.

This rationalization of a specific type of expected behaviour and recognition in an officially multicultural Canada relies on an accounting for a specific universal way of knowing. Out of this expectation flow assumptions for ethical and moral behaviours and attitudes. This way of knowing is a consciousness, defined here as a specifically patterned and nuanced way of making sense of the world and the relationships of objects in it. This consciousness has developed over time and is a culmination that claims for a lineage specific types of choices and decisions that have been made in history. The consciousness and the manner of its formation are captured in an ideology that is self-perpetuating, as it sustains both the consciousness and the ideology itself. The ideology is the glue of the consciousness that is the state and, at times, is seemingly inseparable from the state. Taken all together, the expectations, behaviours, and attitudes make up a dominant culture or way of life. What otherwise would be seemingly random acts are given specific meaning within this ideology and culture. In this regard, we will treat what we call Western civilization as a specific consciousness with a culture and way of life that is based on a specific way of determining good and evil.

Using this framework, the book examines the historical reduction of Blackness to perception as a way of knowing. This is the semiotics of skin colour that almost exclusively erases all other features of the phenomena that are Black and Blackness. This reduction to semiotics is the privileging of an a priori knowledge, where full meaning is already known at the outset. [21] In this way, knowledge that is based semiotically on skin colour is not subjected to cognition or rational thinking, and is therefore non-dialectical, is formulaic, and is even impermeable. This, I will argue, has been a traditional way of "knowing" people with Black skins as Black, a method that multiculturalism promises to jettison from its consciousness and culture.

Specifically, the book seeks to account for why in ethical relations Blackness is ultimately determined solely by the colour of the skin – based on a generality about group nature – and whether it is possible to break the bind that historically associates Black skin with evil, inferiority, exclusion, unenlightenment, and cultural backwardness. It tries to account for the phenomena of Black and Blackness, which are based on analytically derived concepts but are supposedly operating in and meaningful in a world of rational dialectical thought that is itself based on cognition and the extrapolation of this knowledge into abstract laws, rights, and fundamental freedoms. The ethical implications are immense.

And because it argues that it is difficult, if not impossible, to break the semiotic bond between Black and evil in the prevailing consciousness, the book argues that recognition of a group of citizens based solely on their somatic features can only lead Canada into a Hegelian unhappy consciousness – one in which, even with the best of intentions on all sides, the ideals and goals of multiculturalism always appear beyond the society's grasp. In this case, Black and Blackness remain a site for their historically derived legacy of alienation and exclusion, instead of markers of full citizenship, a universal invisibility, and seamless incorporation into the social consciousness that is the nation-state. Tolerance, now presented as the main quality and value of a multicultural Canada – as Walzer suggests, "toleration makes difference possible; difference makes toleration necessary"[22] – appears not to make the Canadian nation-state virtuous, but rather leaves everyone concerned in a state of recognized differences but also unhappiness.

In this consciousness, therefore, a problem of contradictions arises in our understanding of Blackness and Blacks. On the one hand, they are symbolic of an ethno-racial group and, on the other, of a social consciousness that is multiculturalism. That Blacks and Blackness are embedded in the consciousness only seems to deepen the contradictions that can be expressed in the following questions: Is it possible, operating within the existing structure, to achieve a clear break in meaning within an ideology and consciousness that are intended to be self-perpetuating and unchangeable across generations? In other words, can Black and Blackness be given new meanings in the same consciousness and ideology, thereby maintaining Black and Blackness as changeable to a consciousness that is unchangeable?

If this were possible, then it would be practical to transform Black and Blackness into White and Whiteness without any noticeable change to the underlying structure. The answer we shall provide is that there are few clear breaks or revolutions in consciousnesses, but rather an accretion of meaning from one period to another, so that today's meaning of the terms "Black" or "Blackness" will contain the dialectical contradictions from an earlier time. It is because there is no clear break in the development of thought that we tend to see confusion when the universal meaning seems to subsume the particular, and vice versa.

But there might be an alternative that is fundamental to the intent of this book. Perhaps it is possible that the only way to arrive at the assumed goals of a new meaning and ethical relation is to see Black and Blackness as having been historically misrecognized as evil, inferior, and exclusionary, so that reconciliation can only occur by changing the expected way of giving meaning to the world. In this case, the problem can be solved by not only adjusting conceptually Black and Blackness within the prevailing ideology and culture, but also by overhauling the very mechanisms for deriving meaning, which are the ideology and the social consciousness. The latter position raises the issue of whether in the obtaining ethical relations Black and Blackness are not the unchangeable and consciousness and ideology the changeable. By championing the latter view, this book argues that this is the novelty and idealism of official multiculturalism in Canada. This is the beginning of a dialectical movement of power relationships that could eventually lead to what I call genuine multiculturalism – an ideal where

Blackness and multiculturalism are accepted as one in a fully liberal, democratic state.

## BLACKNESS AS FREEDOM, CREATIVITY, AND HUMANITY

Now, on to the second aim of this book. This is to show how Black and Blackness are also ontologically sites of the freedom, creativity, genius, passion, and progress that are the quintessence of human nature. These sites are all tantamount, as such philosophers and mythmakers as C.L.R. James and Ralph Ellison have taught us, to where the spirit that is idealistically the essence of humanity has sought to give itself an embodiment – where over time it has manifested itself in different forms and determinations of freedom and the self.[23] Black and Blackness are the sources of creation. Here we find the infinity of human potential and possibilities for both good and evil. These are the sites promising the fullest fulfilment of all potential, but also, in a practical sense, situations of deepest disappointment, despair, fragmentation, and alienation. It is where anything could happen, and where it literally does, in that what is expected never appears to be realizable in a specific and particular moment.

In this regard, we are dealing with the opposite of essences, fixity, or rational laws. Rather, this is pure indeterminacy, change, and freedom, even chaos or madness as Derrida and Glissant argue,[24] depending on the perspective. This is fullness without a residue, and, so often, its opposite. These are qualities and not idealistic forms as the operative norms, if there could be any such thing as a norm. I am joining in the search of such thinkers, for example, as Thomas C. Holt, Emmanuel Chukwudi Eze, and Lucius Outlaw Jr, who recognize that something important is missing in the current discussion when Blackness is reduced solely to race and racism, or to the externality of the ethno-racial register.[25] That a limit has been placed on Blackness, so that when it is reduced solely to race there remains a surplus of meaning about humanity that goes unexpressed. This is a limit that can only be replaced and overcome by viewing Black and Blackness via the neo-mythic register as well.

Holt, for example, notes that as concepts race and racism continue to be important to our understanding of the world in a common sense way. This is a world where ethno-racially race and racism refer "to the hostility one group feels toward another on the basis of alleged biological and/or cultural inferiority of the other."[26] This is a hostility that in our thoughts is usually manifested as the "exploitation of the labor and/or property of that other (as in slavery and colonialism), exclusion of that other from participation in public life and institutions (as in segregation and disfranchisement) and massive physical violence against that other (as in lynching)."[27]

While it is necessary to recognize the historical importance of these factors in the overall discussion on the appropriate ethical relations within a modern state, something is missing when the debate is limited to only these explanations. As Holt says: "I would argue, however, that such phenomena do not capture all aspects of the contemporary situation and, more importantly, may miss significant changes under way. There are *new* anomalies, new ambiguities, and a *new* ambivalence in contemporary life that our standard definitions of race and racism simply cannot account for, and which even render them somewhat anachronistic."[28] Outlaw for example, is trying to retain in the debate what he finds in the early Du Boisian thinking, namely, the notion that there are salient and valuable characteristics that have evolved out of the social constructions of people in specific groups, so that there might very well be a Black ethos, culture, or way of producing meaning in the world. One way of looking at it is to ask if there can be a value to Blackness without the forms in which it has been restricted historically on the ethno-racial register of meaning. While making clear that it is necessary to "condemn all actions, beliefs, attitudes, and evaluation that make use of invidious considerations of raciality and ethnicity,"[29] Outlaw still wants to hold on to the concepts race and ethnicity as a way of providing meaning in an important way to understanding the world: "I also believe that it is very important that we continue to make use of the concepts of race and ethnie (or *ethnic groups*) and their derivatives (*raciality, ethnicity*) as important resources for continuing efforts to critically (re-)construct and maintain social realities. For in complex societies in which race and ethnicity continue to be factors at the heart of social conflict, it is as urgent as ever that we engage in such projects with careful mindfulness of biologically and culturally constituted social groupings of race and ethnies, though sometimes it will also be important to have little or no regard for a person's or people's raciality and/or ethnicity."[30]

In this book, I want to suggest that what Outlaw and others are searching for can be found in the surplus meaning that is Blackness as creativity, what is usually overflowing any single act of embodiment, and that it can only be located and even fully understood through a neo-mythic gaze. This is where we may conceive Blackness as race plus other finite attributes and extensions. The plus includes all those things that would make a racialized person fully human, defined as a full subject or citizen in today's nation-state. However, when reduced in the current and dominant ethno-racial discourse solely to a racial or ethnic categorization, those presented as Black are still wallowing in an existentialist Blackness that is an embodiment that fails to capture the full extent of what is essentially human. Such beings are robbed of the highest attributes that are common to all humanity. Among these attributes is the creativity that any member of a group achieves and sustains from living with others in a group. This is a production of a culture that comes from shared experiences and the intentions of members of the group to maintain their way of living.

This new understanding is what multiculturalism strives for when it offers ethnicity as a desired will by a group of people to maintain a specific way of life that is meaningful to the members' perceptions of themselves. This is the idea that is captured in the definition in Canadian multicultural policy that ethnicity is a preferred way of life that is an act of fellowship and continued acts of good faith. It is the expression of "a collective will to exist," which makes ethnicity a cultural and political act at the same time, and one of subjectivity and agency.[31] Here the hope of the neo-mythic register is strongly invoked. As Outlaw suggests, the trick is to have a discussion that recognizes what has occurred and why, and to use this information that "will help us to achieve stable, well-ordered, and just societies, norms bolstered by the combined best understandings available in all fields of knowledge that have to do with human beings and that are secured by democratically achieved consensus."[32] The intentions and assumptions behind these categories of knowledge, and why they were developed, hold importance to our understanding of current social realities, such as multiculturalism.

In this regard, this book shows that most of the discussions on Black individuals and Blackness, even with the best of intentions and initial assumptions, tend to be unsatisfactory. Dominated by the ethno-racial register, they often present Black and Blackness as finite and unequivocal categories. In so doing, the discussion never appears to fully capture what is Black or Blackness or what it really means to be Black. From the subject position of those constructed as Black, the authenticity of self-knowledge in Blackness is always missing. When filled with subjective content, these finite positions serve only to provide limits and boundaries on the infinities that are Black and Blackness.[33]

Missing is the creativity to produce something that is new, shocking, boundary transcending, and not stereotypical. Worse, this book argues, the limits that are imposed, even by many of those who identify themselves as Black based solely on somatic and phenotypic attributes, tend to be restricted to the negative aspects and features of humanity.[34] This is usually the case when the neo-mythic register is invoked, but usually in such a way as to make this register subservient to the ethno-racial register and its existential and ontological categories. The result is dissatisfaction all around – a negation of the neo-mythic intentions of multiculturalism.

As a result, this book argues that Black and Blackness cannot be of univocal meaning in social relations. Rather, Black and Blackness, as creations and creative tools, are equivocal in their meaning. Often a particular meaning has more to do with the context and the nature of the social construction than with adhering to one single form or essence across all contexts. It has to do with which of the two registers is deemed most suitable for a given situation. Indeed, in determining what is meant by Black and Blackness, one first has to determine if the definition takes place within a mythological moment that is one of eternal creation, or whether the case is one where everything is reduced to a specific and finite status based on a known context. In this regard, Stuart Hall is right when he talks about the death of the essentialized Black,[35] a myth of modernity, for Black and Blackness are always equivocal in form and meaning, indeterminate, changing, and unfixed. They are always resisting the desires of modernity to impose a single and even unique meaning on Black and Blackness.

## THE MEANINGS OF BLACK AND BLACKNESS

Therefore, as I argue in this book, there can be no single and clear notion of Black or Blackness – which leaves a gaping hole in the fulfilment of the idealistic promise of Canadian multiculturalism which allows for a specific and non-contradictory Black ethnicity. Black is contradictorily what the phenomenon is and what it is becoming, all at the same time. Even if all the people considered to be Black were, contradictorily, constructed as an ethnicity, the term Black would still speak to more than ethnicity. Also denoted by the concept in a common sense way would be notions of status, culture, and the semiotics of skin colour, at a minimum.

This book argues that a novelty of multiculturalism is that it takes what historically and culturally used to be maximums in finite categories and presents them as mere minimums. Charles Taylor appears to have this in mind when he looks at multiculturalism as leading to a politics of difference based on the notion that every individual possesses dignity, an abstract minimum to being human, and the foundation of citizenship: "With the politics of equal dignity, what is established is meant to be universally the same, *an identical basket of rights and immunities.*"[36] So that in a liberal democracy that is multicultural, an individual can supposedly have the choice of starting with a minimum that is the empty content of a finite category or with a minimum that includes all that is known perceptually about the category and identity. Then he or she, as an act of Blackness and multiculturalism, can socially create himself or herself. These minimums are the givens. They are the starting positions. While they are important, they are never so essential that they are considered to include all that is necessary for being human in a particular nation-state. However, if the society is based on the ethno-racial understanding, and aims to privilege ascribed group characteristics, the same individual might find that what are presented neomythically as the minimum are, in a pragmatic sense, the maximum, and allow no room for growth. She or he might be captive of a particular group and culture and can be seen as "free" only to the extent that the group is free. This points to the limits, for example, of racialization and the privileging of ethnic differences as sites not of equality, but of social inequalities.

But among the neo-mythic minimums, in seeming contradiction to any notion of group rights, are those that present the individual, as Taylor says, as possessor of a singular, unchanging identity that can be determined only by the individual. This determination forms the basis for social recognition. It also determines the individual's dialectical other that is the universal recognition of equality where every individual, regardless of her or his identity, is equal and is to be recognized as just a copy of an ideal citizen.[37] Multiculturalism aims for the infinite of the category, placing the emphasis on the unknown, the potential, the probable, and plenitude, and even on the risky as it seeks to constantly extend borders, boundaries, and limits, as it never stops fusing and extending what is a given concept or identity. This is so, as multiculturalism supposedly never stops creation or re-creation. This is the promise for ethical relations in official multiculturalism, one of expanding necessities, and one that can be fully appreciated only through the application of a neo-mythic understanding.

Contrary to the prevailing common sense view that privileges the externalities of the ethno-racial, this book argues that Blackness, of which the somatic is merely a contingent and not a necessary feature, is the natural or pre-consciousness state of humanity. This is so even if, as Frantz Fanon suggests, "lactification" is the condition that humans are always practising. This is where, idealistically, they are trying to escape from a starting position of Blackness, and are seeking refuge in its other, an idealized Whiteness, or lactification.[38] Fanon is not wrong, for such an escape is at the heart of the mythologies that are the bones of the ideology and social consciousness that is Western civilization. Mythologically, the escape is best captured in the Biblical story of the original sin and the expulsion from the Garden of Eden, a site of freedom, of longing, and desire that is captured in the eternal notion of the return in the story of human development.[39] Fanon is merely another of the many in Western thought that sees hope as the idealized Whiteness that liberates, especially from the darkness of despair.

### BLACKNESS, MULTICULTURALISM, AND WORLD HISTORY

The third aim of this book is to account for, and to rationalize, how dialectically a country like Canada has become officially multicultural and what such recognition means in the overall scheme of world history. It argues that multiculturalism is ontological Blackness because it is a form of impurity that produces, and is produced by, creolization, syncretism, and hybridity. It is like the god that created itself out of darkness just to see what it would look like White. Indeed, the book asserts that creolization is what makes Canada truly part of the Americas. It argues that historically Canada has always been a misrecognized creolized space, similar demographically and culturally to what Braithwaite and Glissant suggest as models of creolization.[40]

The book makes two cases for this creolization. One is a cultural explanation, where this creolization is a reflection of the legacy and influence of the physical presence and the philosophies and ideologies of an African experience in the New World. With creolization a hallmark of the part of the world that is now called the Black Atlantic,[41] this region is marked by hybridization and diasporic orientation caused by the commingling of peoples and their philosophies and mythologies from around the world. This book will be looking primarily at what has resulted in the Americas where the peoples and cultures of geographic Africa and Europe have long been pitted in a dialectical struggle. This struggle resulted in a lordship and bondage relationship between those who were Europeans and idealized as White and superior, and those who were African and idealized as Black and inferior. In broaching this, we are beginning with a neo-mythic explanation for these cultures and ethical relations.

The major manifestation of this relationship, its ethno-racial manifestation, was in the institution of slavery whose influences are still most apparent in the culture, demography, and political and ethical relations in what is called the western hemisphere.[42] At one point, which, indeed, is most of its history, Canada disavowed any African influence, presence, or legacy in its body politic. It was to be the sole authentically White, aristocratic, and European nation in a hemisphere that is somatically and idealistically Black and other than European because of its creolization. To do this, Canada had to attempt the erasure of a presence of somatic Blacks from the beginning of colonization. Imaginatively, Canada was denying its neo-mythic Blackness while trying to recreate and recognize itself as ethno-racially White and ethically pure.

Since the 1960s, that position has changed, especially demographically, primarily as a result of immigration from areas of the globe that were previously presumed to be too somatically and culturally Black for Canada, places like continental Africa, and those havens of African hybridized spaces that are the Caribbean, South and Central America, and the United States of America, especially the latter's southern states. The change in position, in a symbiotic way that we will point out throughout this book, contributed to official multiculturalism, which in turn proceeded to concretize the new position as part of the prevailing ideology and mythology. Hence, the contradictions arise when some Canadians still pursue an ethno-racial understanding of Canadianness and citizenship while, at the same time, the state as a collective has supposedly moved to the neo-mythic understanding. The differences from the two registers are simply reconciled through acts of creating newness. This is where the ethno-racial and neo-mythic registers, instead of being in a seemingly dialectical relationship, are reconciled into an understanding of multiculturalism – as a site of idealized or mythic Blackness, and with the neo-mythic as the dominant register.

The second case for creolization is mythological and philosophical in terms of how we make sense of our world. Once again, creolization betrays the influence of Africa and all that was presented as Black in the dominant European thought. Creolization suggests an impurity or a fusing of limits, a crossing of boundaries and sublimation of the contingent into the everlasting and the unchangeable. This, as we shall see, is at the heart of what David Carney calls continental African metaphysics: the idea that our senses betray that ours is a single cosmos that is inhabited equally and temporally by both spirits and carnal beings.[43] Life, then, is a series of changes that ultimately starts in the spirit world or realm of thought, which then becomes immanent to the material world, and later returns again to the spirit world. This is a continuous process of creation and recreation. In the ideal and rational world, spirit has a higher ranking and dominion over the carnal. At any moment, life is a contingent embodiment of the spirit and the carnal, and as such is always impure and creolized as it is neither fully one nor the other, but rather is in the process of becoming something new. It is a composite that, at a minimum, is a dualism.

Indeed, this book argues that it is as creolization and hybridity – based on categories of knowing that I present in this text – that Canada is Black somatically, culturally, and idealistically. These are not categories of race, of ethnicity, domination, or patriarchy. Rather, these are sorts of knowing as perceived pure thought – developed epistemologically within a single consciousness as a way to capture an infinity that persistently eludes the prevailing epistemic limits. They are cognitive. They are exercises in epistemology, but are necessary for a fuller understanding of Blackness ontologically, existentially, and in ethical relations.

Conceptually, these categories speak to the notion that thought or epistemology precedes and imaginatively creates everything – ontology, existentialism, and ethical relations. They are means of positing and refutation that a thinking consciousness must find ready to hand and use dialectically to arrive at truth claims. And this is why, as we quoted Taylor earlier, our discussion starts with a recognition of the role of good, an epistemic categorization, in understanding modern identity. These categories are therefore deemed to be complete in terms of producing a specific meaning. They are necessary to account for a given epistemic claim of the knowledge and nature of what is Black and Blackness. These categories are supported by the argument that for over 3,000 years humans have claimed that they knew/know what is Black and what is White. It also suggests that they know what is good and evil. However, there has never been a single meaning, a pure epistemological category, that has withstood all contestations of what is Black and White. So how can we claim to know with certainty Black and Blackness?

## THE ETHICS OF BLACKNESS:
## LIVING IN THE PRESENT

Indeed, a focus of this book is to show how what we think we know is self-consciously White and Black and our ideas of how we should treat people with differences are epistemologically derived – they flow out of a specific morality and social consciousness. People are not naturally White or Black, do not live a White or Black existence, are not treated as White or Black because of some ontological intention by nature, but because of how they are first constructed epistemologically and then ethically as White or Black in their society. The meaning of Blackness has been equivocal, but always supposedly based on reason.

Therefore, this book sets out that the recognition of Blackness as inherent in the Canadian body politic, and as important to the realization of its future and destiny, is the fulfilment of the quest for freedom. This is a quest that the book shows epistemologically through an examination of slices of social and political thought from periods described as Greek, Christian, and African. They have all been hybridized into a single rational, transcendental ideology that underpins Western civilization. In this case, what we call Greek, Christian, and African is presumably a way of knowing in which the dominant characteristics of a period are associated hegemonically with a specific time and prevailing ethical relations. There is no assumed essence or totalization associated with these generalizations. Here is no single, uncontested view, but rather a privileged one that ends up setting the tone and spirit of the period with which it is associated.

Indeed, these views are associated with dominant thought at specific periods in human history. The thoughts, although dominant, were not exclusive to the period or uniformly accepted, but were themselves contested within the prevailing ethos. However, some thoughts came to be more dominant than others in specific periods. This book argues that this explains, because of shifts in the dominant views, why there are differences in understanding such concepts as Black, Blackness, and freedom as consistent and never changing over time. At the heart of this quest for freedom is the effort to know what is authentically Black, including Blackness in its creolized or composite – and therefore impure – forms of which Hegel speaks in the epigraph to the prologue.

## BLACKNESS: RUNNING TO WHAT WE THOUGHT WE WERE FLEEING

The fourth main aim of this book is to show that the recognition of Blackness and multiculturalism is a contingent moment in history that is at the same time the fulfilment of trends in Western thought that go back to antiquity. This recognition is also a subversion and rejection of this history and the main threads of its social and political thought, in a move akin to turning the world of meaning and understanding on its head. In this new narrative, what were formally presented as evil and slavery are now recreated and repositioned as goodness and freedom. So that while there is continuity in terms of the progressing search for freedom, there is also a revolutionary disruption in terms of how the agents of freedom are now identified, and even in terms of what colour, if any at all, is now given to and expected of them.

The contradiction has severe implications. Since for the good of nature such a carnivalesque moment, when spirit and reason do not rule and evil is masking as good, cannot last forever, the task becomes for Canadians one of how they can change a contingent moment into one of necessity. Yet, there has to be a recognition that the moments of carnival are important, for in them are the sources of creation, ingenuity, and genius, as well as the evil that could destroy the given order. They are the moments that hold the potential for shaping, transforming, and even improving existing society. Yet, such instability does not produce one of the long held goals of human society – constancy and a predictable order to life which is associated with cultural Whiteness as the good.

Such contradictions are inherent to the contingent moment that is multiculturalism, but a moment that is also necessary for Canadian renewal, rejuvenation, and cultural progress. Put another way, as an explanation of their history and a projection of how their history ought to be fulfilled, a task for Canadians is to show how multiculturalism and the uplifting and incorporation of Blacks and Blackness were always intentionally part of the national agenda, even if these intentions had remained hidden for most of the country's history. Another task is to show how any irruption in the old thinking is compatible with the goals of producing a society that is stable, progressive, and just. Indeed, here we are reaching for an ecstatic moment in multiculturalism as Blackness.

This is the idealism that is to be found phenomenologically in multiculturalism as hope: the belief that human beings can always build a better world. And it is for this reason that in examining as if they were physical bodies the consciousnesses that are Black and Blackness we are likely to be involved in an exercise that results in idealistic findings. These results are associated with the hope for freedom as a way of overcoming a Hegelian unhappy consciousness that is usually associated with the contradictions that are so much part of the multicultural lived experience. Idealism is the hope that, in the absence of clear epistemological knowing, that there could be life after death; it is the hope that comes with ethical leaps of faith in dealing with people who are generally positioned as strangers and with unknown qualities.

## BLACKNESS: JOUISSANCE AND THE ETERNAL ACT OF CREATION

When these four particular aims of this book are put together, they create a universal story of how Canada has become Black epistemologically, ontologically, existentially, and Black also in terms of the ethical relations Canadians have with one another and with the wider world – and of how the medium for this Blackness is multiculturalism. As an act of eternal creation, as Northrop Frye suggests,[44] multicultural Canada is constantly returning to the primordial site of creativity, indeterminacy, undifferentiation and beginnings, into a Blackness that is a self-consciousness thinking in the darkness how it can become free and yet take a determinate form.

Contradictorily, multiculturalism is Blackness in the sense that it disrupts the prevailing narrative of Western thought and because it calls for a clear break with the past – a break that is a rupture that is revolutionary enough to amount to a disavowal of the historic claim that Canada was ever a White man's country. In this regard, this book argues that in today's setting, Blackness and multiculturalism in Canada stem from the same root causes. They are an attempt to correct the wrongs of a history that has always presented justice, nation-state formation, and citizenship as exclusionary acts to Blackness.

Blackness and multiculturalism in Canada are now officially acts of inclusion, and this is what makes the discourse in Canada on these two topics radically different, and even exciting, for it offers new potentials for social ordering, socialization, and individual and group actualization. Multiculturalism is a return to the freedom that is Blackness, to a pre-consciousness that is the eternal moment of creation, indeterminacy, and the carnivalesque – this is a moment when the order is always being recreated out of a seemingly endless array of opportunities and possibilities. This is a time when every citizen is the embodiment of Spirit, but, just as importantly, when no individual or group can exclusively be the spirit of the nation, as this spirit cannot be contained and embodied in any way and still be free. It is the moment when the spirit that is citizenship cannot be concretized but can only be discussed in the abstract sense where active and full citizenship is situated in the Blackness and indeterminacy of rights and fundamental privileges, when identity is acknowledged as consisting of a contingent component that is perishable and changeable, but also of a necessary and unchangeable element that at best is merely a universal abstraction. But because it is a return in time, as we showed in the prologue, it is to a higher order, one that is now based on real experiences and knowledge – so that the freedoms and primordiality of the return are not the same as at the departure. There are, indeed, benefits and lessons to be learned from history.

In this regard, multiculturalism is anti-modern or, indeed, post-modern, to the extent that it is a return to the universal by including all in a specific body, instead of the modernist push to exclude, to separate, to limit and place boundaries around, and to know primarily according to atomistic and individual particulars. Therefore, differences are not indications of separateness, but of inclusiveness, for the emphasis is on seeing the forest and not just separate trees. Blackness is the prioritizing of meta-narratives, and the notion that there is always the possibility that we do not yet exist in a just society. Even in one that calls itself a Just Society, there is always at least one group to take us back to a pre-consciousness before there is justice. In this narrative, apart from the First Nations Peoples, this group is, ironically, somatically Black in the Canadian context. For them, as for the aboriginals who are idealistically Black as well, there will always be a need to create a just society, for justice itself must always be raised to a higher consciousness than what exists at any given moment The story about Black and Blackness is ultimately a narrative of modernity acting out of knowledge of history – a way of knowing that should now be based on cognition instead of untested perception. It is in this way that we may discern who should be included in the modern state whose purpose is justice.[45]

# 2

# Blackness: Method, Differences, Perspective

In moving in the four directions outlined in the previous chapter, this book really attempts two goals: (1) a phenomenological study of Blackness, and (2) an explanation of the existentialism of contingent Blackness. The first would be a re-examination or re-evaluation of the "given" when we think of Black and Blackness, that is, of the norm and common sense attributes. The latter yields intertwined rationalizations of how Blackness exists as multiculturalism, but also of how, as a specific ethno-racial category called Black, Blackness exists within a multiculturalism that is perceived neo-mythically as ideal Whiteness, that is, as perfection itself. Given this Blackness within Blackness, and this Blackness within Whiteness, we do well to bear in mind the epigraph to the prologue. It comes from Hegel, whose method we shall borrow for our phenomenology, and is part of his explanation for how apparent truths can become occluded and darkened through common sense usage or when we rely solely on the knowledge gained through our five senses.

There are two main parts to this book, and four sections – three in the first part, and one in the last. The first part, a phenomenology, provides a philosophical explanation of Blackness and multiculturalism. While no meaning is everlasting – whether as a generality or universal on the one hand, or as a particular on the other – the development of Western civilization, as part one will show, has been a conceptual struggle for freedom out of knowing good and evil as unchangeable concepts.

In this part, I argue that civil societies in the Western tradition have been constructed on knowing what is good and on separating good from evil so that the good can be preserved, protected, and carried forward from one generation to the next. The main task of this philosophy has always been how to recognize the good, and how to do so with absolute certainty. In this regard, Western philosophy and mythology always argued that good was knowable, for it was the unchangeable, the same yesterday, today, and tomorrow. In this tradition, it was Blackness that was changeable, for the philosophy contained the notion that through a miracle evil can be contained, banished, or controlled, or transformed into its opposite, goodness and Whiteness. In other words, according to this thinking, out of the indeterminacy of Blackness, change can occur, producing other forms, of which ultimately the essential, irreducible, and unchangeable product of change would be Whiteness and good.

The quest for freedom, this book argues, is really a dialectical struggle between these notions of the changeable and the unchangeable, and of knowing which is which. I argue that eventually, in all matters of ethnicity and race – in a move crystallized in modernity – good came to be associated unchangeably and semiotically with the colour White, and evil with the colour Black. But, in contradiction to this clear separation, according to the same sensibility Black was also deemed as the changeable, as that which can be made into good.[1] Thus, having become, philosophically, a site for freedom, with freedom presented as Whiteness in the ideal, the modern state was nonetheless based on a notion of White and Whiteness that was changeable and equivocal. Such a notion leaves us with a series of important questions. How can we explain such changes that can occur in idealized Whiteness and Blackness? How can there be lasting and certain social relations based on knowing what is good and evil, when the very notions of what is good and evil are never the same from period to period? In this regard, how can the nation-state be unchangeable and perpetual when the very basis on which it is constructed is never stable and changeless?

There is a misunderstanding over what this book shows is now the latest moment in modernity in Western Civilization, multicultural Canada. This is the same ontological being that is struggling for official recognition in most of Europe, Africa, and Asia. What is happening in the European theatre is of utmost importance for it must be made to reconcile with a history that projects Western Europe as the natural home for liberalism and democracy and the unity of the sovereign nation-state. But what is happening in most of Western Europe is technically more a question of developing a peculiar brand of pluralism – where there is a core in these societies of what is deemed to be European or authentically national – and not genuine multiculturalism. In the latter case, there is no unchangeable core that has a position of privilege, dominance, or historic right. Genuine multiculturalism, unlike this brand of pluralism in European and even the United States, is based on radical equality and democracy where every individual and group operates in the public sphere as if having no history or national authenticity but only a present and a future based on questionable filiality and mongrelization. Those in Canada and elsewhere are the latest manifestations of the quest for freedom. Simply put, the quest takes different forms in different times. Greek, Hebrew, various African, as well as Christian mythologies that expressed the syncretism of a dominant view in a particular time have, at various times, contributed to the current consciousness that is Western Civilization. At different times they were the manifestation or concretization, the epitome, of the quest for freedom. However, at no time were they the exclusive manifestations, even though they might have been the dominant ones for our rhetorical purposes.

Dialectically, each new consciousness simply incorporated the previous manifestation conceptually, so that epistemologically very little is ever lost to history. What disappears from view stays on in memory. We are always learning even as the situation and times change. Within what was viewed in a generalized way as unchangeable there was, contradictorily, immanent change. Then on closer examination, we noticed that contained in what was deemed to be the particular that is changeable in the overall generality or universalism was something that was, contradictorily as well, unchangeable conceptually. More questions thus arise. How can we know when either the universal or particular should be treated as changeable or as unchangeable? And without this knowledge, how can we construct lasting and socially just ethical relations?

The second part of the book, as a study in the existentialism of Blackness, provides a socio-philosophical look at how ideas or ideals of Blackness have informed the construction of Western society in general, and Canadian society in particular. This is where we examine what has become of efforts to transfer a way of thinking from the internal neo-mythic register to the external and materialist ethno-racial register. Is it possible to use an ethno-racial register to fully capture what has been given to us neo-mythically as we try to colonize the space that is our past, present, and future?

This part of the book shows how notions of Whiteness as freedom led to ethical relations being based for the most part on ethno-racial assumptions, and how these relations, as political and social acts of inclusion and exclusion, resulted in Blackness coming to be associated with slavery and exclusion. Here, I will respond to the essential question of why a contingent group of people from many different backgrounds, cultures, ethnicities, nationality, all deemed to be changeable attributes – but all sharing one common characteristic, the seeming unchanged characteristic in all of them – come to be identified as Black in a multicultural or cosmopolitan setting.

That common characteristic is the colour of their skin, and as I stated earlier its meaning is semiotically ethno-racial. But is colour of the skin the only, and even the main attribute or quality of what it means to be Black in a multicultural setting? The answer to this question has enormous implications for a society's overall ethical relationship at the nation or state levels. The questions it raises are many. The answers have implications for behaviour and the commitment to living with others in a society that is just. In the Canadian context, for example, this thinking would influence fellow Canadians whose main difference might be that they have a different complexion, and may even influence those with the same complexion. There are implications for the question of how we can know who is truly Canadian, especially when it is considered that historically the unchangeable essence in the Canadian national identity was Whiteness. Has what was perceived as an unchangeable essence changed to now include Blackness, or does this mean that a group socially constructed as Blacks can never become fully Canadian no matter how socially and politically active they may become? Indeed, what are the changeable and unchangeable in the Canadian identity? Is there anything contingent, as opposed to essential and necessary, for identities that are Black and Canadian, and possibly in a way that does not make Black and Canadian mutually exclusive? Overall, then, this book seeks to explain why the importance is placed on somatic features at a moment of supposed enlightenment in Western thought, a moment when all humans are presumably equal, regardless of skin colour.

To these ends, the second part will show that multiculturalism is the latest development in a historic search for freedom, and that this is what Blackness is about in its most recent manifestation. In this way, it will strive for two departures from the current discourse. First, it will show how, as the latest manifestation of our knowledge of Blackness, multiculturalism, with all its shades of skin colours, is a site that contradictorily presents itself as idealized Whiteness, and that it extends the discussion of how what was once presented idealistically as evil and Black is now incarnated in the body politic as good at the neo-mythic level.

Second, this argument departs from, or extends radically, the prevailing thought on ethno-racial Blackness. To this end, this part will be in profound disagreement with much of the prevailing discussion on Blackness, including discussions by some self-identifying Black academics whose acceptance of this label is based solely on somatic features. This disagreement will be on the grounds that most of the current discussion on Blackness within a humanizing project limits the potential and opportunities of those constructed as Black. This is so because the discussion sees the colour of the skin and race as the unchangeable and necessary component of Blacks and Blackness. As an unchanging ontology, race based on skin colour is presented as in the main determining of a Black existentialism, ethical relations, and a Black epistemology.

One of the keys to understanding this book and its four sections is having a sound appreciation for its methodology. In chapter 3, there is therefore a careful explanation of phenomenology and its importance to a critical discourse on Blackness. In this chapter, I also explain Hegelian phenomenology as a unique branch of this philosophical and social science and why the

Hegelian approach is useful for explaining the development of knowledge, ideologies, cultures, and social consciousnesses at specific historical moments.[2] Let us now turn to the sections.

Section I: The first section, consisting of chapters 1 to 4, is an attempt to ground our discussion in the real or lived world as a discussion based in our existence and on our understanding of Blackness. This section explains the significance to an overall understanding of the world of knowing who or what Black and Blackness are at the beginning of the twenty-first century in the Americas in general, and in officially multicultural Canada in particular. In this section, clear distinctions will be made between Whiteness and Blackness as phenomena.

Section II: Here, I will show why a Hegelian phenomenology – one in which the neo-mythic register is emphasised – is necessary to a work that is critical of Blackness and multiculturalism and which speaks to a multi-disciplinary audience. This, in turn, calls for a fuller discussion of the application of phenomenology as a search for fundamental, foundational truths, so that we can explain historical and social developments as social constructs in the life of a people, state, or country. We start, therefore, with an exercise of seeking our answers at the level of the ethno-racial, and follow until the search begins to turn back on itself, and leaves us with many known contradictions that we have not resolved. At this point, we then move to the neo-mythic level to see how many contradictions it can reconcile for us, all the while bearing in mind that it is virtually impossible to collapse one way of knowing entirely into the other. They are syncretic complements of understanding and are often placed in a dialectical relationship.

It is critical to understand that the operative word here is *search*: This does not mean that we will find a specific essence, natural law, force, or any form of totalization. However, the search is part of the refutation method of the social sciences. It allows us to test given hypothesis – such as the suggestion that there is something unchangeable that makes Black and Blackness unique and that determines forever what is good and evil. The search is necessary, even if our aim is to scientifically and systematically negate and even refute such expectations and thinking.

Through this refutation we can get a clear view of the contradictions within a given concept and come to know what it might take to bring about an idealistic reconciliation of these contradictions for a single and common meaning. These steps in our method are important, for the unfurling of the book is contingent on understanding the importance and relevance of the methodology applied. Section II also provides the rationale for having categories of knowledge for Blackness – categories that I will present as somatic, cultural, status related, and idealistic.

Section III: This section discusses the historical triumph of Blackness in an idealized form in the Americas. The context for this discussion is what are perceived as the Black-and-White existentialist twins of modernity – the United States of America and Canada. Here our discussion is about how mythological, philosophical, and even theological notions of Blackness and Whiteness were transformed in sociological relations within the state and into anthropological norms of culture and belonging within a specific group that is a subset of a wider humanity.

Effectively, somatic Blackness is emphasized here so that we can have a better understanding of relationships among nations in what is perceived as the Western ethos, and of relations within a specific culture that is territorialized by modernity's highest ideal, the nation-state. This section starts with an absolute-knowledge discussion of the U.S.A. as Black in an idealized, somatic, and cultural way, but White in status – as evidenced by the White bolts of its military power as the world's sole superpower and with, arguably, the most advanced standards of living. This is Whiteness that has been captured mythologically as the effort to grasp the magic that turns evil into good, Blackness into Whiteness, and allows humans to be separated out of their natural condition of backwardness and darkness into states of progress and advancement.

The section ends with a look at how, historically, Canada became Black idealistically, culturally, somatically, and in status. Here we will examine how the metaphors of Blackness are useful to an explanation of the dialectical development of ideals in Canadian culture. More particularly, we will be looking at the ideal of multiculturalism in the context of a multiracial population and Canada's Free Trade Agreement with the United States. We will also examine the gesturing to Blackness by the Canadian elite that occurred when Canada officially took its full place as a member of the Americas, a region that in Canadian mythology has been presented traditionally as a Black neighbourhood in which Canada was ontologically the sole White house and, thus, an outsider.

Section IV: This section discusses the ethics that are inherent in the dialectics now at work as Canada seeks to fully recognize Blackness. In this discussion, many of the leading theorists on multiculturalism, race, and ethnicity are engaged and their ideas are contested. In this respect, I argue that most critics of multiculturalism have overlooked what is most important to the concept: idealism and hope. This section also includes a discussion of immigration's role in making Canada even more multicultural, creolized, and Black – instead of the White nation that was first envisioned – and the implications for Canada. Here the immigrant is presented as the symbol of hope from the gaze of both subject and object, and as a symbol for the need to take epistemological leaps of faith into the darkness of the unknown. As such, this section deals with multiculturalism as idealized Blackness brought into existence.

This section ends with an examination of the challenge for somatic Blacks to fulfil the promise of multiculturalism: to be transformed into the full Whiteness of citizenship and belonging, or, as Fanon suggested, to become idealized White. Specifically, this is a promise that they can be transfigured, in a more receptive, ethical space, into idealized Whiteness as citizens fully participating in Canada. Even though they are Black in skin colour and even culture, they can become idealistically White through universal human rights that create them fully as abstract Canadians and thus enable them to aspire to elite statuses in Canada. Whiteness, in this instance, can be conjured out of Blackness. This is an odyssey that is true also for so much of humanity that is now considered somatically White but who, like somatic Blacks, are idealistically Black in terms of Canadian citizenship and belonging.

Here, I will look specifically at the Caribbean immigrant in Canada. The discussion at the end of this section will be centred on the socially constructed Black female who is making strides economically in becoming part of the Canadian mainstream – in becoming idealistically White – and is raising the fear of leaving the Black male behind as a social outsider who, in his idealized Blackness, cannot easily be recreated as a new Canadian. This section also looks at multiculturalism as it exists as being idealized Blackness for those who are somatically and often culturally Black because of their somatic features.

Throughout the discussion, there will be one ever-present spectre or shadow: one raised by Hegel. I have mentioned him briefly and have made note of the epigraph that I suggest should guide us throughout the book. A bit more should be said of him now. The Hegelian method of accounting for identity formation and the acquisition of knowledge, which I will explain at greater length in chapter 3, is historical as it accounts for specific developments in history. I therefore situate specific developments that add to knowledge as memory in a specific place and time and in a way that prevents this discussion, and the book, from becoming trans-historical. What is somewhat trans-historical in this book, however, and which I describe in a Hegelian way as a core concern for all humanity, is the search for freedom.

## CLAIMS OF DIFFERENCE

What, then, are the major claims of this book? One of them must be stated forcefully and clearly: This book is different from the existing literature because it is not solely a study or phenomenology of race. Neither is it a study or phenomenology solely of ethnicity. Rather, and importantly, it is a study or phenomenology of Blackness. Here the phenomena are Black and

Blackness: these are consciousnesses that might become embodied and inscribed on some human bodies, but they are also wonders in their own right.

Black and Blackness are thus presented as things that can be examined separately and distinctly from an examination of a human body. Black and Blackness are their own entity. As a result, this book, while a discussion on race and ethnicity, is also more than these discourses. For Black and Blackness are more than just race and/or ethnicity. There is much more hidden in the body and in the concept. It is close to what Theo Goldberg identifies as *ethnorace*, but which he does not give a full ontological development.

Indeed, this book is still more than what has just been said for it also tries to answer the question of what we mean by the term Black in a multicultural country that is a liberal democracy. What do we know of what it means to be Black in a country where race and ethnicity are supposedly contingent and even extraneous characteristics?

This point is crucial, for, as in most discourses on the subject, it is easy to conflate race and ethnicity with Blackness or to reduce Blacks and Blackness to either or both concepts. The novelty of my position is the argument that multicultural Canada, by having a category of full citizens that are Black, by having a society based on rights, and not colour of skin or culture, provides, for the first time in modernity, an opportunity to discuss what is Black and Blackness metaphorically, thus outside of simply a racial or ethnic discourse. Blackness and Black are not just about the sociological and anthropological understandings of relations within a nation and culture. They go further, enabling us to look at how they inform through mythology, philosophy, and religion what is necessary for a good and wholesome state and culture.

Another significant point that this book is making is as follows: Canada is at a unique juncture in history in the ongoing development of Western thought. In the past, Blackness was presented as a reason or justification for exclusion from the state or nation. In making a radical departure, Canada says that Blackness is a reason and justification for *inclusion* in the nation state. Second, in the past, Blackness was presented as an argument to discern who should be dominated, who should be ranked as inferior. Again, Canada breaks new ground by arguing that Blackness is a signifier, not of subjection or inferiority, not even of superiority and inferiority, but of equality. Significantly, Canada seeks to break the bind of determining what is really idealized Blackness and Whiteness by arguing that, essentially and contradictorily, they are the same. Ideal citizenship is contingent on the possession of a body of abstract rights, which means there is no official recognition of culture, semiotic, or status purity. There is only the purity of humanity and the minimums that it takes to be human and Canadian – of being as idealistically Black as humanity but also as idealistically or normatively White as Canada in its mythology. In this regard, while Black and Blackness may be seen as "natural," White and Whiteness – like societies – are human constructions, based on the human imagination, and are social rather than natural phenomena.

The novelty of my argument is that at this point in time, idealistically in the philosophical sense or normatively in the sociological, Blackness and Whiteness have little to do ethically with the colour of the skin, and more with the "rights and privileges" of individuals who in their performances and behaviours are either good citizens or not. Blackness and Whiteness are thus ethical markers. They are not mere epistemological or ontological markers based solely on what is naturally good or evil and on the somatic or cultural. The good and evil on which they are based are, therefore, socially constructed – making Whiteness and Blackness ethical undertakings as well, but in a way that excludes skin colour, place of birth, culture, language, gender, sexuality, and so on, as primary construction materials. This realization flows from the idea in multiculturalism that contingent identities are not important to an individual or group, but that the abstract unchangeable rights are what make individuals both human and citizens within a space called Canada. Theoretically, skin colour does not matter, and where it does this is supposed to be an aberration limited to those who choose subjectively to so identify.

Most theorists treat Blacks and Blackness as race and/or ethnicity. I make the point that this is a study of Blackness in its infinity, neither solely of race nor ethnicity, but inclusive of them, and offering more. It is for this reason that our study ends up utopian, idealistic, and transcendental. Blackness, Black, and multiculturalism can only have full meaning as clear realities and univocal forms in the transcendent. In the lived world, they will have any number of forms and realities as the senses can produce.

As a result, the book argues that, in terms of ethical relations, Blackness is grounded in the mythology of freedom. That is why it is important to emphasize the primacy of the ethical relations founded on freedom in determining how humans treat one another the world over. The ways humans treat one another reflect forms of awareness. They are succeeding consciousnesses, each appearing in a different moment in time, each proclaiming that it finally knows what is Black and what is White. Each claiming that it now knows definitively what is freedom: that it has corrected all past errors of misperception and false consciousnesses. In this regard, this book suggests that Blackness in multicultural Canada starts idealistically and normatively from the position that to be Black is to be also fully human and a citizen, that it is not merely the projection of inferiority onto a specific group of people.

This is a book that both extends and challenges much of the writing by "Black" academics. The book argues that some "Black" academics tend to define Blackness too narrowly – as solely somatic and phenotypic. Missing is the mythological, philosophical, and theological knowledge that adds so much and provides a more rounded picture of Blackness and what it means to be subjectively and objectively Black. In leaving out this knowledge, they are merely reflecting the dominant "White" view and internalizing projected inferiority. When they do this, they limit much that is free and philosophically good about Blackness, such as its creativity, its disruptiveness, its spontaneity, and its genius – features that are common to all humans. In this regard, the book argues that all humanity is Black when viewed from this perspective of full self-determination and a holistic humanity that is essentially equal.

This book also stakes out new ground by defining multiculturalism in Canada as the struggle to bring a group of people traditionally positioned as racially and ethnically Black into the idealized Whiteness of full citizenship. In so doing, members of the group would still lay claim to their idealistic and metaphoric Blackness, which is not the racialized fixed position traditionally projected on them, but an identity that allows them to fully claim all that is human, as well as citizenship in a multicultural space.

Finally, in many respects this is a book of hope for a multicultural Canada. The beauty and novelty of understanding Blackness and multiculturalism as Blackness in Canada are recognition that ethical relations are idealistically founded on "actions." They are culturally embedded performances that are relevant to the moments in which decisions on freedom and morality are made, rather than being actions based on a priori expectations. Whiteness and Blackness are now idealistically determined within a specific culture, rather than predating the culture and being outside of history. Individuals are finally fully free when their rational actions, as acts of morality, make them free in a wider ethical sense. They create their freedom and themselves as free men and women within the state of their choice.

## INTERDISCIPLINARY APPROACH, MULTIDISCIPLINARY AUDIENCE

This book is intended for readers who want to critically engage the construction of society, the ranking and positioning of individuals and groups in society. It is a book which emphasizes discussing and understanding ideas that we take for granted as being grounded in our common sense understanding of the world and its different epistemological categories that are the corner stone of most empiricist research. The concepts that are discussed must be understood before they can be used for the collection of data. Otherwise, they are empty signifiers. To this end, while there will be adequate discussion of empiricist findings, and mainly in the final section, such findings per se or the contesting and validating of them are not the primary focus of the book. This book is intended for those who, in the main, are concerned with ideas, concepts, and meaning in a universal sense, and less so for those who are looking for empirical works that provide the scientific concretization of society.

If only to control the book's length, the footnotes to the chapters contain information that is important to the discussion. They try to deal as briefly as possible with meaningful topics that either cannot be developed fully in a book that is perhaps already too long, or without impeding the flow of the argument by following every possible strand of thought. To reduce the length of this work and still do the subject justice would be an unlikely if dubious achievement, especially in a study that seeks to break new ground in the interdisciplinary study of Blackness. There being a constant need to anticipate challenges from readers who might find the topic and the approach different from what went before, more explanations are required than might otherwise have been the case.

The intended audience is multidisciplinary. An interdisciplinary phenomenological approach is used since the objectives set for this book imply beginning our search for knowledge in the real or material world that is not neatly partitioned into disciplines. However, this does not mean that, in searching for a reconciliation of lived contradictions, that we will not end up in a utopian moment that is multiculturalism and idealistic Blackness. Indeed, this is exactly where we will end up. We must. This utopian moment is a site of hope, freedom, and creativity, and these are the values that have helped humans to survive and to aspire to a time when they would be freed of the social injustices and inequalities that are now part of the every day experience or the prevailing human condition. In this regard, one discipline complements another and informs the collective consciousness. To this end, the book is philosophical in the traditional sense of philosophy as an exercise in knowing for the love of knowledge.

Ultimately, this is a study of how a new multicultural Canada came into consciousness as idealistically, culturally, and even somatically Black. In this regard, it is a story of how, ironically, the aims of modernity – to produce a culturally, idealistically, and somatically White country – were thwarted, and how, instead of Canada becoming ethically and neo-mythically White, it is now Black on all registers of meaning.

Let us now travel down the path of what common sense tells us is Black and Blackness. Out of this discussion, we will develop our first task: the need for clear categories of meaning that also capture, as completely as possible, how the concepts Black and Blackness developed and changed in the mind of the consciousness that is Western thought.

# 3

# Meaning, Understanding, and Knowing

And thus it is of all other species of things, which have no other essences but those ideas which are in the minds of men.[1]

## BLACK AND BLACKNESS: IN THE BEGINNING AND ENDING

In the following, I am going to try to give myself intellectual distance from the phenomena that are myself and the world. I want to take the position that as a consciousness I can step out of myself – and acting as a split but rational personality, can leave behind the physical body that has semiotic meaning only within current social interpretation. Intellectually, and constructed as what might be no more than an ego, I want to arrive at a special vantage position from which, through a neo-mythic lens, I can examine my own ethno-racial history and my strategic positioning across time. I want to achieve this distancing in a way that gives me understanding of myself currently in the wider context of the world around me, a world or existence within which I am concretely both a being that is finite and separate from all others.

In this way of thinking, my body is not the totality of my being or consciousness, and neither is my mind or spirit – my intellectual faculties that allow me to abstract and theorize about myself and the world. Through such a move, I want to see myself purely as thought, as an abstraction, as an entity with a particular knowledge of its past and hopes and plans for a future of freedom. What I deem to be rational is based on the totality of the experiences and rationalization, on the rules and regulations, expectations and fears that make up my history and culture as a unique consciousness. Any differences that I detect should be explained according to this rationalization; otherwise they are meaningless and are absurdities that cannot be accounted for within the consciousness's way of rationalizing. At the same time, I am attempting to recognize myself as a consciousness that is situated in a world or universal that consists of objects in time and space as entities, and as free to reflect on myself and the world in general, but, in the method of this reflecting and reasoning, dependent on what may be termed my cultural biases and expectations. As a self-consciousness that is moral and ethical, I am aware of myself experiencing the world as an external space and of having different opinions and perspectives of the world at different times – and in the process coming over time to internally know myself and the world in this idealistic, transcendental way. In most cases, even though these biases and expectations may come to me as givens from my culture, almost as if they were acts of faith and, therefore, of a high morality and meaning, I like to believe that they are culturally free of taint and that they spring immediately from within me – that as an active and free agent, I can not only think outside of my culture and social construction, but that I can be critical of them – and myself – as well.

In this respect, I want to consider this existence as part of an enclosed system or order, with its own internal dynamics and meanings. The order has a structure, based on its own reason and rationality, from which I am now trying to extricate myself so that for the purpose of this study I can try to position myself as separate and apart from it. In the language of phenomenology I can separate myself as an entity, as that which I consider to be natural and even unchanging, and "bracket" or set aside what might be considered as my social attributes.

Some may say I am simply attempting to withdraw deeper within myself, into my own time. Others may say I am merely attempting the impossible: that any knowledge of myself and of the world would be no more that getting to know a world in which I am, inescapably, embedded as a concrete self. This is the argument of those who say with justification that human beings – indeed, the world, itself, cannot be fully reduced to mere abstractions. It is also the argument of those who claim that meaningfulness for this external world can only be a projection from within me. Yet, I believe that the effort at distancing through thought should be made, for the attempt should be good for a rational understanding that is not based merely on social contexts. Citizenship in a liberal democracy like Canada is based on abstract individuals living as a society or consciousness. If I am an abstraction, then who am I and who is this Canadian that expresses itself as a separate and infinite me? At the same time, Canada in its concreteness is officially multicultural. If I am part of a consciousness that is also concretely Black or Blackness, then, socially, who am I multiculturally? Are the concrete and abstract beings the same, equal, or does one have a privileged meaning and, therefore, existence for me in my totality as a being who is Canadian? In presenting itself as a united and single consciousness, Canada is undoubtedly an exercise in idealism – especially in creating imagined unities between objects and thoughts with specific meaning from either the ethno-racial or neo-mythic registers. As a concrete individual who claims to be at the same time Black and Canadian, and as fully a citizen in a multicultural Canada, I am testing myself as proof of the idealism on which Canada is based. Methodologically, how do I bring together these two strands of meaning and acquiring knowledge in a way that would make me a happy Canadian, or as I call it, a happy consciousness that is neo-mythically Canadian and ethno-racially Black, or even an ethno-racial Canadian and neo-mythic Black? Understanding will be based on the assumptions I bring to the process.

To this end, I want to believe and act as if, as Hegel would suggest, I was seeing the world for the first time, and that, with no prior thoughts on which to shift this knowledge, I am responding to an objective world that includes me. This is a world in which I must rely on my senses to make it known to me subjectively. In this manner, I am taking the world as it comes to me immediately, without mediation whether cultural or otherwise. Without, importantly, the benefit neo-mythically of anything that I know to be good or evil – so that my moral judgment is suspended, if possible. I am starting with a knowledge that is analytic – taken from the common sense of a particular space and time that is this system unto itself. I hope to then proceed to a knowledge that is higher, to a synthetic understanding, and even to a transcendental knowing where everything in the externality of space and the internality of time is reconciled. This is where my sensible way of knowing and my knowing from intuition are united into a specific meaning of myself and the world around me.

So the senses tell me that there are such things in my world that are positively called Canadian, White, Black, and that a spirit of multiculturalism exists as a desire for a specific ethical order that is uniquely Canadian. There are also such concepts as citizenship, fairness, justice, rights, and equality, to name a few, but since these are values, they are not my primary concerns. Indeed, experience suggests that if there are Canadians there are also non-Canadians; if there is not White, there is Black, and if not Black, then White; and if there is not multiculturalism, then there is some form of social integration without the same emphasis on pluralism and justice. These are all picked up by experience as the negatives to the positives of life.

Similarly, there are such negatives as non-citizen, unfairness, non-rights, and even inequalities. Both the positives and negatives come clothed in their supposed truths and universal meanings. Yet, they are supposed to have distinct and specific meanings as well. These are states of existence and being that I must understand. And, just as importantly from an ethical perspective, I must see in a final moment of understanding if there is any connection between them. This understanding of the relationship is the source of my expectations for a relationship that I may judge as ethical. This is where what I learn on the ethno-racial register will inform my actions as prescribed by the neo-mythic register. Here, I turn to Hegel in the *Science of Logic* to set up the situation for me: "Further, in the beginning, being and nothing are present as *distinguished* from each other; for the beginning points to something else – it is a non-being which carries a reference to being as to an other; that which begins, as yet is not, it is only on the way to being. The being contained in the beginning is, therefore a being which removes itself from non-being or sublates it as something opposed to it.

"But again, that which begins already *is,* but equally, too, *is not* as yet. The opposites, being and non-being are therefore directly united in it, or, otherwise expressed, it is their *undifferentiated unity.*"²

In this and the following chapter, I shall show how knowledge of Blackness and Whiteness are given to us and that even our common sense understanding of what Black and White are must start with "given" concepts that come out of our mythologies, culture, and dominant ideology. I shall now trace how this way of knowing Blackness as a consciousness that is recognized as Black must go through three distinct stages in coming to fully know itself. The first may be seen as a mere consciousness produced by sense-certainty. This is when knowledge is supposedly based on the senses and common sense. Then it becomes reflective. This second stage is where it has certain knowledge of the self in the world and uses this knowledge as it tries to makes sense of the world. Third, it grows into reasoning. Here the self-consciousness explains the way the world is and its position in the world – but this time from a position of supposedly knowing everything about itself with absolute certainty. In the next chapter, I shall show how common sense offers us very little certainty in understanding what is Black and Blackness, and instead drowns us in contradictions.

### REASONING WITHIN REASON: WHY UNDERTAKE THE STUDY

Accepting the above, I therefore want to be a consciousness that goes through three main phases of growth and thought: stages of consciousness, self-consciousness and, ultimately, reason – the latter is where I even present myself as the quintessential Canadian, one who knows with what may be termed absolute certainty in the Hegelian sense what it means to be Canadian, Black, and multicultural at this moment in Canadian history. Actually, it is in the reflection and reasoning that I can come to know myself as part of the Canadian consciousness.

Phenomenologically, I want to begin with an examination of a socially constructed Black body to find out, not if there is an essence of the body, but of its quality – Blackness. In all its many permutations and determinations throughout history, has what we may call the Canadian consciousness or what it means to be Canadian consistently shown up as Black, particularly in this moment of official multiculturalism? In searching for this essence, I will be searching here and throughout the book for what Kolb reports Hegel as calling an inner foundation for an outer manifestation: "The immediate being of things is thus conceived under the image of a rind or curtain behind which the essence lies hidden ... There is therefore something more to be done than merely rove from one quality to another, and merely advance from the qualitative to the quantitative, and vice versa; there is something permanent in things, and permanent is in the first instance their essence."[3] In this case, this essence is my own Blackness over which I supposedly have subjectivity and agency.

More than that, I will be operating under the claim that I can be objective, both in the sense of viewing my self and its Blackness as ethno-racial objects, just like any other object in the world, and in the second case in the desire to do these examinations systematically. In the latter case, I am going to eliminate or reduce emotions, prejudices, and any received learning that are ways of knowing which do not stem directly from my personal experiences gained through my examination of my self and its Blackness.

With this in mind, and as I have indicated, I will be making the assumption that we live in a rational system – or one that tries to be rational. Indeed, with its level of rationality having evolved over time, this system has attained the highest level of rationality that has ever been. This rationality, as I will argue in this book, is a consciousness of ourselves as these beings who think they are idealistically White.

This analysis that I am offering is based on a specific approach to explaining history – on the acknowledgement that the world as it exists is rational, the product of a connected series of efforts to produce a specific social order based on rational thought. This is the notion that our rational system or social order has its own internal logic of development, and that this logic can be examined in such a way that we can trace a series of important developments and come to understand the formation of this consciousness, which is really ourselves at the latest point in human development. This tracing can be carried out by looking at what happened in specific moments. These moments are like eras, coming with their own philosophy, approaches, and social engineering. In this sense, then, some developments are necessary for the explanation of how this rationality was achieved and is being preserved, while other developments are merely contingent – almost the equivalent of happenstance in the lifespan of this rationality. Tracing these necessary and rational moments allows us to follow how the spirit or consciousness developed over time. We can also glean which specific forms it took, which ones it abandoned, and what from any period the consciousness deemed important enough to bring forward from that moment to the next.

Two points are worth noting. The first is that under this internal logic, all historical developments are not equally important. Some are deemed to be *necessary* or more important to the understanding of this consciousness. They are absolutely essential for understanding the historical development of this rationality. The other point is that some developments are merely contingent or secondary at best. We may recognize these contingent moments in the overall development of the "world history."[4] Contingent events, developments, and even personalities are not deemed as important to the explanation of the final forms taken by the consciousness, and hence rationally. Of course, there is always the likelihood that what I might perceive initially as a necessary moment might turn out to be merely contingent when tested against the system's own internal logic. Similarly, what might have been taken to be merely contingent might, on later examination, prove to be very necessary to understanding this narrative of development and consciousness formation. Indeed, one of the major claims of this book is that the Blackness that Western thought has always deemed to be contingent to its becoming idealistically White does not stand up to its own logic – for the consciousness has never been able to escape from its natural Blackness. Rather than being a contingency, Blackness is the necessity or essence, as such, of this consciousness.

Primarily, and in the final rational stage of the three stages mentioned earlier – the first two being consciousness and self-consciousness – what I am going to rely on is the total amount of knowledge that I have acquired over my life, a knowledge that I will now use in this journey to look out on my environment and myself and to discern what kind of narrative there might be to my life. In doing this, I am setting myself up as that pure ego that has a body that is Black, and an ego that can try to separate itself from the body and this Blackness. I am aiming for rationality – for a way of accounting for why social relations are the way they are at this moment in time. This would be an explanation of how reason has worked itself out over the years to arrive at the good that is the society that now exists. Indeed, as John Russon explains in *Reading Hegel's Phenomenology*, I am aiming for an Absolute reading of history.[5]

If I pull off this expedition, I will be a self-conscious ego that is as purely thought as I can get. The body and Blackness would be objects that this ego can dissect, poke around at, and place in a specific historical context in the hope of gaining cognitive knowledge about each. If I pull it off, and chances are I will not, I would achieve the cognitive objective of modernity – pure objective self-knowledge, enlightenment, or, as we shall call it in this book, rational and idealized Whiteness.

Second, by assuming I am solely a thinking being, I am also working on the basis that starts with a recognition that the world not only consists of other beings or objects besides me, but that there is a nexus between my mind and body in the first instance; second, between me and the other individual objects in the world; and, third, between individual object members, one with the other, and in a way that might not include me. The world, therefore, is relational in existence and meaning. Somewhere in the mix of these three assumptions are the qualities and quantities that make Blackness a phenomenon, one that in turn can affect me and other objects, and is in turn affected by me and the other objects in the world. What I am attempting to do is to find out how I can know anything. For by setting myself up as a self-conscious ego, I am assuming certain knowledge of myself and my Blackness that is based on intuition. By assuming that there are other cogitative and non-cogitative beings in the world, I am assuming that I can know of them through the certainty of my senses by how they help create ideas or confirm intuitions or perceptions in my mind. I am also acknowledging that social relations are ethical and important to the subjects and objects of this world in which they exist.

However, intuition and sense certainty are forms of perception – they are knowledge that I have received and not what I have discovered, tested, and demonstrated as real according to the standards of proof I set myself. Ideally, I would like, through systematic proof, to ascertain demonstrative knowledge, where my intuition and sense certainty produce a refutable and more certain truth of myself, Blackness, and the world, and of whether the rational and mediated images of myself, Blackness, and the world map perfectly to what exists empirically in nature. This demonstrative knowledge would be absolute when I have filled in all the gaps in my knowledge and understanding by tallying up all the experiences I have learned over the history that is my lifetime.

My reasons for doing this examination are threefold. First, as stated earlier, I am a self-identified Black man living in multicultural Canada. I want to know myself and my positioning in my country. I want to see myself in the world. And I want to do it from the vantage point of any other citizen to understand and even appreciate how she or he would see me. Just as important, I want to concentrate on Blackness as a quality and substance in my life and in the lives of those interacting with me daily in a specific ethical relationship. I want to see if how I am *seen* would have any bearing on how I am *treated* and *positioned* in society.

Second, I want to look back on history, including my experiences both in Canada and elsewhere, to discern a subjective narrative of what it really means to be Black, and whether, in my contingent position, within an unchangeable notion that is the Canadian state, being Black or being Canadian is my most important ethical characteristic. Working on the assumption that I now have more knowledge of what its means to be Black than at any other time in life, I want to locate points in the past when I might have misrecognized Blackness and its other, Whiteness.

Third, in a systematic way, I am applying a Hegelian phenomenology that will have implications later in the book for explaining how the notion of an all-knowing spirit – this spirit being the central thought of what is commonly generalized as Western civilization – would come to recognize, at this point in time, that it can only inhabit what has historically been defined as a Black body. This is what I will be referring to when I talk about the spirit of the times and present it as a self-conscious ego caught up in a quest for freedom, hoping someday to be embodied but still be free-spirited. This spirit, as the repository of all knowledge and experiences, is a social consciousness, and individuals like myself are individual embodiments of it. In a Nietzschean sense, it is our will to power, a will that ultimately is idealized Whiteness, perhaps giving a new meaning to the terms White and Black power.[6]

## WHITENESS, REASON, AND RATIONALITY: BLACKNESS'S OTHER

In its rationality, for it to not see itself as Black and fragmented, and that these characteristics are the materials it must use to produce an ethically White society, would be for this spirit to continue to misrecognize itself. This would mean that, alas, this spirit is not fully enlightened, that it does not yet have perfect knowledge, and that it is not free. Certainly, it would not yet have an absolute will to power. In other words, this would be for the spirit to continue to deny its reality and true existence. It would not be recognizing its forms of being that are rationally exercises in otherness by thinking, contrary to the evidence presented, that it is White, enlightened, has absolute knowledge, and that it has ceased to inhabit a body that is as backward, primitive, and Black as all other humans. Importantly, that this spirit, in my case, inhabits a body that is also somatically Black is purely coincidental and, in terms of our discussion, is one of the most contingent of all ontological possibilities. However, this was clearly not the case for most of Western history. The colour of my skin was taken as the full extent of my being. So, I am assuming that there can be changes within these consciousnesses over time.

And so, because of changes, immediately we run into a problem: what are White and Black *always*? Are they features of the soma, cognitive ideals, class, gender, race, religion, ableism, sexuality, or some idealized form of culture that mythologically has been presented as mainly primordial, Black, and undifferentiated into the Whiteness of perceived progress, development, modernization, and ultimately power and freedom?

And what is true for Western civilization and modernity, I will argue, is also true for Canada as a specific condition of this Western consciousness and what now embodies the Canadian spirit – multiculturalism. In doing this, I will be indicating that to have full knowledge of such terms as Canada, Blackness, multiculturalism, freedom, belonging, and citizenship, we must see them as infinities. They are the purported embodiments of an eternally restless and uncontainable spirit. This is to go against the grain of our regular discourses, where we have been discussing them as if they are, indeed, self-contained finite concepts with clearly discernible and acceptable meanings, with precise limits, boundaries, and definitions.

Cornel West makes gestures to this point in *Race Matters* by trying to get us to think of race, which is merely one component or quality of Blackness, in a way that removes the limits. He states that these limits, whether social or economic, have historically blinded us to a fuller discussion on race and, I would add, to the bigger and more all encumbering question of Blackness. The full effect of race "is difficult to grasp because most of us remain trapped in the narrow framework of the dominant liberal and conservative views of race in America, which with its worn-out vocabulary leaves us intellectually debilitated, morally disempowered, and personally depressed."[7] I would say that we are trapped exclusively on the ethno-racial register, and limited to our social constructions. Some of the best examples of this are found in the recent discourse on international terrorism, where differences in ideology have been reduced to mainly somatic, phenotypic, and cultural determinations on the ethno-racial register, to a Black-and-White discussion of us and them, good and evil, the civilized and the barbaric.

Indeed, even in limiting the discussion to race, we would not be grappling with, or as West would suggest, grasping, the full implication of what we are dealing with in a bigger frame: with Blackness and how we can determine socially what is good and evil, and what should be included and rejected from the state. We would be excluding conceptually all the good stuff that, as West argues, is central to the basic humanness of everyone as constitutive elements of our social lives: notions of inclusion, hope, empowerment, full citizenship, and creativity, to name a few. We would not, in my view, understand Blackness through our neo-mythic register. And we would not understand what went into the "social" construction of what is now accepted unquestionably as the social. The goal in this book, therefore, is to show that finitude can neither fully contain nor exhaust infinitude, yet, as fungible concepts, the finite must be included in the infinite, and the infinite must also incorporate finitude.[8] The ethno-racial register must be complementary to the neo-mythic, which, in a circular motion, must be part of the ethno-racial at a higher level, which must also be part of a higher neo-mythic level ... and so on. This spiralling staircase is part of what we may call the Hegelian ladder of higher knowledge, and, most important, of ethical values.

This approach points to the need for a careful categorizing, at every stage, of what is Black and Blackness, and an explanation of how these categories came into effect over time and how they may have changed over time. Ultimately, I will show how, in attempts to effectively capture the infinity of meaning, we arrived at the privileging of what I call idealistic Blackness in ethical relations as the ideal way for people to recognize themselves within the world. This is where people are defined primarily not by their contingent appearances, such as with ethnicity or race, but by what is considered to be necessary and universal for their existence or *beingness* – citizenship rights and fundamental freedoms that, owned by individuals as abstract property, give subjectivity and the highest claim to humanity within specific ethical orders.

This analysis will also allow us to raise some initial red flags about the roles played by those assumptions and intentions that are inherent in our discussion of the being that is human but also Black, Canadian, and free. Here we are reminded of the following claim by Michael Ignatieff: "As a cultural ideal, nationalism is the claim that while men and women have many identities, it is the nation that provides them with their primary form of belonging."[9] This means that their primary form of belonging must be socially constructed, even the very notions of what are good and evil, what is citizenship, and what are the best ways to treat fellow members of this social construction. Indeed, it is in the nation-state, an ideal carved out of the rest of humanity, that men and women are idealistically White or Black, good or evil, citizens or otherwise. Culturally, they are evaluated on the neo-mythic register. Here, we are talking about a humanistic project that aims to perfect the human ideal and which takes place within a civil society. This chapter contains a discussion of what I will later explain as idealized Blackness, which defies our common sense way of knowing and is one of four categories for knowing what and who at the somatic level is Black, but not necessarily who or what is good or evil.

## WHAT THEN ARE BLACK AND BLACKNESS REALLY?

Everywhere, Blackness is in the world. Just about everyone we encounter is simply Black, just like the stranger in our movies and mythologies, if only because we can never have absolute knowledge of another. This is as true now at the beginning of a new millennium in our Western civilization of philosophical enlightenment and technological advancements as it was at the beginning of time. And most likely this will be the case, if the received narratives hold true, at the purported ending of history, when everything in our imagination – along with all those continuous news channels the world over – are supposed to fade eschatologically to Black, if only because there would no longer be such a thing as news as there would be no further changes, or at least none of note.

In the end, inevitably, we are merely returning to what we fled from at the beginning but always misrecognized.[10] Here we are addressing the metaphors of Black and Blackness: we can already hint that, as happens to a cliché when it is worn, there is no longer precision in the use of these metaphors or vivid images of what they represent. Black and Blackness have been conflated to represent many things and many ideas, some of which are still mythological and ideological, others being purely sociological, such as Black ethnicity, families, criminality, and cultures, and supposed to carry a specific idea within society.

Apocryphally, and mythologically, this return is either an act of redemption, reconciliation, and self-fulfilment when the human race is at peace in its natural state, or it is an exercise in ultimate damnation, when the world is most alienated from what it knows to be a better condition or state.[11] In this latter case, we are concerned with mythological and even theological Blackness. Indeed, we only have to listen to the dire warnings of the fundamentalists in any religion or political grouping to know the extent of our Blackness and how we can escape it, if we are enlightened enough to try. Indeed, we only have to listen to how our political leaders the world over discuss the Blackness and barbarism of terrorism and compare it to the freedom and civilization of "our" way of life that is so threatened by an indeterminate Blackness. In this sense, everywhere the world over, there is much discussion about who is Black mythologically, and what behaviour makes one ethically Black or White.

Such discussions are natural. For Black is idealistically the colour of humanity and, despite the best efforts of virtually every country to negate this by fading to White, mythologically Blackness is humanity's natural state and condition. Black and Blackness touch every human. They are central to her or his effort to bring order out of all the eternal surrounding chaos and to prevent what order there is from returning prematurely to Blackness. They are crucial to her or his understanding of the world and efforts to conserve or reformulate it as civil – as what is presented perceptually as White. Blackness and Whiteness are crucial to our understanding of the making and perseverance of any social order and any civil society.

The problem for many of us is that our common sense tells us something different: it leads us to believe that we can intuitively separate humanity into different groups, that we can place human beings in a hierarchy of importance, and that we can tell with certainty the behaviour of specific groups and how they differ fundamentally. In Western societies, we can believe this because our epistemology is based on the mythology of a rational transcendentalism, and also because we have developed patterns of ethno-racial categorization that are now part of the Western consciousness. In this common sense regard of received knowledge, we are arguing that we can know humanity at its most atomic levels and through this knowledge can separate out of this universal Blackness those who can be, or have been, transformed into a racially superior group. These are the ones who have advanced to a higher level of humanity that makes them almost humans no more, but brings them closer to having membership in a race of beings that philosophically, anthropologically, and historically have always been called gods.

Here we have the discursive beginnings of a racialized association with Blackness. It is that which is considered to be imperfect, inferior, ungodly, and even exclusionary. Racialized Whites are the opposite. They have become racially White, even if ethno-racially every other thing about them looks like the rest of humanity, even if they must continue to exist in a world of Blackness and chaos. But since we all act so much alike and seem to aim for the same things, how do we know if we are among those who strive to be of a higher racial grouping, with its perfection and godliness, or if we are among those who are still the truly Black, those remaining most trapped in the natural, uncultured, and even uncivilized state Whites have supposedly left behind? And, if part of the Blackness, in our perception is it possible for any of us to escape such primitiveness? As Emmanuel Eze explains, there is a dominant strain in Western thought which holds that "racial 'blackness' and 'whiteness' are indeed original and primal qualities attendant to acts of perception: the 'black' person need not be actually black – as the 'white' person need not be white. The African or African-descended person is deemed black not necessarily because the skin color is black, just as the white European is white not by virtue of his or her skin color. It seems that beyond what is given in cognitive or rational apprehension, the modern mind, through known processes of the constitution of its aesthetic experiences, *sees* 'black' and 'white' of peoples or individuals."[12]

"Your hands can't hit what your eyes can't see" is a well known phrase in diasporic Black philosophy – indicating that seeing is not all there is. I would like to relate now an anecdote that helps explain the claims in this book that idealistically all humanity is Black and that we are most human when we accept and celebrate our Blackness. This contention holds whether we consider humanity as the family that consists, at a universal and neo-mythic level, of beings the world over that we call humans, or at the particular or ethno-racial level of nations, states, and countries when we cull specific groups of people out of the expanse of humanity and set them apart in territorial boundaries, as distinctly different in culture and sovereignty – as no longer Black like those outside their territory and culture, those that they have come away from. This is Blackness very much in the same way that Greeks of antiquity saw the barbarian in terms of status and culture, and the Hebrews their unclean and gentile. Indeed, who is Black and what is Blackness?

The anecdote, then. For a long time, I have been writing and reflecting on issues of Blackness. In the last while, particularly, I have been studying

Blackness and Canada as a significant part of the Americas and as a way of life or culture developed in the Atlantic. I have always started from the position that I am Black, and proudly so. Anyone looking at me, I assume, should have no doubt about this identity. The image in the mirror told me as much. And, following what Eze says about how our cultures and civilizations teach us to see, I had no doubt that what anyone saw and what I saw, reflected, and felt amounted to the same thing: recognition of who and what is really me, my humanity, my Blackness. To this, I was fully reconciled, even if some might be tempted to say that I was at home and accepting of merely the obvious and the incontrovertible. The question then follows: is this obvious identity a signifier of a specific type of behaviour and of a distinct way of seeing the world and finding happiness in it?

In other words, I am asking if Blackness is cultural, something that I must have learned, and that I learned so well that a specific form of behaviour this specific learning produces is now second nature to me. Perhaps I was socialized Black. *Is* my Black skin a foolproof indicator of my authentic Blackness as a specific and even unique consciousness? Here, I am debating whether or not my Blackness is somatic, something that is ontological and which determines me, something over which I have no say or freedom. Or is it that I am Black because in a socio-economic sense I am among those who have traditionally been excluded from what was intentionally a White state, one of those who has traditionally suffered from a lack of social mobility and denial of social justice in this land? In this sense, I am wondering if my Blackness is a social positioning, something that I can escape from if I can make it into the class of elites and aristocrats. Is Blackness a quality ascribed or can it be achieved or even rejected as a goal in life? Does an identity produce a culture or a culture the identity, so that the way I am treated in society and the ways that I treat others and react to them are directly tied to my identity as a Black citizen, or as a citizen who happens to be Black, to how I am seen and perceived, and not so much to my state of being a citizen? The one common element of the questions raised is what or who is truly and interchangeably Black and, by extension, White? The answers have ontological, epistemological, and existentialist implications. They go to the heart of ethical relations that result from the prevailing ideology and practices in the prevailing social consciousness.

Just the very thought of my Blackness has always given me reasons for celebration. To my way of thinking, Blackness is creativity and life: what is necessary to get through this moment and into the next. It is what is not fixed, what is flexible, and what is new. It is freedom. As an unbridled creative force, it is pure negativity, always trying to remake the world into something new and different. In its purity, it is potential that is limitless. And it is lawless, a sovereign unto itself, absolute freedom as an ideal.

Idealized Blackness is every baby at the moment of birth, that transforming moment when the infant begins what St Augustine describes as a journey that is a life of deaths that is a death of life that hopefully leads to the Whiteness of eternal life. This is before the infant becomes idealized White, cultured, and civilized on the way to eventually dying as a partially attained potential. In this regard, we are all born idealized Black. In the end, idealized Blackness is what remains, a reminder of what we cannot, or could not, achieve while still remaining human, of what we could not achieve in one lifespan. It is a measurement of alienation in the world and the deficit between the lived reality and the dream of self-actualization. Blackness is what we would have to give up to overcome ourselves and to become higher beings. It is the recognition of finite limits as boundaries in a cosmos that is imagined as functioning as a single unit and with unlimited potential. Mythologically, this infinity is everlasting and incorruptible and White; the finite is the human nature within this universe; idealized Blackness is the inevitably premature arrival at these boundaries and the need to be constantly pushing back the boundaries and the limits, to be gradually claiming more of the potential by extending the boundaries, and to see and grasp for the infinite that is immanent in every finite moment and being.

In my mind, idealized Blackness is also the cultural act of civilizing, for it is freedom within a specific history, and it is youthfulness, specifically for those naive days before the act of living seemed to weigh me down with the cost of living, of simply surviving as part of the human tragedy that is the daily passing of time and loved ones, of mortgages and angst on the job, of diminished love and hope, of interminable disappointments, and of achievements that are at best tainted and hollow because they are only fleeting and temporal. It is the freedom before I became who I am and then discovered that my becoming was simply a series of restrictions on my initial freedoms. Each new identity I took on appeared to have come with new responsibilities that limit my freedom to be simply irresponsible, spontaneous, and living a life of abandonment. Usually the colour of my skin seemed not to matter, as I noticed many others with different colours of skin who found themselves similarly restricted and constrained through society's need to socialize all citizens in a certain way and to place them in a social order. In all cases, this socialization was the price we all paid for living in a society whose aim is to treat us as if we are idealistically or normatively White. Socialization is the Whitening process.

Apart from an identity, for me Blackness has been my culture or social existence. This means a special way of living and making sense of the world, one that emanates from having to deal with this specific environment that is the stage for the human tragedy of simply trying to survive in an unreal, ever-changing world. This is a culture that, although temporarily Black at its most basic level and orientation, has one thing in common with all other enlightened ways of life: we who were the products of this way of life hoped for a transformation out of some aspects of this Blackness. We wanted to fully achieve our potentials, possibly even including that of living forever either physically or in memory because of our worthy achievements. In either case, we would be Black no more. If not in this life, perhaps in another, but we will be Black no more. We want to recreate ourselves by bringing Whiteness out of darkness, by becoming in body and soul idealistically White.

That this transformation in status never occurs fully and, equally, that still we never fully give up hoping that it might were further confirmation of our universal Blackness. This approach was as much our quest for the Holy Grail of Whiteness as it was for any other groups of people. This was a quest captured spiritually in every song, in the most holy of hymns or the most debauched of calypso or blues pieces. It is there in our gospel music and in jazz, reggae, hip-hop and any combination of these types of music whose strong pounding rhythms captured our heartbeats. This was a music that seemed to pump through our bodies the hopes, fears, and tribulations so necessary for our living, as critical to our survival as the heart pumping our blood in our veins and arteries.

Blackness was in the music of our lamentations in the face of an unyielding fate, the tyrant that makes us look so small, fragile, and temporary. It was also in our joyousness because of our uniqueness among all beings, a distinctiveness that comes from being so small, fragile, and temporary, from the tenacity of always struggling with the tyrant even though we knew the almost certainty of losing. And Blackness was in our dancing, definitely in the jumping of the waist of every young girl beginning to sense the creative power budding in her awakening sexuality, in the wiggling of the hips of every young boy, in the gracefully swaying movements of the older folks, in the celebration of life that is the creation of life and the ending of life in the hope for survival, in a new creation that is every moment and, therefore, everlasting. As an individual, coming out of a specific history with its tragedies and achievements, I looked forward to the day when, on a specific level, we would be Black no more, even when contradictorily, at the same time, I would be Blackest yet existentially in the taunting of any tyrant or slave driver.

Such was my worldview or perspective. This was how I made sense of the world and it is through these lenses that I gave voice to hopes and fears that were the Blackness of life in general. I thought I knew what is Black, what it is to be Black, and I thought I knew simply because I lived it in a recognized way. Blackness makes me proud. It is what I run away from but end up running towards: the beginning and the ending that, at least in appearances, are mythologically the same. In my experiences, Blackness was not only the contradiction, but the act of contradicting and being contradictory. But knowing all this, I thought that epistemologically, I was White, even if I remained Black ontologically and existentially. Through knowledge I had received the elixir that would transform my status into the status enjoyed by those who are White ontologically and existentially, and this transformation would be the passport for my entry into a land where I would be treated as idealistically White. From a standpoint of knowledge, in a practical sense, this kind of thinking and its certainty of knowing that informed my being and worldview only showed that I was Blacker than I thought and in ways that I had not yet recognized, even if I was still proud in this contradictory world.

Invariably, as part of the act of coming into a reflective self-consciousness, this pride takes me back to the genesis that is those early teenage days at Christ Church High School in Barbados. With me in the darkness of those classrooms are the Black faces of Maurice, Anthony, Cedric, Winston, Wayne, Carl, Lloyd, Mark, Arthur and, of course, Clifton. In my mind's eye, these classrooms are always dark: the colour of the cool shade that was typically the refuge from the broiling, bright Whiteness of the tropical sun outside. There, in this Blackness of the shade, and of youth and celebration, a group of us is always assembled. This is in the heady days of an era marked by the Winds of Change, the Black Power movement and national independence that are the everlasting spirit of what it means to be a part of so-called Western civilization, especially after the Second World War, and specifically as part of the universal blossoming of freedom from the 1960s onwards. We would sing with much gusto: "Say it loud, I'm Black and Proud." Then, in this darkness that also allowed us the creativity that is the ability to change, amend, add on, and to subvert and reject as freely as we wished, we would include words that were not officially part of the 1960s James Brown lyric: "Say it easy, I'm White and greasy."

These things I remember spiritually from those times: idealized Blackness as the pride, creativity, and natural talent whenever heavyweight champion and draft dodger Muhammad Ali won a boxing match; when James Brown and other soul brothers and sisters sang and danced on the world stage; when the West Indies won an international cricket match; when the Barbados cricket team won the regional Shell Shield series; when a Senegalese Dance troupe visited our part of the world or a Mahalia Jackson arrived with her Christian message of hope and redemption; when one of us in the classroom won anything, which usually meant that we had survived another day at a school that socially even in Barbados never ranked among the elites; when we hid with impunity in the darkened classroom from the face of the school rector, Rev. Johnson, or to avoid compulsory attendance at the religious service in the establishment church with its White stained-glass images of Jesus and a host of angels and saints, a church that was *next door* to our school but miles and eons away in our acceptance.

And equally, I remember our improvisations about Whiteness and how we hurled the word White, as an invective, at opponents of Muhammad Ali, for regardless of skin colour they were simply White and Uncle Tomish for entering the ring against this Black god. We hurled it with equal force at any team that tried to defeat our regional or national cricket team. And we hurled it, like a White bolt of lightning, at the entrenched system that we knew we would have to deal with some day: the day when, never to return, we left the safety of the darkened classrooms for the wider world.

This was a world with two distinct paths from our classrooms. One was at home, just beyond the schoolhouse, where we had to adapt to, and later contribute to changing the oppressiveness of rules and regulations that we associated with a system produced by those Whites who had long kept people like us in bondage. These rules were a legacy of the crippling and suffocating Whiteness that treated our Blackness as unequal and inferior; this, in our spirit of independence and freedom, was what we had to change. Alternately, there was the Whiteness of the greater universe, made up of several supposedly more enlightened and rich countries, where some of us would spend much of our lives as immigrants, as outsiders in someone else's country, in places where even we thought we *naturally* did not belong because of our cultural Blackness, our poverty, and because of the history encoded in the colour of our skin. The Blackness of our behaviour was what naturally made us out of place in such a setting. Yet, in a sense, we knew we were part of a worldwide state of Blackness that linked us to members of a family in just about every part of the globe – one big family that was Black ontologically, and in particular, not just because of our universal humanity, but because of an African ancestry. Blackness was diasporic, the scattered seeds of humanity: international and local at the same time. And our particular embodiment of it came on a rainy night on 30 November 1966, when symbolically we seized our freedom as an independent and Black nation-state.

Yet, in our minds, it was possible to transform, just like all those "White" fighters that ontologically looked exactly like Muhammad Ali, but were not as genuine as he was; or just like all those professionals and elites "born and bred" and living among us, who looked like us, but were, in our infallible estimation, other than Black. Just like all those, of these we had heard much, who had come from among us and in a transformation made themselves into successes in the wider world. The few of them who have achieved such status were transfigured: they were like us in spirit and physical appearance, but they no longer had to endure the existence that was so typically ours. They remained Black inside even if they lived White in a White man's country. Their Whiteness served as the beacon on the hill that attracted every one of us taking the second path out of our own Garden of Eden.[13]

Indeed, change was possible, but not all change was good or welcomed. Some changes were even too Black for us, for, contradictorily, they made some Blacks look and act White. In a false consciousness produced by living in an unreal and contradictory world, they thought themselves White. Such is the circle of infinity, where finite White and Black endings are in a Hegelian sense the merging of one into the other. And in our world such transformations were evil and social death, no different from the seeming pathological illness inflicted on a Miriam in the Hebrew mythology that was now fully ours, or on Constantine the Great, in another part of the same tradition that was also as much ours. A baptism in water was the culmination of the healing of Constantine's body from leprosy and his spirit from its primitive Christian unbelief. This would be a "double health [that] shalt thou receive, first for thy body, and next for thy woeful soul; both alike shall be made whole."[14] This was a healing first in respect to the ethno-racial register, and then, secondly, with respect to the neo-mythical. Similarly, what was foretold in a dream, according to the legend, became reality or a double transformation when Constantine acted, when his morality was translated into action through his seeking baptism by water: "As the holy rite began, a great light like the sun's rays shone from heaven into the place, and upon Constantine; and as the sacred words were being read there fell now and again from his body scales like those of a fish, till there was nothing left of his horrible disease; and thus in baptism Constantine was purified in body and soul."[15]

To be White and therefore greasy or ethically slimy was a matter of personal choice, of knowing what is right and wrong, and of personally deciding to side with the wrong group, of the need for spiritual healing and reconciliation, of standing in the need of prayer. In the end, a Black skin did not matter as much as the inner pride, as the intentions, the good will and the good heart of the neo-mythic register. Blackness was an issue of morality – of being morally right by choice. Yet, perversely, morally right could also be Whiteness, for such was the message in the contradiction or miracle that is supposed to be the genesis of Western thought.

For was it not true that Blackness and a Black skin were at the very heart of the Christian mythology of Western civilization, this Blackness that is at the beginning of the civilizing process that is the legendary quest for the Holy Grail? For was it not Joseph of Barimacie who, legend has it, caught the blood that flowed out of the side of the Christian Messiah in the bowl from the Last Supper in Hebrew and Christian mythologies – an act that led to the ultimate transformation: that of the bowl into the cup that shone brighter than any other light, and as a horn of plenty was capable of giving believers the best of food and drink, so that they lived in a land of milk and honey in this life; and that of the physical complexion of Joseph, who instantly "turned black from sorrow, (as) he collected the blood in the holy vessel"[16] – a transformation that was completed when he became Joseph of Arimathea, the "born again" new man, that according to the legend, was imprisoned for his actions. "To him Christ appears with His vessel, in a great light, and instructs Joseph, telling him of his love to Him he shall have the symbol of His death and give it to keep to whom he would; He then gives Joseph the great, precious vessel wherein is His Holiest blood."[17] Blood that when dried turns Black, unless, and until, it is transformed by a miracle that, as we shall see, is a double transformation that is so important for the idea of Whiteness and the idealistic reconciliation as presented by the Christian philosopher Hegel.[18] (This was the representative of Blackness that received instructions from the Christian Messiah that he should construct a second table, this one a replica of the table at which Jesus and his disciples had their last supper, the one that gave the Christian Church the concept of the Eucharist, the idea of a transformation that was total and complete once it assumed the Whiteness of doctrine. But it was a concept, nonetheless, that remained sufficiently Black in its potency to initiate the Schism in Renaissance Europe that led to a historic fracturing of the mythologically White body of Christ into doctrinally White and Black parts – a break that led directly to the position of a specific Protestant church *next door* to my school.)

But at the beginning, it was different; there was an understanding in which Blackness and Whiteness were reconciled in the same beings, in the man-god Jesus, the Messiah, and in his servants. These utopian reconciliations were acts of Blackness, for they subverted the existing order, were miraculous in their undermining of common sense and the historic notion that only White is pure, what is pure is White, and that any hybridized or mixing would only succeed in making White Black. As the legend of this beginning says, the hybridized man-god had instructed that "Joseph is to sit where Christ sat at the Last Sacrament." Thus seated as head of the Christian church, Joseph then named things so as to give them common sense meaning and he administered to all the people. And to "sinners (who) ask the name of the vessel," he answered, "it is called Graal ... hence we call this the Story of the Grail, and it shall be henceforth known as the Grail."[19] Thus, we have here another story, myth, or legend of how a specific order or Whiteness was brought out of Blackness.

The third time that the table would be set for a "final supper" was for King Arthur and his Knights of the Round Table, but this happened only after Joseph had become the Apostle of Britain, leading to another conversion that would have significant impact on the history of Anglo-Saxon literature through Arthurian romances, and on Western culture in its quest for a civilizing talisman.[20] This conversion, too, would lead directly to the Christ Church Anglican parish church being situated next door to my school – my school being run by the Anglican church.

We knew we were part of that civilization each time we looked at the images of the monarchs of Britannia that ruled the seas and were of direct lineage and filial connection to those claiming Joseph of Arimathea as, at least, their spiritual progenitor. It was a legacy that also took us back to the commonly accepted beginning of Western history, the fall of Troy. Looking out from our classroom, it was impossible to escape the symbolic importance and connections that we had just next door in the local representatives of the Church of England. Even in those not yet fully conflicted days, we knew that our identity depended on knowing not only who we were, through having a sense of history, but just as importantly on knowing who or what we were not. We had to know ourselves as Others, as well. We had to recognize our bondsmanship in a world where we were not always the lord. Ours was a syncretic and ideologically impure existence. It was a history with a master narrative, but one punctuated with discontinuities and minor narratives sometimes running parallel, but in many cases in opposition, to the dominant. At times, it was a history that itself was a rejection of the dominant narrative, or it at least tried to force the dominant one to tell a different story, with different meaning, while using the same accepted events, norms, and projections about the ending of history.

This was how we made sense of the world, when we sang either legitimate or illegitimate lyrics, when we acted White or revelled in our Blackness. Christ Church high school and church, Barbados, the Caribbean, North America, and Canada were all part of such a world, part of the same system, all part of the same Atlantic painted in the same civilizing colour scheme and responding to the same rules, regulations, and categories.

Our Blackness was as much a sign of the vigour of humanity as that captured in the legendary return to good health by a Miriam or a Constantine the Great, in the redemption and transformation of a St Augustine and of all those legendary people that gave us the legacy that is Western civilization. We knew all this based on what others taught us as part of an overarching master narrative and we confirmed it by how we lived. Such was our world in Black and White. Or so I thought. V.S. Naipaul paints similar expectations and ways of making sense of the world as an entire system, with us as colonials in it:

Very soon I got to know that there was a further world outside, of which our colonial world was only a shadow. This outer world – England principally, but also the United States and Canada – ruled us in every way. It sent us governors and everything else we lived by: the cheap preserved foods the islands needed since the slave days (smoked herring, salted cod, condensed milk, New Brunswick sardines in oil); the special medicines (Dodd's Kidney Pills, Dr. Sloan's Liniment, the tonic called Six Sixty-Six). It sent us – with a break during a bad year of the war, when we used the dimes and nickels of Canada – the coins of England, from the halfpenny to the half-crown, to which we automatically gave values in our dollars and cents, one cent to a halfpenny, twenty-four cents to a shilling.[21]

Naipaul was describing life in his native Trinidad a generation before my time, but a world that was still so common an experience throughout the English-speaking Caribbean in my time. Indeed, as Glissant suggests, supposedly figuratively and, at times, even literally we were all on the same plantation, this extended *encomienda*:

Just how were our memory and our time buffeted by the Plantation? Within the space apart that it comprised, the always multilingual and frequently multiracial tangle created inextricable knots within the web of filiations, thereby breaking the clear, linear order to which Western thought had imparted such brilliance. So Alejo Carpentier and Faulkner are of the same mind, Edward Braithwaite and Lezama Lima go together, I recognize myself in Derek Walcott, we take delight in the coils of time in García Márquez's century of solitude. The ruins of the Plantation have affected American culture all around.[22]

In this regard, moving to Canada should have been like going from one room to another in a giant tabernacle or mansion with many rooms; going from the family room to the bedroom, with, as every cultured and civilized person knows, there being different types of behaviour and expectations for each room. The change occurring in a twinkling of the eye, or in the amount of time it takes to get from one room to another; a transformation that occurs *en route*, in the in-between, that is completed as the transom is crossed. Whatever the room, it was part of the same house that Blackness built as part of a mighty colonial empire. This thinking informed the greater part of my expectations upon arriving in Canada. That it was not so, nobody had told me. And these unfulfilled expectations and perceptions produced the Blackness and the personal meaninglessness that was part of my Canadian experience. This was part of the process that brought me into a reasoning consciousness, one that sees itself as a rational being that is a Black Canadian fully aware of the world all around and the necessary developments and points along the way that culminated in this particular moment.

My problem started when I realized that the presumed common set of rules was not common at all. This world was not my home. In the rooms were alienation, angst, dread, and the unwholesome and sickening feeling of being thrown in the Heideggerian sense into an unfriendly world. My Blackness in a Canadian setting seemed to be associated with more negatives than positive, with more of what I would consider to be the evils of Whiteness, from being even too Black for my liking, than with the goodness that I had expected of the world back in the comfort of the darkened school room. This was a problem not only for Blacks like me who were immigrants and had our earliest acculturation and education elsewhere. I found out that the same existence and experiences of homelessness were common to those Canadians who were born and bred in Canada, but who were treated as inferiors, called into a finite Blackness that signalled they, by their nature, did not fully belong in Canada either.

None of the rooms in this mansion was theirs. In them, they were expected to be the servants only, never fully the ones with entitlements and privileges; they were not deserving of entry into the rooms of leisure, unless to work there in an alien and alienated space. Neither in any meaningful numbers were they to be seen in the boardrooms and classrooms of politics, finance, influence, and academia. These were rooms that were not built with them in mind as genuine occupants. And the reason that they did not belong was because they were deemed to be Black and, therefore, racially inferior and worthy of exclusion from a society that was White in aspirations and soma, if not always in enlightenment.[23] The proof of this Blackness and inferiority? The Black colour of their skin.

Coming out of the darkness into this light produced for me a reversal of what I had long expected: this was a different kind of Blackness and it was not like the case of the foes of Muhammad Ali living in Black skins but behaving White; this was not like the Black middle and upper classes that I grew up watching and who were socially White. This was a Blackness that amounted without residue of meaning to inferiority, to an existence that is based on the belief that some Black people are mostly White, happy, and useful when held at a lower ranking in society, or simply excluded from the wider community of humanity. At the same time, I was experiencing a different type of Whiteness: Canada, after all, was not as fair and just to all people as portrayed internationally. This land of Whiteness was at heart and by its actions ethically Black: it was not the heaven of equality and fairness in how it treated all groups that reside under its sovereignty.

In Canada, I was noticing that many people whose actions were consistent with what was considered to be an enlightened and White country could not shake the notion imposed on them by others that they were too Black to be fully Canadian. This was so even when, by just about every cultural standard, they should be enjoying the full rights and privileges of being unquestionably Canadian. They were excluded, not because they sought to exclude themselves, but because the majority deemed them too Black culturally and somatically and treated them in a manner that, in terms of status, would not be fitting for those who fully belong in the society. This was the way that members of this group were forced to live.

The explanation for this inequality was the colour of their skin, an argument that in my formative years seemed to go against the transformation of all those Black-skinned people into White and greasy by personal choice and behaviour. This was a transformation of Blackness to Whiteness that was not part of my history, culture, or expectations.[24] I could not readily explain how, in the twinkling of an eye, good got transformed without its volition into evil, how knowledge became debased as ignorance, how cultural sophistication could have no social currency. This was opposite to the accepted norm of evil transforming itself into good by availing itself of the healing promised in our creed. In this understanding, good was everlasting: if it was the natural state at the beginning there was no possibility of change. Good could not become evil, for good was unchangeable. Unless there had been the miracle of a mythical fall – which by its nature would require our complicity. If only because it was not a natural state, only evil could be made into good, just like the White light that inevitably fades to darkness or Blackness. Yet in Canada many that I thought were already good – deemed to be good, that is, elsewhere in our common tradition – were transformed into symbols of evil. That symbol was universal: the Black colour of their skins. Such backward evolution was not part of the civilizing process that taught me that what I was witnessing was a Whiteness so morally Black that it was heinous and a curse on humanity – an example of the very ethical Blackness all humanity was fleeing.

Indeed, I had always thought that collectively in the world that I inhabited that who and what is Black and who and what is Canadian were general knowledge. Now, in a changed moment and space, I was Blacker than I thought: for I realized that cognitively I knew very little about the transforming process that, in a civil society in North America at the ending of the second millennium, could turn Black into White or White into Black. I did not know of those magical drops, of which Ralph Ellison writes in *Invisible Man*, that allowed Spirit to turn jet Black paint into White that was beautiful and not simply frightening.[25]

I later found out, like just about everyone else, that we were wrong about what we thought we knew. It was not based on what we assumed to be enlightened knowledge; rather, it was based mainly on perception. We know very little with certainty and predictability – and this is one of the main arguments of this book – an argument that suggests that all of us are indeed Black, for we are human beings. Cognitively, ethically, and mythologically, Blackness is the natural colour and behaviour of humanity. And, in a way that seems to defy what our common sense tells us, Blackness has very little to do with the colour of the skin. Yet, at the same time, it seems to have everything to do with skin colour, as attested to by the many "mixed race" Canadians of presumed White and Black parents who find themselves without the choice, without the ability to determine whether they are Black or White, but who are simply told they are Black and treated as if they are fully Black. It all has to do with the register we use in trying to gain understanding.

In addition, the Canadian government has determined that a group of people – regardless of where they were born, how much money they have, what languages they speak, what religion they practise, and whether they are gay or straight, highly educated or not – are simply Black in a primordial way. They are recognized by the Canadian state as forming an ethnic community that is Black, so that if they were born and bred in Italy, France, Germany, Britain, or any part of the Americas, unlike others born with different colour skins in the same places, their ethnicity was no longer Italian, French, German, British, or that of any other part of the Americas, but simply Black. Indeed, the ethnic group called Black contains some Ghanaians who in their homeland would call most members of this new ethnic group *obruni* or *White men*, while reserving the term Black or African for those coming to Canada directly in space and time from the continent of Africa and having Black skins.[26] That members of this Black community are products of Western civilization and modernity seemed not to matter in terms of their imposed identity and treatment, and their positions of exclusion within the Canadian state. For some, Whiteness or Blackness was not an entirely subjective and moral issue, but an objective, ethical one as well. It was viewed as being beyond the individual's control and choice: it was imposed by another or by the dominant group in a tyrannical affront to the rights of self-determination.

This was not the case of other groups, not the case primarily of those who are considered the natural heirs to the history of freedom that is Western civilization and thought, and to the entitlements and freedoms attached to this inheritance. How, then, can two different groups of people that share the same inheritance receive separate and distinct treatment? Is this another instalment in the inimitable tragedy that is at the heart of the metaphysics of Western civilization: the story of the brothers fighting for a father's or lord's blessing and inheritance? He that gets the blessing is White and he that goes without is Black? A story that is as old as that told about Cain and Abel, of Ham and his brothers Shem and Japheth in Noah's Ark, of Joseph and his brothers, and of the warring brothers Eteocles and Polynices in the Greek Tragedy *Antigone*. Who, then, exactly is Black, what exactly is Blackness, and is this problem peculiar to Canada or is its form in Canada merely a manifestation of a colourful way of thinking within a specific yet wider history, intent, or order?

## SPIRIT AND CATEGORIES OF BLACKNESS

What I am raising here is the equivocal nature of that thing and spirit we call Black or Blackness. The same thing, I have found out, is the case for what we call Canada or Canadian. Both are infinite and resist all-inclusive definitions, the types we seem to need for common sense understanding.

The same is true, I guess, for what we call American and the Americas, and what we call White. Trying to pin down what we really mean when we speak and think of these concepts became part of the genesis of this study. The search led me on two paths: one that is universal, in searching for a general description and definition of Blackness. The second is a way of explaining a particular way of life in a specific place, in a broader context that is the Americas – that land mass that from at least medieval times was seen as the bridge in the Atlantic between Europe and Africa, on one side, and Asia on the other. Within that bridge, I focused primarily on one area, Canada.

In undertaking this quest, I am specifically examining Blackness in Canada and what it means to be identified as Black and Canadian in a multicultural country that is a liberal democracy. I am looking to explain race, racism, and ethnicity as acts of philosophical history in Western thought that are efforts to get beyond the presumed evils of finite limitations imposed by mere common sense, even if in so doing we try to act according to an accepted or common sense way of knowing. Historically, Canada was presented as a White homeland, in much the same way as were South Africa, Australia, New Zealand, and the proposed segregationist states in the United States of America. Canada, as a product of modernity, was situated philosophically as the European or White homeland in the Americas. Even as a multicultural country, it still purports to be a country founded by two European, or White, peoples or nations. In this way of thinking, we may cognitively view White and Whiteness, on one hand, and Black and Blackness, on the other, as two universals that are mutually exclusive. They may be viewed as the opposite ends of binaries, where the two can never meet.

However, as officially multicultural, Canada has recognized that it is unintentionally Black and not as White as is still imagined in some quarters. My inquiry seeks to explain how mythological and philosophical attitudes to Blackness still inform lived experiences in Canada. How they do so even though, cognitively, we are required to imagine that Black and Blackness are now merely particulars – different forms of determination – of a universal that is Canada. This is to say that a Black Canadian is effectively as much a part of the Canadian universal as a White Canadian. In this regard, black and White are meaningless determinations of this Canadian universal. Both are effective manifestations, determinations, or construed essences of the same consciousness. This is where Black equals Canadian with no surplus or deficiency of meaning, so that the particular is equal to the universal. In this sense, this is the point of satisfaction and ethical well-being, where the consciousness knows itself absolutely as a particular that is a universal and as a universal containing different particulars – all of which are essential and necessary to its understanding of itself. This understanding is necessary to its quest for one or more particular identities that say universally "I am Canadian" and I am absolutely free, regardless of any particular manifestation.

How do we really know who or what is Black and what is the natural and happy state of Blackness? And while it seeks to explain Blacks and Blackness in terms of the positives and negatives they have experienced traditionally, this book makes the claim that Blackness and being Black is much more that merely race, racism, and ethnicity. Indeed, it argues that there is so much more that is Black – so much creativity and ingenuity, so many passions and freedoms – that efforts to reduce Blackness into nice packages on the ethno-racial register have always been disrupted and disproved. Likewise, there is so much more in those human beings who, in being reduced to and encaged in categories of Blackness that have always restricted them, have been stripped of all their potential in being human.

As a way of understanding the experiences of this group of people, I am arguing phenomenologically for four categories of Blackness: (1) the idealized, (2) the cultural, (3) the social, or status, and (4) the somatic. This is how Blackness manifests itself in the dominant view of Western imagining. This is how we *see* Blackness, in other words, how in our everyday life we perform in our seeing: our seeing is not so much an unmediated translation of the outer world but rather how we perform what we have been taught, and are expected, to perform socially through our seeing the right way and making the right inferences from what we see. The categories are the expression of a consciousness that over time has come into absolute knowledge – and understanding of what it means to be Black and Canadian, and what it takes to now have an identity that is the quintessence or latest expression of freedom.

Phenomenologically, our seeing confirms the primacy of perception.[27] As the empiricist John Locke long argued, and as others have expanded upon, as the epigraph opening this chapter shows, essences are real only in the mind. This is the only place where concrete matter that are infinites can be reduced to finite groups constructed ethno-racially around some primary characteristics that are deemed to be necessary for the group's assembly. But even with these constructions, which are the mental amalgam of simple ideas to form complex ones, there can be no certainty of knowledge as to what are really the necessary and contingent components – as is the case with all composites that are at a minimum dualisms.[28] I explain that under such circumstances the meaning of Blackness in the modern state is equivocal, in that it has no essence or univocality, but instead a specific definition depending on the moment and circumstances. This approach examines how these categories were developed ontologically, epistemologically, existentially, and ethically in Western civilization, and how they were applied in the Americas, primarily in Canada.

In layman's terms, I am looking at what forms Blackness is supposed to take to make it undoubtedly Black, what knowledge we have about Blackness and what is Black, what is naturally a Black way of life so that Blacks are happy in their cultural Blackness, and, finally, what kinds of meaningful and just relationships should exist between those who are known to be Black and those who are not. The latter is important in a world where those who are supposedly known to be Black are also considered racially inferior and are usually powerless.

In undertaking this examination, the book accounts for the primacy of the somatic, of Black skin, in common sense meaning and of perception as the methods for identifying individuals constructed ethnically as Black in a multicultural country. The theory for four ways of categorizing Blackness analyses how somatic features became analogous to good and evil, how they became racialized signifiers of superiority and inferiority, and how they developed as a way of determining certainty and predictability of knowledge – according to cognition, perception, affectivity, and motility – about humans in the modern state. I make this examination within a specific context: this is the notion that modern states are predicated, as Taylor has suggested, on knowing what is good and evil, with the intention of achieving an idealized Whiteness where a select group of people are sheltered from the evils of the wider world.

Modernist states are products of Western civilization and thought that have produced a specific way of life that gives a peculiar meaning to human existence. This idealization is part of an ideology that is so deeply ingrained in Western societies that the idealization and ideology are virtually unnoticeable on the surface. Western thought idealizes specific ways of living and of treating people, as individuals and as groups, in order to ensure the happiness of all.

At the heart of the mythologies of Western civilization is the notion of a transformation or transfiguration producing a rebirth or creation: this is an act of idealized Blackness, for defying common sense explanations, where miraculously Blackness is turned into Whiteness, but in anticipation of an ultimate return to a more purified Blackness which aspires to be spiritually White, with this aspiration never turning into reality. A peculiar definition of Whiteness is when any group or individual assumes that it has achieved that to which it aspired, there being therefore no further changes towards Whiteness. This is a fixed and fossilized position, a static utopianism and idealism: it is a finite category, a rigidity that is death, that is an absolute ending from which there can be, in the Western mythology, no resurrection or transcendence of boundaries to the common sense. This is what happens when some countries and cultures define themselves as so separate and distinct from the rest of the world, through their technological and other social developments, that the difference is as clear in a common sense way as is Whiteness from Blackness, and gods from humans.

Modernist states are generally based on notions of a homeland, an idealized place where a special group of people have natural rights of membership or citizenship. In this homeland, individuals share risks to try to preserve their achievements across generations. This is part of the notion that each generation's task is to achieve a little bit more of the elusive Whiteness that will result when all human potential – the Blackness inherited at birth – is completely used up. These bits of Whiteness, the achievements, are held up, preserved, and carried forward as knowledge and culture, as the building blocks for an enduring civilization that aims for the eradication of Blackness. The hope is to achieve freedom that is orderly, stable, and neither capricious nor marked by arbitrariness. This translates into happiness and long life for the people and their institutions, and this hope is embodied in the modernist state as the spirit or core values of its people.

Once it is brought into being, the state is deemed to be perpetual and unchanging. Such attributes and the state's continuing success are based on knowing and recognizing those who are fully committed to the preservation of the homeland and those who would destroy it. The state becomes, in the prevailing ideology and mythology, a White body. It must be preserved and venerated. In the mythology, it should be untouched and unspoiled as any Odysseus's Penelope, Lavina awaiting her Aeneas, any wife encased in her chastity belt awaiting her returning knight of the Crusades, or any White *belle* of the Southern American states – a symbol of purity for only a small elect chosen out of the rest of humanity and having undergone the transformation into a never changing Whiteness or citizenship. This is the case whether the task is to know who is the terrorist that might destroy the society, the immigrant demanding full acceptance into the society but who might not be trustworthy, the guest-worker who might be allowed to live in the state but is prevented from participating fully, or the citizen who has uncontested rights and entitlements. Only those who are fully members of the state are White. All others are Black, culturally, idealistically, and socially. In a country like Canada, for a long time, they also did not belong because of somatic Blackness.

There is a reason for this. Mythologically, Western societies have been imagined as gardens of purity and enlightenment that have been carved out of a wilderness or Blackness that is the rest of humanity in its natural state. Those that belong have traditionally been imagined as White, possessing unchangeable purity, goodness, and cultural enlightenment. The primary determinant of belonging is not the outer feature, such as colour of the skin, but an unwavering and unchanging commitment and good intent to

the ideals of the society. Those that do not share these inner qualities are imagined as Black, as the Other. This is generally the stranger, the unknown, the
corrupter, and even the evil harbinger of chaos and an untimely physical
death. Meaningful existence in modernist states, in Western civilization, is
still based on knowing who is Black or White and what is Blackness. In this
sense, Canada is typically a Western modernist state with a worldview on
Blackness that is informed by the mythologies underpinning Western civilization. Existentially, Blackness and Whiteness, therefore, have always been
more than the colour we see physically.

These issues came home to me in a big way when I returned to university.
How did Blackness fit into a country like Canada that supposedly, viewing
it as part of its body politic, gave official recognition to an ethnicity that is
Black? In one of my courses on immigration and settlement, my professor
and I searched extensively for documented material and academic treatment on the Black immigrant experience in Canada. We did not have much
success. Even though we did unearth some materials on Blacks and immigrants, much of it was non-academic. Indeed, all the literature that turned
up started with one common assumption: that Blackness was essentially the
colour of the skin or of African ancestry.[29] The discussion was either
anthropological or sociological. Almost nothing was said about the mythological, philosophical, and theological understandings of Black and Blackness. In this regard, Blackness became the acceptance of a Eurocentric
determination that came fully into vogue in modernity.[30] A significant component of Black and Blackness was missing from the prevailing discourse.
Something similar occurred in an early course in political philosophy.

It was only when I started to read extensively on modernity and the
absented presence of some groups in the social consciousness of many modernist states that I started to realize what was happening. In one context,
Blackness in modernity was a signifier of the excluded and the other. The
history of modernity is generally told through the eyes of the included and
is for the included. This history is usually the narrative of the vanquishing
of the Other and how the Other must be held at bay. The included are
members who are already part of the notion so central to democracy of we-
the-people that has power, recognition, and acknowledged presence in
modernity's state. The narrative about nation-statehood is about achieving
Whiteness. The history of Blackness is what is implied would have happened if good did not triumph. This history of Blackness and modernity is a
struggle by those constructed as Others and Black for recognition and
inclusion. Theirs is usually the unwritten narrative in modernity, that
which is considered counterfactual and a counter narrative.

Yet, in this new knowledge was a glaring contradiction: was it not the
same modernity and its aspiration for enlightenment that produced such
states as Canada, the United States of America, France, and Haiti, and was

it not the same modernity, granted in its later states, that was marked by the Winds of Change, the Black Power movement that was part of the civil rights struggle in America, and the independence movement that were all part of a genuine desire and quest for freedom that is the hallmark of modernity? And did not this same modernity produce a consciousness in Canada called multiculturalism, which was trying to use a category of citizens called Black as a vehicle for inclusion – not exclusion – in a liberal democracy that aims to be a just society?[31] And did the quest for freedom and the production of a new consciousness not have their beginnings first in mythological, philosophical and theological discourses about the meaning of life in general and what ought to be the ideal condition for the human state? In a real sense, only a very small part of the story of modernity was being told and that story was coming from a particular point of view and perspective, thereby further limiting its universal appeal and inclusiveness.

But if Blackness was a measurement of exclusion, as a Black man I also knew that it was a signifier of a way of life or behaviour. Even within modernity, Blackness seems to change with the context. The main product of modernity was supposed to be rationality. Reason was supposed to be the highest order in civil society. Reasonable people would easily discern Whiteness from Blackness and, through their moral imperatives, act appropriately. Race and racism, according to most common sense arguments, had no real basis and place in a multicultural country like Canada. Race and racism were irrational, part of an unenlightened history that Canada has now repudiated officially. Once again, even when exploring race and racism, only a small and limiting part of the modernity story was being examined.

Yet, most indications were that reason and rationality were missing in the Black and White debate of who belongs in Canada and who should have full rights and entitlements. This is particularly true if a sociological and anthropological argument is used to define Blackness and race. Most economic statistics paint a dismal position of the groups constructed as ethnically Black in Canada.[32] Members of this group, by just about every standard, still do not appear fully to enjoy the good life in Canada. Like that of the aboriginal peoples, their existence still seemed to be more so at the mercy of a tyrant or terrorist called race and racism than were many other groups once held in this slavery and having since escaped this Blackness into the Whiteness of acceptance in Canada. Indeed, were not the aboriginal peoples considered Black idealistically, culturally, and even somatically, and in terms of status worthy of exclusion in the White Canadian state? Reasonably, what were the implications of being called a Canadian Black and what are the expectations of this Blackness? Is this an inflexible categorisation with an over-determined existence?

Indeed, what does it mean to attempt to reduce Blackness to finite categories and what are the realities of such a lived experience in Canada? I shall now highlight the existentialism of finite Blackness and the implications of ethical relations based on such limitations. In so doing, I shall be showing how, ultimately, Blackness came to be equated solely with the colour of the skin.

# 4

# Common Sense Blackness

## *Existentialism, Epistemology, Ontology*

I recall a somewhat rowdy conversation with some friends in Jamaica nearing the end of my post-graduate studies. All of us were somatically Black, of a mature age, and supposedly middle or upper class. The scene was in what was recognized universally as a Black state aiming to become a Black modernist nation. By this I mean that it clearly aspires for what I call idealized Whiteness in this book, but has a somatically non-White population. We were sitting in a restaurant that was frequented mainly by the social elites. More than once, some of us remarked upon the fact that so many of us at the table were professionals that had gone through the alchemist bowl of social transformation that was the University of the West Indies.

The aim from the 1960s onwards was to take poor children from islands throughout the region and to provide them with opportunities for secondary and tertiary education in the hope of producing a class of somatic Blacks that behave and live no different from the somatic and aristocratic Whites who had ruled the region for several centuries. This reflected belief in a social justice based on meritocracy as a way to escape into existential and ethical Whiteness. We, as representative of that class of cultural Whites, were served that night with a deference by the owner and her waiting staff that indicated that socially we were not as Black as the workers, certainly not on the same level as those who brought us our drinks and food, and anticipated our generous tip, definitely not on the same level as those shadowy figures begging for money, food, and drugs on the outside just a few streets away.

Yet, somatically, we all looked alike. In this respect, I am reminded of the statement by Marcus Garvey, the Jamaican-born "messiah" who preached African and Black upliftment worldwide. Garvey was making an important distinction between West Indians who have somatic Blackness as a primary identity and others who are White inside Black skins. Commenting on the opposition he faced when he started his Universal Negro Improvement

Association in Jamaica, Garvey stated that "men and women as black as I, and even more so, had believed themselves white under the West Indian order of society. I was simply an impossible man to use openly the term 'negro'; yet every one beneath his breath was calling the black man a negro."[1]

To many of his early detractors, Garvey was not only Black by skin colour but by behaviour and even social standing. In the United States of America, Garvey was also Black by citizenship, something that led ultimately to his physical expulsion from the US as a deportee.

As the evening wore on, the laughing and loud talking from our part of the restaurant were more noticeable, setting us apart from quieter, more acquiescent eating at nearby tables. At one point, one friend said, "But, look at us, we are all behaving *soooo* Black," a comment that succeeded only in self-consciously generating more unapologetic laughter among us. In this context, I knew that the comment had nothing to do with skin colour, and neither was it pejorative, for as a little boy growing up in Barbados I remember my grandmother telling me I should not behave Black, and I remember her disapprovingly describing someone acting like a proverbial Black hat with a red rose on it – which meant simply awful behaviour that was out of place and cultural context. This behaviour by the group of professional, upper-class somatic Blacks in Jamaica, was no different from what we see on television every spring break, when the elites of what we term White societies in the Americas escape from the routine and prison of academic conformity for a week on the wild side. This is when they descend into Blackness, a site from which they will quickly arise and be transformed as soon as they board the planes, boats, trains, and cars that take them back into the Whiteness of normal society and conformity. This is the Blackness of the carnal. It was a behaviour that we would not repeat in polite society, such as when we returned to work, went to church, or hopped on a plane and headed back to the presumed Whiteness of Canada.

The same is the case of the legendary experience of so many affluent tourists of all colours and complexions who arrive in the Caribbean for two weeks of fun that are usually forbidden back home – an experience that is quickly filed away in the darkness of memory only to be fetched up occasionally and usually under the most controlled circumstances. But for a moment, the descent is delicious and intoxicating, as powerful and alluring as any of the carnivals that are so endemic to the Americas – the illicit times when the given order is subverted and turned on its head, the brief respite of bacchanal carnival when reason is dead and passions rule, when the White tyrant of Greek mythology Apollo gives way to the licentiousness of a Black Dionysus, when the Black Eliohem of the Hebrew tradition stands in glory over the White Yahweh, and when in the African tradition Eshu takes on one of his/her many disguises and stretches the boundaries of freedom by simply conflating and mixing up what is White and what is Black.

Yet, I knew that in a different time and place that the remark about our Black behaviour might be misconstrued and even deemed inappropriate regardless of the intent. Such manners would not be seen as carnival, as an accepted aberration that has clear limits, for in Greek, Hebrew, and African mythology we know that reason and Whiteness are the norms. They are the colour of humanity's resurrection and transformation after the darkness of the descent or fall into licentiousness – White being the colour of the other than human, the claim of the elect, the saints, and their thrones and horses in Christian mythology. This carnival of licentious Blackness, by its very nature and definition, cannot be permanent. Universally, whether they exist in Port of Spain, Rio de Janeiro, London, Toronto, or New York, or in New Orleans either as the famed Mardi Gras or Bourbon Street night life, carnivals, as the epitome of acting *sooo Black* and of the indeterminacy or Africanism of Eshu, cannot be ordained as the natural and lasting order in Western civilization or any other civilization. Order, supposedly, must be imposed on the disorderly for the common good.

For otherwise to happen would be to engage in a Blackness that is socially unacceptable, a Blackness become so Black that it is White in much the same way that every geographer knows that too far east becomes west, too far north, south. This is the message behind the African American adage "The Blacker the berry the sweeter the juice, but if too Black it ain't no use"[2] – a determination of culture and behaviour based solely on somatic features. Every human, while having the option, as Toni Morrison says, to play on this Black side, must just as quickly retreat back into the conformity of the White light of order.[3]

In Canada, from time to time, I would be invited to appear on radio and television to present the Black point of view or perspective. In many cases, it was often assumed that it would be negative, contrary, angry, and even disruptive. It was assumed that, naturally, I would be speaking out against, contesting, and even subverting the prevailing order. I was expected to behave Black, to always perform on a stage that, even in normal times, was permanently *carnivalesque*. This is, as Appiah asserts, part of the thinking on collective identity that gestures not only to recognition of the authenticity of a specific identity but to how individuals of that identity should behave. "It is not that there is one way that blacks should behave, but that there are proper modes of behaviour. These notions provide loose norms or models, which play a role in shaping the life plans of those who make these collective identities central to their individual identities; of the identification of those who fly under these banners."[4] This includes the expectations that are harboured about Black and minority literature in Canadian studies, where those considered outside the mainstream are usually quoted only in the sense that they are contesting or negatively trying to refute the prevailing order. Seldom are they invoked in the sense that they are also suggesting positive possibilities for the order, even if they are indeed asking for changes.

But were such appearances the same kind of Black behaviour that I was exhibiting in a moment of abandonment and frivolity in the Jamaican restaurant? Indeed, I even once had a radio talk-show to give the Black perspective or Black voice. Often television producers would expect me to perform that way, occasionally coaching me in pre-interview interviews and in commercial breaks to act appropriately. In their estimation, life was forever carnival for me, or for the point of view I was supposed to be representing.

Sometimes, it would be assumed that, naturally, I would want to perform or speak on a specific topic even if publicly I had shown no previous interest in the topic. One case in point was the horror in the voice of a producer for the *Pamela Wallin Show* on CBC Newsworld who had invited me to be on the show for a discussion on the issue of how society should handle violent youths that were socially classified as young offenders. The implication across the land was that many of these young offenders were somatically Black and were universally part of a somatically Black community in Canada. Indeed, a policy in Ontario in the 1990s of three-strikes-and-you're-out that penalized youth deviants by expelling them from schools and other socializing institutions was generally taken to be aimed primarily at somatically and culturally Black youths. The invitation-cum-summons came with the full expectation that I would want to appear on the show to give the Black side. When I pointed out that I had never given much thought to the issue, and more so that I had never written or spoken publicly about the matter, I was still invited to participate. The producer argued that there was a need for the show to have the optics of a representative of the Black community responding to charges by the somatically White author of a book on this issue. She was extremely miffed when I further declined. There, she said, was the chance of providing balance on the show, and we in the Black community should not keep griping that we were not given a voice on that particular medium.

Later, I noticed another Black performer on the show. His appearance, I was most certain, had nothing to do with having expertise on the issue, but rather with the colour of his skin and the behaviour that was expected to be consistent with those sharing the same colour skin. This was the Whiteness of political correctness, of a misguided search for balance that relied only on somatic appearances, that is so ethically Black. His was a status of permanent carnival and of supposedly representing a specific way of life that was invariantly the pageantry of difference and nonconformity. Again, who is Black and what is Blackness? These are questions of epistemological value, for how can we know what is hidden behind the skin, what we cannot physically see, even if we can mentally? Traditionally, as part of our knowledge, we have always hoped to achieve the perfect reconciliation of what we think a thing or person to be with what that thing of person thinks itself to be. Seldom do we have a perfect match. Frequently, the outer shell or husk is a poor guide for knowing the internal qualities and intentions that are "hidden."

To this end, I am reminded of times when even among those who identify themselves as Black, that this identification was not enough. There was always the Blackness of ambivalence to take into account. A few years ago, I and two other Canadian writers took to dubbing ourselves "The Griots" and embarked on a series of readings that started out in Ontario and took us to Manitoba, British Columbia, and Nova Scotia. We chose the name Griots because it spoke to our "African" background and because we were representatives of the ethnic community that multicultural Canada calls Black.

The aim of this 1997 tour was to highlight Black-Canadian literature, to draw attention to the contributions of Blacks to Canadian history and literature, but primarily to bring to light the new works that the Griots had just published. Barbados-born Austin Clarke, Montreal-born Mairuth Sarsfield, and yours truly were the Griots. Trinidad-born, Dionne Brand participated in some of the Ontario readings. Academic and author George Elliott Clarke, who was born in Halifax, would join Austin Clarke, and Sarsfield, and historian Dr Sheldon Taylor in taking the Griots tour to the United States.

The final stop on the Canadian leg was perhaps quite appropriately in Halifax, which from the inception of Canada in the late eighteenth century was continuously associated with a Black Canadian presence. On the final night, the readings at Dalhousie University were followed by a question and answer session. Someone put the question to us: what were our real identities – Black writers, Caribbean writers, or African writers? In other words, the questioner asked, in the case of Clarke and me, did we see ourselves as Africans or as Caribbean? The questioner, to much approval from the audience, said this was an issue of intense importance to the Black people of Halifax.

Austin Clarke argued that if there was an essence to his Blackness he could not see it going back further than his native Barbados. Even then he would not accept an essence of Blackness. If that were the case, someone asked, can there ever be unity among Blacks in Canada? I argued there was need for such unity and for the recognition of a common experience, and that in the quest for this Holy Grail of commonness it might be necessary to search for an essence of Blackness that would take us back to Africa. Ultimately, I conceded, I would have to go deeper than my Bajan roots to find such uniqueness, thereby going beyond Clarke, to find the common element. Essences, commonness, community – indeed, who or what is Black, particularly in a Canada with a particular history? In that moment, I think Clarke had the clearest idea of his identity.

Needless to say, the discussion resolved nothing, while making apparent so many contradictions in our common sense understanding of these matters. It could not, beyond proving the obvious: Black and Blackness are equivocal in our world and we run into problems when we try to pin them down to a specific and determined meaning. At one time, they are universalizing concepts; at another, they speak to peculiarities, parochialism, and insularity. This does not mean that the exercise of searching for a meaning did not have ethical relevance. For it was part of an intractable discussion among those who are constructed socially and politically as Black, among those who know themselves to be Black, over who is really Black. In this case, it is an argument over who existentially is genuinely Black-Canadian: those who have a lineage of several uninterrupted generations in Canada or those who have arrived most recently but have acquired the right to be presented as Black Canadian by acquiring Canadian citizenship, by identifying themselves as Black, or by claiming a lived experience that is only common to those who are seen by the wider Canadian society as Black? On that night, the answer was elusive – for it stemmed from seemingly irreconcilable positions based on the notion of who is unchangeably Black and who is also unchangeably Canadian. Again, seeing these concepts in the common sense way told us precious nothing that was meaningful.

Still, there are times when Canadian society, like societies everywhere, has deemed specific people to be Black in actions and character. It may even associate those actions and characteristics with skin colour. Such is the case, at the time of this writing, with a dispute over the question of racial profiling by police in Toronto, Canada's largest city. This issue broke onto the public agenda in the publication of a series of articles in fall 2001 by the country's largest and most liberal newspaper, *The Toronto Star*, in which it was claimed that Toronto police have consistently practised racial profiling of Black Canadians. The newspaper stated that, compared to other Canadians, Blacks in Toronto are more likely to be stopped by police, are more likely to be charged by police, and are more likely to be held overnight in police custody. How did the newspaper know this and, as it was not the first time the issue had surfaced, what was new in its reporting? There had previously been several reports, ranging from official investigations to commission reports claiming the same thing. In addition, several people described as representative of the Black and African communities had made similar claims with little attention or results.

The *Toronto Star* argued that what was newsworthy was its reliance on a database compiled by the police themselves. These statistics were based on people who came in contact with the law – people who were described as Black, Brown, or Other. According to the newspaper, Blacks were those whose skin colour indicated they were of African ancestry and Brown was for those who were East Asian. Others were Caucasian Whites. It is interesting to note that this classification of people was not much different from the way census takers were instructed to categorize Canadians in 1901. Then, as Constance Backhouse states in her book *Colour-Coded: A Legal History of Racism in Canada, 1900–1950*, the Canadian government had determined: "'The races of men will be designated by the use of "w" for white, "r" for red, "b" for black, and "y" for yellow.' Missing was the colour brown, which was sometimes linked to race, but including it would have mucked up the short-form letter categories, leaving two 'b's in a polyglot of confusion."[5]

To ensure no confusion of any kind, as Backhouse notes, the federal government gave this very clear explanation to the census takers on how they should apply their method: "The whites are, of course, the Caucasian race, the reds are the American Indian, the blacks are the African or Negro, and the yellows are the Mongolian (Japanese and Chinese). But only pure whites will be classed as whites; their children begotten of marriage between whites and any one of the other races will be classed as red, black or yellow, as the case may be, irrespective of the degree of colour."[6] Recalling the epigraph from Hegel, it would seem that Whiteness was what the several layers of darknesses did not cover up.

The difference between now and then is more than 100 years. The difference is supposed to be reflected in an attitudinal change, where if people are identified by colour, race, or ethnicity it is supposedly done to include them in society, and not to leave them out.[7] A century ago, Canada was clearly and officially a racist country, where people were categorized based on an imputed essence or ethnicity that showed up primarily in the colour of their skin, and they were treated differently because of this classification. Today, Canada is officially a multicultural country where colour of skin is purportedly meaningless in the way the state's institutions and agencies deal with citizens, residents, and visitors. Yet, the belief persists that there is an ethnicity called Black, even if the First Nations people, and the Japanese and Chinese are no longer called red and yellow in polite society. As was the case for the census takers a century ago, how do the police know who is Black and does being Black translate into a special and unequal treatment in Canada?

Stung by the criticisms, the Toronto police chief responded that his force does not maintain statistics based on race, that it does not treat Blacks differently from other citizens, and that there is no racial profiling of Blacks. But can this be true in all cases? Is it not true that historically in our imagination all suspects, deviants, lawbreakers, terrorists, and criminals were Black even if all those considered Black were not suspects, deviants, lawbreakers, and criminals? As the police pull over a motorist, does that person not immediately transform into Blackness, and is it not the job of the courts to determine the individual's Blackness or Whiteness? When a police officer challenges someone without good reason or treats a citizen unfairly, is not the officer being Black, especially in actions, and regardless of his or her skin colour?[8]

The social and political history of state formation, of the acceptance of public will, and of conformity have long been discourses in Blackness. Historically, plenty of examples abound. As Iris Marion Young has noted, in nineteenth-century discourse in the US, women, Native Americans, Blacks, Jews, and homosexuals were used interchangeably as examples of "uncultivated passion" and "wild nature" that comprised a Blackness which sat in opposition to the Whiteness that was "civilised republican life."[9] This is a point that was further emphasized by Mason Stokes in his book *The Colour of Sex: Whiteness, Heterosexuality and the Fiction of White Supremacy*.[10] Is not this the same kind of thinking that in Europe from the Renaissance on led to the expulsion of criminals to places like Australia, the US, and Barbados as part of penal sentences?

Indeed, conceptually, are not all immigrants idealized Black and have they not always been so from the beginnings of xenophobia, acquiring a cultural and status Blackness that usually remains until they are transformed through the Whiteness of citizenship? In this regard, popular Australian writer David Malouf seems to be mining a rich epistemological vein when he suggests in his novels that Australians are native and therefore idealistically Black, meaning that their nativeness, while it cannot make them somatically Black, does make them Black in culture and status.[11] Making his own distinction in his lament *Song of Lawino*, East African writer Okot p'Bitek argues against the Blackness of things foreign or White or European in his African society that is struggling to maintain its authenticity.[12] And to prove the universality of this point, even among those constructed as Black, so too was this distinction made by the Guyanese West Indian N.E. Cameron as early as 1929 in his book *The Evolution of The Negro* of those whose Blackness is not limited strictly to the colour of their skin or African ancestry.[13]

Indeed, some of the efforts by journalists and columnists to deflect criticism of the Toronto police officers' racial profiling sought to draw attention to the presumed very Black behaviour of those citizens constructed as ethnically Black,[14] the line of argument being that members of the "Black community" were not co-operating with the police. Scores of them would witness a homicide and refuse to come forward as witnesses. This, as the columnists and police suggested, was very Black behaviour – that which is unsuited for the proper behaviour of citizens in a civil society. The norms of citizenship included co-operating with the police to keep evils out of society or contained in places where evil cannot do greater damage.

And there was the norm of ensuring that the criminally deviant members of the society were brought to justice, so that the perpetrators received their just desserts, and the victims sensed an attempt to repair the injury. Collectively, these norms produce the Whiteness of a civil society. To act otherwise, the argument goes, is to court a return to the Blackness of a state of nature and the chaos that is the hallmark of such an existence. As columnist Christie Blatchford suggested in the *National Post*: "What this means ... is that the modern-day cone of silence has spread far beyond the criminal associates and relatives of the various gunmen – in other words, those with an interest born of blood and loyalty in keeping mum – and infected a significant segment of the otherwise law-abiding public."[15] And she further quoted the lead detective investigating a double murder as saying: "'They (witnesses) ought to try knocking on a family's door at three in the morning to tell them their kid was gunned down in front of hundreds of people and the police haven't a clue what happened,' he said despairingly. 'If this hear-no-evil, see-no-evil continues, one day it will be their doors we're knocking on.

"'Then,' he said, 'it's mayhem.'"[16]

To be a part of the society, and not to abide by the norms, was simply to be culturally Black in a way that has nothing to do with the colour of the skin. Yet, it is a Blackness that is ultimately reduced to the somatic in this instance. That those behaving so Black were also somatically Black and tended to be Black in social status was a choice of theirs that prevented them from becoming idealistically as White as any other citizens.

Then there are the following two examples to confirm the point that in Western thought all deviants and nonconformists are Black, ultimately making a link between Blackness that is idealistic, cultural, status related, and somatic. Indeed, these are cases that begin the documentation of the reduction of Blackness in all respects to the somatic, thereby making even more finite the definition of Black and Blackness.

In the year 1570, churches in England were required by the king to read a homily on obedience and the proper behaviour of a subject. Obedience to the law of the land was an act of Whiteness that God intended as part of creation when God called light out of darkness. This order was predicated on a descending order of creation, with God at the top, followed in order of lesser importance by his angels, humans, lesser creatures that were without reason, and inanimate objects. This is Whiteness in keeping with that of the Book of Revelation with its many references to the elect and saints dressed in White or associated with White horses. But within the human order, there was a natural order also, for as long as God was the king lesser humans were to recognize that "all kings, queens and other governors are specially appointed by the ordinance of God."[17]

The matter of obedience is then addressed. "And as God would have man to be his obedient subject, so did he make all earthly creatures subject unto man, who kept their due obedience unto man so long as man remained in his obedience unto God. In the which obedience if man had continued still, there had been no poverty, no disease, no sickness, no death, nor other miseries wherewith mankind is now infinitely and most miserably afflicted and oppressed."[18] As the homily stated, human existence was a tragedy because Blackness or sin had entered this world or natural order and had subverted and corrupted it.[19] "But as all felicity and blessedness should have continued with the continuance of obedience, so with the breach of obedience and breaking in of rebellion, all vices and miseries did withal break in, and overwhelm the world. The first author of which rebellion, the root of all vices and mother of all miseries, was Lucifer, first God's most excellent creature, and most bounden subject, who, by rebelling against the majesty of God, of the brightest and most glorious angel is become the blackest and most foulest fiend and devil, and from the height of heaven is fallen into the pit and bottom of hell."[20]

The linking of Black and Blackness with subversion, and with the state as a natural White order, would become potent forces in English and British history. Such was the case, as E.P. Thompson notes in *Whigs and Hunters: The Origin of the Black Act*, in the eighteenth century. At this time, *bands* of people painted their faces Black, emphasising the somatic, to signify a characteristic change from one of obedience of the law of the land to that of rebellion. It also signified a necessary change, for given the Blackness of a meagre existence, to obey the law of the land would have meant to become destitute and soon unable to keep human body and soul together. The *Black Act* was passed by the English parliament in 1723. Its main purpose was to make a number of acts of rebellion punishable by death. As Thompson says:

The main group of offences was that of hunting, wounding or stealing red or fallow deer, and the poaching of hares, conies and fish. These were made capital if the person offending were armed and disguised, and in the case of deer, if the offences were committed in any of the King's forests, whether the offenders were armed and disguised or not. Further offences included breaking down the head or mound of any fish-pond; maliciously killing or maiming cattle; cutting down trees "planted in any avenue, or growing in any garden, orchard or plantation"; setting fire to any house, barn, haystack, etc.; maliciously shooting at any person; sending anonymous letters demanding "money, venison, or other valuable thing"; and forcibly rescuing anyone from custody who was accused of any of these offences.[21]

In both cases from English history, Blackness is an act of morality that can either be good or bad, depending on the lens through which it is seen. If the perspective is that of overthrowing a natural God-given order, then it is seen as evil. Therefore any act against a morally upright and constituted

government or order is Black and wrong. But there is also the other meaning, where Blackness speaks to the creativity and triumph of the human
spirit against tyranny in any form, whether it is hunger or the authority of
an evildoer, or in Sartre's case, the creator himself. In this case, Blackness is
good, for it subverts and overthrows the Whiteness that is evil. It is for this
reason that groups of people in the British Isles still paint their faces Black
to participate in folk music events with a special historical significance.
One such group, the Welsh border Morris group, offers this explanation on
its Web site:

Border Morris is one of several styles of morris dance, which today include
Cotswold, North-West, Molly (East Anglia), Rapper (North-East) and Long-sword
– each associated with an area of England ... The border Morris dances were
mainly performed in the winter by farm labourers and fishermen (on the Severn) as
a means of earning a little extra money when work was scare – it was a form of begging, and as such it was illegal. This is usually offered as the explanation for the tradition of blackened-up faces as a means of disguise.

However, people have been painting their faces for a long time, and this may not
be the original explanation. Blackened faces were used as a form of disguise in the
"Rebecca Riots" in South Wales in the 1830's, which were a protest against toll
roads, which also involved men dressing as women. They may have been revived
following the Minstrel Shows of the early 19th century. Did the face blacking continue through the Puritan era following the Civil War? How was it treated following the Black Act of 1723 which treated face blacking as an intent to commit a
crime, with harsh penalties?[22]

By this way of thinking, Robin Hood would have started out as acting
Black or performing Blackness, but would later have been transformed into
the Whiteness of acceptance and correctness. Similarly, every mass murderer, every tax cheat, and every playground bully is undeniably Black,
regardless of skin colour, until he or she becomes a hero. Black is the colour
of the intent of all those who would bring death into the garden that every
nation and state claims itself to be as a civil society. It is the colour of the
hearts and intentions of all those who have the ability to do harm to the
people as a collective. It is the disguise of all those deemed to be in the service of death and evil, the natural colour in Western mythology of the four
horsemen of death.

Black is the colour in Western thought of the devil who would not abide
by an all-powerful and all-knowing God, but who sought to deceive, disrupt, and destroy the order that is ordained by whatever is the most and
highest good in the universe and in the state or nation. Similarly, all those
Black-skinned police officers and soldiers, every Black-skinned security
guard that died in protection of the state and order is undoubtedly idealized

White and is venerated as such in the Whiteness of memory which is the accepted and official version and narrative of how a people in a specific place and time achieve the Whiteness and enlightenment of a civil society. If this is what Black and Blackness has always meant traditionally, who then is really Black, and how do we know before the fact who is likely to exhibit the Blackness that is marked by the actions of those who ought not to belong to a free and civil society?

Indeed, in the early years of a new millennium in Western society, in what is called Christendom, Blackness seems to be everywhere. This is as it has always been, even from the beginning of time and, seemingly will be, till the end of time. This Blackness is there in the movies when an ET phones home or in any of those science fiction movies that are always premised on the arrival of evil from somewhere in the galaxy in our garden that is Earth. These evildoers come from the land of the Unknown and they approach with a Blackness in their hearts – if they have any – that is aimed at disrupting our normal life and destroying our civil societies and civilizations. But the invaders are culturally and even somatically Black in another sense: in their several heads, the weird body parts, the manner in which they are grotesquely constructed with excessively large eyes, hands, heads, and too many limbs – in general the complete opposite of what are the norms of human creation or evolution.

These tales of fantasy are no different from those that have always been told of creatures from the dark, the lagoon, or from a place that was described as Dark Africa. This is the Africa, that from the beginning of Western civilization, was presented as the heart of darkness, a place populated in the view of Herodotus with troglodytes or in the view of Pliny, the Greek geographer Ptolemy, and in the early Middle Ages the *Etymologiae* by the Seville bishop Isidore with a host of unusual creatures. As Peter Mark shows in *Africans in European Eyes: The Portrayal of Black Africans in Fourteenth Century Europe,* Africa and the Black people found they were seen by the European gaze as strange and even non-human. Bishop Isidore, for example, "populated Ethiopia with fanciful creatures, all derived from earlier writers. He wrote of Sciapods, whose one huge foot was used as an umbrella to shade them from the sun. He mentioned the 'Blemmyae' of Libya who had no heads, and whose eyes were in their chest, and he described other monstrosities."[23]

Or, in this imagination, Africa the land of the unknown was the place of strange religions and morals. There was a race of Black men who worshipped a dragon, according to the Spanish author Ramon Lull in 1283. There were the Moors and Muslims of northern Africa during the Crusades. And, according to Enlightenment thinkers as diverse as Hume, Kant, and Hegel, Africa and the Black people to be found there were the antithesis of the enlightened and civilized European.[24] Later, these images and fantasies will be incorporated through writers like Christopher Marlowe and William Shakespeare in the construction of norms of European and English citizenship in such a way that the monsters were presented as non-European, non-English, and uncivilized. They were Black in skin colour, intent, and behaviour. This much we can bear in mind when watching another episode of a *Star Trek*–like series, the latest invasion from another world, or the appropriately coloured somatically Black ET phoning home.

It is for this reason that when scientists with the Science Museum in London claimed in fall 2004 that they had discovered the remains of a proto-human – described as "a new species of hobbit-sized humans who lived about 18,000 years ago on an Indonesian island – they presented a picture of what was effectively a minute Black-skinned homo sapiens. Apart from skin colour, the being was "black" in other ways: it was presented as uncultured, uncivilized, and not yet fully human, even if it was presented as physically fit even at an advanced age, a characteristic more typical of the prototypical American capitalist who must survive in the Blackness of a state of nature of "all against all." The press release noted: "the partial skeleton of Homo Floresiensis, found in a cave on the island of Flores, is of an adult female that was 3 feet tall, had a chimpanzee-sized brain and was substantially different from modern humans." Ironically, the accompanying drawing was of a naked male, penis and all.

In this way, these TV shows and movies, in firing up the imagination, and by drawing clear distinctions between good and evil, are laying claim to a long legacy of Whiteness and Blackness. Similarly, Blackness is present each time we hear of a movie that is raking in the cash at the box office – the latest attempt by some investor to end up in the Black with profit as the reward for her or his effort. Traditionally, profits have been Black – gifts from the Greek god Hades, or Roman Pluto, ruler of Blackness and the underworld – as a sign of disapproval by major religions for a specific way of life, especially that of people involved in what was seen as usury or money lending. But Black is also the colour of the tax collector and of the highwayman, of the pirate and those still involved in blackmailing, blackballing, blacklisting, or those Black Hand members of such criminal and terrorist secret societies as the Mafia and the Camorra – all those reprobates of civil society that are usually hauled off to prison in a Black Maria or some such van used for transporting prisoners from police courts to jails. All those really in league with Hades or Pluto.

Why is knowing who and what Black and Blackness are important? Put another way, why is it necessary to understand the equivocal meaning of the words Black and Blackness in our modern cultures or civilization? I am arguing that this knowledge is important because it will help bring a clearer understanding to how some people are treated within states and nations and to why this treatment might not be consistent with how the group expects to be treated. It may be that those with the power to hand out the treatment feel that they are doing the best they can and that their intentions are to help rather than hinder, and find themselves instead in a position where their treatment brings charges of inequality and unfairness. Meanwhile, on the other side, those that it seems should benefit from the special treatment find themselves appearing as ungrateful in the eyes of their benefactors. This is particularly true of several countries where race and racism are part of the main discourse, and the parties placed in a binary opposition seem unable to extricate themselves from this bind even when they act with the best of intentions to do good for the other side and for themselves. This is the case when, as a collective, the main parties involved and the goodwill they endure amount to what Hegel calls an Unhappy Consciousness.[25]

This allows us an analysis of Canada through which it becomes possible to understand the group of people commonly called Black Canadians as unhappy consciousnesses, as living in states of interminable and intractable Blackness. They are unhappy and to a large extent do not know why. The originality of my discussion is that they are unhappy, unintentionally, because of idealistic assumptions based on perception and lack of knowledge: they all think they are White in all categories except the somatic while others *see* and recognize them as Black, based on perception and the somatic.

Neither side is aware of this, as each side strives to be recognized as White. Perception and somatic Blackness are at the heart of this unreconciled unhappy consciousness. This is particularly the case of somatic Blacks from the Caribbean who believe they are idealistically White and highly skilled immigrants that have been recruited for being among the world's brightest and best. Many of them think they are White idealistically, culturally, and in status; yet in Canada they live a socially Black existence and are perceived as Black.

It is, therefore, for this reason that it became necessary to argue for the four specific categories of the idealized, the cultural, the somatic, and status for understanding Blackness. In this regard we are beginning to map new terrain, as I have not found this kind of category-centred discussion elsewhere or in one place. This is also why we should discuss what it means to be Black, who is Black or can be constructed as Black, what kinds of existence come with Blackness, what kinds of ethical relations Blacks should have with themselves and others, and what can be known about the happiness or abilities of Blacks.

Here again, in approaching Blackness through an epistemological framework that looks at categories of perception, cognition, motility, and affectivity, I am mapping new areas in the Canadian context. In examining Canadian multiculturalism according to these frameworks, we propose a particular and perhaps original approach to understanding who is a Canadian and who may claim full citizenship in the Canadian state.

These original approaches, however, are grounded primarily in philosophy, sociology, anthropology, cultural studies, history, and religion – among other disciplines. In doing all this, I am reminded of the thoughts of the famed phenomenologist Martin Heidegger, and of his prescription to how we should try to come to terms with equivocations in our thinking and views of the world, such as those we have encountered in trying to understanding common sense Blackness. He was dealing specifically with the question of knowing what is truly essential and necessary from what is contingent and inessential on the issue of the substance of beings that are created and finite and that are creators and infinite.

In both cases, the substance or essence of one was projected analogously onto the other, so that one being or appearance that is merely an ontic was deduced to be the same for all beings and was therefore ontological to all beings. Writing in his seminal work *Being and Time*, Heidegger says

What is here intended is substantiality; and it gets understood in terms of a characteristic of substance – a characteristic which is itself an entity. Because something ontical is made to underlie the ontological, the expression *"substantia"* functions sometimes with a signification which is ontological, sometimes with one which is ontical, but mostly with one which is hazily ontico-ontological. Behind this slight difference of signification, however, there lies hidden a failure to master the basic problem of Being. To treat this adequately, we must "track down" the equivocation *in the right way.* He who attempts this sort of thing does not just "busy himself" with "merely verbal significations"; he must venture forward into the most primordial problematic of the "things themselves" to get such "nuances" straightened out.[26]

The method that Heidegger suggests is phenomenology. Let us now turn our attention to a fuller discussion of the aims and perspective of this study and for an explanation of the methodology on which its arguments rest.

# SECTION TWO

# Theoretical Frameworks

# 5

# Blackness and Goodness

## Frameworks of Study

In this chapter, I will present two frameworks for viewing Blackness and its binary other, Whiteness, in what I have been calling Western thought in referring to a peculiar system that is rationally self-contained and has been developing syncretically throughout history. This is a system where we want to know in terms of universals, both in the hope of arriving at synthetic a priori forms of knowledge, but also as a way of explaining that seeming x-factor, the supersensible element that influences ethical relations with different people and groups. This factor is always part of the system, in subjects, objects, and relations in the system, but is usually not explicitly stated or considered as given. It is seldom deduced empirically, yet is considered indispensable to reasonable thinking in this system.

The first framework makes use of four categories of Blackness and Whiteness: the somatic, status, culture, and the ideal. These are, importantly, categories of knowing rather than categories of social phenomena, such as race, class, gender, citizenship and so on. These categories will allow us to pull away from the basic perceptional way of knowing that relies on common sense. This is where, as noted in the previous chapters, we start with taking things as they supposedly are or, as received knowledge, they are given to us. We aim to move on to a higher level of knowing, where we try to resolve the contradictions that plague our thinking at the common sense level. Indeed, we will be trying to rise from what Hegel calls primary or analytic cognition to synthetic cognition – the latter being a necessary step for our moving on to what he calls dialectic cognition. This is where we have an understanding of the objects of our study as universal concepts or absolutes that express themselves, seemingly contradictorily, as particulars.

When we arrive at this point – if we ever can arrive – we will have left the world of perception for that of pure cognition. At this level, we will recognize that objects, rather than being the static and unchanging beings that common sense expects, always come to us in a form of *becoming*, where they are positioned as universals and particulars on a slide scale. On the ends of this scale are the binary positions of the concepts fully realized and actualized: on one end the *being* and on the other end the being's *other*, with the being presented always as the opposite of the other. Just as warm water takes either hot or cold as its positive being, and in so doing automatically takes the negative as its other, the actual or realized lukewarmness of the water is a mixture of both hot and cold. They can be seen from one side as the positive and its other and as the complete opposite from a different perspective. Yet, regardless of the view, in the specific moment the actual lukewarm water has not changed, whether we see it as hot becoming cold, or as cold water being heated up. It is on its way to becoming at either extremes cold or hot, and in a practical sense, it is also neither hot nor cold, but lukewarm – a bit of hot and cold combined.

It is the same with such concepts as Black, White, multiculturalism, Canada, Canadian, and citizen, to mention only a few of the concepts that we want to know as objects in this study. This is why a major link in the understanding of these concepts phenomenologically is seeing the world in categories of analytic thought.

The second framework presents four ways of looking at Blackness and Whiteness: ontologically, existentially, ethically, and epistemologically. These are the prerequisites for a third framework that I will develop in chapter 7 to analyse how, through the application of phenomenology as a search for perception, cognition, affectivity, and motility, we understand Blackness in Western society, and what we can know symbolically and analytically from the Black body.

These frameworks will help us understand Blackness and the placement of those traditionally defined as Black in Western societies. They will also help explain casual living, and such historic moments in the dialectical struggle between good and evil as what occurred in New York City in the fall of 2001, as I shall discuss in chapter 10, it being a specific moment of change on the neo-mythic register. The analysis in this chapter now begins with a look at the evolution of Blackness in Canada as part of the international phenomena of Blackness produced by Western civilization and the high point of this culture, modernity.

## BLACKNESS AND WHITENESS: CHANGEABLE AND UNCHANGEABLE

Blackness, even in multicultural Canada, has multiple meanings, frustrating any attempt to determine Blacks according to a fixed and specific set of attributes, as is the official classifying practice in a country that claims to be a multicultural liberal democracy. Yet, as Canadian literary theorist and cultural historian Northrop Frye argues, Canadians have always had a fixed or seemingly unchangeable notion of what Black is. "Early Canadian writers were certain of their moral values: right was white, wrong black, and nothing else counted or even existed."[1]

Such was and is Canada's original good, an ontological one that was based from inception on a functionalist creed or ideology emphasizing law, order, and good government *a mari usque ad mare* – based on moralistic norms of good and evil bounded in a territory from sea to sea. This is how, as a consciousness, Canada sees itself, its component parts, and its place in the world. As Frye argues, this is not a collective state of mind that encourages the challenging of standards, norms, or already decided philosophical questions.[2] This was a cosmological ontology based on the uplifting of clear and unchangeable notions of idealizing Whiteness, civilization, progress, and the good, in opposition to Blackness, primitiveness, degeneracy, and evil.[3]

But by the beginning of the twenty-first century, there was a new element in this argument. Will Kymlicka offers, for example, that for sociological and public policy purposes, "our society remains racially divided [as it always has been] but the fundamental divide is less and less white/non-white and more [somatically] white/black."[4] Kymlicka is speaking indirectly of how Canada has proclaimed a good that is no longer based exclusively on moral issues or a Kantian sense of the intelligible, but has come to rely on somatic and cultural features to divide Canadians into groups that are equal, superior, and inferior to one another. This is a good that is situated fully in the world and which does not acknowledge that there are different ways of knowing. This way of knowing is based on the separation of the "inner" and the "outer," of the real and the pretend, but is nonetheless an acknowledgement of the social reality that is the lived embodiment of the diversity of people and cultures that are Canadian.

Change has entered the Canadian ideal. In this case, Whiteness is associated with superiority and Blackness with inferiority; Whiteness with acceptance and Blackness with exclusion; Whiteness with wholesome Canadian liberal values, Blackness with the foreign and an undesirable "subculture." Generally, equality is a matter of tolerance, where a subject that is usually White confers recognition on a lesser one that is normatively Black. Blackness and Whiteness are no longer exclusively "colours" of the heart, as a moral site for goodness or evil. They are markers of status or class for deciding who is deserving of and entitled to benefits and privileges in a nation-state that still sees itself as morally White.

Colour of skin is still, however, the main and unchangeable signifier of this racial categorizing. This is an ethno-racial way of knowing that apparently stands in the face of the *changing* received knowledge of who is a Canadian according to Canada's understanding of its mythic essence. This awareness might be the case where the unchangeable is the empirical and sensory manifestation of Canadians as opposed to the usual expectation that the unchangeable would be Canadian as a concept unto itself. As Kymlicka argues, moral issues in Canada are now complicated by shifting colours of ethnicity because of "considerable historical variation in people's perceptions of who is 'white' and who is 'black.'"[5] Shifting perceptions over the colour line have made it possible for groups that were once Black to become White and to gain equality of status in society. "I think that Latin Americans are increasingly seen as white by many Canadians. Perhaps some day the Japanese and Chinese will be seen as white as well."[6]

The same, alas, as Kymlicka argues, is not true for those whose skins are Black, and who might have been born and acculturated solely among those groups fast becoming White, that is, those having made it into the idealistic preferred position. Thus, as less emphasis is placed on religious or cultural difference, Arabs and South Asians, as well as Muslims, Sikhs, and other non-Christian religions appear to be becoming White for Kymlicka.[7] "The term 'visible minorities' presupposes that, for sociological and public policy purposes, these non-white groups are closer to the 'Black' side than the white. But in reality many of these groups are coming to be seen as (almost) white. The term 'visible minorities' may be blinding us to this important trend."[8] There is still a real and finite boundary, even within Canada, between those deemed to be ethno-racially Black and those who are considered to be genuinely Canadian. In many respects, the concept Canadian does not in its infinity include those who are purportedly racially and ethnically Black. Also, we must acknowledge that Kymlicka was writing before the world-shaking 9/11 terrorist incidents, the results of which, among others, made Muslims, Islam, and peoples from the Middle East idealistically Black in Western countries. This, too, was before police forces in Canada arrested dozens of Middle Eastern men and boys – all of the Muslim faith – as a purported crackdown on "home grown" terrorism. This, too, is an indication of how what was once deemed to be White can be "discovered" to be actually Black.

In Kymlicka's narrative, Canada is still the epitome of moral goodness pitted in an ontological struggle with Blackness, associated in the Canadian imaginary with evil and chaos. As in earlier times, the epitome of the threatening disorder was the presence of ethno-racially non-White people, but previously they were excluded from official recognition in the Canadian narrative. These were mainly people excluded from the social, cultural, and political life within the Canadian territory, or were people from non-preferred or "Black" spaces around the globe looking to immigrate to Canada. In the later development, chaos is still Black but is acknowledged as having an official presence in the Canadian cosmos, a presence that could grow even bigger because of an increasing need for immigrants to populate Canada and because of an immigration policy that, technically,

does not select new Canadians according to explicitly ethnic or racial characteristics, but tries to return the selection of immigrants to a more neo-
mythic register.

Canada's good as a multicultural nation, therefore, consists of two distinct parts of the same tale: in the first, as captured by Frye, Canada is a
White and homogeneous nation-state with no place officially for Blacks; in
the second, it is a country in which citizens and residents are conflictedly
divided into two racial categories, White and Black, to decide who gets official de facto recognition in the polity. Full entitlement, rights, and belonging are reserved for Whites; Blacks have a second-class status and are
constantly struggling to be recognized as full citizens. In this analysis, it is
worth pointing out again that Black and White are moral and normative
attributes, not only features of the soma. Frye and Kymlicka are speaking
of the same phenomenology of Canada and Canadianness, but from different perspectives. Conceptually, they offer finite, if different, views that are
dialectically parts of the infinity that is now multicultural Canada.

Even though Canada claims officially to have shifted away from the earlier ontology, the inferior existential experience of those constructed as
Black indicates that Canada may remain wedded to an essentialist ontology
that was handed down fully formed by the intellect of its two mythological
founding peoples. This was the ontology that originally reduced Blackness
solely to skin colour and to the culture of those whose skin is Black. The
notion of good, from which all things spring, has not changed, even though
the materials available for the creation of the Canadian state from inception have never been changeless, uniform in their purity, and White.

Within the current thought and expression of who is a Canadian, the old
ontology remains present, though hidden. As Kymlicka notes in *Politics in
the Vernacular: Nationalism, Multiculturalism, and Citizenship*, over time
some groups that were deemed to be culturally Black and somatically
brown have become White for sociological and public policy purposes in
Canada, leaving it ambiguous and unclear if there is a fundamental difference between somatic and cultural Blackness, a difference that decides who
is Black in status in Canada:

It is an interesting question how exactly we should describe this phenomenon. Are
Asians and Arabs in Canada (or Coloureds in South Africa) in fact being perceived
as "white"? Or is it rather that whites continue to see "brown" people as non-
white, but now draw greater distinctions amongst different kinds of non-white
groups, emphasizing the difference between brown and black? Put another way, is
the fundamental racial divide between whites and non-whites, so that being accepted
in Canada requires being seen as white? Or is the fundamental divide between
Blacks and non-Blacks, so that being accepted does not require that one be white –
one could be brown, yellow or red and still be one of "us" – so long as one is not

Black. I am not sure how best to analyse this phenomenon. But it seems to exist, and I think it has potentially serious consequences for the integration of Blacks in Canada.[9]

What we have embarked on is a phenomenological reading that addresses the questions raised by Kymlicka and other liberal pluralists about Blackness in modern thought. It will describe a search for a good or bad essence of Blackness that, over time and specifically in modernity, has proven futile. This futility is the dead end of meaning, in terms of knowing with certainty the attributes of humans, a dead end to which this search for certainty has led Western civilization, in the universal, and Canada, in the particular. This is the belief that the colour of a person's skin, primarily if it is Black, has a transcendental significance, that colour of skin can be equated to an ethnicity or that it can be used to discern a racialized positioning in a social hierarchy.

A phenomenological reading of Blackness shows that it consists of too many categories for it to be portrayed as having unequivocal meaning, for the claim that all people whose skin are Black, are in fact, Black, or that those whose skins are not Black cannot be Black. Contrary to the view of Frye's early Canadian writers, there is no single definition of Blackness, just as there is no single and permanent common sense meaning of the good. Both the good and Blackness, as universal categories, have to be placed in a context for a specific meaning, and they must have an other against which to be judged.

CATEGORIES OF BLACKNESS

Throughout the history of Western philosophy and political thought, attempts have always been made to reduce what we can know about the world and ourselves to synthetic categories. The results of this synthesis are taken to be pure categories of knowing and understanding. We recall Claude Lévi-Strauss's comment in *Structural Anthropology* that humans are by nature classifiers: we have to place objects and phenomena in categories so that we may know them with any certainty, and so we may bring meaning into our world.[10] Indeed, as Kant argues in *Critique of Practical Reason*, in approaching any concept and to determine its causality or freedom, "I soon see that since I cannot think without a category, I must first seek out the category in reason's idea of freedom."[11] How we categorize is cultural, given to us as part of a social imagination. It is how we expect the world and experience to conform to concepts and notions that start within us, but which are necessary for us to make meaning of the world. This is a way of knowing the world through a series of categories or representations where our experiences in the world are a representation of what we think, and think we know.

In this way, as Stuart Hall argues in *Representation*, we believe that through a series of representations we can generalize between the universal and particular.[12] This is not done so much as an act of totalization and homogenization but to allow us to deal with society and its members as abstractions and groups within a larger group or universe. This is the case, for example, when the modern state seeks to treat every citizen equally or when it decides that some people ought to be treated differently and be discriminated against positively or negatively. In either case, sociologically, societies try to reduce themselves to categories within a broader unit, each a recognized finite extracted from the larger infinity that is the society, and constructed around some a priori element that is ascribed or said to have been achieved but held as common to the group.

Aristotle gives us a method for determining categories as a means of acquiring epistemic knowledge. This is a process that has been built upon since Aristotle's time but which remains the core of category formation and recognition.

Things are said to be named "equivocally" when, though they have a common name, the definition corresponding with the name differs for each. Thus, a real man and a figure in a picture can both lay claim to the name "animal"; yet these are equivocally so named, for, though they have a common name, the definition corresponding with the name differs for each. For should any one define in what sense each is an animal, his definition in the one case will be appropriate to that case only.

On the other hand, things are said to be named "univocally" which have both the name and the definition answering to the name in common. A man and an ox are both "animal," and these are univocally so named, inasmuch as not only the name, but also the definition, is the same in both cases: for if a man should state in what sense each is an animal, the statement in the one case would be identical with that in the other.

Things are said to be named "derivatively," which derive their name from some other name, but differ from it in termination. Thus the grammarian derives his name from the word "grammar," and the courageous man from the word "courage."[13]

Later, Immanuel Kant, as the father of modern transcendentalist philosophy, built on Aristotle's thinking. In Kant's *Critique of Pure Reason*, categories are essential for a synthetic understanding, one that is dialectical and is the intended marriage of pure intuition or thought, and empiricism based purely on the senses. As he states, this synthesis of the many things or objects into categories, and whether in thought or through these senses, "is the first requisite for the production of knowledge, which, in its beginning, indeed, may be crude and confused, and therefore in need of analysis – still, synthesis is that by which alone the elements of our knowledge are collected and united in a certain content, consequently it is the first thing on which we must fix our attention, if we wish to investigate the origin of our knowledge."[14]

This understanding of categories as being pure products of reason, and as a basis for a phenomenological study, was later taken up by Hegel, who in turn provides a model for our own examination. In this regard, these synthetic categories are necessary for us to understand the phenomena given to us through our senses in space and time. As subjects, we impose our categories on these objects as a way of classifying time chronologically and in a way which enables us to detect truth and changes, or what are the changeable and unchangeable in these objects. Indeed, the categories are limited by our imagination.

Epistemologically, Black and Blackness are by the above definition equivocal and often known or perceived through derivation and analogy. There can be no single meaning that covers all circumstances and contexts. I want to suggest four specific ways of reading Black and Blackness cognitively:

1   as **appearance** or the **somatic,** based racially and genetically on the colour of the epidermal skin layer that is perceived to be encoded with values that signify good or evil. This has become the predominant way for discerning who is Black in modern society, but it is a category that is so open to misunderstanding that from the outset one has to deliberately decide to set aside the notion of skin colour as the sole and absolute determination of Blackness. One aim of this discussion is to show how the perception of Blackness as amounting solely to skin colour has become so ingrained in Western thought that at times it appears unshakeable and, consequently, has become one of the biggest issues in anti-racism discourses when the participants do not (or cannot) see beyond the superficiality of skin colour. One of the ironies – and difficulties – of seeking to determine with certainty who is Black is the frequency with which the matter always returns to skin colour as the sole voice of Blackness. In this regard, skin colour sticks out falsely as Black and Blackness a priori. The somatic is the primary category under the ethno-racial register.

2   as **status,** which usually translates in the sociological and anthropological as referring to (a) the low class status of those who are least skilled and, in Marxist theory, are considered the proletariat; (b) a struggle against that status by seeking participation in power, social justice, and influence as a democratic right or entitlement; (c) the force behind the struggle as disruption and subversion; (d) the reversal of that status, and the success of the struggle to obtain recognition as being among those who rule, and recognition as individuals; and (e) ultimately, a social and legal marker of ownership of rights or of property, or in this case the lack of them, of which the highest form in a liberal democracy is ownership of the self. In the Hegelian

analysis we shall apply, this category is representative of the bondsman position and its situation in a lordship and bondage ethical relation. Status is a category found mainly under the ethno-racial register.

3 as **culture**, based on (a) a particular cultural expression associated primarily with Africans and their descendants and with the celebration of the body over the mind, the present over the future, and the temporal and earthly over the everlasting and spiritual; (b) creativity, anti-formalism, non-conformity, and the questioning and rejection of the given and the established; (c) passion and desires, the root of that cultural expression and, also, as the projection onto Blacks by the opposing expression of White reasonableness; (d) chaos and death that disrupts everlasting life and order, as a continuation of that White projection; and (e) evil, especially when disruptive of the given, the formulaic, and the established order. This category is also expressive mainly of the ethno-racial register.

4 as **ideals**, an evaluative category made up of the supposed best of all the other categories, formulated through attempts for a common mythological, philosophical, and theological view of the world. It takes into account the preferred positions of the three previous categories and establishes them as ideals of Blackness that translate into (a) the opposite of a pre-ordained ontological good; (b) what is morally and ethically wrong, but which translates existentially into (c); (c) what is truly human and creative; (d) creolization, hybridity, and syncretism; and (e) sociologically, what is usually presented in the dominant discourse as deviant, abnormal, and pathological in social construction. This category is found mainly on the neo-mythic register, and it is that against which all other categories are subsequently adjudged. In this sense, ideals can mean more than what is striven for but also what have been present as the norms of perfection.

Similarly, the four matching readings for White and Whiteness are:

1 as **appearance** or the **somatic,** based racially and genetically on the colour of the epidermal skin layer that signifies good or evil perceptually

2 as **status**, based on (a) an aristocratic class with more skill, wealth, power, and entitlement; (b) those who do not need to struggle but participate fully in the power elite and who achieve social justice and are influential; (c) the force to counter disruption and subversion; (d) those who put down attempts to reverse that status; and (e) ultimately, incontestable ownership and rights, particularly those of the self in a liberal democracy. This is the equivalent in our analysis of the lord's position in the Hegelian lordship and bondage ethical relation.

3 as **culture**, based on (a) the universal definition of what constitutes a cultural expression; (b) reason; (c) order and life that is everlasting and unchanging as opposed to temporary and transitory; and (d) what is good

4  as **ideals**, an evaluative category based on cosmological and essentialist
   notions of goodness and perfection as the preferred position of the other
   three categories. It refers to (a) the ontologically divine; (b) the pure and
   uncontaminated; (c) the culturally and existentially fixed or formulaic in
   terms of presenting an ordained or singular method for achieving a good
   that never changes; (d) absolute cognition and full knowledge epistemologically; (e) ethically, as justice, happiness, and self-sufficiency; and (f) the
   normative and even natural in the dominant discourse.

In presenting these categories, we must be extremely mindful of the following caveat: idealized Blackness and Whiteness are what is "given" to us
by culture out of our myths and moral education. At any given time, they
are the binaries in our social imagination. These myths carry and produce
the concepts that from within us give reality meaning. In this sense, Black is
all that is the "not-I" or identified negatively as the other of consciousness.
This is the same consciousness that posits itself positively as I and thinks
itself White. It is the "I" that it is – the I am, with subjectivity and agency.
All others are the collective "not-I" of this consciousness. If the concept I or
Canadian is the subject, then the "not-I's" are the objects that stand against
the real meaning and the self-determination of the concept.

## CANADIAN WHITENESS
## FROM BLACKNESS

In Canada, a Canadian has traditionally been defined subjectively as
White. All other groups were seen by this consciousness as the "not-I,"
those who are not, for whatever reason, genuinely Canadian. This was as
true over time for the Black-skinned peoples as it was for the Chinese,
Ukrainians, South East Asians, Filipinos, First Nations peoples, Jews,
Romanians, Slavs, and others. Indeed, this was the lived reality for all those
not defined conceptually as White.

Therefore, if they were all different representations of the "not-I" of consciousness, then, phenomenologically, by representation they were also not
White idealistically. Thus, they did not correspond or even cohere in the
actual world to the good as thought and imagined. Therefore, if they were
collectively "not-I" and non-White, they were all Black – and here we must
remember that Blackness is indeterminate. It is, as Hegel says, the vacuity
of the "night when all cows are black." White and Whiteness in modern
thought were determinate and morally free. Speculatively, then, in a holistic
way a Canadian consciousness always aimed to be White, but as history
and dialectical reasoning will show in later chapters, it has always found
itself to be represented by the "not-I" of the concept for good. Canadian
consciousness has always found itself not White, but Black. In this recogni-

tion of identity – or the lack of denial of such recognition – is the story of a multicultural Canada coming to see itself in a true light – in a proverbial burst of sunlight.

The other three ways of reading Blackness and Whiteness – through the somatic, culture, and status – are empty signifiers, especially when seen through the gaze of the ethno-racial register. We have to be always pouring the idealized meaning into them in order for them to be coloured as they are. This meaning may take different forms depending on differences in time and space, in other words the context or situation. These three categories are really just representations of the idealized concept in its infinity and entirety; they are the determinate forms that we use to make lived experiences meaningful to us.

In many respects, these categories are present in much of the dominant Western literature, although they tend not to be recognized specifically as different and named categories of understanding. In addition, each category is not always perceived as essential or necessary to Blackness. Depending on the social, political, and historical contexts, a category might be considered to be accidental for Blackness. Or, as has been the case for some time now, one category – as with the somatic – might be deemed the essential, and all others contingent.

For example, Holt notes how eventually race or Blackness is reduced to biology and genetics, what I call the ethno-racial, but that this leaves the discussion incomplete, especially for those who, from a common sense perspective, have mixed ancestry. "I am black because I am descended from black people – notwithstanding the fact that some of them were actually white. However much we acknowledge the fiction, traces of the old biological idea linger."[15] Holt exposes the "fiction" of any social construction of Blackness that is based on the somatic and phenotypic as analogies for that which is natural to these categories. He then turns to exposing "another ambiguous and fraught concept – culture."[16] But this culture or new racism, so described in the literature because of a purported shift away from biological determination, also falls short of capturing everything, and is often conflated back into the old biological notion of race. As Holt argues: "Whatever their putative racial or ethnic identity, the inhabitants of Western late-capitalist societies confront powerful forces that dictate allegiance to the same fundamental culture, notwithstanding variations on or even occasional opposition to its main themes. Thus the culture concept abuts 'the social' and 'the ideological,' which produces its own ambiguities, leaving it no more capable of doing the work of race than biology."[17] If we add idealistic to Holt's "social" and "ideological" – and recognize as he does that it is a product of Western thought – we can find in Holt's analysis categories of knowing Blackness and Whiteness that amount to the somatic, the cultural, and the idealistic.[18]

As another example, Mills sets his task in *The Racial Contract* as being to explain, "the most important political system of recent global history – the system of domination by which white people have historically ruled over and, in certain important ways, continue to rule over nonwhite people."[19] While Mills has somatic, cultural, and idealistic or normative White-ness and Blackness in mind, undoubtedly one of the main challenges he set himself was to explain the dominant relationship in this, depending on per-spective, idealistically Black or White system – effectively to spell out status Whiteness and Blackness and how it shapes and limits the real life experi-ences of those who are somatically (biologically), idealistically (ethics, rights, justice, abstraction), and culturally Black or White (as expressed in the life-styles and dominant or subordinated conditions under which some people live). As he brings together these four categories – without naming them as such – Mills explains: "The 'Racial contract,' then, is intended as a concep-tual bridge between two areas now largely segregated from each other: on the one hand, the world of mainstream (i.e., white) ethics and political phi-losophy, preoccupied with discussions of justice and rights in the abstract, on the other hand, the world of Native American, African American, and Third and Fourth World political thought, historically focused on issues of conquest, imperialism, colonialism, white settlement, land rights, race and racism, slavery, jim crow, reparations, apartheid, cultural authenticity, national identity, *indigenismo,* Afrocentrism, etc."[20]

As Holt puts it, what we are doing is showing that "there is no question, then, of defining race and racism (or, for that matter, ethnicity) and follow-ing them as unchanging entities through time. It is rather a question of see-ing how historical forces shape and change the meaning of these terms over time and space."[21] Indeed, we are examining, ultimately, the one thing that supposedly remained unchangeable over time and space and which was reduced existentially to finite subgroups, of which race and ethnicity are merely two. That concept, in its infinity, is Blackness and its conceptual other, Whiteness.

Here I am setting the groundwork to examine Blackness in four ways: through the ontological, existential, ethical, and epistemological, in a man-ner that corresponds loosely to what I have defined as the four categories of Blackness – the somatic, culture, status, and the ideal. It is helpful to show how the different ways of looking at Blackness complement the categories, and vice versa. I shall do this by examining, first, how the four categories can be explained ontologically and existentially, and, second, how they can be explained ethically and epistemologically.

In each case, I will also present what is the ideal, read neo-mythic, position ontologically; existentially; ethically; and epistemologically. In all cases, it is necessary to make a distinction between the individual and the general pop-ulation as bodies, one that is personal and the other that is collective, but both having different ontological and existential features and experiences. In the end, this discourse settles phenomenologically on these questions: What can we know about the body, whether that of an individual or collective, and what truths do Black bodies reveal? What then is Black and Blackness, if these words are not merely meaningless labels?

Through ontology, we see a world that is made up of dichotomized opposites of Blacks and Whites because of somatic features. An individual is born White or Black based on the colour of the skin. Collectively, societies are White or Black in this Manichean or dualistic world where even mixed "race" people are idealistically positioned in Western philosophy and mythology as Black or contaminated from a pure White. Existentially, these individuals, separately or collectively, produce a culture. They live in societies where they are positioned in a hierarchy of binary positions.

## WHITENESS AND BLACKNESS: EUROCENTRISM

In a Eurocentric cosmos, somatic Whiteness is placed at the top and somatic Blackness at the bottom. But in the lived experience, it is a hierarchy that is not based solely on the somatic and other factors, such as cultural traits, which influence the position in the vertical hierarchy. This accounts for the creation of class in the collective body, and the superior or inferior existences that are associated with a specific class. Thus, those who might be deemed to be subversive, disruptive, or deviant, and even if they are somatically White, will be positioned at the bottom as Black. Those who are conformist, accommodating, and accepting of norms, even if somatically Black, are perceived as White and placed morally and ethically at the top.

Idealistically, those of the leisure class and those who have power in society occupy the top positions in Western societies. Technically, they are the White gods of their society. They have full rights and entitlements to the best of their society and to full protection from the society. They enjoy the best of life and endure less of its drudgery. On the other hand, the idealistic Blacks are those in the inferior positions, those who do not live the life of leisure or power. Rather, they are the producers for the leisure class and they are the ruled.

Existentially, the cultural Blackness and Whiteness also results from the creation of culture and the forms of culture that are created. The forms of culture that individuals and groups produce are best viewed on a horizontal continuum that shows human progress towards the ideal of a stable, predictable, and fixed existence or social order. One extreme point is marked by the creativity that is necessary for human progress. This is the point that represents the creative, the subversive, and the deviance that produces the geniuses that are constantly pushing societies to higher levels of achievement and progress.

Without them life would be static, but orderly. Without this, life would be as close as possible to a static, and even dead, utopia. However, this point is also associated with the immature, primordial, primitive, and irrational culture that is still in the process of being fully formed. It is marked by the dynamics of life. This point is represented in mythology by Blackness. Idealistically, this corresponds to chaos, instability, and disruptions in the extreme. Yet, it is the site of pure and free creativity, and of creation itself.

The opposite extreme position is marked by civilization, defined as a fully developed and formalized culture, supposedly a fixed and unchangeable place where there is no need for further progress. This, as Frye would suggest, is the garden that has been brought out of the bush as a place and attitude of difference and defiance. It is the garrison and its mentality in a desert.[22] This point is discernible through order and the preservation of this order. This is the Whiteness of civilization, where disruptions are not welcomed, where the passions must be controlled, and where reason is enthroned and rules are based on the authority of natural and rational law and order.[23] Idealistically, this spot corresponds to the paradisiacal and idyllic, where there can be no greater good, and where any disruption would be only to move backwards towards chaos or a lesser good. It would be degeneracy, heading towards the Other, or the binary opposite to progress and civilization on this sliding scale. In our mythology, ironically, this ideal of perfection is the kind of Garden of Eden from which any being must escape to become fully human.

The ethical category asks: what is the appropriate way to treat individuals and groups based on their ontological/somatic characteristics and on an evaluation of their cultural/existential positioning in the social order? This is not a value-free evaluation. It presupposes that there are fundamental and inviolate norms of behaviour, an ethical idealistic Whiteness, based on well-recognized notions of good and evil. These ethical arguments presume a patented way to change those who by the four categories are Black into the Whiteness that is part of the prevailing mythology that informs the culture and ideology of a people. This mythology depends on two clear concepts: first, that there is Blackness that is changeable and, hopefully, transient culturally and in status, and secondly that it can change into a Whiteness that is unchangeable and idealistically good.

Indeed, in the Biblical mythology, it is Blackness and not Whiteness that is eternal and ever-present. Whiteness, as light, comes into being out of the darkness and eventually returns back into the permanent that is Blackness. This inversion of White coming out of Black is an important point of this book: a chaos-like Blackness that is changeable and unpredictable is the only constant in this order, the only perceptually unchangeable. Mythologically, such a role is not given to an unchanging Whiteness. Only the unchangeable, which is Blackness, is foundational and real, for it is not subject to change because of differences in perspective, gaze, knowledge, bodily functions, and cravings. The unchangeable is the Platonic form, always the same a priori and a posteriori, in the beginning and at the ending. It is analytic and not subject to dialectical negation or refutation, as is the case with that which is changeable and epistemologically Black – in terms of always falling short of perfect knowledge or understanding.

It is a process akin to Marx's suggestion of the double reversal, which in *The German Ideology* he says is necessary to correct the effects of ideology by standing the presumptive thought process on its head and inverting perceived causes and effects. This is an ideology that produces a widely held notion that Black and Blackness are degradations of White, rather than that White and Whiteness must have Black and Blackness as its origin, and perceptually, its ending also. While it cannot change, this good or Whiteness can be revealed by doing something similar to what Hegel suggests in the earlier epigraph for this book's prologue, by peeling away that which is changeable: the many layers of darknesses or Blackness that naturally hide what is esteemed in Western thought as the *real* thing.

In this regard, we must be extremely mindful of an admonition given to us by Kant about an overreliance on categories of understanding as necessarily leading to a synthesis of thought and empiricism in the lived world.[24] Seldom is this the case, and ultimately the value of what we know is imposed with one way of knowing, the neo-mythical as we call it, usually dominating another (the ethno-racial). In most cases, this dominance occurs subconsciously, willingly, and systemically, as continues to be the case with the dominant mythology, ideology, or intuition.

## BLACKNESS IN AN ETHICAL FRAMEWORK

For philosophers, alchemists, magicians, politicians, educators, criminologists, and others who have practised statecraft from the earliest times, the trick to this conversion is to move with surety and full knowledge from an unreal position that is changeable, because it is unstable, uncertain, and unpredictable to another unchangeable position, but one which in Western thought is presented as stability, certainty, predictability, and everlasting freedom and life. This is a transformation in an idealistic manner that is no different from the mythology of death and rebirth at the heart of the rational optimism that can be found in the dominant Greek, African, and Judeo-Christian roots of Western civilization. This is the foundation of what we are terming the neo-mythic register.

Such a radical transformation occurs when the sinner in her or his Blackness is turned into the Whiteness or purity of forgiveness, when the elect is

changed from the temporal body of pain and suffering into the everlasting
state of bliss in the land of milk and honey, and when in the Christian
Eucharist the wine in the chalice representing the Holy Grail becomes the
blood of Christ and the bread His body. In Western thought, even if discredited in some modern circles, such change from the changeable and malleable
to the unchangeable and fixed was presented as occurring only mythologically, through transfiguration or the revolution of a radical rebirth or recreation that can only occur in a site of pure and unbridled creativity.[25] This is
one order giving way to a radically different one.

This is an ethical relationship that is predicated on achieving good
through a personal and collective release from the Blackness that is chaos
and death, or the bondage that is near death, to the Whiteness of everlasting life, good government, order, and freedom. This release comes through
the transformation or transfiguration from Blackness via what I shall call a
double determinacy.[26] This conversion or rebirth is presented in Western
thought as a three-phase process: the starting position is the permanent but
changeable status that is the human tragedy of a living death that is bodily,
perishable, and Black; the first transformation occurs in death or purgatory
as the moment of transfiguration, when the old dies, thereby allowing for
the first real change; the third stage is the final determinacy or rebirth into
freedom and genuine reality, as idealistic and everlastingly White.[27]

This notion of double determinacy is so like the double healing and con-
juration that happened to Constantine to make him Great. As a framework, it may help bring us to a deeper reading of the significance of such
nation-state markers of inclusion as ethnicity, race, and class that are characteristics of moving from a primary state of Blackness to the ideal of
Whiteness in Western thought. This is analogous to the double determinacy
that immigrants, for example, must undergo to become fully Canadian
citizens.

One area where the double determinacy proves a useful tool is in examining how the modern state discerns who are citizens with full rights, privileges, and entitlements and who are, at best, strangers or visitors among the
citizens. The double determinacy decides which individuals, from out of a
universal population of billions of people in the world, have a right to call
themselves citizens of a particular country, whether it be Canada, the
United States, Britain, South Africa, or those dots for islands that are the
several sovereign states of the Caribbean. In Canada these rights of citizenship are meaningful in a very practical sense. For example, under the *Canadian Immigration and Refugee Protection Act*, only Canadians and First
Nations Peoples have a right to enter or re-enter the country.[28] All others
appearing at Canadian ports of entry are assumed to be strangers or foreigners until they show proof of citizenship, and thereby claim the inviolable
right of belonging to and having ownership in the state. The *Immigration*

*and Refugee Protection Act* of Canada makes this point clear: "Every Canadian citizen within the meaning of the *Citizenship Act* and every person registered as an Indian under the *Indian Act* has the right to enter and remain in
Canada in accordance with this Act, and an officer shall allow the person to
enter Canada if satisfied following an examination on their entry that the
person is a citizen or registered Indian."[29]

Once this primary determination is made, a second is activated. It decides
social Whiteness and Blackness among those who have already transcended
to the primary level of Whiteness out of their primordial Blackness. This
second stage within the nation or state determines who are the elites that
ultimately enjoy power, leisure, and the freedom of thought. The second
determinacy in its physical and outer manifestations is usually according to
what we are calling the ethno-racial register. Internally, it is according to
the neo-mythic.

## CITIZENSHIP: RIGHTS AND ABSTRACT WHITENESS

In Western mythology, the elites are the Adams of the world in their gardens. They are White, with a Whiteness that has nothing to do with the colour of their skin, but rather with their placement in society. They are not
the socially Black members of their country: for they are not those whose
function in the state is to work and produce, those who do not enjoy fully
the fruits of their labour, those who do not own all their capital, and those
who must be directed by and held accountable to more elite groups.[30]

The prevailing view in most liberal democracies is that, before the eyes of
the state, there is no second level of determination, for all citizens are created equal. This equality is what makes them social and is that through
which they are perfected to become the idealized human product in this
social arrangement. Through this socialization, how they are determined
and recognized on the ethno-racial register is deemed, from a ethical perspective, as less meaningful than how they are imagined under the neo-
mythic register. The rights that are recognized and protected in this society
are deemed to more important than any that might have been given to them
by nature. The equality section of the Canadian Charter of Rights and Freedoms, for example, makes this point a foundation of the state: "Every individual is equal before and under the law and has the right to the equal
protection and equal benefit of the law without discrimination and, in particular, without discrimination based on race, national or ethnic origin, colour, religion, sex, age or mental or physical disability."[31]

This, as we shall see, is akin to the Platonic creation of Whiteness in the
ideal and mythic state. In this regard, everyone is created White within the
state, and any tinge of Blackness is a drop or fall from this created status. If,
indeed, there is a second determinacy, the argument goes, this is based

solely on merit – and occurs in places where the state is blind and unknowing – for it is a determinacy of and through social justice in a way that is rational and even mechanical. If merit were, indeed, the main arbitrator, the change would still be neo-mythic, even if this determination would be deemed as not essential to a basic life of equality in the state. But when issues such as perceived race, ethnicity, and culture are considered, understanding moves to the ethno-racial register. Where there might be a difference at the state level is in the determination of who is primordially Black and who is primordially White, those who by their very nature and social construction start out as changeable Black or unchangeable White. This shows up in the Canadian Charter of Rights and Freedoms, when it switches from a neo-mythic register to explain citizenship to the ethno-racial as an attempt to recognize differences and levels of inequality – of status Blackness – that exist in Canada. The switch is made almost in the same breath, with the clause on neo-mythic Whiteness as equality followed immediately by the ethno-racial determinations and acceptable means of correcting inequalities. The Charter states: "Subsection (1) [of the section quoted above] does not preclude any law, program or activity that has as its object the amelioration of conditions of disadvantaged individuals or groups including those that are disadvantaged because of race, national or ethnic origin, colour, religion, sex, age or mental or physical disability."[32]

In the first category are those born into the special culture. For them the transformation first occurred in the past when it made their ancestors White, and the Whiteness was then handed down to them from generation to generation as an unbreakable and unchangeable legacy. This is a filial relationship, making the beneficiaries the "natural" sons and daughters of the nation-state. As the progeny of those that have already been transformed, they do not need in a Platonic sense a second change, for they are already White. Their Whiteness is already incorporated in their blood or in the culture that produced them as fundamentally White and belonging. In this case, reliance is on the outer manifestations, for the radical change that made them good occurred earlier, and it can be assumed that good never changes – and that it is whole, with the outer and inner the same.

All those with such a history, culture, and tradition are already White in their own eyes. This is the Whiteness that translates in citizenship that is *jus sanguinis* – or the right passed on directly through blood lines. In the second group are all those that are not so born, who come from a different place and time, are Black, and will enjoy only what status, rights, and privileges are benevolently extended to them by the unchangeable Whites of society. This is a citizenship or Whiteness achieved through change, through adaptation, or by taking on a new nature, a citizenship attained through *jus soli* – by the right of naturalization.[33] They do not have a "natural" filial relationship, but can be "adopted" into the family of the good. Supposedly, they will be accepted and recognized as full family members, no different from the "natural" inheritors, even if the "adoptees" look ethno-racially different from all others. This is akin, as we shall see, to the Aristotelian model of moving up a hierarchy with ever lighter shades of Black until pure White, or full naturalized citizenship, is achieved. In this regard, there will always be doubt about the authenticity and genuineness of this good, for the outer may not very well reflect the inner. Indeed, our two registers of understanding might be antithetical.

However, few liberal states can sincerely boast of not having this division among citizens along the lines of social Whiteness and Blackness, of not having first- and second-class citizens either because of the colour of skin, ethnicity, aptitudes, religion, gender, sexuality, or a host of other perceived essences which modernity has given to specific groups. Some citizens might be recognized as idealistic White on the neo-mythic register but are given a different determination that positions them as unchangeably Black on the ethno-racial register. Indeed, specifically in the Canadian setting, this double determinacy becomes meaningful in examining, first, the placement in Canadian society of immigrants, primarily those from Third World countries who are considered somatically and culturally Black, and First Nations peoples, who face the same construction as Third World immigrants, and, second, when they have become Canadian citizens, what reasonable limits should be placed on them that other "traditional" or *jus sanguinis* Canadians do not have.

Determinacy remains an issue in Canadian life, for it is part of a mythology inherent to the dialectic of freedom in Western thought and on which the Canadian state was founded ideologically. This founding belief states that, on one hand, Canada is officially multicultural where, under the constitutional equality provisions, no particular group has official dominance or primary recognition, where there are no differences between citizenship acquired *jus sanguinis* or *jus soli*. On the other hand, the belief also claims that Canada has two founding nations that are, for all intents and purposes, in a practical sense the power elites, and are fully and unchangeably White Canadians. They are still the "natural" citizens and other groups the "adoptees." As the first citizens, their behaviours are the reference of Canadian history, citizenship, and plans for the future, and everyone else is expected to recognize this primacy and dominance, and conform to it. This might be the case even though Canada supposedly does not expect assimilation, but rather integration and pluralism, at the ethno-racial level. Unstated, perhaps, is that at the neo-mythic level Canada expects assimilation and an unfragmented unity for state formation purposes.

In general, the ethno-racial register determines daily existentialism. This is why the Canadian Charter allows for what it calls affirmative action programs that at the neo-mythic level appear to contradict the ideal of oneness and unity but at the ethno-racial level are a practical recognition of differences and inequalities. Because ontological Blackness is associated with evil and the undesirable who does not belong, the result is an inferior positioning in society for members of this group. Existentially, those positioned as producing Black culture are treated as evil and not good for societies that believe they have attained levels of perfection that can only be threatened by the disruptive. Idealistically, especially in a country like Canada that defines itself as a liberal democracy with the rationalist Charter of Rights and Freedom, each individual would be treated as a rational moral agent that is free and intends good. Such agents act out of good faith to themselves and others. They expect to likewise be treated in good faith, where they are always given the benefit of the doubt, always held as innocent until proven guilty, and always viewed as intending to be good in their thoughts and actions. As Lewis Gordon argues, to do otherwise is to treat them in bad faith, ethically.[34] However, issues of good faith, as with most issues measured on the neo-mythic register, are usually those of "becoming," something that can only be reconciled fully in the transcendent or imagination, whereas the ethno-racial register speaks of already being, of things as fully formed objects and subjects as they are in the here and now of the material world.

## WHITE NIGGERS: BLACK HUMANITY

Some other individual or group does not determine the individual's morality under the neo-mythic register. Every moral individual, regardless of the person's somatic features and level of perceived cultural development, would be treated as White culturally, and her or his status in society would reflect this recognition. That some individuals are denied the opportunity to move from a lower status to a higher would be viewed as immoral and as keeping moral agents in bondage. In this case, it would be in bad faith to assume that members of this group do not intend good, and to therefore make them stereotypically and unchangingly evil and disruptive. An understanding of the ideology that produces norms of good and evil in Western civilization, and the reasoning behind what is held as the norm of a fully-formed and perfected society, thus helps us understand the status and classes of those who are treated in society as Black, and inferior, and as White, and superior. To this end, the neo-mythic is predicated on the becomingness of freedom, and on a subjective that is based on agency and knowledge on its way to becoming complete. The ethno-racial is not, and this is where the conflicts or contradictions over equality of citizenships may be explained.

In deed, such analysis presupposes for both registers, for consistency, a knowledge or epistemology of Blackness and Whiteness. How do we know how specific individuals or bodies of individuals will behave? Traditionally, Western societies have tried to organize humanity based on what is known about the behaviour patterns of different groups. This determines what faith is placed in them. Those who behave rationally and thoughtfully were positioned as White; those who were passionate and supposedly irrational were Black. But how could anyone know with any level of certainty who is White and who is Black, since issues of rationality and passions are internal to the individual's body and can be known only with certainty after the person has acted? How can we know without profiling and categorizing them racially and otherwise and running the risk of acting in bad faith towards them? John Burbidge provides an excellent explanation of how this process works, and how ultimately reason, in the form of an epistemology or official narrative, indicates which categories are essential and necessary and which are accidental and contingent:

To assist in defining the procedures for determining choice, reason introduces a further set of categories by which it organizes its concepts and ideas. Those that merit attention are called the essential, while others are called accidental. These two are defined as: those characteristics without which the object would be something else, and those which could be changed without affecting its character. The essential, then, are necessary for any adequate reflection; the accidental are contingent. The categories of necessity and contingency follow from that operation of reasoned thought which refers to actual existents. As the distinction used to determine which possibilities should actually be thought, they are however to be given content from that which is independent of the thinking process.[35]

Reason, as we should note, is another way of saying the neo-mythic register, and to act reasonably as a way of understanding is to privilege this register over the ethno-racial. That we tend not to do this most of the time might speak to the reasonableness of our ethical relations and of the challenge that reason can face when it runs up against a perception or way of knowing that is non-dialectical and non-synthetic, such as what is provided by the ethno-racial register.

Ultimately, epistemology suggests that, idealistically, the ontological beginnings of individuals are the best indicator of how an individual or groups of individuals can be expected to act. Those who were ontologically/somatically Black, and second, those who were culturally/existentially Black, were deemed to be epistemologically Black and their ethical treatment was based on this evaluation. Epistemology is, in fact, captured by senses and outer manifestations of the ethno-racial, rather that being held to a purported higher judgment of the neo-mythic. As a form of determinacy, ethically, an individual or groups of individuals are determined to be either inessential and therefore not necessary to the state, or deserving of recognition within the state and good faith in their ethical treatment. In this case, judgments presented via the ethno-racial register are supposedly validated as ethical according to standards of the neo-mythic register – thus making evident the contradictions present in understanding the given existence.

These determinations are the basis of race and racialization. However, this idealism has failed to address those groups who consider themselves to be over-determined by their skin colour, and who see themselves as full moral agents seeking acceptance and recognition in liberal democracies. Their over-determinacy means they are stuck on the ethno-racial register, which gives them a specific and unchanging being. It thus prevents them from moving to a higher rational neo-mythic register where they would not be stereotyped and fixed and would instead always be in the process of becoming. A proper idealistic position is to assume that the behaviour of humans cannot be predicted formulaically, and that humanity consists of moral agents with different levels of creativity and with different notions of what good and evil are. Yet, the opposite is what epistemological categories presuppose.

Blackness, even though codified as an ethnicity in Canada based mainly on somatic appearance and assumed cultural characteristics, implies more. Blackness is the epitome of the body as human or not godly, as contingent and inessential to the state, either as an individual or as a community hoping to produce or create, as is more appropriately the word, a civilization or a specific culture. It represents an existentialist position when compared to that of the gods or humans who consider themselves to be godlike, and ethically as inessential when compared to the good, the essential, and the everlasting.

This would account, for example, for the notion by some Québécois that, based on status and culture, as Pierre Vallières says, they are *White Niggers of America*.[36] The term "White Niggers" might sound contradictory only because of a long-held perception that a sub-human species called Niggers in Western thought had to be somatically Black. Vallières is referring to status, culture, and idealism as Blackness, as Quebec French were placed in an inferior position in terms of status and culture vis-à-vis English Canadians, who Vallières positioned as White. His argument was that Québécois live a Black and inessential existence, and would continue to do so until they were transformed idealistically into Whiteness, acquiring the same status and position as the English in Canada, or until they created a new country with its own sacred time and space and to which they would be essential and non-changing. Only through a revolutionary break would Québécois move from the perceived slavery of an ethno-racial determination to a state of becoming that privileges the neo-mythic. They would move from a position of being automatically treated in bad faith to one of being treated in habitual good faith in their own essentialist country.

Similar notions are at work in Noel Ignatiev's *How the Irish Became White*, where he discusses the changing status over time that resulted in greater social, economic, and political acceptance for Irish immigrants in North America.[37] As Kymlicka states: "It is important to remember that until well into the twentieth century, Eastern and Southern Europeans were viewed as separate 'races,' and indeed sometimes even as 'black.' The idea that all Europeans belong to a single 'white' race is comparatively new."[38] Indeed, the ethno-racial register is often presented as a child of modernity, whereas the neo-mythic register is hoary with age. Blackness as fully determined according to both registers is not, therefore, essentially skin colour.

## STRUGGLE OF BEINGS: GODS AND HUMANS

What I am doing here is to locate this discussion of how we attempt to know what is Black primarily in the Greek and, to a lesser extent, African and Hebraic mythologies and philosophies that are the bedrock of Western civilization. Here again, it is worth repeating that we are talking about a dominant thought in a consciousness that may include other views and positions. What we are isolating is the dominant position in these mythologies and philosophies. Dominant Greek mythology, for example, associates purity, reason, reflection, essentialism, and order with Whiteness; and impurity, irrationality, passions, contingency, and chaos with Blackness. Originally, these were not associated with somatic characteristics, but rather with approximations of the attitudes in all humans.

These mythologies, either individually or syncretically, as in the Americas, produce binaries of Whiteness/Blackness, essential/contingent, and goodness/evil that result in the dialectical struggle for freedom and recognition. First, the myths posit the idea that a force that is good by nature, acting in good faith, and the creator of all things good made the universe. This is an ontological explanation that is Greek and Christian in orientation and which reached its apex in Medieval times with the European Crusades and the search for the Holy Grail – the magical transforming cup, filled invariably with nectar and ambrosia, milk and honey, or the blood of Christ that was the reward for those deserving of an everlasting life along the lines suggested in sacred and mythological texts from the Bible back to ancient philosophers like Plato. As Glissant states, this thinking is based on the idea of filial relationship, one that was established by the god or gods of the state and then handed down to later generations,[39] somewhat as *jus sanguinis*.

However, well into the Renaissance and even the early stages of modernity, this ontology placed humans in a chain of being that, as Arthur Lovejoy states in *The Great Chain of Being*, presumed an orderly and Aristotelian hierarchical creation of the world and a creator of the world.[40] Ontologically in this view, humans have a special ranking between the most important position, occupied by the creationist force and followed by ideal-istically White and other beings of almost the same status, and the least important act of creation. This positioning determines the kind of existence humans endure, for they do not have the status White existence of the creator who has dominion over them – which raises the question of whether, if by their very nature they have been created by a higher force, humans can be free. It was a positioning that was so firm and durable that it could only be changed in a revolutionary way, for in this order Black was always Black and White was White. If there was any leeching of Blackness into Whiteness, the product was Blackness, not some variation of Whiteness.

This was so because Whiteness was a clear, homogeneous, and unitary category, and what, in Hegel's epigraph on darknesses, light, and pure water, we aim to reach. It was unchangeable, having distinct borders and boundaries that shielded its purity. Blackness, in contrast, consisted of various forms of degradation. These included the marginal degradation of Whiteness, starting from the miniscule contamination through such things as one drop of Blackness, to an extreme Blackness that had never undergone any change from its primitive first status. In the latter state, this was an unchangeableness that was idealistically the least desirable, but which I shall show was traditionally associated most closely with the tragedy of human existence and what it means to be Black. In modernity, these presumed ontologies were crystallized into racial categories, where humanity was supposedly separated by natural attributes into groups of the good or evil, the included or excluded, the superior or inferior, and, in terms of the state, the essential or contingent, and the free or slaves.

At the same time, humans were given dominion over everything else of a lower ontological ranking. Relatively speaking, by analogy this made them idealistically White or more godlike in status when compared to their ontological inferiors. A similar argument was offered epistemologically to explain White and Black differences in creation. At one point in the history of the world, according to the Christian tradition, evil re-entered the picture after having been banished into the darkness that was not part of creation. It arrived in a disruptive way, seeking a new and different creation and ensuing order, threatening to return the world to the chaos out of which it was originally created.

Since then, there has been an ongoing struggle for good to re-establish its claim and dominance, with good eking out a fragile existence in a sacred land surrounded by hostile evil forces. Humans are part of this "eternal act of creation," with, as suggested by Northrop Frye, some of them good and some evil, but each thinking of him- or herself as naturally good, and each aspiring to achieve the same status as the gods that have dominion over humans.[41]

Those that are deemed good by fellow humans are mythologically presented as White and free, and so come into full possession of liberal rights;

the evildoers are traditionally Black, even in African cultures, including the syncretized African Christianity. This concept can be traced back to the etymology of goodness and evil, or White and Black, from the believed creation of the world out of darkness, to its becoming situated within specific people in nation-states which are committed to creating a common good for their members, the chosen people of a specific god.

The second, existentialism, is a commentary on the lived experience of humans in a world that is explained in, Greek, Hebraic, and African mythologies as tragic, naturally enslaved, and tending towards decay and destruction. Particularly in Greek mythology, this is a struggle partly internal to humans, as they have to combat base bodily desires in the hope of eventually escaping the corrupt world for the more enlightened realm of wisdom and the gods. This is a struggle between the evil and good wills in humans, wills that are described mythologically as innately Black, like the horses drawing an ever lustful and polygamous Jupiter or Zeus. For the creation of a rational order, these passions have to be subjected to a more reflective and smarter reason that is innately White.

Therefore, the gods, who have total control over their passions, are Whiteness and reason, and can steer a straight path to a reasonable and predictable ending. They are the epitome of freedom. But similar controls must be placed on the passions of the gods, for while they may be merely playing, the actions the gods take can be detrimental to human beings. A thunder bolt could kill many human beings, as could a flood, or a hurricane, caused arbitrarily by the gods. For humans to hope to complete the journey of life at a predetermined place and time – the place in mythology that is marked by everlasting freedom – the gods should not intervene unintentionally or should do so only when specifically requested to.

## STRUGGLE OF WHITENESS AND BLACKNESS

In this thinking, for the cosmos to work properly as a system and attain its virtue, Whiteness or reason must be the master over Blackness or the body's passions. This is difficult, for humans are by nature emotional, a direct result of having a body that has seemingly unquenchable appetites and must be fed and tended constantly for its survival. When appetites are at their sharpest, or when they are satisfied, the body endures pain or enjoys pleasure. In the Greek mythological tradition, since the human body abhors pain and loves pleasure, it is by nature a prisoner of the emotions, desires, or appetite – which means that it is deceiving itself if it comes to believe it is choosing pleasure rationally.[42]

However, this would be true only of a world based on sensations and slavish cravings.[43] The seemingly rational choice of taking pleasure over pain would, in effect, be irrational in a world that allows for transformations. It would be based in the unreal desire of the body for momentary survival at the expense of enduring the pain that is necessary in order for the individual to be transformed into a better being that is genuinely rational. This irrational desire for pleasure supposedly resulted in, and from, a slave or bondsman disposition that was natural and unchangeable. In this regard, the relationship between Whiteness and Blackness is to be viewed as a covenant among rivals, with each seeking to make itself the lord and the other the bondsman. In the prevailing narrative, idealistically Whiteness should be the lord and superior and Blackness the bondsman and inferior. However, even then the covenant would be unstable, so much more so than if the relationship were a social contract for example.

Thus, in choosing pleasure over sacrifice, the body would be settling for a lesser good, and even a possible evil, instead of the ultimate good that comes through pain and sacrifice. In this regard, the body is changeable and inessential to the "real" and unchangeable part of the being. Spirit is everlasting, but the body dies, which allows for a new creation, as the old gives way to a presumptive new existence that is spirit only. Therefore, the body is contingent and inessential; spirit is its opposite – the everlasting. The body is idealistically Black and the spirit White. Rational thought, or Whiteness, thus frees the slave from a dependence on pleasure and the abhorrence of pain, but not without rebellion by the body. There would remain a contradiction, however. Yet, it is the desires – satisfied by pleasure – that are the source of creativity, the essential ingredient for the creativity that is necessary for, as Frye suggests, this continuous act of creation that is human existence.

It follows, then, that the Blackness of the body and the Whiteness of reason or the gods are always in a Manichean lordship-bondage struggle for freedom  – the freedom in reason's case to be always godlike and White in behaviour and status; the freedom of Blackness to feed an addiction for what might momentarily bring pleasure, but which, in the long run, could be evil for the body, by keeping it trapped in a dystrophic world that is also based on a specific behaviour and status. Blackness, then, has to be kept in tutelage to a superior and paternalistic reason that knows what is best for the body because reason operates from a transcendentalist position that is free of the corrupting influences of the body.[44] Therefore, the idealistic – unlike the other three categories of Whiteness – is in the realm of the transcendental, whereas the other three are creatures of a lived, material world of bodily sensations.[45]

## FREEDOM OF THOUGHT AND ACTIONS

Third is the ethical on which is based the notion that humans have free wills that allow them to discern good and evil and to act appropriately in their dealings with one another. Those who act out of evil intent are presented as idealistically Black and acting in bad faith, and those who intend good as idealistically White and acting in good faith. Humans thus need to attain the position of Whiteness to become rational enough to make the right decisions when choosing between good and evil. A rational person, according to Plato, would do only what is good, so that to act evil is a human lapse, best explained as a fall from the goodness intended by the creator into a primordial Blackness.[46] For its part, African mythology argues that while humans have free wills their destinies are pre-determined before birth, and evil can arise when individuals ask their ancestors to intervene in daily affairs to thwart the destinies of the living.[47]

Fourth, epistemology indicates the human appeal to knowledge for an understanding of what is good or evil and who is likely to have good or evil intentions. A subject coming into full consciousness of knowing itself and what is good for it would know that Blackness is evil. However, while it might then wish to escape idealistic Blackness, a subject that has come to understand itself will be confronted by its having been defined as Black by a more powerful being, and will therefore know that it is limited in its ability to escape Blackness. These limits produce a special type of existence, one in which this "subject" is not free to determine her or his status in a sacred land. But this is a Blackness recognizing that it is part, and even representative, of the human condition. It is not a godlike existence where the individual would have dominion over herself or himself and over all others in an ontological ranking.

This is Blackness exulting in the self-identification of being Black somatically, and similarly in the creativity that is so central to humanity's existence, a creativity that is based on the recognition and celebration of passions and desires that can only be manifested bodily. This is the recognition that to be of and in an unchanging world of pure Whiteness would be to experience the worst form of death, annihilation, or static utopia, as there could be no further transformation or hope of rebirth. In this regard, Blackness subverts the existing mythologies where Whiteness is a preferred good by arguing that the lived experience is truly human and should be celebrated for what it is. Freedom is the ability to create oneself in one's image – an act of idealized Blackness as the created being is never static or fully completed as it is always in the process of being created.

# 6

# Ideology That Privileges
# the Somatic

Ideology, according to Terry Eagleton, is "literally, the study or knowledge of ideas; and as such it belongs to the great dreams of eighteenth-century Enlightenment that it might somehow be possible to chart the human mind with the sort of delicate precision with which we can map the motions of the body."[1] Theories of ideology are attempts to explain why men and women hold certain views and to provide a method for the examination of possible links between the way people think and their social reality.[2] It is, I shall argue, the glue of the supersensible element, holding together what we are calling Western thought, of which official multiculturalism is its latest manifestation.

But as Northrop Frye explains, ideologies are consciously created,[3] and as Foucault observes, often violently imposed.[4] They result from choices, and usually idealized preferences that start with some supersensible notion of good and evil. As Charles Taylor states in *Sources of the Self,* historically, there has always been some notion of "the notion" behind the development of identities in Western thought.[5] Ideologies are constructed by active imaginations out of a mythology, and its attendant metaphors, that seeks to explain the world from a specific perspective. Once this way of life is accepted and asserted, it stays in place and provides the framework through which to view existential issues. Its duty is then to replicate itself, often without drawing attention to itself. In this respect, it remains largely internal.

Mythologies are at once the stories and the methodology of how humans – or in a specific society, an exclusive group of them – preserve, put away, and carry forward what they have learned in the past and, what on reflection, they deem to be good and necessary for their future well-being. They are also a means of reconciling the outwardly irreconcilable. As Frye puts it, "an ideology is a secondary and derivative structure, and that what human societies do first is make up stories. I think, in other words, that an ideology always derives from a mythology, as a myth to me means *mythos*, a story or narrative."[6]

These myths, handed down from one generation to another, are to a large extent stories about how order or idealized Whiteness and good was established in the world and how humans found themselves in a cosmos or self-perpetuating system in which they are usually at the mercy of forces beyond their control.[7] The story of how the ancestors conquered these forces of evil or idealized Blackness and the perceived non-being of indeterminacy, or came to an arrangement with them, becomes the text for teaching survival techniques to ensure that the gains of the past are preserved for the present and future. These narratives place in a meaningful sequence a series of events within the life of an individual or nation-state, starting at some pre-creationist moment and ending in the undetermined future with the acquisition of a full consciousness through perfect knowledge. This is a story that supposedly starts in the transcendent and ends there.

Myths, or the storylines, according to Frye, are not intended to argue truths as verifiable facts or scientific principles, nor, in the strict historian's observation of facts, are they intended to provide a clear relation between causes and effects. What we can learn from Frye is that myths are not supposed to be reducible to the ethno-racial register of meaning. Instead, they are the explanation after the sifting of possible causes and effects within a specific narrative to ascertain the most plausible explanation. They seek to provide a unique understanding, one that is rational and supposedly unchangeable over time. This way they provide a comprehensive and universal explanation – rather than proof or pure determinations – of all that has happened since some alleged beginning of time. Myths are, therefore, truths in the absolute sense of addressing issues in the natural or socially constructed forms, with a view and perspective unclouded by human frailties. As Frye explains:

Two categories of stories crystallize in most societies. At the center is a body of "serious" stories: they may be asserted to have really happened, but what is important about them is not that, but that they are stories which it is particularly urgent for the community to know. They tell us about the recognized gods, the legendary history, the origins of law, class structure, kinship formations, and natural features ... The less serious stories become folktales, travelling over the world through all barriers of language and culture interchanging their motifs and themes with other stories ... The more serious stories, on the other hand, become the cultural possession of a specific society: they form the verbal nucleus of a shared tradition.[8]

We thus have an explanation by Frye of what we have been calling the neo-mythic register, the so-called serious stories, and of the ethno-racial register, or less serious stories, and each register's attributes and usages.

Metaphors, Frye argues, allow humans to *hear* and to *see* the myths as they are played out in the retelling or in the living that is the continuous creation. They provide the structure within the mythology. Metaphors are acted out through rituals and practices in a manner that affects behaviour and in a way that brings predictability and stability to collective living. They are the precursors for social justice as entitlement to a right of belonging, linking subjects and objects in a semiotic relationship, intertwining them as one within a specific context and moment. In this regard, the subject and the object in this relationship reflect each other, but the reflections are read according to a predetermined ethical agreement, and through predetermined codes that give a peculiar reading to the subject and object, thus binding them in a unique relationship.[9]

As Frye explains, metaphors are ways of seeing and hearing that help link the real with the unreal, the actual with the past and the expected, and the methodology for explaining the links. Along with mythology, metaphors reify and encode an ideology that explains how "the present becomes a moment in which ... the past and future are gathered."[10] Within this pattern of thinking and perceiving, "it becomes clear that myth is inseparable from another verbal phenomenon, the metaphor."[11] Metaphors become the bridges between the ethno-racial and neo-mythic registers, and by definition, they are also part of the neo-mythic explanation.

As Frye sees it, "the myth does to time what the metaphor does to space."[12] The first collapses the interval between events, making them one, but also transfers internality to an externality; the latter shrinks the space in which events occur, separating subjects and objects and translating what may be the externality of the so-called physical or natural world into a series of beliefs, an ideology and internal understanding. Together, they collapse time and space into an ideology that explains a single continuous moment, a continuous lived experience over generations that includes at the same time a constructed beginning and an anticipated ending, all occurring within the same place. Together, they reconcile the two registers of understanding, but in a syncretism that can happen only "mythologically" in the transcendent.

Mircea Eliade suggests in *Myth and Reality* that the resulting ideology provides a paradigm for consistent interpretation of the past, present, and future within a given cosmos.[13] It is through this paradigm that problems are solved and the world is given consistent meaning. This is the idealistic explanation of a plan by the assumed regulator of the universe for a specific people, a plan executed within a specific place and time, the secrets of which are revealed moment to moment but only to the initiated, to those who have rights of belonging and entitlement, to those who are entitled to and live steeped within the myths and the obtaining ideological structures. Eliade explains that the following can be said about the structure of myth:

"(1) [that it] constitutes the History of the acts of the Supernaturals; (2) that this history is considered to be absolutely *true* (because it is concerned with realities) and *sacred* (because it is the world of the Supernaturals); (3) that myth is always related to 'creation,' it tells how something came into existence, or how a pattern of behavior, an institution, a manner of working were established; this is why myth constitutes the paradigms for all significant human acts; (4) that by knowing the myth one knows the 'origin' of things and hence can control and manipulate them at will."[14] Myths, therefore, provide an explanation of how the structure of the cosmos works and how it should work in the future. In this regard, myths provide the explanation and rationale for why things are the way they are, and also why this is appropriate and even necessary for having a specific lifestyle. Myths provide the ideological structure on which the society is built.

But as Frye argues, ideology consists of a Black and White struggle between what he calls primary and secondary concerns, and this struggle provides "the growth of an ideology in society" based on the pursuit of what is deemed to be good and meaningful for a particular way of life.[15] The effect of this growth is the creation of a social capital to be shared by all deserving members of the group or nation. Those with an undisputed and full claim to this social capital are fully citizens of the nation-state that was brought into being concurrently with the creation of a sacred time and space. This capital – or "sacred space," "navel of the earth" with "a superabundance of reality" – is what Eliade describes as central to the paradigms of what is reality. Subsequently, the supposedly "natural" social order as well as "every construction or fabrication has the cosmogony as paradigmatic model."[16]

Here, we are reminded of Burbidge's argument that reason determines among all the various categories it has constructed which are necessary and essential and which are accidental and contingent. This first category consists of Frye's primary concerns, and the contingent and accidental his secondary concerns. The first is what we call the ethno-racial and the second the neo-mythic. Frye's primary concerns deal with survival issues, such as "concerns for food, for shelter, for sexual relations, for survival"[17] – those appetites that rational transcendentalist thought associates with the passions, desires and enslavement. The secondary concerns are those of preference resulting from rational thought, consisting of big picture universals of what does and should obtain. Underlying Frye's argument is the following reasoning: "Primary concern is based on the most primitive of platitudes: the conviction that life is better than death, happiness better than misery, freedom better than bondage. Secondary concerns include loyalty to one's own society, to one's religious or political beliefs, to one's place in the class structure, and in short to everything that comes under the general heading of ideology. All through history secondary concerns have had the greater prestige and power. We prefer to live, but we go to war; we prefer to be free, but we keep a large number of people in a second-class status, and so on."[18]

Thus, following Frye's explanation, concerns are primarily culturally and idealistically Black in orientation and secondarily culturally and idealistically White and, as he describes them, "based on rationalism."[19] Both are locked in a dialectical struggle for freedom and recognition, but generally secondary concerns are sovereign over the primary. It is a struggle between feeding the body and feeding the mind. "One cannot live a day without being concerned about food, but one may live all one's life without being concerned about God. At the same time one hesitates to rule out the conscious and creative concerns from the primary ones."[20] And it is a struggle about attitudes to life and about status, whether bodily desires, issues of bodily survival, should always have a lower importance than those of the mind. For as Frye argues, primary concerns are not about "indicat(ing) a higher level of culture" but are about enlarging consciousness "to get at least a glimpse of what it would be like to know more than we are compelled [to know]."[21] In this regard, then, in most of our understanding of concepts we are trapped on the neo-mythic register even when we think we are invoking the ethno-racial. Therefore, ideologically, the important register for understanding daily living, and such things as racism and ethnocentricity, is not the ethno-racial that is changeable and malleable, but the seemingly unchangeable neo-mythical. In the beginning, then, and in a Hegelian sense, was the Word and not, as postulated by Marxists and ethno-racialists, the materials.

Just as there are these two categories of concerns, there are also primary and secondary mythologies, with comparative statuses and claims. "Primary mythology," Frye claims, "sees the environment in terms of the human impulse to expand into it. The chief instrument of this expansion is metaphorical identification."[22] Secondary mythologies provide structure in society by attaching "what is imagined to the ideals of some ascendant group or class," so that, in general, primary mythology tends to be anthropocentric and secondary to be ethnocentric.[23]

In this framework, depending on the prevailing perspective or ideology, societies are idealistically Black or White. In societies with a strong sentiment of nationalism, patriotism, and civic identity, as Frye suggests, the secondary concerns generally trump the primary: in such societies, Whiteness, by implication of this argument, therefore has higher status than Blackness.

This struggle between concerns is basic to our philosophical construction of idealistic Blackness and Whiteness, as I argue them, and as an explanation for how such concepts are sociologically imposed on society. In this regard, as Frye attests, every society is a planned construction of Whiteness based on a rational, specific good for an elite group of people made White by being plucked from the rest of humanity. Within this elite group, there might be an additional aristocratic stratification but, as a collective, the group in its universal consciousness is generally elite and aristocratic, as among the most elite of the human family, to all other nations and states.

Still, this idealism always has to account for the residue of humanity, all that was left behind after the choice or creation. It also has to rationalize that simply remoulding or reformulating old material – including the elites and the residue – does not necessarily change the fundamental nature of the material, even if it gives it a new identity and a new space and time in which to live. Based on Frye's argument, in reality, in the choice of Whiteness, Blackness is seldom left behind, for conceptually Whiteness as an infinity needs an other for identity and to recognize it in its new home and identity. This is an exercise in subjective false consciousness. As Frye explains: "I have often enough insisted that every human society exists within a cultural envelope that separates it from its natural environment: that there are no noble savages, and no men sufficiently natural to live in a society without such an envelope. Most people call this envelope an ideology, which is accurate enough for fairly advanced societies. The word *ideology* suggests argument as well as ideas, because of the Hegelian principle that every proposition contains its opposite."[24]

Frye's turning to Hegel for an explanation of the mythological unfurling of society as a struggle between Black and White concerns – what Frye defines as primary and secondary concerns and mythologies – is not surprising. For Frye's argument is that metaphor and mythology produce an ideology that is a sort of ladder which allows humans to explain and rationalize how throughout history they have endeavoured to become White and godlike. This ladder is similar to Eliade's theophanies, for it implies a stairway between humans and their gods that in most mythologies is let down and drawn up from heaven at the pleasure of the god. Humans cannot build these ladders and stairways on their own; otherwise, because of humanity's imperfect knowledge, they would be no more than Towers of Babel that the gods of Christian and Hebraic mythologies would have to destroy so that humans would forever remain dispersed among the ethno-racially determined states and cultures, rather than in one single nation-state, determined neo-mythically and ethno-racially.

In the end, such a ladder or stairway is an acknowledgement that gods reveal to humans only what they desire to disclose, pealing back levels of darknesses, and that this is one of the obstacles humans face in ascending the ladder to absolute knowledge – a knowledge that would allow humans to know themselves and their gods perfectly. Frye explains the concept of the ladder, which at its most perfect development is as much a tower as well: "Hegel's *Phenomenology* is called a ladder by its author, but it is really a tower or mountain stood on its head, its apex the concept that can hardly be found between subject and object, but steadily broadens until it becomes absolute knowledge. Such a structure could not exist in nature, only in thought, and perhaps only in Hegelian thought at that."[25]

With such an introduction, faint praise and all, we shall now turn to Hegel in the next chapter for an explanation of how ideology – based on mythologies as an important feature of history – is the working out of an eternal struggle between Blackness and Whiteness. Along with trying to understand Hegel's formal explanation of how the dialectics of history work, we will take a look at an explanation of how the types of paradigms described by Eliade and Frye are established and dethroned. In this regard, we will compare the work of Thomas Kuhn,[26] who offers an ethno-racial explanation, with Hegel's neo-mythic rationalization in the hope of accounting for the stops and starts of history and for the hold of ideology in human imagination, especially in modernity and Western civilization.

Here, we will be arguing that there are no clear and profound breaks in human history as suggested by the likes of Althusser and other structuralists, but rather that ideologies are accumulative, accreting from one period to the next, and culminating in the latest manifestation.[27] On this view, ideology is like a humanistic organism, growing and dynamic, rather than the mechanical, static being that the ethno-racial register suggests. In the third section of this book, it will be relevant to keep in mind Frye's metaphor of a ladder that is a tower when we consider the World Trade Center Towers and how they, like the Biblical Tower of Babel, have become important symbols of the American mythology about the fight between good and evil.

## BLACKNESS: EXISTENTIALISM OF WESTERN THOUGHT

All the arguments I have advanced so far on Blackness would eventually become concrete as the ideological basis for Western European thought. This ideology is based on mythological and philosophical thinking where Whiteness is constructed as signifying primarily cultural differences, and as a mark of progress and sophistication. In a practical sense, as well, this is Whiteness as a reflection of the world seen and understood in binaries that can be placed in a hierarchy from good as the idealistically most desirable to evil as the least, and which corresponds to a range having European culture at the top and African at the bottom. The cultural association with Whiteness and European would also become the basis for deciding issues of class and even caste in a world consisting of European and other cultures.

Ultimately, the colour of the skin would come to bear cultural inscriptions that also decide status, but this was a status that was first based on presumptions to know naturally who is good and evil, either from skin colour or an innate culture. In this case, and specifically in the Americas, Blackness is primarily based on value judgments in memory and history accumulated by different segments of humanity, one claiming Europe and the other Africa for primordial beginnings.

The existentialist experience of Blackness is also lived by those, primarily of African descent, who realize that they are constructed as outsiders in a power relationship, but who are using their creativity to unfix themselves from this perception and to subvert the prevailing norms and orders imposed by Eurocentric thinking. The escape from these racial and cultural inscriptions that result in status difference is made into an idealism that offers different views: into an "existentialistic" Blackness recognizing that humanity, in its most basic and "essentialist" nature, is Black, or changeable, for it is a race of humans with desires and passions in a body that is corrupt and will decay; and recognizing that, because of the diversity of humanity, it is impossible to cull a pure and homogeneous group of people.

All of which means that the creationist moment necessary to produce a pure and uncontaminated people cannot happen, because by necessity, starting with materials that are all ontologically Black, the component parts for Whiteness are not available. Causally, such a nation or state can only be brought forth out of what already exists, which is Blackness.[28] To create a pure and uncontaminated people would otherwise require a radical transformation of the existing materials, a transformation that usually occurs in mythology when gods or superhumans intervene in history in revolutionary moments that restart creation. In this sense, too, Canadian multiculturalism is Black, for it was not caused mythologically by some god re-entering human time to create a new, pure, and radically perfect order; it was simply an attempt to refashion an order that was already deemed Black and whose materials were already judged to be idealistically Black. The hope of multiculturalism is that humans will create from the available materials a Whiteness that the mythological gods never did, but a Whiteness, because of human nature, that can only exist fully in another world – that of the gods.

This impasse results from the idealistic definitions of Blackness and Whiteness, where Blackness is presented as a dystopia of irrationality, pluralism, and disorder in opposition to a utopian Whiteness that is rationality, purity, and homogeneity. This suggests that at the heart of idealistic thinking is the notion that Whiteness in the form of an ideal, harmonious society must be brought out of the chaos and disorder that is Blackness. This Whiteness is an ontological marker that occurs ironically and even paradoxically only through change, in a creationist moment akin to when the gods or superhuman beings create such a cataclysmic break that a sacred space and time is cleared and the people are transformed into the Whiteness of the elect. This would be impossible for any human, for ontologically Whiteness is supposedly unchangeable.

Blackness, then, is also the existentialist reality of living in an unreal and tragic world – in the Christian tradition, of awaiting the Messiah, the redeemer, or life after death to free the individual from the human travails that are bodily in nature. Whiteness comes then to be associated existentially with a superior status or culture due to that culture's progress and development – an attainment typified ethno-racially by European culture that was first deemed by Enlightenment European thinkers to be the best.[29] According to this same binary thinking, Blackness comes to be associated ethno-racially with underdevelopment and primitivism – traits that Europeans thought they saw best embodied in Africa and Africans. This dystopia of so-called backward existences becomes a utopia in this thinking when Blackness becomes Whiteness, not necessarily somatically, but in culture and ultimately status.

Whiteness and Blackness are binary opposites within the structure of a society established on an idealist ideology that suggests social justice should be based on merit and entitlement. Under this ideology, only the good has entitlement, and entitlement can only be distributed according to knowledge of who is deserving. Western Europeans would ultimately come to dominate Western society in power relations with other groups. In this power relation, Europeans defined themselves as White in colour and character and placed themselves at the top of the hierarchy. They would also claim an unbroken filial relationship with the "true" gods of creation. Whiteness, therefore, is distilled from Blackness.

In their domination, Europeans situated Africans – constructed as Black by culture and skin colour, as the stepchildren or adoptees of the true gods or children of different and lower gods – at the bottom under this arrangement. Then, they developed ethno-racial societies based on social, political, and economic agencies and institutions that were structured to maintain this order as a desired good for society. This power relation was often masked under pretence of being knowledge-based, or an appeal to the ethical norms, rationalism, and understanding of the neo-mythic register. And because it is a synthesis, and by its very nature and definition hybridized, syncretic, and creolized, it would show the inherent ambiguities, tensions, and anxieties of trying to reconcile different conceptions into a single definition. In this regard, then, the very concept of enlightenment, as Whiteness, functions as a myth, as do various modernist doctrines of transcendence, as well as religions.

It thus follows that a way of life – of knowing good and evil, White and Black – based on enlightenment is also based on myth. Part of the problem of existing in a world that is at heart mythically Manichean is to separate the myth that is fiction from the myth that is knowing. And this is where, as Marx would argue, ideology blinds us into thinking that the effect is the cause, and we end up living in a distorted world where we accept Whiteness as unchangeable and Blackness as ephemeral.

## WHITENESS, BLACKNESS, KNOWLEDGE, AND DEATH

The dominant ethos of Western civilization has been built on claims to subjective knowledge, as Enlightenment philosophers like Kant, Hegel, and Marx argue.[30] The aim is to produce self-consciousness as this enables a subject to fully know what she or he is capable of doing and of becoming. Limits and boundaries must be clearly known, and a free subject would be able to desire and achieve what can rationally be expected, given the limits. However, Western civilization in a generalized way also endeavours to achieve objective knowledge, so that a subject can know with high levels of certainty whether the other or stranger – anything that is not her or him – is essentially good or evil in intentions. Primarily, this knowledge is deemed useful for a subject seeking to ascertain if the other would limit or even take away the subject's freedom. The greatest fear of the subject is that an other might be the personification of death, the one thing that mythologically has long been presented as the ultimate limit and boundary on a subject's life. This is a knowledge that is acquired through the objectivity of the ethnoracial register.

Death is the finite point at which the subject ceases to be a physical being, or where the exterior limits are stripped away.[31] The subject disappears into infinity, an eternity of epistemological nothingness, or into a spirit world reserved for ancestors, deities, and memory, as suggested by African, Greek, and Hebraic mythologies. Therefore, the moment of death is also one of creation, an ending that is the beginning of a new order. However, these mythologies also suggest that individuals are entitled to enjoy a fruitful life, and, in the case of African mythology, to attain the predetermined limits negotiated in a pre-life stage with the creator.[32] This is the inviolate right and freedom to live within chosen limits and boundaries. In a lordship-bondsman relationship, only the regulator of the universe should decide an individual's temporal limits.

Where the individual is free by volition, only she or he can set the limits of her or his exteriority; only the individual can freely impose finitude on herself or himself. Therefore, premature death is an evil, in the form of a premature limit or imposed finitude, and it is effectively anti-human for those who see it as an attempt to thwart the destinies and fates imposed by their gods.[33] Similarly, anyone believed to be in the service of death is an agent of evil, a tyrant looking to enslave the free by nature and virtue. Humanity's quest, as the dominant thought in Western civilization has it, is presented as the pursuit of goodness and life, and doing so in order to identify those who might be allies or enemies in this endeavour.

In this respect, therefore, what is presented as Western civilization is based on the ability to discern Whiteness and Blackness, goodness and evil. This is a search for the freedom to live in one's own peculiar time and space, rather than that imposed by someone else, another whose notion of the good, the pursuit of it, and of human limits might, in reality, be evil. Blackness, then, came to be associated with the stranger or outsider who would introduce change, more specifically unwelcome change leading to something that is unknown and unspecified, a change that is death and should be feared because it is an imposition of a finite boundary not freely chosen. This need for setting apart could be seen as the genesis of what would later be known as segregation, and even Apartheid, in presumptive Western civilization, all based on the idea that it is possible to separate the clean from the unclean, the elect from the non-elect.[34] Therefore, Blackness, as a projection of idealistic Whiteness, has to be resisted, rejected, excluded, and/or subjugated in a state constructed idealistically on principles of Whiteness. Such a construction privileges notions of the separateness of an elect group from the uncleanness that is the rest of humanity, and on the basis that such a construction is dedicated to the achievement of the only meaningful good there is.

In this regard, the dominant stream of Greek mythology in this putative Western civilization, and the dominance of Western European thought in this civilization, both place heavy emphasis on epistemology. Western society, as we understand it, is based on knowledge, and ultimately the search for cognizance would become privileged over definitions of Blackness that are ontological, existential, and ethical, because the latter are hidden characteristics of humans. Cognizance, then, becomes based on a perception, which must be taken into consciousness and subsequently negated in order to produce a higher level of knowing. This is a normative, rational way for a free agent to behave. However, such a knowledgeable person seldom gets beyond the immediacy of having to respond to issues of life and death, of Whiteness and Blackness, when it is confronted by a threatening situation or a moment of aporiatic change facing the very point where finite categories are recognized. Blackness, as perception, based on the privileging of epistemology, thus became a marker of the skin, and was encoded with knowledge about an objectivized group in a power relationship.

As a highpoint of this generally accepted Western civilization, modernity, the current historic era, promised a foolproof way of knowing, in contrast to knowing where the emphasis was placed, as the dominant Greek thought did, on the object of knowing. This was an appeal to science based on a repeatable and falsifiable method as the ultimate rational way for discerning good and evil, what would protect and extend human life and what would shorten or endanger it. This method would be the Whiteness of rationalism, based on the knowing of laws that regulate nature, and the unemotional and therefore "scientific" application of these laws mythologically without fear or favour. If there was a natural essence for all things, as the dominant Greek thinkers and Medievalists believed, then it was not the essence, per se, that was going to be proved, but the method, and being verifiable, the ethical laws of behaviour would then be based on this proven method.

## BLACKNESS BY ANALOGY: THE SEMIOTICS OF SKIN

How then, in the absence of genuine and non-refutable knowledge, did Blackness become associated in late modernity primarily with somatic features, to the point where the three other categories – the idealistic, culture, and status – have been reduced to the somatic as a purported way of knowing with certainty? At different times, Blackness can refer, among other things, to cultural knowledge, to specific ideals and statuses, and to somatic characteristics and phenotypes, all of which help produce a moral framework for explaining the positioning of Blacks as an ethnic group in North America.

But as Appiah notes, by the nineteenth century in Western thought, most Western scientists believed that, ultimately, the somatic and phenotypic were fair representations of the innate qualities of a finite group or specific people. These scientists, and then lay people, came to believe that "racial essence accounts for more than the obvious visible characteristics of individuals and of groups – skin color, hair, shape of face ... For a racialist, then, to say someone is 'Negro' is not just to say that she has inherited a black skin or curly hair: it is to say that her skin color goes along with other important inherited characteristics – including moral and literary endowments."[35] This was Blackness identified ultimately as culture and reduced to race, the ranking of people based on presumed superiority and inferiority of their qualities and status. As a philosophical or sociological undertaking, however, such a ranking always fails to capture the fullness of the object that it seeks to explain. The question "What is fully Blackness?" can only elicit an equivocal answer.

Yet, Blackness exists as a phenomenon and as a spirit, idea, or notion in Western societies. Blackness, as a quest for understanding humanity, is always like the body, as Merleau-Ponty says in *Phenomenology of Perception*, giving up knowledge about itself only reluctantly, and in layers.[36] The truth is never fully known. And wisdom and enlightenment that is known in one moment can be negated in the next. This is why, even on the ethnoracial register, notions of Blackness have become so uncertain, unclear, and problematic, and why, ultimately, in a power relation, subjects who construct themselves as White regard, as a matter of faith, objects with Black skins as both morally and culturally Black. It is not that they know with certainty that these others are evil, primitive, childlike, and without knowledge, but that they perceive them to be that way. Their belief, therefore, becomes the basis for a social construction that makes Blackness a "reality" in ethical relationships.

And neither do they really expect every individual to behave according to his or her group's presumed stereotypes and characteristics. But, in the absence of knowing the individual's virtues and intents, they must treat her or him based on what their faith tells them. For a subjective consciousness does not have absolute knowledge and must rely on signifiers to initiate a perception of what sense to make of the world and the objects in it.[37] Being uncertain, the neo-mythic register must shift understanding to the external ethno-racial register in its search for symbols and signs that it can then translate into myths and metaphors.

What lies at the heart of the resulting ethical relations, therefore, is not the Whiteness of reason and knowledge, but rather the Blackness of belief that is grounded in the phenomenological Blackness of faith and intentions. These perceptions as full knowledge are themselves based epistemologically on the prevailing ideology and mythology. What is meaningful about this way of knowing is that there is an inversion at work, where certainty is not based on the empiricism in daily living. This is so even though the attitude is that it is "natural" reality or the empirical that leads to the social realism – when in fact there is really no such progression.

Blackness is not univocal but equivocal, which means that it never has a clear, unambiguous, or determined definition. This means that meaning and understanding are always in a dialectical relationship between the neo-mythic and ethno-racial registers and within the registers, with the neo-mythic, in the form of reason, trying its best to come up with a final and unchangeable determination. Similarly, no meaning is "natural" or essential, but rather has to be constructed. Blackness is like the Hebraic God that is changing and learning through new adventures and development. It is the antipathy of Hellenic gods who are fixed in their ways and know the extent of their powers. These gods are pure essences, following laws that are inviolate and unchangeable. Thus, when a finite understanding is imposed, it is through derivation, as Aristotle suggests, or analogy, where the meaning is noted more for what it represents than for its exactness.[38]

Analogy, as Palmer explains, is theory developed to explain the existence of God, or infinity, an ontological examination for a creator of the universe that starts by examining the evidence or the data of what is known and is available for examination.[39] This is where we search through the externality of space for metaphors that can give us clues to the internalized myths, ideology and, ultimately, appropriate ethical relations. Put another way, and in the context of understanding the use of our two registers of knowing, the ethno-racial is irrationally used to determine the neo-mythic meaning, and what is hidden on the neo-mythic register. No single or finite bit of information is conclusive on its own, yet it is useful for what it portends and what it adds to the wider explanation. Bits of information are important if they are derivative of their source, so that working back through the derivation we may arrive at the root of the first principle from which every action originates. In this way, the goal is to be able to explain God, in the commonly accepted Greek and Christian traditions, by a specific word; and even though it might be inexact, incomplete, and inconclusive, the finite word or category is to stand as a meaningful reference. God, as a good being or intention, can be derived from good works and actions: this means that God understood as a concept through the neo-mythic register can be known through forms that are understood and recognized from the knowledge provided exclusively by the ethno-racial register.

The word is an acceptable metaphor for what is known, but also for what is yet to be fully defined, traced back, or, as Heidegger would say, phenomenologically "uncovered" and revealed as a form of discovery.[40] This is a theory of knowing based on faith, which, in the absence of full knowledge, is often broken down by analogy into two supposedly finite concepts: hope and despair. They are the dialectically opposed pair that is most obvious in faith, with good faith usually associated with hope, joyous anticipation, and affectivity, and bad faith with despair, despondency, and melancholia. As a way of explaining specific existential and ethical relations, this understanding starts, epistemologically, with perception, a known truth or self-certainty that knowledge will be proven and never refuted, for, ironically, the result of the search is known in a Kantian way a priori.

The examination starts with the notion that infinity, in Kant's argument a god, or in our case a specific type of human subject or object that is to be defined and certified, exists. Proof is only a matter of collecting data from which the known inferences can be made. These data are the works of the god or human archetype: for by their actions they are confirmed, since in belief the god or archetype already exists irrefutably. Their actions and works reveal their intentions and their characteristics.

According to this reasoning, a good universe can only be the work and intent of a good god; similarly, the evil of humans or a branch of the human family can only be the work of an evil mind with evil intent. This, however, is contrary to the characteristic of the Hebraic god, who is capable of both good and evil, a god that can create, but who can also destroy with a flood and can order the genocide of specific ethnic groups. However, in the dominant Greek and Christian traditions, through an association of the work with the intent, we can phenomenologically determine the god or human type bit by bit by comparing the latest knowledge about the actions or creation of the creator, but the result would be just as expected. Ultimately, the fullness of the concept supposedly can be reduced to a symbol or caricature. Put another way, what should be presented only as a representation that at most can only be partial becomes fully representative of all there is to the concept. But even then this might become a job too big for the symbol

or representation. In this case, the descriptive words might have one or
more meanings, some literal and borrowed or derived from known and
fully determined cases: the symbol would now have to give the same meaning on both the ethno-racial and neo-mythic registers, even though the
registers might be speaking to different attributes of the concept. One standard and dominant meaning might be read exclusively according to a specific
register. Other meanings are implied or based on a perceived relationship that
allows one register to represent the other. As Palmer explains the Greek and
Christian approach: "We may infer that if some statements about God are
somehow established we need not worry too much what these statements
really mean. They will not mean exactly what they say, yet we cannot say
what else they mean, for we have no better words; but we can be sure that
real meaning – the truth behind them – is entirely satisfactory."[41] But, needless to say, this inference is not proof, but perception. At best, it might be a
very close approximation of the fullness of the concept; in the worst case it
might be way off the mark. For no specific form on the ethno-racial register
can be expected seriously to capture the full infinite of a concept that can be
fully understood only by knowing fully both its neo-mythic attributes as
well as those that are testable according to the five human senses. Indeed,
there is always a surplus of meaning if only one register is used, in this case,
a residue that spills over from the form recognized on the ethno-racial register. Usually, what is left out is what the senses cannot easily comprehend;
usually what is added beyond the ethno-racial understanding is simply a
projection or estimation of what analogy tells us might be present but not
recognized by the senses. But this projection is merely a product of the
understanding produced solely by the ethno-racial register. The projection
is what has been mediated in our minds to account for what might be missing – it is not based *per se* on what is being experienced but rather on what
our minds tells us to anticipate, the guess to fill in the blanks that are the
unknown. This guess could just as easily result in hope as it might in
despair, for either approach would be based on faith or the lack of it. And
faith is what is left when knowledge is absent, epistemology is silent, and
we still have to make an ethical decision. Using the ethno-racial register as
the sole way of knowing would be to severely limit, and even stereotype,
the concept in its fullness.

## SYMBOLS: IDEALS AND LIVED EXPERIENCES

Such is the story of how in modernity segments of humanity, with their
neo-mythic and ethno-racial attributes, were ultimately reduced to a specific meaning solely on the ethno-racial register. That reduction was to
show that all of their humanity could be adequately captured by one form
and expression on the ethno-racial register: the colour of their skin.

This is the case for the infinity Blackness in an epistemology such as that on which what is commonly accepted as Western civilization is based, an epistemology that privileges cognition and semiotics and structuralism, where there is usually a hidden and wider meaning behind the metaphors and signs that is applied in daily living.[42] This is an understanding that starts from the ethno-racial register of signs and phenomena to arrive by analogy in the neo-mythic. In effect, this is the argument for what Umberto Eco in *A Theory of Semiotics* calls quite appropriately, as it applies to Blackness, the theory of the lie: "A sign is everything which can be taken as significantly substituting for something else. This something else does not necessarily have to exist or to actually be somewhere at the moment in which a sign stands in for it ... If something cannot be used to tell a lie, conversely it cannot be used to tell the truth: it cannot in fact be used 'to tell' at all."[43]

This is so because we should remember that this sign is opened to ethno-racial knowledge. "Truth" is evaluative and therefore neo-mythic Whiteness. What value is told by the sign – a different process – is ethno-racially determined, and neo-mythically is neither good nor evil in itself. Therefore, as Eco is suggesting, the lie is when meaning on one register is used analogously to explain attributes that are fully knowable only on the other and competing register.

With these categories established and explained, we are now in a position to map how issues of Blackness and Whiteness, in general, inform identity formation in the philosophically and sociologically constructed Western civilization, primarily in the Western hemisphere or Americas. These notions of how the infinities of concepts can be captured fully in a being determined ethno-racially decide such issues as citizenship, belonging, democratic participation, and entitlement. Ultimately, they became the main signifiers of who has a right to be included in the modern nation state – and all were and still are predicated on philosophically predetermining what is good, and *then* implementing plans to recognize those beings and expressions of good and evil.

In making a differentiation between the two registers of meaning and their sociological results, we are also providing a general analysis of the historical legacy of modernity, an era that ushered in such modern notions as the state as a social and political consciousness of a people; of democracy as the notion of who among the people have the right to rule within the state, that sacred space and time; of liberalism with its conceptions of inviolate individuals and collective freedoms; and of racism as the suggestion that humanity can be divided, based on the analogies that begin with the ethno-racial register, into unique and distinct groups that can be placed in a neo-mythic hierarchy ranking from superior at the top to inferior at the bottom. The key to this understanding is to appreciate how what started as concepts

– ideas and ideals best expressed on the neo-mythic register – came to be implemented as bodies and beings recognized solely by their positioning on the ethno-racial register and its chain of being. We will also show in the final section of this book how sociologically Blackness came to be associated and embodied, through a category of people, with the somatic. This Blackness was associated with slavery, bondage, and the contingent or peripheral in the dominant notion of what should be the modern state.

But before going forward in our study of Blackness in general, we will first examine some concepts in the specific, primarily as they are localized in the Canada that is a product of this perceived Western thought. These include an examination of how people who are constructed as Black are positioned in an imagined Canadian nation state and what accounts for this positioning. This is a Canadian sovereign state that conceptually, at inception, was presented in opposition to its neighbour, the United States of America, with early Canadian thinkers presenting the US as the epitome of Blackness, however constructed, but primarily because of its sizeable Black and African population.

Both countries would start with specific philosophical and mythological notions of what is good and of who the good people are. Sociologically and anthropologically, they would attempt to produce a society that could only create this predetermined good, for that would be the society's sole metaphysical function. One of the results of this attempt was systemic racism from the mixing of those predetermined as good with those predetermined as evil, from mixing those that, in the pre-creationist moment, were supposedly by faith intended for inclusion with those deemed by faith as candidates for exclusion. If Eco is right that analogy works on the basis of the lie, then perhaps the best test of this theory is the lie of common sense: that all people with Black skins are ontologically and anthropologically Black, or that those with White skins are not also Black.

## BLACKNESS AND CANADA: A THEORETICAL FRAMEWORK

First stated in the introduction, my goal is to explain the quest for personal and collective social mobility and for social justice, which, as identifiable goods in society, are best typified in the struggle for democracy and inclusion. It is a study of how those who have not been defined as good all along have fought to change this definition and their social position that resulted from an original designation, or mythological sin.

As Charles Taylor suggests in *The Politics of Multiculturalism*, this is a struggle for subjective recognition and inclusion by a group of people that from the inception of the Canadian nation were excluded from the Canadian mainstream and from power.[44] This is one of the things that the Canadian state has in common with its neighbour to the south. Both nations are inheritors of the legacy of modernity, a memory of racism and segregation based on racial and cultural characteristics, and both claimed in their pasts to be implementing a model of nation-state development that was pioneered in England.

The latest "original" but democratic version, which was the "latest" working out of the mythical register in terms of the ethno-racial, was established around the 1650s with a new order based on clear and separate roles and limits for an executive, the common people, and an aristocracy.[45] This model came with specific aims and outcomes planned into the system – based on the system's inherent mythological and ideological ideals. And it had specific notions of who should and should not belong among the people and the aristocracy. Even if the resulting social order with its inequalities was not sociologically heaven on earth, philosophically it was still deemed to be most desirable, the closest possible reconciliation of the concept and existence in this world.

A schism in the English state located in North America led to the creation of two pretenders of this legacy in what would become the United States of America and Canada. For a while, both countries initially followed views that were almost diametrically opposed as they were based on different ideological notions of the aims of society. This occurred when the two countries were subjected to a determination on the neo-mythic register and each came up with a different ideal of the good – of what philosophically was the legacy they had inherited. On the other hand, a different understanding emerged from the ethno-racial register, where the outer manifestation of these goods that were supposed to be different internally were of the same form and determination. Both countries started from the same manifestations of good as White, based on the categories of knowing that are the somatic, the cultural, and status. On the ethno-racial register, both countries presumed a finite good and Whiteness, and these were considered to be holistic and unchanging – a position that was counter to their understandings through the neo-mythic register. This was particularly the case regarding what commitments the state should have to the people and what responsibilities the people should have to the nation-state. One of the things these collectives – Canada calls its form of being ethno-racially a confederation and the US a union – took in common from modernity was the ideology of racism. This is the idea that humanity is made up of groups of people who are distinct culturally and politically, and that these groups can be placed in a hierarchy from most superior to most inferior.

Another thing they both inherited from modernity was the notion that Blackness, whether decided by colour, culture, geography, religion, or nobility of lineage, was the preserve of all those unworthy of inclusion among the people that would form liberal democratic states. In a state constructed neo-mythically to produce a specific good teleologically, there could be no official room for Blackness, by any measure, according to this belief. There could only be an absented presence, a form of being that phenomenologically is felt, as Sartre suggests, but not seen or acknowledged.[46] So that even if there is a physical presence, it is still absent through lack of official recognition.

In the rivalry between the US and Canada for discerning the truly White, Canada took the neo-mythic stand that Whiteness entailed noblesse oblige, a responsibility that translated into communitarian notions of peace, good government, and order against the Blackness or seemingly unlicensed freedom and individuality in the US. This was a view that when adjusted to the ethno-racial register offered that the somatically Black body had no place or privileges sociologically in a body that intended to be a good the state defined as White and European.

Ultimately, seen as the body, the colour of one's skin would become the main marker for deciding who should be shut out of these states, or if one were allowed in, it would become the explanation for why some people should be positioned only on the society's periphery. In this respect, we see here the primacy of the ethno-racial register and the expectations for assimilation in the human material provided for the state's formation. Seeing, as Eze is quoted earlier in this book, was privileged as an act of knowing; perceptually what was seen was considered to be the real or analogous of the hidden "real" that is the genuine, the essential, and unchangeable. Knowledge of who should be formally included or excluded was reduced to skin colour – to the ethno-racial register also having to do the work of the neo-mythic register. In this regard, when people with Black skins were excluded this was based on a position they supposedly took on the ethno-racial scale of being. This position was the equivalent of being placed at the bottom of a hierarchy based on the supposed superiority and inferiority of groups of people, but also based on estimations of whether the groups are naturally good or evil.

These nation-states started with strong and firm notions of what was good and bad ethno-racially for the nation-state. Neo-mythically, both saw Blackness in its many forms as bad for nation-building. Both turned to the ethno-racial register as an assimilationist tool that made all shades of non-White simply Black – as a tool that also reduced any perceived differences in what was presented as Black and White to seemingly objective markers and signs. Indeed, the nation-states often associated Blackness with degradation ontologically of the purity of Whiteness, as evil, or existentially as the embodiment of badly needed labour, as only a partial good. But this was a meaning for Blackness that was merely a projection by those who felt they really knew truth as Eco suggests. Instead they were relying analogously on the outer representations as signs to indicate both the external and internal characteristics and values of a specific group of people. On these precepts, two opposing nation-states were founded in North America, both of them claiming initially to be the sole neo-mythic heir of the spirit of enlightenment and modernity. Both also initially identified the other as modernity's usurper, and as Black in spirit and, as Canadian elites thought of the US, even Black in body.

But change happened along the way. The United States of America underwent change of historic proportions that forced it to re-examine the race-based foundations on which the nation-state was established. This occurred, first, in a bloody Civil War that ended in 1867. A century later, a second development of liberation occurred in the Civil Rights Movement. These developments resulted in the official jettisoning both of racial perceptions and attempts to create a White homeland. This approach is best exemplified by various forms of affirmative action to bring African-Americans fully into the nation-state and to offer them opportunities for social mobility and self-actualization. This was an attempt to adjust perceptions and understandings acquired through the ethno-racial register to be consistent with changes in the composition of the good at the neo-mythic level. As an act of creation, this was an intervention by the fathers of the nation to transform a group of people long defined as ontologically evil or only partially good and to bring them into the mainstream – it was an attempt to make them, even though still ethno-racially Black, as idealistically White as all other groups.

The result was that somatic and cultural Blacks were reconstituted as fully good and belonging in the American state, and they were idealistically released from a caste-like status of inferiority. The good of the state was redefined to officially include Blackness in all its forms. According to this thinking, while the United States was questionably White idealistically and in status because of the inequalities that still existed, these positions having been derived on the neo-mythic register, it was unquestionably Black in culture and somatically, as determined under the ethno-racial. Equally, it should be noted that these moments of creation were idealistic, pregnant with hope, and lacking the despair that preceded them. Indeed, moments of creation and rebirth are phenomenologically the spirit of hope being placed into a new body. Canada has not had change of this proportion or as fundamental.

As Frye suggests, such radical approaches to social and political issues are not part of the Canadian thinking of what conceptually is Canada.[47] It is too revolutionary for Canada and might even be foreign to Canadian conception, as the apparatuses of the state have not developed in a way that would enable them to deal with such ruptures.[48] The moment of multiculturalism in Canada offers the idealism of a creative moment that might still be available for the seizing.

The argument, therefore, is that the fundamental problems of race relations and denials of social justice will exist as long as the neo-mythic and

ethno-racial registers are not reconciled. Also, there is the question specifically of social mobility, primarily for somatic Blacks, but for other minority
groups as well. That the accepted physical manifestations of what is deemed
social justice are not readily available to all Canadians might reflect a failure by Canada to fix all the cultural structures that existed before the
arrival of the new creationist moment that is conceptually official multiculturalism. The old types of human materials out of which the state will be
refashioned have not undergone the necessary and magical change that in
Canadian mythology and theology would make them new. They have not
undergone the double negation as we have discussed. Instead, the old materials in the state institutions and agencies still produce and perpetuate
Canadian racism and inequalities. Phenomenologically, the new body with
the new spirit of social equality, a just society, and with social mobility as a
main manifestation of this quest for justice has not yet fully emerged from
its nativity canals even though the crown has been showing for some time.

This argument goes to the very heart of being and becoming a Canadian,
and of feeling both fully accepted and that one fully belongs. These are
issues deep within the historical dialectics of belonging, acceptance, and
recognition – issues of freedom – that are played out daily in the lives of
Canadians, especially in the discussion on immigration. Much of this discussion is about how many immigrants and refugees should be allowed into
the country, how these newcomers should be placed strategically in society,
and about what limits should be imposed on them, especially over how
readily their professional and educational qualifications should be accred-
ited.[49] This is a discussion dominated almost exclusively by meaning associated only with the ethno-racial register, for it is mainly about physical
characteristics and positioning in a hierarchy of belonging, and seldom
about the values of immigrants and Canadians. This is so even though on
the neo-mythic register it has been determined that, in a general and universal way, immigration is good for Canada, and that a diversity of immigrants is in the nation-state's best interest.

One of the most restrictive limits is that placed on expectations, where
only a few immigrants are expected to ascend the Canadian ladder of success, and only partially and slowly, if at all.[50] Rather, immigrants are
expected to sacrifice themselves for the immediate benefit of the society as a
mark of gratitude for becoming Canadian, and then for the benefit of their
future generations.[51] This is a dialectic of hope by mainstream historical
Canada that turns out to be a dialectic of despair, the phenomenological
other of hope, for those that would become the new Canadians. Both sides
are dealing with the same social phenomenon, and both are viewing it from
radically different finite positions and gazes.

The result is a conflict of perceived goods: the good of the state, which
needs foreigners mainly for their labour, money, and other forms of social

and financial capital, and that of the good of immigrants looking neo-mythically for full acceptance in the Canadian nation-state in return for their social capital and commitment to Canada. The first good offers only a reduced form of citizenship with proscribed boundaries and limits on achievement; the second is a demand for full acceptance and participation – or what is called deep and moral citizenship[52] – that offers the freedom of full self-actualization and social mobility. Such a citizenship offers the fullness of hope and the negation of despair.

In turn, this conflict results in Canada's failure to fully meet, on a continuous basis, the annual demands for immigrants that would keep the economy growing and ensure the economic viability of social security programs. For immigrants, the failure is reflected in the inability of newcomers to receive social mobility as quickly as they expect. Actions taken by either side to satisfy a perceived good on one register lead to an evil on the other – thereby leaving contradictions in understanding and an absence of unity between the two registers, and the nation-state as an unhappy consciousness.

The result, existentialistically and ethically, in their social, economic, and political lives, is inequality between Canadians by naturalization and Canadians by birth, especially those of the latter who have traditionally been constructed as White and/or European in Canada.[53] The problem is the situating of finite boundaries in such a way that they both fully contain the infinities that are Canada and the immigrant, but also express the full extent of faith as both hope and despair.

Other theorists have produced eloquent examinations of the inequalities and lack of social justice that result in marginalization in the Canadian space. Traditionally, they tend to explain inequalities based on race as being (a) a product of social practices;[54] (b) foundational to Canada's early history;[55] (c) the by-product of shifts in power relations over the course of Canadian history;[56] and (d) the specific version of Canadian racism, which stems from the very definition of Canada at its inception as a "white man's country.[57] They have relied almost totally on the ethno-racial register for an explanation, and they have always presented this as being a problem with a system that is not working as efficiently as expected.

## SYSTEMIC WHITENESS, BLACKNESS, AND INEQUALITIES

My argument, in contrast, is that the system is working as well and as rationally as it was intended to, and as well as the dialectic within the infinite concept of Canada inclusive of all the conceptual oppositions and contradictions. Ironically, the system is working too well to be compatible with the new spirit, expressed ideology, or mythologies of current times. My argument is that the very foundation of the system or structure is faulty, because it is based on recognizing and imposing finite limits on what, with the benefit of greater knowledge, turns out to be infinite and changing. The system was founded on meaning derived through the ethno-racial register that was then used analogously to estimate what should be good and evil as determined on the neo-mythic register. As it turns out, meaning cannot be limited in a finite way to either of the registers: it must be common to both, and thereby infinite, or neo-mythic in the end. The problem is that too often the finite concepts limit themselves to expressing only one part of the dialectic, to the hope or the despair, and do not include both parts in the same notion. The systems, as captured bodily by the major nation-state institutions and agencies, have not kept pace with the changing meaning of who is a Canadian and belongs in Canada—a meaning that over time has captured more of the neo-mythic meaning of who or what is human and has come to rely less solely on ethno-racial meanings and their projections.

These contradictions result from using old analogies developed under an ethno-racial register as the basis for arriving at reasonable and rational understanding through the neo-mythic. There are contradictions because there is no normative good and ethically White way of reconciling the knowledge of the two registers, or of placing that of the neo-mythical at the higher and elevated level. In this regard then, the solution must transcend the registers, as the neo-mythic would suggest, either by going back to the original before the creation of time and history, or jumping ahead to another time when the irreconcilable can be reconciled mythologically.

What are now considered inequalities and inequities were once measured as the good of society on the ethno-racial register. Using this register, some people might still consider this to be the rational and most desirable outcome. As Emmanuel Levinas argues, the good is always already, even if it must later be renamed or redefined[58] if we are to be guided by a new register of meaning. This is where we start with the mythology, ideology, or ideal and then try to give it bodily expression. However, we later discovered that the wrong bodies were created for they in their exclusivity were never able to fill all that we intended by the idea of the good. To adequately explain racism and other forms of social, economic, and political inequalities requires a historical analysis that goes back to a primordial dialectical struggle between good and evil, and the resulting preference for good over evil, the acceptance of valorization and hierarchies, the symbolizing of evil with somatic Blackness and goodness with Whiteness, and how these notions became ingrained in the memory that is History. In so doing, we would be examining how evaluation of the concept led to its becoming truncated via stereotypes and analogies so that it could represent only parts of its being. To get a more complete picture, we would need to reattach to the prevailing finite concept the parts that were left out, or were not chosen, to be part of the preferred definition that now obtains. Also, we may need to free them of projections that in our sense certainty we have placed on them. Such an analysis calls for a careful examination of how early myths about good and evil still inform today's transcendentalist ideology. In this way, we may understand some of the "truths" to which Eco alluded.

Different outcomes in Canadian society, even if normatively ascribed, might only come about through a restructuring of the society, through a moment of such infinite proportion that it would require a mythological return in cyclical time to the ritualized moment of creation.[59] The ethno-racial register might be given the task of discerning difference and diversity. However, evaluative questions of equality and other ethical issues should be reserved for the neo-mythic register, with clear understanding that the entire system, the concept of multiculturalism, does not rationally assume that difference is de facto inequality.

Existentially and ethically, this would be a return to the earliest moment when the good was defined, and this good would have to be replaced for it to be valid for all who now call themselves Canadian. The definition of what constitutes the good of the Canadian society would have to be reconstructed and society would have to be reconstituted along the lines that can expect rationally to lead to the elimination of social inequalities, which is the pre-ordained good of the existing rationalist discourse. This is so even though history has taught us that ideals, like dreams, never come true. The idea and the action never work in synch: the result is always, as Plato suggests, a poor copy at the very best. Still, the dream or the ideal is the blueprint, the philosophical explanation for the sociological developments that would emanate from this plan.

The other option might be to try to change society's transcendentalist idealism, virtually an impossible task in light of 3,000 years of the development and entrenchment of this idealism as an answer to the apparent purposelessness of life and the human tendency to nihilism in the acceptance of meaninglessness in life.[60] Redefining the good and taking a new path to this goal would require a rewriting of Canadian history, a painful exercise that the United States has undergone. Such a rewriting calls for recognition dialectically of specific moments or ruptures in a national narrative – idealized as junctures or breaks in time – that are marked by struggles between competing conceptions of the good, with only one side winning.

Before going any further in this examination of Blackness as a Canadian particular, I want to further spell out the methodology and what should be established epistemologically as proof that this argument can be sustained for the four categories of Blackness. This will help us understand the Hegelian explanation of the unhappy consciousness, an act of conscious evaluation – I am claiming that conceptually Canada is a self-conscious ego – which, with the benefit of time and hindsight, realizes its despair and Blackness from imposing limits on the limitless and repeating the unintentional consequences. Here it finds itself caught in a bind where the knowledge and understanding from the neo-mythic and ethno-racial registers are in conflict, often producing contradictory meanings and unequal social relations. Such an approach will help as we shift the discussion in part from the mainly ontological, on to the epistemological, and, then, ultimately, to the prevailing ethical and a wider discussion on multiculturalism.

We will attempt a phenomenology of Blackness, starting with what is given to us through the externalities and phenomena of the ethno-racial register. We will then search the register, according to the categories of knowledge that we have identified, for evidence of internality, for an essence or force that is unchangeable. Using the evidence, we will try to see if we can arrive at a mythological essence, that on which the neo-mythic registry is based. We will be successful if we are able to collapse the neo-mythic and the ethno-racial into one register, with one univocal and unchanging notion of Blackness to match that of the given Whiteness. This would be evidence for a claim that the ethno-racial register can be used, ultimately, for an assimilation process. Through it, all differences and diversities, all those hidden attributes, characteristics, and unknowns – might be reduced and homogenized on a single register. Ethical relations could be based solely on the ethno-racial attributes. Ethical relationships would be reducible in their entirety to semiotics, to the non-synthetic understandings or mere perceptions that our senses can determine.

If we are unsuccessful, we will have an explanation of why, even with the categories of Blackness that we have identified, Blackness still remains equivocal in meaning and ethically a leap of faith. We would have an explanation of why Blackness is much more than skin colour or a specific lived reality commonly called Black culture. And we would know why meaning must move beyond the analytic product of perceptions and the privileging of the assimilative to synthetic understanding, with the implications for diversity and differences that are automatically implied, and even, ultimately, to the transcendent absolute where the diversity and differences themselves are ethically reconciled. More than that, we are likely to gain much knowledge from examining why, after a well-intentioned search, we would be unsuccessful at producing a single and univocal meaning for Blackness and Whiteness from the two registers.

# 7

# Phenomenology, History, and Paradigms

What matters is this: to recognize in the semblance of the temporal and transient the substance which is immanent and the eternal which is present in it. For the rational (which is synonymous with the Idea), in its actuality, also embeds itself in external existence and thus manifests itself in an infinite wealth of forms, appearances, and figures, shrouding its core in a multi-colored rind.[1]

## LESSONS FROM HISTORY

This chapter continues the argument that a rationalist ideology, in thought privileging the neo-mythic register but in action that of the passionate and assimilative ethno-racial register, underpins Western society. This is an understanding of society as both a complete system of its own and as a specific way of finding meaning. Canada and multiculturalism are embedded in and intrinsic to this system, and because, analytically, the two registers are not always reconciled, the system itself contains equivocal notions of Whiteness and Blackness as ways of making sense of daily life. We have accounted for this historical development through Frye's explanation of the role and potency of myths and how they are inherent in the later philosophies that shape our perceptions, including those that we now think to be at the heart of multiculturalism. We have also seen that these perceptions seem to clash with those given to us by the ethno-racial way of making meaning.

The perceptions produced by either register are in turn the blueprints that are used sociologically and politically to construct and structure a society based on the goals of achieving reason, stability, and certainty. In our way of thinking, again given to us by the neo-mythic, societies are sites of justice and of all those things we call the common good – in effect, as I shall argue, a place of happiness in a general sense. The goods are what supposedly make the difference between our living in civil societies and simply existing in states of nature, there being in the latter no law and hence no justice or rational happiness. Here again, these attributes of social living are taken from the neo-mythic register, as the fulfilment of efforts at human perfection, and in the end this register is the tool we use to evaluate our actions and even the perceptions that flow from the complimentary ethno-racial register.

The perceptions, values, and evaluations from the rational neo-mythic register are the bones and sinews around which public policy is wrapped in the hopes of producing a mythological structure that outlasts times – and thus becomes everlasting and unchangeable. These perceptions also determine what should be good about the society and how, idealistically, these discernments can be used to make individuals and groups happy within this culture that is produced through a life in search of freedom. Similarly, the perceptions help qualify those who are best suited to benefit from this arrangement, who will help improve and expand the structure and who will be happiest in such an environment. Philosophically and sociologically, these are issues of culture and the so-called civilization, of nation-state formation and the intended outcomes that are anticipated for those living in a particular time and space, and in the collective pursuit of a good existence.

In moving from how mythologies become philosophies of state formation and from the ensuing positions of individuals within the collective, I will juxtapose Frye's analysis with the explanation by Hegel of the dialectic of freedom as the engine of speculative history that is current multicultur-alism. I am thus beginning to shift my argument from being primarily one of establishing ontological and epistemological consciousness for Black and Blackness, to emphasizing issues of cognitive certainty and of good ethical relations. This will include a discussion on Hegel's existentialist view of the human struggle for perfection and greater understanding of the self: one in which the pages of happiness are blank in the book of life, and where individual heroes, after basking in momentary glory in the creation of new-ness, of Blackness becoming White, are often shortly eaten up by the very system they produced or initiated. We will be paving the way, ultimately, for a discussion of how multiculturalism is ethically a Hegelian unhappy consciousness, of why it is a sight of melancholia and lament – and how this unhappiness results cognitively from the irreconcilability of the two registers of meaning that we are studying.

Some readers might find this analysis to be something of a detour on their way to the later discussion on the ethical relations that comprise multiculturalism. However, I think there is still much to be mined philo-sophically, sociologically, anthropologically, politically, and culturally from having a detailed explanation of the unhappy consciousness and its genesis. Such an explanation is crucial for an understanding of my reasons, for example, for stipulating that the unhappiness is rational and results from a quest for the good – not, as some would suggest, from bad faith or mali-cious actions by those who intend evil and slavery for others instead of goodness and freedom.

In particular, I am in disagreement with those who argue, primarily from an "anti-racist" standpoint, that racism and ethnic inequalities are intentional evil and knowing acts of bad faith. There is much in the ethno-racial literature to suggest that the solution is to "educate" bad-minded individuals not to misrecognize individuals so that the "bad-minded" become aware of the unintentional effects of their actions and thinking.[2] To me, this is the same as saying that individuals should not rely solely on the meaning given to them by the ethno-racial register. My argument will be that the educational process must not only be at the level of the individual but must be system wide, for the unhappiness is a systemic phenomenon that has to be explained through the two registers of meaning, so that contradictions *intentionally and rationally* produced by them can be reconciled in the society itself.

The re-education, I argue, has to be a question of ethics, of evaluating what society holds to be good and wholesome; in doing that, we will be privileging the neo-mythic register. This evaluation can only be acceptable to all when we all return to the departure point of a new beginning by first of all asking ourselves what kind of ethical relations we want to have, how they should be manifested in society, and what the goods of that society should be determined as being. This is what I argue is epistemologically at the heart of multiculturalism in Canada – a site where in a quest for freedom and happiness there is little memory, history, and reliance on the externalities and objectivities associated primarily with the ethno-racial register as a primary way for a good ethical life. But first allow me an indulgence to provide a rationale for what I am proposing. This is important. In an exercise in phenomenology, how we are making the examination and why we are doing it, in terms of expectations, are just as important as the examination itself.

## UNHAPPY CONSCIOUSNESS, MULTICULTURALISM: DIALECTICS OF HISTORY

It is my argument that unhappiness in human affairs, as marked by a quest for genuine multiculturalism, occurs seemingly for no other explanation than that such unhappiness is what the amoral dialect of history needs in order to move on. The actions and determinations of this dialectic by themselves are neither good nor evil – they become such only after they have been evaluated on the neo-mythic register. This is a story of the failure of humans in general to achieve satisfactory affectivity and motility either within or outside of civil society. Affectivity determines what makes members of a society happy, and motility is a way of indicating what makes these members most useful to the society and themselves. In a functionalist way, it might be difficult to achieve affectivity and motility as what might be good for society might not be good for some individuals. Some might still feel that because of their functions in society that they are not fully actualizing, that they are not achieving personal social mobility, even though the wider society might be benefiting. Yet, by the way the society is structured to maximize the common good, much might be gained by society from limiting the affectivity and motility of individuals or specific groups. This is the classic argument between liberalism with its emphasis on the affectivity and mobility of the individual or minority groups, and communitarianism and socialism with the latter two privileging affectivity and motility for the happiness of the wider group in general. In this respect, then, as history has shown, freedom is always licensed, as is individual happiness and self-actualization. Here, I argue my reading of Hegel that suggests that the spirit of freedom is Black; that Blackness is the primordial, undifferentiated condition of humanity, or the "night in which all cows are Black," and that ontologically Blackness is a kind of creolization or composite made up of layers that occlude Whiteness.

But there is another way that I am using Hegel: as providing a mechanism for ascertaining what Blackness genuinely is and who is genuinely Black. This is the phenomenological search, one that aims to find the salient and analogous characteristics that are essential to effectively and systematically explain a group or person objectively. These are the characteristics that allow us to make some concrete sense when we talk in general about such universal things as groups, cultures, and civilizations. What is the necessary condition for these generalities to make cognitive sense? For a group, culture, or supposed civilization to remain unchangeable and perpetual, reason tells us that there must be necessary and permanent conditions, maybe eternal laws or essences, that keep them forever unchanging. So far, neither in the social nor natural sciences, have we found these eternal conditions, but this has not stopped us from generalizing almost to the point of totalizing individuals into groups. Whatever it is that necessarily makes a group Black, this same condition is also what makes the individual Black. Simply put, then, what is the essence, if there is one, that makes an individual Black?

Multicultural Canada operates on the condition and understanding that there are Black groups and Black individuals. This is why we have to continue the search for what is indeed the heart of Blackness, for either there are groups that are Black and unchangeably so, or there are no such groups. It might also be the case that there is no univocality for the Black individual or for Blackness. Alternatively, it may be that there is an essence of Blackness, but that it is something that rather than being static is part of a process of becoming – of a struggle or quest to attain an identity that is freedom.

As C.L.R. James suggests, this essence in a Hegelian dialectical sense is a *movement*. It is a process of becoming and occurs through successive negations of forms. These negations occur when each new form proves not to be the essential expression or determination and has to be replaced by a later expression or determination. Therefore, this essence can be seen only through a series of changes, with no single expression quite capturing the being of Blackness, but all of them in some way adding up to an absolute picture of what is and what is not the essence of Blacks and Blackness. Here we are examining, effectively, the full range of the ethno-racial register, and this is before we even subject its determinations to an evaluation. Still, if only to continually refute them, we must test the bodies or forms for these eternal things. Thus, as there is a perceived certainty or univocal acceptance in Canadian law, for example, of what Blackness is and who is Black, we need to test this too.

Phenomenology continually restarts with ostensible certainty and then takes us on a pathway of despair as each successive sense of certainty dissolves in turn into doubt. The accumulated wisdom that develops produces, not demonstrated knowledge, but truer wisdom as a science of experience among ethno-racial determinations. In this regard, what is initially plain to see – that which is readily apparent – comes through the application of dialectical logic to reveal itself as contested. It then allows the apparent certainty to reappear in a new guise yet to be unveiled, but propelled onwards by the quest for semiotic truth beyond appearance. Ironically, it establishes wisdom, not as the Whiteness of an abstract disembodied truth, but as Blackness, as the very process of turmoil and struggle, as the appearance of the dynamic of Spirit. In this way Whiteness, especially as an idealistic static utopia, is subverted in the search for it as the Holy Grail.

Phenomenology is an attempt to disabuse us of doubt and to take us into certainty through a series of proofs that produce demonstrated knowledge. In this way, we come to know that the category with which we are dealing is a faithful representation of the infinity that has been reduced to this finite grouping.[3] In this case, and throughout this book, we will be searching ethno-racially for the essence – the ultimate law or non-reducible quality given by nature – to Blackness and to what really makes Black Black. This would be a definition that transcends time and history, for it is a concept that is supposedly everlasting and unchangeable. And it would tell us what to look for and to expect in contingent bodies that are Black and that appear from time to time in society or Western thought. Indeed, we may even want to ask the question: are Black and Blackness contingent or necessary characteristics and properties, especially in a multicultural setting? To this end, it is worth repeating that we do not expect to find the essence. What we will most likely find is the "process," a way of discovery or uncovering, as Heidegger calls it, that enlightens us and helps us to move beyond perception to cognition.

By doing a Hegelian search and applying his existential, ontological, and epistemological explanations of Blackness, I am hoping to provide a final piece in the framework for how we should read for Black and Blackness within Western thought and to explain why multiculturalism is idealistic and cultural Blackness. Instead of an essence of Blackness, I am hoping to illustrate a series of connected manifestations. These are what Hegel calls the shades, one stage and manifestation succeeding another along a sliding scale of determinations, with the previous retaining a presence in the subsequent. It thus follows that the sense of Blackness and multiculturalism will be manifested in time and historically as forms rather than as essences, eternal laws, or necessary conditions. Therefore, were we to generalize, it could only be in the strict sense of dealing with universals, or classes and types of determinations, that are made up of particular forms. Generality can be made only in specific contexts and in moments that seldom reoccur in the same form or as the same spirit.

What we may know about any particular has to be located in a specific context that is its own time and history, but which is just one of many different contexts that form the overall universal condition. In this regard, any particular has to be relative to something else, which might generally be another particular in the universal or the universal itself. In recognizing this, we have built into our system protections against totalization and homogeneity as even at its most universal level the body we are studying would be a composite and syncretic.

In trying to seize the phenomena, we protect their heteronomy, creolism, and impurity on the ethno-racial register. We can use this method to study multiculturalism and Blackness either as particulars on their own, as separate particulars in a universal, or simply as universals that consist of diversity and differences – universals that are formed in the night when all cows are Black. This is where we see multiculturalism as being akin to Hegel's *multi-coloured rind*. It is where Canada appears across time as an unchangeable – the rational concept that is the state – but where the people are the essences of this state. In this case, therefore, the essences have been changing over time. It is multicultural and demographically very diverse.

The image of Canada – the rind, appearance, expression, or current determination of the state – is its multicultural faces, voices, and cultures, these all being measurements of the ethno-racial register. The supposedly White essence can be seen in the many attempts at peopling Canada, starting with the initial intention that Canada would be mythologically a White man's country and would be idealistically, culturally, status-wise, and somatically White. The multicultural rind of Canada, or the husk and hue as Hegel calls it elsewhere, is the non-White that is presented as the negative expression and determination of Canada. Therefore, multiculturalism, as idealistic and cultural Blackness, reifies both multiculturalism and Blackness ethno-racially. We can also make a case that with the changing demographic profile of Canada, existential multiculturalism is also reified somatic Blackness too.

This framework allows us to benefit from the Hegelian analysis of what we have established in the universal as Western thought as a search for freedom. This is the quest by a self-consciousness, who I will argue is Black in Hegel's description, to become White and free. However, and regardless of its ethno-racial determinations, it is eternally finding itself in bondage and unable to make the desired transition to perfection. In effect, a Hegelian search for the essence of Blackness is a search for Whiteness, for the hope is that the search will reveal that Blackness is the counterpoint to the search for essences, for it is the dynamic process itself of undermining essentialist thought. This explanation will help us account for the self-conscious ego's recognition, as we track its quest for freedom over time, that its freedom includes knowing who it really is, and why it would misrecognize itself as White and having a particular essence, when epistemologically, ontologically, and existentially it is Black. Finding no essence, the search will show that the self-consciousness can only be Black idealistically.

But I will also argue in this chapter that history does not move progressively and teleologically. The self-consciousness may not come to know and accept its purported essences and Whiteness in a progressive series of ethno-racially determined events. There are disruptions and moments of rethinking that lead to changes in approach. These changes can be benign, such as a tinkering with the process, or revolutionary, when even the very theories on which such assumptions of transformations are made are rejected and replaced. The self-consciousness can choose to remain in a state of false consciousness and even try to create conditions that confirm it in its self-deceit. Or the self-consciousness may subsequently change its mind about what it thought and how it behaved at various points of the series of historical events. It might tell itself that it might have indeed been Black ethno-racially and/or neo-mythically at earlier points, but that it subsequently introduced radical changes to liberate itself from the Blackness it despises. At this latest point in modernity, it might be willing to admit it was Black at some point, but that it has succeeded in the most recent moments in bringing Whiteness out of Blackness.

Here, Hegel argues ethically not only for recognition but for a reversal to correct the wrongs created in the name of an earlier good. To this end, I will examine what may be termed the more populist interpretations of Kuhn's *Paradigms of Knowledge*, where paradigms of knowledge are explained as being particular goods in specific moments.[4] Kuhn explains how these goods are established, entrenched, and possibly refuted, and how ethno-racial determinations take on the tone and of neo-mythic meaning and so gain popular acceptance. Here, we should read these goods and paradigms as specific points in the development of the Hegelian self-consciousness. Kuhn's explanation was originally intended for scientific knowledge, but, as others have found, it holds epistemological implications for the rest of society.

Finally, I argue that both Kuhn and Hegel are trying to account for the creativity that is necessary for human progress. This is a creativity that is often at odds with cultural fixity.[5] In my reading of Hegel's *Philosophy of History*, I argue that Hegel falls just short of naming finitely this necessary creativity and subversion as ontological and ethno-racial Blackness, but does describe it as having a specific hue, and in an idealistic sense, a multi-coloured rind. I read this as suggesting that Hegel, in the preface of the *Phenomenology of Spirit*, believes that Spirit of freedom is idealistically and, when embodied, culturally Black.[6] This I deduce from Hegel, along with noting his attack on Reason, which I believe Hegel views as what I call idealized Whiteness that as a false consciousness can be evil masquerading ethically as the good.

### PHENOMENOLOGY: METHOD AND EXPLANATION

This is what the philosopher Paul Weiss says of phenomenology: "A pure phenomenology tries to look at everything without blinkers and without illusions. It tries to put aside all concepts, all theories, all demands of practice, and to attend to what is before one. Distortions, additions, errors, and qualifications can, it thinks, be avoided if only one would enter into experience in a truly catholic, open-ended, neutral spirit, in innocent honesty."[7] Weiss is describing a way of knowing that allows individuals to go beyond appearance to ascertain the quality of things and objects as they really are – what we may call moving metaphysically from the assimilative eye of the ethno-racial register to a final position among the diversity of thoughts and opinions allowed on the neo-mythic register. But it is a method that calls for the individual to set aside much that she or he already knows, for the observer must be eternally open-minded and conscious so as not to impose received knowledge – so as not to impose from the neo-mythical. For it is a method that seeks to know "the thing" or phenomenon solely as it presents itself to us, and in such a way that nothing that we attribute to the object is a projection of our knowledge onto it.

In the classical form of phenomenology, the searcher is attempting to go beyond perception in order to reveal hidden knowledge, that which epistemologically is still in Blackness and unenlightened, to go beyond perception in order to arrive at cognition or the full truth. This is in keeping with the task Heidegger sets for this branch of philosophy: "Phenomenology must develop its concepts out of what it takes as its themes and how it investigates its objects. Our considerations are aimed at the *inherent con-*

*tent* and *inner systematic relationships* of the basic problems. The goal is to achieve a fundamental illumination of these problems."[8] This is what the empiricist John Locke, for example, calls demonstrative proof that leads to revealed knowledge on which reason can be based. This is a phenomenology in the Cartesian tradition, one that is slightly different from Hegel, where the aim is to disabuse us of doubt. This is the phenomenological method used by the likes of Husserl, Heidegger and Merleau-Ponty, and which we gesture to in our attempt to demonstrate that the affectivity, motility, and perception of what is Black, Blackness, and multicultural can be reduced to pure cognitive knowledge. Here again, we are expected to find that, because these concepts are infinities, they cannot be reduced to what in effect would be an essence or single meaning.

This search and the expected outcomes are fraught with difficulties, for as individuals we must be aware of social and cultural conditionings – the ideologies and mythologies discussed in the last chapter – that have already given us a peculiar way of thinking and of making sense of the world. Such is the received knowledge that shapes our intuitive perception, the knowledge that comes from our self-certainty about ourselves and our surroundings. It must be bracketed from the process. In a common sense way, we are products of our society, and the knowledge and attitudes that we have are informed by received knowledge. A phenomenological study brings us to question much of the ideological explanations that are already incorporated in our sensible world.

It is for this reason that a phenomenological reading is often, especially on the ethno-racial register, against the grain, that it challenges common sense assumptions and tries to get to the intentions behind actions. Such a reading is often attempted in a way that seems to jar against prevailing thinking, approaches, and conclusions. Phenomenology thrives on doubt or skepticism, in the belief that there is always something fundamental that is missing in the explanation, something that might be discerned by changing the gaze of the subject, and therefore that existing knowledge is incomplete and that claims to absolute certainty must be withheld. Theoretically, an infinity of gazes would produce an infinity of knowledge. However, the hope is that with each new gaze what is gained is a new way of looking at "old" problems.

Each new look adds something new to what was previously known according to the ethno-racial register, so that each new gaze, the examination of each new slide of the object or body, helps produce a deeper knowledge that takes us closer by analogy to when all truths are revealed. "Phenomenology," says George Dyer, "is a descriptive process. It does not 'prove' anything, but rather lets us see what is really there by removing distortions and camouflage. Existentialism is similarly analytic, but what is analyzed is human existence."[9]

The object of this search – the epistemic or idealized Whiteness, ironically, as evaluated on the neo-mythic register – has traditionally been at the heart of modern philosophy. As Reinhardt Grossman explains in *Phenomenology and Existentialism*, philosophy has always been predicated on the principles of *individual things* and *accidental properties,* and the assumption that often they are parts of the same object. These properties have been translated into substances and accidents, or what are generally viewed as the necessary and the contingent. In our study on Blackness and multiculturalism, we shall refer to them as the unchangeable and changeable. Accidents depend on substances for their existence, whereas the substances, as universal beings, can and would exist even if the accidental or contingent form that they take never happened. Here, we should bear in mind Frye's discussion about primary and secondary concerns that shape our existence.

Objects and materials are supposed to be made up of these two parts and when they are undifferentiated they are a combination of both the necessary and the contingent. This is an undifferentiating that, epistemologically and ontologically, has been presented as a primordial and pre-consciousness Blackness, what obtains before there is a separation, or a distillation to produce the White essences that are pure knowledge out of the accidental and contingent that is ephemeral. As Grossman states: "From this point of view, one may say that a substance has two kinds of property, essential and accidental properties. The essential property is part and parcel of the substance itself; it determines the inner structure of the substance. The accidental properties, on the other hand, are added on to the whole, compromised of matter and essence, in such a way that the substance would be what it is, this particular kind of thing rather than that one, without the accidental properties."[10]

Therefore, a search for the essence of an object, be it a so-called Black individual or group or a culture called Blackness, is an attempt to ascertain what is the unchangeable, natural, or necessary component. This is a search that approaches the body in general as a dualism, one part essence and the other part the form that it takes in a particular historic moment. In our discussion, we will be searching for two essences per se: one the changeable, the other the unchangeable. In this way, we will be able to analogously arrive at what in Western thought has been presented as the qualities of a never-changing good and those of a changeable evil.

The question, however, has always been how to know what exactly is the unchangeable and changeable. How should we handle the doubts that always arise over truth claims? The answer is to develop a critical method, one that tests and rigorously challenges every claim, that, in effect, subjects every neo-mythic evaluation to another round of ethno-racial determinations or to a higher absolute way of knowing – a superior neo-mythic examination. This critical approach, as Richard Zaner argues in *The Way of Phenomenology,* is at the heart of modern philosophy, going back to

Descartes's notion that humans are "thinking beings" that are embodied in contingent structures.[11] How does the part of the body that thinks get the unthinking portion to act? Is there a clear cause-and-effect interaction between the two? Are there laws that govern these actions so that the mind can always get the non-thinking part to react the same way every time by following the same procedures? Are there laws that can explain the essential and necessary characteristics as the two parts of the dualism? Or, in the absence of the full knowledge on which laws can be based, is there enough knowledge available on which probable laws can be fashioned, where behaviour with high levels of certainty can be expected rationally in much the same way as if it were governed by immutable laws? Again, here we are trying to ascertain if there is a rational basis for power, for one object lording over another, or whether they should be treating one another as equals.

But once again how can we *recognize* what is unchangeable and changeable? This is a problem as each object can be made up of several distinct parts and diverse properties, even though some of them may be classified as necessary and contingent. But which of these parts and properties are essential and which are the laws that determine this necessary condition? These are questions that must remain foremost in our mind in our discussion of Blacks and Blackness, for as descriptions of humanity and human actions these are concepts or notions of infinities. This means that they are concepts that contain inexhaustible properties and ways of being. How do we place a boundary or limits ethno-racially around these properties and qualities in a way that captures faithfully their infinities? And once we have limited the properties and qualities to finite sets, what are the requisite bundles of properties, and do they change from time to time or according to given circumstances? How do we ascertain the unique relations between the various components singularly and collectively, and, further, how do we discern which components are the essential and necessary elements in the set and to the relationships – those which allow us to make meaningful and new mythical evaluations, such as those for ethical relations?

Another problem that Descartes tried to figure out is how his search for knowledge could produce something that is "indubitable."[12] Here we are concerned with two types of laws: (1) those that explain intention, so that the thinking mind gets the non-thinking component to react exactly as it intended; (2) those for testing whether the initial thought is pure in that it captures the essence or truth of the thinking being and how it acts.[13] These add up to laws that know the difference between sense perception, that which is received from outside either via a received culture or the personal sensations, and intuitive perception, that which is presumed to be genuinely known and unchangeable, but which can only be ascertained from its hidden form through a diligent search. Importantly, this is a search that, as Weiss suggests, and as Husserl claims, calls for the bracketing of the objective world or the sensations of the unthinking part of the dualism that is the human body. To do this we must perform a phenomenology, as Grossman puts it, that "reveals to us truths about essences." This is a phenomenology, an eidetic reduction, that "inquires into the structures formed by essences," and "its method, tentatively speaking, is eidetic reduction."[14]

This, Grossman argues, requires the kind of phenomenological consideration that consists of a *reflection* on consciousness – something that can happen only on the neo-mythic register. The thinker must reflect not only on her or his thoughts, but on the very act of thinking itself. This would allow us to reflect on what we know and how we come to know what we claim to be truth or unequivocal. This means there is a high level of critical introspection, the self-conscious ego having to know itself as a thinker and as a product of its own thoughts. Secondly, this approach strives for the idealistic – for knowledge of infinities can be had only in a transcendental way, by knowledge going beyond the perceived limits of human reason. This is why in the final section of this book we will examine multiculturalism as a moment of pure idealism that in the absence of epistemological proof is surrender by the body to hope. This is an ecstatic moment of liberty. It is pure idealism: a moment when the self-consciousness is all Black because it does not know who or what it is and what it can become. Most importantly, this is a carnivalesque time when knowing these things does not really matter. Only the joy as opposed to despair is what matters in this in-between moments, this point being both a perceived end of history and the beginning of a new history.

Our approach aims to understand a world that is a universal but which can be known and appreciated only through particulars, for that is what essences are and what laws explain. Phenomenology helps us to understand a world that is based on transcendental idealism, on the notion that there is a regulator or structure to the world, that this structure is knowable in part as an analogy for the whole, and that this knowledge can be reduced to essences and to both natural and, in the absence of full knowledge, probable laws that are the basis for hope. This knowledge will help us discern what is good and evil and which actions would be either in harmony with or alienated from these laws and structures.

### LAWS OF PERCEPTION, COGNITION, MOTILITY, AND AFFECTIVITY

As Merleau-Ponty presents it, phenomenology is a study in hermeneutics to discover the truth or essence of a body.[15] This starts with the privileging of cognition, of the need to reduce everything to an epistemology of what can be known about the subject under study. In this approach, the body is seen in a Manichean way: what is not known is hidden and in darkness and what is known and understood has been brought to light, into consciousness through cognition. But as Merleau-Ponty suggests, cognition is only one of four methods for probing the body for hidden secrets. These include (1) the *cognitive,* based on the notion of the mind operating in the light reflecting on a dark body; (2) *perception,* based on the senses and producing only analytic knowledge that is already dependent on recognition of the body's soma and its ontological characteristics; (3) *affectivity,* based on emotions and passions that stem from an inquiry into the somatic and cultural evaluation of the body with a view to determining how the body should be treated ethically; and (4) *motility,* based on discerning the practical usages of the body, and carried out through an evaluation of the somatic and class or social status features of the body under study.

Ultimately, the aim is to map all elements of the body, so that perception, affectivity, and motility are generally reduced to cognition as assessed via the ethno-racial register. Western philosophy gives primacy to cognition, mythologically, as enlightenment, as the idealistic point when the body becomes fully known and transparent, with nothing hidden from the light, with the body brought out of its primordial darkness. Cognition is the unchangeable that we hope to achieve. Perception is what we start with as the unchangeable. Since both cannot have the same identity in this context, then one must be changeable.

Generally, as earlier empiricists like Locke and others suggest, perception is positioned idealistically as changeable and cognition as unchangeable. The end of the dialectic would occur when perception and cognition are equally unchangeable, by perception in the final stages taking the form of cognition. Until such a time, perception, affectivity, and motility – because they are not epistemological – are considered to be exercises in darkness, primarily because they rely on the senses and less on a detached rationalism that is outside the world and is ideally free of the effect of emotions and passions.

Perception, for example, is an ontological enquiry through soma and presumed race, but it is based primarily on intuitions of an a priori nature. Affectivity is based on the emotions and the passions and is ideally aimed at producing an ethical answer on how the body should be treated and positioned in a relationship with other bodies. The enquiry into the affective is usually through the somatic and cultural frameworks, areas generally perceived philosophically as dark. Motility is based on the practical use of the body and is an exercise in deciding what kind of existence is best suited for the body. This is an existentialist approach through a somatic and class analysis and is also an exercise in perceived darkness.

But there are some paradoxes in this schema. Cognition is usually presented as the rationalism of the human mind, the understanding of what has been brought into the Whiteness of light. The aim of the exercise in cognition is to acquire knowledge, or light, but this tends to be a futile exercise as the body that is cognitively Black produces only partial truths or contextualized knowledge. Epistemologically, cognition is supposedly dialectical and a synthesis that is a composite of knowledge and values arrived at after reflection. Ontologically, it is supposedly a Whiteness, intended to be absolute knowledge. Instead, it produced impurities, as bits of Blackness are always present. Indeed, we may argue with greater authority that only bits of Whiteness, both ontologically and epistemologically, can be discerned. A society that is based on knowing both pure subjects and pure objects ethno-racially runs into trouble, especially where subjects need others to confirm the truths of the subjects' and objects' determinations. This is the case where truth is presented as being outside the subject and the other, as the embodiment of the truth, as pure negativity for the subject. It is virtually impossible for the subject to fully know the other and, therefore, even itself. Thus, as it is questionable what, indeed, a subject can know with absolute certainty, this system that is based on acquiring full objective knowledge has a paradox at its very heart.

And there are also other paradoxes that are produced through perception, affectivity, and motility. Perception is never negated nor affected dialectically by subsequent actions, as it is produced by the senses based on what is already known by the sensor as sense certainty. It is ethno-racially derived and not subject to reason, if it is perception. This means that the existing knowledge is analytic, limited only to highlighting the contradictions and sameness in classes and forms. If they are based on the somatic, perceptions about the body start in darkness and can only remain in darkness. Affectivity is also faced with a paradox: it is supposed to help generate an ethical order, but this order can only be based on cognition, on what is known to be morally good and evil, something that cannot be known a priori or before the ethical act in question occurs. Yet the affective is intended to help in the decision of how to respond to an other before the other acts. A similar paradox exists for motility: the ideal existence for the other is based on some knowledge of what is morally good and evil and what is virtuous for this other.

In the end, the affective and motility may be approximated so that how an other is treated is based on partial knowledge that is a false consciousness or perception, in a practical sense on notions that the skin colour or the cultural behaviour of the individuals provide meaningful information about them and should decide ethical relations with them. Similarly, motility, based on knowledge, ends up being adjudged in a relationship where specific classes or people of specific skin colours are deemed to provide the requisite knowledge that determines their usefulness in society.

As a search for an essence, the exercise thus appears to be circular and a failure: a search for knowledge based on what is already known. The result is a continuous exercise in darkness, as through perception, affectivity, and motility the body refuses – indeed, is unable – to give up the White knowledge of cognition, and it therefore remains in a state of darkness. It follows that a civilization that bases its progress on cognition and epistemology is unintentionally stuck in darkness, its ethical relations that affect the lived experiences of others and subjects being based on assumptions and perceptions. The human body, already existing in a world of darkness, remains Black – with neither subjects nor objects ever fully known.

Finally, in the way Merleau-Ponty describes phenomenology, as a scientific method in itself, it is effectively an act or attitude of Blackness, as it seeks through reason while knowing full well that the search will inevitably fail in its quest for essences. Phenomenology, therefore, can only be idealistically and culturally disruptive and disorderly – challenging accepted orders, norms and paradigms, and the accepted wisdom of the day. This penchant for challenging, the act of rationally negating the existing, is basic to what Hegel calls a science or a systematic way of studying history and philosophy. This Blackness is creativity, a recognition that perfect knowledge, like Whiteness, exists only in the transcendent, or epistemologically in the mind – an idealistic but illusive goal that remains forever present as the unfulfilled promise in each layer of the human body that is uncovered and examined.

Still, it is a search that gives meaning to human existence, for its guiding motif is the good, the perfect form against which all achievements and constructions are measured. In this regard, then, phenomenology is an existentialist ontology: a search for an essence or Whiteness through the material that is available. That material is the body, usually presented in the philosophical language perceptually and cognitively as a composite that is dark, primitive, natural, and unknown. Phenomenology, as a systematic search, does not start with the notion of a cosmological ontology, of an essence that already exists, that is good, and which is unchangeable. It searches for the good, placing emphasis on the method and not the outcome, per se, of the search. The essence is not the focus that decides the goodness of the body or material; rather it is the body, as discovered in phenomenology, that analogously explains the essence. Therefore, an exercise in phenomenology is an exercise in Blackness through a search for ontological Whiteness.

But since we know these laws and essences as revealed out of the body or consciousness by searching it, any actions that we take in our ethical relations with one another would be free acts by a self-consciousness knowing what is right and wrong and knowing its limits. That is the ideal: to have the answer for how to treat one another and what societies we should build by ascertaining through our knowing who or what is essentially good or evil. Such essences have not yet been found, and, as Grossman states, perhaps cannot be: "Every such [mental act by a reflective self-conscious-ness] has two poles. There is the act itself and then there is its object. But the object is a noema. Beyond these noemata, transcending them, lies the non-mental world. This world is forever beyond the grasp of conscious-ness. On the other end, behind the world of mental acts, hides the 'pure ego.' It, too, transcends the direct grasp of consciousness. Both the self and the world are beyond our reach. But in the middle, between the two, dwells consciousness in splendid lucidity."[16] A main point that Grossman is mak-ing, one that is fundamental to phenomenology, is that context matters and that, even with the context or acknowledged social construction, full cogni-tion as epistemic and ontological Whiteness on the ethno-racial register is never attained. This is an important point in Hegelian phenomenology, as it is always how we behave morally and ethically in our negotiated space that determines our colour, and whether we fit into a category determined as White or Black at that specific moment. Even as exercises in pure thought, our categories of Blackness are always returned to the contextualized.[17] Our registers of knowing and understanding cannot be reduced totally one to the other, even if we try to conflate categories of knowing and to limit the concepts.

We shall now look at a specific type of phenomenology that is associated with Hegel and what it says about truth claims, about the pure or self-con-scious ego as it tries to understand the world, and about the lucid conscious world in which we think we know what Black and Blackness are.

## HEGEL'S PHENOMENOLOGY

At the heart of the Hegelian phenomenology is the notion of the concept. This is the idea that thought and epistemology precede ontology and being. Even more importantly, they are all preceded by the ethical. In this regard, what we deduce as concepts and beings are usually infinite thoughts, which we are trying to limit by definitions in a way that make sense for common usage. In a common sense way, we are trying to collapse what is partially neo-mythic to a never-changing meaning on the ethno-racial register. But in so doing, we end up with contradictions, for the infinite must include its finite category and more – we can never fully exclude the neo-mythic. There will always be traces of it, and it will occur as an absented-present. Indeed, as Hegel argues, the infinite concept includes what has been posi-tively asserted about it, as well as what has been so negatively. It is made up both of what is revealed and acknowledged and what is hidden, of both the inner subjectivity and the outer exteriority or objectification of both intu-itive and sense certainty perception. Cognition is always elusive.

This leads to another major component of the Hegelian method: the working of dialectics, the way of negating and transcending self-referential limits within the same concept or body. This working dialectically emerges as demonstrative knowledge primarily through the ethno-racial register. It is based on history and the negation of both the seemingly unchangeable intuitive perception, and the changeable perception based on the senses and experiences in the world. But if nature is real, then it is the natural or unchangeable component of perception. Either way there is a paradox of knowing that in the Hegelian sense is reconciled in demonstrative knowledge, or in reason through deliberation and mediation.

The Hegelian rationale is that in the end even the much-vaunted reason is merely another form of perception. Reason can only appeal to what has been established a priori as the good or ideal. This good or ideal has been established before the deliberation started, which means that it must exist prior to the rationalization, and in perception and social embeddedness. Therefore, even as reason, knowledge would be back in the world of perception, making judgments that are consistent with the previously determined moral and ethical determinations. There seems to be no way around the fixed neo-mythic way of evaluating.

Dialectics can come in three main forms of limits and boundaries: (1) as contraries in a binary when such opposites as hot and cold, good and evil, high and low are both included in the concept but in a way where one part is privileged as the unchangeable over the other; (2) as two independent component parts that come together to form a unity, such as in the manner where night and day are different parts of the same twenty-four-hour period, or where males and females make up the full complement of citizenry, so that to talk of the entirety is to include both components conceptually, but with neither component claiming to be the essence of the composite, complex form, or idea; and (3) in a complementary manner where they are two parts of the same concept and are needed for a single meaning, such as space and time, or nihilism – where there is almost a totality of despair and a minimum of hope or enthusiasm – this recognition is made through the paradoxical recognition of there being in a single unity two equal essences that are both unchangeable.

Examples of how the dialectics work can be found in our concepts of freedom, which includes the binaries slavery and death, and of death itself, which includes the opposites despair and hope. Together, they consist of the *totality* of human existence, of its coming fully into being in the same way that night and day form a twenty-four hour day or cycle, and together, as complements, all parts are components of the single totality that is the concept and must be taken into account to decide the *quality* of a resulting existence. In each of the three groups, the dialectics operate on the edge, where there are limits to what the positive or negative as the unchangeable and changeable parts of the concepts mean, and where the other takes over.

Where the other takes over, it is a point of negation, where one merges into the other. Where one destroys and completely wipes out the other is a point of refutation, for Hegel something that rarely happens. Negation points might occur in the three given cases where good and evil rub up against each other, when night begins to give way to day, and where there is an implied space that gives an implied time. Therefore, at the point of negation the other is included liminally in what is presented as the finite of the new concept or consciousness. The old is not destroyed, but sublimated in the new form.

The act of trying to understand a concept, such as Black and Blackness, is to see how finite boundaries that are placed around them eventually become negated as one limit gives way to another within the given universe. This means that the categories Black and Blackness cannot be complete, as the finite categories are constantly being negated dialectically. Seen then as infinities, conceptually Black and White will include each other as the negatives to their positive identities, although in a finite form one of them would be dominant and the other sublated. If this is so, there arise the attendant problems that we can never know what bundle of attributes and properties make up Black and Blackness through an identification solely of what appears positively, and, second, that we cannot find an essence, unchangeable, or necessary condition or component of Black and Blackness without a search for the hidden or unknown. As infinities, they cannot be reduced meaningfully to finite categories – there will always be an excess of meaning, what cannot be captured by the limiting definition.[18] In our discussion, however, we are trying to understand the second category of dialectics, where the ethno-racial and neo-mythic registers are equally valid components for ethical meaning. Indeed, like Hegel, by searching supposedly for the efficacy of the ethno-racial register, we end up showing the importance and the necessity of its compliment, the neo-mythic, if we are to arrive at a meaningful understanding. In the end, the two are simply intertwined and suggest the third category of knowledge where one way of knowing needs the other for a full picture. Therefore, in our discussion we will be looking at the three forms of dialectical movements: those that are inter-register, or contained between different points on the ethno-racial and neo-mythic registers; those that are intra-register, or between the registers themselves, with binaries comprising separate and complete entities; and third, those where the registers are intertwined, such as in the search for motility and affectivity for ethno-racial determinants that are also supposedly already evaluated as good or evil on the neo-mythic register.

In his seminal work, *Phenomenology of Spirit,* Hegel applied his method of a search or a quest to explain how an infinite that is God appears in the world, and how it takes different forms throughout history by expressing itself through the three types of dialectical movements. At no point is the form final, but merely the most recent manifestation of a spirit that, even then, still remains fully unexposed. However, any given form has a precursor, an ontic that places it in its historical context, and which allows us to know God ontologically and historically in a limited way that is a string of ontics. This idea of having a historical relationship does not presuppose that the contingent manner in which we meet the infinite at any moment is unchangeable and everlasting. Indeed, Hegel argues that the *Phenomenology of Spirit* is really the story of at least two infinities trying to determine themselves over history, trying to know themselves as finite particulars of concepts. This is the infinity that is God, in its many different forms, and that of freedom, which developed as a form that contextualizes and gives meaning to the contingent determination of God. This is a story of a spirit that resides in both the neo-mythic God and the ethno-racial humans and is trying to know itself over time and taking specific forms at specific moments of time. One spirit tries to create the perfect human *being*, the other sprit tries to *become* God. As both human and God, neo-mythically, they want to achieve a concept and being called freedom, or rather, neo-mythically, freedom wants to express itself as ethno-racial beings that are God and human, but keeps finding beings that appear to be composites of both beings. It is a story of, as Aristotle had suggested, knowing equivocally and through derivatives or analogies.

This spirit is self-consciousness or an ego – but, importantly, it is an embodied ego that thinks it is an essence or Whiteness. This means that, Grossman suggests, this ego must come to terms with three different realities: (1) that which is presented to it and is a projection of its knowledge or perception; (2) the hidden which it is in the process of discovering, but a world that is unknown, indeterminate and has within it the realms of infinite possibilities and gazes; (3) the hybridized or syncretized world that is a third space between these two, where some things are known and some are unknown, an intersection where there is a history and memory of the past and desires and expectations for the future. This moment is the present – the contingent and necessary moment for the past and the future respectively.[19] One of these third spaces is the world of a creolized Canada called multiculturalism.

One thing is common to these worlds, and that is the wish by this self-consciousness to know itself fully, in a way that is absolute and where there are no doubts and gaps in knowledge, and in a manner that removes all contingencies by converting them into necessary laws. This is an act that must involve the mythical genesis of the concept. But this is virtually impossible unless the concept can limit itself to something that is concrete and has an exterior – something that can be recognized on the ethno-racial register. This it cannot do, because, as a concept, it is infinite, which means that no matter how many finite or ethno-racial determinations it has gone through,

and how much memory and knowledge it has acquired from each manifestation, there will always be one or more that are still available. This is so
because diversity of beings and the constant state of simply becoming are
essential to the neo-mythic register.

And if there is another determination, the spirit can never be complete
and be fully known until it has exercised that choice. But to do so, would
only lead interminably to discovering even more infinite possibilities. There
would be an infinite progression. This leaves knowledge, identity determination, and ethical relations as open-ended concepts which in turn, subject
to their inherent dialectical nature, causes them to appear in different forms
at different moments. Neither can be a category that exhausts all its possibilities and potentials. As a result, the self-consciousness will never know
with absolute certainty. However, it can acquire some knowledge and memory from reflecting on the different stages and forms that have developed
over time, and on how the finite levels have given away to others in an infinite sequence. Therefore, the dialectical is historical and continuing. There
can be no end to history, as this would be akin to finding the absolute determinate point on the ethno-racial register that exhausts all possibilities on
the neo-mythic – something that reason tells us is not possible. Any dialectical movement and its outcome would be evaluated according to some ideal,
against some notion as Taylor states that is the "good."

By not knowing with certainty either this ideal or its determinant form,
this self-consciousness must come to accept by the standards set for epistemology, where complete knowledge is Whiteness, that it is always in Blackness. This is so because it can never be in complete fullness of knowledge,
that which, since the beginning of modern philosophy, has been associated
with Whiteness and light, with the end of history where there is no longer
any need for additional knowledge, and when the dialectic of freedom
peters out on its own. The Hegelian phenomenology suggests that at any
speculative moment this self-consciousness is in false consciousness, for it
tends in a backward glance to always believe that it has arrived at the end
of history. It positions and places itself as the ideal and perfect – with everything before now evaluated as less than ideal or perfect. It always believes
that while it was once Black it is now White. Only with time and in a subsequent repositioning to a new position, and therefore ideal, does it realize
that the previous position also was in Blackness. Each movement on the
ethno-racial register produces the same result, the same errantry of Blackness recognized as Whiteness. This is a very important point for the ethical
understanding of multiculturalism: it often views itself as idealistically
White, but on closer examination it is riddled with contradictions, so that it
is really idealistically Black.

Two things flow out of this. At the most recent point in history, we can
look back with the fullest of knowledge that is now available to us and

realize that in the past we were Black in behaviour and culture, for we made decisions based on the best knowledge available to us, thinking that we were White and enlightened. Now, we can pass judgment on ourselves and argue that we were misinformed, ill-informed, or simply wrong and even evil – that we were still culturally and idealistically Black as we had not yet escaped fully the primordial human condition of ignorance into the Whiteness of enlightenment. This is an ethical lesson we can learn from history – a lesson that comes to us through the reason of the neo-mythic register. We can now look back from our privileged position on this register and say that what we thought all along was an ethno-racially unchangeable White body was, in effect, Black and changeable.

The second thing we can do is to change our glance to be forward looking. This also will cause us to doubt our Whiteness. For we would come face to face with all the seemingly inexhaustible combinations, possibilities, and potentials that are awaiting us, all of which we must exhaust before we can claim to fully know what it is to live in what is essentially a determined indeterminacy. We are in the Blackness that is the end of our epistemology and what history and ethics teach us, even if we are still not yet at the end of history. In this regard, we would still be closer to the primordialism out of which we think we have come than to the end of history. How, then, do we deal with the future, and what rational decisions can we take that would also provide a "truthful" meaning in the common sense world of passions, assimilation, and the ethno-racial register? Here, we are using the dialectics between registers – of ultimately determining what is truth, and then using the dialectics that hold both registers as equal parts of a system that produced one knowledge or cognition. We are now in a position to see how such understandings can be ethical.

The false belief that there is a never-changing that has been found in human history is a Whiteness that has been applied to understanding, and which accounts for Eurocentrism. This accounts for the primacy of the Whiteness that is associated with the privileging of European thought within Western civilization. Inwood explains:

Hegel here applies one of the principles expounded in his logic, that inner and outer, subjectivity and objectivity, stand in direct proportion to each other. As Europeans detach themselves from the world and delve inside their own minds, they can to the same degree master the world instead of being simply buffeted by it ... He cannot, he believes, fully understand what human beings do or why, say, Europeans behave differently from other human beings, unless he explores their thought, their "categories." What is it about human beings that makes them operate differently from cats and dogs? What is it about Europeans that impels them to explore the world? What is so special about the Christian religion?[20]

As Hegel suggests, his phenomenology is based on a logic that allows a consciousness to become three parts, one each for its past, present, and future, thereby allowing what the consciousness deems to be its true self to reflect on what it has done in the past, what it has produced, and where it is going. Only some point in the future is White, but there might be seemingly infinite Blackness before reaching it; the ego, however, must know from experience and knowledge what was the unchangeable Whiteness in the Blackness that is now the past and in the present which is categorically so indecisive, syncretic, and ambiguous. This, it does by searching for its essence, what have been, are, and will be its unchangeable characteristics in all past, present, and future manifestations. However, only in the reflection does it come close to recognizing what it has really become, and to realizing that historically it has no essence or epistemological and ontological Whiteness, and that, indeed, its actions are based on only an approximation of full knowledge.

Whiteness can only be ethically derived from knowing and then making free choices. This means that in every determination of knowledge – in which, for example, good and evil, Black and White, are made – there is always something missing. And what is lacking could very well be that which is essential for determining an infinite bundle of these concepts. What we may provide to fill in the blanks in knowledge might merely be our best guesses – mere projection with no empirical basis. We shall now look at Hegel's argument that historically both good and evil have been changeable, if only because they are based on the shifting sand of morality, which in turn is based on the uncertainty of infinite knowledge, and that, indeed, this changeability that has always been ascribed to Blackness has been at the heart of human progress towards absolute knowing. Historically, then, Blackness has always been and will remain with us until the end of infinity. Indeed, even if it does not produce idealistic Whiteness, the ethno-racial register can still teach us a lot.

### HEGEL'S EXISTENTIALISM: PHILOSOPHY OF HISTORY

What can be discerned by pouring through the entrails of history, the wreckage of humanity, is that there is a central aim to the revelations of the Spirit: freedom. As Hegel posits in *Philosophy of History*: "As the essence of Matter (the opposite of Spirit) is Gravity, so, on the other hand, we may affirm that the substance, the essence of Spirit is Freedom. All will readily assent to the doctrine that Spirit, among other properties, is also endowed with Freedom; but philosophy teaches that all the qualities of Spirit exist only through Freedom; that all are but means for attaining Freedom; that all seek and produce this and this alone. It is a result of speculative philosophy, that freedom is the sole truth of Spirit."[21] Hegel argues that "the History of the world is none other than the progress of consciousness of Freedom; a progress whose development according to the necessity of its nature, it is our business to investigate."[22] But, as he notes, this notion of freedom, "without further qualification, is an indefinite, and incalculable ambiguous term; and that while that which it represents is the *ne plus ultra* of attainment, it is liable to an infinity of misunderstandings, confusions and errors, and to become the occasion for all imaginable excesses – has never been more clearly known and felt than in modern times."[23] Also, as Hegel suggests, it is necessary to view the revelation of Spirit as a struggle between "a principle in the abstract, and its realization in the concrete"[24] – in the first place what we may call the neo-mythic and in the second case the ethno-racial. According to our understanding, history, then, is a search by this presumed dualism that is spirit and body to attain rationalist freedom, the autonomy to know what it is ultimately capable of becoming and knowing, including the cognition of what are its absolute limits. History, also, is the story of how, in a lordship-bondsman relation, body and spirit have had to settle for licensed freedom, while aspiring for the moment when either can achieve a liberty that is unlicensed. History, then, is the epistemology, the gains, retreats, and stalemates on these fronts.

Hegel suggests that a meaningful study of history would reveal such a struggle and the way that humans have tried to capture in national or official explanations the story of how humanity came into being and what is its likely ending. The development of nation states, what we have come to call sacred times and spaces, as the embodiment of a specific spirit and culture, is one of the ways mythologically that Spirit has revealed itself over time. But the clear implication is that nothing static can hold this ever-moving and inquisitive Spirit. It is constantly breaking free of any efforts to contain itself. Rather, as Hegel suggests, the anathema of Spirit is containment or limits, in our case of being trapped on the ethno-racial register, for that is what it is trying to escape most of all. Spirit wants to be defused, diversified, and containing differences – by nature its essence appears to be the indeterminacy of being and becoming of the neo-mythic register. However, its embodiment as the material that it needs to work through has a different intent: it wants to be contained, for, dialectically, in no moment is the dualism finite and contingent. This is the only way it can be recognized on the ethno-racial chain of being. Therein lies the beginning of the struggle between spirit and material for ascendancy, for the expression of a separate understanding of what freedom is. Here is how Hegel explains this struggle:

It is a result of speculative Philosophy that Freedom is the sole truth of Spirit. Matter possesses gravity in virtue of its tendency towards a central point. It is essential composite; consisting of parts that exclude each other. It seeks its Unity and therefore exhibits itself as self-destructive, as verging towards its opposite [an invisible point]. If it could attain this, it would be Matter no longer, it would have perished. It strives after the realization of its Idea; for in Unity it exists *ideally*. Spirit, on the contrary, may be defined as that which has its centre in itself. It has not a unity outside of itself, but has already found it; it exists *in* and *with itself*. Matter has its essence out of itself; Spirit is *self-contained existence*. Now this is Freedom, exactly. For I am dependent, my being is referred to something else which I am not; I cannot exist independently of something external.[25]

    In one form, the unity it seeks is within. In another, it is external. In one form, it is assimilative, hierarchical, and stereotypical; in the other, it is diverse, different, and unfixable. Yet, Spirit and body must find a unity that is always acceptable to both. The inner unity must match the outer. For Hegel, this contradiction captures the dilemma of human existence, the struggle for a rationalist freedom that can never be attained in the concrete existence. Freedom cannot be unlicensed: individuals and nation states can only be truly free when they are in full self-knowledge or self-consciousness, thereby, paradoxically, as infinites, knowing their limits. Such a point is when they not only know what they want to become, but when they know how to become the idea: they can see and hear beyond their physical limits. This knowing is as much of what they cannot become as it is about what they cannot know analytically. Only then would their rational thoughts and their desires be in sync and fully reconciled. In Hegel's words: "I am free on the contrary, when my existence depends upon myself. This self-contained existence of Spirit is none other than self-consciousness – consciousness of one's own being. Two things must be distinguished in consciousness; first, the fact *that I know;* secondly, *what I know.* In *self* consciousness these are merged in one; for Spirit *knows itself.* It involves an appreciation of its own nature, as also an energy enabling it to realise itself; to make itself *actually* that which it is *potentially.*"[26]

    This is a dialectical struggle, the explanation of the system behind human history and its primordial quest for freedom, with this freedom being situated epistemologically between intuitive and sensory perception and being the necessary knowledge for any action to be free. It is a struggle that produces an idealistic form of self-centred Blackness – freedom – with its penchant for creativity and its inextinguishable quest to break through boundaries and limits. But this is now dialectically, and paradoxically, a freedom that wants to be seen as idealistically White in a higher consciousness.

    In turn, this idealistic Blackness produces for the spirit or self-conscious ego moments of cultural Blackness or self-doubt. This is best exemplified by a way of life that is a commitment to freedom itself and to the treasuring and enjoyment of the moments of freedom that existentially are constantly

under attack. Spirit feels torn because of its commitment to both perceptions – to accepting intuitive perception as an a priori, while acknowledging that sensory perception has the right to challenge this analytic position
with real world experiences – yet having to privilege one at the expense of
the other whenever it makes a decision or takes action. Without vigilance,
these freedoms could quite easily be eradicated in a flash of White light that
produces conformity, fundamentalism, and unquestioning loyalty, and the
privileging of one group of people over all others. Spirit, torn between the
meanings of the two registers, ethically finds that it does not know rationally how to act in a "truthful" way: it is an unhappy consciousness.

# 8

# Blackness and Speculative Philosophy

What, then, are the ethical lessons that we can learn from this history that leaves us with a future, that is an ethical and epistemological dead end for pure meaning, that is really just another point in a never-ending history predicated on changing determinations on the ethno-racial register? What does this tell us about what we should take with us for our leap into the future – into the epistemological Blackness where we hope to be the ethical Whiteness within this darkness? What should we expect of multicultural-ism today, and possibly in the future?

As Hegel argues, history is humanity's reassessment of the extent of its knowledge, of what it passes on through time as memory, as the lessons learned from the dialectical struggle of history. These are truths and shades of self-consciousness gleaned from specific moments, what with practical judgment and reason should be preserved and raised up. This is a working of memory, of knowing, through an appeal ultimately to reason, what is good and what is evil, what should be carried forward from one generation to another, and what should be excluded.

But what do we really mean by history? Is it simply the narrative of a chronological order of determinations in search of a fixed and successful manifestation on the ethno-racial register? Is it, neo-mythically, the eternal search by the mythological spirit for a determination that exhausts all pos-sibilities; or is it the number of times the spirit has had to return into inde-terminacy? In the latter case, this would be a history of errantry, of a seemingly endless series of failures. Or is history some combination of the working out of these two registers, and necessarily a bit of the mythological and a bit of the ethno-racial?

Memory is the idealistic link between a past that in the present is unknown, because it has ceased to exist bodily or materially, and a future that is unknowable, because it has no physical existence and its being can only be an act of faith or hope. But this history can often be truncated and smoothed over, so that the moments of disruptions and discontinuities – the changing dialectical movements – are neatly explained, and even erased from the official history or memory. In the official narrative, and even on the ethno-racial register, the excluded remains outside memory. Its determinations and manifestations do not count. But as thinkers such as Michel Foucault and Homi Bhabha suggest, memory results from a dialectical struggle between the included and excluded, between those who have written and are part of the national narrative and those who are constantly disrupting the narrative by demanding to be written in, to become part of the wider self-consciousness.[1]

These are the particulars in a Hegelian phenomenological universal or body. As Bhabha contends, the excluded are arguing for "an ambivalence in the narration ... that repeats [itself], uncounselled and unconsolable, in the midst of plenitude,"[2] that aims for a primordial freedom that is Blackness with its endless potentials and possibilities to offer at every contingent moment always a new opportunity for a new beginning with a new narrative. And history filters the past through the lenses of the present – and from the position of a supposedly fixed, mythologically complete and unchangeable White order. It stacks the results according to the objectives of the historians or of the institutions and agencies the historian observes.

Hegel had earlier seen the dangers in this type of memory that eradicates and refutes the movements on what I call the ethno-racial register: "A history which aspired to traverse long periods of time, or to be universal, must indeed forego the attempts to give individual representations of the past as it actually existed. It must foreshorten its pictures by abstractions; and this includes not merely the omissions of events and deeds, but whatever is involved in the fact that Thought is, after all, the most trenchant epitomist. A battle, a great victory, a siege, no longer maintains its original proportions, but is put off with a bare mention.[3] Indeed, in the preface to *Phenomenology of Spirit*, Hegel suggests that the thinking of such a history presents a danger for knowledge and memory. People of one generation may be tempted to believe that the current version of the truth is the absolute and to ignore the earlier "shades" of truth that have contributed to this realization. When compared to the ideal, or the later wisdom of knowledge, these shades are the erroneous manifestations of the mythical Spirit. This truth is held to be fully determined and unchangeable, even while at different moments what is presented as the truth appears to be constantly changing. It is, Hegel suggests, like looking at a seed and not seeing that at one moment it is a seed but that with time – a time that is captured in the seed – its potential will be revealed, all in different stages, each stage negating while building on the previous, each one the latest manifestation, but part of a single unity of truth that is built on the various stages of the past and those that are to come:

The more conventional opinion gets fixated on the antithesis of truth and falsity, the more it tends to expect a given philosophical system to be either accepted or contradicted; and hence it finds only acceptance or rejection. It does not comprehend the diversity of philosophical systems as the progressive unfolding of truth, but rather sees in it simple disagreements. The bud disappears in the bursting-forth of the blossom, and one might say that the former is refuted by the latter; similarly, when the fruit appears, the blossom is shown up in its turn as a false manifestation of the plant, and the fruit now emerges as the truth of it instead. These forms are not just distinguished from one another, they also supplant one another as mutually incompatible. Yet at the same time their fluid nature makes them moments of an organic unity in which they not only do not conflict, but in which each is as necessary as the other; and this mutual necessity alone constitutes the life of the world.[4]

This development results from engaging in what Hegel calls critical history, a series of dialectics based mainly on contraries and complements, the incorporation of myths and the latest manifestation of Spirit but only from the perspective and momentary consciousness of the writer. These expressions of forms of history and memory "consist in the acuteness with which the writer extorts something from the records which was not in the matters recorded."[5] For, as Hegel further explains, "here we have the other method of making the past a living reality; putting subjective fancies in the place of historical data; fancies whose merit is measured by their boldness, that is, the scantiness of the particulars on which they are based, and the peremptoriness with which they contravene the best established facts of history."[6]

This is more often associated with the ethical relations that are known as the national life, which, as Hegel argues, stands

in close relation to the entire complex of a people's annals; and the question of chief importance in relation to our subject is, whether the connection of the whole [of history] is exhibited in its truth and reality, or referred to merely external relations. In the latter case, these important phenomena (Art, Law, Religion, etc.) appear as purely accidental national peculiarities. It must be remarked that, when Reflective History has advanced to the adoption of general points of view, if the position taken is a true one, these are found to constitute – not a merely external thread, a superficial series – but are the inward guiding souls of the occurrences and actions that occupy a nation's annals. For, like the soul-conductor Mercury, the Idea is in truth, the leader of peoples and of the World; and Spirit, the rational and necessitated will of the conductor, is and has been the director of the events of the World's History. To become acquainted with Spirit in this its office of guidance, is the object of our present undertaking.[7]

But then along comes a revolutionary moment, a war of irreconcilable difference, the yin-yang of history that results primarily from a dialectic of opposites. Such as when the fixed position on the ethno-racial register appears too limiting and meaningless and there is pressure for change. This is when the existing form or manifestation of spirits cannot contain the fullness of the spirit of the times. What we are left with, in the absence of the efficacy of the ethno-racial register, is the neo-mythic – that which has not yet been tested in time in such a way as to successfully produce a finite and meaningful determination. This is to return to a moment of infinity, to use Levinas's term, and this calls for the rewriting of history.[8] This is the deconstructionist aporia all over again, and the decision out of the aporia, is a decision that rewrites history. This is a moment of discontinuity as suggested by Foucault and Bhabha. In this case the "history" as truth has to be amended and even rewritten to, as Hegel says, "quicken the annals of the dead Past with the life of to-day. Whether, indeed, such reflections are truly interesting and enlivening depends on the writer's own spirit. Moral reflection must here be specially noticed – the moral teaching expected from history; which latter has not infrequently been treated with a direct view to the former."[9] This new life can only come ethically from the neo-mythic world.

Hegel suggests that these irreconcilable moments are when Spirit and body are so wide apart on what constitutes freedom that there can be no hope of bringing them together. "The universal Idea exists thus as the substantial totality of things on the one side, and as the abstract essence of free volition on the other side. This reflection of the mind on itself is individual self-consciousness – the polar opposite of the Idea in its general form, and therefore existing in absolute Limitation."[10] Spirit and body appear to each other as separate self-consciousnesses. There appears to be no meaningful way to reconcile the ideals of the ethno-racial and neo-mythic registers in the same forms or times. Here, the meaning that comes from one register is always inexact for explaining what is occurring on the competing register. The two meanings are in a dialectical struggle with each other and can only be reconciled by moving the action and meaning to a different, and hopefully, higher level. So history, as the story of the existing and idealized social order, is urgently in need of change and movement. How then can there be the agreement that is necessary for the formation of a civil society and for deciding the roles that should be played in a state?

LORDSHIP AND BONDAGE: DECIDING SOCIAL ORDER

In the following, I shall present two opposing readings of Hegel's *Phenomenology of Spirit* to explain the formation of societies. These two readings offer significant applications for understanding the lordship and bondage ethical relationship that resulted in a multicultural Canada, as a social order, becoming ethically an unhappy consciousness. Knowing this "history" of becoming can open the way speculatively for us to find a way out of this unhappy consciousness.

The first reading suggests an external battle in nature between individual entities that, in their purity of thought, see themselves as fully developed and all encompassing and as having no room for others. Analogously, this is intuitive perception lording over sense certainty as knowledge. We can read this as a dialectical choice between the differences that occur within either of the two ways of life and social meaning associated with our registers. Eventually, existentially and epistemologically, the differentiated differences from the registers that seek to supply a single meaning must confront one another. This is necessary if the desired social order should have a single prescribed way for handling differences. Usually, there is a battle for dominance within the already agreed upon social system, a struggle that results in a master-slave relationship. This fight is to receive the recognition produced by the specific register, so that those, for example, who are determined as a specific group on the ethno-racial register would be in competition with those similarly determined, but occupying a different position and placement. Those considered as different would struggle among themselves within that register for the official acclamation that they hold the dominant position. One group and its way of life must triumph over another; the other group, recognizing that it must do a master's bidding, agrees to enslavement as the price for maintaining its culture and mores. In this analysis, one group is clearly recognized as the master and the other as the slave, but this is according to a culture that is already determined.

This is the view that is shared by theorists like Alexandre Kojève in *Introduction to the Reading of Hegel: Lectures on the Phenomenology of Spirit*, who views the dialectic as driven by fully-imagined or finite combatants that are initially nose-to-nose and unwilling to yield.[11] This is a battle entirely on the ethno-racial register, but for me it is a battle that does not move on to the double negation of Blackness that produces evolutionarily or systemically an ethical Whiteness. Instead, one is forced to yield and becomes the slave and the entity that is alienated in its labouring for the pleasure of the master. Inadvertently, however, through this alienation it is also producing a culture and civilization. There is no ethical evaluation of this battle. Undoubted in this context, is that the slave is Black idealistically, and in culture and status; the master is White in status, culture, and idealistically. This is the argument on which Charles Taylor builds his classic on multiculturalism, *The Politics of Recognition*, an argument that has been accepted in the literature as a seminal explanation of the politics of multiculturalism and diversity in civil society in general, and, in the particular, as the widely accepted explanation of multiculturalism in Canada.[12]

The second explanation is associated with the recognized Toronto Hegelian School, as explicated in Howard Adelman's "Of Human Bondage: Labour, Bondage, and Freedom in the Phenomenology."[13] Its main point is that ethical relations start out as a quest for the reconciliation of differences, even in thought, but end up with one component *temporarily* dominating the others. If there is a choice in this way of life, it is between registers, between different ways of recognizing and evaluating differences, with each offering a contrary way of life and meaning relative to the other.

This struggle is *intra*registers, and not *inter*register. This struggle is within the same consciousness, like a conflicted person. This intraregister version positions the beginning of civil society as a struggle internal to humans over which modes of life are necessary and good to civilization. This is a struggle ontologically and epistemologically to define infinities. It is a struggle in which humans have already acknowledged their diversity and plurality, and their alienation – all forms of idealistic Blackness. The ethno-racial register and its latest manifestations of history have already been taken into consideration, but something necessary – as a value system – to civil life is still missing. The dialectical struggle is one that comes out of contraries, initiated by oppositions but with the knowledge that one of the binaries is unchangeable, or in ethical relations is the unchallenged lord. It is a struggle for meaning on the neo-mythic register, for determination of what is good and what is evil.

Reconciliation at the analytic or common sense level would lead to the assimilation of differences, and ethically to what has been described in philosophy and the social sciences as a social contract. But all the parties involved know this can only be a temporary band-aid solution to the handling of differences as an issue of equality. This would be an agreement among the parties involved. Contrary to this view, the Adelman explanation suggests that ethical relationships are covenants – between beings or consciousnesses that begin embedded in their differences, and have no way to reduce these differences to a single common way of life that would also recognize these inherent differences. They are differences between groups or individuals that are already radically different, but who must come together and live socially. They value and assert their quest for equality differently, if only because equality has different meanings for them. No matter what relationship they find themselves in, they are ethically unhappy, and they are struggling for change. So that to them, whether tyrant or subjected citizen, they are always advocating a change within the order. But such change would appear meaningless within the order, or even incompatible with the system itself, if the order were to remain unchangeable. Therefore under this covenant, even the order – the state in a setting of multiculturalism – is at the heart of the contestation over differences and equality.

As a result, one or more differences that form a consciousness in themselves become dominant in the wider way of life. They represent the wider way of life hegemonically, and they do this by claiming that they have the authority to determine the neo-mythic register in terms of the ethno-racial register. To do this they establish norms and behaviours that can be situated and differentiated on the ethno-racial register and they claim neo-mythically that this is the perfect order in terms of meeting the goals and desires of both registers. Needless to say, because there are still differences embedded in the neo-mythic register, those who find themselves in a dominated situation, in a form of slavery, are ceaselessly trying to overthrow the "dominance" and establish a new one.

This is the story of why, neo-mythically, human beings, and even their gods, are supposedly always looking for a new covenant, for an end of history as determined by the existing covenant and played out in the common sense of the ethno-racial register, and the beginning of a new history under a new covenant that incorporates more of what the individuals construe as proper in the neo-mythic order. And we must remember that one thing that is endemic to covenants, and not to social contracts, is the idea of change – it is expected that as the parties come into fuller knowledge they will have to amend the covenant. A social contract, on the other hand, usually involves fixity – where what is agreed to in the past or present is expected to obtain in the future in a non-changing relationship, and where any attempt to introduce change is tantamount to cheating.[14]

This is the covenant story told so well in Du Bois's notion of the double consciousness, where those who are deemed to be somatically and culturally Black want to see themselves as idealistically White and full in their freedoms as are the dominant groups that have claimed somatic and cultural Whiteness on the ethno-racial register to be the norm of the society. Certainly, what Du Bois had explained as the existence of somatic Blacks and Africans in the Americas, primarily in the US, was not a social contract into which they had placed themselves as the dominated, but a covenant in which they had found themselves, in the Heideggerian sense, thrown into and which they had to struggle from within to change. Moreover, under the neo-mythic register, while their struggle and their desire for a different recognition of difference was ethical and good for them, it was, as seen through the eyes of those with the power in the covenant, deemed unethical and as having the intent to destroy the latest and best social order in history. When changes are introduced under the covenant, we start the process of hybridity and creolization. Du Bois wanted this change to operate along the lines of the ethno-racial register – on which his liberalism as a struggle for recognition is structured. However, in the end he was really asking for more – for a radical change to liberalism itself, something he could only appeal to through the neo-mythic register.

My argument is that understanding multiculturalism in Canada as a covenant, not as a social contract, is central to understanding the differences experienced by those who are considered phenomenologically Black and those considered phenomenologically White. For, if it is a consciousness flowing out of the dialects of a covenant, multiculturalism is by definition ontological, existential, and ethical Blackness, rather than the mythical Whiteness that is assumed under a social contract where everyone has been assimilated into a unity, and their differences are wiped out, at least contractually. This, then, is an ethical question that goes far beyond the recognition of difference, as it questions the very determinations of liberal rights and liberalism. It also speaks to how these experienced differences are managed and what the ethical standards are for governing them. Key to this question, therefore, is where the ethical standards that determine good behaviour and treatment come from – and we see they are not natural to either of the registers, but have to be constructed in the heat of the struggle and imposed by the dominant on the supplicants. Therefore, multiculturalism is always questioning the legitimacy and historicity of the prevailing liberal rights, questioning the authenticity of the state itself, and proposing a new covenant. The result is always new moments of syncretism, hybridity, creativity, and creation. Bit by bit, the bondsman achieves some desires by getting the Lord to incorporate the bondsman's ideals into a social order. So that the social order, a state for example, would itself be, technically, always under construction. For the parties that will inhabit it, the order would never be fully formed, would always be a work in progress. The culture that emerges would be creolized and hybridized – a mixing of the desires, ways, and attitudes of all the contending parties operating under the covenant. Life under the covenant would be eternally dynamic – and Black with potential, creativity, and possibilities.

## MULTICULTURALISM: STRUGGLE FOR MEANING BETWEEN REGISTERS

What prevails in multiculturalism, ethically, is not an arrangement among equals on the ethno-racial register but one among those who see themselves as becoming equals on the neo-mythic register. It is also a complex order where diversity and differences are accepted, where evil and good can coexist, where Blackness and Whiteness in all their categories are recognized without dispute. However, the recognition and the ethical relations are expressed through the ethno-racial register – this is where one of the differences is deemed to be analogous to the good on the neo-mythic register and all other differences and diversity are deemed the not-good.

Human beings know that a power higher than themselves exists and that it does not recognize them as equals. This is the recognition of differences in being itself – not as where neo-mythically there is a difference between gods, or at the ethno-racial level where there is a difference between all beings that are human, or between humans and godlike beings. This difference is akin to that of comparing ways of life – emphasizing the motility and affectivity most suited to gods and human beings. These are genuinely differences of types and kinds. This is the same kind of difference that practitioners of race and racialization assume, as they in effect claim they can detect on the ethno-racial register where different groups of human beings, as specific types or kinds, are fundamentally different from other kinds and types within the same human family, or race.

In this case, human beings also know that they are deemed on the ethno-racial register to have a finite determination, yet they want to escape this and live as if they have all the potentials of becoming that reside on the neo-mythic register. They want to bring about a switch or change in registers – qualitatively, in types and forms – or to reconcile them so that both registers equally describe their beings. Existentially and epistemologically, what we are talking about here is analogous to both intuitive and sensory perceptions recognizing that neither is, in today's vernacular, "the man" or the truth. There must be an appeal to a higher level of knowing or understanding – to demonstrative reason in which resides unchangeable truth. This is an appeal to the neo-mythic for a fuller meaning of life.

First, existentially and epistemologically, this mythological power that has the ability to physically extend life is neo-mythic and is not only supposedly White but sets the norms for the acceptance of Whiteness. It determines what is necessary for Black and Blackness to be converted into an unchangeable White and Whiteness. This force, in an assimilative and stereotypical way, recognizes humans as being determined as Black in culture, status, idealistically, and, perhaps, even somatically, too. The power lives supposedly according to the neo-mythic register but evaluates human beings according to the ethno-racial. It maintains the neo-mythic for its own evaluation, and the humans would like to avail themselves of this treatment – where they may be recognized not as finite beings but as gods.

Second, human beings know that within them there is ontological diversity, captured by analogy in the two forms of perception: one side of them thinks, and it thinks that as a thinking being it is infinite, superior, immortal and like a god in every way; the other side acknowledges that it is perishable and finite, that it has needs, desires, and appetites, that it must do and make things to satisfy its passions, and that it is the opposite of the everlasting god. The first is intuitive perception, the second is perception based on experiences from living in the material. In this sense, human beings are, therefore, culturally and idealistically White and Black at the same time – paradoxically, providing both intuitive and sensory perceptions all at once. When they are restricted to a determination on the ethno-racial register, humans therefore feel cheated of their full potential.

In both scenarios there are problems. In the first, human beings in their cultural Blackness want to become gods and to be acknowledged as White but the Lord in this myth does not give them this recognition. In the second scenario, in its already perceived Whiteness, the mind of the individual does not accept the culturally Black body as its equal. The perceived solution in both scenarios is the sacrifice of what is deemed to be primordial, primitive, impermanent, mortal, and impure – sacrificing, as Hegel says, the perceived husk of humanity to preserve the presumed essence of humanity, its godlike Whiteness. It gives up as a burnt offering what the ethno-racial register considered to be its determined form in the hope of gaining acceptance for its potential to become greater than the ethno-racial register would allow. This is the putting away of the changeable and contingent for what is unchangeable and necessary in order to live happily and mythologically ever after. Epistemologically and ontologically, Whiteness is therefore privileged in the idealistic sense over Blackness, the body, and the changeable.

But there are also practical and ethical implications. In their alienation, human beings must make an existential choice about their own affectivity and motility: they must decide how they can be most happy and congenial with one another, and how they can idealistically use one another in the fullest and yet most satisfactory way. This is a decision about which of their many virtues or characteristics are ontologically and existentially essential and unchangeable, which they should develop and carry forward into a civil society, and which, as the unnecessary and changeable, should be excluded or, at best, confined to an inferior status or class.

These virtues are bodily and they are the passions of human creativity, and the decision is to elevate specific "natures" as abilities and virtues over others in a secondary determination of Whiteness and Blackness. Since human beings in their ontological and epistemological Blackness and alienation are incapable of making a decision about what is pleasing to God, they prepare a table of their virtues that is a representation of the best they are capable of producing in body and thought – on both registers – on their own. Then, they offer the fruits of their labour or body to the god in them, or to what they perceive as the Lord. What the Lord chooses of this offering would be deemed as indicative of the specific form of living – in extremes, labouring or leisure, for example – that the Lord finds most worthy and pleasing – in effect what the Lord knows to be essential, necessary, and unchangeable for a White existence for human beings.

The one out of the many possibilities that is chosen would become archetypal for humans seeking reconciliation between lord and bondsman, or preferably, on the neo-mythic register between lord and lord: it would become the method that humans should adopt in their bid to become godlike, idealistically White, and to become the embodied reconciliation of body and spirit. It would become analogously the finite representation of the infinite and, epistemologically, of the demonstrated reason that keeps both intuitive and sensory perceptions in check. The choice would become the preferred way of life, and, supposedly, both inwardly and outwardly human beings would be reconciled through the choices made for them by a higher mediator.

On a wider scale, the Lord's choice among the competing sacrifices would be the archetype of the society where God and humans would be fully reconciled, where humans would live in the pleasure of God and would be recognized as equal to gods. In their hope for reconciliation with God, human beings, therefore, produce or transform their virtues and passions into their work and, thereby, into their society of choice. They produce the very best that will then be offered as a burnt offering to the Lord, all in the hope of attaining an affective relationship with their Lord, and then, on the basis of this relation, in order to create a society that will produce the optimum affectivity and motility among human beings. They sacrifice the best of the fruits of their body to the Lord, symbolically giving up their bodies through what was produced by their strength and sweat, and, abstractly, by their imagination and creativity. They sacrifice the outer for the inner, and their desires for everlasting life and goodness. The choices presented to the Lord are, on one hand, those fruits physically produced by the body, ethno-racially; on the other, those produced as thoughts and wishes, internally, and as measured more appropriately by the neo-mythic register.

The Lord chooses, and in so doing inevitably alienates some elements of humanity, because human beings have many virtues and create different cultures and objects, such that there is no affectivity and agreed upon motility. Another bind for the Lord is that no choice can be for all time and reconciliation only lasts for its moment before it too falls prey to its own immanent dialectical nature. Existentially, even the Lord is destined to a tragic and unhappy experience as a mediator between the two conflicting parts of human beings.

Epistemologically, for example, the Lord chooses the gifts that are bodily determined – in the estimations of human beings, incomprehensibly privileging the limited ethno-racial register for humanity. In so doing, the Lord seems to reject those gifts of purity, well-being, and aspiration that are internal and associated with the neo-mythic register. Instead of the choice leading to reconciliation, in the first case, with God, and in the second case, within humanity, it leads to further alienation and estrangement and, ultimately, as told mythologically in the Biblical story of Cain and Abel, to further disruption in the family of humanity. This result is in itself an outer expression of the internal conflicts over good and evil within the dominant force. The Lord, thinking it is pure mind and ego, cannot understand why it has to be embodied, but recognizes that it is only through a body that it can be creative and enjoy the fruits of its and others' labour. Notions of good and evil can only be expressed and shared in a practical sense – they must have some determination on the ethno-racial register to make sense in a social relation – but so determined, something is always lost or missing.

A good example of the differences in registers that we encounter daily is what happens to immigrants when they arrive in Canada. They enter into a covenant: they know that the social order that is Canada already exists; they know that Canadian citizens according to the law of the land are positioned as superior and that non-Canadians, that is immigrants, are inferior and Black in this social order. In this respect, on the neo-mythic register, Canadians are idealized White and the immigrants are non-White, or Black. On the ethno-racial register, Canadians are idealized White, while the immigrants – including the somatic Whites – are Black in culture, status, and even soma. There is no chance of the immigrants entering a social contract as equals, or as idealized Whites on either register. Immigrants would be entering a social order as inferiors, but with the also agreed upon hope of eventually becoming equals, a status they would achieve by ultimately claiming the same Canadian citizenship as everyone else. They enter the existing arrangement in a bondsman's position, where there is already agreement that the immigrants are inferior (citizens versus non-citizens) according to both the neo-mythic register and (cultured Canadian versus those of another culture and even race) on the ethno-racial register.

But the immigrants are constantly "cheating" creativity: they are not seeking to transform fully into the ideals or Whiteness of Canada and Canadians, for to do that would require them to "sacrifice" or give up much that they already consider as meaningful to their true being and identity. Indeed, they are hoping to change Canada and to get it to incorporate some of their ideals. The difficulties arise for the immigrants when Canada appears to block the way to equality or neo-mythic Whiteness. This can occur by maintaining that because the immigrants and native-born citizens are ethno-racially different, they can never achieve the neo-mythic equal of full citizenship that everyone has agreed is the good of the social order they had all agreed upon. At the same time, as the lords in the piece, Canadians would be expecting the non-Canadians to do the biddings of the lord, and to ultimately be transformed into the likeness of the lords – thereby expecting the non-Canadians to sacrifice all that is virtuous for them.

So, the struggle continues: native-born Canadians expecting the immigrants to change to the "Canadian way of life" and to even accept a second-class citizenship because of a difference on the ethno-racial register that is an agreed indication of inferiority. The immigrants are forever "cheating" by trying to change not only themselves and the Canadians with privileges, but in the process helping to produce a new culture, a new history for Canada and a new Canada itself.

In societies where the mythic White lords still dominate, there exists the kind of pluralism that was once practised in Canada and is now in vogue in Europe, the United States, Australia, and elsewhere – where the immigrants are expected to "respect" and transform into the likeness of their hosts. Since the 1960s, Canada has been the site of a struggle where the bondsmen can force concessions out of the lords of the piece – so that social order has been pitched into even greater existential Blackness. This is the lordship and bondage struggle that shapes multiculturalism in Canada, and which gives the Canadian version a slightly different hue from the pluralism of elsewhere.

ETHICAL HISTORY: ENTRENCHING LORDSHIP
AND BONDAGE

The lordship and bondage struggle I have just explained became the archetype of ethical relations from the supposed beginning of history that centuries later informs what would become Western civilization. This is where the Whiteness of personal intuition is privileged over the sensory awareness of knowing, where thinking is privileged over labouring. Ironically, in the building of societies the ethno-racial register with its fixity and presumed certainty has been privileged over the potential but uncertainty of the neo-mythic. This kind of struggle leads, unintentionally, into an unhappy consciousness – where the goals for the different participants might be the same, but, because of different methods, the outcome is never what was anticipated or expected. This leads to the recognition that, while they might be guided by their understanding of the two registers, members of societies can only build societies based on the materials that are available to them – they must use a determination based on the ethno-racial register. For, neo-mythically, like Cain, unless they can present materials that embody their wishes and hopes, there is really no choice open to a lord, as its choice has to be expressed materially. We might want to bear this point in mind when we think of the history of Canada and how it was intended to be a White man's country. Because of the country's reliance on immigration for the materials to make this society and to express this neo-mythic desire, Canada has had to make do with less-than-desirable materials in terms of the immigrants that were available. Instead of a White man's country ethno-racially that would meet its neo-mythic desires, Canada, in practice, has always been a non-White country – for such were the materials available to it. Intentions do not always produce the intended goods.

Civil society, even with the best of intentions, becomes a moment without reconciliation because it is based on contradictory motives: of striving for limits while hoping to be free of all limits, as Fanon suggests, of seeking idealized Whiteness while remaining Black culturally, in status, and even somatically. All of these are an outer expression of an internal conflict over good and evil. As Hegel says, "The Limitation originates all forms of particularity of whatever kind volition wills itself; desires to make its own personality valid in all that it purposes and does: even the pious individual wishes to be saved and happy."[15]

Human beings, constructed out of the two registers, cannot accept within the same body or state the limits projected by one side on the other, for even in the sacrificing of the body, the mind is still not accepting of the body and the body is not happy with the outcome of its efforts. Yet, they must exist in a civil society that strives to be happy and self-sufficient according to the ideals of both registers. In reality, they are an unhappy consciousness, living in a moment of pretend happiness, which is ethically and evaluatively an unreal and untruthful world that could be disrupted at any moment. Often, in terms of self-knowledge, the participants might have no clear idea of who they really are: for there is no resulting happiness from their actions, and when they are unhappy they do no feel they have attained that level of authenticity that would make them feel they really know and understand what is good for them.

## UNHAPPY CONSCIOUSNESS: BLACKNESS AND MULTICULTURALISM

So begins mythologically a new post-choice dialectic, this time one of lordship and bondage on which the covenant is based, but in an impure world, in a "third space."[16] In this setting, "each is for the other the middle term, through which each mediates itself with itself and unites with itself; and each is for itself, and for the other, an immediate being on its own account, which at the same time is such only through this mediation. They *recognize* themselves as *mutually recognizing* one another."[17]

But this struggle for self-knowledge does not end in civil society as initially constructed and, similarly, there is a continuation of the struggle that is internal to the individual as it wrestles to fully know itself as body and mind. The lordship and bondage struggle results in two specific movements. Each is a return into ethical Blackness – into an assimilative position where the ego or self-consciousness thinks of itself as fully determined according to one or the other register exclusively, where it is abstractly one or the other. There is no diversity or composition within the individual being. This rejection of one of the two registers is a rejection of known epistemology and recognized ontology for a leap of faith, a belief in a one-sided hope or nihilism.

The first movement is where the individual withdraws into a reality of believing that nothing that happens in society affects its essence. In this way it states explicitly that the ethno-racial register has no meaning, so that while it may live in an alienating world it can be free in thought. It relies for meaning totally on the neo-mythic and becomes a stoic. In this case, the individual realizes that physically she or he is not free although she or he can be free in thoughts. This is where the individual reduces her- or himself to an abstraction, to a universal being who possesses the rights and entitlement of the society. This is idealized Whiteness, or what multiculturalism hopes to become, based on such things as the privileging of constitutional rights and freedoms to define citizenship – on the essence and necessary elements for effective citizenship. "The freedom of self-consciousness when it appears as a conscious manifestation in the history of Spirit has, as we know, been called Stoicism. Its principle is that consciousness is a being that *thinks*, and that consciousness holds something to be essentially important, or true and good only in so far as it *thinks* it to be such."[18] As Pierre Elliott Trudeau, the purported father of Canadian multiculturalism, states:

The very adoption of a constitutional charter is in keeping with the purest liberalism, according to which all members of a civil society enjoy certain fundamental, inalienable rights and cannot be deprived of them by any collectivity (state or government) or on behalf of any collectivity (nation, ethnic group, or other) ... They are "human personalities," they are beings of a moral order – that is, free and equal among themselves, each having an absolute dignity and infinite value. As such, they transcend the accidents of place and time, and partake in the essence of universal Humanity. They are therefore not coercible by any ancestral tradition, being vassals neither to their race, nor to their religion, nor to their condition of birth, nor to their collective history.[19]

But this rationalization of the world, where the individual is free in thought while her or his body remains in bondage, proves untenable, especially when the individual tries to test the perceived freedom at a personal level, in a world patterned on the determinations also of the ethno-racial register, and is rebuffed. Stoicism fails to capture fully the desires of humanity – the result is still unhappiness.

This leads to the other development in the lordship and bondage ethical relationship. It results in the humans giving themselves over totally to living in an alienated world, to taking the position that the neo-mythic register is meaningless, that there are no eternal values, and to the belief that even if they are free to think, such action is meaningless because humans are unable to create what they really want. This is the multiculturalism moment, when people with Black skins, for example, realize that they are always determined by the outer or bodily appearances, and not by colour-blind and unemotional abstract rights, laws, and constitutional freedoms. Contrary to what Trudeau and others may say, they are trapped tragically on the ethno-racial register. Liberal recognition is better than no recognition but it is not entirely satisfying. Worse, it may be expressed objectively as tolerance for them and they may appear subjectively to be ungrateful for not accepting the tolerance.

As sceptics, operating only as determined on the ethno-racial register, they accept that it is the contingent manifestation that matters and not some presumed law of necessity. So they act Black, according to the script expected from having a Black body or perceived ethnicity or racialization. They give up, or are forced to be identified with, the other human characteristics and desires of becoming that are associated with the neo-mythic register. Their notions of the self are expressed ethically in the material things that might bring them happiness, with seemingly little respect for any values or permanent institutions or agencies. These are the sceptics, who privilege the survival of the body as necessary a priori for the very embodiment of Spirit, for without a body Spirit is ineffective on its own. Therefore, sceptics, often at the expense of the mind, go over to feeding the body and keeping it healthy, for in a practical sense civil society and existence depends on accepting the alienation exhibited in the affectivity and motility of the material that is available at any specific moment, and not only on the essences and generalities or abstractions.

In trying to claim personal rights and privileges in the society, the individual has thus become a sceptic, where as Hegel says "the [abstract] thought becomes the concrete thinking which annihilates the being of the world in all its manifold determinateness, and the negativity of free self-consciousness comes to know itself in the many and varied forms of life as a real negativity."[20] This attempt also comes to futility and unhappiness, as the sceptics, in asserting their individuality and personality, find that they must still present themselves in universal terms that are meaningful only as abstract thought. Believing he cannot escape being perceived as Black, he acts Black, suppressing the individuality of his being, and surrendering to the abstract idea of how Blacks act.

The individual oscillates between extremes of stoicism and scepticism, but fails to become fully free: its notion of full freedom remains unchanged, but only as a thought – the very thing that started the dialectics of history. In this process, the individual's determination as a free person is constantly changing and is never reconciled with the unchanging notion or ideal of the good. In this regard, such individuals in society are riddled with internal contradictions on points of identity, where, as Hegel suggests, the differences between stoicism and scepticism become somewhat like a game between two children trying to catch each other in a contradiction. Hegel is worth quoting at length on this:

In Scepticism, consciousness truly experiences itself as internally contradictory. From this experience emerges a *new form* of consciousness which brings together the two thoughts which Scepticism holds apart. Scepticism's lack of thought about itself must vanish, because it is in fact *one* consciousness which contains within itself these two modes. This new form is, therefore, one which *knows* that it is the dual consciousness of itself, as self-liberating, unchangeable, and self-identical, and as self-bewildering and self-perverting, and it is in the awareness of this self-contradictory nature of itself.

In Stoicism, self-consciousness is the simple freedom of itself. In Scepticism, this freedom becomes a reality, negates the other side of determinate existence, but really duplicates *itself*, and now knows itself to be a duality. Consequently, the duplication which formerly was divided between two individuals, the lord and the bondsman, is now lodged in one. The duplication of self-consciousness within itself, which is essential in the Notion of Spirit, is thus here before us, but not yet in its unity: the *Unhappy Consciousness* is the consciousness of self as a dual-natured, merely contradictory being.[21]

This struggle also shows up in society in the quest for an ethical world in the universal and for social justice for individuals. In this regard, justice is presented ethno-racially as the ability by an individual to assert his or her individual difference, while at the same time neo-mythically receiving all the rights and entitlements that are offered by the state to all members. As Trudeau states in suggesting that Canada must not only be multicultural but a liberal democracy: "The liberal philosophy sets the highest value on the freedom of the individual, by which we mean the total individual, the individual as a member of a society to which he is inextricably bound by his way of life, and by community of interest and culture. For a liberal, the individual represents an absolute personal value; the human person has a transcending social significance."[22]

This leads into contradictions over ideals, or what ethically is idealized Whiteness. As Hegel says, in this case, the universal ethical world can only be an abstraction. Individuality and personality have disappeared in it. "The ethical realm is in this way in its enduring existence an immaculate world, a world unsullied by any internal dissension."[23] On one side, such a state is brought about in the relation between individuals or groups determined according to the ethno-racial register. Here individuals lose their individuality before the law and are treated equally in abstraction as assimilated and abstract "things" of a specific kind or type to which the society has a duty. "In it there is no caprice and equally no struggle, no indecision, since the making and testing of law has been given up; on the contrary, the essence of ethical life is for this consciousness immediate, unwavering, without contradictions."[24] But that is only part of the equation, for the individuals in society are, by nature, inclined to be always asserting their individualities and their differences, to aspire to neo-mythic evaluations.

To this end, the individual appears to be governed by two contradictory laws: one that treats it abstractly as just another member of society, as one of a specific type or category of being, and the other that demands that it not be treated as an unequal individual fully formed and unique in its own goodness. This is a situation similar to where somatic Blacks demand that they be recognized as no different and no less equal than any other group in society, but at the same time cultural and status Blacks demand, through such things as affirmative action and others rights of equity, that they be treated as different and recognized as more deserving specifically because of their cultural and status Blackness. Idealistic Blackness is an attempt to reconcile these two positions in one body that is Black somatically, culturally, and in status.

The individual is caught up in a question of determinacy: is it an individual with its own passions and desires that must be fulfilled for it to be happy; or is it a member of society that must be treated equally as any abstract citizen for it to be happy? The individual is in the dilemma of being finite and infinite, contingent and necessary, Black and White at the same time. This, as Hegel says, highlights the "pathos" of the individual that is governed by two different demands for freedom: one involves the personal freedoms that are developed in a state of nature and brought into civil society. The other is a form of government that is developed in civil society on the basis of common interests and equality between all members of the society. This, as Hegel states, is the same discussion between stoicism and scepticism and the resulting unhappy consciousness – the idealistic Blackness of despair that is brought on unintentionally by the self.

This is a point, as we shall see, that goes to the very idea of identity and belonging in a modern state like Canada and explains why it matters so much for immigrants and minority groups outside the mainstream to *feel* accepted in Canada, and that they are, at the same time, capable of achieving their dreams for social mobility. By social mobility, I mean the ability of an individual, as a rational dualism consisting of desire and labour, as determined according to the neo-mythic register, to transform herself or himself into whatever she or he desires – into his or her notion of idealized Whiteness on the ethno-racial register, and vice versa. This is a transformation into the idealized person, in the particular, or the idealized "thing," in the universal, that is the object of her or his aspiration. As the object of the individual's desire, such transformation must occur freely through the individual's labour. Lack of social mobility is the equivalent of living in bondage, marked by the inability, or imposed restrictions on an individual, to freely act on her or his desires in a realistic hope of achieving them. Multiculturalism is about trying to reconcile different orders – and not simply about reconciling and recognizing differences within an accepted a priori order. The task for multiculturalism is to construct an a priori that would be the basis for the leap of faith into the future, where none of the competing orders dominate.

The demand to feel accepted speaks to the stoicism in the social outsiders, for it satisfies the need for recognition, in the abstract sense, that they are part of the universal: they are fully Canadian as can be attested to by having an undifferentiated citizenship. At the same time, their quests for social mobility satisfy the scepticism in them: they want to be self-actualized as individuals and to fulfill the dreams that they brought with them into the Canadian civil society. The appearance as an unhappy consciousness also explains why mainstream Canada may feel suspicious about immigrants, especially those *demanding* recognition as a given rather than waiting to *earn* it – a process that could be time-consuming, lasting generations, and amount to the acceptance of self-denial.[25]

These contradictions arise, in a practical sense, every time a new immigrant arrives in the country. At its most idealized, the dialectical struggle between stoicism and scepticism is a first step before entering a new level of consciousness, one of acting and behaving without second thought about full acceptance as a Canadian citizen, while at the same time looking for assurance that the state would but put obstacles that hinder the individual's efforts towards social mobility.

This dialectical struggle lasts until the immigrants is *acclimatized* or *Canadianized,* which means entering ethically into a lordship and bondsman relationship, one that in a practical sense is determined historically according to the ethno-racial register. Usually, this determination entails settling for less than the immigrant had imagined as her or his potential under the neo-mythic possibilities for determination, but also in the best of cases receiving more than Canada had originally intended. Recognition is conferred from an other to a subject or from one subject to an other. The solution to the unhappy consciousness that is multiculturalism requires as a first step recognition of how this unwanted ethical relationship arose through a process that is deemed to be extremely rational and well intentioned.

This is recognition of what there is about the immigrant that is changeable and contingent and worthy of being discarded or converted into a Canadian nature, and what there is already in the immigrant that corresponds to the Canadian nature that must be developed into full citizenship. Ontologically, the immigrant, as a composite, is made up supposedly of essences and accidents, or the unchangeable and changeable, and to become fully Canadian the unchangeable must be separated out. This can occur either by changing the immigrant's unchangeable nature miraculously into a Canadian unchangeableness, or this essence must already be the same as the Canadian unchangeableness, but like the flower in Hegel's seed, is initially hidden away and has to be developed.

## BLACKNESS: THE CONSCIOUSNESS OF HUMANITY

This, then, is the ending of one struggle between Whiteness and Blackness and the start of another between the same two combatants, both of whom have their own notions of Whiteness. Indeed, a closer look at Hegel's description of what is happening cannot but show the colour, and even essence, as a non-Hegelian would say, of the combatants as Black and White: "What still lies ahead for consciousness is the experience of what Spirit is – this absolute substance which is the unity of the different independent self-consciousnesses which, in their opposition, enjoy perfect freedom and independence: 'I' that is 'We' and 'We' that is 'I'. It is in self-consciousness, in the Notion of Spirit, that consciousness finds its turning point, where it leaves behind in the colourful show of the sensuous here-and-now and the nightlike void of the supersensible beyond, and steps out into the spiritual day light of the present."[26] Here, Hegel is describing a cosmology with two combatants whose "essences" are from two seemingly different spheres, one earthly and bodily, the other divine and spiritual – both of which must somehow seek conciliation in a unity that is a "We" but in such a way that both sides have autonomy and recognition. They are struggling for a specific ontology in this cosmos, each looking to put itself at the top and the other, if present at all, at the bottom. This decides their statuses. Existentially, Hegel portrays the side that is associated with the body and sensuousness with darkness, and it is from this world that the Spirit retreats in its lordship and bondage relationship. Spirit retreats into a spiritual or abstract existence where it feels safest, into a place that is its natural homeland of Whiteness and the spiritualism of daylight. From there, it plans its next foray into Blackness, while knowing from the epistemological records that are the memory of its master and slave struggle that Blackness exists as a formidable opponent.

But Hegel also suggests that the temporary moment of reconciliation in the lordship and bondage struggle is of a form where consciousness is a "We" that is also an "I," suggesting that in this idealism the reconciliation can only be in Blackness, since Whiteness, by its own definition, its own self-identity, is purity and singularity. It cannot be an "I," ethno-racially. In addition, Blackness has as its idealism both diversity and a unity that stretches across the spectrum. By self-definition this would have to include the absorbing of any purity, in this case the "I," according to Hegel, and making it impure by contamination with all other colours, for the "We" is a unity of impurities and heterogeneity.

The aim is to arrive at an absolute, which for idealized Blackness is total darkness and for Whiteness is absolute light. But that is what started the problem in the first place: Whiteness mythologically realizing that it exists as a creative force in darkness and that it needs to be recognized and brought out as separate and apart. White stipulated that it was good for this recognition and separation to occur. That good was mythologically called day and what was left was called night, dialectical opposites within the same system. Each of which mythologically was good in itself. Indeed, this appears to be a practicable compromise, as mythologically and onto-logically, neither an existence of all light or all darkness, of all day or all night, would be acceptable to even Spirit itself – for in such a situation, it would be trapped in total unhappiness because it would no longer be creative, or it would no longer have a specific form.

Such was the case before the supposed beginning of time and a seemingly bored Spirit started to amuse itself by playfully transforming itself, endeavouring to find out the range of goods, in terms of distinct embodi-ments, it is capable of becoming. Mythologically, this is a Spirit recognizing that, in its darkness, it needs to reflect on itself, to the point of becoming fully enlightened about itself. To this end, Spirit realizes it must become both the light that throws light on itself and the darkness that takes on forms and can be recognized through them. It aspires to add Whiteness to its Blackness. This initiates an ontology that runs into trouble once Spirit finds that the good it has created becomes a prison, preventing it from mov-ing on to other creations, for the creation has become the sole model for all future copies, thereby even limiting the creative process.

It is a good, then, that became culturally fixed and determinate, placing a limit on the creativity of Spirit and the realization of its full potential. A fur-ther problem developed when humans, as the mechanism through which Sprit transforms itself, decided that a specific good was the ultimate good, and sought to close down the creative process. In doing this, they associ-ated the preserved and uplifted good with cultural Whiteness and those desiring another structure or cosmos with cultural Blackness, thereby, in effect, and even unconsciously, delegating any further powers of creation to Blackness for the created world was deemed, from a White perspective, as already being the most perfect. In this thinking, Whiteness had already been created in its fullest potential.

Hegel argues that "to comprehend the absolute connection of this antith-esis (of how, in this case, ideals unravel) is the profound task of metaphys-ics."[27] He says understanding history rests on a realization that "if men are to act, they must not only intend the Good, but must have decided for themselves whether this or that particular thing is Good. What special course of action, however, is good or not, is determined, as regards the ordinary contingencies of private life, by laws and customs of a state; and here no great difficulty is presented."[28] At this point Hegel has entered a momentarily reconciled world of idealism where freedom in some pro-scribed form exists – for there were gains made in past struggles – and where individuals know who they are and accept their statuses. They are fully reconciled as the "I" in the "We" and they are full moral agents, with the freedom to discern what is good and evil and to make conscious choices. But this is a good that comes already through reflection and consensus, and comes to later movements and moments as perception rather than as dialectic knowledge based solely on the unique circumstances. This is a good that when evaluated itself is found to be contradictory, not as one truth appearing everlastingly good but instead as a good that has become an evil – yet these now contradictory evaluations arise from similar actions or determinations on the ethno-racial register. This is akin to Bhabha's suggestion that national narratives have to make room for particularistic narratives, those meta-narratives that strive to convey in the diversity a unity that, as we said earlier, "repeats, uncounselled and unconsolable, in the midst of plenitude."

But even then Hegel suggests that in moments of apparent reconciliation the struggle for freedom continues. The existing freedom is still culturally too constrained, this time by the wishes of the collective proscribing the actions of the individual while the individual is trying to do whatever he or she wishes: "Each individual has his position; he knows on the whole what a just, honourable course of conduct is. As to ordinary, private relations, the assertion that it is difficult to choose the right and good, – the regarding it as the mark of an exalted morality to find difficulties and raise scruples on that score, – may be set down to an evil or perverse will, which seeks to evade duties not in themselves of a perplexing nature; or, at any rate, to an idly reflective habit of mind – where a feeble will affords no sufficient exercise to faculties, – leaving them therefore to find occupation within themselves, and expend themselves on moral self-adulation."[29]

But existentially and epistemologically, the history of what humans have learned of History's lessons is abysmal: "The History of the World is not the theatre of happiness. Periods of happiness are blank pages in it, for they are periods of harmony, – periods when the antithesis is in abeyance," which as Hegel says never really happens.[30] Hegel notes that humanity has not learned that "it is useless to revert to similar circumstances in the past. The pallid shades of memory struggle in vain with the life and freedom of the Present."[31] Hegel claims that there are some major reasons for this unhappiness; one is that Spirit is often projected in the dominant Christian thought of the West as being by nature and essence goodness, so that the ultimate working of Spirit and Freedom is good. Similarly, humans, even with the best of intentions, can produce corruption on the one hand, while on the other they can produce good results even when such is not the intent. Hegel then observes that "reason is the Sovereign of the World; that the history of the world, therefore, presents us with a rational process."[32]

Mythologically, these two sides – those of good and of evil – of Spirit are forever in contention. Humanity's corruption and the decay of empires are due to passions of humans to fulfill their individual needs, talents, and interests.[33] The result at any given time is that humanity, as the embodiment of Spirit, is living in a false consciousness even as the Spirit attempts to attain absolute self-consciousness. Existentially, the result is human unhappiness and alienation from the ideal good. The object, recognized phenomenologically, is unhappy and feeling alienated; its affectivity and motility are not fully known.

This unhappiness is existential and also epistemological. It is idealized Blackness. As Hegel puts its, "but even regarding History as the slaughterbench at which the happiness of people, the wisdom of States, and the virtue of individuals have been victimised – the question involuntarily arises – to what principle, to what final aim these enormous sacrifices have been offered."[34] Even the vassals of Spirit, those that become the heroes for managing to capture the spirit of their time and to become the handmaidens of History, are not happy in the ethical relations that exist. These are the great men, as Hegel called these main actors, who, in a higher state of consciousness, are ahead of the rest of humanity. For a while they enjoy the position of self-satisfaction in achieving a dream or ideal, in providing leadership, and in momentarily enjoying their creativity, but "if we go on to cast a look at the fate of these World-Historical persons, whose vocation it was to be the agent of the world spirit – we shall find it to have been no happy one. They attained no calm enjoyment; their whole life was labour and trouble; and their whole nature was nought else but their master-passion. When their object is attained they fall off like empty hull from the kernel."[35]

Indeed, Hegel suggests that these "great men" – those so recognized universally by one register but striving for the good as seen by a different and revolutionary order – are usually fated to be destroyed by the very Spirit or reason that used them; primarily because of their very nature, of being able to give in totally to passions and creativities and to escape the bonds of Reason. They would not be contained in a bondsman role. Epistemologically, this is a carnivalesque moment that is the triumph of sense certainty over both intuitive perception and/or demonstrated reason. For life, indeed, is a tragedy and apparently all the greater for great men. Whereas, as Hegel says, the genuinely happy man or woman is the one who recognizes limits and the dangers of being in control of the emotions, yet such a happy person creates very little, as she or he finds happiness as determined on the ethno-racial register and settles for that. The genuinely happy person must accept her or his Blackness while still striving lukewarmly for idealized Whiteness. Because they create little, it is assumed by Hegel that they can never escape this Blackness even though they may process according to the definition they take for such from any of the competing registers. "The Free Man," Hegel notes, "is not envious, but gladly recognizes what is great and exalted, and rejoices that it exists,"[36] perhaps in the transcendent only.

Sensory perception submits to reason. Idealized Whiteness triumphs and rewards, therefore, with a happiness that flows out of a mediated freedom – out on an idealized Blackness.

## HEGEL'S BLACK SPIRIT AND SPIRIT OF BLACKNESS

There is another reason, ontologically, for this ethical unhappiness. It stems from the passions and desires of humans and the question of whether these passions and desires should always be in submission to the rule and sovereignty of reason through man-made laws. Effectively, this is the ethical relationship that questions the existential appropriateness of the lordship and bondage relationship and, epistemologically, the submission of intuitive and sensory perception to demonstrated or revealed proof for ultimate knowledge on what is proper for action. Humans, by their supposed nature, as subjects also coming into a self-consciousness, are not happy to remain in a lordship-bondsman relationship.

Indeed, as Hegel explains, it is only in this rebellious state and in giving in to their impulses, intuitions, and bodily emotions that humans are most creative. And, ironically, it is when they are most creative that they are most helpful to a Spirit that cannot create without the help of a body. So while Spirit is by nature struggling to create good, humans are inclined to do things for their own good that Spirit in its non-body existence might consider evil. However, when it comes into full consciousness later, Spirit may, in fact, discover that what it thought was evil was really good, as the human or the sense perception suggested, and that what it had determined to be good was also evil, just as the Other had suggested. Laws developed in society and intended as good may, with time, turn out to be evil according to a later evaluation. The result can only be known after the event, when judgment can be made on whether the actions were those of an unchangeable reason that is always good or of changeable and flawed emotions, which may be good or evil. It can only be identified when human beings and the godlike being agree that what happened was good, as this has to come after the fact for both types of beings. For as Hegel says:

It is only by this activity that that idea as well as abstract characteristics generally, are realised, actualized; for of themselves they are powerless. The motive power that puts them in operation, and gives them determinate existence, is the need, instinct, inclination, and passion of man. That some conception of mine should be developed into act and existence, is my earnest desire: I wish to assert my personality in connection with it: I wish to be satisfied by its execution. If I am to exert myself for any object, it must be in some way or other *my* object. In the accomplishment of such or such designs I must at the same time find *my* satisfaction; although the purpose for which I exert myself includes a complication of results, many of which have no interest for me. This is the absolute right of personal existence – to find itself satisfied in its activity and labour.[37]

Individualism and emotions are central to understanding the workings of humans. This suggests that it is true that such personal gains as social mobility, self-actualization, and recognition are the epitome of freedom for humans. Within the context of a search for freedom, such individualism has clear democratic implications. This is how individuals receive meaning from a world that, as Hegel says, has been their slaughter board over time. Meaning, even if defined at the universal level, must have a personal interpretation for it to be good and worthwhile; it must be based on the satisfaction of passions and desires which are sharpest and most determined when individualized. Reason has to be embodied and contextualized. As Hegel notes: "We may affirm that *nothing great in the world* has been accomplished without *passion*. Two elements, therefore, enter into the object of our investigation; first the Idea, the second the complex of human passions; the one the warp, the other the woof of the vast arras-web of Universal History. The concrete mean and the union of the two is Liberty, under the conditions of morality in a State."[38]

Hegel is pressing an important point in the discussion on the philosophy of history and sociology: he is making a radical departure from previous philosophers and sociologists that condemned the Blackness in creativity, and the ethical Blackness that is the future and valueless until it has become the past. For the longest of times, philosophers and social scientists tended to diminish the creativity inherent in the passions and desires of humans. They always suggested that this creativity is, by nature and essence, evil and has to be rigidly controlled. This was because the creativity produced change within a given form or system, refusing to accept the given limits and boundaries. For these philosophers and social scientists, passions had always to be in the tutelage and bondage of a sovereign or Reason, for unbridled creativity could lead to chaos, too much impermanence, and a threat to a mature culture or civilization. In taking an opposing view, by rejecting the very notion of essences, Hegel was departing from such thinkers as Plato, St Augustine, Hobbes, and Kant, who saw very little that was good in human passions and suggested the building of societies based on the good that holds the passions in slavery.

Kant, for example, argues in *Foundations of the Metaphysics of Morals* that freedom consists in coming into the unchanging Whiteness of Enlightenment through liberation from the tutelage of an external tyrant.[39] But this enlightenment occurs through an internal process of willingly enslaving the individual passions to a friendly tyrant called Reason, thus leaving the individual permanently in the grip of a moral code that allows for no spontaneous outbursts or flashes of creativity that challenge the governing code. Not so, says Hegel. Indeed, in a criticism of the Enlightenment in *Phenomenology of Spirit*, Hegel argues that it is this *passion*, a cultural Blackness, for reason and the pure principles, which was misnamed Reason, that led to terror and ultimately the loss of freedom in modernity. The problem was not passion or reason, per se, but the rigidity of believing in the desirability of living in a fixed unchanging state or system – by our categories, a culturally White existence – a fixity that is maintained passionately but in a manner where the objects of the passions are drained of their passions. The passions should not be disabled permanently either by making them too licentious or keeping them too firmly in control. The passions must have freedom of movement within reason.

But even in giving a meaningful role to the body and passions in this struggle for freedom, Hegel seems stuck in his effort to arrive at a precise definition of this phenomenon. As he says:

Passion is regarded as a thing of sinister aspect, as more or less immoral. Man is required to have no passions. Passions, it is true, is not quite the suitable word for what I wish to express. I mean here nothing more than human activity as resulting from private interests – special, or if you will, self-seeking designs – with this qualification, that the whole energy of will and character is devoted to their attainment; that other interests (which would themselves constitute attractive aims) or rather all things else, are sacrificed to them. The object in question is so bound up with man's will, that it entirely and alone determines the "hue of resolution," and is inseparable from it. It has become the very essence of his volition.[40]

It is my argument that there is such a word or concept, one that was in popular metaphysical usage across Europe in Hegel's time. Hegel has not named it as such in this context, but he has described it. For the thought it represents, the description alluded to in the words *hue* and *essence* as Hegel quotes others describing it, is ontological and even somatic Blackness. Passions that are the driving force, indeed the maker of history, are Black culturally and even somatically.

This is the same hue and Blackness that the British poet John Milton was thinking about when he wrote in *Il Penseroso* (1.11–16):

But hail thou Goddess, sage and holy
Hail divinest Melancholy
Whose saintly visage is too bright
To hit the sense of human sight,
And therefore to our weaker view
O'erlaid with black, staid Wisdom's hue.

Similarly, Shakespeare wrote in *A Midsummer Night's Dream*, a story based on the magic that causes binary changes so that hate becomes love and evil goodness, "O grim-looked night, / O night with hue so black / O night which ever art when day is not!"[41] Hegel would have been aware of the writings of both Milton and Shakespeare and, indeed, he often sang the praises of Shakespeare's works, particularly his tragedies, which Hegel referred to in *Phenomenology of Spirit*.[42] Heidegger seems to signal a similar conclusion: that in the Hegelian system, and in his idealistic philosophy and metaphysics in general, sprit is somatically Black and its works of negation are culturally Blackness. Writing in *The Question of Being*, Heidegger noted that those who find it necessary to "think through the basic fundamental structure of Hegel's metaphysics, the uniting unity of the *Phenomenology of the Mind* and the *Science of Logic*" would make a discovery: that "the fundamental character is 'absolute negativity' as the 'eternal force' of reality, that is, of the 'existing concept.'"[43] These are the passions that cannot be determined on the ethno-racial register, but by their nature must be recognized and valuated on the neo-mythical.

Indeed, this is the point at which we return to the epigraph from Hegel at the beginning of this book: "One cannot express oneself too strongly ... regarding the conceptual barbarism which applies the category of *composition* ... even to light, and makes brightness consist of seven *darknesses:* one might as well say that clear water consists of seven sorts of earth."[44] Here we have Hegel spelling out not only what he thinks is one category of Blackness but also what he thinks it is useful for. In this case, as Inwood notes, Hegel is hostile to the Newtonian notion of what light is and expresses his preference for Goethe's theory of colours: "The preference is in part an aesthetic one, but the point which primarily worries Hegel is the gulf between more and less general concepts and theories, and between concepts and theories of any kind and concrete individuals."[45]

Darkness for Hegel is the layers that hide the light; or, to put it another way, the light is achieved by phenomenologically peeling away, as it were, layers of darkness until the light is revealed. Darkness is the composite, the creolized, the hybridity, not the light, the purity of the clarity – which can only shine through when the darkness is removed. This statement is worth reading in its context in the *Phenomenology of Spirit*, where indeterminacy is essentially "the night when all cows are Black," and in regard to his later statement that the essence of the virtue of individuals is known in their acts. In their movements, in the peeling away. As Hegel says: "Action alters nothing and opposes nothing. It is the pure form of transition from a state of not being seen to one of being seen, and the content which is brought out in the daylight and displayed is nothing else but what this action is in itself."[46] Commenting on this, Paul Franco says that for Hegel "action is understood to consist simply in making this original or implicit nature explicit and actual, in translating it 'from the night of possibility into the daylight of the present.' It is only through action, Hegel tells us, anticipating Sartre's assertion of the priority of existence to essence, that an individual learns who or what he really is. Nor can the deed or work that results from such action be said to be good or bad; it simply expresses the original nature of the individual, and beyond that no other standard is relevant."[47]

In other words, all actions are composites of good and evil by agents who are composites or hybrids of spirit and body. They are all Black, culturally, idealistically and, based on the prevailing hue, possibly even somatically. For as Hegel has shown, in agreement with the empiricist, none of the concepts of identity we have been studying, such as Canadian, citizenship, and multiculturalism, can be of a White essence. This is so because they are composites and complexities. They are infinites. There are no essences. Therefore, phenomenologically, they are Black epistemologically, existentially, and possibly even ontologically. The question arises if in power relations they should be treated as Black as well, thereby imposing an inferior status on them, or on some of them. The question becomes problematic for it speaks to an ethical relationship built on a constructed and complex social consciousness, which could be based on either a false consciousness or full consciousness. This awareness must be given by a consciousness that might very well be ethno-racially Black, even if it thinks it is White. Getting from a false consciousness, which is cultural and idealistic Blackness, to full consciousness can only occur over time, making everything Black until enlightenment or idealized Whiteness is achieved.

I shall now show how an explanation of Black and Blackness through a Hegelian phenomenology and philosophical explanation of history can help us to understand the thinking of Western thought and how it established "known" ways of privileging meaning from time to time – and in our current multicultural moment.

## RUPTURES AND MYTHOLOGIES: HISTORY'S EXISTENTIAL BLACKNESS

In the last quarter of the eighteenth century, the period that spawned modernity, there were reasons for celebration and lamentation throughout the Americas. This was the kind of setting in which Hegel saw the spirit of the times coming into consciousness, a spirit rising out of the ether of an earlier death, but only to linger for a moment before its embodiment too would start to decay. It is a spirit that captures the fears and expectations of a people at a specific moment. Often it is symbolized by and embodied in the individuals who manage to capture these aspirations and hopes in such a way that the individual comes to be identified with the times and the spirit of the people. Often it is the story of at least two sides, born of the same history and traditions, but one representing the old direction of history, and the other the new.

Like the intuitive and sensory perceptions in the body, both sides are caught inextricably in a conflict of irreconcilable differences that can only be solved through a battle to the death of one side and its ideas. There must be a death or simulation of one in this struggle where supposedly the old is master and the new the slave – and a victory nonetheless – for there can be no reconciliation except in a later lordship and bondsman's relationship. Ultimately, the side winning this struggle imposes its will to power by creating a charter myth based on its victory for the proposed social order, by making the world in its likeness, and still more so by attempting to vanquish its enemies, and by even writing them out of, erasing them, from the official narrative by positioning the vanquished mythologically as evil and unworthy of mention in a story exclusively about the triumph of good. If the conservative forces of the old order win, they then resist the changes that are pushing society and human development in a direction other than what prevailed. Here the charter myth would have an earlier beginning, and in it the losers would be positioned mythologically as the evil that tried and failed to destroy the existing good. Or, if the winners are the progressive forces, they then embark on a new direction toward some nirvana and the end of time. The two sides are needed to fully grasp the infinity that is the sprit of the times. Whether, in victory or defeat, it is there that both sides come to recognize how much they need each other. For it is at the expense of the other that the victor and powerful is able to impose hegemony in the name of the good as it defines it.[48]

The result could be a shift in society's thinking, something that Hegel calls a new consciousness, or what Thomas Kuhn argues is a paradigmatic shift with the resulting hegemonic conditions being imposed ideologically on the world and on how people should react and behave in given circumstances. While Margaret Masterman shows in *The Nature of a Paradigm* that Kuhn gives many definitions for paradigms, what is relevant for us in his discussions is his attempt to explain the process by which a specific way of thinking can arise, come to dominate a discourse, and become ingrained in human behaviour such that it provides all the solutions to all perceived problems.[49]

However, it is possible for an established paradigm to be overthrown by a competing one if the recognized paradigm is unable to provide acceptable answers to emerging problems. This is a dialectical development of knowledge, and it is an explanation for how mythologies can implicitly influence ideologies from which they are derived, and how, in turn, these ideologies, based on "paradigms" of behaviour and thought, can validate or refute challenges to what can be construed as normal behaviour within a specific cosmos or worldview. At the same time, we should excise some care in the use of paradigms that are based on Kuhn, given their ambiguity and inde-terminacy.

Masterman notes that Kuhn's use of the term paradigm can be confusing, primarily because his argument for paradigms results "from the fact that Kuhn has really looked at actual science, in several fields, instead of confin-ing his field of reading to that of the history and philosophy of science, i.e. to one field."[50] Masterman identifies twenty-one different meanings for *paradigm* as used by Kuhn. But when the bulk of the scientific definitions are stripped away, there remain a number of meanings that can be usefully applied to a philosophy and sociology of history and are useful for under-standing mythology and how these meanings contribute to making ideo-logies such a potent force in everyday life. In an analysis of Kuhn's paradigms, Masterman concludes that

when [Kuhn] equates "paradigm" with a set of beliefs, with a myth, with a new way of seeing, with an organizing principle governing perception itself, with a map, and with something which determines a large area of reality, it is clearly a metaphysical notion or entity, rather than a scientific one, which he has in mind. I shall therefore call paradigms of this philosophical sort *metaphysical paradigms, or metaparadigms;* ... Kuhn's second main sense of "paradigm," however, which is given by another group of uses, is in a sociological sense. Thus he defines "paradigm" as a universally recognized scientific achievement, as a concrete scientific achievement, as like a set of political institutions, and as like also to an accepted judicial decision. I shall call para-digms of this sociological sort *sociological paradigms.*[51]

Sociological paradigms explain behaviour that happens out of percep-tion within a specific system or order and without an actor first taking a pending action into consciousness. This is when what is done is done with-out consciously resorting to and applying a theory on which to rationalize a priori the course of action or behaviour. "By following these (paradigms), successful problem-solving can go on: thus they must be intellectual, ver-bal, behavioural, mechanical technology; or any of these; it depends on the type of problem which is being solved."[52]

This notion of sociological paradigms is akin to Eagleton's suggestion that ideology is a look at why people hold certain ideas and why they act and behave unquestioningly according to specific beliefs, why they act mainly out of habit and less out of consciousness.[53] Indeed, these paradigms are practical knowledge, as opposed to the merely theoretical. This is where the game of life is played without the need to refer to the official rule book, in this case the underlying mythological, to see if everyone is playing fairly or even playing the same game.

Similarly, the idea of a sociological paradigm fits also with Frye's expla-nation of ideology as being a way of behaving and acting that can best be explained through references to mythologies that explicate the conditions in which individuals find themselves acting and performing.[54] Society's formation, as an internally regulated system or order, is according to these mythologies whose attendant concerns try to explain the reasons for life and the methods for maintaining life. This, in practice, makes mythologies, and the ideologies that they produce, sociological paradigms as these concerns can lead to and thus explain the stratification of humanity. Perhaps, this is what Eliade has in mind when referring to mythologies, and the rites and rituals in which they are constantly constructed, as operating within a paradigm of how the world used to operate, how it operates now, and how it ought to operate in the future.[55]

Masterman argues, in a second regard, that Kuhn was also thinking of paradigms behaving in a way that further satisfies Eliade's suggestion that mythologies, as paradigms, offer solutions to and explanations for the existential problems of human beings within the accepted order. This is where Kuhn saw paradigms as also being philosophical in nature, leading Masterman to conclude that "the primary sense of 'paradigms,' clearly, has to be a philosophical one; and the paradigm has got to exist prior to theory."[56] In this regard, a paradigm is a tool for solving problems in a way that a successful outcome is known, or can be fairly estimated, beforehand.

On this is built the notion of proofs and refutations as a form of dialectical negation. The basis of paradigms is implied probabilities that amount almost to laws of cause and effect. Analogously, they are the intuitive perception of epistemology that is accepted as if it were demonstrated reason. Masterman interprets Kuhn as saying that science depends on philosophy to establish the framework for scientific tests and to provide the lenses and perspective through which to view the outcomes. In this case, paradigms are established in a dialectical way: a new thought arises out of an old school, challenges and overthrows the old way of thinking, then behaves according to a specific script or map and solves problems according to its specific theoretical approach, and is then itself challenged by a new paradigm. If the latter succeeds in replacing the old, exchanging the known order for another and different one, there is a paradigmatic shift that could be revolutionary in scope and effect. Or it might only bring a minor distinction, or the equivalent of a social rebellion, in which case the old paradigm is not shifted but realigned and remains essentially still in practice, though in a modified form. In this regard, Kuhn's definitions of paradigms seem in keeping with Hegel's argument for a systematic or scientific way of interpreting history and philosophy.

There is much discussion on whether Kuhn's paradigmatic shifts and Hegel's new consciousness are compatible. The concerns that they are not similar stem from the rapidity and suddenness of the change that occurs. Hegel suggests that radical change is a result of forces building up over time until they can no longer be contained and they burst loose. Kuhn puts less emphasis on the history of the change for his paradigmatic shifts, suggesting that the period of incubation can be quite short, just as it can be long. However, both Hegel and Kuhn emphasize the hegemonic forces that must secure the success and permanence of the new consciousness or paradigmatic shift, and it is this emphasis on hegemony, on the ideology, that is useful for our discussion. George Psathas in *Phenomenology and Sociology* seems to support this commonality between the approaches described by Hegel and Kuhn:

What Kuhn refers to as a "paradigm shift" does not occur in an instant as does the *Gestalt* switch (e.g., the drawing that appears either as a vase or as two faces). "The transfer of allegiance from paradigm to paradigm is a conversion experience that cannot be forced." Yet the shift from one paradigm to another is possible, as evidenced by the fact that new paradigms are created by those already familiar with the existing ones of normal science. Whether it is fruitful to attempt conversions can be argued. Our view is that the presentation of a variety of problems, each being studied from a phenomenological perspective, can stand as evidence of the possible contributions of a new paradigm. Those who are engaged in research on the same topic from different paradigm perspectives can thereby make more informed decisions about the value of a phenomenological approach to the study of the social world.[57]

For Kuhn, each paradigm, whether in the sociological or philosophical sense, represents specific principles that govern a way of life with the system's own truths and authenticity, with its own specific rules for expression and recognition that exist in and form a specific tradition. Occasionally something comes along that cannot be contained in this tradition. According to our categories, each paradigm shift is an exercise in cultural and idealistic Blackness; and each privileging of a paradigm is an exercise in the attainment of idealistic and cultural Whiteness.

Speaking of natural science, but in what could just as easily be applied to the science of knowledge, Kuhn notes that "the extraordinary episodes in which the shift of professional commitments occur are the ones known ... as scientific revolutions. They are the tradition-shattering complements to the tradition-bound activity of normal science."[58] Having overthrown the old paradigm, the new one installs itself, develops its own traditions and ways of doing business until it is itself challenged by a new paradigm. But in the meantime, the newly enthroned paradigm will cement its hold. It will eventually reach the point where, for the individual practitioner, "acquisition of a paradigm and of the more esoteric type of research it permits is a sign of maturity in the development of any given scientific field."[59] The point would soon come, when supporters of the new paradigm would

begin to act as if they were in possession of the authentic method for finding truth, rather than as someone trying to point the misguided in another
direction. They would force others to conform to their way of thinking and
to act according to the new traditions. In any case, either of the old or new
orders must decay.

Alternately, a compromise solution might be reached, a negotiated agreement with each side accepting its symbolic death as a prerequisite for containing hostilities within the agreed boundaries of a neutral space. Here, the
combatants live in a pretend world between two contradictory orders, with
supposedly no hostilities, but where ambiguously the different forces try to
exist according to their own rules as well as those negotiated by the enemy.
This results in new tensions within the paradigm or consciousness. Here is
another example of a Hegelian lordship and bondage covenant.

But as Kuhn and Hegel suggest, the hostilities do not cease. It is rather
that their forms of expression change and become disguised in their conceptual sublation. This situation cannot continue forever if the quest is for
a paradigm that is finite, for it would be contrary to the natural tendency
for day to eventually follow night, for all humans to move towards the light
that is knowledge and self-consciousness, and for all matter and ideas to
strive unceasingly for their true, authentic, and distinctive appearances.
Short of an abject surrender or a total victory, it becomes impossible and
seemingly unnatural to live according to two sets of laws, especially when
one set is aimed at negating the full effects and intentions of the other. The
struggle continues surreptitiously below the surface in the heart of the infinite, once in a while erupting like a volcano to show what lies beneath.
Indeed, such a third space, as Homi Bhabha suggests in *The Location of
Culture*, becomes an area of contestation as boundaries are drawn, erased,
and redrawn in subsequent negotiations.[60] Limits are never permanent, but
always contested. This is so, even though the entire area is supposedly one
of compromise, one with clear boundaries and certain limits.

Eventually, as Hegel suggests, the differences from living according to
two sets of rules form two different orders or systems – those representing
the essence and soul of the side now thwarted in its bid for full expression
and recognition, and those from compromising with the enemy – will create so much tension that they must be released for the good of all. Even war
is more desirable than the situation of duplicity and hypocrisy that
obtains.[61] When this happens, the possible solutions involve a resumption
of full hostilities in a battle once more to the death. There would be a violent renegotiation of the rules of compromise, or the destruction of the contested area so as to limit the possibilities of this space becoming an irritant
on its own to the combatants.

Another solution calls for the parties in the struggle to realize the horror
to both sides of forcing reconciliation. This is where shared mythologies are

useful. By creating a belief of common kinship and a shared future, mythologies help ease the tensions and may even unify the warring parties. This argument rests heavily on the notion that perhaps there are no authentic and real worlds aside from the physical ones and that it is an injustice to all humanity to force any human being to believe in a world held as an ideal. In this respect, as lived experiences, mythologies act routinely on the same level that reason does epistemologically through intuitive and sensory perception in the acquisition of fuller knowledge.

At the beginning of modernity, these two ideas – both of rupture to start all over and of a mythological bonding of disparate peoples – were at the heart of the philosophical debate that spawned the American Revolution, a time when unreconciled forces led to open hostilities and the ultimate triumph and vanquishing of sides. Even within the revolutionary camp there were competing ideals – visions of a very different assimilative order and system. What would become the dominant view favoured the creation of a new consciousness, a paradigm, that would result in the creation of a new country.[62] It was believed by those of this view that allowances should be made for as many people as possible to live in their own world with none forced to conform to another's view. This would mean no hierarchy of values and no good or evil. Neither would there be absolute knowledge about anything, as each revelation would amount to absolute knowledge for the given moment, but for that moment only.[63]

This means, then, that there exists the possibility of a compelled resolution whose dialectical forces are at work and the ideal solution – if there can be one – would be to allow the forces to remain unreconciled. This is recognition that, essentially, life is play, with many particular and individuals players within the overall universal one. Life and the necessity for play should be allowed to *play* themselves out – signalling a hands-off approach by individuals who would no longer try to guide and even force the dialectic forces to behave in a particular way. This means recognizing the eternal play between Whiteness and Blackness and that it is for the individual to find a place and position within this revelation.

As the history of humanity teaches, such a position of accommodation has rarely been taken in power struggles. But in the end such radical thoughts should not be discounted, for they might hold the seeds for what may be termed genuine multiculturalism, where in a plural liberal democracy the very obvious aspects of a cultural struggle for dominance by one group are removed or abated and freedom and democracy reign. This would be a genuine multiculturalism or cosmopolitanism based on the mythology of shared experiences that stem from the recognition of Blackness and its dialectical fight with Whiteness, for there will always be a subversion of constructed worlds that are based on ideals of purity and essences, and are, thus, mythologized. Human nature is based on death and decay on the ethno-racial register; on the need for a constant series of rebirths and hybridizations if the resulting social order is to be measured as everlasting on the neo-mythic register; on the belief that the gods or superhumans, often in the form of artificers, are constantly reincarnating themselves and recreating the world. Immigrants, too, can represent, and are representative of, this death and rebirth, but more particularly of the potential to transcend accepted boundaries and limits.

Each time an immigrant arrives, as with the unknown that comes with the epistemologically Black stranger, it is possible that mythologically a superhuman has just appeared, a new incarnation, and this time in the specific example of a Canadian. In this way, every newcomer from outside the particular system, even if still from within the wider universe, symbolizes a clash between orders and systems. One question that arises is whether immigrants actually do come from outside the system, in terms of representing specific and different orders, or whether, as in the case of former British subjects in the Caribbean, Asia, and Africa, they are representative of one global system that produced Canada and their native countries. Kymlicka argues in *Finding Our Way* that these immigrants are of the same order – they are already for the most part neo-mythically liberals who want to come to a country like Canada that is a liberal democracy.[64] I agree with Kymlicka, that, particularly from the Caribbean and other British Commonwealth countries, immigrants believe they have been determined both ethno-racially and, significantly, neo-mythically in the same order that produced Canada. (Other commentators see them as bringing a completely new order.)[65] The question then becomes one of how they should be positioned and what places they should take on the ethno-racial register so that their placement is consistent with the rational determination that they are already liberals.

It is my argument that the mythologies that explain or shape the existing ideologies should take these breaks and irruptions into consideration. This is why the mythology of genuine multiculturalism is necessary. For at one and the same time, it idealistically seeks to transform Blackness into Whiteness as an exercise in essentialism, while acknowledging the existentialism of Blackness as a given. Under this arrangement, because of the acceptance of plurality and heterogeneity, one person's worldview, itself an expression of Blackness, and especially if it goes against the grain, would be as valid and authentic as any other. This would be so because there could be no prior claims that are beyond negotiation and even negation. Of course this would also then mean accepting the risk of chaos and the constancy of conflicts, the essence of idealistic Blackness. But all that would be needed would be rules commonly agreed upon, and constantly updated and renegotiated, on how to handle differences without resorting to force and dominance. This would mean constantly readjusting the terms of the covenant to recognize dialectical changes and to accept fuller and updated expressions of such ideals as the good, citizenship, and justice. Such an arrangement might lead to a civil society that is also a "third space," a space that itself is not contested but rather is a refuge or safe area for handling disputes. This might lead to acknowledging the beauty of living in a world of relativism, a world of democratic justice and of Blackness while hoping for Whiteness.

Having come to the end of this section on the theoretical frameworks for this study, it is now time to turn to the Canada that emerged from the dialectic struggle in modernity between Blackness and Whiteness. Section four will thus trace, through my four suggested categories, the development of Blackness in Western thought. I will start with the view that was dominant to the Greeks and show how a combination of Greek, Hebrew, and African thought was syncretized in the Christian ideology that is the basis of the Western world's intuitive perceptions and dominant paradigms. It was on this ideology that modernity was erected and subsequently presented as the latest effort and truest fulfilment of the quest for a good life, as where humans can be transformed from their Blackness into the Whiteness of gods.

# Blackness: Quest for Whiteness in Western Thought

# 9

# Greek Mythologies and Philosophies

White is the colour most proper for the gods.[1]

But if the things we have named are also things good in themselves, the account of the good will have to appear as something identical in them all, as that of whiteness is identical in snow and in white lead.[2]

## BLACKNESS AND GOODNESS: MYTHOLOGY AND PHILOSOPHY

In this the third section of the book, I begin mapping philosophically and sociologically the movements and structural manifestations of the spirit of freedom in the dominant strain that we call Western history. In this way, I will present a path and explanations that allow the self-conscious ego that is reflecting on itself to rationalize that, at the beginning of a new millennium, it is idealistically Black, and that the spirit of the times is trapped in a world that is culturally and somatically Black. First, a quick word on my methodology as it applies to this section.

To start this inquiry, we will begin by looking at the contradictions over the meaning of Blackness at the beginning of this millennium in Western mythology, a point that is now taken to be revolutionary in modern history – a moment which the then president of the United States of America George W. Bush qualified as a paradigmatic shift in the struggle between good and evil, and a moment which, at the time of writing, is still reshaping the geopolitical map along revolutionary lines of Blackness and Whiteness.[3] From this example, we can examine the changeability of good and evil as defined according to one register, but expressed in the materiality of another.

Moving backwards from this point in time, we shall then search phenomenologically for an assumed universal essence or natural laws that were necessary for this historical moment to occur. As usual, we are not going to find it. But to be scientific, we must search for it nonetheless. For already in the writing of history, this moment is not presented as contingent – an accident or aberration – but as a necessary development and manifestation for the dominant spirit of the world to know itself, and for humanity to know the fundamental difference between freedom and slavery.

Starting at this juncture in time, where the self-conscious ego thinks it is as close to absolute knowledge as it has ever been historically, we shall then trace our way back through the developments that led up to this point. In so doing, we will also be looking at how the self-consciousness ended up in a Canadian setting as a particular shade in a wider universe, specifically as the Hegelian unhappy consciousness that is multiculturalism, and which I categorize as idealized Blackness.

This will provide us with the opportunity to show how the three frameworks that we developed in the last section help us understand the equivocal meanings of Blackness over time – meanings that were derived from examining merely slices of the basic African, Greek, and Hebrew mythologies that are at the foundation of the transcendent rationalism that is the ideological underpinning of a system or order long called Western civilization. And here, we point out again, that because we are examining slices we are never totalizing or homogenizing. Phenomenologically, we expect to find bits of Whiteness within the Black slices. Or from a supposedly White and enlightened perspective, we hope to find no residue of Blackness in these White slices that capture these mythologies. Once again our view will be refuted, and from a Hegelian phenomenological viewpoint only the search itself will be meaningful.

In doing this, it is worth reiterating that I am simply teasing out approaches and specific thoughts that eventually coalesced into the dominant ideology that is commonly called Western civilization. When these choices were made, obviously, other competing options as specific particulars were eliminated, and while in a Hegelian sense they remain present in the prevailing consciousness, they are sublated and often reduced to invisibility. They will have what is called in Sartrean phenomenology an absented presence.[4] To the extent that we recognize their physical or ethnoracial absence, we will be tracing what accounts for the visible but dominant minority in Western thought. This approach is necessary and has to be spelled out as fully as possible; otherwise, it would be extremely difficult to show the radical departure and irruption – the privileging of a narrative that was usually rejected in Western thought – that is peculiar to multiculturalism in general, and Canadian multiculturalism in particular. Multiculturalism is an attempt to achieve the impossibility of having the cake and eating it too: of claiming a heritage that arrives out of the specific way of thinking that is Western thought, but at the same time rejecting as extremely flawed the very basis on which these decisions and choices were made. Multiculturalism in its pure form is idyllic and is an intended dynamic utopia of idealism: a rejection of the concreteness of the past for the insubstantiality of the future.

In this section, I will examine how those presented as the ancient Greeks viewed Blackness and Whiteness in their mythology and philosophy. I will argue that the dominant view was intended, epistemologically, to discern what is good and evil, what was godlike and what was base. This discernment was intended to take place within a framework that saw human existence as a struggle for freedom and, teleologically, as a quest to break the control and arbitrariness of physical death over individuals. Ontologically, within this framework, humans were positioned as fragile and as the inferior playthings of powerful tyrants, including the gods, Nature, and even powerful humans. In one version of the mythology, humans were gods with immortal souls in a previous life, but they fell because of a weakness and impurity that reflected a "madness" stemming from base desires. The godliness of a previous life that was the soul was implanted in a human body and remained there for several life cycles until the soul was made pure again and was released to return among the gods.

In this mythology, the soul is reincarnated in several human forms until it is pure enough to return to its godly state. Failure to make good in one life is rewarded with relegation in the next to a lower rung in the human chain of being. Ultimately, if the transgressions do not stop, the soul could be implanted in a "brute beast,"[5] as determined ethno-racially, a category of being that is the binary opposite of the gods in their purity, knowledge, and Whiteness. Also in this mythology, any purity from the previous life that remains then appears as a "White" plumage or outer appearance that attests to the individual's temperate nature and is a signifier of those humans that are godlike in spirit.

The lack of godliness, the innateness of the pleasures and uncontrolled passions that forced the gods to fall from the celestial realm to earth, shows up in a plumage that is Black as a mark. This is a mark, not of godly spirit, but of passions, of even the brute beast in nature. As a word of caution, this analysis is not intended to show that the ancient Greeks were racist in the modern sense where knowledge is assumed of inferiority and superiority based on the colour of the skin. Indeed, it is worth repeating that our task is to examine Blackness – which might have led to the modern conception of race – but not race itself. For Blackness, as even with the Greeks, is more than what we now view as being fully conceptualized in race.[6] This is too limiting for the infinite concept that Blackness is. Before mapping out how the sections shall unfold, let us have a quick overview of what the Greeks did think about Blackness so as to provide neo-mythic and ethno-racial contexts for this section.

## BLACK BEASTS, WHITE LORDS

As Plato states, in recounting a myth in *Phaedrus*, the aim of humans on earth is to get back to their previous godlike status – to shift from the ethno-racial to the neo-mythic register. An individual's existence on earth should be "after the manner of the god in whose company he once was, honouring him and copying him so far as may be, so long as he remains uncorrupted and is still living in his first earthly period."[7]

Ontologically, humans existed in extreme as two binary types according to this mythology: those who were first-round fallen gods on their way to being restored to their previous glory and purity; and those who were beasts and were corrupt and evil and trapped in this debasement for several life cycles. In the first group resides the memory of the previous godlike existence. Within its members are temperance, reason, and wisdom. On the outside, their bodies are "beautiful" as a testament to the partially tinged purity of their previous life. Those who are most evil, whose vision of the mystery of the gods is long past or whose purity has repeatedly been sullied, cannot appreciate the beautiful and cannot know what is good. Of such an individual, Plato states, "wherefore he looks upon [beauty] with no reverence, and surrendering to pleasure he essays to go after the fashion of a four-footed beast."[8]

The dominant Greeks were among some of the earliest in classical thought to come to terms with the notion that humans strive to be free, and that freedom's antithesis is slavery. For them, freedom, at the collective level, was the ability to escape the chaos and darkness that epitomize the dangers inherent in Nature, and which were thought to be always pressing down on human settlements and threatening to wipe them out. At the individual level, liberty mythologically was the ability to escape the arbitrariness, capriciousness, and unpredictability of not having choices, of simply living according to the dictates of a tyrant. Such a despot could be a god, fate, or Nature, but it could make life or death decisions about humans. The struggle for freedom took form in the individual having to contend with forces that were greater than her or him. Death was the epitome of slavery, coming as it usually does without choice for the individual, and always pending. Freedom was the ability to have choices: those of a group of people in the relentless battles against the cycles of death in Nature, and those by individuals within groups of humans for self-actualization and self-determination.

Collectively, the Greeks of this view looked for an insurance policy that would ensure the survival of individuals as groups, but in a way that was more than a mere survival that could be blotted out at the whim of some tyrant. One result of this quest was the development of politics and civic participation in a state. As Cynthia Farrar states in *The Origins of Democratic*

*Thinking: The Invention of Politics in Classical Athens:* "A self-governing community enabled men to act to secure the ends they desired, to express their autonomy, and by its operation ensured that the social order was such as to preserve the liberty of its members. The political and social interaction characteristic of a self-governing community fostered those capacities and dispositions essential to the preservation of the autonomy of all citizens, their security against tyranny and exploitation."[9]

Classical Greeks, so defined, discussed what was the ideal form of life that would allow individuals to live as freely as possible with one another in a society. This was a significant philosophical development, one which sought to evaluate the choices available to humans, but it was a philosophy that did not fully negate the preceding mythological explanations of human ontology and the tragedy of survival. By becoming political, these Greeks were not only discussing questions of epistemology, but of existentialism, and of moral and ethical relations too. Ivan Hannaford says in *Race: The History of an Idea in the West* that politics, as developed by these Greeks, was intended to release humans from the tyranny of Nature and that of fellow humans: "Politics was the highest end of human activity, and philosophy was the key to its understanding. In politics and philosophy rested the alternative to rule by demigods, intellectuals, priests, soldiers, entrepreneurs, sojourners, aliens, and capricious self-seekers, provided the political arrangement was based on *good* thought, *good* laws, *good* education, *good* arms, and *good* people bonding together by the practices of law and citizenship."[10] The key, therefore, to survival and freedom was discerning and knowing a priori what was unchangeably *good* or, borrowing from mythology, what the gods intended to be naturally beautiful and good. Good and goodness in the dominant Greek philosophy would come to be associated with beauty, and with the expressions of Whiteness and Blackness developed in the mythology. Good and goodness would be associated with purity, well-meaning goals, justice, and reason – all of which would be presented as the characteristics of a god, who, like the demiurge in Plato's *Timaeus*, planned to do good when it created the universe. Good, in this regard, came to be associated with the idealized Whiteness of a good god. As Plato states in the *Republic*: "Then god, being good, cannot be responsible for everything, as is commonly said, but only for a small part of human life, for the greater part of which he has no responsibility. For we have a far smaller share of good than evil, and while god must be held to be the sole cause of good, we must look for some factors other than god as cause of the evil."[11] The opposite of goodness was idealized Blackness, which was associated cosmologically with irrationality, ugliness and evil and, existentially, with the human condition.

For Plato, Blackness was the larger of creation, indeed that from which the created came. Blackness was not the creation of the god that intended to make a world that was pure, beautiful, and good. Therefore, epistemo-logically, knowing what was good was, analogically, to know what was godly and pure, and created out of Blackness; knowing what was Black was to be cognizant of evil and the ungodly, of that which had never been touched or shaped by a creative and just god. The laws that govern society to protect humans from tyranny and chaos, Plato suggested, must be as if they were god-given; and their objective should be to produce the same kind of created good out of the eternal Blackness that a good god would wish for and did attempt at a different level. The laws and regulations in a society that intended to be good should be framed as if they had been cre-ated by a god – by one that would bring only good out of what was not good already. "Then our laws laying down the principles which those who write or speak about the gods must follow, one would be thus: *God is the cause, not of all things, but only of good.*"[12] Blackness was uncreated, or if created had an older lineage and a beginning that was primordial to good.

In this way, a society that was idealistically White, based on laws akin to those of a god, would produce a White culture or civilization that was fully free – a good life and existence that a good god would wish for its creatures that were brought out of slavery or Blackness. But at the same time, philos-ophers like Plato and Aristotle were concerned that an idealized society should not be so disruptive as to leave individuals uprooted in Nature, which becomes the site for the newly created order. Any society that humans carved out of Nature would be established and then preserved according to specific laws and regulations that must be followed continu-ously. Otherwise, the society would fail and the order would return to a state of Nature, with the entire process reverting to the neo-mythic Black-ness that was Nature. In this way, Nature epitomizes analogously those parts of God's creation that were already partially good but in need of human perfecting. The societies that are brought out of Nature this way are ethno-racially tender plants in their supposed neo-mythic Whiteness: they would need nourishing and tender care; otherwise they would die and return to their pre-created state that was of a natural order of its own.

Therefore the laws and order of creation were different from those of the uncreated and Blackness. These two orders were conceptually and dialecti-cally of a single unity made up of the created and the uncreated, Whiteness and Blackness, the ephemeral by nature and the everlasting, together form-ing a single universe with neither part being the essence of the universe. Each was supposedly of a separate essence, order, and natural laws, even if incongruously the two finites existed side by side and always in tension.

As Farrar argues, in the dominant ideology of the Greeks, there was also a state of mind that was captured in the thought of philosophers like Plato and Aristotle who worried about the escape from a natural social stratifica-tion – one that flowed naturally out of God's created goodness – that occurs when individuals seek personal freedom and self-actualization without regard for a natural or idealized good.[13] Such an escape would be Black neo-mythically, as it is intended to subvert the goodness of a well-meaning creator. It would be Blackness pitted in a battle with good, with God's plans, with Whiteness. In this respect, Whiteness would exist within Blackness like a cultivated garden in a wilderness.

## MAPPING THE REMAINDER OF THIS SECTION

Now that we have provided an initial contextualization of my argument, let me explain how it will unfurl. This section will show that while there were distinctions ethno-racially among humans made on the basis of colour, these differences were not originally judged as being morally significant. They had nothing to do, originally, with neo-mythically discerning who was good or evil and, analogously, who was ethically superior and inferior, and by derivation physically so. Indeed, while the dominant ancient Greeks were concerned with knowing good and evil, this was to find out more about the inner and hidden qualities common to all individuals and not to gain knowledge about placing groups of people into stereotypical, one-dimensional categories of good and evil. That would come later when, especially during the Enlightenment, some philosophers and political scientists would read into Greek mythology and philosophy justification for racial categorizations based on notions of the inferiority and superiority of specific groups of people according to presumed natural characteristics. They would try to support an order constructed solely on the ethno-racial register by appealing to the goodness that should come only from determinations made neo-mythically. This presented a big ethical challenge, especially for those caught in the inauthenticity of existing between registers. To this end, they had to order the ethno-racial system so that it mapped on perfectly to the order required by the neo-mythic.

The quest, associated in the dominant Greek mythology and philosophy with a journey to the teleological end of freedom and a life of leisure, was to discover if an individual was inherently good or evil, and whether specific individuals were likely to be good or bad for humans living in a society. The good inside the individual was a virtue, but that was more a characteristic of motility and affectivity that was indicative of how existentially useful different people might be in a society and how happy, responsive, and responsible they would be with one another.

I will argue that through their mythology and philosophies, these Greeks were concerned with the creation of an idealized state, where White was, as Plato says in *Laws*, the colour most proper for adorning the gods. I will read this as symbolic of the purity of gods – a different type or form of being than humans. Blackness was intended as a signifier of human nature, in opposition to the power and often enlightenment of the gods who knew with certainty their powers, their role, and the meaning of their existences. I will argue that the Greeks were concerned primarily with how to bring happiness to human existence that, perceptually for them, was always threatened by collective devastation and personal tragedies. This was akin analogously to creating Whiteness out of Blackness. These ancient Greeks wanted to know how humans could triumph over adversity not only in this life but also in the legacy that is left in death.

In this section, my analysis will deal with six issues of Blackness. Pursuing a circular argument, but arriving at a higher level of knowledge than from where we started, I will show how freedom underpins discussions on Blackness, but more so how mythological notions of who or what is Black inform the philosophy and politics of state formation. I will thus argue that it is impossible to separate the mythology and philosophy that are presented in idealized ethical relations for how societies should operate as proposed in dominant classical Greek thought. This applies equally to discussions on justice, social mobility within the state, plurality and diversity, ownership of property, who can become a citizen in an ideal state, and how societies can create lasting happiness.

I will begin by first examining how these Greeks accounted for somatic and phenotypic Blackness, and in doing so I will arrive at an ontological and existentialist explanation of this human characteristic. This argument will show that, epistemologically, somatic Blackness was associated primarily with perception and cognition of who was truly human. Somatic Blackness originally had no meaningful ethical implications of how one human should treat another; in modernist terms it was not a racial signifier. Instead, it gestured to a relationship between defenceless humans, on one hand, and powerful gods on the other.

Second, I will look at Blackness as culture, and again I will provide an ontological and existentialist explanation. Here, I will be dealing with the Whiteness that is produced by what I shall call, based on Plato's mythology in *Phaedrus,* a double determination of elitism. The first determination is of a group of people who in their presumed godliness create a separate culture and civilization – one whose goal is as good as if it were designed and produced by a god – by setting themselves apart from the beasts that were the rest of humanity. Through this separation, they become, as a collective, the elites or virtual gods of humanity. They are the elites who come together as families, clans, and states to achieve their highest actualization or intended good. This is an achievement and a goal that is not available to those who are not members of this grouping and culture.

The second form of determination is social and occurs within the body politics of the culture. This is a determination of who, based on their innate godliness, is good enough to belong among the elites of humanity's elites.

This is very much like the arrangement in the main Greek mythology, where there are classes of powerful gods and of lesser gods – but all gods, nonetheless – with all being separate and distinct from humans. In the human realm, these elites would thus be those humans whose souls are virtually those of gods, who, so doubly determined, would be the equivalent of the human gods in a society of lesser godlike beings. They would live the life of pleasure and contemplation. They would not work and they would be, for some people, those who are most entitled to the good life that results from freedom. The doubly determined elites would be the ideal citizens in an idealized state. In status, as society's upper crust, they would be White.

Those who are not so determined are presented as Black, in the first place as the rest of humanity that did not make the first cut in the separation of humanity. They were not created out of Blackness, for they are still Black. Within the separated society, the site of the first determination, they are those who are chosen by way of a second determination for an inferior status, even if they are still considered superior to those left out of the state. They are thus Black in culture and in status through this double determination. First, they are Black culturally because they are not among the near-gods created out of the available materials in a specific state. Second, within the state, they are Black in status because they are not at the apex, among those whose souls are the most godly and most superior of human souls.

Third, I will look at idealized Blackness in existentialist and ethical frameworks, and argue that knowledge about this category is based on perception and cognition of what roles in society some people are best suited for and what responsibilities an individual should have in order to be happy.

Fourth, I will analyse Blackness as a marker of status, and here I will strive for an existentialist and ethical explanation. I will examine how the Greeks thought specific people should be positioned in society based on judgments of their goodness or evil, their rational or irrational nature, and whether they should have social mobility. Significantly, the somatic was an irrelevant signifier for social placement. Here, I will argue that, epistemologically, this category depends on cognition, motility, and affectivity for meaning, of knowing what is good for the society, for the individuals seeking happiness and self-actualization in a reconciliation of the social and personal. This argument will show how Whiteness was associated with reason and rationality, and how Blackness was linked with passions and irrationality.

I will then look at how the dominant Greeks decided issues of belonging based on two distinctive models of citizenship. These were the models employed in deciding who had the right to leisure and the good life in a state that is free of tyranny. The first was an early version of what would become in modernity *jus sanguinis*, where sociologically and anthropologically the individual is tied by blood to a homeland or to a sacred land with a sacred time, and is, therefore, thought to be ethnically part of a civic consciousness and cognition. The second is *jus soli*, epitomized by the immigrant or alien seeking inclusion in an ethnic grouping through naturalisation, through actively learning the cultures and mores of the people.

Knowledge in these models is based mainly on perception and the imputed motility and affectivity of both the *natural* and converted or *naturalized* members. For the Greeks, both models assumed different kinds of ethical relations for those constructed as outsiders or as culturally Black. These are the ethical relations that governed the type of trade and foreign relations that were conducted on a collective state to state basis, how foreign individuals were to be treated and, on entering the Greek city-state, into what class and status they were to be placed and positioned.

Finally, I will look at how death and rebirth figured into Greek mythology and philosophy as part of the human lived experience, and the types of ethical relations that can be expected in a culture that over generations seeks to transform what is human, temporal, corrupt, and subject to decay into the good, pure, and everlasting; how Blackness through its death can become White, and how death can transform White into Black again. This is a culture where the death of Blackness was morally and ethically good and welcomed; and the death of Whiteness morally and ethically evil and undesirable.

In all six areas of discussion, I will present Whiteness and Blackness as firm concepts in the prevailing classical Greek thought. Moral determinations depended on the relationship between these two concepts. These were ethical relations in which the good was directly associated with reason, beauty, the preferred, the superior, and Whiteness. In contrast, the death of Blackness was welcomed. Evil was associated with all that was the opposite of White, just as, in *Philebus*, Socrates claims, in a discussion on who is moral and good, that slavery is associated with pleasure and acting immorally.

As Socrates says, in general, all humans have good and bad sides to them, and in that sense they are all the same. Each human is thus a sort of microcosm of the dominant Greek universe with the created and good living next to and in tension with the uncreated and primordial evil. But as Socrates indicates, there is also difference in sameness, and the differences within the same category can be polar binaries. "As, of course, colour to colour. What man are you!" Socrates says in an attempt to move his discussion from the general to the specific, from the neo-mythic to the ethno-racial register. "Certainly, in respect simply of its all being colour there will be no difference, but for all that everyone recognizes that black is not merely different from white, but in fact its absolute opposite."[14] It is the uncreated, that which is without an essence and an order based on laws, that must become everlasting for the good state to remain perpetual. In the next two chapters, we shall look in greater detail at somatic and phenotypic Blackness in mainstream Greek mythology and philosophy.

Finally, the fourth chapter in this section will look at the African, Hebraic, and Christian influences in modernity. These are not geographic or other forms of totalizing essences; rather, they are dominant views that were held by different groups at different points in what we now call Western history. Sometimes, these different views were in competition with one another and instead of yielding one to the other merged into a new syncretic thought.

Once we have finished this search that is analogous to a journey, we will have completed the first part of this book, having paved the way for the second part in which we apply a Hegelian analysis to multiculturalism, and see the latter as producing a specific ethical relationship in a particular moment of speculative history – one when the dialectics of history are temporarily at rest, when momentarily the finite and the infinite appear reconciled in a single concept. And we shall start this explication from a position that we perceive as being, in terms of enlightenment, the highest that the dialectic of history has thus far produced. It is a positioning that provides us with the intuitive knowledge that is most central to our understanding of the prevailing circumstances, and it might very well be that of pure cognition or demonstrative reason. From this vantage point, as a self-conscious ego, we can give a backward glance at all the shades and forms that have made us historically Black, but which have in this moment of fuller knowledge made us as idealistically White as we have ever been.

# The Cunning of Blackness

Every so often, it becomes necessary to see things starkly as Black and White, as a choice philosophically between good and evil. In our time, one such juncture is widely believed to have occurred on 11 September 2001. This was another proverbial day of infamy and Blackness in Western civilization, when socially-constructed evil struck in the guise of terrorists at the symbols of Whiteness and goodness. What happened on this day is a story that explains Blackness in the four categories that we have developed – those of the somatic, cultural, status, and idealistic – and their counterparts for Whiteness. It is a story of the Blackness or Whiteness of the ethical relations that produce either the happiness or despair in our daily lives at this particular moment in modernity.

Before the eyes of the world on television, hijackers flew the second of two of humanity's most sophisticated pieces of technology into two gleaming towers, producing a second fireball in the blue sky over New York City. The attack by the first plane was captured by amateur video, one of the ubiquitous wonders of our time that is so much a part of the dominant mythology of individual freedom. Along with the second attack, it was played over and over on televisions and in theatres until the destructive endings were seared into the prevailing memory and narrative. These were the proverbial shots heard around the world in a renewed war between elemental claims to being good and knowing evil and how both good and evil are constructed and reformulated in time and context. This act of terrorism, as opposed to an assertion of retribution, and the place of its manifestation were meaningful: they were intended as an attack on the bastion of what is commonly accepted as Western civilization and its way of life, for that is what the towers and the city had come to epitomize and embody internationally. This was an attack on a land and time that were already ruled with a specific notion of what is good and how it was created out of the ever threatening Blackness.

The attackers were intent on interrupting, or even producing an irruption in the unfolding of the good that was being expressed as and through an American history that had started unfurling 225 years earlier with the beginning of modernity. With its claims to secularism, modernity was the start of the latest era in Western civilization, an era in which one of the chief participants, the United States of America, preordained and created good by its founding fathers, was to bring freedom to the Americas, or the New World, and then, ultimately, leadership to the free world. Indeed, the founding fathers had suggested that the United States would become the White beacon of light for the rest of humanity that was still in its uncreated world of darkness.

Its Whiteness would set the country and its people apart from the rest of humanity that remained prostrated in its darkness of underachievement, backwardness, and even slavery. Such affirmation was the good on which the United States was constructed and which was being challenged in a universal dialectical struggle between this good and its opposites or pretenders. Such is the mantra about the Manifest Destiny of the United States of America and the American Dream that is repeated at just about every state function of note.[1] For, universally, not everyone agreed that the constructed good of the American founding fathers was adequate for the rest of the world, or even for the United States of America. Opponents argued that the founding fathers had merely reshaped the existing evil material into a more acute form of evil and Blackness and that the White light of creation and good had yet to shine on their handiwork.

In their view, America the good was still awaiting its birth or construction. In its undifferentiated way, they argued, America was not godly. Those of this mind included such people as the spiritual leader of Iran, Ayatollah Ruholla Khomeini, who in December 1986 seemed to capture the disdain for the US, especially among Muslim and Middle Eastern countries and residents, by calling it "the Great Satan." Neo-mythically then, this was a struggle for freedom of choice internationally, a worldwide struggle between symbols of good and evil cast in their philosophical White and Black clothing, with the two sides inverting each other in claims, perspectives, and anthropological and sociological gazes.

Only a short distance from the towers that were attacked is the famed Statue of Liberty, a monument in American folklore to the eternal quest for freedom that is the essence of human nature. For ages, it seemed that this statue in its Whiteness had been one of the enduring symbols of a new land, a new life, and a New World to all humanity. One narrative and perspective claimed this was a symbol that had acquired meaning and status around the world, its spirit even travelling to Tiananmen Square, China, a country with a different concept and folklore of freedom. For it was to stop the worship of the "Goddess of Democracy" in June 1989 that the People's Liberation Army sent tanks and troops to reportedly kill a sizeable number of people giddy with the intoxicating dream of freedom American style. But America was perhaps best celebrated as a refuge, a mother earth figure symbolically rising out of the ground and the water of the nearby Atlantic Ocean to gather the peoples of the world together that they may be reborn, irrevocably changed, and set on a new idyllic course. As the country and western music icon Willie Nelson sings:

> Give us your tired and weak
> And we will make them strong
> Bring us your foreign songs
> And we will sing along,
> Leave us your broken dreams,
> We'll give them time to mend
> There's still a lot of love
> Livin' in the Promised Land.[2]

This is the place, presented as proof to the world, where there are ideals and a created good worth dying for in the hope of rebirth to a better life. It is a symbol of the good that comes through change:

> Livin' in the Promised Land,
> Our dreams are made of steel,
> The prayer of every man
> Is to know how freedom feels
> There is a winding road
> Across the shifting sands
> And room for everyone
> Livin' the Promised Land.[3]

Also only a short distance away from the towers was the United Nations with the flags of every nation of the world, symbolizing the diversity and plenitude of humanity, of variety and difference in oneness, of hope for a better world, of change. By the same gaze, this is the United Nations that was born out of the ruin of a global world war only a generation earlier, a conflagration that shook Western civilization to its roots and unleashed some of the most unforgettable barbarity of humans on humans.[4] This is a symbol of rebirth through reclamation of the Whiteness of life that had reverted into Blackness but which, recreated, was still a fragile entity. As such, this concept reveals a Christian spiritual thinking that is itself a syncretism of dominant themes in earlier African, Greek, and Hebraic mythologies.

Out of the ashes of desolation comes a hope or Whiteness that destruction shall be no more. This is the United Nations, so closely modelled on the philosopher Kant's ideal of a way to ensure perpetual peace on earth, a body that transcends national boundaries and sovereignties, but pledges to respect these same boundaries and sovereignties, that is the symbol of international hope, the belief that humans cannot again flirt with the Blackness that risks annihilation of the entire race or even of any one specific group. The United Nations: a hope for the future and rebirth; and by the same token a reminder of the uninvited death and destruction that is always potentially only a moment away. The United Nations represents humanity in all its Blackness and Whiteness; but it is a United Nations that is symbolically a great White hope.

In a particular sense, however, it was the City of New York, the ethno-racially determined financial capital of the world, created with its many languages, cultures, and frenetic lifestyles, and the World Trade Towers that remained most prominently associated with the attacks. This is perhaps so because not only the physical assets of the city, the buildings, were targeted, but also its human capital: the very polyglot of people that inhabit the buildings and walk the city's streets.

The multiplicity of ethno-racial identities and neo-mythic dreams totalled up to the very spirit of what the United States of America had come to symbolize, and to how it had kept the promise of the prophets or revolutionaries from the epic moment in history that is the American War of Independence of 1776. Indeed, regardless through which set of eyes and from which perspective, one thing was clear: in this struggle between good and evil, good always wins. But, as the events in New York showed, it must be a changing good, one that I argue allows Blackness to become White, the kind of idealism that Frantz Fanon spoke of in his seminal text *Black Skin, White Masks.*[5] It had to be a good according to somebody's imagination, and only that special person or group of people in its freedom can determine if the accepted good is really good or, indeed, evil under a mask.

## WHITE SPIRIT: BLACK BODIES

In a Hegelian sense, the aftermath of the attack was a propitious moment when Spirit and body within the same system were reconciled and even recognized as a unity, a kind of moment that tends to last as long as the proverbial blinking of an eye, but which leaves epic change in its wake. In this reconciliation, the self-consciousness thought it now had absolute proof that it had become White at some point in history. Domestically, the people of New York and the rest of the United States, if opinion polls are the judge, were of one voice in condemning the acts as evil. But there was also international reconciliation, which means that the dominant world opinion thought itself White, and the destroyers of the centres still existentially, ontologically, and epistemologically Black.

Can we please have a moment of silence?
That's for my niggaz doin' years in confinement
And for my soldiers who passed over, no longer living
That couldn't run whenever the reaper came to get 'em
Can we please pour out some liquor?[6]

Indeed, this pouring of libation as a ritual of African spirituality tells a lot about the existential Blackness of life and about what has happened since what has come to be known the world over as the event of 9/11, of how evil attacked the good, how the good counterattacked evil and drove it from office, and how the good appeared in its victory to change in evil, just like its enemy. In this way, according to this narrative, nothing changed: many of the home boys on streets around the world and in various neighbour-hoods still continue to face the despair of death and imprisonment. The truth: that life will always be filled with Blackness. Or there is the other narrative: that on 9/11 good attacked evil, did some damage, before it was driven back into the remotest places of the universe, where it struggles to survive but mainly in the hearts of a few committed men and women, watching and plotting while evil continues what appears to be an inevitable march. In this case, too, existentially nothing much seemed to change. The truth: that good must still be worth dying for – even by those who still want to live.

And can we please have a moment of truth?
For soldiers and troops away with helmets and boots
And families back home who pray they make it home safe
Hopin' that they don't get hit with a stray or missiles.[7]

What is the truth, even when you see it before your eyes? 11 September 2001 appeared to be one day when truth was true and evil was obviously not good. Beyond that everything else since then seemed covered by a veil of Blackness – the same veil that appeared to return to cover the world after the white light of a seemingly apocalyptic moment.

Back in 1776, when the American founding fathers made their choices, the spirit of the times that gives an era or civilization its character and iden-tity appeared unreconciled. It was seeking to split the United States of America from an extended British family or empire that included the Brit-ish North American territories and other colonies in the Caribbean. In two centuries, this "family state" would shatter ethno-racially and even neo-mythically: first by the breaking away of what would become the United

States of America; then again, with the separation of Canada as an independent country; and, finally, into several smaller splinters that became independent states in the Caribbean.

Each splintering was a mythological intervention of sorts, akin to the creation of a new sacred space and time that occurs in legend at the beginning of a new era. In this case, each of the new states had come to be out of a reformulation of the first principle materials that were at one time moulded into an extended British state that straddled the Old and New Worlds, the ancient and modern. But on 11 September 2001, as if with one voice, the people and governments in Britain, the United States of America, Canada, and the Caribbean were reconciled in their condemnation of the attacks as acts of evil. From that day forward, they have all struggled together to neo-mythically reconfirm the original good – ironically, a good that in its first writing marked an irruption of a previous initial good that produced the very good that was under attack on 11 September. The big question in 2001 was whether the good would now have to be rewritten and re-chosen yet again.

The World Trade Center towers, in the glory of their ambiguity of change and permanence, had with time become even more potent symbols of this American good: of the financial success of the New World, of particularly a land where an elite and almost godlike people enjoy the highest standards of living in the world. But they were symbols also of a country whose people, according to the religious purists of the major religions of Christianity, Islam, and Judaism, had lost their sense of morality and goodness.[8] Indeed, as Charles Taylor suggests, much of what had come to be venerated as good and a created Whiteness had become *desacralized* and *disenchanted* as Western society put less emphasis, or none at all, on "the heightened presence of the divine in certain privileged places, times and action," and as humans became more fully aware of themselves and their powers and potentials.[9] This is a Blackness that at some point had been transformed into Whiteness without everyone recognizing or accepting such alchemy.

The perfectionists or fundamentalists on both sides of the good-evil divide, especially those troubled by the desacralization and disenchantment of the mythical origins of the universe, wanted to offer a different good or Whiteness to replace the prevailing one. This was the other contradictory perspective regarding what is essentially good and White, and what is still evil and Blackness. They wanted purity and conformity to come out of the Blackness they saw covering all of America. For, in their eyes, they saw the inhabitants of this country living in a profane land and thinking they were the aristocracy of the human family, a people who dared to call their capital and its seats of government the Capitol, seemingly flying in the face of the gods of old, appropriating a name traditionally associated with the heights of Mount Olympus where over the ages the immortals of Greek and

Roman mythology resided.[10] Indeed, ironically, the fundamentalists on the other side from the Americans did see the towers as analogous of the neo-mythic good, but they did so for a different reason from those looking for the ending of one order and the beginning of another.

LIVING WITH SYMBOLS: A PAST THAT IS
A PREFERRED FUTURE

This modern day Capitol Hill was fully recognized the world over as indeed a filial seat of power for the gods, man-gods capable of unleashing thunder-bolts from the skies more deadly and destructive than those of any Jupiter, Jove or Zeus.[11] This was a Jupiter that in Greco-Roman mythology Venus described to her son Cupid as the "dark monarch, who rules the realm of Tartarus"[12] and travels in a chariot "drawn by dark horses"[13] long associated in ancient mythology with the passions and desires.[14] And the Capitol is also a clear reference to the Capitoline Hill, one of the seven hills on which Rome was built, but also the site for the temple of Jupiter, which housed the mythical books that contained the destinies of the Roman state.[15] Capitol Hill in Washington, the supposed capital of the free world, was the centre of what was imagined both neo-mythically and ethno-racially as the filial successor to the supposedly greatest of all modern orders – the Roman Empire.

This was Rome of old that through its progenies was destined to rule the world and, according to mythology, Rome whose legacy and destiny had been chosen as good for the United States of America by its founding fathers. This real power over life and death was the preserve of the world's sole Super Power, not only economically, but militarily, and culturally as well. This was a power that is best symbolized physically by the World Trade Center towers in New York City and their equation with money. But it was also the military power associated with the Pentagon in Washington – the other site of success for the terrorists on that eventful day – and the omnipresent spirit of US worldwide media outlets, such as ABC, NBC, CNN, and others that brought the images of destruction to the world in almost real time. These powers were in that moment the reserve of a nation undeniably Black and creole in its orientation.

For critics and supporters alike, New York City, in the particular, and the United States, in general, had become the epitome of St Augustine's New City. This was St Augustine's attempt to codify a way of life that reconciled the main strands of African, Hebraic, and Greek traditions into a single syncretic religion at the most recent beginning of what would be termed Western civilization and that has so far culminated in the American Empire. His efforts would eventually provide the underpinnings for an ideology that is the foundation of the city, state, and nation that has become one of the most syncretic in human history, and, as such, would become the explanation for why a specific good was chosen, why a specific land was chosen, and why a specific people were chosen from among the rest of humanity for special treatment.

American born, American raised, American made

Every time I hear the wind I think a slug went in
I'm checkin' my chest, holdin' my head
Catchin' my breath, watchin' my back
Smokin' this grass, beatin' my dick, thinking of ass
I don't know what they broadcast, the newsflash is fake
Every day I'm feeling like you, I wanna escape
And if y'all feelin' like me, y'all niggas just say:

My country shitted on me (My country)
She wants to get rid of me (Naw, never)
Cause the things I seen (We know too much)
Cause the things I seen (We seen too much)[16]

St Augustine's Christianity would come to provide an explanation for the working out of this specific good through a specific history and legacy. A history based on the Hebraic notions of a contractual beginning and ending along a linear continuum, but still accepting the African and Greek notions of an eternal time played out in cycles, as creation repeating itself through different affirmations, through various rituals and practices of the different stages of life, death, and rebirth that are all parts of a continuous existence.[17] This is an ideology that suggests there are separate worlds of spirit and the incarnate: one of Whiteness, purity, and order as alluded to by the Biblical prophets, Greek philosophers, and African diviners;[18] the other of Blackness, a world of the body, of corruption and denial, of impurity and darkness, as also alluded to by these same prophets, philosophers, and diviners.

In this scheme, based on these entrenched philosophical underpinnings, the spirit world is superior and more desirable to that of the bodily and lived existence. The spirit world is the home of the creator of the cosmos, the saints, patriarchs, elders, and ancestors who are of a superior knowledge that makes them infallible and immortal. These spiritual beings are the regulators of the universe, prescribing the destinies and lots of humans in a contract with them that is recorded in memory. And when these deities leave their world for that of humans, as mythologist Mircea Eliade suggests, they do so through the "theophanies" and doorways of the sacred land they gave to special people who are careful to observe the boundaries between the land of the sacred and elect, and that of the unworthy and outcasts.[19]

Each city of god in major mythologies must have its totem, stairway, or axis that acts as a ladder from the underworld of death and memory, through to the lived world, and on to the world of the unseen – the ladder that makes humans into gods, and allow gods to become human. Outside the cities of god or sacred places lies the other world of Blackness, that of fallible humans, who from time to time must uphold their part of the contract through deference, and by worshipping and appeasing the inhabitants of the higher world. Within the world of the infallible will be the sacred, but separate and distinct from it, is an enclave of Whiteness constructed for the occasional sojourn of the powerful non-beings or spirits and for those beings on their way to becoming godlike in disposition.

New York City had its World Trade Center towers, the phallus-like theophanies that symbolized the act of creation into goodness and transformations necessary for maintaining the links between the visible and invisible worlds. St Augustine's quest for purity – what he associated with a pure Whiteness of God – and for attainment of a superior world even here on earth came to form the religious basis for the rationalist idealism that is so central to the way of life that came under attack. This is a brand of transcendentalist idealism that has been locked in a dialectical struggle against proponents of a different ideology, culture, way of life, and religion. And even though there is the doctrine of the official separation of church and state in the United States of America, and even though Canada and Britain may deny the existence of any such religious overtones in their daily political life, there is no doubt that transcendental idealism, as a secular religion or ideology based on cosmos-creationist myths, is the very foundation of these societies. This idealism explains and validates their chosen good and the route to attaining it, and is the very spirit that roams through their World towers, parliaments, cultural institutions, and sporting arenas.

Applying the motif of St Augustine, critics and supporters alike could argue that New York City and the USA had either become the newest Babylon worthy of condemnation for its Blackness as home of the scattered tribes of humanity or, according to its boosters, had become the New Jerusalem to which St Augustine aspired, the mythical heaven of Whiteness and enlightenment on earth, the created good that left Blackness behind, or the closest humans have ever got to such an end.[20]

While for some there might indeed be a New York state of mind where, as the song says, if you can make it there you can make it anywhere, there are also hip-hop artists with a different view of New York:

It's like a jungle, out here
So much struggle, out here
And my dream's still unphased
Greed still the cousin of death

Always feels like always somethin' farther time
In the streets of New York

New York, New York, New York, New York oh
State of mind (New York City)
New York, New York, New York, New York oh
State of crime (New York City)
New York, New York, New York, New York oh
Big dreams (New York City)
New York, New York, New York, New York oh
Big schemes[21]

For its critics, including the hijackers of 11 September, this city was by analogy a neo-mythic site of bodily passions and lust of the flesh: it was the embodiment of the Great Satan of the Qur'an locked in a struggle to the death with the One and true God, or their version of it. The United States of America had supposedly turned its face away from the purity, and Whiteness, and piety of reason and had fallen prey to the lust and desires of the body. As godless entities, the towers were symbolically no different than the Biblical Tower of Babel built for the worship of humans rather than God – the same sin that, in Christian mythology, caused the initial separation of God and humans when Adam attempted to become a god in as much as he identified with and aspired to mirror God in his sense of disembodiment. These modern Towers of Babel were not true theophanies, for they were intended as one-way ladders: for humans to ascend to the heights of gods forever leaving their humanity behind; and not for gods to become like men before returning to their natural state of godliness.[22]

They had to be destroyed so as to make humans humble and pious, to keep them in their natural position, in the lordship and bondage relationship, a pose captured by the French sculptor Auguste Rodin in his appropriately bronze-coloured Adam. This is the image of the first man captured in the ethno-racial, depicted in this new world-dominant ideology as caught in the first knowledge of shame. This is humanity made to be eternally crestfallen and bound to the earth, rather than aspiring to the heavens. Therefore, in this respect, the towers were non-Christian in their symbolism, for they did not symbolize human perfection to all, an irony that was apparently lost on the attackers.[23] A different gaze would suggest that phenomenologically with idealistic Whiteness defined as Islamic, it would not matter that the towers were symbolically non-Christian, for in such a view all religions that are not Islamic White are simply part of the indeterminate Blackness that is the other of Whiteness. This is how one side of this dialectical struggle was projected by the Western media: as the evil-doers in the good-versus-evil paradigm.

WHITE RELIGION: BLACK LIVING

For supporters of America, the symbols were of a land, as Taylor says, somewhat *desacralized* and *disenchanted* mythologically,[24] of human redemption and even promised pristine happiness and hope, where humanity in all its diversity and plenitude, in its many languages, faults, and fears, could enjoy life, could try to forget the mistakes and tragedies of human existence. This is a picture of the same Adam of Rodin's imagination, of a man pulling himself up from the mire and mud of the earth, but a man who also recognizes the joys and challenges of being the colour of the dust of the earth and is conscious of the inevitable transformation back into this source from which he originated. It is an image of enjoying the moment, of enjoying the narcissism of savouring and celebrating bodily pleasures by loving oneself. Such is the image of an archetypal man escaping from the limits inherent in the lordship and bondage relationship, never having fully accepted them as permanent, or yet hoping for an escape rather than succumbing to the despair of having his actions eternally licensed. It is therefore quite appropriate that Rodin chose bronze ethno-racially as the material out of which to create his Adam, for this Blackness was the colour in the prevailing ideology associated with the human phenomenon and its tragedies.

New York City and the USA had become ambiguous symbols of good and evil, of the created and primordial, of Whiteness and Blackness. The land that provided their physical limits and boundaries was the centre of the world; what it stood for in terms of human development was under attack in September 2001 by those of a different ideology, which by definition and perspective of the good they assaulted, meant they were of evil intent. Eliade draws the following analogy: "Since 'our world' is a cosmos, any attack from without threatens to turn it into chaos. And as 'our world' was founded by imitating the paradigmatic work of the gods, the cosmogony, so the enemies who attack it are assimilated to the enemies of the gods, the demons, and especially the archdemon, the primordial dragon conquered by the gods at the beginning of time. An attack on 'our world' is equivalent to an act of revenge by the mythical dragon, who rebels against the works of the gods, the cosmos, and struggles to annihilate it, 'our' enemies belong to the powers of chaos."[25] As Eliade shows, in the prevailing paradigm that supports Western civilization, the dragon of chaos is a symbol "of darkness, night and death."[26] In the opening years of a new millennium, the attacks on the USA thus became the starting point for the newest phases of the epic battle between good and evil, between life and death, and between idealistic Blackness and idealistic Whiteness.

New York City and the World Trade Center towers on the morning of the terrorist attacks were also symbols of another type of Blackness, the cultural – of hybridity and impurity, of the indiscriminate mixing of people without concern for beliefs in racial purity and segregation based on the Whiteness on which the nation was founded. This was a city that as a unity was a composite, consisting neo-mythically of the several darknesses of which Hegel wrote and of barbarous people, like Plato's brute beast, who were considered by so many different standards to be culturally Black in behaviour. The United States, and New York in particular, had long ago strayed away from the dominant Western ideal of Whiteness. While in no stretch of the imagination was nor is there yet full equality between Black and White Americans, at least there is a sense that opportunities have been improving for people who are somatically Black.[27]

Almost forty years earlier, the city and the nation had undergone a rebirth resulting in the acceptance ethno-racially of somatic Blackness. This necessitated a complete rewriting of what the good of the nation was and who was to be listed as being among the good people. Instead of each recognizing itself as intentionally White and primarily English in descent and language at inception, the city, state, and nation now recognized a neo-mythic "melting pot" of differences: of colours, ethnicities, races, nationalities, lineages, diasporas, and cultures. It was a melting pot that could not fully dissolve every difference in a brew of absolutes. But it appeared to have created a reconciled spirit of a diverse community, a different kind of absolute, where differences, as Hegel argues, are indistinguishable in the darkness of night, when, as the saying goes, "all cows are Black."[28]

As initially reported, the attack on the World Trade Center towers killed about 3,000 people. With nationals and citizens from some seventy countries among the dead, it was as likely a cross-section of people as would be represented by any United Nations.[29] Death made no distinction between nationality and citizenship, between immigrant, refugee, and native born. And neither was there discrimination on lines of class, gender, sex, religion, or other markers of identity and difference. A seemingly premature death claimed some of the richest and most powerful individuals conducting business as well as low status security guards and cleaners.

## WHITENESS AND PURITY; BLACKNESS OF DEGRADATION

But at the same time, New York was also a symbol of impurity in a different way. It epitomized the opposite of the pious city promised at the beginning of the historically constructed Western civilization, the place that would be the home for immigrants and refugees, but only for a special and elect group of people who were entitled to the good life.

In *The Aeneid*, the poet Virgil described such a city of grandeur and world dominance, the home of an exclusively White people, all descendants from a single racial ancestry without cultural and somatic purity.[30] The task of the writer of *The Aeneid* was to "sanitize" Roman history, to make it establishment White, in a way to validate the rule of Emperor Augustus and his claim to the natural leadership of a special group of people that were naturally different and set apart from all other humankind. Emperor Augustus was seeking to prove demonstratively that he was doubly determined, ontologically, to be the Whitest of White in his culture.

Virgil would trace Augustus's lineage and legitimacy back to the Trojan hero Aeneas as the supposed founder of the Roman nation that was destined to rule the world, and that was the supposed moment of creation for the Whiteness that is called Western civilization. Ironically, for this Whitewashing of the official narrative, Augustus turned to a man who was not Roman born but became a citizen of Rome through naturalization, and who, judging by the only known portrait of him in the Bardo Museum in Tunisia, looked somatically Black.[31] Idealistic, this narrative was of the mythical return to a Garden of Eden in the Christian tradition, the place of creation when Whiteness first occurred, and a final resting place of bliss for the weary, outcast, and downtrodden.[32] Aeneas, the hero of the band of refugees, had prayed to his god to

> Give a resting place
> To the sad relics of the Trojan race:
> A seat secure, a region of their own,
> A lasting empire, and a happier town.
> Where shall we fix? where shall our labour end?
> Whom shall we follow, and what fate attend?[33]

And the oracle had advised, if not promised, in reply:

> Go, seek that mother earth
> From which your ancestors derive their birth.
> The soil that sent you forth, her ancient race
> In her bosom shall again embrace.
> Through the wide world the Aenean house shall reign,
> And children's children shall the crown sustain.[34]

Aeneas had imagined that this was to be a home for the refugees fleeing the sacking of Troy, one of the first epic battles that marked seemingly the first mythological beginning of Western history. This was to be a special land, for a special genealogical people: a land given to them by the gods, a land for those who were White, pious, European, and good; and not those who were Black, lascivious, African, and considered in this mythology as evil. It was the neo-mythic land of order and purity on which a European civilization with its own culture would be based, a society for which Aeneas rejected Black Carthage and Africa and the possibilities of a hybridized and mongrelized race of people that would have emerged from the joining of the Latin race with those of Africa and Asia. He would not create a White goodness or state that befits the creations of gods out of the materials offered to him in Africa. He would thus leave Africa still technically uncreated and still in the Blackness of non-creation of which Plato spoke.

As captured in the early writing that *The Aeneid* is, the very foundation of so-called Western civilization is a rejection of ethno-racially determined Blackness, which it associates with the undesirable whether through colour, lineage, or culture.[35] It is the story of how what once was Black as sin could be made through an act of creation as White as pure snow. In the case of Aeneas, it was Blackness represented physically by the African Queen Dido in Libya, then home to a technological culture superior to that of the Trojans, and the kingdom offered to Aeneas if he should marry Dido and stay in her kingdom. But Aeneas could not physically create a new White lineage of Godlike people out of her Black body, even if he mixed his spores with this uncultured earth.

As Virgil describes the plural society of Africans and Tyrians that Aeneas saw upon his arrival in Africa:

The prince with wonder sees the stately towers
(Which late were huts, and shepherds' homely bowers),
The gates and streets; and hears from every part
The noise and busy concourse of the mart.
The toiling Tyrians on each other call,
To ply their labour: some extend the wall;
Some build the citadel; the brawny throng
Or dig, or push unwieldy stones along.
Some for their dwelling choose a spot of ground,
Which, first designed, with ditches they surround.
Some laws ordain; and some attend the choice
Of holy senates, and elect by voice.
Here some design a mole, while others there
Lay deep foundations for a theatre
From marbles' quarries mighty columns hew,
For ornaments of scenes, and future view,
Such is their toil, and such their busy pains,
As exercised the bees in flowers' plains.[36]

This was the ethno-racial and neo-mythic blackness that existed naturally, which was not created or brought into being by another that was good and intended good. Although Aeneas "admired the fortune of the rising town, / The striving artists, and their art's renown,"[37] he had to forego these and other wonders of this Promised Land of somatic Blackness and cultural Whiteness that were offered to him in marriage. Instead he sought a new land of lesser achievements, of somatic Whiteness and cultural and status Blackness, believing that his god had promised not just a city or a country but a world to dominate and to make White in their image. For the god had

> [P]romised once, a progeny divine
> Of Roman, rising from the Trojan line,
> In after-times should hold the world in awe
> And the land and ocean give the Law.[38]

New York, outwardly, looked like the most perfect incarnation in the particular of Aeneas's dream. It looked like the future that had been foretold in the great books on the future stored away in Roman times. Indeed, it had become the apex of a culture that was started by those in Europe who had claimed not only a direct lineage to, but inspiration from, Rome and, by extension, to Aeneas and his rejection of Libya and Africa. They had created a mighty empire out of what existed in its natural Black state. But inwardly it was not so perfect, for it met few of the requisite conditions for purity that Virgil and others at the beginning of Western civilization had established for the chosen city. It was too mongrelized. It was a composite, not a purity or single essence. It had become, effectively, more like the multicultural city that Aeneas had rejected than the one Aeneas thought the oracle had promised him. It had achieved its Whiteness without losing its Blackness, something that Aeneas and so many philosophers after him had considered impossible.

For in their eyes, only Whiteness was associated with goodness, and only evil with all forms of life and development that were not authentically White. If good were to appear as Blackness, then a magician or evil genius would have to have been at work. This was the reality of the myths that explained goodness and evil in terms of Whiteness and Blackness in daily life: only through the intervention of the supernatural could Black become White.

### MYTH AND SOCIAL ORDERING: WHITENESS OUT OF WHITENESS

Indeed, a similar point was made in 1929 by Gerald Heard in *The Ascent of Humanity*, in which he gave an account for what he presented as the historical and anthropological rise of individualism, and explained this rise as the attaining of a new consciousness where the individual turns upside down what was previously considered to be the common good. In societies without conflict, Heard argued, the individual is submerged in the wider community. As individualism places the good of the individual above that of the group, in effect creating a conflict within the group, in such societies individualism brings an end to the pre-consciousness in which the individual saw himself or herself as secondary to the wider group. As Heard states mythologically: "It has often been urged that magic cannot but be black, for essentially it is the individual's unhallowed effort, a conscious turning-away from the group practice which is religion, to seek, like Balaam, the prostituting wizards, 'enchantments in the wilderness.'"[39]

Otherwise, the world would have been reduced to being unreal. Nothing could be known with authority and nothing could be predicted with certainty. How otherwise could one explain that goodness was flowing out of Blackness? – a question that the terrorists sought to answer in the argument that what was elevated as goodness was de facto evil and had to be destroyed for the good of humanity. It would seem, then, that what has been proven, ultimately, is that the matter is not one of good and evil being created but rather of the morality that determines how specific acts and instances become good or evil.

The World Trade Center towers and New York City had become the fulfilment of the central promise of the Hebraic and Greek/Roman traditions that had produced such a mythological city – a place that was a paean to Western civilization, the capitalist ideology, and its inherent, and at times only thinly disguised, Judeo-Christian religion and resulting rational transcendentalism. This is a Western civilization based on the search for freedom by immigrants and refugees, of people eternally looking for freedom, in a place where the individual can worship his or her god and make children that, as a newer generation, would take humanity's quest of becoming gods closer to completion. At the same time, at the heart of this tradition is the notion of a "True God" and of the purity of a civilized culture symbolized by the hearth and the divinity of a woman, whether a Penelope in Homer's *Odyssey* or a Lavinia in Virgil's *The Aeneid*. These symbols in their purity are White, the home and place for the ideal creation through mixing of a specific spore with the right land. This was the opposite of the Blackness of dispersion and diaspora.

But, at the same time, this is a model of civilization that for its creativity must rely on the temptress, on all the modern day Eves of the Biblical legend, and the Queen Dido of Virgil's time. In their Blackness, they ensure the continuation of a specific race of people by providing the negative idealism, the evil that is rejected and is the opposite of the good that must be chosen. It is a Western civilization based on knowing and authenticity, as Virgil suggested when he got Aeneas, the hero of his piece and to whom the gods promised a new city for the redemption of his specific race, to acknowledge that his original city was destroyed through deception.

Sin had arrived when the people lost their piety, when they allowed strangers of different spores within the gate. The people of Troy had defended stoutly against the Greeks until they let down their guard and found themselves in an unreal world where nothing could be known with certainty and where life had become unpredictable and unstable. Blinded by compassion for a stranger, they believed his story that the Greeks were in retreat and allowed, on his word, the proverbial Trojan horse inside their fortified gate. In no time, the city was destroyed, the king and noble lineage destroyed, the women raped and captured, and only a small band of refugees, with a few household gods to protect them, were left to roam the seas looking for the safety of a new land and home.

> With such deceit he gained their [Troy's] easy hearts,
> Too prone to credit his perfidious arts.
> What Diomede, nor Thetis' greater son,
> A Thousand ships, nor ten year's siege had done –
> False tears and fawning words the city won.[40]

The people of Troy that were to build the cities that would eventually produce the Roman Empire learned their lessons, at least for a while. So continued the traditional fear, and contempt, of the stranger. This is an ancient form of xenophobia, based on the idea that the stranger or immigrant cannot be trusted. This is a fear that was captured in Greek history, where even in the world's first known democratic city-state, Athens, citizenship and the right to vote were assured only to those whose parents were both Athenian. This was to ensure no mixing or contamination of the clean with the foreign unclean, which might otherwise subvert the commitment to democracy. But even then in the establishment of the mighty Roman Empire that came to represent the initial fulfilment of the Trojan's quest, the descendants of the lineage of Aeneas had fallen. They did not remember the lessons of this earlier period and did not protect themselves from deception as they should have learned or recalled from an earlier period. Following the loss of the Roman Empire, as exiles a second time the Trojan people would argue through their descendants that Rome had fallen because of deception. It had taken in too many strangers with their diverse gods and values, including the Christian god as the new Trojan horse.

As Arthur L. Little Jr argues in *Shakespeare Jungle Fever*, this notion of deception and fear of diversity would become central to the notions of who should be included, and specifically who should be excluded, in the models for the nation-state of Western Europe.[41] These ideals were eventually transplanted to the settler colonies in the Americas – reproductions that were based primarily on homogeneity or assimilation, or ultimately on the exclusion or genocide of those deemed distrustful and inauthentic. Little argues this was particularly the case with the forms of English nationalism that developed in the Renaissance. Traced through English dramatists like William Shakespeare[42] and Christopher Marlowe,[43] these models of nation-building influenced the then British possessions in the Americas. They expressed a national mentality or consciousness that was partly developed out of the fear that dealing with foreigners, as traders and eventually as a colonized people, would destroy ethnic purity in the same way that plurality had destroyed the Roman Empire, which empire colonial England was claiming as its natural image As Little argues, for the prototypes of states that were Venice and other European states, accepting diversity and difference was akin to opening the gates of the city to the proverbial Trojan Horse. "More important, Venice, with its extensive cultural and racial plurality – its own brand of multiculturalism – would be seen by the English as (in this respect especially) a less chastised state. England fantasized bringing to fuller fruition the imperial and cultural vision of a classical Rome. Present-day Rome may have been England's danger 'above all.' But its decisive difference from Protestant England made it less a mirror through which early modern England could glimpse itself."[44] This was the model of nation-building that began unravelling in 1776 with the separation of a distinct American nation out of the British Empire. It is a model that, similarly, became the reference for later nation-building in the former British possessions of Canada and the Caribbean.

### CREOLIZATION AND HYBRIDITY: BLACKNESS OF KNOWING

Finally, the attacks on New York underlined something else: they showed how deeply seated and accepted are the theology and the mythology that are the foundation of so-called Western civilization. As Hegel suggests, as an explanation for how instinctually we make sense of the world, "we should have the firm, unconquering faith that Reason *does* exist there; and that the World of intelligence and conscious volition is not abandoned to chance, but must show itself in the light of the self-cognizant Idea."[45] This is an idealism that suggests that even if its workings are beyond the limits of human understanding, there is an order and rightness to the affairs of the cosmos, that there is a master regulator at work, battling the forces of darkness and evil for its innate goodness to triumph and to be manifested as light in the world.

From this light, according to the myth, springs all that is good, because this regulator is good and can only produce what is good. For as Hegel explains of this reasoning, "it is only an inference from the history of the World, that its development has been a rational process; that the history in question has constituted the rational course of the World Spirit – that spirit whose nature is always one and the same, but which unfolds this its one nature in the phenomena of the World existence. This [rationality] must, as before stated, present itself as the ultimate *result* of History."[46] This is a rationalism that is central to the African, Greek, and Hebraic traditions that provide a view of the world. As Henry explains in *Caliban's Reason*, African philosophy and mythology are largely transcendentalist:

The stories of African origin narratives are about the creative agency of this unmanifested spiritual world, the real hero and sustainer of creation. Although the created and uncreated worlds constituted a unity, the African ego imposed the binary marking of its linguistic capabilities on the difference between spiritual and material or created worlds. Not surprisingly spirit was positively marked in relation to nonspirit and so came to represent a higher and more desirable order of existence. This binary can be usefully compared to the Platonic binary between the world of being and that of becoming. The former is a spiritual world of eternal ideas, a world that always is. The latter is a world of changing forms that is always becoming but never really is.[47]

The attack on the World Trade Center towers and the aftermath are perfect illustrations of this rationality that is produced by history. Within moments of their happening, the attacks were condemned as evil and contrary to the good of civilized society. Governments and religions of all types and hue, contrary to the professed secular belief in a separation of the two estates, were joined in a common alliance against the enemy. For as Eliade says, "sometimes the religious conception of the world still persists in the behaviour of profane man, although he is not always conscious of this immemorial heritage."[48] Non-Christian groups were just as quick to condemn the actions of the evildoers, perhaps indicative of another change – the recognition of a single society but with a plurality of gods. This point was emphasized by philosopher Juergen Habermas in a speech days after the terrorist attacks when he accepted the Peace Prize of the German Publishers and Booksellers Association in Frankfurt. He noted that in a time of avowed and even official secularization, the terrorists and the wider international public shared a unity in the terrorist attacks:.

These suicidal murderers, who turned civilian means of transport into living missiles against the capitalist citadels of Western civilization, were motivated by religious convictions. For them, those symbols of globalizing modernism were the embodiment of the Great Satan. But we too, the universal eyewitnesses to these "apocalyptic events," were moved to Biblical imagery by what we saw on the TV screen. The language of retribution used at first (and I repeat, at first) by the U.S. president in reaction to the events resounded with Old Testament overtones. Synagogues, churches and mosques filled up everywhere, as if the blind attack had struck a religious chord deep within the innermost core of secular society.[49]

The resulting fight, led in the first instance with the immediate responses of the United States, Britain, and Canada, would eventually emanate from a collective world consciousness. This cementing of a common bond between these three countries was not always the case. Indeed, at the start of modernity that would shape the modern world and result in the pre-eminence of the United States of America in global affairs, these three countries had splintered off from the same colonial, imperial beginnings. Now, just over two hundred years later, they appeared headed for a reconciliation that seemed geared towards what some might see as the original position at the beginning of modernity when what would become the United States of America and Canada were part of the same political system.

Then some of the British North American colonies were, seemingly, seeking release from infantile tutelage into the freedom of national aspirations, of a more mature *Mother* country that was Britain. First, the colonies that would become the United States demanded to be released from this tutelage or bondage. Much later, Canada would go the same route, but in so doing return much closer in relations and identity to its erstwhile sibling. At the beginning of second millennium in Christendom, the spirit of the times and of world history appeared to be reconciling the members of this old family. This is a reconciliation that appears to have severe implications for each of these countries, for their separate and individual identities and senses of belonging, domestically and internationally. What, then, can explain how the world in general, and Canada and the United States in particular, have arrived at this point?

The images presented by the US and Canada as they reacted to the potential transformation of society in response to the terrorist attacks – whether the old good would be replaced by an evil from another time and space – provide studies in Whiteness and Blackness at their most basic. The two countries provided contrasting examples of primordial images of goodness. The image of America on the television screens around the world and at home was of a social reconciliation to Blackness – the full spectrum of humanity as self-consciousness. This is a Blackness that fundamentalists – in their rational, ideational Whiteness – abhor for its lack of purity, its hybridity, plurality, and licentiousness, and its open celebration of such diversity.

It was a Blackness that in reconciliation appears, at least on the surface, to refute established Western philosophical notions on the epistemological meaning of Blackness, where it is defined solely based on perceptible somatic and phenotypic characteristics. In contrast, what appeared on television was a Blackness based on ontological and existential definitions, on humanity in the universal clothed in its fullness of human experiences, on creativity that is a prerequisite for changes and transformations, and on the struggle to enjoy and regenerate life while existing in the constant shadow of death. Pointedly, it was the symbolic rejection of the primacy of an epistemology based on knowing good and evil that is ultimately reduced to the ambiguity of skin colour or other somatic features. For the America on display was Black in the material or bodily sense, too: this was reflected in the colours of the people and the reality that people from just about every nation and state had full entitlement to the sorrow of the occasion and the protection of the state.

But it was also another view of Blackness, as not somatic any longer, but instead as a performance between the good and evil that is inherent in the world. This is best illustrated by the then presence in the American leadership of two African-Americans in powerful roles, Secretary of State Colin Powell, the son of Jamaican immigrants, and National Security Advisor Condoleezza Rice, the descendent of those who generations earlier were chattel slaves. This cultural Blackness was also there in the presence of leading cultural icons, from television talk show hosts participating in leadership roles in religious services, to various singers leading public events in the singing of the American anthem, from Americans of all colours and cultures explaining their fears, apprehensions, and hopes through the national media.

A generation earlier, based on cultural but ultimately their somatic characteristics, Blacks would not have been playing such leading roles in the affairs of state. Indeed, it is questionable if they, and people constructed like them somatically, would have felt as personally violated by the attacks, taking them as a violation that placed them innately and intimately within the bosom of American institutions and agencies. Indeed, it should be remembered that the original drafter of the Constitution of the United States never expected that he would have seen a day when somatic Blackness was no different from what made the All-American boy or girl. For Thomas Jefferson, who became the third US president, had written that somatic Blackness could not be turned into idealized Whiteness, that there could be no effective mixing and melding into a single state of those who were Black and White culturally, somatically, and socially.

These were peoples naturally different by just about every measurement, as different as two distinct races of people with their own distinct and natural notions of freedom, government, and state. Jefferson had argued that "deep rooted prejudices entertained by whites; ten thousand recollections, by the blacks, of the injuries they have sustained; new provocations; the real distinctions which nature has made; and many other circumstances, will divide us into parties, and produce convulsions which will probably never end but in the extermination of one or the other race."[50] As K. Anthony Appiah argues, "for Jefferson the political significance of race begins and ends with color."[51]

In this regard, Powell and Rice were acting White in the mythological sense, for in their ideology they were on the side of reason and rationalism.

Indeed, we might remember that for a long time afterwards, both Powell and Rice were the butt of jokes among African-Americans over the purported Whiteness of these Black-skinned government officials. And they were White in another way: they had the power of the gods of that specific sacred time and space called the United States of America. This is Blackness based on good and evil – on specific norms of moral and ethical behaviour that transcend an epistemological appeal to the immediacy of skin colour, such that US President Bill Clinton, although somatically White, in his exuberant celebration of the world and the flesh, would be presented with a straight face, even by those self-identifying as Black, as the first Black president of the United States in allusion to the triumphs and foibles of his humanity.[52]

The outcome of this dialectic, imposed by plenitude of differences and the diversity in humanity, contrasted with the image of Canada, which, despite the plenitude of colours and its claims of official multiculturalism, as a country still equates in terms of practical entitlement with somatic Whiteness. Canada is still ontologically and epistemologically at the level of perception. Canada's image was that of the absence and powerlessness of those that were historically constructed as Black and epistemologically associated with somatic features. All the government officials, the people explaining the ensuing crisis in the media, the people collecting donations, and the images of the soldiers going off to fight terrorism had one thing in common – an absence of anything but the somatic Whiteness that is the preserve of a privileging of knowledge as defined by the so-called founding fathers of the nation.[53] This is the image of a country that has not yet found it necessary to rewrite and redefine its founding myth of who and what are good and therefore entitled. This was the image of a country being pulled in two irreconcilable directions: one still tied to a legacy that privileges somatic, cultural, and status Whiteness; the other of a country struggling to live up to the promise of freedom and the acceptance of somatic Blacks.

### BLACKNESS AS SOMATIC AND PHENOTYPIC

According to the dominant strands of Greek mythology, ontologically, the people of Africa lived at the eastern end of their world, a place where the gods went frequently for recreation making humans their playthings, and the Greeks for trade and knowledge. One of the earliest Greek historians, Herodotus, says in *Histories* that Egypt was located on a gulf that "penetrated from the sea that washes Egypt on the north, and extended itself towards Ethiopia; another entered from the southern ocean, and stretched towards Syria; the two gulfs ran into the land so as almost to meet each other, and left between them only a very narrow tract of country."[54] In regard to what we are calling the ethno-racial register, Herodotus also notes that this region included Libya, Syria, Arabia, Ethiopia, and an inner land mass with different climates, geography, and soils from which the Nile River originated. Indeed, Herodotus argues that Egypt was a cradle of civilization for the known world of his time, and suggests that the Greek gods were first named and worshipped in Egypt or Libya: "Almost all the names of the gods came into Greece from Egypt. My inquiries prove that they were all derived from a foreign source, and my opinion is that Egypt furnished the greater number ... Of [Poseidon] they got knowledge from the Libyans, by whom he has always been honoured, and who were anciently the only people that had a god of that name ... Besides these which have been here mentioned, there are many other practices whereof I shall speak hereafter, which the Greeks have borrowed from Egypt."[55]

There were specific somatic and phenotypic characteristics to the people of that region. Herodotus notes of the Egyptians and Ethiopians, in particular, "they are black-skinned and have woolly hair, which certainly amount to but little, since several other nations [in the region] are so too."[56]

According to Greek mythology, the people of this area were made ontologically Black-skinned because of the excessive passions and the vainglory of the unreasonableness, not of themselves, but of a human-god, Phaeton, who was born to the sun god Apollo by the nymph Clymene.[57] Like other humans in the Greek cosmos, the people of Africa shared one common existentialist characteristic: they were the playthings of the gods, including in sexual relationships, which led to the creation of the category of beings human-god. Syncretic and creolized in nature, the human-gods could mediate between the gods and humans as they were neither fully one nor the other. However these were also alienated beings, as they were without a clear essence and were often questioned about their authenticity and belonging.

The people of Africa suffered mythologically like all other humans for the gods' irresponsibility. Originally, the colour of their skin was not Black. It was because of a tragedy caused by the licentious gods, and which almost led to the destruction of all humanity, that the colour of their skin would change and become Black. As the following story will show, the change in colour was meant as a sign of what happens to the human blood, humanity's lifeblood really, when humans are left at the mercy of the gods and fates.

According to the mythology, every day Apollo would ride his fiery chariot with two horses across the sky, always taking care to follow a straight course and not to venture too far north or south off the beaten path. Teased by his friends on earth to provide evidence that his father was Apollo, the human-god Phaeton approached the sun god and asked for proof of his lineage. Apollo said he would grant Phaeton any wish, simply because he was his son, and that would be proof enough of his divine lineage. Phaeton asked for the right to drive the sun's chariot to play at being fully a god. Nothing Apollo could say persuaded his unreasonable son to accept a lesser wish, so Apollo decided to give his offspring some tips on how to make a safe journey. Apollo told him that the key to a successful passage was to control the passions of the horses and to steer a reasonable course: "If, my son, you will in this at least heed my advice, spare the whip and hold tight the reins. They go fast enough of their own accord; the labour is to hold them in. Keep within the limit of the middle zone, and avoid the northern and southern alike. You will see the marks of the wheels, and they will serve to guide you. And, that the skies and earth may each receive their due share of heat, go not too high, or you will burn the heavenly dwellings, nor too low, or you will set the earth on fire; the middle course is safest and best."[58] But the youngster, immature and irrational, addicted to the mythological passions that were the cultural Blackness of humanity, was unable to control the horses, and the animals, freed of the firm hand to which they were accustomed, "dashed headlong, and unrestrained went into unknown regions."[59] The heat from the sun melted the snow caps on earth, parched crops, scorched trees and plants, destroyed great cities, and consumed their people to ashes. "Then Phaeton beheld the world on fire, and felt the horrible heat. The air he breathed was like the air of a furnace and full of burning ashes, and the smoke was of a pitchy darkness. He dashed forward he knew not whither. Then, it is believed, the people of Aethiopia became black by the blood being forced so suddenly to the surface, and the Libyan desert was dried up to the condition in which it remains to this day."[60]

Even the gods felt threatened and called a speedy meeting to discuss the fate of the cosmos. Sensing that the whole universe would plunge into chaos, Jupiter shot a thunderbolt that struck the chariot. Phaeton fell to earth with his hair on fire, like a shooting star consumed by its pleasures and burning up in the earth's atmosphere. Such was the lesson for vainglory, but also for immoderate and unthinking behaviour that wiped out sections of humanity from the face of the earth. Such was the result of an action that was not taken out of reason, but was governed by the emotions.

Ontologically, one of the permanent marks of this indiscretion was the ethno-racial colour of the skin of those humans that survived the devastation. Inscribed on their bodies was the warning of the fragility of human life: a message and reminder to all humanity of humanity's precarious nature. The colour of their skin would, cognitively and perceptually, act as a reminder to all humanity of the devastations for humans that were the likely outcome when gods fooled around and became unmindful of the effect of their actions on humans. It was a reminder of the fragile existence of humanity and how floods, fire, or pestilence that could just as easily be caused by the gods or unbridled human irrationality could easily wipe out the species in its entirety. Such was also the outcome when humans become unmindful of their fragility, their limits, and boundaries and behave, as the human-god Phaeton did, as if they are gods. It was also a reminder of what happens when humans forget their cultural, status, and idealistic Blackness – as epitomized by Phaeton in his irrationality, age, ignorance, and compositeness from being hybrid human and god and therefore without a pure essence – ignore their own limits, and act as if they are fully White, as rational, mature, and all-knowing, that is, as the essence that was Apollo.

In my assessment, Blackness of skin came to be the marker of humanity, of its innocence and its fragility, but also of how humans can be prone to misguided behaviour. It is a warning sign of humanity's origin and aboriginality, of what could have been left of humanity at the gods' discretion, of what had been left, and of the task that is all humanity's, to preserve and develop what was saved. It is the signifier that human beings still are not yet gods, even if they aspire to this goal. Here, we see that the colour of the skin is still seen within a single register, that of the neo-mythical; this is before the ethno-racial that differentiates between beings is introduced in modern thought.

Human beings, guided solely by their passions and desires, could do great harm to their own cause. Those who bore the marker of the gods' indiscretion and human complicity in this act represented all of humanity, culturally and symbolically, by the colour of their skin. Such was not the preserve of a specific group, as in this mythology those who received Black skins had nothing to do with what caused the blackening of their complexion. Indeed, they were the only identifiable group that survived the destruction and, who, in a primitiveness that is innate to all humans that aspire to a lasting civilization, would be responsible for human preservation and development. They simply exhibited the human condition of suffering, often unfairly, at the hands of arbitrary gods and fates and of those humans who behaved as if they were fully gods.

It is important to note then, as Herodotus indicates, that the somatic and phenotypic features of the people of this region held little ethical and moral significance for the Greeks. This point was born out obliquely by Aristotle in *Politics,* when he suggested that during his day one of the most effective forms of governments was in Carthage, on Africa's northern coast. Aristotle says that the Carthaginian institutions were excellent. "Many of their arrangements work well for them, and it is an indication that their constitution is well organized that the people willingly stick with the way the constitution is organized, and that no faction even worth talking about has arisen among them, and no tyrant."[61] The others with ethno-racially determined "excellent forms of government," according to Aristotle, were the Cretans and the Lacedaemonians, both of which were European states. They had managed to take an idea and ideal that are expressive of the neo-mythic register and express it satisfactorily, in Aristotle's mind, as an ethno-racial determination. It is worth noting that Aristotle made no reference to somatic or phenotypic features in discussing these states, the citizens, and their governments.

I shall now move on to show how Blackness, as culture, came to be viewed as a double determination of elitism based on the notion of a culture that is created by a people in the wake of one disaster, while anticipating the next. Blackness will be presented, mythologically and philosophically, as the inability to escape from such an entrapment of being Black and human into the Whiteness of an everlasting culture of knowledge and of self and communal preservation.

## BLACKNESS AS CULTURE

In *Timaeus*, in telling the story of the creation of humanity as part of the cosmos and placing this creation in the context of memory and history, Plato – reportedly a neo-mythic son of Apollo like Phaeton[62] – reports that there were several creations and devastations of humanity by Nature or the gods. Plato makes the point, in *Timaeus*, that the Ancient Egyptians were more conscious of the human struggles for survival than were the Greeks. This point was supposedly emphasized in a discussion between the Egyptian wise men and Solon, also one of Plato's ancestors.[63] Solon would go on to be venerated in Western civilization as the person who brought order and peace to the Greeks after disastrous fratricidal warring. Solon helped develop a prototype of a social order based on the rule of law which limited inequalities among citizens. In Athens, he helped ensure one of the earliest democratic moments in Europe and he provided rules and regulations for the best government that he thought possible. But this was a democracy that only applied to 10 per cent of the population, as it excluded foreigners, women, slaves, and children who had a foreign parent. As Agard says in *What Democracy Meant to the Greeks*, Solon, who was an aristocrat by birth, came to be called the father of Athenian democracy, but this name might not be a true reflection of his lasting achievements:

First he cancelled all debts which involved the security of a man's person, and made it illegal for such security to be asked or given thereafter. He proceeded to fix limits on the amount of land that any one person could own and restricted the display of wealth. From a fragment of his writing we gather that he considered an excess of money to be the root of at least many evils. These economic reforms were a moderate sort, satisfying neither the rich who wanted debts paid in full nor the poor who demanded a complete redistribution of land, but they were adequate to remedy the acute disbalance of Athenian economic structure. His political reforms were also moderate, but they carried far-reaching implications. Office was still open only to the upper economic orders, but the poorest class was now given a voice in the election of officials and participation in courts which reviewed and judged the acts of the magistrate.[64]

According to Plato in *Timaeus,* Solon had gone to counsel with the wise men in Egypt for insights into the functions and order of the universe so that he could apply this knowledge to the Greek states that he was hoping to bring out of the chaos of internal conflict. As Plato recounts:

Thereupon one of the priests, who was of a very great age, said O Solon, Solon, you Hellenes are never anything but children and there is not an old man among you.
    Solon in return asked him what he meant.
    I mean to say, he replied, that in mind you are all young: there is no old opinion handed down among you by ancient tradition, nor any science which is hoary with age. And I will tell you why. There have been, and will be again, many destructions of mankind arising out of many causes; the greatest have been brought about by the agencies of fire and water, and the lesser ones by innumerable causes. There is a story which even you have preserved, that once upon a time Phaeton, the son of Helios [Apollo], having yoked the steeds in his fathers chariot, because he was not able to drive them in the path of his father burned up all that was upon the earth, and was himself destroyed by thunderbolt.[65]

In *Timaeus,* the location of Egypt at the mouth of the Nile is associated with life and redemption, for it was the Nile in this mythology that saves civilizations from the devastation of time as epitomized by flood and fire. The following extensive quote of the wise men replying to Solon shows that while it would later be read as a place of cultural Blackness based on geographical and environmental influences, Egypt was then considered one of the places in the cosmos that was habitable to humans in all seasons and times:

We are preserved by the liberation of the Nile, who is our never-failing saviour. When, on the other hand, the gods purge the earth with a deluge of water, the survivors in your country are herdsmen and shepherds who dwell on the mountains, but those who, like you, live in cities are carried by the rivers into the sea. Whereas in this land, neither then nor at any other time, does the water come down from above on the fields, having always a tendency to come up from below, for which reason the traditions preserved here are the most ancient. The fact is that wherever the extremity of winter frost or of summer sun does not prevent, mankind exists, sometimes in greater, sometimes in lesser numbers. And whatever happened either in your country or in ours, or in any other region of which we are informed – if there were any actions noble or great or in any other way remarkable, they have been written down by us of old and are preserved in our temples. Whereas just when you and other nations are beginning to be provided with letters and other requisites of civilized life, after the usual interval, the stream from heaven, like a pestilence, comes pouring down and leaves only those of you who are destitute of letters and education, and so you have to begin all over again like children, and know nothing of what happened in ancient times, either among us or among yourselves.[66]

The Egyptians, as Plato saw them, were wise enough to know about what happened to the Ethiopians and to the Libyans by the Phaeton fiasco. However, they did not mention the somatic characteristic of any of the peoples involved in retelling these stories. Instead, they spoke about the culture and civilization that were preserved in the garden of this creation while those of other regions had perished. Solon was reminded of the civilizing history that was all humanity's but which had been lost to his people. Indeed, the suggestion is clear that, existentially and epistemologically, the human experience is one common to all people. Civilization is the effort or quest by all humanity to maintain human life in the face of innumerable perils.

Civilization was presented in *Timaeus* as based on knowledge that was experienced cognitively and recorded. Societies, in this respect, made conscious efforts to record what they knew, to preserve it, and to carry forward knowledge by sharing with other societies. Particularly, in language and sentiment similar to that of Virgil's *The Aeneid,* the Egyptians recounted for Solon a glorious past that was that of the Greek people and which had, just as importantly, sprung out of the land and been carried on through bloodlines. But like Aeneas and all the patriarchs before him, these special people had forgotten their history, and this ignorance was part of the reason they had an immature culture and could not achieve the Whiteness of the civilization that had been given to them in the mythology by the goddess Athena.

As for those genealogies of yours which you just now recounted to us, Solon, they are no better than the tales of children. In the first place you remember a single deluge only, but there were many previous ones; in the next place, you do not know that there formerly dwelt in your land the fairest and noblest race of men which ever lived, and that you and your city are descended from a small seed or remnant of them which survived. And this was unknown to you, because, for many generations, the survivors of that destruction died, leaving no written word. For there was a time, Solon, before the great deluge of all, when the city which now is Athens was first in war and in every way the best-governed of all cities, and is said to have performed the noblest deeds and to have had the fairest constitution of any of which tradition tells, under the face of heaven.[67]

This knowledge asserts that, existentially, human existence, in the main, was an experience marked by fragility of life and the lived recognition of how, every so often, Nature and the gods were prone to arbitrarily wiping out large sections of humanity. In this respect, the remnants of the devastated people were forced to resume their quest all over time and time again. They begin in Blackness as uncivilized, uncultured, and illiterate – just like humans at birth. Only the memories of what other humans had achieved, and the lingering dreams of attaining what earlier humans had set as their quests, would spur on this residue of humanity in this vale of tears. And that quest will be pursued relentlessly until the next devastation, when the group that survives is forced to start all over again. In this way, a cycle of death and rebirth continues.

Even if Plato places in the Egyptians' mouths the notion of their inferiority based neo-mythically on Athens having previously produced the "fairest and noblest race"[68] and a history of achievements that was superior to theirs, the Egyptians, as an ontologically identifiable group in *Timaeus*, were ethno-racially favourably disposed. Perceptually, they appear to have been culturally reconciled with nature so that they prolonged the periods between deaths. The Egyptians had taken some of the sting out of nature; they had domesticated it and had learned how to control and channel the forces of nature for humanity's benefit. But at the same time, they were also wise enough to keep records of human achievements, perhaps just in case the gods wiped them out too, or in case, as with Solon, they had to share their knowledge with a group less fortunate than themselves.

Plato seems to be suggesting that early Egyptians had an existence that made them self-sufficient. They existed in a well ordered and preserved cosmology, such that their culture and their status were not considered inferior to those of any other group of that time. They also had an epistemology that was the envy of other people, a history that explained plausibly the beginning and ending of the cosmos, and from which others could learn. As Plato argues, the Egyptian sages told Solon that the same goddess Athena was responsible for the Egyptian and Athenian civilizations, for the same goddess "is the common patron and parent and educator of both our cities."[69]

There were other instances when Plato also referred ontologically to the wisdom of those that would eventually be known only as Black based on somatic features or geographical and cultural associations with Egypt. In *Philebus*, he credits another Egyptian for a godlike ability: "The unlimited variety of sound was once discerned by some god, or perhaps some godlike man; you know the story that there was some such person in Egypt called Theuth. He it was who originally discerned the existence, in the unlimited variety, of vowels – not just 'vowel' in the singular but 'vowels' in the plural – and then of other things which, though they could not be called articulate sounds, yet were noises of a kind."[70]

Plato's language is noticeable for its existentialist tropes: mentions of age, the childlike and the immature, primitiveness, and the divinity-inspired social order founded on a natural separation of various groups based on their elitism and social rankings. These would become the attributes of those who are members of the elect, those of a sacred time and place: that is, of the civilized nation whose function is to preserve and enhance human existence between devastations. But if a people were carved out of humanity to form an idealized White state, does this mean that all members would be equally White? In the next section of this chapter, I will illustrate that while the citizens of the state might be White compared to the rest of humanity, the mere fact that they are human was taken by classical Greek philosophy to show that there would have been an admixture: some members of the society would remain almost as culturally backwards as the rest of humanity, while other members would be the cream of the new elites. In this respect, the elites would be discerned by the innate virtues that make them good or evil, idealistically Black or White. Thus, we shall now examine how Blackness and Whiteness were treated in Greek mythology and philosophy as analogous to evil and good.

## IDEALIZED BLACKNESS AND WHITENESS

In *Phaedrus,* Plato equates life to the struggle mythologically and analogously between two horses and a charioteer who wants to steer a middle ground of proportion and control that would lead to a long and happy life. One problem is negotiating sexual passions and desires that could make individuals unruly and unmindful of their teleological good: to find a life partner with whom to find happiness through a long and productive life and, after death, to resort fully to the status of a god. The idealized aim is to control excess desires, which could lead the team of charioteer and the two horses astray, if the horse with the penchant for unruliness and a tendency for unbridled emotion has its way:

Now of the steeds, so we declare, one good and the other not, but we have not described the excellence of the one nor the badness of the other, and that is what must now be done. He that is on the more honorable side is upright and clean-limbed, carrying his neck high, with something of a hooked nose; in color he is white, with black eyes; a lover of glory, but with temperance and modesty one that consorts with genuine renown, and needs no whip, being driven by the word of command alone. The other is crooked of frame, a massive jumble of a creature, with thick short neck, snub nose, black skin, and grey eyes; hot-blooded, consorting with wantonness and vainglory; shaggy of ear, deaf, and hard to control with whip and goad.[71]

This time it is not reason, as in the god Apollo or an immature Phaeton, that has become unreasonable and unpredictable in its actions, but the passions that drive human life towards its final goal. In this case, the author Plato is directly linking the passions, ugliness, unreasonableness, and crudity with Blackness – the predominant colour of the unruly horse. Indeed, Plato calls this horse evil.[72] The White horse is "beautiful" and of the right temperament and spirit, and is amendable to the instruction and guidance of a charioteer with reins, just as a good soldier is to a commander. The outer looks of beauty or ugliness are intended to reflect the inner beauty and ugliness in the respective horses. For, as Plato suggests, the outer qualities are a reflection of a soul that is divided into "three parts, two being like steeds and the third like charioteer."[73] As Plato says, in each human "there are two sorts of ruling or guiding principles that we follow. One is an innate desire for pleasure, the other an acquired judgement that aims at what is best." Both of them are held in governance by a charioteer of sorts that is reason.[74] The two horses would react in markedly different ways at the sight of beauty, goodness, and purity. This is the godlike form which the body and soul as an entity aspires towards teleologically, and is epitomized by a male horse that, according to Plato, is in the presence of its beloved: "The obedient steed, constrained now as always by modesty, refrains from leaping upon the beloved. But his fellow, heeding no more the driver's goad or whip, leaps and dashes on, sorely troubling his companion and his driver, and forcing them to a monstrous and forbidden act, but at last, finding no end to their evil plight, they yield and agree to do his bidding."[75]

In this analysis, knowledge of the godlike qualities of the early Phaeton myth is now discerned by outer characteristics, somatic and phenotypic Whiteness, while those of the misguided Phaeton are transferred to Blackness, not as an unintended result of an action but as the cause. The results, analogously, are the data that can be used to infer the goodness or evil of the artificer, who in *Timaeus* intends to do good. The charioteer, like an Apollo, is reason and sovereign over the two parts of the souls – what Hegel would later interpret to be the arrangement for a lordship and bondage relationship.

To this end, Plato is associating reasonableness, beauty, honour, and civility with ethno-racially defined Whiteness – the predominant colour of the White horse, making a link that starts out as cultural but which would become a somatic and phenotypic signifier of inner goodness, or evil, as well. As Plato states, the significant feature of the horses that draw the chariots of the Greek gods is their wings "and more than any other bodily part it [a wing] shares in the divine nature, which is fair, wise, and good, and possessed of all other such excellences. Now by these excellences especially in the soul's plumage nourished and fostered, while by their opposites, even by ugliness and evil, it is wasted and destroyed."[76] Indeed, the gods that fall to earth as humans are pulled down or carried astray on the wings by "the heaviness of the steed of wickedness."[77] While the White horse might have some spunk in it, as attested by the blackness of the eyes, by its nature it is more disposed to be guided by reason – it is not itself rational – because its primary colour is White, a colour that is, as Plato argues in *Philebus*, the primary signifier of inner goodness.

Plato says the key to completing the journey is the role played by the charioteer, which is to say the role of reason within the soul. It must control the spirit of the White horse and the passions of the Black horse. For this reason, the two horses are wisely yoked together by the god. In the story Plato tells, the charioteer needs the passions of the Black horse to drag along the more temperate White horse, while the same controlled spirit of the White horse is also necessary to act as a brake on the excesses and enthusiasm of the Black one. The Black horse will act unreasonably, would be incapable of hearing and learning and, therefore, would not be able to be taught, either by itself or anyone else, to act reasonably. It could not be redeemed by civilizing influences to which, by nature, the Black horse is impervious. The horses of spirit and passion are therefore yoked together to allow reason, through its control of spirit, to steer and guide:

The driver, with resentment even stronger than before, like a racer recoiling from the starting rope, jerks back the bit in the mouth of the wanton horse with an even stronger pull, bespatters his railing tongue and its jaws with blood, and forcing him down on his legs and hunches delivers him over to anguish.

And so it happens time and again, until the evil steed casts off his wantonness; humbled in the end, he obeys the counsel of his driver, and then he sees the fair beloved is like to die of fear. Wherefore at long last the soul of the lover follows after the beloved with reverence and awe.[78]

As Plato argues, Reason, as symbolized by Whiteness, must be the god, sovereign, or charioteer that controls base desires associated with Blackness, and do so by imposing limits and boundaries, in the case of the two horses by keeping Blackness yoked to another less passionate horse. Both Plato and Apollo thus offer the same advice: Reason, marked by moderation, must be in charge to avoid chaos and destruction. Apollo had suggested that the whip should be applied sparingly, but there was the need for a tight rein on the horses so that the chariot with its three parts would not go astray. Plato is in agreement: Reason, as the charioteer, must be firm; otherwise an unreasonable sovereign, freewheeling passions, and too much temperance or spirit will endanger not only the cosmos, but even the gods as well. This is what happens when humans step beyond their bounds and do not respect moderating limits, and which explains, as Plato says elsewhere, the need for law and order: "For that goddess of ours, fair Philebus, must have observed the lawlessness and utter wickedness of mankind due to an absence of limit in men's pleasures and appetites, and therefore established among them a law and order that are marked by limit. You maintain that she thereby spoiled them. I assert that on the contrary she preserved them."[79]

However, in the stories about the horses, one with erotic passions and the other with courage, Plato suggests that the charioteer can only bring the Black horse under control through a strong hand on the reins. She must struggle frantically in a battle of strength, and not intellect, to physically subdue the passions of what is essentially a "wild" and uncultured horse. This is wildness, as I shall show in succeeding sections, that can only be "cured" or controlled in a civilizing society whose aims are to produce individual happiness and collective self-sufficiency. The White horse has already been acculturated, as is a soldier, to being directed and controlled and is amenable to guidance by a firm rein only.

Plato is arguing that, epistemologically, there is a knowledge that can be acquired from the colours of the horse, and by the description of their bodies, about how they can be expected to behave:

So when they lie side by side, the wonton horse of the lover's soul would have a word with the charioteer, claiming a little guerdon for all its trouble. The like steed in the soul of the beloved has no word to say, but, swelling with desire for he knows not what, embraces and kisses the lover, in grateful acknowledgement of all his kindness. And when they lie by one another, he is minded not to refuse to do his part in gratifying his lover's entreaties; yet his yokefellow in turn, being moved by reverence and heedfulness, joins with the driver in resisting. And so, if victory be won by the higher elements of mind guiding them into the ordered rule of the philosophical life, their days on earth will be blessed with happiness and concord, for the power of evil in the soul has been subjected, and the power of goodness liberated; they have won self-mastery and inward peace. And when life is over, with burden shed and wings recovered they stand victorious in the first of the three rounds in that truly Olympic struggle; nor can any nobler prize be secured whether by the wisdom that is of man or by the madness that is of god.[80]

In sum, then, Plato's analysis has provided us with a particular look at how some classical Greeks discerned what the good and the evil are in human beings. The question that arises is how humans must live together in a society so that it allows them, like individuals that consist of the mythical charioteer and two horses, to live in a land of peace and happiness. This would be an existence that, like a journey, would be marked by justice based on temperance and knowledge of good and evil, but also on the creativity induced by passions, so that, at the end of the journey, "her charioteer sets his steed at their manger, and puts ambrosia before them and draught of nectar to drink withal."[81] We shall now discuss how these thoughts informed discussions on moral and ethical relations in a society whose aims, idealistically, were to produce justice for individuals as a group, and to allow them to return ultimately to a godlike existence. Thus, chapter 11 picks up this discussion with a look at the works of Plato's student, Aristotle, who represents further developments in classical Greek thought on Blackness and Whiteness.

# 11

# Blackness

## *Status, Citizenship, Death, and Rebirth*

### BLACKNESS AS STATUS

Aristotle argues that by their very nature, humans are, in terms of affectivity and motility, political creatures and must live gregariously to achieve their highest virtues. Idealistically, they can only hope for justice in a civil society and it is only in a civil society that they can expect to achieve happiness, which is the highest good for individuals. For it is by living this way that humans create and share a common good of becoming self-sufficient in their material needs and happy in their spiritual well-being. In such a way, Aristotle claims, is the good of society established, and this is the good to which society must work if it is to be just. On this view, the city-state was the highest attainment of humanity's living, for it provided rules and a constitution of governance. "Since it is evident that human beings have the same end, both individually and collectively, and since the best man and the best constitution must of necessity have the same aim, it is evident that the virtues suitable for leisure should be present in both. For, as has been said repeatedly, peace is the end of war, and leisure of work. Some of the virtues useful for leisure and LEISURED PURSUITS accomplish their task while one is actually at leisure, but others do so while one is at work. For many necessities must be present in order for leisure to be possible. That is why it is appropriate for our city-state to have temperance, courage, and endurance."[1]

Therefore, within this construction there is order and predictability, created and ordered idealized Whiteness, as opposed to chaos, unpredictability, and arbitrariness. This is the civilizing order which the Egyptian sage had described to Solon as "natural" and which Plato held up as the ideal arrangement developed for humans by a benevolent god. Everyone was in his or her place based on his or her virtue, and in Aristotle's case, based on his or her strength, youth, and wisdom as appropriate for a given task;

everyone had recognition in some form, but recognition that in this social order is based on a rigid functionalism. For, as Aristotle says: "We see that every city-state is a community of some sort, and that every community is established for the sake of some good (for everyone performs every ACTION for the sake of what he takes to be good). Clearly, then, while every community aims at some good, the community that has the most AUTHORITY of all and encompasses all the others aims highest, that is to say, at the good that has the most authority of all. This community is the one called a city-state, the community that is political."[2] Aristotle emphasizes that humans are found in their natural state in a community, of which the state as a conscious act of creation is the highest form – the Whiteness that has to be brought out of the primordial or universal Blackness of all humanity. It is in a community that humans develop to their fullest potential: "[A] city-state is among the things that exist by nature, that a human being is by nature a political animal, and that anyone who is without a city-state, not by luck but by nature, is either a poor specimen or else superhuman. Like the one Homer condemns, he too is 'clanless, lawless, and homeless.' For someone with such a nature is at the same time eager for war, like an isolated piece in a board game."[3]

This is what separates the citizens that are the socially created humans in their idealized Whiteness, those who have the right to live within, and to the protection of, the state, from the others, the barbarians of supposedly another clan, laws, and homeland.[4] Aristotle also suggests a "civilizing" or rationalizing aspect as goals of this creation of living in states – thus to temper appetites for war, sex, and food, an overindulgence of which would not be appropriate for the common or individual good. An extension of this argument is that cultures that are developed into homelands by specific clans under their own laws can be learned, for they are not instinctual but habitual. Education, then, is an act of creation making humans enlightened or civil out of their naturally uncultured primordial state.

For Aristotle, there is an educational component to culture and civilization, for as memory it elevates humans from living only according to base instincts. They can thus acquire knowledge and wisdom in the state. In this way, civilizing is tantamount to accepting reason and to becoming rational by learning. Aristotle argues that this arrangement is natural, and that the aim of the state is to be so *organized* and human affairs so arranged that justice flows naturally within this created entity. Individuals, as the embodiment of passions and appetites, must die metaphysically, must forsake their idealistic Blackness, to be reborn as civilized and rational members of a community. They must enter into a lordship and bondage relationship with the state as the lord, as the retainer of memory and knowledge of what is good, civil, and idealistically White and as, paradoxically, the unchangeable in the obtaining ideology. This is so because the prevailing ideology seeks, in a Marxian subversion of the real by unreal as the permanent condition, to develop a culture and Whiteness that is eternal, so that the state continues from generation to generation and becomes perpetual. For this to happen, what was once perishable must be transformed into a permanency and unchangeableness. Aristotle explains:

Anyone who cannot form a community with others, or who does not need to because he is self-sufficient, is no part of a city-state – he is either a beast or a god. Hence, though an impulse toward this sort of community exists by nature in everyone, whoever first established one was responsible for the greatest of goods. For as a human being is the best of the animals when perfected, so when separated from LAW and JUSTICE he is worst of all. For injustice is harshest when it has weapons, and a human being grows up with weapons for VIRTUE and PRACTICAL WISDOM to use, which are particularly open to being used for opposite purposes. Hence he is the most unrestrained and most savage of animals when he lacks virtue, as well as the worst where food and sex are concerned. But justice is a political matter; for justice is the organization of a political community, justice decides what is just.[5]

In terms of social ordering, Aristotle's reference to a god as an entity not in need of civilization is important, for elsewhere he argues for the aspiration to a god-likeness through the acquisition of knowledge. However, and significantly, Aristotle is arguing that the seemingly unchangeable god outside of society must die in order to be reconciled and repositioned in the state as a citizen, as an enslaved or even defanged god. Outside of society, a god is Black; it is part of the unchangeable essences captured in the unpredictable nature of life. Here, we see a similarity with the later suggestion by the empiricist types of modernity that, epistemologically, perception has to submit to demonstrative reason for the acquisition of real and unchangeable knowledge.

In *The Metaphysics*, Aristotle argues for a divinity, which comes from knowledge, as providing the ultimate freedom "and for this reason it is justice that its acquisition would not be thought to be human."[6] This knowledge/divinity is acquired by those who have the time and the leisure to study "for the uselessness" of just knowing causes. Aristotle argues that knowledge that comes through the arts was discovered not by those looking for pleasure but by those of leisure. He maintains, "that is why it was in Egypt that the mathematical sciences were first developed, for there leisure was available to the priestly caste."[7] Later, he suggests an ideal social order based on knowledge as the highest attainment of humans. Only when they have acquired wisdom do humans, as perceptually in Greek mythology former gods, transcend the need for civilizing influences. It is then that they have become civilized, perfected virtuously, and, paradoxically, godly – the latter as a higher level of attainment than the previous godliness that had to be surrendered for amelioration, corrigibility, and justice. Therefore, in status and culture, Whiteness is what a civilized god becomes.

In a statement reminiscent of Plato's philosopher-king in *The Republic*, Aristotle argues that "for the wise man should not be instructed but should instruct, and it is not he who should obey another, but rather the less wise should obey him."[8] In placing the development of mathematics in Egypt among those who survived the various floods and genocides of humanity by the gods in Greek mythology, I argue that Aristotle, like Plato, gives recognition to Blackness as the natural order and that it is the original material out of which civilization must be fashioned. This is particularly the case where Aristotle discusses, existentially and ontologically, who should by nature be slaves and what should be the treatment of citizens in his ideal state. For example, Aristotle does not believe that herdsmen or farmers should be citizens, become perfected specimens or White gods: "As for the farmers, ideally speaking, they should be racially heterogeneous and spiritless slaves, since they would then be useful workers, unlikely to stir up change. As a second best, they should be non-Greek subject people, similar in nature to the slaves just mentioned. Those who work on private land should be the possessions of the owners; those who work on the communal land should be communal property."[9] Aristotle seems to be suggesting, using Plato's horses analogy, that herdsmen should idealistically be those with the temperament of the White horse. They would be owned by the state and they would work specifically on state-owned land. Reason, as idealized Whiteness, will make sure that the civilized herdsmen achieve their fullest virtue by becoming idealistically as White as possible. But ultimately, citizens of the ideal state could settle for farmers of the Black horse temperament, in which case they would already be of an inferior class and could be treated differently from the norm for even regular herdsmen. The question, as we shall discuss next, is whether in this Aristotelian model it is possible to separate Blackness and Whiteness in a human state, and whether there is here an argument for inequality based on the perceived nature of these groups.

Thus, is Aristotle suggesting that justice is doled out equally even in a civilizing state ruled rationally by laws? He is not. Aristotle does not believe that all humans are equal, not even within the constructed civil society, for he argues that even in their most natural state, humans have a hierarchy of worth. "Those, then, who think that the position of STATESMAN, KING, HOUSEHOLD MANAGER, and MASTER of slaves are the same, are not correct."[10] Further, he says, there is a hierarchy among homelands with their different clans and laws, noting that it is not natural for Greeks to be slaves to barbarians, a clear implication that Greeks and their states are superior. However, according to Aristotle's way of thinking, Greeks could keep slaves, who tended to be from other clans and homelands.

Culturally, then, the Greeks were White and people of other clans Black. This was also the presumed natural order for social or status Whiteness and Blackness within the Greek state. Important too is Aristotle's hierarchy: since ontologically Whiteness is purity and cannot be differentiated, it cannot then be divided into a natural hierarchy. This is what can happen, however, to Blackness, as it becomes differentiated in stages and hierarchies. Therefore, Aristotle's hierarchy of citizenship as expressed on the ethnoracial register would suggest the primacy of a single White class of citizenship at the top of the hierarchy, with different forms of Black positionings below – thus an array from the highest White content at the top to the lowest at the bottom. This would be a good precursor for differentiation somatically based on shades of colour, as will eventually be found in the Americas where there is a creole power elite. It would also explain differentiation in citizenship in modern states based on class, race, or ethnicity, with the somatically Black proletariat at the bottom.

Indeed, even in the Greek states, everyone was not equal in terms of citizenship, and even if a citizen, citizenship did not automatically bring equality. First, citizenship came only to those with a Greek mother and father, making citizenship, as a claim of entitlement to the good of the state, directly dependent on an undiluted lineage or bloodline. Citizenship, in this case, becomes a racial characteristic as much as an ethnic one, for it presupposes that one bloodline is superior to all others and that mixing of blood can lead to contamination.

Second, citizenship in this society based strictly on functionalism, as captured in the analysis by Plato and Aristotle, does not translate into equal entitlement. Some people, based on higher and different roles in the society – which was in turn predicated on the individual's innateness to perform a role – had greater claims to the good of the society than those of an inferior rank or of a base nature. This leads to the awarding of full and second-class citizenship, with each level enjoying different privileges and entitlements, some being active participants in the society, others passively performing what is required of them. For example, women were not the equals of men in the polis. They did not, for example, participate in government, not even in the Athenian democracy. Yet, such inequality was deemed necessary for the proper functioning of this society envisioned by gods.

In Aristotle's world, some people are natural rulers; others are naturally slaves. A monarchy best typifies oligarchy, where the rule is hereditary, or, as was the case in Rome, was by the ascension of one member of the aristocratic class to the position of first among equals. As Aristotle proclaims, this is how society is naturally organized and the law administered to maintain these divisions. Men thus rule their households and lord over their wives, non-age children, and their slaves. Slaves are only useful for the master's pleasure and to help him to maintain his lifestyle. Similarly, "the relation of male to female is that of natural superior to natural inferior, and that of ruler to ruled."[11] Here, we have a clear racial definition – where the neo-mythic good and evil are translated into ethno-racial determinations at the physical and objective level.

Summarizing his point, Aristotle says that "it is evident, then, that there are some people, some of whom are naturally free, others naturally slaves, for whom slavery is both just and beneficial."[12] But the question of justice and station in life did not stop there: it extended as well to natural born nobles and the aristocrats, those who, for Aristotle, were naturally superior. These were the people that were best suited to be the full citizens and rulers of the state, for they had time, leisure, and wisdom from their natural inclination to decide matters of state. They were free of bodily desires: for they were rich and could satisfy their passions until they were satiated. Therefore, freed of the edged appetites of passions, they were likely to be more rational, and therefore be the best citizens. We may remember this differentiation when we consider how Canada selects future citizens out of the undifferentiated mass of humanity, by searching for those who are "naturally" the brightest and the best in this aboriginal state and by creating new Canadians out of them.

This was justice, as Aristotle saw it, for it was rightly based on recognized inequality produced naturally by virtues. Power, therefore, should be given to those that are naturally superior, even if they are a minority in the community. However, Aristotle recognizes the "natural" inclinations of the excluded to have power and argues for a power sharing relationship as a compromise: one where, in a semblance of democracy, the natural rulers govern in alliance with those who are not. Therefore, he acknowledges the pragmatism of a dualism, not because it was natural to the city-state, but because it was the most practical: reason would still have a chance of ruling, even if the passions in their false consciousness believed they were in control: the wise men in the ruling group would have the task of keeping the passions in check. Ontologically, power should thus be of mixed essences, making it a hybrid or composite with no singular essence, per se, and making the exercise of power existentialist Blackness.

Before Aristotle, Plato had raised some of these issues and had similarly stated that all humans were not equal. From him we can see how the elites of the ancient Greeks viewed the placement of individuals in the state and whether there could be individual social mobility in an ideal state. Plato, through Socrates, argues in *The Republic* that society exists because the individual cannot go it alone successfully: "the individual is not self-sufficient, but has many needs which he can't supply ... And when we have got hold of enough people to satisfy our many varied needs, we have assembled quite a large number of partners and helpers together to live in one place; and we give the resultant settlement the name of a community or state."[13]

In this arrangement, people produce for themselves and one another, with the virtuous man using all his talents to produce his best for the common good. Thus Plato, in asserting the rationality of self-sufficiency in a community of four people in a state that provides basic needs for its members, asks: "should the farmer provide enough food for all four of them, and devote enough time and labour to food production to provide the needs of all four? Or, alternatively, should he disregard the others, and devote a quarter of his time to producing a quarter the amount of food, and the other three quarters one to build himself a house, one to making clothes, and another to making shoes? Should he, in other words, avoid the trouble of sharing with others and devote himself to providing for his own needs only?"[14]

The answer Plato supplies is that this should not be the case, for "we have different natural aptitudes, which fit us for different jobs," and by extension different roles in society. People are to fill specific roles in society, the best roles being reserved for those suited to them by nature. There is therefore no escaping one's position, no social mobility of moving from one role to another. Roles are thus predetermined by nature, a state of being that by aptitude makes some better as slaves, some as masters, some as rulers, and some as members of a leisure class. Virtues are essences that socially determined people's Whiteness or Blackness in Plato's ideal society. Eventually, Plato's state, as it grows and prospers, would have needs for luxuries and other amenities. But as it grows, one thing would remain the same: people would be allowed to produce only what they do best, this being the formula for the creation of idealistic and cultural Whiteness: "Well, we forbade our shoemaker to try his hand at farming or weaving or building and told him to stick to his last, in order that our shoemaking should be well done. Similarly with other trades, we assigned each man to the one for which he was *naturally suited*, and which he was to practise throughout his life to the exclusion of all others, and so become good at his job and never miss the right moment for action."[15]

What is true for the craftsmen, Plato suggests, is also true for all others in their various stations of life: a soldier should be the best at soldiering; rulers are those naturally best at ruling; law keepers those naturally best at keeping the law. This is classic functionalism, based on individuals possessing assumed singular and undiluted virtues or essences that determine their roles and positions – their motility and placement – in society. Using this perception of natural virtue, the state may then "assign" a trade or positioning in society to individuals or groups based on a perceived knowledge. This formula thus determines who should be created within this idealized White space as status White and who as its opposite, status Black, and be accorded a corresponding position in the hierarchy based on the needs and desires of the state.

Aristotle seems to open the door for an element of choice, suggesting that rational beings would do what is rationally best for them, such as limiting their activities to what they do best and by putting the general interest of the community ahead of their own, as typified by the political compromise by the aristocrats in a democratic state. People, then might not be created unchangeably White or Black in status. They can move from status Blackness to status Whiteness in an unnatural development or they can move from a Black status up to a higher White one. This being the case, social mobility is idealized Whiteness based on status as it can lead to improved circumstances. Aristotle is, therefore, arguing not for a pure essence, but for an existentialist Blackness that translates into idealized Whiteness through intentions and actions. Here, then, there is an element of volition and freedom. Plato, on the other hand, imposes rigid restraints: people are allowed to do only what they produce best and are forbidden from attempting anything else. They are unchangeably Black or White in culture and status when they are created in the state. In his idealized White state based on essences, there is no personal choice. All personal activities must be for the common good only.

Plato presents another argument for the civilizing influences that come from living in a community, arguing in *The Republic* for the selective breeding and educating of a select group of citizens called the guardians and the carefully educated philosophers, who would be best suited by nature and virtue to rule. Here, again, we see concern for creation as a phenomenologically Whitening act: as bringing good and wholesomeness out of the undesirable circumstances that went before the creation. Plato argues that inequality – based only on ability and therefore not some mythical equality – should be the criteria for justice. This means a state based on each according to his worth, as defined by the ability to contribute to society. Therefore, in the Plato-Aristotle world the individual is recognized for the role she or he is best capable of performing; not for the power best held by a class of people specially selected to be rulers and free of individual ambitions.

One of the biggest points of contention was the disagreement between Plato and Aristotle over ownership of personal property. This goes to the heart of social mobility and is the anathema of social functionalism. Possession of personal goods was seen by Plato as a significant way to disrupt social order as it privileges individualism over the collective – and thus makes some people Whiter than others, or rather creates a collective poor or class that owns no property and is status Black in an idealistically White state. This would not happen because of any change in the essence of Whiteness to Blackness but because of an unnatural social construction, the idealized Blackness of property acquisition.

Once again, Plato is concerned with idealized Whiteness dying unnaturally and returning to an idealized Blackness – this time by the creation of a socially lower class of people without the new cultural Whiteness of property. Aristotle, in contrast, argues for private property, primarily to avoid dissension in society and to allow a degree of meritocracy, a reward for those who do become White whether by aptitude or nature – all of which would be allowed for the general good of society, however, and not for personal aggrandisement. He wants a natural death that leads from the decay of Blackness to a higher form that is idealized Whiteness. Aristotle was more concerned with the creation of social Whiteness through property ownership in comparison to Plato's worry that property ownership leads to a relapse into Blackness and a negation of the initial White creation that should be a perpetual order not subject to human intervention. Therefore, while property ownership for Aristotle was liberation into Whiteness and the creation of those who are really worthy of becoming White, Plato saw it as slavery, where those created White may end up being misrecognized in a false consciousness as Black in status and therefore be deemed inferior beings though they are not.

For Plato the biggest problem with wealth acquisition, therefore, was that the wealthy and poor would be alike in one respect: equally they would be producing nothing and the society would not be self-sufficient. As Plato puts it: "Then we come to the worst defect of all [in society], which makes its first appearance in this form of society ... That a man can sell all he has to another and live on as a member of society without any real function; he's neither businessman nor craftsman, nor cavalryman nor infantryman, but merely one of the so-called indigent poor."[16] Individualism would lead to a form of social mobility that was unnatural, for it would be based on personal wealth and not on natural attributes that are distributed unequally. By extension, this was an argument against the notion of merit as based on virtue, as this thinking frowned on the belief that an individual using his or her talents for personal gain did so purely out of self-interest and not for the common good of the society.

Aristotle argues that there is a basic difference between acquisition for the good of a household and the acquisition of personal wealth. One is natural and the other is not, as wealth should not be acquired simply for the status of ownership but for the leisure and quality of life that it produces for the individuals. Wealth for leisure is to be encouraged and wealth for aggrandisement discouraged. Personal wealth in the form of money that is acquired simply for its sake is unnatural because money is unlimited, abstract, and its usage can change daily. In this sense, money is conceptually an infinity with no singular essence, virtue, meaning, or purpose. It is not finite enough for a society that is clearly intended to be finite in its construction, choices, and goals. Money should be a means and not an end to a common good, Aristotle says, and human virtues are about the common good. Wealth undermines the virtues of a society. If acquisition of wealth went unchecked, individuals would spend their lives in pursuit of money, rather than in pursuit of the good life that a certain amount of money would help in achieving. Aristotle says: "For the end of courage is not to produce wealth but to produce confidence in the face of danger; nor is it the end of generalship or medicine to do so, but rather victory and health. None the less, these people make of all these into forms of wealth acquisition in the belief that acquiring wealth is the end, and that everything ought to promote the end.

"We have now said what unnecessary wealth acquisition is and why we need it. We have also said that the necessary kind is different, that it is a natural part of household management concerned with the means of life, and that it is not limitless like this one, but has a limit."[17]

As much as he feared the disruption to social life and natural order by the accumulation of property, Plato, and to a lesser extent Aristotle, also feared an ideology that they saw as capturing this disruption – democracy, especially its dialectical tendency to equality based on individualism, and linked to which is the notion of the individual's ownership of her- or himself as personal property. Plato's arguments are explicitly anti-democratic, and thus represent not the ancients as a whole, but an oppositional, aristocratic tendency in the Athenian democracy. Plato's was adamantly against popular or participatory democracy, especially the type he witnessed in Athens. This is not representative democracy, where office holders, trained in government and mindful of the gravity of making decisions, could make rational pronouncements.

Plato, speaking through Socrates, felt there was no consistency in the method of the popular government in Athens. As he saw it, on any given day decisions of state could be made simply and arbitrarily, based, in the first place, on the quality and inclinations of the people that actually turned up for the meeting, but secondly, and more significantly, because of the passions exhibited in arguments and how a passionate orator could prey on the fickleness of the listeners and, ultimately, decision-makers. For him, participatory democracy was not rational and deliberative, but primarily responsive to sensory perception and to an inferior intuitive perception because of the social standing and qualities of the majority. It was in this context that he likened the statesman to the ship's captain, inaugurating all the metaphors about the "ship of state." Plato maintains that the natural form of government, oligarchy representing status and cultural Whiteness, gives way to democracy when it is corrupted, especially by individualism, "as a result of lack of restraint in the pursuit of its [individualism's] objective of getting rich as quickly as possible ... Because the rulers, owing their power to wealth as they do, are unwilling to curtail by law the extravagance of the young, and prevent them squandering their money and ruining themselves; for it is by loans to such spendthrifts or by buying up their property that they hope to increase their own wealth and influence."[18]

This concept is similar to that of modernity's one-drop-of-blood rule that Blackness is the corruption, even in the most minute manner, of pure White, with individualism being the one drop of blood. The problem for Plato is that democracy means freedom or liberty, and bound up in this idea is the notion that people can escape their station in life and that even the vulgar poor and uneducated might aspire to rule. Further, because the majority of citizens are uneducated and uncouth, that is, Black in culture in terms of not being aristocratic and noble, the majority is always likely to be swayed by orators and the best speakers, rather than by knowledge and careful consideration. They are likely to be irrational. Indeed, Plato mocked democratic rule in Athens, the one Greek state where it was practised consistently. He laughed at the drawing of lots from a pool representing a fair cross-section of Athenians to decide rulers and judges and at the gathering of large numbers of people to vote on state matters.

In *The Republic*, with palpable sarcasm, Plato tells the story of a ship at sea – thereby developing the metaphor of ship of state – and asks if it made more sense for all the oarsmen, in full individual liberty, to row in whichever direction they pleased or to row in one direction under the sage knowledge of a captain. Indeed, Plato's discussion of what happens on this ship of state betrays not only his thoughts on the importance of knowledge but also on the "uncivilized" manner in which business would be conducted if left to the rabble. The overzealous oarsmen are no different in behaviour and the need for a restraining hand than the Black horse of another tale. He argues:

The crew are all quarrelling with each other about how to navigate the ship, each thinking he ought to be at the helm; they have never learned the art of navigation and cannot say that anyone ever taught it them, or that they spent any time studying it; indeed they say it can't be taught and are ready to murder anyone who says it can. They spend all their time milling round the captain and doing all they can to get him to give them the helm. If one faction is more successful than another, their rivals may kill them and throw them overboard, lay out the honest captain with drugs or drink or in some other way, take control of the ship, help themselves to what's on board, turn the voyage into the sort of drunken pleasure-cruise you would expect. Finally, they reserve their admiration for the man who knows how to lend a hand in controlling the captain by force or fraud; they praise his seamanship and navigation and knowledge of the sea and condemn everyone else as useless.[19]

The result, as Plato sees it, is sheer anarchy and chaos – so similar to what happens when in another Socratic story the Black horse of unreason gets its way – in place of the natural order of government, the type that in

*Phaedrus* Plato praises for its reasonableness and predictability. Moving to the allegory of a ship of state is only a short distance from Plato's thought about the horses and the chariot. Both the ship and the chariot are on a journey with a clear teleological ending. There is a cosmological good that must be maintained.

And this, Plato argues, can only be achieved if reason is in control, rather than the passions, whether these passions be represented by the idealized Blackness of human bodies, the somatic Blackness of the unruly horse, or the cultural and status Blackness of a majority of people, of the lowest classes, swayed by passion and not reason. The goal can be achieved only in a lordship and bondage relation with the society's virtuous few as the lords and rulers and the unreasoning majority held in bondage for the good of the entire society.

How then could there be justice based on unnatural ability – based on recognition of individuality and common citizenship only? Indeed, Plato paints a very contrasting picture of rule by the philosophers, as idealized Whiteness. Through a life of leisure and elitism, philosophers "have the capacity to grasp the eternal and immutable, while those who have no such capacity are not philosophers and are lost in multiplicity and change, which of the two should be in charge of a state?"[20] Natural government for Plato would be class based, an administration by those elites who would have had the training and the time and leisure to be trained.

As Plato argues, democracy is good for diversity, "like the different colours in a patterned dress, making it look very attractive," but on closer examination it is a chimera, something to attract women and children with bright colours that are ephemeral and illusionary. The colours they see are not the real, but a pale copy. The truth is hidden from them by the various hues and the Hegelian "darknesses" that obscure pure light. For humans would see the beauty and the sublime in any pattern – and by extension the flaws in a democratic government based on diversity – if they were free of bodily pleasures and could see the goodness of rationalism, like the gods who are governed by reason. They would see that the colours are not equal in their beauty, and that a democratic government is not just. Democratic government based on this diversity is undeliberated reason, making it merely perception.

Aristotle is in agreement with Plato that democracy can be a perversion of good government, but only if it is based on the protection of power and not on justice and a common good, the White order that was good as intended naturally by the gods and by humans. For example, democracy can be a perversion in a situation where the majority owns property and the minority is poor. Then the majority would simply be a tyranny in a democracy if they rule so as to protect their property rather than to create a situation that is for the good of all in society: the few have authority in oligarchies and many in democracies, a result of the fact that everywhere the rich are few and the poor are many ... What does distinguish democracy and oligarchy from one another is poverty and wealth: whenever some, whether a minority or a majority, rule because of their wealth, the constitution is necessarily an oligarchy, and whenever the poor rule, it is necessarily a democracy. But it turns out, as we said, that the former are in fact few and the latter many. For only a few people are rich, but all share in freedom; and these are the reasons they both dispute over the constitution."[21]

In general, however, Aristotle is more willing to allow individuals personal freedom in his ideal state that is ideally a plural one and, in this regard, he disagrees with Plato's suggestion that private and family property should be abolished. Aristotle gives the following reasons for his disagreement with his teacher: the abolition of private property would create communal rule with the aim of making all citizens absolutely alike in an attempt to create a unitary state. Yet, as Aristotle argues, Plato's state, even while trying to eliminate differences, would be based on functionalism in which people are placed according to their different natures and virtues. This would create a contradiction in purpose. More so, Aristotle notes that there is a virtue in diversity in a city-state, and indeed, that it is because of this diversity itself and the need to protect plurality that it is necessary to create a state in the first place: "It is evident that the more of a unity a city-state becomes, the less of a city-state it will be. For a city-state naturally consists of a certain multitude; and as it becomes more of a unity, it will turn from a city-state into a household, and from a household into a human being ... Hence, even if someone could achieve this, it should not be done, since it will destroy the city-state."[22]

Another argument that Aristotle raises for individualism is that private property can help alleviate dissension among members of the state. There is little interest by members of the society to take care of collective property, "since what is held in common by the largest number of people receives the least care. For people give most attention to their own property, less to what is communal, or only as much as falls to them to give."[23] Aristotle uses this same argument to discredit the Platonic idea that men should share women as common property and that children should be fathered in this way. Such a development, Aristotle says, would destroy natural affections in the family between wives, children, and fathers.

Aristotle suggests that it would be best to allow individuals to own private property, including abstract ones such as money and affections, primarily because humans are selfish. This is to be expected "for the love each person feels for himself is no accident, but is something natural." Second, people are happy when they own property privately and are able to generously share it with friends, rather that having joint ownership of property to encourage the equal welfare of all members.[24] Finally, Aristotle argues that it is only through education, and not by enforced cohesion, such as the abolition of property and the provision of strict moral laws, that a diverse group of people can be made into an effective city-state.[25]

Thus, making a strong case for the individual and private choices in an ideal state, Aristotle proposes different ways of making a determination within the state of who should be adjudged to belong to specific rankings in the society, who should be among the elites and who, as Plato says, should be the indigent or Black in status. Society, therefore, must be deliberative, and this comes in a democracy where there is a trading-off of positions and powers, reflecting an intended commonality of all society's diverse elements.

The difference between Aristotle and Plato will become even more acute as we consider the primary issue in making the first determination of elites or Whiteness: this is the matter of citizenship, of who should be entitled to belong to the state, to have entitlements, and to assist in the state's administration. We shall now turn to a discussion on this issue and how the classical Greeks, through their mythology and philosophy, discussed issues of belonging in the state – of who can be included and made White, and who should be left out and left Black, both culturally and in status, with the rest of humanity. Within this discussion, the chief question I shall deal with is whether or not there is evidence of some classical Greeks having felt it possible for Blacks to become White after the cosmological creation has begun and Blackness and Whiteness have already been defined philosophically and politically.

### IDEALIZED BLACKNESS:
### CITIZENS AND STRANGERS

Mainstream Greek mythology has many stories about new beginnings that forced members of the same family, group, clan, or state to make hard choices. Often they are about the inclusion or exclusion of an Other who comes from outside the limits of the grouping, or of all the Others that are various minorities in a diverse group of citizens. This is the process for turning Blackness, in terms of culture and status, into idealized forms of Whiteness that have already been defined cosmologically.

Often, these stories are also about immigrants and refugees, those who must seek out and explore a new land where they will have to confront the devils of the unknown and unfamiliar. In these stories, somatic and phenotypic Blackness or Whiteness is seldom an issue of moral or ethical significance. These are stories about the dialectics of hope and despair, of being seen hopefully as a potential ally and even a missing member of the group, or the despair of being tricked into willingly accepting a tyrant and even death from without. Epistemologically, it is the hope that comes from realizing that intuitive and sensory perceptions are the same as deliberative reason, or the fear that reason will prove them to be false consciousnesses at best and even ignorance at worse.

The migrants in these stories are leaving a world of cultural and status Blackness, from among the barbarians in Greek mythology, with the hope of living in the Whiteness of a specific civil society.[26] Usually, they must make a journey so that they can learn about themselves, about the lands they enter, about Nature and uncivilized time, and about what transformations are necessary for them to become White. In this way, they become conscious of their difference – for example, ethnically, culturally, or religiously – from others. In most cases, they end up as strangers in a strange land, Blacks in a White man's country, unsure of their abilities to understand the customs of the people and the dictates of Nature. The only consolation they can hold onto in these journeys is the faith that it would be folly of a receiving people to harm or reject a stranger without giving the foreigner a chance to prove his or her worth.

To not give such a chance is to risk mistaking Whiteness for Blackness, and vice versa, based solely on sensory perception, and to therefore risk that the stranger is actually a superhuman in disguise, and capable of inflicting untold harm and damage if offended. The stranger thus became symbolic of the Blackness of Nature that is the epistemologically unknown, an absence of knowledge that creates problems for discerning what social and ethical relations the society should have with the stranger. For what is perceived as Black could be, in essence, White. But how was anyone to know who was essentially good or evil?

This was an enigma of knowing for the Greeks. Homer tells of Odysseus returning home, dressed as a stranger, indeed even in the rags of a beggar, the ultimate in cultural and social Blackness for that time.[27] This stranger is not recognised. He is not allowed to claim what is justly his, whether his property, his life, or the affections of his wife, the woman that is symbolically at the heart of his culture. This stranger is underestimated, and rejected: exemplifying the limits of epistemology and knowledge. As a result, the elites or those living off the fat of the land and unjustly consuming that to which they are not entitled, suffer the wrath of the stranger and are justly slaughtered. Other times, the mythology tells us the newcomer instead appears as an indigent, but carries in the womb or in the genes the materials that would make the stranger the mother or father of the deliverer, of the one who would liberate humanity from all physical hardships that blight human existence and even from the ultimate bondage, death itself.

These are categories of people that should unchangeably be part of a state that is committed to the good of such liberty and to all people who share this goal. Such people would be strangers only by accident of birth and socialization, and otherwise, essentially, members of the state. At the same time, *The Iliad of Homer* tells several stories of bad people who appeared as good, and therefore White, but turned out to be the opposite.[28] Such is the story behind the Trojan horse. These are all stories of the stranger as possible death or Blackness: the death of the Subject that confronts this unknown and unidentified being; or as the Messiah or saviour, the arrival of a White carrier that would usher in the era when death shall be no more and tears shall cease to flow, death having been vanquished.

In the first case, this would be the experience of a Blackness that remains the Blackness of death for elites and their contemplative life of leisure. In the second case, it is the story of Blackness that becomes Whiteness, which supports and preserves the life of elitism and leisure by freeing humans from the bodily constraints of having to work and produce and, eventually, of dying. In the third way of viewing this example, it is the story of Whiteness that is, in effect, Black in accidental disguise: if as it turns out the stranger is really an agent of good and not, as originally perceived, of evil. From these three examples, the limits of epistemology can have negative or positive effects. Only the context will decide which is good and which is evil. The ethical question for a Subject was therefore how to treat a stranger who might not be what she or he appears or claims to be. How to know whether the stranger is good or evil?

In *Laws*, Plato captures a specific approach by classical Greeks to strangers. But Plato is ambivalent at best, in viewing the stranger as marginally good or White. At worst, he is xenophobic, viewing homogenizing strangers as innately inferior, backward, immoral, and Black. On one hand, he states that the gods protect strangers in much the same way that they protect citizens of his ideal state;[29] but on the other hand, he would not allow foreigners to have permanence or full entitlement in his ideal state. They would not have entitlement, for example, to the leisure life of retirement, to partaking of the ambrosia and draughts of nectar that are the just rewards, as he explains in *Phaedrus*, for the deserving, for those who successfully arrive at the end of an arduous, rational, and controlled life.

Plato suggests that the ideal state should be formed out of a social contract of sorts along ethnic lines and that the agreement, in respect to such things as property rights, should be consecrated by an oath before the divine. This would make the state, by analogy, as good as if it were produced cosmologically. The ideal state should thus be based on the rule of law and the respect of agreed contracts. The limited rights of foreigners should then be protected in civil society in the same way that God in Nature protects them. "For Zeus the god of common clanship is witness to one of these sanctities, Zeus protector of the stranger to the other, and when the wrath of these powers is awakened, deadliest hostilities ensue."[30]

To this end, the rights of citizens and foreigners should be recognized as legitimate, but they should also be seen as separate and distinct from those before the construction of the state and as God had ordained them. In *Laws*, Plato seems more intent on a social contract among members of the same clan, the freeborn and aristocratic who were Greek by birth and lineage. He was very clear that strangers and immigrants should not become citizens. Indeed, Plato is emphatic that immigrants and their children should be forced to leave after a fixed period of time: "Remember that they (immigrants) will not, as a rule, live to an old age among us, or make themselves a nest where others of their own type will be bred up to be naturalized in our country."[31] To avoid this happening, Plato suggests that foreigners should be handled in a manner that befits their status as outsiders. In ethical relations, they should be positioned as inferior. Having taken such a position, Plato is thus proposing that the ethical relations governing immigrants be based epistemologically primarily on perception, with little cognition, of the affectivity and motility of the stranger.

Any foreigner who pleases may become a resident in the country on certain express conditions. It shall be understood that we offer home to any alien who desires to take up his abode with us and is able to do so, but he must have a craft, and his residence must not be prolonged more than twenty years from the date of his registration. He shall pay no personal dues as an alien, however small, beyond good behaviour, and no toll on the transaction of sale and purchase, and when the period of his stay has expired, he shall take his property with him on his departure. Should it be his good fortune, during this period, to have distinguished himself by some signal service to the state, and have hopes of satisfying the council and assembly of his claim to an official prorogation of his departure, or even to lifelong residence, he may appear and plead his case, and any claims of which he can convince the state shall receive full satisfaction. For the children of such aliens, providing they posses a handicraft and have reached an age of fifteen, the period of residence shall be computed from their fifteenth year. When one of them who fulfils these conditions has completed his twenty years, he shall depart whither he pleases, or if he prefers to remain, he must obtain permission as already provided for. At a man's departure, the entries which previously stood against his name in the magistrates' register shall be cancelled.[32]

This means that strangers would be chosen to stay in the state based on a specific virtue or essence but would never be effectively integrated or assimilated into the idealized Greek state. They would have rights and entitlements, but these would not be of the same level as those of native-born Greeks. Ontologically, foreigners enter the state as inferior, and they will be most useful solely as producers and workers. They will never be allowed into the leisure class of contemplation. The most effective use of their body will be to produce more producers and inferior people. Existentially, happiness for them is merely to exist, even if in an inferior relationship, in a state that is superior to their native homeland. Epistemologically, their bodies would therefore always remain Black and outside of the collective consciousness.

Indeed, in his proposed model, later to be modified in political thought as *jus sanguinis* that privileges the bloodline in citizenship, Plato is excluding from citizenship children born in Greece to non-citizens. He is rejecting the notion of citizenship that would later be called *jus soli*, a version of which was supported by Aristotle, where simply any child born in the sacred time and place that is the recognized state can claim citizenship. The latter model also provides for non-nationals to acquire citizenship by learning the culture. Under *jus sanguinis*, Whiteness remains incorrigible, unchangeable, and immutable in a unitary state. *Jus soli*, by definition all that is not *jus sanguinis*, is a Whiteness that allows admixture of Blackness to create an off-White through the blackening of the pure. Idealistically, in a very diverse and plural society, the kind that was defended by Aristotle, *jus soli* could be entirely Black. As we shall see, there are significant traces of this thinking in Canadian immigration policy at the beginning of the new millennium as Canada searches for new citizens from among strangers who are by virtue "the brightest and best" and determines whether they are entitled to full Canadian citizenship.

Plato's views, ever those of an aristocrat, were in keeping with those of official Greece. This was the case even in "democratic" Athens, which Plato criticized repeatedly for the limits on citizenship entitlements that Athens placed on aristocracy and for the powers it gave to some of the lower classes. In *The Origins of Citizenship in Ancient Athens,* Philip Brook Manville states that the Athenian democracy took the notion of citizenship as an infinity very seriously and did not debate lightly the limits, boundaries, and responsibilities of citizenship:

The analogous term for citizenship in Greek (politeia) can have similar legal (passive) and social (active) meaning, but it is much less easy to draw distinction between them. That is because the status of membership in the Athenian community could not really be separated from the role the citizen played in it; politeia appears in text as "the condition and rights of a citizen" but also as "the daily life of the citizen," with both senses often implied at the same time. For the classical period, it is difficult to talk about a purely "passive" meaning of politeia, that is, as an abstract legal status, because Greek citizenship was defined by the active participation of citizens in public life. An illustration of this often-stated point is provided by the procedures outlined in Athenian decrees granting citizenship to foreigners. In the fifth and fourth centuries, all such decrees, even those only "honorary," always included the proviso that the recipient be enrolled in a tribe and a deme, the membership corporation that (after the Kleisthenic reforms of 508/7) comprised the bodies of actual and practical involvement in the state.[33]

Manville argues that Athenian citizenship was based on a ranking, first, among native and non-native, and then on another ranking within the polis between the aristocratic and the poor, and between males and females. This is what I call the double determination of the elites that leads to a privileging of social Whiteness. Manville adds: "Except for the small percentage of foreigners granted Athenian citizenship by decree (which entailed its own criteria and formal procedures), the citizens of the polis were native Athenian males who had reached the age of eighteen, and who had been duly registered in the same local Attic village unit, or deme, to which their fathers belonged. That registration embodied a formal and multistepped process. Candidates were scrutinized by fellow demesmen to ensure that they were eighteen, freeborn, and legitimate with regard to the lawful marriage of two Athenian parents."[34]

Indeed, all demes were not equal and even within these groups individuals were ranked differently. Excluded from membership in these exclusive clubs were foreigners, resident aliens, and slaves. For example, foreigners could not marry Athenian women, could not own land, and needed a licence to conduct trade. Those who wanted to remain permanently in the state had to pay a yearly tax, but even then were still prevented from marrying an Athenian. However, residents were required to do military service and to pay taxes. Slaves were treated as property and could be bought and sold. Native Athenian women could claim citizenship but only "through their relationship with a father, husband, or other male relative who acted as their master and guardian in all important affairs." Athenian women could neither own nor inherit property. Male children of two citizens, as Manville suggests, were treated like Athenian women until they came of age.[35]

Plato acknowledges that it would be impossible for his ideal state not to have trade and diplomatic contact with foreign countries. While he could accept within limits trade, diplomacy, and travel for tourism, he could not agree to the full mixing of people in a common citizenship. Mixing would undermine the rights and entitlements of citizens.

Now free intercourse between different states has the tendency to produce all manner of admixture of characters, as the itch for innovation is caught by host from visitor or visitor from host. Now this may result in the most detrimental consequences to a society where public life is sound and controlled by right laws, though in most communities, where the laws are far from what they should be, it makes no real difference that the inhabitants should welcome the foreign visitor and blend with him, or take a jaunt into another state themselves, as and when the fancy of travel takes hold of them, young or old. On the other side, to refuse all admission to the foreigner and permit the native no opportunity of foreign travel is, for one thing, not always possible, and, for another, may earn a state a reputation for barbarism and inhumanity with the rest of the world; its citizens will be thought to be adopting the ill-sounding policy of exclusion of aliens and developing a repulsive and intractable character.[36]

In keeping with his view, even in the construction of states, mixing of essences and virtues is undesirable as a social good. Plato does not want a society that is a social composite, with differences and diversity within, instead of the idealistic purity that he thought Nature intended. Similarly, Plato's analysis betrays deep suspicions about foreigners and immigrants and their ability to not only corrupt physically through bloodlines, but culturally through the moral debasement of citizens. This is particularly true of those immigrants who are not in control of their passions – one of the requirements for functioning effectively as a citizen in Plato's idealized society. This society would thus run according to a very strict morality code.

I say it is the law's simple duty to go straight on its way and tell our citizens that it is not for them to behave worse than birds and many other creatures which flock together in large bodies. Until the age of procreation these creatures live in continence and unspotted virginity; when they have reached that age, they pair together, the male with the female and the female with the male their preference dictates, and they live thereafter in piety and justice, steadfastly true to their contract of first love. Surely you, we shall say, ought to be better than the beasts. But if, alas, they should be corrupted by the example of the great mass of other Greeks and of non-Greeks as they learn from their eyes and ears how all-powerful so-called free love is among all, and should fail to win the victory, I would have our curators of law turn legislators and contrive a second law [to shame citizens into controlling their lust and sexual indulgences].[37]

Aristotle takes a different tack on the issue of citizenship, culture, and morality. He notes that in many states foreigners hold office and are subject to the laws of the land. He argues for a simple definition: "someone who is eligible to participate in deliberative and judicial office is a citizen in this city-state, and ... a city-state, simply speaking, is a multitude of such people, adequate for life's self-sufficiency."[38] Aristotle acknowledges that this definition is useful primarily because it is workable and practical. For example, he notes that it was tradition to decide Greek citizenship based on whether both parents of the child were Greek. But Aristotle says such a definition creates problems: "Some people look for more here too, going back, for example, two or three or more generations of ancestors. But quick political definitions of this sort lead some people to raise the problem of how these third- or fourth-generation ancestors will be citizens ... For 'what comes from a citizen father and mother' cannot be applied to even the first inhabitants or founders (of the city-state)."[39]

There is also an even bigger problem than defining the fidelity of citizenship based on lineage and blood as Aristotle states: this is the matter of how to decide citizenship in the practical sense if the city-state is founded after a revolution or a radical change and must include people that were previously slaves and foreigners, how to fill offices of state with those worthy to hold such offices at a time of population decline, and how to recognize and reward non-citizens holding office in the state. For Aristotle, citizenship is dependent on the peoples' will to live together in a state. It does not have much to do with the location of the state, how many people live in the state, who founded the state, and whether the state is split over more than one jurisdiction. Maintaining that the ideal state must be diverse by incorporating those who subscribe to the aims of the state, Aristotle argues, in a radical departure from Plato, that citizenship should be as changeable and as flexible as the people within the state, and that there can be no essence to the state, even if it may have a socially constructed virtue and social good as its goal. As he asks rhetorically:

But when the same people are inhabiting the same place, is the city-state to be called the same as long as the inhabitants remain of the same stock, even though all the time some are dying and others are being born (just as we are accustomed to say that rivers and springs remain the same, even though all the time some water is flowing out and some flowing in)? Or are we to say that human beings can remain the same for this sort of reason, but the city-state is different. For if indeed a city-state is a sort of community, a community of citizens sharing a constitution, then, when the constitution changes its form and becomes different, it would seem that the city-state too cannot remain the same. At any rate, a chorus that is at one time a comedy and at another in a tragedy is said to be two different choruses, even though the human beings in it are often the same. Similarly, with any other community or composite: we say it is different if the form of the composite is different ... But the name to call it may be different or the same one whether its inhabitants are the same or completely different people.[40]

However, Aristotle suggests that since there are several different types of political constitutions and states there should be several different forms and levels of citizenship according to the nature of the state. Some, who might be granted citizenship under one constitution, and even because of a specific economic context, might not be granted citizenship in another. This is particularly the case, he says, for democracies that admit some foreigners, and children whose mothers only are citizens, and children whose parents are not married. Democracies should decide on the citizenship that is

best suited to their particular situation, rather than make citizenship conform to previously agreed ideals. In this case, the process of granting citizenship should be open, which is not always the case when elites see other
people as their means, or simply have a need for them, to maintain their
existing way of life. Aristotle points out the hypocrisy of such an approach:
"Nevertheless, since it is because of a shortage of legitimate citizens that
they make such people citizens (for it is because of under population that
they employ laws in this way), when they are supplied with a crowd of
them, they gradually disqualify, first, those who have a slave as a father or
mother, then those with citizen mothers, until finally they make citizens
only of those who came from citizens on both sides as citizens."[41]

Such arrangements are exercises in deception, Aristotle says, for some
citizens would be of lower status than others. Indeed, some so-called citizens would effectively be "disenfranchised aliens" because they are intentionally and deliberately excluded from the honours and consciousness of
the state. In practice, despite the rhetoric of equality, some citizens would
be no better than strangers or aliens. When the elites or the privileged class
conceals such exclusions, the aim is to deceive their fellow inhabitants in
the state.[42] This issue of deception also gestures to the kind of ethical relations that can reasonably be expected in the state whether it is diverse or
unitary, which brings us to our next question.

Leaving now the differences between those who belong and those who
should be excluded, we may next ask, What should be the ethical relationship between individual citizens, and between the state and individual citizens? Greek mythology dealt with such social relations by telling stories of
warring brothers: the most unlikely of enemies, who in a seeming fit of
madness or chaos, kill one another. This is the tragedy of how brothers
become strangers to one another, either in thought or action, for being of
the same flesh and blood, they should have no difficulty recognizing one
another. They are not an entirely unknown quantity. Indeed, they are the
closest thing to a copy of each other, being essentially of the same essence:
but a copy that might still be deceptive and inauthentic; a copy that philosophically can be at best only a copy in a world of expected absolutes, finality, hierarchies, and valorization.

Importantly, they may be copies that do not share a common essence or
virtue, who can be determined differently based on their social constructions as individuals and on their intentions and actions. Even if there is idealized Whiteness in a state, might Blackness not still exist in the way that
members treat one another, and in their behaviour in general? Epistemologically, in terms of Whiteness, can everything be known about two or
more people who perceptually share everything in common – with a degree
of certainty that would allow for a confident prediction of their future
behaviour?

Greek mythology suggests that even brothers can be strangers, for in the end who can be trusted with absolute certainty? Who can one have absolute faith in for the protection of one's life and property – with the things that bring meaning to an individual's life, rather than to a collective interest that resides in the family or the community? And if this is true of those sharing a common bloodline, what can be said of those related only constitutionally and by design? This is a story that questions the adequacy of knowledge to determining what is good and bad and as the basis for a moral code of personal behaviour and ethical relations. Knowledge, the mythology suggests, is still unknowing and unknowable. Any order or society constructed on knowledge and certain recognition is suspect and fatally flawed, and will be unnatural. This raises the question of justice and its entitlement, especially in regards to those considered to be Others in a pattern of knowledge already constructed by a Subject.

These tensions were typified by the choices outlined in the Sophoclean play *Antigone,* when two brothers took up arms against each other in a battle to decide who should rule the coveted land.[43] The main theme of *Antigone* is the choice the sister, as a member of the immediate family, had to make over the question of honouring a brother deemed dishonourable by the state. Which limits should she observe: those of the state or of her family? Which limits and boundaries were natural? As a member of the family, and particularly in Hegel's analysis as the handmaiden of divinity, Antigone should have been bound by a code that suggested she place her family before the state. This was the "natural" or White order that should have had priority for her and she should have been willing to violate only at her detriment. She did and paid the supreme price for this decision.

But I think there is another issue in this tragedy: what is the commitment of the nation or state to the man or woman, who, in making a *choice* for the state, sacrifices his or her old self to maintain the state and help it prosper? This is the situation of someone who is Black in culture and status making a choice to become White, and what freedoms the individual should have to carry out this transformation. The state is a different construction of order compared to the family, but, as Aristotle argues, it is still a natural order. Yet, at the same time, it is constructed, unlike the family, and is therefore not automatic for everyone and is based on exercised choices. It must be constructed at a specific moment, for it must be purposely brought into consciousness. In the family, individuals, as siblings, are born into Whiteness – this unchangeable ethical relationship with family members.

The family is nature expressed ethno-racially through biology and is choiceless as determined on this register. But in *Antigone* we are looking at a different method for achieving Whiteness, one that is not based on the naturalism of being determined White by family or lineage and translating this

Whiteness into power and entitlement in the state, but rather a Whiteness that is based on the natural virtues and abilities of individuals, regardless of their lineage, and produces a creolized type of belonging and entitlement. In the latter case, acceptance and belonging is based on the innate ability of the individual to contribute, function, and sacrifice herself or himself for the collective. Let us remember that this is the Whiteness that Antigone rejected, but a Whiteness that is the ideal of the state. Put another way, Antigone and the state saw each other's Whiteness as idealized Blackness. Important to this discussion is that they are reacting to the same event or ethical imperative – yet they see the event through seemingly different lenses, as White according to one perspective and Black from the other.

What happens in the public sphere of the state is distinctly different from what can be expected in the private sphere of the family. Perspectives and social positions matter to the determination of good and idealized Whiteness. In the state, members are brought into Whiteness, primarily through consent in the way they express their desires. Idealistically and ontologically, Whiteness has to be brought out of Blackness and, philosophically, choices entail moral and ethical responsibilities and consequences. In terms of the family, this is an argument that applies, at most, to the level of the extended family, which is a composite of the national and the constructed or adopted, and how the individual can be rewarded and reconciled in an area of activity that is beyond the family and is governed by different rules.

Responsibilities to, and from, the state are different from those to and for the family: the state is neo-mythically determined, the family biologically so on the ethno-racial register. Responsibilities and commitment to the state must be constructed and reconstructed moment to moment, unlike those of the family, which are conferred once and always on the individual, and begin with birth and extend to the dead. The main consequence of not acting responsibly towards the state is the chaos of Blackness that is the ruin of the state and a return to a state of nature and chaos. Whiteness is achieved through acting, and this is true even for those who by *jus sanguinis* have been born into the state: Ethical goodness is not solely belonging, but acting in defence of the good, and identifying with the good through works. For as we see in the Antigone tragedy, that the two brothers were born into a particular state is not as important as their intentions and good will towards the state and for what it stands. Theirs is the story of determining the true patriots, the soldiers and workers in daily living, including those who are willing to die for a good that did not come naturally to them at birth, but to which they have wilfully chosen to belong, that to which they have transferred allegiance and good intentions. This is an issue that we shall bear in mind when we are thinking of modern citizens whose attachment to the state is by choice, particularly the choice of an immigrant.

The state's promise was quite clear in *Antigone*: those that sacrifice themselves in the service of the state will be rewarded and honoured; those that raise their hands against the state or harm it will be excluded, banished, and dishonoured even in death. It will be as if the latter were never born, so excluded will they be: they will be segregated into the memory of the damned, where, in fact, there is no memory. Metaphorically, they will be exterminated and returned to the Blackness of non-being. What should the state do when its loyalties clash with those of the family or private interests? Who should be the judge of White and Black when there is a clash between ideals of Whiteness and Blackness? For the tragedy of this case is that there is a no single definition of Whiteness and Blackness, or of evil and good. Indeed, there are polar differences in perception and cognition: what the state says is Black, the family calls White; what the state calls White, the family calls Black. There is a radical difference in perspective.

Such is the dilemma not only for Antigone, but also for her uncle Creon, the King, who has a public task of ensuring the survival of the state. At the expense of making them violate family traditions, the state imposed a different and perhaps higher calling on the combatants and on itself. Let us remember, too, that the action required by the state is a public bodily one, not the private reflection of an idea, but something done in the public sphere and not in the privacy of home and hearth. This was a promise, as Plato says, that was witnessed by the gods. Therefore, under the highest possible obligation in the culture, the king had to keep his word to the two brothers and to society: one brother to honour as culturally White and the other to deem disreputable or culturally Black, while preserving the state even at the cost of destroying his family. The king could act only one way and be culturally, idealistically, and most importantly, ethically White. This was so even if the king, as a member of the Antigone family, had a different personal perspective from the one required by the office he held. In his capacity as king, he could only be a Black member – now called a Black sheep – of the personal family. An alternative would be for the king to declare, as would be done today, a conflict of interest, acknowledging his Blackness and indeterminacy – a course of action that in the idealized Blackness of living in a specific time was open to neither king nor traitor, uncle nor sister, if they were to be true citizens.

Ontologically and epistemologically, this is yet another story of the eternal struggle between goodness and evil, between Black and White – a struggle that starts with the very perception of what is what, and how different groups may have different perceptions and perspectives in a diverse society. This is the ontological and epistemological challenge of Whiteness and Blackness. However, there is an equally challenging problem ontologically, epistemologically, and ethically even if there *is* agreement on definitions of Whiteness and Blackness: what is the process for turning Blackness into

Whiteness and what can be discerned in terms of affectivity and motility of those going through the actual transformation? We shall now turn to these issues, and to the ethical relations that might ensue from an analysis of the process of Whitening Blackness or Blackening Whiteness.

## ARISTOTLE AND DEATH: BEYOND PERISHING

Conventional Greek mythology treats death as the end of one experience and the beginning of another. It is a liminal point. Epistemologically, death is the entering of Blackness, the limits of knowledge and consciousness, the other and unconscious part of the conceptual existence of being. The person moves from the real or finite world into the ethereal, which, cosmologically, is at the bottom of an axis that begins with heaven on the top and the world of human experience as the intermediary. This human world exists in time and is supposedly working towards its teleological natural ending as specified by the gods or whoever is the master of earthly fate. Human beings are caught in time: that of the universe and that of the personal. The mythology also suggests there are times when gods come to earth and live as humans, die and go to the ethereal world, and then return to their places of residence.

However, for human beings determined on the ethno-racial register physical death is the ultimate tragedy, the end of time, when the god of death, Thanatos, ends personal time. Since humans tend not to enjoy justice in their time, are they likely to find it when they have been transformed into the non-physical? Does their death mean that injustice will always prevail? If they do not get justice when they are determined dominantly by the ethno-racial register, will they get it when they slip into a Blackness of becoming and determination of the neo-mythic? Aristotle and others of his time suggest that humans can triumph over injustice, the tragedy of the gods, not only by going to another world that is just, but by maintaining a legacy in the one from which they have departed. They can remain alive in this world through family and friends, through a legacy or trace in the community. This is a filial justice based mainly on external expressions of subjectivity. As Aristotle says in *The Nicomachean Ethics*:

If we are to look to the end, and congratulate a man when dead not as actually being blessed, but because he has been blessed in the past, surely it is strange if at the actual time when a man is happy that fact cannot be truly predicated of him, because we are unwilling to call the living happy owing to the vicissitudes of fortune, and owing to our conception of happiness as something permanent and not readily subject to change, whereas the wheel of fortune often turns full circle in the same person's experience. For it is clear that if we are to be guided by fortune, we shall often have to call the same man first happy and then miserable; we shall make out the happy man to be a sort of "chameleon," or a house built on the sand.[44]

For Aristotle, the question of what is the true legacy of the individual matters because, ultimately, the only thing that is lasting about an individual is his or her virtue, for this is what the individual contributes to the supremely happy. The individual who is noble and virtuous makes the best of whatever is given him or her, whether it be a general facing defeat but deploying his or soldiers to make the most of the circumstances, or an individual battling life's misfortunes and one day to be claimed by them. Aristotle makes the distinction ethno-racially and in an objective way between something to be praised and something to be honoured. Praise is reserved for human actions, not for that of gods. Thus, individuals may be praised for specific virtues, for example bravery, strength, and being fleet of foot, all of which are judged by human standards. Honour is reserved for the gods, and is to be considered neo-mythically. Aristotle thus notes that "no one praises happiness as one praises justice, but we call it 'a blessing,' deeming it something higher and more divine than things we praise."[45] He comments further: "We may draw the conclusion from the foregoing remarks, that happiness is a thing honoured and perfect. This seems to be borne out by the fact that it is a first principle or starting point, since all other things that all men do are done for its sake; and that which is the first principle and cause of things good we agree to be something honourable and divine."[46]

There are three points to carry forward from this section: First, Aristotle privileges happiness over justice in this world as a goal in itself; so that if an individual's life is filled with misfortune, but he or she remains resolutely happy, that individual has contributed to the social good of society; he or she has triumphed in his or her time. Second, in the face of such misfortune, one would have to be a god to remain happy, and this is an implication of Aristotle's: either happiness is a gift of the gods or the happy person is, indeed, a human-god. Third, recognizing and remembering the contribution of those who lived, suffered, and died, all in the quest of happiness, society is elevating such departed to godlike status.

Thus, there is in fact justice after life and the evil gods do not triumph in the end. There will be reconciliation: humans can achieve happiness in their lifetime and justice in the hereafter by bestowing happiness on those coming after them. Justice – and happiness – can thus be attained. Whiteness is therefore accomplished idealistically through the existential Blackness that is death. And happiness, therefore, is a feature of idealism to be attained in the transcendent. Happiness, of which justice is a mere part, is thus to be measured on the neo-mythic register, an act that according to the prevailing Greek thought as exemplified by Aristotle privileges the neo-mythic register of becoming over the ethno-cultural of being. In other words, this is the dominant view that will inform Western thought, where death is the evil represented by finite limits ethno-racially, but a good marking new beginnings and possible justice on the neo-mythic register. However, on either register death is Black and the return is to Blackness – even if the reasons and values might be radically different. Ethno-racially, death removes the individual from a position on the chain of being and makes this individual a non-being, a return to the Blackness of infinity and indeterminacy. On the neo-mythic register, death is a point of change and as a transfiguration point it has to be positioned on the only part of the sliding scale between evil and good where change is allowed. As we indicated in section 2, all points but one on this sliding scale are non-White, or Black. White and Whiteness occupy that one spot on the register; the one point where everything is changeless and static. Therefore death as a site of change is positioned in Blackness, and this is no doubt why neo-mythically in Greek mythology both Thanatos, the god of death, and Hades, the god of the underworld where the dead go, are somatically Black.

A clear implication is that individuals should gracefully accept their lot in life and be happy – for their reward will come later, and if not for themselves then for members of their community. Therefore, it is important that even after death they should not be seen as chameleons, as those who did not really contribute to the culture of the state by diligently working to improve the common lot of society and, in so doing, help humans defeat the gods who are so prone to inflict disorder and premature ethno-racial death on humans. In this sense, even though it is ethno-racially inevitable, death can be a human victory at the universal level – even when it is an obvious tragedy at the personal level. Everyone adds a bit to the good fortune of humanity as it moves forward in time to its natural and perfect end, the individual bits lasting and not as impermanent as shifting sand. The same thing would apply ethno-racially to a state and its culture: it will be remembered long after it is gone should personal death arrive and find that the state has achieved self-sufficiency, thereby making its independent members happy, thereby ensuring an "everlasting" life for the community, if not for specific individuals. Indeed, as long as the state neo-mythically meets these goals, creating goodness for all through such things as self-sufficiency, it is more likely to prosper than die. However, a society whose members are not happy would be most tragic, for even after the tragedy that is certain death – either of individuals or of the state itself – there would be nothing worth honouring. Such a state would disappear into Blackness instead of being revered in the Whiteness of memory and enlightenment, just as the Egyptian wise men told Solon in Plato's *Timaeus*.

In this and the previous chapters, I have shown that in their mythology and philosophy the ancient Greeks had clear notions of Blackness and

Whiteness. These were moral positions of extremes between good and evil, between utopia and dystopia, between the elites and the indigent and between citizens and foreigners, between those who perish and those who live in memory. However, there was one type of Blackness that did not have a moral meaning: somatic and phenotypic Blackness. Somatic Blackness had meaning only in the universal sense of a lordship and bondage relationship between beings that are powerful, perfect, and immortal – the gods – and beings that are powerless, imperfect, and mortal – humans. Somatic Blackness was instead a symbol of the lowly status of all humans when compared to gods and how vulnerable humans were existentially. Later, as Herodotus suggested, it would be associated with people of a specific region but would still have no moral significance. In modernity, any morality based solely on somatic and phenotypic Blackness as natural ethnic and racial categories was the result of having read such categories back into Greek mythology and philosophy at a later date. We shall now discuss the depiction of Blackness in Christian mythology and philosophy.

# 12

# Slavery and Death

They will walk with me dressed in white, for they are worthy. He who overcomes will, like them, be dressed in white.[1]

The heart of light is black, as has often been noticed.[2]

The white man – white because he was man, white like daylight, white like truth, white like virtue – lighted up the creation like a torch and unveiled the secret white essence of beings.[3]

## BLACKNESS IN THE CHRISTIAN NATION-STATE

The next two chapters argue that what we call Western civilization, with its well-developed epistemological concepts of Blackness and Whiteness and of good and evil, is founded on a syncretism of Greek, Hebraic, and African mythologies into mainstream thought. The creolized Christianity that resulted from this mixing would selectively choose to emphasize aspects of ontology, epistemology, and of ethical relations from the three separate mythologies to explain a Christian worldview in which evil was seen as constantly threatening the created good and Blackness as eternally pitted against Whiteness's quest for survival. As a result of this thinking, the social order that is itself the product of an idealistic creation has always felt threatened by the chaos that is found in Nature and is aboriginal to this way of life.

Epistemologically, the resulting worldview privileges specific notions of who is White and Black somatically, culturally, and by status or class. In its idealized form, Whiteness became a discussion on who is created or made anthropologically a new species of humanity with the rights and entitlements for membership in what would become the Christian state. Those that did not have these rights were consigned sociologically as Black. Built into these concepts of Whiteness and Blackness are ontological and ethical relations to explain the positioning of specific groups within the social order and how groups of people should existentially be positioned, placed, and utilized effectively to ensure the perseverance of social stability. This positioning determines and is determined by such ethical norms as the political, economic, and other forms of social well-being that establish the perceived correct way for people to live together in a society whose goal is the good as idealistic Whiteness.

Within this sociological perception, Whites were positioned and placed politically as internal to the state, and were thus included in it. They were useful and necessary to the state for its very maintenance and preservation. Blacks were positioned and placed as external or excluded. Their motility or usefulness to the state was incidental or contingent, or at best relegated to a secondary supporting role of ensuring that important members of the society are free to carry on their functions of nation-state construction. The first group was assimilated into a fully reconciled unity with recognized members of the state and were permitted to claim a common citizenship and identity. Those that were constructed as epistemologically or ethically Black were existentially excluded from the main life and purpose of society, or they were integrated on the society's margin or periphery. They were denied recognition as full members of the state.

In the Christian nation-states of modernity of north-western Europe, whose models of state formation were transplanted in European colonies in the Americas, somatic Whiteness and Blackness would ultimately become the primary determinant of inclusion and belonging as part of the continuing evolution of Western civilization. In this regard, the English version of state formation, what would later become an imperialist British model, would be imposed as the dominant approach to state formation through force and power in the Americas. It would be transported pre-packaged and idealistically prefabricated with its ready-made ideals of Whiteness and Blackness that were specific notions of who should be a citizen of the nation-state. In this example, all forms of Blackness – with the somatic becoming the primary finite signifier of Blackness – were excluded from modernity's most idealized ethical relations and from what was seen as the apex of this era, the nation-state.

This and the following chapter show that while there is a claim to strong Hebraic traditions in Western thought, a stronger case can be made for the development of specific modernist institutions, such as race and slavery, from Greek mythology and philosophy than from the African and Hebraic. Greek influences are therefore accorded greater weight as eventually determining the existential experiences and moral and ethical relations in the New World. In these chapters, I argue for at least a third dimension to Western thought – that some African mythologies were incorporated in Western thought in two specific ways. The first is through the notion of human existence being part of a holistic experience that involves the mixing of the living and the dead, humans and gods, the visible and the invisible in a single community whose existence is continuous and cyclical. This is an idealistic composition that produces no clear essence or light, but rather, in the Hegelian sense, the several *darknesses* and barbarism of creolization, hybridity, and ideological syncretism. Although there were other mythologies and philosophies incorporated in this syncretic thought, I will limit my discussion of the "Other" mythologies and philosophies to the so-called African merely to emphasize the point about somatic and cultural impurities that, according to the ethno-racial register, are inherently part of Western thought. Second, I will use African thought to emphasize the point that, contrary to established narratives, so-called African mythologies, philosophies, and people have contributed significantly to the neo-mythic understanding of the Americas as being in their entirety a creole space.

In this respect, human beings, departed ancestors, and their gods are part of nature and co-exist in ideal harmony within nature. Good is the idealistic, existentialist condition of human beings. Evil arrives when there is a disruption in harmony, and the result is chaos. I will show that, in what is termed traditional African mythology and philosophy, covering parts of the continent south of the Sahara and south of Egypt, notions of good and evil were constructed within society and were dependent on human action and agency. Good and evil were not primordial to human existence in these mythologies; good was not created out of evil but existed along with it in a contrarian dialectical relationship.[4] Constructed by modernity ironically as the primordial matter out of which idealistic Whiteness is created, Africa is big geographically and encompasses many distinct mythologies and philosophies.

I will show the influence of competing African notions that suggest good and evil are primordial to human creation and are locked in an endless battle to overthrow or maintain the good that is not of human creation but which is natural and as everlasting as evil. These views are contained in the Manichean religion of North Africa and they would be fused with Greek ontological notions of good and evil in Christianity and ideas of how good can be created in the embodiment of a nation-state that at its extreme idealism is a singular, homogeneous, "White man's" country. At the other extreme, the evil that remained after the creation of the idealistic good, was the indeterminacy and the Blackness of heteronomy, difference, diversity, and pluralism. We now call this multiculturalism.

The second approach came through the influence of North African theologians who revived and reformed Christianity by overlaying African and Greek mythologies and philosophies on the Hebraic history and traditions that undergird Christianity. Hebraic mythology gave to the construction of supposed Western civilization the notions of covenants, contracts, and commandments as a basis for social order and nation-state formation. This is seen in the incorporation of monotheism and the concept of history that devolved from the idea that a single god created everything in the universe out of darkness, but that this god was actively involved in the here-and-now of human existence and remained within the world.

## RATIONAL REGULATOR: WHITENESS IN BLACKNESS

In the dominant Western thought, there is a rational regulator of the universe. Parts of this god's creation were humans and Nature as separate entities, so that in Hebraic mythology humans and their gods were not totally embedded in Nature, but were involved in a constant lordship and bondage struggle for dominion. In Hebraic tradition, God had dominion over humans and, through a never-ending fight, over Nature, the latter being undifferentiated matter that possessed only opportunities and potentials for creation. As a separate entity, God could also work through them. As the active agents for God's eternal act of creation, humans were thus pitted in a struggle to claim dominion over Nature. In addition, humans had fallen from their godlike purity back into evil, and they and God had agreed to ethical relations based on agreements, covenants, and commandments that kept both sides in check and allowed for an existence based on agreed notions of what was good and what was evil. With good and evil idealized, norms and laws were then created or constructed within these agreements.

Humans thus govern their relations with one another through specific laws and agreements, in the same way that the covenant and commandments bound God and humans to behave appropriately according to defined standards of what were good and evil. The laws, regulations, and traditions that emanated from this existence informed the ethical relations of the human family and made it possible to discern the appropriate moral and ethical behaviour. The result of this struggle for mastery in an already constructed order was the concept of history: of a people struggling to achieve dominion and liberty, and of aiming to become ultimately good, defined as idealistically White. But this is a struggle that is explained as happening within creation, and not as the mainstream Greeks suggest, a battle between primordial goodness and evil that predates creation and is constantly trying to overturn the results of creation. The struggle happens in time and is history itself.

As with the traditional African philosophy, social relations in the Hebraic mythology came out of a specific culture that was a created social order. Culture resulted from, and was influenced by, historical events in a post-construction moment. Cultural Whiteness was not presented as a way of achieving an ethical relation based on pre-creation ideals that came out of a seemingly interminable struggle and which had to be fulfilled in history. As Irving M. Zeitlin states in *Ancient Judaism*: "Nowhere, in the Bible, either in the primeval legends of Genesis or in the prophetic and poetic literature, is there the faintest suggestion of a force, a condition, or principle that is prior or superior to Yahweh. Neither is there the slightest indication that other autonomous principles exist in the universe. What we find in the biblical literature is that ideas which had originally emerged in a polytheistic culture have been radically transformed. They are no longer 'natural' forces but historical and ethical concepts."[5]

Dominant Hebraic tradition suggests that good and evil, White and Black were created by the same god, but a god who at times, caught in moral and ethical binds, does not know what is good and what is evil. Cultural Whiteness and Blackness are reflections of obedience or disobedience to the norms of society and the rules that govern them: they are moral and ethical. Idealistically, to obey is to be White and to disobey is to become Black as sin. Yet, there are times when, as in the Garden of Eden myth, disobedience leads to life and greater recognition of humanity, when good comes out of disobedience and evil comes out of obedience, so that what was normally viewed as idealistically and culturally Black is White and what was White is Black. Blackness and Whiteness are not fixed but based on contextualized choices; they are primarily ethical, and in them there is no ethical, epistemological, or existential significance placed on the somatic or ontological Blackness and Whiteness. Zeitlin emphasizes this point:

In the Scriptures the beginning of everything is of course, the supreme will of Yahweh. A supradivine force is unthinkable. In the garden of Eden we find not a primordial monster but a serpent. Evil comes to the world not from the netherworld or some other autonomous sources, but from sin – which presupposes choice, the attributes of free will with which God has endowed mankind. In this way evil is transposed from the mythological to the moral realm. Evil, far from being a primordial principle, is, like everything else in the world, created by God. As an episode in the creation of the world, evil is part of its history, resulting from man's disobedience. Therefore, all the struggles of the Pentateuch are, without exception, social, moral and historical.[6]

In a bid to explain differences between various groups, European Christians in what became the New World, while claiming to be the direct descendents of the Greeks, turned to Hebraic tradition for justification of their ethical relations with other groups and even for proof of the ontology that they read out of their "ancestral" Greek mythology. In so doing, because Africans were determined as Black somatically, culturally, and by status, European Christians ignored African mythologies and traditions as meaningless, ill-informed, and unimportant to the polity and to the fulfilment of the concept of history that they took from the Hebraic tradition. They tried to erase African philosophies from the national consciousness.

Their efforts would fail, as the mythologies and philosophers would remain physically present within Black members of the state. This would result in a lordship and bondage relationship at two levels in the Americas: physically, between the socially and idealistically constructed Black and White members of the society, and culturally between the mythologies and philosophies that informed the cultures of those constructed as White or Black. As a powerful counter-argument to this dominant view in Western ideology, I offer, through Black or African mythology and philosophy, the celebration of indeterminacy and the unpredictability of life that is embodied in the West African god Eshu.

At the same time, in their bid to account for differences in society, European nation-state builders read the Hebraic literature through Christian lenses, thereby, in some cases, radically reinterpreting Hebraic thought to make it conform to the syncretism required in Christianity. The result was a search for a Greek-like essence in the Hebraic mythology, leading to the claim that specific passages in the Bible supported the notion of inferior and superior races – of Blackness as essentially evil and Whiteness as good – just as the Greeks had suggested. Unwittingly, as a result of these dialectical relationships, European Christians were helping develop, from their positions of power and influence, a syncretic and creolized culture in the Americas, something that was the complete opposite from what they intended.

Similar ambivalent effects of the ideological syncretism are illustrated in African or Transatlantic slavery in the Americas and its cultural legacies throughout the region. Syncretism, as an active agent itself, holds important existentialist lessons and produces its own types of ethical determinants of who is Black and White, what is good and evil, and how societies should deal with individuals as social creatures. Here, we are reminded of Orlando Patterson's assertion that physical slavery is the equivalent of social death, a meaningless existentialism.[7]

But what is death and can there be mental and physical deaths? Is there a difference between a death in which Blackness passes into Whiteness and that when Whiteness becomes Blackness? Is death metaphorically an act of creating, but one which captures an ecstatic moment of freedom? Is it an improvisation, possessing an array of choices, a plenitude where good can be defined any way one pleases, or where there are no rules, boundaries, limits, or social scripts. And if so, does this make the creator absolutely free, limitless, and all powerful? And is not death the first negation of citizenship and membership that is necessary for a second negation of that finite limit to account for full membership among the select that are fully White in Christian theology?

## HEGEL: BLACKNESS, WHITENESS, AND AGAIN BLACKNESS

As the Hegelian scholar Alexandre Kojève maintained, a combination of Greek and Hebrew/Christian thought offered the West a form of cosmopolitanism as the ideal of state formation. First brought forward by Alexander the Great, through his idea of binding all the peoples of the world into a single state, it was then taken up by the Pauline doctrines of the New Testament. As we shall see, this is the syncretism that breathed new life into Christianity and ultimately Western thought at a decisive moment in their history – at a time when they turned to Africa and somatic Blacks for an infusion of creativity in these orders. As Kojève states: "What characterizes the political action of Alexander, distinguishing it from that of all his Greek predecessors and contemporaries, is the fact that it was directed by the idea of *empire*, that is, a *universal* state, in the sense at least that this state would have no limits (geography, ethnic, or otherwise), *given a priori*, nor any *pre-established* 'capital,' that is, a geographically and ethnically *fixed* nucleus destined to dominate politically its periphery ... Moreover, by obliging the (enemies) Macedonians and Greeks to enter into mixed marriages with the 'barbarians,' he certainly had in mind the creation of a new ruling class which would be independent of all rigid and *given* ethnic support."[8]

Kojève said of Alexander the Great that "instead of establishing the domination of his *race* and letting his *Fatherland* reign over the rest of the world, he chose to dissolve the race and do away with the *Fatherland* itself."[9] Without so naming it, Kojève was pointing to one of the first prototypes of the multicultural state.

The other prototype for the modern state, and for multiculturalism, was the Christian church, which Kojève acknowledged is very different at one level from the idea of a state, properly speaking. However, he suggested that this model is based on "the *philosophical* idea going back to Socrates which, when all is said and done, acts *politically* on earth and which continues today to determine the political acts and entities aiming at the actualization of the *universal* state or empire."[10] What was taken from the Christian model were the ideas of intention, as an analogy for desires, that is fully actualized in the beyond that was either heaven or hell. For Kojève, the whole story of the new political cosmopolitanism resulting from these two models was based on a Hegelian lordship and bondage reading of history as explained earlier, or what Kojève called a Master-Slave narrative:

For St Paul there is no "essential" (irreducible) difference between the Greek and the Jew because they both can BECOME Christians, and this not by "mixing" their Greek an Jewish "qualities" but by *negating* them both and "synthesizing" them in and by this very negating into a homogeneous unity not innate or given, but (freely) *created* by "conversion." Because of the *negating* character of the Christian "synthesis," there are no longer any incompatible "qualities" or "contradictory" (= mutually exclusive) "qualities." For Alexander, a Greek philosopher, there was no possible "mixture" of Masters and Slaves, for they were "opposites."[11]

Greek mythology would also come to heavily influence Western society's approach to knowledge, putting greater emphasis on the rational and the cognitive, and less on the senses and what cannot be easily explained by cognition. However, as we shall see, rationalism presents idealistic problems for societies. The primacy of rationalism in the Americas would result from the privileging of Greek thought, as incorporated in a specific branch of European Christianity as a continuation of Hebraic thought, over the African mythology and philosophy.

But this is not to argue against African and Hebraic influences on modernity, especially as read through Westernized Christian eyes. Indeed, my argument is that in turning to official multiculturalism, Canada was returning to the earliest roots of Western thought, a time before specific narratives and ethnic groups were privileged. Therefore, this move towards multiculturalism was recognition that Canada specifically, and Western thought generally, had never been able to live up to one of the main boasts of modernity – that it could bring light out of darkness and White out of Blackness. That project, especially as the prototype for social justice and other forms of ethical relations, never materialized. Multiculturalism is an official recognition that Canada and the body and system of thought and materials that produced it in time have always been Black, and will most likely forever be so, whether neo-mythically or ethno-racially.

## HEGEL AND SOMATIC BLACKNESS: CAN A BLACK SCHOLAR BE HEGELIAN?

Before moving on, it is necessary to clarify a point that some scholars have raised about the theories and method of Hegel and a Hegelian phenomenology as applied to somatic and cultural Blacks in Africa. They might question the offering of what on first reading might appear to be a unified mythological field that is defined ethno-racially as African. In a sense, this is one of the problems presented to us by modernity, and it is present even in modernity's construction of the entities and concepts called Africa and Africans, especially as these are supposedly also inferior to Europe and Europeans. Indeed, some scholars argue that Dogon, Yoruba, Fon, Akan, or Egyptian mythologies are separate and distinct unities.[12] There is a danger that states of pre-consciousness and self-consciousness as entities are framed within cosmogonies, theodicies, and discourses of destiny and fate, and of separation and reconciliation that bear little or no connection to Blackness and Whiteness ethno-racially, even if they do neo-mythically. Again, I argue that such is the legacy bequeathed to us from modernity and its one-sided way of searching for meaning.

In this respect, I invite readers to consider Dogon, Yoruba, Fon, Akan, or Egyptian mythologies as states of pre-consciousness and self-consciousness framed within a universal quest for freedom and self-determination, rather than as elements in a discussion on destiny, determinism, and predetermination within a particular cosmology. It is not a difference within a single system or order of cosmologies that I am concerned with, as much as the differences between accepted orders, or those that in the Hegelian sense are said to be given to us in common sense meaning. It is precisely because of this difference – between that of cosmological or theodical determinism and my postulated individual quest for freedom – that the odyssey to and from Africa can be completed. In this way, we can reconfigure Whiteness and Blackness in a non-somatic rather than the racist way suggested by those of the ethno-racialist discourse and those schooled in the neo-mythic register.

A second point bears emphasizing: this is to reiterate that I am not writing from an essentialist point of view, where there are single meanings to Black, Blackness, and multiculturalism. My approach is of a self-consciousness who rereads and rewrites history in the light of subsequent developments and later knowledge. This is why I start with the determination of categories and then try to find their genesis so as to find an a priori meaning. In so doing, while I am using a Hegelian method, I am also starting from a position that recognizes some earlier flaws in Hegel's thinking – where as a man of his times Hegel was unable to escape the somatic racism of the nineteenth century. This is particularly the case where Hegel looked at the homogeneous place given to him by modernity as being a place with no consciousness and where the dialectics of history were not yet present. Hegel was steeped in the racist myths of his time, and at times the ethno-racial understanding overshadowed the findings of his dialectical process. However, these shortcomings in Hegel do not wipe out his genius in providing us with a dialectic method that helps us explain Blackness and Whiteness within a world history. This is the Hegel that none other than C.L. James fawningly calls a "maestro,"[13] that Du Bois, Fanon, and so many Black and African thinkers have incorporated into their works,[14] and whose approach Judith Butler says is central to understanding the modern discourse on race and identity.[15]

### BLACKNESS:
### AFRICAN TRADITION

Blackness, viewed idealistically in Western thought through the perspective of the Other, is celebration of the subversion of purity and of modernity's claims to essentialism. It seeks to dethrone the enthroned order that ceases to represent just another method to achieving ends and instead becomes its own end. Blackness emphasizes the continuous construction process that is a part of cultures and nations that are always works-in-progress. It privileges this ever new construction over what has already been constructed and is now fossilized.

In Blackness, good is always in a process of becoming, always undergoing the never-ending creation that is so vividly captured by Frye in his claim of an eternal act of creation. This moment is always the now, the in-between time that has passed with its notions of good that phenomenologically proved to be misrecognized Blackness as Whiteness, and a future state when a self-conscious Whiteness would have been brought fully into creation. It is the irrepressible spirit that reveals itself in human existence as disruptive, irreverent, and carnivalesque, for it is always rejecting the good or perceived Whiteness of the past as inadequate, while trying to create a new good of the future by using radically different assumptions. Blackness, and the death it symbolises, is a striking moment of creation.

As Aimé Césaire, a pioneering proponent of *Negritude,* suggests in *The Tempest,* Blackness comes ontologically in the representation of the African god, Eshu, the trickster and the epitome of sexuality and licentiousness, of uncontrolled fertility and creation.[16] Eshu turns up at the wedding feast uninvited, intent on disrupting the new order in its most fragile moment of birth, by creating different and even unthinkable possibilities by pressing the limits and boundaries of the existing order.

On the day of the wedding, he makes the bride get into the wrong bed, so that on this very day of creation and purity, uncertainty, disappointment, and even death are the unwelcome guests. This is a story of a god playfully not knowing its limits and using every opportunity to create something that is, if not socially constructed as good, by its nature just different. So is the presence of the unknown, whether good or evil. The gods barge in, sneering, misbehaving, and self-indulgent simply because humans are powerless against them.

Human beings have no special status, for they are just like anything in creation: an order that can be overthrown as part of the search for newness, difference, diversity, and another uniquely new order. Most of all, as elements in the dialectical dance, they privilege the body over the mind with their licentious and sensual behaviour: they know that human beings are commanded to reproduce themselves and to be plentiful, if only because a collective death that is physical is always hovering and rules are not always a protection or guarantee. They choose the body because it is the material they must use to recreate or create new possibilities and orders, some that even the mind might not have created in imagination. They privilege pleasure over rationalism, although they acknowledge through the use of proverbs and wise sayings that rationalism is important epistemologically.[17] Césaire captures these sentiments this way:

Eshu can play many tricks,
Give him twenty dogs!
You will see his dirty ticks...
Eshu is a merry elf,
And he can whip you with his dick
He can whip you,
He can whip you.[18]

This is a moment of everlasting creation so aptly described by Toni Morrison as playing in the dark. And, as Eshu shows, creation should be fun and enjoyable for the creators, and for the liberated subjects alike, even when the latter exist in the shadows of pending doom and chaos that is natural to their existing order. This, however, is the only order that the created beings really know, for in it they will always be the playthings of the likes of an Eshu or any ethno-racial form arbitrariness and capriciousness will take. In *The Signifying Monkey*, Henry Louis Gates Jr notes how Eshu (or Esu or Esu-Elegbara) in his numerous African-American permutations has become a trope for Blackness in African-American literature and mythology:

Scholars have studied these figures of Esu, and each has found one or two characteristics of this mutable figure upon which to dwell, true to the nature of the trickster. A partial list of these qualities might include individuality, satire, parody, irony, magic, indeterminacy, open-endedness, ambiguity, sexuality, chance, uncertainty, disruption and reconciliation, betrayal and loyalty, closure and disclosure, encasement and rupture. But it is a mistake to focus on one of these qualities as predominant. Esu possesses all of these characteristics, plus a plethora of others which, taken together, only begins to present an idea of the complexity of this classic figure of mediation and of unity of opposed forces.[19]

Eshu epitomizes the uncertainties and vagaries of life – a natural and irrepressible order that cannot be contained in any social order constructed by human beings. This is at the same time a blessing and a curse – a gift of the gods that comes in the form of change and indeterminacy. This is the Blackness to which Appiah gestures in his discussion on the need for the unaccountable, for luck, and that which cannot be planned in Western thought and in the basic system that undergirds Western society and its infinity of finite identities. It cannot be planned because it emanates from the creation process itself, not, markedly, from the creator. "Capitalism – like life – is full of such unfairness: luck – from lotteries to hurricanes – affects profit. And we can't get rid of all unfairness; for if we had perfect insurance, zero risk, there'd be no role for entrepreneurship, no markets, no capitalism," and no individualism, either.[20]

## AFRICAN EXISTENTIALISM: IDEALS OF WHITENESS
## AND BLACKNESS

In *Soul of Darkness,* David Carney says, of what he calls traditional African mythology and philosophy, that change through the transcending of finite boundaries and limits is central to traditional African metaphysics:

Change is the essence of African metaphysics, of existence, as exemplified in the human life cycle, and every significant event in the life of an individual and the community is celebrated or commemorated by appropriate rites and activities. Thus, the following are celebrated

(1) At the community level: preparation of the fields, sowing, harvesting and storage; hunting and fishing; house construction; etc. All these activities follow the natural cycles – seasons, phases of the moon – and are celebrated with rites appropriate to each.

(2) At the level of the individual: birth, puberty, initiation into the adult community, marriage, good fortune, misfortune, illness, death and bereavement, each accompanied by its appropriate celebration or "rite of passage."[21]

Existentially, every human being is an embodiment of a spirit with a personality of its own. In addition, the individual has a *psycho-personality* that "inhabits the separate minds of the person's intimates; that is to say, an individual's personality creates a duplicate image of itself in the minds of those with intimate knowledge of that individual from personal or close contact, such as family members, friends, or associates."[22] Therefore, there are three phases in the human evolution: one, as a spirit from God or the ancestors that arrives in the visible world with its destiny already preordained; second, as an embodiment for the acting out of the destiny and plan; and, third, as an embodied-spirit-personality, which continues to have an indirect influence in worldly affairs, and only through the immediacy of the embodied spirit.

At physical death, the embodiment disintegrates, leaving the spirit and the psycho-personality still alive; thereby creating a new entity that is no longer physical. Ideally, during the first stage, the individual would live a long life growing in wisdom, so that prior to physical death that person would become as wise as possible for him or her and receive status and social justice that comes with being elevated to the rank of an elder.

Carney states that "death, however, is not an existential disaster to, and for, the African."[23] This is because death is not a negation of existence and it is not finality.[24] In a Hegelian sense, it is part of a continuum, a dialectical movement that is akin to a new birth of sorts. It is a new act of creation, of bringing a new or higher good into existence out of the prevailing evil. Neither is it intended ethically as justice and reward for a life of denial in pursuit of a greater good. Death is a natural aspect of living, an act of re-creation of the good in one order so that a new order and its own idealistic goodness and Whiteness can come into being. It is another distinguishing of movements in being. As Carney states: "Death deprives the living only of the *physical* companionship of the deceased who continues, nevertheless, to exist as 'living dead' – psycho-personality – and eventually as depersonalized spirit only, all this side by side with the biologically surviving members of the community in the first phase of existence. Thus death is merely the gateway to pure personality (psycho-personality) and to spirit."[25]

Individuals can move through different ranks in their lives, eventually arriving at the highest social ranks, and expected level of happiness, that the society can confer. Their happiness and justice comes in the here and now and lives on with them in the memory of them. This is akin to Hegel's notion of the various shades that are memory and are rolled into the latest manifestation of a specific consciousness. Indeed, we are reminded here of Hegel's idea that we are always in the process of becoming, a positioning which as we may recall is a determinate spot on a sliding scale with coming-to-be on one end and ceasing-to-be at the other. In this way of thinking, for Hegel there can be no clear beginning or ending, but merely a circular movement of one part of the scale sublimating the other, in much the same way that, as we may further recall, lukewarm is a mixture of cold as much as it is of hot – its other or the supposed nothing of cold.[26]

In the second stage as suggested by Carney, the individual who has passed over to death – or in the Hegelian sense is sublimated – is living only as a memory, and is "physically" among the recent dead, those who are at the lower level of the pecking order among the ancestors. This second stage will last until the last person to remember the deceased has died, until all memory of the physical likeness of the individual has faded. "Hence, from the metaphysical point of view, it is to the advantage of every individual to have as many children as possible in order to maximize the number of those who will prolong the individual's second stage."[27]

Here, again, the emphasis is placed on change and growth over time, on an eternal act of creation, as identities are transformed and acted out as always a production in progress. Higher levels of perfection are achieved with time, but an individual's time is finite and so it is that perfection, and the ideal of Whiteness, cannot be achieved in an individual's time. At the end of the second stage, only the spirit of the individual remains, at which point it joins fully the past community of ancestors and moves to a higher level of influence that increases based on the length of the physical death, as if the dead adds to its storehouse of wisdom what it has acquired since its physical transformation.

With the three stages being conceptually one single cosmos, and the dead and living part of the same ecosystem, honour in this system is based on

seniority. A long age indicates the accumulation of wisdom, which is carried over into the recent dead, and these recently dead are not as wise as the
distant ancestors. This is like the suggestion by Aristotle that honour and
blessing are neo-mythically derived. Such wisdom would come as the
recently dead age into the distant ancestors. As Carney adds: "the African
existential view of death thus contrasts with that of ancient Greece and the
Occident, where death is regarded as a transitional link between two
existences or existential worlds, one phenomenal (empirical or sensate), the
other noumenal (non-empirical or non-sensate). For the African there is
only one existence."[28]

   In the traditional African mythology and philosophy, the earth is a cosmos created by a god who left the world to run according to its internal
dynamics and with little interference from the deity. To this end, God, as
the initial creator, appears to be remote from traditional African life, in the
same way that with time humans become ancient ancestors and become
increasingly remote from the daily activities of the living as they fade in
memory. While God created a universe that is innately good, evil is a
human construct that is caused when an individual imposes a change on
another. This might be in the case of death when an individual causes the
premature transformation of an individual from among the living to the
dead. "Evil is thus an attitude of unreceptivity to, of unacceptability of
change – or, by general transference, whatever militates against the individual's current condition, integrity or happiness. When, evil is, at the same
time, *objectively* the essence of existence in its unchanging changingness
and, *subjectively*, the negative human reaction to such change."[29]

   However, it bears noting that the Greek, Hebraic and African mythologies that concern us accept the notion of ancestors who have an interest in
daily lives, either directly or through memory, whether it is the ancestors,
the fathers of Israel, or the Greek heroes – all of whom found themselves
acknowledged universally in Christianity and the dominant ideology of the
West as saints, founding fathers, and defenders of the faith or nation. This
came about through an act of re-creation when North African religion was
infused into Christianity, primarily through the directions of St Augustine,
around the fall of the Roman Empire. Later re-creations occurred through
the further integration of traditional African mythologies and thought,
captured in the creative institution of physical African slavery that became
the bedrock for the development of the Americas.

### ST AUGUSTINE: FINDING WHITENESS IN BLACKNESS

St Augustine by birth was what is now familiarly called ethno-racially an
African, and was perhaps the leading member of a group of theologians
responsible for the syncretism that blended mainstream Greek, Hebraic,

and African influences and mythologies into the Christianity that in the fourth century of Christian history provided the ideology for the socially constructed consciousness that Western civilization is. In so doing, St Augustine helped redeem Christianity and helped it transcend its youthful limits. As Eliade says in *Sacred and Profane*, at the point of St Augustine's intervention in its development, Christianity was under "violent attack" as an immature and poor example of a religion when compared to those of the "pagans" among the Indians, Greeks, and Egyptians.[30] Its future did not seem assured, as it appeared to be caught in the status and fixity of finite contradictions and ambiguities. Paradoxically, Christianity was like the symbolic good that was created out of Blackness and was struggling to survive the efforts of its mother-like Blackness to reclaim it. Psychologically, Christianity had to mature and become responsible for itself, to the point of struggling to overcome the very nature out of which it was created.

Eliade further notes: "The outstanding figures in the Christian counterattack were the Africans Minucius Felex, Lactantius, Tertullian, and Firmicius Maternus, and the great Alexandrian scholars Clement of Alexandria and Origen. Eusebius of Caesarea in his *Chronicles*, Saint Augustine in the *City of God*, and Paulus Orosius in his Histories *dealt* out the last refutation to paganism."[31] They would revitalize, re-mythologize, and refashion Christianity, causing it eventually to spread out of Africa to Western Europe, where it would become transformed into a religion that was somatically and culturally White on the ethno-racial register. Later, this idealistically and even perceived somatic White religion would be brought back to Africa, where it would be used to infer status: those not deemed to be Christian would be made inferior and those not of the same standards as Europeans would be deemed primitive and representative of that from which Whiteness and good were culled.

St Augustine embodies the struggle for Blackness to become White. Idealistically, St Augustine presented himself as a sinner born in Blackness who, through a Christian conversion or rebirth, became White, and of a Whiteness that is reserved for those who are the deserving and entitled inhabitants of a New Jerusalem in the Biblical Book of Revelation. "Who will grant unto me that Thou wilt come into my heart and inebriate it, so that I may forget my evils and embrace my one Good, Thee?"[32] St Augustine was born physically in Tagaste, Carthage, in North Africa. In *Augustine: His Life and Thought*, Warren Thomas Smith describes St Augustine's father, Patricius:

Patricius Herecules was probably a small man, quite dark, "swarthy and with quick black eyes." His background was doubtless that of the Berber or moors – most of the citizens of Tagaste were of Berber stock – the oldest race in North Africa. Before the time of Egypt's pharaohs these Berbers inhabited much of northwest Africa ...

They were people tending to be short of stature, of dark complexion, wide shoulders, narrow hips, of nervous personality and energetic temperament. If this is an accurate portrait of his father's people, would it not give a reliable clue to Augustine's appearance and personality? It is rather well established that Augustine was a small man physically.[33]

His somatic Blackness seems not to be in doubt, but, generally in his time, neither was it of any moral or ethical significance. St Augustine acknowledges that at various moments in his life he was Black culturally and socially, in terms of living in the darkness of what he called paganism and unenlightenment until he was brought into the light through a Christian conversion. He started out as a Manichean traditionalist believing that the world is divided between forces of good and evil and that these combatants are pitted in an eternal battle that informs everything in creation. When he became a Christian, he preached against the paganism that he saw around him and lifted up Christianity as the only true religion. But this was Christianity with a difference, one into which he had infused both neo-Platonist teachings from the Greek and Manichean notions of good and evil. This led to a stoicism that would allow Christians to live in a hybrid world of good and evil while striving for a non-worldly city that was an idealized purity where the good soul lives. This is the idealized place, as we recall from the Platonic dialogues, of forever feasting on the nectar and ambrosia that became the Christianized milk and honey of an afterlife Heaven.

Carol Harrison writes in *Augustine: Christian Truth and Fractured Humanity* that Augustine was what we call ethno-racially an African and originally a member of the Manicheans, who believed everything in life flowed from an eternal conflict between good and evil.[34] This conflict was the act of creation. He helped reposition Christianity by reconstituting it through borrowings from Hebraic and other "pagan" traditions and mixing them with neo-Platonist Greek philosophy. The new life infusion came in an appeal to reason idealized as a disembodied Whiteness. He accomplished this by privileging the mind over the body, a philosophy he took from the Greeks, and infused this way of thinking in the Hebraic mythology. In so doing, Augustine idealistically positioned reason as wisdom – phenomenologically White, spiritual, and godly – unlike the bodily world of human sin and lusts, and spiritual death. As Harrison states: "Wisdom is like the intellectual light of mind – Reason draws on Plato's allegory of the Cave and the analogy of light: some can look at the sun directly, others are blinded by it and seek out the shade, needing to be gradually accustomed to its brilliance by first looking at objects upon which it shines, then, as the light intensifies, upon shiny objects like gold and silver, fire, the stars, the moon, the dawn, and then perhaps finally the sun."[35] But this is an escape into the Whiteness of wisdom that comes at a great price: self-denial of the body and a self-hatred for the Blackness in humanity. It was up to St Thomas of Aquinas to reintroduce the body and existentialism to Christianity.[36] Key to St Augustine's theosophy is hope: a final rebirth or re-creation into idealized Whiteness, a negation and rejection of the old self. This is a rejection of the Blackness of daily living. We shall return to St Augustine later to show how his ideas were taken up in modernity, particularly in the Americas. It is enough to say, at this moment, that the religion St Augustine handed to what we now call Western civilization was predicated on the notion of hope as an idea that humans can have faith in a future that they do not know.[37] They can trust in a redeemer to keep a promise to deliver them. And this deliverance amounts to another birth or re-creation. Hope is then a metaphor for re-creation. Epistemologically and ontologically it can only exist and perform in Blackness. Therefore, it is also ethical Blackness.

## ST AUGUSTINE'S LEGACY: WHITENESS OVERCOMING BLACKNESS

The dominant Christianized mythology that borrowed from the Hebraic and Greek traditions would come to inform notions of nation and state formation and who should have entitlements within the state. Moral and ethical relations would be developed based on a reading of the Bible as a revealed truth that was intended to exist for the good of Christian nations. This was particularly true of the English, and then British, nation, which would adopt a Christian worldview, first at home, but later in relations with other peoples around the world. This was the case in the cultural agencies that helped shape national institutions for the construction of the nation-state and notions of patriotism and love of country. And this was also the case in terms of how the Europeans, particularly the English, viewed others with Black skins, and how they imagined them as fitting into their nation-state. In their Christian mythology, they started with the perceived Greek association of somatic and cultural Blackness with evil, and then sought justification in the dominant Hebraic mythology.

Christian mythology saw a battle between Blackness and Whiteness in their idealized and cultural forms at the heart of Hebraic tradition. It was manifest in the very conception of God: whether this supernatural being was good and evil at the same time; whether this dualism was all goodness as represented by a singular concept of Yahweh, or also a god of potential evil and disruption as was Elohim in the Hebraic tradition. This god, that in the early Biblical narrative appeared to be struggling with itself, seemed to be giving conflicting demands and commands, but eventually came to be reconciled in a god of goodness as Yahweh.

In the first five books of the Bible, which appear to be an amalgam of different mythologies, there are other seeming contradictions, such as the order of events in the creation of the cosmos, when and how the first man and woman were created, and how the selection was made for those entering the ark before the flood. At different points the narrative states that God created man and woman at the same time, then that God created man and shaped woman out of a rib from man. According to one part of the narrative, the selection for the ark was made based on the clean and unclean, while in another section it claims that the selection was based on species, with male and female members of each species acting as representatives. And, significantly, the difference appears most poignantly in the seemingly contradictory commands that God gave to humans: go forth and populate the world, but do not have sex.

This same moral and ethical ambiguity is true of the struggle between the many nomadic tribes that would be carved out of the rest of humanity to become the redeemed nation of Israel. This is why the creation narrative, and particularly the story of the Garden of Eden, is central to this mythology, for in the Christian imagination, they deal with issues of conflict, of deciding moral and ethical relations, and of knowing who is good and evil. The creation mythology in the Hebraic tradition is a question of limits and boundaries and of a dialectical struggle to be free of the limitations while recognizing that there is a consequence for such freedom. And it is the story of how a specific social order – a particular way of existence – from among all other alternatives imaginable, came to be naturally superior and most desirable. Mythologically, this is an explanation of how Whiteness came out of the indeterminacy and plenitudes of Blackness.

It is also a rationalization for how choices should be made to bring about this order and then preserve it. In this story, a creator also discovers change through the potency of actions, of trying to implement a thought and being unable to control the action once it has begun. This is a change whose Whiteness or Blackness can be known only on reflection – only after the event – so that it becomes a challenge for this creator to know in a pre-creation moment and through thought only what will be the ensuing good or evil. For once the act is committed there might be no chance of changing what turned out to be an evil into a good, for the damage would have been created already. Eventually, Yahweh and Elohim would recognize that they are the opposite sides of the same face. As pure thought, they are both good and evil, which means that whatever they would create would be a reflection of whether it flowed from the good or evil sides of the same beings. Accentuating the positive as part of the dialectic of hope resulted in the privileging of Yahweh and the sublation of Elohim in the resulting dominant conception of the infinite God.

## WHITENESS AS CHOSEN, BELONGING, CITIZENSHIP; BLACKNESS AS OTHERS

Finally, there is the notion that Israel, as a chosen people, was created or transformed out of Blackness, from among a people that are somatically Black, particularly the people of Ur among whom the Israeli patriarch Abraham lived, but who were also Black idealistically, culturally, and in status. This is an example of a special group of beings transformed out of the Blackness that represented all humanity, into the Whiteness, in the Christian mythology, of a specially elected who were saved through the intervention of their god to make them as an intentional act of creation lesser than gods but superior in status to the rest of humanity.

This was a different reading compared to the main Hebraic tradition, where such an honour was often considered a greater burden and responsibility. In the Christian mythology, the good is a life where there is no conflict, no Blackness, but a symbolic return to a Garden of Eden and its idealized Whiteness that ontologically and existentially is a static utopia. In this way, whether the good is the pronouncement of a Hebraic god of creation after calling forth light from darkness and chaos, or the good of a Platonic demiurge who intended that all creation be good, it is interpreted as being the same.

As Derrida says in *Khora*, this is not only a question of recognizing limits, but also of contesting them, and of not knowing beforehand which of the possible actions are good and bad, but in the face of death being willing to try what is rationally the best choice. [38] In *Khora*, Derrida is trying to get us to return intellectually, before making ethical decisions, into the Blackness that is supposedly a pre-creation moment, a time so similar to that of Plato's demiurge in the *Timeaus* before the creation of the universe. This is the same recognition of even a seemingly omnipotent maker of the cosmos realizing that by creating a perfect world it had to impose limits, boundaries that cannot subsequently be changed if the idea of perfection is to remain meaningful. It is the realization of the seeming contradiction that even God, in all its power, wisdom, and goodness, in creating itself and its handiwork, also created a master for itself in subjecting itself to limits and the idea of perfection. The master having created the perfect social order in all its pristine Whiteness finds that it must subject itself to the lordship of the order that it has conceived – such is a story for all those individuals who come together to create a social order that is a country or state and then have to submit themselves to governance by their creation. [39] This is another example of a Hegelian lordship and bondage relationship, one that is played out within the self as a distinct unity, rather than as a struggle between two competing and distinct selves. One implication of this struggle is that even a god or demiurge might eventually find itself in bondage to that which it has created – for example, the citizen who has to live within the boundaries and limits set by the state.

Even God has to be a dualism, what it is and what it is not, so that depending on the context even God is good and evil, but until it acts is neither, and even more importantly, it is also ineffective and powerless. Therefore, Blackness, as that moment before action starts to create Whiteness and good, is phenomenologically neither good nor evil. It just is what it is without a moral or ethical value. This epitomizes the ideal position of living in a value-free world that has no consequences and, therefore, no responsibilities. But once God acts, all is changed: there are consequences; either good or evil is created; something is lost and something is enslaved. Conflictedness, with an assumed and specific moral value, as a new state of Blackness is now created out of the Blackness of innocence and playful naïveté.

Through limits, through action, God thus created of itself both a bondsman and the bondsman's own lord, unless the very first principles of creation where good is created by good in a Platonic sense were violated and the process begun all over again. This is a limit that would ensure the static and even statism if the opposing views were not constantly negating each other. This is the *aporia*: as Derrida suggests, a position of no choice that is either clearly good or clearly evil, or as Hegel suggests, a juncture where a choice has to be made between irreconcilable positions, each of which, in the given situation, is neither correct nor wrong, as each is a recognition of a boundary, and a juncture where life has to be the only real choice. Good and evil, then, are not natural: they are social constructions given to us by our culture. Such is the mythological story where free-will human beings with self-determination "wake up" to find themselves being refined into idealized products of their culture – by what they are supposedly creating. They find that they might not be as White as they thought.

This is analogously God as an infinite self-consciousness who realized that before creation and the start of history the world was without form in its Blackness, but acknowledged that it was also a lifeless state of nature. It was a static utopia. A universe without life was bad and once this moral idea came into consciousness, dialectically this evil of lifelessness had to be destroyed. Phenomenologically, then, goodness arrives as a value through the act of thinking. Thinking, therefore, thinks it is White and that it fully knows what is good and evil. At the same time, God as pure thought wanted order, to be without conflict. But life by its very nature is change, the eternal act of creation, and life too is the awareness of finite boundaries and limits. How can affectivity that is certain be anticipated in life? For once the process of creation has started, the affectivity of the social order and of those within it might have, even unintentionally, been predetermined. Either as lord or bondsman, God was therefore unhappy, dissatis-fied, and alienated.

These opposites had to be resolved and, paradoxically, this could only happen by disrupting the status quo to find out what would be the effect and the new outcome. By choosing change and life, God selected a favour-ite out of its two options for itself. But even then the morality outcome was unknown until action was attempted. Would the product be good or evil? Would the outcome still be *natural* – that is consistent with the very laws that give the universe shape and form? There had to be a concrete test case: it had to be contextualized and materialized based on social relations. In this case, the now conflicted god had to turn its back on the Blackness of the world without form but, seemingly contradictorily, in so doing accepted its own Blackness as the living component of the dialectic: in other words, in striving to create a perfect world with its order and limits, it had created imperfection too. It had created not only the positive identity, but the not-what-it-is identity as well. However, in the Christian mythology, God loses the indeterminacy of the Hebraic tradition, and becomes good, unchanging, and idealistically White. God becomes one-dimensional and almost finite conceptually. Ironically, in this way of thinking, it was change that produced unchangeability – something that could not undergo further change, something that was the end of the line, a death that was a dystopia for a being that is supposedly inquisitive by nature and now had to exist as if it had exhausted all possibilities of knowing itself and its powers to cre-ate. It had arrived in a static utopia, where epistemology is complete and ontology fixed and known.

In the Christian interpretation of the Garden of Eden myth, ontological Blackness can be read through Eve, the woman who would eventually induce the rational man Adam to sin. Eve is presented as the embodiment of passions, or of a primordialism that would show her as not fully reason-able, for she was not reasonable enough to reject the temptation of the less rational creatures in the cosmos. This is why in the myth, Eve is presented in a primitive condition, as speaking to the snake that is seen mythologi-cally as the epitome of the uncivilized and irrational, and as a henchman of evil and death. But in a conflation of Christian and Hebraic traditions, if Eve is not rational, she is yet wise enough to recognize the human condition of finite limits: that someday she and her husband will die, that they can only live on through their children.

Therefore, they must procreate, it being the only way they can transcend their finitude: they must recognize their Blackness while aspiring for White-ness, and the passions are thus made essential for the continuation of life. With the help of the snake that is archetypal of the male body, she induces Adam into the act that is necessary for procreation, holding a rationalist Adam to the recognition that he must also be a practical person for his own survival. In this regard, the passions triumphed over Adam's rational Whiteness – epistemologically, this amounts to what the empiricist of modernity would idealistically call evil on the scale of perception trumping reasoned thought. The result was that the archetypal woman Eve, through her creativity and willingness to disrupt the existing order, ensured the survival of the human race. Eve in her idealistic, cultural, and status Blackness is the dominant subject in this creation story.

But there are other examples in the early Hebraic narrative that appear to support the contention that the first humans were ontologically Black. For instance, the creator made them out of the dust of earth, a point that would be later illustrated so ably, as we saw earlier, by the French sculptor Auguste Rodin in his bronze *Adam*.

Then there are the examples in the post-Eden narrative of women continuing to act and be symbolically Black, particularly those women who created a "race" of humans by copulating with the angels. The result was the creation of a race of demigods, much like the god-humans of Greek mythology and Hegel's god-humans that are the heroes in the dialectic of freedom. Hybrids and composites, as we have discussed, do not have an essence of purity. Therefore, these demigods by nature had to be Black, the purity of God contaminated by the impurity of humans. Alternately, they were idealistically Black because they were now fully separated from the primordial Blackness of humanity. This was so even thought they had godly Whiteness within them. Still, we must remember that neo-mythically, any mixture of White and Black is really Black on the sliding scale; similarly, on the ethno-racial register, a union of superior and inferior beings always results in the creation of what might be the equal of the inferior, but necessarily the inferior creation of the superior being. In modernity, we have seen these concepts producing what have been termed half-caste, half-breed, bi-racial – where the children of socially unequal partners are deemed to be from the culture and identity of the partner in the lesser position. Hybridization, the mixing of two distinct beings, is ontological Blackness and the process that creates it and perpetuates itself is cultural Blackness.

## BLACKNESS: AS NATIONAL HYBRIDITY, CREOLIZATION

In the dominant Western mythology, producing such a class of hybridized people as discussed above is an attempt, once again, by women to break the barriers and limits between finite and infinite, especially those epitomized by the so-called great chain of being which suggests a formulaic and functionalist construction for the universe. Women were thus like Eshu seeking to see what would become of mixing strange and seemingly incompatible alloys.

Second, Adam's lineage appeared to be somatically and culturally Black, particularly Cain after he had killed his brother Abel: a deed for which the punishment was Cain's forced departure from civil society – the then site of Whiteness – and his return to a life of lawlessness and chaos in the Blackness beyond the gates of the city, having to wander the world as a traveller, a nomad in a desert. This was a Black experience both culturally and in status. So placed at the dictates of nature and the fates, Cain cried out to God for relief and God consented, by giving him a mark of humanity – somatic Blackness – that was to serve as protection.

Arthur S. Peake explains in *A Commentary on the Bible*, "So Yahweh mercifully sets a visible mark on him, not to identify him to all men as the murderer Cain, but to warn any who may desire to kill him that sevenfold vengeance will be taken for his death."[40] This somatic feature would be picked up in Christian mythology to explain "the curse" of Black skin that was imposed on a specific branch of mankind, a curse that existed through lineage and bloodline. Cain becomes the founder of cities and of civilization, an achievement that would make him culturally White and not Black, something that showed that not only did he have to use the materials at hand but he also had to apply his godlike imagination and creativity. This notion of Black skin as a signifier of a curse would again reappear in the story of Cham, the son of Noah, as a philosophical explanation that Blackness, by its very nature, was unreasonable, disproportionate, and disruptive and had to be controlled – usually by Whiteness. In this respect, we see a parallel with the Greek mythologies, which explain Black skin as a signifier of the human condition, first of humanity's struggles against the gods, but eventually as a marker of primitiveness and irrationalism.

But this was not always the case. Mythological references to the people of Kush and Egypt, "races" or nations of people that were noted in the main for their Black skins, are a case in point. In *Before Color Prejudice*, Frank M. Snowden Jr points to the Old Testament references to the Kingdom of Kush, "an independent country, economically and politically important, extending from Syrene far to the south of Egypt, one of the geographical extremes of the world."[41] This location is important because, as Snowden shows, things Black were not associated with exclusion from the every day Biblical life, even if they were treated as foreign, unusual, and even undesirable. Black was simply a human sign of difference, without any specific cultural, social, or political value or ranking. It was read in accordance with the neo-mythic register and not the ethno-racial that would come later.

Such was the dilemma created of this specific union. "Moses married a Kushite woman and when, Aaron and Miriam rebuked Moses for this, 'the anger of the Lord was roused against them, and he left them; and ... there was Miriam, her skin diseased and white as snow.'"[42] In this instance, it was almost as if in contrasting Black and White the Biblical God was associating the elevation of Whiteness with death and that of Blackness with life.[43] Snowden sums up how the people of Kush were then viewed: "In short, in the Old Testament Kushites were looked upon as one in a family of nations, a people whose color in the eyes of both God and Moses was of no moment – ideas that were to figure prominently in the early Christian view of blacks."[44]

Indeed, the argument over Moses's choice for his bride can be taken a step further to indicate that in the Hebraic tradition God disapproved of difference based on somatic and even cultural characteristics. The Hebraic God sided with Moses against Miriam and Aaron, which seems to indicate that God saw no negative significance in his servant marrying a woman of another colour and culture. Perhaps, ironically, to make the point that skin colour does not really matter morally, Miriam's punishment for speaking against God's servant Moses was limited to affecting only the surface or top layer of her skin, for the word in Hebrew means "peel off." The disease produced a type of White scaling for about a week. It was not one of the more pathological sicknesses, such as leprosy, that in the Hebraic tradition turned the body deathly White deep in the flesh. In this thinking, the inflicting of Whiteness is intended to turn an individual idealistically and even culturally Black, with Whiteness becoming a signifier of the unclean – an anathema to the purity and preservation of the culture and society. The question, it would seem, thus becomes one of whether or not the specific Whiteness is pathological.

In Miriam's case, Whiteness was presented positively as a temporary punishment that fell or peeled away after she had endured a period of exclusion from society, for this sickness was in the form of boils and scales that would fall off. She would be cured in seven days, the amount of time that must pass for an unclean person to be restored to cleanliness. In the Hebraic tradition, a distinction was thus made between the Whiteness of a degenerative disease and the Whiteness that is caused by a swelling or eruption of the skin as a symptom of becoming temporarily unclean – or idealistically Black. The deeper and incurable skin disease was different from the scales and boils. It was more of a threat to the household and society. In Leviticus, the Lord had instructed Moses and Aaron on how to differentiate the gravity of skin diseases that generically were all called leprosy: "the priest shall examine the disease on the skin of [the sick person's] body, and if the hair in the diseased area has turned white and the disease appears to be deeper than the skin of his body, it is a leprous disease; after the priest has examined him he shall pronounce him ceremonially unclean. But if the spot is white in the skin of his body, and appears no deeper than the skin, and the hair in it has not turned white, the priest shall confine the diseased person for seven days."[45]

## NEW SOCIAL ORDER: WHITENESS AS IMPERIAL, BLACKNESS AS COLONIZED

As we saw in section 1 of this book in regard to the Roman emperor Constantine, early Christianity would borrow this image of healing from the Hebraic tradition. However, the negative connotation of cultural and somatic Blackness would hold sway in Christian mythology in the conception of who or what is good and evil and who should be a member of civil society, particularly of the European social order that reached its apex in the European nation-state. Writing in 1578, George Best, for example, offered the explanation that somatic Blackness was a stain on a branch of humanity that indicated God's eternal displeasure with those so marked. This happened, he explained, during the Biblical flood when Noah imposed an order on his sons that they abstain from sex:

Which good instructions and exhortation notwithstanding his wicked sonne Cham disobeyed, and being perswaded that the first child borne after the flood (by right and Lawe of nature) should inherite and posssesse, he contrary to his father's commandment while they were yet in the Arke, used company with his wife, and craftily went thereby to dis-inherite the off spring of his other two brethren: for the which wicked and detestable fact, as an example for contempt of Almighty God, and disobedience of Chus, who not onely it selfe, but all his posterite after him should bee so blacke and lothsome, that it might remain a spectacle of disobedience to all the worlde.[46]

With this approach, we are seeing the collapsing of the ethno-racial and neo-mythic registers in order to provide a meaning that, significantly, supports a system that has already come into being. In some cases, the curse was associated with Cain's killing of Abel, and occasionally this mythology and that of Cham's disobedience were actually conflated. An example of this is the rationale given by Azurara, the chronicler of Prince Henry the Navigator, that somatically Black Moors (Mahomedans) were slaves "because of the curse which, after the Deluge, Noah laid on his son Cain."[47] Otherwise, the question of colour was dealt with as an indication of sin and having fallen from grace. According to the Christian mythology, the world was Black and ugly and loathsome because of its sinful nature, a Blackness that was always in dialectical opposition to the Whiteness and brilliance of Revelation's New Jerusalem in the Bible. "Augustine asks who are meant by the Ethiopians; and answers that all nations are Ethiopians, black in their natural sinfulness; but they may become white in the knowledge of the Lord."[48]

Elliott H. Tokson indicates in *The Popular Image of the Black Man in English Drama, 1550-1688* that stereotypical images of Blackness and the

African from the pre-modern period informed the way members of the English nation saw themselves and their relationship with other groups, especially those that were African and Black.[49] Most of the raw material for the negative images of Blacks came from early travel reports, from fantastic voyages of discovery in strange lands to discover strange peoples and cultures, travel accounts that were informing the European imaginary of Blackness and Africa as late as the twentieth century. These voyages continued with modernity, leading to the civilizing and colonizing of other peoples, to the mapping of both natural terrain and humans, and to the building up of images of virtue and stereotypes by which to identify non-nationals as inferior. As Tokson states:

When history produced a need for white men to react to black men, the already highly developed and persistent tradition of the wild man offered itself as one source of ready-made concepts that would result in two images of the wild man and the black man sharing the same essential quality. That quality, a "raw, unpredictable, foreign" force of lust and destruction … originates in some "basic and primitive impulses" that are "hidden in all of us, but are normally kept under control." The unfortunate consequences of such impulses are not directly felt when they result in the creation of imaginary monsters like the hairy wild man whose existence always remained a fictive one. But when the fairy tale creature helped shape the image of black-skinned men, his qualities were imposed on real human beings who would enter and remain in the historical experience of Western culture, and who would suffer from the unfair transference of such qualities.[50]

As Tokson and others show, the images of somatic Blacks as evil and cursed, and unreasoned and unruly, would play themselves out in many forms. On the stage, and in popular folklore, this would take the form of the somatically Black demons that were the jealous Moors, the Satanic barbarians that killed simply for the love and pleasure of killing, and the Black and evil despoilers of virtuous women and nations. In *Othello and Colour Prejudice*, G.K. Hunter, for example, indicates how constructed images and stereotypes of Blacks were part of Renaissance England and Europe, images that were maintained in modernity. These were constructions in which the ethno-racial register was presented as proof of the neo-mythic, rather than as a complementary or different way of finding meaning. As Hunter states: "As *candidus* had combined the ideas of white skin and clear soul, so the word *fair* served to combine the ideas of beauty and whiteness. Black remains the adjective appropriate to the ugly and the frightening, to the devil and his children, the wicked and the infidel. In the medieval romances, the enemies of the knights are usually Saracens, often misshapen and monstrous (eyes in forehead, mouth in breast, etc.) and commonly black … The habit of representing evil as black-faced or Negroid had also established itself in a pictorial tradition that persists from the Middle Ages through and beyond the sixteenth century."[51]

These were the uncivilized, oversexed, most basic, and naturally biological of beings, producing the kind of animalism that was the dialectical opposite of what humans mythologically aspired to. Rather than being those of gods, these traits were consistent with those of the most debased humans. Their behaviour typified a licentious, spontaneous approach to life that respected no boundaries and accepted no limits – a behaviour, that as with the Biblical fall, was constantly chancing death and persistently resisting the latest constructed social order. These were not wholesome characteristics for the nation-state, or for the protection and preservation of the life created with the construction of a new nation and with the culture it was producing. These were examples of what came to be seen as a slave mentality, a virtue that ultimately translated into a lordship and bondsman relationship between somatic and cultural Whites and Blacks. This would become the main rationale for the institution of African slavery on which the Black Atlantic, especially the Western Hemisphere, would thrive.

Ultimately, these forms of finite Blackness came to be associated with those who were identified as natural allies of death, with those who, by their very nature, should be excluded from among the company of the selected. Eventually, this form of Blackness would be symbolized most by those people that were called Negroes, the most basic and uncivilized of humanity. The somatic marker for Negroes as a race would be their black skin. Modernity brought all these identities together and merged those of the outsider, the rejected, and the despised into the African – thereby beginning the construction of a nation of Others based on the supposed naturalness of their race, as indicated and revealed by their corporeal characteristics and their attendant preconceived natural behaviour.

This attitude towards Blackness – as being representative of the excluded – would inform the culture of those who called themselves English, including those English living in the provinces of Canada and various English outposts in the Americas who continued to see themselves as an integral part of the English "race" – a nation of people that were the most civilized in the world. On other stages, these imagined ideals based on the presumed differences between so-called races of people would be played out in physical and chattel slavery, colonialism, and rigid racist stratifications based on skin colour. These were countries deemed inferior by those groups that, under specific national identities, treated themselves as gods and all others, especially those with dark skins, as evil and Black. As Fanon attested: "In Europe, that is to say, in every civilized and civilizing country, the Negro is the symbol of sin. The archetype of the lowest values is represented by the Negro."[52]

This differentiation is central to the history and cultural legacy of Europe to which Canada and Canadians, for centuries, claimed an inheritance, and which they fought to maintain in its purest and most essentialist form. Particularly in the Americas, Canada was supposed to be the homeland for Whiteness at its purest, the place where the best of humanity was set aside and moulded into a nation that was as separate and distinct from the rest of humanity as was Blackness from Whiteness. It is a manner of thinking that even remains at work in multicultural Canada, where it can be seen in an immigration policy that selects for inclusion in the Canadian nation only the idealistic White members of humanity, those now identified as possessing the highest levels of social capital in terms of skills and education. Initially, the Whiteness of the specially elected was based on having English blood. Later it came to mean having European blood. This was an approach that at different moments of discontinuity in Canadian history privileged Whiteness as being characteristic of English and European lineage, culture, ethnicity, natural disposition, and colour of skin, and it came even to apply to geographical considerations.

## UNCHANGEABLE BLACKNESS: SOMATIC BLACKS AND BELONGING

Throughout this discourse, one thing remained unchanged: the notion that Blackness represented the undesirable, even if the primary characteristics of Blackness changed according to the given moment and the reason for the discourse. In all cases, Africans and their descendents were typical of this Blackness and supplied its core identity. Conceptually, the idea came to include other groups as well, even Europeans perceived by the dominant as being of lower standing and cultures. At the beginning of the twenty-first century, immigration would be based on selection criteria that offered entry to only "the brightest and the best" from around the world. Whiteness at this time was thus based on a points system that prejudged how well the new immigrants would fit into a country that was at heart still racially White, where in practice power was still held by a mainstream that was constructed based on the perceived natural characteristics of a European White race. Yet, paradoxically, it is a country that in theory aims today for an idealized Blackness epitomized as the Whiteness of official multiculturalism, of multiculturalism as the privileged social and political good and national creed.

# 13

# Ethno-Racial Bondage

We shall take a closer look in this chapter at the quest for freedom within an ever-changing lordship and bondage relationship that is the underpinning of Western aspirations and thought. Slavery, as Orlando Patterson argues, is the other to freedom: to talk about one is to speak indirectly about the other.[1] As Patterson further states, freedom has meaning only in comparison to bondage, whether physical or social.[2] Indeed, whether of a people or of an individual, slavery was anathema to the Enlightenment that spawned modernity. In the ideology that came to dominate Western life, liberty meant, in practical terms, consent freely given and, when appropriate, freely revoked.[3] An array of thinkers in African, Greek, and Christian mythologies had hotly debated this issue, with most of them condemning human bondage.[4] But often these condemnations started with the rationalist notion of a free will, of having the right and ability to imagine a good, and then the unfettered ability to attain or receive the fruits of liberty. If physical slavery is the ontological and ethical opposite of freedom, liberty's epistemological expression is hope – the faith and expectations, that in the absence of certain knowledge, still drive humans on towards this presumptive liberty at the end of history. Hope, then, more than anything else, is at the heart of freedom – the misrecognized White light as Derrida states in one of the epigraphs to the previous chapter – for hope starts as a ray that in its primordial Blackness aspires to become White.

In the three mythologies of concern to us, liberty was at the heart of the concept of self-determinacy, whether of an individual or group of people; it was the belief that humans should endeavour to control their fates; it was ultimately a hope. As such, it was believed that humans should aim to be totally and absolutely responsible for their fortunes and destinies. This meant being able to claim sovereignty and with it asserting the ultimate right to self-ownership and self-determination. It meant taking full responsibility for all the transformations and changes that occur in a life. To this end, even today much of our discussion on the meaning of citizenship within a Western social order is still within the context of choices between liberal individualism and civic responsibilities:[5] under liberalism the individual or a minority group is the master in the lordship and bondage relationship with the state and other groups; under the civic the individual or minority group is the bondsman, but one who suffers under a benevolent lord. Both concepts are supposed expressions of freedom – even giving us ideals of what we have come to call the First World and Second World, when during the struggle for dominance within the West the body of thought known as liberalism represented the First World and the body represented by the socialist or communist camp was deemed to be Second World.[6] The reason that liberalism was deemed to be of a higher order was the assumption in modernity that the free individual was the highest expression of liberty. In this way, individuals were assumed to have choices in ethical relations, the chance to determine what good should come out of any of their metamorphoses, including having, idealistically, a direct say about the ultimate transformation that is death.

Indeed, from the beginning of the history of the Western social order, humans have used rituals to incorporate into their lives the death of finite positions and the hope of transcending them into something higher and morally better. Death and hope, the Blackness that is negated for Whiteness, go hand in hand as identical twins. As Eliade states, initiation rites from physical birth to death, and the ritual expectations of what happens next, are based on the idea of change, that humans are constantly in the process of changing from one state to another, that they are forever enduring small deaths and resurrections on their way to the ultimate death.[7]

And this is seen through the life cycle that begins with the baby in the womb and ends with the disappearance back into the tomb that is earth – a series of transformations beyond finite limits and boundaries. The rites that celebrate these changes can be divided into two types: those of puberty "by virtue of which adolescents gain access to the sacred, to knowledge, and to sexuality – by which, in short, they become *human beings;* and second, specialized initiations such as confirmations and adult baptism, which certain individuals undergo in order to transcend their human condition and become protégés of the Supernatural Beings or even their equals."[8] As discussed earlier, such a process is a double determinacy or double negation of the human condition. The human life is thus made up of a series of "deaths" or tragedies and "resurrections," each of which is tied to the human condition or to the hope and probability of transcending it.[9]

Death is valuated as an essential moment in the existence of the Supernatural Being. By dying ritually, the initiate shares in the supernatural condition of the founder of the mystery. Through this valuation, death and initiation become interchangeable. And this, in sum, amounts to saying that concrete death is finally assimilated to a transition rite towards a higher condition. Initiatory death becomes the *sine qua non* for all spiritual regeneration and, finally, for the survival of the soul and even for its immortality. And one of the most important consequences that the rites and ideology of initiation have had in the history of humanity is that this religious valuation of ritual death finally led to the conquest of the fear of *real* death, and to belief in the possibility of a purely spiritual survival for the human being.[10]

But human beings acknowledge that, in the lordship and bondage relation in which they exist, they do not have a real say about the ending of their physical life. Even though they may mimic death and try to prepare for it, they do not have meaningful choices; they do not know when death will arrive. Neither do they as individuals know with absolute certainty what death *is* since they have never experienced it.

Death is an individual experience that is as unique as every individual, and can only be truly understood a posteriori – after the change: it cannot be rationalized effectively. Death is the limit of critical thinking, which is based on a priori concepts and even demonstrative proof of reason, what the mind can imagine and wills the body to achieve: the collective epistemological experience. Beyond that limit is infinity, the unknown and unknowable as pre-thought, where thought can be, and generally is, as Kant suggests, of the impractical and unpragmatic, of antinomies.

For the living, therefore, death imposes a gap in knowledge. Into this abyss, humans place hope, a mental theophany that becomes a mystical bridge allowing humans to cross from one side to another, from among humans to the gods and ancestors, from the physical to the spirit world, from the finite condition to infinity.

### LIFE AND HOPE: BLACKNESS TO WHITENESS

Hope is the key element, in the prevailing Judeo-Christian tradition, that has historically been presented as the only measure that gives meaning to human existence. Promising continuity between the present and the future, it is the constant that transcends the most ultimate and most indeterminate of limits. This is the hope that is captured so poignantly in the Christian hymn "Amazing Grace," which, like so many of the ritualistic Black and blues dirges of African Americans, is a song of joy that if robbed of its infinite hope by restricting it to a finite or contingent moment at the side of a grave becomes a mere exercise in nihilism and despair. Unfettered, it sings of the hope of re-creation and rebirth.

Ontologically, hope is the idealistic belief that human beings need have no fear of returning to a time of possible chaos for they will reach the ideal point where they will be free of fear. The good that created the cosmos will exist in the afterlife, and in a Hegelian sense they will be at one with it, in a final reconciliation that negates the evil of the original separation or fall. Phenomenologically, then, hope is idealistic Whiteness, but existentially it is Blackness, which, in the end, makes it Blackness.

But hope also has its existential features: by linking philosophy and mythology, as a promise of justice, it is the pledge in the here and now that death, the tragedy that is human life, will some day end. It is the promise that human beings will not have to look to a hereafter for justice: they can achieve their ideals without going through a transformation into an unknown. Hope connects these ontological and existential needs by allowing human beings to hold onto the intangible, but through faith, in the absence of epistemological proofs – through that which cannot be proven empirically or dialectically, that which escapes both analytic thought and the senses as well. Fear of death will thus be eradicated at that point when humans have achieved perfect knowledge: not only of what they are as beings, but of what they will become through every transformation in and from life. Hope is the spirit that acknowledges the presence and certainty of an infinity – that goes beyond the need for analogy – and as such it is also idealized and cultural Blackness.

Hope enters human experience as an entity on its own through mythology, thus transcending ontology, existentialism, and epistemology. It is not simply a belief, but a faith based on optimism, on an idealism that says the universe is in the hands of a good regulator who knows and understands rational change – who has an understanding that surpasses human knowledge. It is the answer to existential angst of life in the absence of full knowledge. This is the response to the argument, particularly in the Greek and Christian mythologies, that life is universally short, harsh, and full of pain, that the gods, in all honesty, could only give humans two nihilistic bits of advice. "The definitive wisdom of Silenus, the satyr companion of Dionysus: the best thing is not to be born – the next best is to die soon."[11] Perhaps, in the context of our wider discussion on Blackness and its positioning in the cosmos, it is worth noting that ontologically, in Greek mythology, Sileni are wise creatures, well-known drunkards, and Black in complexion, and because they were man-beasts, they were hybrid and composites – all of which makes them idealistically and culturally Black.

And from the dominant Hebraic and later Christian mythologies there is a notion of punishment and retribution that hangs over insolent humans for, as St Augustine says in *Concerning the City of God against the Pagans*, "the condition of human beings was such ... [that] if disobedient [to God] they would be justly condemned to punishment of death."[12] So that, as St

Augustine argues, life is either a living death or a death while living.[13] In the latter case, life is also meaningless unless lived according to imposed rules, those that come to us neo-mythically and also trumped those from the ethno-racial register. Hence, there is no rational unfettered freedom, except when the individual willingly agrees to the limits, placing himself or herself in a position as where the limits and boundaries can be viewed as being self-imposed. Death is the ultimate test of Whiteness and Blackness, of how idealistically the latter can be transformed into the former, of the ignorant wanting to enter the Whiteness of perfect knowledge and everlasting life. In this respect, death is the ultimate lord ethno-racially. Human existence is an ongoing lordship and bondage relationship. In it humans acknowledge that death will triumph some day. But in a covenant with this lord, they try to live in such a way that, through their thoughts or actions, they will not cause death to speed up its arrival. All the while, and through their mastery of science, technology, and wisdom, humans are plotting for the day when death shall be no more – when the lord will be overthrown and the bondsmen would now be free neo-mythically and ethno-racially.

But with such an existence, there is also the realization that ontologically Blackness and Whiteness are inextricably bound. Writing in *Correlations in Rosenzweig and Levinas,* Robert Gibbs refers to the image of rays of White light emanating from the kingdom of God in Judaic,[14] and I would argue Christian, mythology to illuminate and redeem the entire cosmos, and which have as their source a heart of darkness: "A bright star shines its light outward while it burns within, but the foundation in thought of this ultimate star must be an introversion. The very motion of light outward would be introverted with a motion of light inward, and the brilliant fire would be introverted into a stillness, an absence of all energy. This star turned inside out we now know as a Black hole ... If the star of redemption is the positive product, the result of exploration beyond pure thought, then in pure thought (Reason) ... must construct its opposite, the Black hole."[15] Indeed, again as Derrida concurs, as stated earlier: "The heart of light is Black, as has often been noticed."

Whether given by the gods or individuals, hope was thus the one way out of the meaninglessness and temporality of human existence. If life as existentialist Blackness itself was a tragedy – founded on the realization that ultimately all life, ideas, and loves that are common to humans must die and decay – hope was the intended tragedy for tragedy itself, the dialectical negation of a negation, the promise of diminution and possible eradication of those forces that inflict hardships on humans. Therefore, the future as hope, as a leap of faith, as an end to our epistemology, must by definition be constructed according to the neo-mythic register. It has to come in the transcendent.

Coming out of the main Greek mythology, hope was thus the human way to get even with the vindictive and conflicted gods who had no compunction about making humans their playthings to push, pull, and abandon in any which way it pleased them, or to treat them as benign, half-witted children, and, ultimately, to devour them with the dialectic of time. For traditional African mythology, the hope is for a transformation that allows an individual to pass into the world of the ancestors, to a higher existence where humans and spirits exist side by side in the same world, as was the original plan at the beginning of creation.[16]

However, this universe or existence is made up of parts visible and invisible, with the invisible and aristocratic order having power over the lower and visible part. A lordship and bondage relation exists, then, between those members living ethno-racially as humans and those existing as spirits – of both the ancestors that have lived and died and those spirits that have yet to be transformed into future human beings. In an order that is good, humans live under a covenant where the spirits are the lords, and they agree to intervene directly only under specific conditions or when humans appeal, as in prayer or through various rituals, to the spirits' help. Similarly, in Christian mythology, hope is at the basis of conflict management,[17] in the belief that a sovereign will protect individuals from arbitrariness and bring stability and predictability to their lives. It is behind the notions of fair play implied in a social contract, as discussed by Locke[18] and Rousseau,[19] for example.

Because physical death comes, according to the predominant mythology in Western thought, like a thief in the night, or even in the next moment, it ultimately prevents human beings from transcending their human imperfections and weaknesses with certainty. They seldom can transform into an existence as higher beings, such as gods experience in the Greek traditions. Such a transcendence depends on the power that only the gods have neo-mythically. This is the power over death. With only the gods knowing the future, if only in the sense that there must be a future, theirs is a world without end – conditions do not change for them. Time, for the gods, if it exists for them, is not finite, even if there are temporal periods when they may intervene in human affairs. Secure in this knowledge, these unchanging gods can proceed with the production and creation of wondrous works that give meaning to their existence. They can make mistakes and correct them as part of the revelation that is always part of the act of creation, that – borrowing from Christian thinking – is a continuous cycle of births and rebirths, and is central to the unfolding of the universe and is caught in the arrival of the next moment. They have time to play and to indulge themselves, as they do not have to worry about producing the necessities of life – all in a losing battle to keep death and a transformation into the unknown at bay. Instead, there is play in which every moment is a new one arriving from an endless plenitude of options. Therefore, it is dangerous for human beings when gods play with them: for a mistake by the gods can doom the finite beings – humans would have no second choice to recover from harm that might even be unintentional. For this reason, humans enter into covenants under which the gods agree not to play with them as long as humans perform certain rituals that are acts of praise or efforts to keep the gods in good spirits. In this way, human beings help keep the gods in check; both the gods and these lesser beings would clearly know what is expected of them and the boundaries within which they can operate. In Greek mythology, in the ensuing lordship-bondage relations, the gods do not face the daily personal repression of their desires and wishes for pleasure that is so intrinsic to the making of human culture and civilization. To this end, the gods would give up freely the options of playing with other beings that are, contradictorily, so much like gods and at the same time so primitive in their folly for wisdom as to be capable of amusing the higher beings. The hope for humans is that the gods would continue to respect the provisions of the covenant, even when humans are caught cheating, and that this hypocrisy of sorts would continue until the moment when the gods suddenly realize that the humans were equal to them – they would become, as it were, citizens of this state that would now be free of further change. For humans, the good of creation would now be complete; the creative process would have produced what a creator or demiurge that was good had originally intended. Equality as the desired good would be fixed for all times, as unchangeably good and White, and even the gods would not be able to change this new rule of Nature. The new humanity would be one of idealized Whiteness, even for those who might be somatically and culturally Black.

Hope, then, is humanity's aspiration to be godlike; it means freedom, which means choice. Human existence is normally without meaningful choices and lasting freedom because of the drudgery of staving off death. So that humans, instead of ascending to higher beings like the gods, find themselves by nature tending to descend to the lowest levels of the cosmology, those of the beast of the fields, the fowls of the air, the fish of the sea – to be no different from the bees and the ants – who, according to the Prometheus legend, at least knew the moment of their death and what death is.

In Greek mythology, human beings were to have dominion over these lesser unthinking animals, just as gods had dominion over human beings. That was to be the natural order, one that would not have to be constructed. Human beings were also endowed with divinity in the form of reason, the fire given to them by the gods in the Greek tradition of Prometheus, the same spirit that in the Hebraic tradition is the breath of God captured in bodies brought forth from the nothingness of the earth into the likeness of God. Humans received reason, but lost knowledge or clearsightedness about the reality of their ultimate transformation. This was the natural ordering of the Greek universe, where human beings would use the gifts handed them by the gods to eventually ascend the cosmological ladder to be among those that live forever.

## DEATH AND THE HUMAN IMAGINATION: LIMITS AND REPETITIONS

But this is a cosmology based on contradictions: human beings as both material bodies and as spirit with the breath of God; human beings as the makers of fire but still living like animals and capable of making the most irrational decisions; human beings as capable of the clarity and pristine authenticity of reason but living in a world that is fake and without reason. Ultimately, physical death as presented on the ethno-racial register brings human beings physically, not to the higher level, but to the lowest. It takes them back to the first principles that are the laws that govern them – back to the dust from whence they came – rather than allowing them to escape the slavery of their nature. What was true of death also applied ethno-racially to its philosophical ally blindness, especially to intellectual sight-lessness – considered a mark of the uncivilized even by human standards. Humans, who are capable of achieving the sight and understanding of gods, are inevitably brought low to the Hades of those without light, without hope, and without a future. That was one interpretation that came out of the pre-modern world and resulted in a commingling of Greek and Hebraic traditions.

The only future with certainty to human beings is that of the nothingness that comes from the inevitable ticking away of time and passing of history; and, as a greater indignity, usually they do not even know when this igno-minious future will begin. For while death, epistemologically, is a transfor-mation of being into nothing or non-being, in terms of matter; human minds cannot fathom such an experience of not knowing what happens at the moment of death, particularly their physical death.[20] Neo-mythically, they think they cannot die physically, cannot seemingly run up against a limit with no other form of becoming. As a result, humans fear death ethno-racially;[21] for them it is like being sucked into a great Black hole epis-temologically, and they have only the hope of finding a White light emanat-ing from its centre. Death is thus the point at which the senses fail and where, as Kant argues, pure reason breaks down, so that what is left is hope of some mythological cosmic good. As Robert Gibbs says in *Correlations*:

Philosophy has always been up to its neck in the fear of death, but never admitted it. The philosopher, the one who fears and thinks, refuses to face his own death. But in order to deny his death – that "unthinkable annihilation" of himself which he can only fear – the philosopher insists that reality is identical with thought: what he cannot think [death] cannot be. In a grand evasion of his own fear, the philosopher denies the object of this fear: death is absolutely nothing. His own death becomes a mere separation of a body from his soul, which cannot die, likes Socrates imagining the philosophical conversation continuing after death. But in order to accomplish this denial, the philosopher must undertake the totalizing philosophic project: know it all. If he can only think everything, can know it all, can complete the system, then in that moment of completion he will have proven that death is absolutely nothing (because it will have no place in the system).[22]

Indeed, Kojève argues that Hegel was the first philosopher to complete the system conceptually through the continuous working of the dialectic of knowing, so that there can be no real limits within his system of thought. In this regard, Hegel's analysis is very similar to traditional African thought, as suggested by James Snead in *Repetition as a Figure in Black Culture*.[23] Once a limit is established, it falls under its own weight, because inherent in the thought are the currents that would extend the old boundary. One's death is only a step to another consciousness, so that idealistically there is no end of time, history, or transcendence into Whiteness. Limits and boundaries, as do freedoms, are constantly appearing and being replaced systematically. Technically, then, there is no permanent death idealistically, even if there is a transformation that causes a physical disappearance. Gibbs brings in Hegel on this score: "Hegel expressly denies that there are limits to thought, by claiming that the very process of limitations displays the overcoming of that limit. This is much the same as the 'bad infinity', which for Hegel is the impossible attempt to separate the infinite from the finite. Thus whenever we place a limit on thought and assert that beyond that limit lies the infinite, Hegel challenges that we have, through such thinking, already reappropriated that infinite and transcended the limit. Hegel's 'true infinity' is one that is present in the finite."[24]

It is difficult for individuals to imagine their personal non-existence as both body *and* spirit. For this reason, while they know and can accept that the body will expire and decay, they cling to the hope that the spirit, as Socrates suggests, will not only live on but will have a more "realistic" experience. Similarly, as idealistic philosophers such as Plato, St Augustine, Descartes, and Kant[25] suggest, memory that is instilled in the mind diachronously reminds humans of an existence before the acquisition of a body, an existence that is pure thought and not dependent on the body.

Whatever its consequence on the spirit, physical death involves a transformation that produces a loss: that of the body and its senses and pleasure. As measurements of existence in the present, they are not subject to possible false memory. In return, their knowledge does not offer anything concrete, nothing akin in practical terms to the butterfly metamorphosing out of death's cocoon. This lack of knowledge ethno-racially is one of the reasons for humans' ever constant attempt to subvert death and its control over them, why for centuries they have looked to the arrival neo-mythically of hope, and not death, as the thief in the night, as the stranger arriving in the next moment. Hope would be embodied ontologically in a messiah: ethno-racially a teacher in the Hebraic tradition, but in the Greek and Christian mythologies a human-god who had slipped the surly boundaries of human existence, the person who would commingle the essence of the gods into a human body, container, or vessel. Existentially, hope would be in all those humans fighting to extend life on earth, and to reach the point when "death shall be no more." This is where, in the neo-mythic view of the world, the ethno-racial and neo-mythic registers could be reconciled in this life.

## DEATH: PART OF AN ETERNAL CYCLE

The other notion at the heart of modernity was neo-mythically that death was a beginning, the removal of corporeality, materialism, and all the earth-bound matter that keep the other part of the dualism – the soul, the idea, reason incarnate – from reaching its natural heights. Only by shedding the human body could there be freedom from the shackles of time, history, human emotions, and fear. Only then could humans soar to the heavens, to the levels of the gods, and even begin to live as they do. This, too, is an expression of faith in hope, of hope based on a leap of faith. Human death, then, became the pre-requisite for a rebirth as gods and for the full revelation of all purity, authenticity, and truth. This was a thought that reached back to Platonic and Socratic discussions on the liberation in death of the individual's "soul" into its natural state – a soul that was in existence before the materializing of the body, soul as the original and indestructible idea of form that lives on after the body is gone. As Socrates argues in *Phaedo*, the truly good exists in another world than this and it is only by releasing the soul from its enslavement in the body that humans will transcend this bond to become as good as gods. As David White explains in *Myth and Metaphysics in Plato's Phaedo*, Socrates's arguments mean that,

if the gods are in some sense higher than men in a metaphysical hierarchy, then Socrates' conviction is justified, if the gods are not subject to conditions that could affect their goodness in the way that the goodness of men is affected [by their bodies]. Such disruption for men could occur only in this life. As a result, if there are good men in the afterlife, it is possible that the goodness of good men is similar to the goodness of good gods. This possibility would locate men and gods on the same metaphysical plane (at least with respect to the prediction of goodness) and opens up the further possibility that there may be something higher in a sense than both men and gods.[26]

As White explains, "Socrates then concluded that he has 'good hope that there is something in store for the dead, and, as has been said from long ago, something better for the good than for the wicked.'"[27] But what was Socrates's proof? He had nothing concrete, only hope. He had only a myth on which to base his presumed ethical relationship. This is quite an admission from someone who had devoted his life to searching for epistemological truth, for absolute knowledge and certainty. His was a life dedicated to a search for essences and reason as the only real truths. But was this the truth according to the ethno-racial register, the neo-mythic, or a combination of both? As these senses of the body may mislead, he had decided to place his faith in the rational only. In the end, he chose to rely on a hope that is based on two expectations: (1) that the soul exists after death; and (2) that there will be justice, with the good and the wicked distinguished and rewarded appropriately.[28]

Thus, death is not annihilation; it is a reward, a rebirth as a better being. But, ironically it is the tragedy of Socrates and his search for absolute knowledge that he is ultimately reduced to a hope that is a leap of faith, that is mythical rather than epistemological. As Derrida points out, there is a significant difference between dying and perishing, with the latter suggesting an absolute erasure, no legacy, no trace. Antigone, in the Greek tragedy, tried to save her dead brother from perishing: she tried to preserve his legacy.

In this sense, death comes with a further promise of justice, for it turns responsibility into a human requirement and a trigger for dispensing rewards and punishment. Gods and infinite time can be irresponsible for their actions because there is no capital punishment for them. This is why they can be amoral or, even by human standards, immoral. They do not have to be mindful of good and evil, and they do not have to be consistent in their actions, for nothing can stop them from being everlasting. Even Prometheus, bound to the rocks, can only wish for the liberation of death – the ultimate human experience. For even if he suffered the death of humans, he would die knowing his gift and legacy would continue even if he were no more. Humans would live better experiences, and they would live to talk about him. He, too, like so many humans who struggle against evil and death, would live in human memory – in effect he will live again but in a different existence.

Unlike gods and infinite time, the main characteristic of humans is that in their finitude they face death at every moment. Every decision is crucial and is technically a matter of life or death. Every decision is contingent, with the individual's death the ultimate contingency. Indeed, the seemingly most insignificant action or choice can produce the most severe consequence for humans. Yet, even in these contingencies there is an unchangeable law at play: there is a cause and effect attached to humans and their thoughts and actions. In the end, humans can lose life, thereby losing themselves through a transformation into something unknown. Unfortunately, humans might be the cause that produce this ending – and that is why in so many societies the truly evil were those in the service of death, such as murderers and marauders. This is why the stranger arriving as the unknown and often thought to be in league with death was feared and, ironically, even killed physically or, as Patterson would argue, through social exclusion.

For it to maintain the good of creation, every human action has to be predicated on maintaining life, at least until that point when a human decides freely to give her- or himself to death. Supposedly, this latter should be the point where, as Homer suggests, for the lucky and the just, every facet of life, every choice and benefit humanly possible, has been squeezed out of living. She or he would have arrived at the limits under the prevailing lordship and bondage covenant. Every action thus has to be evaluated for its contingent and necessary components, as choice should result in life or in the hope of making the contingent that is life as necessary and unchangeable as life's dialectical opposite, the law that is death.

### WHITENESS IN BLACKNESS: KNOWLEDGE, DEATH, AND FREEDOM

In choosing the infinite life, the kind of death, if not its moment, is also being chosen – that of a happy and satisfied being awaiting an inevitable transformation – or, in effect, not positively chosen through the negation of one law by another. As Jaspers argues, the wise person lives the way she or he wants to die.[29] He argues that this is how wisdom should teach humans to triumph in the existentialism produced of the lordship-bondage dialectical struggle for freedom. Viewed positively, the wise person lives so that living is not contingent, but that death would be unnecessary. Otherwise, death, the only certainty or law, is inflicted as the natural default. This can be a physical death or a death from a loss of choice and responsibility – a rigidity that empties life of meaning.

As an array of Western philosophers and sociologists from Plato and Aristotle to Derrida argue, freedom is escape from the fear of death that is inherent in limits and finitude. This is part of the argument for hope and optimism even in the face of death that was advanced by Socrates in Plato's *Phaedo.* After a life devoted to finding the truth, Socrates was left with a seeming deathbed "repentance" of sorts: that of recognizing that the truth or essence of phenomena in human life is unknowable and unknowing. Only gods know essence, because they are pure reason, pure soul, are unsullied by the body and its conflicts and fears over pain and pleasure. Only gods have an essence, because they are unchangeable, for anything that is changeable is a composite by nature and cannot have an essence. In their Whiteness, idealistically, gods as essences are free from the needs of biology, freed of the accident and contingency of being a dualism. In conversations with his followers and fellow philosophers, and hours away from his own death – technically at his own hands for the ultimate philosophically in free choice – Socrates acknowledges that reason and rationalism can only go so far as an explanation. The only certainty to life is death, Socrates offered. Thereafter must come a leap into mythology, into a constructed story that explains a beginning and an ending to human existence within an overall plan for the cosmos.

This is transcendental idealism, a leap into a world of belief and hope: into something that is non-bodily, non-sensuous, and unprovable by reason or perception, an area where the dialectic is silenced, where empiricism does not provide full answers, but neither, also, does pure reason. This is the limit of human understanding either through the senses or through intellect or reason. This is a leap into the great beyond, into a transformation that signals a disruption of a sacred time and space, a moment when the old order gives way, and in this case time and history end – the one point where there is no lordship and bondage relationship in freedom. This is the opposite of what happens in the creation myth where order with its inherent limits is brought forth out of chaos in order to introduce stability and predictability. The leap is a return to chaos, ontologically, without a clear notion of good, except in the form of a wish.

With such a leap of faith, the dialectical struggle would have come to an end, with Spirit, in the Hegelian sense, producing the final *coup de grâce* to body, or reason to perception, in the lordship and bondage stage of this struggle. Such a prospect is frightening for the body in the Hegelian analysis, for there would no longer be a reason for its existence. Spirit would have exhausted its need for a specific vassal through which to create and to test its potential. Body would perish in this Whiteness of absolute freedom for Spirit. Freedom would be idealistically abstract and unchangeable.

David White points out in *Myth and Metaphysics* that Socrates makes a distinction between dying and death: "Taken abstractly [the distinction] exemplifies the difference between process and product. Thus dying refers to the process of dying, a process that, for the philosopher, does not occur just at the end of life but rather is ongoing throughout life itself. To understand dying is to study the sense in which living and dying are coincident and coterminous ... In contrast, however, death is a state in which the soul is fixed, at least to a certain degree. The state of death, the end result of the process of continuing dying ... is that state where body and soul are separated from one another, each then existing 'alone by itself.'"[30]

Socrates would not run away from death, as his followers suggested even as late as the appointed day of death, and he would not resist its seeming inevitability: he would self-administer his poison and lie down quietly while death takes and transforms him. He would not cringe and lose his humanity – the acceptance of death – in the face of its presence; rather he would look to defeat death by transcending his limits to a higher and more glorious existence as an infinity. There, he would be truly free, truly indeterminate; but because he has knowledge his would not be a return to the base indeterminacy of Blackness, but to epistemological and ontological Whiteness.

What Socrates offers is thus the truth or hope that a true philosopher – one who has attained the highest levels of purity and life, and who has trained the soul to prepare for a separation from its body – should live a life that was an acceptance of death. The philosopher should face his or her bodily demise courageously, freed from the bodily pleasures that would make it crave and even beg for life. The true philosopher would be willing to risk giving up temporal life to attain the good in the afterlife, in everlasting time, since in Socratic mythology, that is where the ultimate good will exists. As White says: "If Socrates has this sense of courage in mind, then he is understanding it in relation to pain, pleasure, and fear. The assumption seems to be then that the philosopher's decision to embrace this distinctive kind of living with death is the most courageous act a human being can perform. For the philosopher, death continually animates life; thus, if the philosopher lives his life as a living death, then he must be courageous about the uncertainty of the outcome of life throughout the duration of that life."[31] The ultimate goal, and, hence the meaning of life, whether for an individual or a community, is the avoidance of an untimely death or a death not freely accepted, or better yet, not chosen.[32] This is the notion of freely choosing death in the hope of a better afterlife, of freely putting away that which has become tiresome and contingent for that which is always new and everlasting. An indication of how death figured in Western imagination can be seen from the way Canadian Prime Minister Arthur Meighen wrote of the symbolic death (retirement from public life) of his predecessor Robert Borden in an introduction to Borden's memoirs. Meighen writes: "There are those whose desire it is to bid farewell to the things of earth in the full flesh of their everyday activities, to drop, as it were, beside the forge. Others plan their journey in the hope of a restful eventide when the weary but rewarded traveller can stroll leisurely along the glades, conscious of having wrested something of victory out of life, and looking back in unspoken pride on the storm-torn terrain over which he has fought and toiled."[33] Indeed, the dominant mythologies in Western thought tell us that this ideal of which Meighen was speaking is the preferred forms of affectivity and motility in this rational, idealistic culture. Death must be anticipated: but life should be marked by a victory that might be no more than the struggle itself against death. And at the end of the struggle, instead of running away and hiding, humans should take a leap of faith, serene in the belief that the approaching transformation is another step on the way to liberty.

As humans must die, the ultimate justice for them would be to die on their own terms, when they are ready. Failing that, perhaps, this death is now best achieved in an Alzheimer-like end of life, when the body is seemingly too old to care about death, far less to recognize or resist it. This is a merging of a finite limit into an infinity in a most natural way – one in which there is virtually no knowledge, yet the previous moment was pregnant with the absolute knowledge of the self-conscious ego that is seeking its liberty from a Black human body. Odysseus offers such an ideal:

> There is an island, called Syria, you may have heard of it,
> Lying above Ortygia, where the sun makes his turnings;
> Not so much a populous island, but a good one, good for
> Cattle and good for sheep, full of vineyards, and wheat raising.
> No hunger ever comes on these people, nor any other
> Hateful sickness, of such as befall wretched humanity;
> But when generations of men grow old in the city,
> Apollo of the silver bow, and Artemis with him
> Comes with a visitation of painless arrows, and kills them.[34]

Similarly, in *Timaeus*, Plato talks about a peaceful death coming at the end when the human body falls out of harmony with the cosmos, a transformation that is presented also as a reclamation by the cosmos of the individual. This brings us to modernity and its expressions of freedom as a triumph of life over death.

One way for meaninglessness to enter the lives of humans, especially the lives of those who are still wedded in a Socratic sense to the pleasures of life, is for the individuals to resign themselves to a deathlike experience. Here, instead of accepting death as a future event, they surrender to its immediate presence. Instead of it leading to living to the fullest, such an acceptance of death is tantamount to existing at the pleasure of an other, a pleasure that it is not humanly possible to influence. This is a person incapable of even influencing the direction of the dialectics of life and time. Such is the slave who realizes that his or her life can be lost at the hand of some other. Such is the case when death is represented ethno-racially in the presence of an other and the subject has no way of resisting. Justice presupposes that if humans make the right choices, they will at least be rewarded with continued life and its freedoms of choice. Issues of right and wrong can only be metaphysical human concerns, as right equates to life and wrong to death. A denial of justice would offer humans no rewards, either in life or in death, for making what they think is the right decision.

The alternative is to choose death, if only in the hope of escaping the living death of a life without justice. This is why Arendt argues that for the ancients an honourable death was preferable to an ignoble surrender,[35] why Aristotle and others contend that slavery is a mentality and some people were by nature weak and slaves. Issues of social justice, acceptance, and recognition are thus issues of life and death in modern society. Slavery and freedom, despair and hope, life and death, finite and infinite, even if they are opposites, are all dialectically parts of the same infinite concepts. Multiculturalism hopes to capture the positive elements of these dialectics. But what happens in practice might be different from the ideal, for instead of striving for a life that is limitless, multiculturalism, itself, can often be found in a dialectical relationship with its other – with what would negate the intent and assumptions of multiculturalism by imposing a finiteness characterized by limits, unchangeableness, determinacy and the privileging of the status quo. Those hoping to negate this prevailing order find themselves in bondage and having an existence that for them is thus characterized by despair and ultimately social death – by what is not positively multiculturalism and its promise of hope for justice.

In the case of Canada, existentially and metaphysically, these dialectical relationships highlight the fear of the powerful and the mainstream of a death that could result from the entry of, and disruption by, cultural and idealistic Blackness in their perceived White spaces. Such an entry would lead to death of the existing way of life, with its time-tested systems and functionalism, and with the replacement of them by the unknown. Many in mainstream Canada sees immigrants, especially those who are somatically Black, as harbingers of death. They do not see them as representing hope of a rebirth or a transformation into a greater good.[36] The immigrants are not messiahs, but devils and harbingers of an apocalypse. In this regard, mainstream Canada has lost the optimism for human existentialism that is imbedded in its rational transcendental ideologies based on Greek and Christian mythologies. It sees death only for finite limits and not as part of the infinity of existence. Or, alternately, mainstream Canada selectively picks from these mythologies those elements and characteristics that look at death as slavery and an unwelcome imposition, something over which the subject has no control, and associates them with specific groups of people. In either case, the fear of death paralyzes Canadian society so that it runs away from the hope that has always been read into death, as merely a transformation to a higher level as part of a systematic approach to existence. It does not, as philosophers from Plato through Jasper and Derrida argue, willingly accept death, but instead lives life in such a way that death becomes a natural part of living. Death, life, and change are, therefore, inextricably bound in the Blackness of the human condition.

## SLAVERY AS SOCIAL DEATH: EXISTENTIAL BLACKNESS

Freedom is a neo-mythic synonym for hope, a reason for living. Its antithesis: death, the existential dread. In Western civilization, one of the unkindest deaths is to suffer a fixation that denies the individual the chance to change socially, to determine her or his next manifestation in the next moment, and to transcend finite boundaries. This fixity is a denial of hope: it is being robbed of participation in the human quest to some day become fully free and idealistically White. Such denial was the kind of death that was imposed on a group of people who were considered by nature to be slaves idealistically, culturally, and socially because of their somatic Blackness. And even when chattel slavery was abolished, the group of somatic Blacks continued to be held in this bondage, one from which, as Fanon says, they were always fixed in limits and boundaries, and denied self-determination. This is the kind of fixation or social death that multiculturalism would try to overturn and thereby liberate the enslaved from this imposed finitude into a freedom of plenitude, self-determination, and self-identification.

As Orlando Patterson argues, sociologically slavery is social death with the slave transformed into the working dead, a revelation that he found at the heart of the dialectical discourse from antiquity to modern times.[37] "I had gone in search of a man-killing wolf called slavery," Patterson says, and "to my dismay I kept finding the tracks of a lamb called freedom."[38] This point is also supported by Hannah Arendt in her argument that freedom started out as a "biological" liberty, whereby humans of certain status and class were freed from the daily concerns of survival – what Locke and Frye call primary concerns – when they started to live as they imagined gods did. And through this point a contrast can be made between the idealized and natural outcomes that are presented in the Greek, Hebraic, and Christian mythologies as most desirable: to live in a land with ambrosia and nectar in the Greek tradition; of milk and honey in the Christian tradition; and of natural water where the rains fell plentifully and brought forth abundance in a place that in the Hebraic tradition was the Promised Land, and which was presented as the site of liberation from the "bondage" of relying on irrigation for household water and agriculture in Egypt.

This was a transformation into Whiteness in idealism and in status. These aristocratic humans had enough food, clothing, shelter – the necessities of life – and the freedom that was embodied in leisure – the pursuits of the gods. They even had lesser beings, humans still trapped in the primitive Blackness, through which they could continue their creation. For they only had to give the word, just like Spirit, and a body would create it for them. They decided what was good and what should be good; lesser beings abided by their notions of what is good and what will be good in the future.

The lesser beings were the slaves, the bodies in a Hegelian lordship-bondage analogy. As lords, they concerned themselves only with secondary concerns, as Locke and Frye suggest.

This was also Whiteness in the idealized form: an order of life that was deemed good by this aristocratic group and worthy of preservation. Anyone trying to change this order would be disruptive and idealistically Black, because they would be trying to exchange one good for another, one that this aristocratic group saw as akin to the death of their lifestyle, and the beginning of a way of life that was unknown to them. This was a death that was feared, one that came in the form of darkness. Here we are reminded of Hegel's analysis of individuality, creativity, and that hue and volition of experiences that are always in a struggle with forces attempting to restrain or even thwart them in their intentions. For the slaves, this Blackness was liberation and creativity – it provided them with hope of a new way of life, a transformation that could be worth taking. And it provided them, in the Hegelian sense, with the opportunity to make history.

As Patterson argues so effectively, freedom can only have full meaning when it is compared to its diametrical opposite, slavery or death. Freedom is coming into full consciousness for the enslaved, fully into objective knowledge of itself as, somehow, always enslaved in life. This is the knowledge that the subject is an object for a higher subject, and that there are limits and boundaries imposed, not by the lesser subject as a rational being, but by a higher and more powerful sovereign. Sociologically, slavery typifies the ultimate in social exclusion, short of physical extermination and genocide. It is of being of one system or order, while others are of a different system or order. For, it might even be argued, to take away the freedom and the spontaneity of choice that is the ultimate expression of humanity is to reduce a person mentally and psychically to nothingness. That is a kind of death or even genocide when practised on a wide enough scale. Freedom is the hallmark of liberalism and democracy in Western civilization and its roots are firmly planted in the flight away from slavery and death.

As Patterson says in *Slavery and Social Death*: "Freedom was generated from the experience of slavery. People came to value freedom, to construct it as a powerful shared vision of life, as a result of the experience of, and response to, slavery or its recombinant forms, serfdom, in the roles of masters, slaves, and nonslaves."[39] Patterson explains that this is why freedom first appears in history as freedom from some form of bondage as opposed to freedom to do as the individual pleases. Slaves were imprisoned in an ethno-racial determination that left them without the hope and ethical values of the neo-mythic register. As slaves, their humanity was constructed one-sided.

This is why, Patterson argues, women and somatic Blacks are usually, as a specific group, in the vanguard for physical freedom and for primary concerns. In the past, they were enslaved in societies constructed around goods that were based on patriarchy and/or racism. The first level of freedom may be seen as arising from a master and slave relationship, and the second as resulting from a lordship and bondage struggle, each as a different level of consciousness and of knowing. In the first, both parties believe that they are free and their growth can come only at the expense of the other; in the second, one of the parties gives up its freedom, but not the desire for liberty, in exchange for life. Each level produces its own unhappy consciousnesses, those who have to make the decision to act and risk the death of the body, or to not act and risk the death of the spirit in the dualisms that are humans. Similarly, Frantz Fanon writes in *Black Skin, White Masks* of a kind of spiritual and idealistic death, the sterility and lack of choice born of an intellectual alienation created by middle-class society: "What I call middle-class society is any society that becomes rigidified in predetermined forms, forbidding all evolution, all gains, all progress, all discovery. I call middle-class a closed society in which life has no taste, in which the air is tainted, in which ideas and men are corrupt. And I think that a man who does take a stand against this death is a revolutionary."[40]

The revolutionary in this case is Black, and the middle-class status is Whiteness. This is a mismatch, where Blackness appears out of place; Whiteness is a harsh and suffocating master or lord. In this case, Blackness has to be creative to break out of the rigidity of Whiteness as perfection and to continue the creation process by bringing to an end this "bad infinity" of Whiteness.

In this section, I looked at how notions of Whiteness and Blackness in Western civilization were developed through a syncretized Christian view of good and evil. Christianity was a creolization of African, Hebraic, and Greek traditions with the Hebraic Bible used as a tool to confirm notions of Blackness and Whiteness that were first presented in Greek mythology and philosophy. African thought, treated as a form of Blackness, received no official recognition in the modernist states that were developing in the Americas. However, the African influence remained potent in these societies, even if unrecognized. I shall now provide an explanation of how this hybridized view based on the epistemology of Whiteness and Blackness became the prevailing ideology on which the Canadian nation-state was founded. This ideology influenced how groups of people were automatically included or excluded from society, what roles they played, and what rights and entitlements they had. It also decided their usefulness to society and what levels of happiness they could expect through their automatic placement and positioning in the society.

The second part of this book, then, starting with the fourth section of my argument, presents the case formally for four categories of Blackness that are present in Western thought and the imagination of state formation.

Having developed and explained the case for the two distinctive ways of finding meaning in an ethical relationship and of understanding humans ontologically, the first part of this book is now completed. We shall turn our attention now to tracing phenomenologically how Canada became officially multicultural as a form of idealized Blackness that aspires for Whiteness by promising universal hope. In so doing, part two will also examine the ethical implications for all the diverse and different groups now recognized as inseparably part of the Canadian body politic.

# PART TWO

# Canadian Blackness and Identity

# 14

# Multiculturalism and Blackness

## DIALECTICS OF CANADIAN BLACKNESS

This chapter takes a closer look at what is still the goal in the Canadian nation-state, that of achieving A Just Society, an ideal state where Canadians can live in peace and happiness with themselves and the world. We shall examine it as a paradigm and as an idealized consciousness of hope that provides the framework for Canada's ideological acceptance of Blackness. The chapter studies in greater detail, as part of the continuing dialectic of freedom, the inner contradictions that result from Canada's self-conscious recognition of itself as multicultural, idealized, and culturally creolized Blackness. The contradictions were embodied in Pierre Elliott Trudeau, the rationalist intellectual who, as a Hegelian great man of history, was prime minister of Canada from 1968 to 1984,[1] and whose government was the parent of the ideology embodied in *A Just Society*.[2] Trudeau said the following of the ideal to which he aspired, and which was so comprehensive a break with the past that it is worth quoting in full:

The Just Society will be one in which all our people will have the means and the motivation to participate. The Just Society will be one in which personal and political freedom will be more securely ensured than it has ever been in the past. The Just Society will be one in which the rights of minorities will be safe from the whims of intolerant majorities. The Just Society will be one in which those regions and groups which have not fully shared in the country's affluence will be given a better opportunity. The Just Society will be one where such urban problems as housing and pollution will be attacked through the application of new knowledge and new techniques. The Just Society will be one in which our Indian and Inuit population will be encouraged to assume the full rights of citizenship through policies which will give them both greater responsibility for their own future and more meaningful equality of opportunity. The Just Society will be a united Canada, united because all of its citizens will be actively involved in the development of a country where equality of opportunity is ensured and individuals are permitted to fulfil themselves in the fashion that they judge best.[3]

Trudeau's goals were to recognize as limitless a new phenomenological spirit of Canada, one in which the country and its citizens were constantly being reconstructed, according to the times in which they exist. As part of the eternal moment of creation, they were to be forever responding to changing environments, to the changes within themselves, and in the cultural identities they accept and project. As individuals, they were to be contingent, taking many different forms in the name of ethnicities, but as a collective spirit they were to be unchangeably and "essentially" Canadian. This restructuring was part of a Nietzschean type of "overcoming" of a nihilism born from the awareness that there were no discernable essences in the being or beings historically called Canada and Canadian. In place of this absented unchangeableness, Trudeau tried to substitute an unchangeableness based on values, thereby aiming for a peculiar type of existence that is Canadian. "A country," Trudeau argued, "is something that is built every day of certain basic shared *values*. And so it is in the hands of every Canadian to determine how well and wisely we build the country of the future."[4] Ironically, in a country renowned worldwide for its aesthetic beauty – for example, viewed as gifts from nature, the pristine lakes and rivers, the snow-capped mountains, the rolling prairies – nothing Canadian would be deemed to be natural; everything meaningfully Canadian would be socially constructed and transformed to meet the dreams of those who happened to be living in this land of natural wonders. In this scheme, what would really matter would be the people and how they create a social and physical environment to ensure their survival and happiness. Canadians, then, would be constructed by Canadians out of whatever materials first appeared. They would be shaped according to a specific ethic that dominates a nation-state carved out of the natural landscape and peopled by citizens produced out of a uniquely Canadian consciousness.

Trudeau felt this goal could be achieved because Canadians were to be constructed unchangeably around specific universal rights and freedoms that are embedded in the mores and values of a particular people in a particular space and time. While the people were contingent in their ethnicity and races – in the outer and finite identities – they were necessarily Canadian because they possessed the spirit or values that are unchangeably Canadian: a commitment to hope for the improvement of humanity, and recognition that humans should always choose life and hope over limits and death. Freedom should amount to the ability to change that which is contingent, such as ethnicity and racial characteristics, to giving up these finite ascriptions but remaining authentically Canadian by embodying the spirit of justice and fair play that are the aspirations of an idealistically White ethical order based on justice.

Existentially, in Trudeau's analysis, states and individuals die in one moment to be reborn as states and new individuals in the next – the only things unchangeable in this process being the universalism or generality of the concepts that are the state and individuality. In times of change, which in Trudeau's view are continuous, only the abstract ideals of Canada and Canadians would remain unchangeable. The specific materiality or contingency of what Canada is or who Canadians are would be continuously unfixed and changing.[5]

In this section of the book we are looking at the contradictions that are embodied in Trudeau's idealized Blackness as a goal for Canada. They are an examination of the sacrifice of the Black body to achieve idealized Whiteness. I will make the argument that in keeping with this goal Canada has come to terms with idealized, cultural, and somatic Blackness by recognizing that the Canadian body is multicultural, and in international affairs, a middle power. This was the answer to Canada's unhappy consciousness internally and internationally that Trudeau put forward.

In a Hegelian sense, Trudeau presented the Canadian body as the mediator that could be sacrificed for the love of humanity, linking the unchangeables that were the concepts of Canada and humanity with the changeables that were the separate nations and states. However, especially internal to this body itself, Canada has only gradually been coming to terms with somatic Blackness as an authentic expression of identity. Somatic Blackness had always symbolized the Hegelian other in the Canadian dialectic of freedom, with the unchangeable in perception being somatic Whiteness.

I will look at how Blackness broke down dialectically, primarily through differences of recognition and acceptance in *realpolitik*. In this regard, multiculturalism was nothing but idealized Blackness epistemologically: the Black hope of creation that gestures towards idealism; the Black method of creating, where the outcome is never known with certainty and, even if another form of Blackness results, there is still always the hope that finally the creator will get it right and bring pure idealized Whiteness out of Blackness.

RATIONALISM AND LAWS: BLACKNESS AS WHITENESS

Trudeau was the epitome of contradictions, with all of them resulting in the legacy of an unfinished "Just Society" that Canada has carried into the new millennium. As his editor Ron Graham notes in *The Essential Trudeau*, the prime minister embodied all the contradictions that were Canada:

For counterbalancing the strong provinces with a federal government, he was branded as a centralist – even though he argued in favour of strengthening the provinces in the 1950s and gave them unprecedented resources in the 1970s. For counterbalancing the strong corporations with a strong state, he was branded as socialist – even though he opposed the nationalization of Quebec's hydro companies in the 1960s and entrenched the rights and freedoms of individuals in the 1980s. His efforts to strengthen Canada vis-à-vis the United States were confused with the ethnic nationalism he so adamantly opposed in both English-speaking Canada and French-speaking Quebec. His lifelong devotion to multiculturalism as a key to social tolerance, democratic pluralism, and individual fulfillment was twisted to appear like a ploy to undermine the two-nations theory of Confederation, a ruse to capture the immigrant vote, a sop to Western Canada's pioneer communities, and an argument for collective rights.[6]

The contradictions were produced through what Trudeau recognized as a dialectical struggle for freedom between the forces of individuality and those of tyranny, with, ultimately, the rights of individuals as recognized in liberalism and democracy being what is at stake. The most meaningful lesson of history is that it points to the paths of liberty and away from tyranny. "The great lesson to draw from revolutions is not that they devour humanity but rather that tyranny never fails to generate them."[7] And, as Trudeau argues, one of the greatest tyrannies in modern society is blind faith in an ideology – particularly what he calls cultural nationalism – that presents certain unassailable "truths" which nonetheless must be backed undemocratically by the threat of violence. "This is the seed of totalitarianism and dictatorship" that is best marked by terrorism in civil society.[8] As Trudeau explained:

In the normal course of life we are subject to many constraints, and we do not hesitate to impose others on ourselves if need be; we are able to accept them as mechanisms indispensable to our life, as the framework of our liberty – for liberty is not without form. And the price of our liberty may be a momentary surrender of one's personal freedom. This is undoubtedly the highest price we can pay for liberty, next to giving our life itself. But liberty is worth this sacrifice. With the love which gives it life, liberty remains the most difficult conquest for humanity. Liberty can thrive only if consciously nurtured; liberty is never won for all times; liberty never sleeps.[9]

Trudeau positions the dialectical struggle, and the contradictions that exist within Canadian society, as grounded in the state. Within the state is the conflict produced by individualism. As we noted, neo-mythically, individuality does not lead automatically to inequality, as does a determination on the ethno-racial register. The state is a determination in a physical sense on the ethno-racial register as it is determined to be different in its form collectively from all others. The individual is determined neo-mythically and without evaluation as being simply another fully formed object among all the many in a given space. What we are analysing here is the struggle of a liberal democracy, one in which Trudeau starts his analysis by positioning the individual as the unchangeable and as predating the state. This is a struggle in which the individual acknowledges that the state must be multicultural first and foremost if there is to be any chance at happiness for its citizens. For Trudeau, it is the individual that makes the state: while the individual is unchangeable, the state is changeable, and, as Trudeau argues, has no essence of its own for it exists only in the will of individuals to live together.

As Trudeau explains, both liberalism and democracy, by privileging the sanctity of the individual, while at the same time proposing an orderly way of bringing individuals together in a rational state where the majority view dominates, are the products of a dialectical process. However, liberalism and democracy are themselves subject to their own internal contradictions and dialectical differences. These contradictions must be mediated through counterweights, mechanisms that are moderate in nature, in order to avoid the extremes that in the Aristotelian manner produce tyrannies and corruption of government and power. In the case of liberalism, this struggle is between what Trudeau saw as tyranny in the form of freewheeling *laissez-faire* capitalism and what he approvingly called personalism, a kind of communitarianism:

Personalism essentially said that the individual, not the state, must be supreme, with basic rights and freedoms, because the individual is the only moral entity, the only one who has significance. But, granted that, we should view the individual as a person involved in society and with responsibilities to it. In other words, sovereign individuals can get together and co-insure each other against the accidents and hazards of living in society. This co-insurance is exercised through the welfare state, by helping those who cannot help themselves. I found personalism a good way to distinguish my thinking from the self-centred individualism of *laissez-faire* liberalism (or modern-day neo-conservatism, for that matter) by bestowing it with a sense of duty to the community in which one is living.[10]

In a democracy, the struggle is neo-mythically between the tyranny, as discussed by Plato, in the form of freewheeling direct democracy and the more rational and deliberate form of government that the Aristotelian Trudeau calls ethno-racially participatory or representative democracy. The latter calls for sober reflective thought, deliberation, and leadership by politicians to keep at bay the chaos and tyranny that comes from people coalescing in a majority at a given moment and thoughtlessly acting on the whims of the moment. To this end, Trudeau is a strong supporter of parliamentary democracy, a system of majority participation in government that makes it possible to look at issues holistically and try to resolve them comprehensively. This is in preference to a system that "contributes to a climate of fear, encourages negative manifestations of the human instinct for survival, and invites tribalism and lawlessness." The result of the latter would be anarchy and a Hobbesian state of nature existence. "In this kind of environment there is no safety, no order, and no protection for the unpopular, for the minorities, or for the weak."[11]

In the ethno-racially determined representative democracy, which Trudeau argues is best suited for civil society, it is incumbent on leaders, such as parliamentarians, to be informed. It is also the responsibility of leaders, acting with reason, to go against the majority view when doing so is for the collective good. However, even in this discussion, Trudeau creates new contradictions. On one hand, he positions the individual as sovereign, and cites this as the reason for his incorporating into the Canadian Constitution a Charter of Rights and Freedoms[12] that recognizes what he considers to be the fundamental minimum, the unchangeable, of what it means to be human. On the other hand, however, he also neo-mythically gives this same sovereignty to the majority in the state – and thereby gives the same evaluative quality to two seemingly different and even contradictory forms and types in a world where differences between types are most important. Similarly, while preaching the centrality of individuality to good government, he argues that the majority of individuals in the state are epistemologically Black by tendency, in that they exist in a state of lacking full knowledge and enlightenment. It is only the reflective and rational statesman produced on the neo-mythic register who has the Whiteness of knowledge. This Whiteness and Blackness must be held in balance in an ethical relationship that is destined to remain epistemologically and existentially Black while aspiring for a transcendental rational Whiteness.

Through these approaches, Trudeau established new epistemological benchmarks for what is good and evil – benchmarks that were beset by their own contradictions. These benchmarks have their greatest meaning as universals that are unchangeable. Ideally, the only moral agent, the individual, decides them. Yet, these measurements of morality would try to incorporate particulars and to govern over changing circumstances. This change is central to the dynamism of progress, creativity, and liberty. Trudeau states: "The first visible effect of freedom is change. A free man exercises his freedom by altering himself and – inevitably – his surroundings. It follows that no liberal can be other than receptive to change and highly positive and active in his response to it, for change is the very expression of freedom. Clearly, though, a liberal can neither encourage nor accept indiscriminate change by indiscriminate means."[13] The benchmarks Trudeau proposed offer a methodology for a way of knowing with certainty, which is to appeal to reason and rationalism in groping towards intellectual Whiteness. Yet, they also acknowledge the darkness in which all human endeavours must occur and that methods and formulas, by their nature, seldom deliver what is discerned. In Canada's case, a good example was the attempt to produce a White man's country through the selection of ethno-racially White people to become Canadians – a failure that Trudeau had to deal with when he came to power and for which he offered the solution of multiculturalism.

Indeed, Trudeau positioned the state and its constitution, the instrument that brings the state into being, as perishable and bodily, while the individual that consents to the constitution is not, except in the physical sense. "No nation is eternal. The glue that holds it together, the thing that makes nationhood, is the free will of a sovereign people to live together."[14] The state is, therefore, malleable and totally dependent on the changing moods of the individuals who form the majority in the state. While arguing that there can be no guarantee that a state will last forever, Trudeau says that it is the changeable wills of the people that make up the state. "So the modern state is a pluralistic society whose citizens must come together on the basis of their citizenship, as individuals with equal rights and mutual tolerance, not on the basis of their ethnicity or background or religion. Otherwise, it's a self-defeating principle."[15] Indeed, Trudeau argued that the role of the state is to produce laws that enjoy the consent of individuals in the state and to educate individuals to become good citizens – people who know their liberal and democratic rights and responsibilities. Trudeau argued, then, that the values on the neo-mythic register are unchangeable, while the different forms and types on the ethno-racial register were changeable, corruptible, and subject to physical death. "The state cannot and must not make laws that do not tally by and large with what the citizens want; if it does, they (citizens) will defy its laws, until the time comes to overthrow it. The real purpose of laws, then, is to educate the citizens in the common good, and persuade them to behave in the public interest, rather than to command and constrain."[16]

But even in this struggle within the state, Trudeau acknowledged that there are contradictions. For example, while individuals have the right to change the constitution this is a right that they should not exercise too freely and without deep and profound forethought. In this regard, this freedom should not be unlicensed. The only solution for a possible paralysis of inaction that can result from being free but not free enough to act indiscriminately, is for the creation of counterweights – rational rules and procedures that, through the collective will that is the state, temper the excesses of individuals towards anarchy, and lawlessness, tyranny, and totalitarianism. Once again a lordship and bondage relationship is offered as the ideal solution to these radically different ways suggested by the two registers of meaning for determining what is Canada and who is a Canadian. Equally, lawlessness and totalitarianism are evil: the first is too much Blackness and the other too much Whiteness. The solution is a creolization and hybridity that allows for some Blackness in Whiteness as this permits creativity and genius within an orderly society, or some Whiteness in the form of order, stability, and predictability in Blackness that is the spirit of change and progress. There could be no magic formula, for any unchanging formula would itself become an imposition of tyranny.

The only tyranny that would be acceptable would be Enlightened Reason, the willing submission of all individuals in the state to specific rules and procedures, to methods and guidelines that are known in advance, and to an unrestricted good will by all parties to work for the good and well-being of everyone as individuals and collectively as a state. This enlightened reason, ontologically, had to be constructed through a general good will that is a composite of the hopes and intentions of the people in general. This is the genesis and reason for a constitution.

This supreme law does not pre-date the state, yet a constitution is the very necessity that makes the existence of a state possible. Individuals are free, but they need the collective will to guarantee their freedoms as unchangeable and not subject to particular contexts. This is the view of Trudeau and why he gave Canada a Charter of Rights and Freedoms that is based on unchangeable universals. Yet, Trudeau acknowledged that, contradictorily, context and moments do force reason to be pragmatic and to settle for a lesser good. This occurred when he agreed to what is called the notwithstanding clause, which allows provinces to indicate that there are times when universal rights can be overridden for the collective good. In this thinking, it is the collective or the state that is the unchangeable, not the individual as previously asserted. Similarly, in fighting for a strong central state, it was Trudeau who appeared as the "White knight" fighting against the dialectical pressures towards fragmentation and cultural liberalism, especially in the issue of Quebec sovereignty.

Ironically, Trudeau argued that the commitment to reason must be defended with passion, the very aspect of human nature that reason was supposed to keep in check. Here again, while he privileges the neo-mythic register as the ideal and legislative force, he argues that its success depends on understanding and approaching the system as if it were an ethno-racial creature.

It may be that in the sources he used there lies an explanation for all the contradictions in Trudeau's thought. Trudeau borrowed heavily from Western mythologies and philosophies, at points arguing that his views on the state and the happiness and motility of the individual were Aristotelian in orientation.[17] Trudeau also drew heavily on Plato[18] and leading philosophers and mythologists in Western civilization.[19] These were the role models for his vision of a happy state. In adopting these models, he perhaps unwittingly incorporated in his thinking the equivocation over Blackness that is inherent in Western thought. Blackness, even in Trudeau's highly rational world, still maintains the four major forms of the idealized, cultural, status, and somatic – and out of this equivocation would spawn many of the contradictions in Trudeau's liberal democracy as a plural or multicultural state.

A significant legacy of *A Just Society* at the beginning of a new century is Canada's slow progress towards fully coming to terms, in the domestic body politic, with one significant form of Blackness. This is the form that is still regarded epistemologically as the quintessence of Blackness, the somatic, and which seems to be confirmed rather than negated, contrary to expectations, as a result of the machinations of *A Just Society*.

Phenomenologically, in Trudeau's thinking, two things matter to produce this Blackness. First, Canada is simply one part of a wider universe that is made up of the many states and nations in the world. It is part of the changeable in a body where other nations, because of their size, power, and might, position themselves as the unchangeable. Mythologically, they consider themselves as having attained the highest levels of purity and enlightenment in human development. In the second case, Canada is presented as an independent body, with different parts and segments that are not always fully reconciled. As a result of contradictions based on the differing perspectives of the universal and the particular, Canada presents itself as fully Black on the international scene. It appears fully reconciled internationally in its idealistic notions of what good and evil are and what Black and White are epistemologically. This was exemplified, for example, in Canada's decision to join forces with the United States and Britain at the beginning of this new century to fight international terrorism. This was a battle against a force that was presented epistemologically as evil and Black, based on the more indeterminate notions of what good and evil are, rather than on somatic features, which were used as the basis in the past. This is an evil that has no essence. It is instead determined by specific choices and actions which are predicated on limiting the choices of others, and primarily by imposing premature physical death.

### REWRITING THE NARRATIVE OF WHITENESS

Trudeau's leadership also caused Canada to take practical steps towards recognizing Blackness internationally. This occurred through improved and more equitable relations with African, Caribbean, and other Third World countries after Canada officially made itself a multicultural country with official recognition of a Black ethnicity. The recognition of Blackness was translated, pragmatically, by reforming Canada's immigration policy to make it more universal in nature and less nation-specific, a move that led to a major increase in somatically Black immigrants to Canada from the Caribbean and Africa. This immigration led to increased visibility for a minority of people whose ancestors were associated with Africa, and who, historically, had received little or no official recognition in Canada until then.[20] In all these cases, Trudeau was making Canada Black idealistically, culturally, and even somatically. "My approach to international relations was really based on my approach to the Canadian community. The community of mankind should be treated in the same way as you would treat your community of fellow citizens. It was an idealistic approach, as opposed to a *realpolitik* approach. I felt it was the duty of a middle power like Canada, which could not sway the world with the force of its armies, to at least try to sway the world with the force of its ideals. I wanted to run Canada by applying the principles of justice and equality, and I wanted our foreign policy to reflect similar values."[21]

There is also another feature of the ethical relationship between the so-called First and Third Worlds that Canada tried to change. It stems from a legacy of colonialism, when the colonials of the First World held the people and nation-states of the Third in bondage. By the 1960s, while many Third World countries were claiming full political independence as mature states and nations, the rivalry between the North and South continued through the North's almost insatiable appetite for the South's resources. One of these resources for which Northern demands would continue to grow was human: the need for a continuous stream of immigrants, not necessarily intentionally to populate the First World, but were so to carry out the functions in states and nations that were reserved for those that were not the leisure class. Canada would move to the forefront by opening its borders fully to peoples of the world as immigrants and as refugees. With time, Canada would come to be seen as a model nation for the way it accepted refugees fleeing physical death in their native countries and hoping for a rebirth in a new country.[22] In selecting which of the world's people would qualify for inclusion in the Canadian nation-state as full citizens, Canada adopted a points system. Intended as an objective evaluation of the suitability of people for acceptance, the points were based on a universalizing code that technically de-emphasized ontological and epistemological differences between the peoples of the world. Through these actions, Canada was signalling internationally that humanity has no essence and that, phenomenologically, Canada, like the rest of humanity, was epistemologically Black. Further, it was demonstrating at the international and universal levels that Canada was reconciled in a new consciousness based on the acceptance of epistemological Blackness.

This was particularly the case in Canada's advocacy of new ethical relations based on universal egalitarianism between what came to be known as the First and Third Worlds. The first group consisted of those countries long construed as White idealistically, culturally, somatically, and in status by virtue of being situated in the northern hemisphere, being more technologically advanced, and offering their citizens some of the highest qualities of life. Ontologically and epistemologically, this group was dominated by European nations, those heirs to the civilization that claims a legacy that stretches back to the Greeks and Romans and who subscribe to a transcendental rationalism based on Christian mythologies. Existentially, this group was perceived, by those with power, to be the closest that humans have come to living like gods in their existence. Theirs was a lifestyle that set them apart. It differentiated them as White and different cosmologically from the Blackness that was the rest of humanity. In their ethical relations, humans who were not members of this elite group were perceived to be best suited to be the producers and workers for the society. Nonmembers of this group were historically presented as the most alienated, unfulfilled, and unhappy peoples when left to their own devices and without the tutorship of the First World.

The second group consisted ethnoracially of those countries and people long positioned in Western epistemology as culturally and somatically Black, and who at different times were deemed to be backward, technologically less advanced, poor, and biologically inferior. Members of this group were all, in essence, that the First World was not.

Trudeau spoke of the need for an equitable world: "We must aim for nothing less than an acceptable distribution of the world's wealth. In doing so, the inequities resulting from the accidental locations of valuable geological formations should no more be overlooked than should the present unequal acquisition of technological and managerial skills. Nor should we be reluctant in encouraging those willing to help themselves."[23]

In international relationships, Canada from the 1960s would move to the forefront in the battle for a new epistemology and ontology that would result in more humanitarian ethical relations between the rich and leisure class of the North and the poor of the South. Here Canada was caught up in a contradiction: Canada was historically part of the North or First world, yet it sought to identify with the Blackness of the South by trying to change the material existence of these non-Canadians through improved relations between the North and South. Canada, idealistically, endeavoured to produce an international ethical relationship that was based on improving the existence of those that, mythologically, have always been presented as Black idealistically, culturally, and by status. That a significant portion of the people whose existence would benefit from the new ethical relations was somatically Black appeared coincidental and inconsequential. This insignificance, with regard to the colour of the skin or phenotypic characteristics, seemed to be in keeping with the early Greek, Hebraic, and

African traditions that underpin ethical relationships in the Americas. This was a contradiction that was best captured in the international relationship between Canada and apartheid South Africa. In leading the international charge to end racial discrimination in South Africa, Canada had ended "a special relationship," turned its back on a traditional friend and ally, and was repudiating a system and social order to which it had contributed much, helped establish, and nurtured.

However, Canada is still only gradually coming to terms fully with somatic Blackness, a feature of discernment on the ethnoracial register that is supposed to have no value on the Trudeau-imposed, dominant neo-mythic register. This gradual acceptance remains a legacy of modernism that transcends the death and rebirth from Canada's unhappy consciousness in the 1960s. This is a Blackness that, culturally and ontologically, situates Canada in the Black Atlantic and as a significant partner in the Americas. It is also a finite category of Blackness in which Canada acknowledged that it was not, and would most likely never be able to be, a superpower.

Based on this understanding of itself, Canada accepted, epistemologically, being relegated to an inferior position in status relative to the superpowers of the day. But this was not perceived as a powerless position, for with this acceptance came the realization that Canada was positioned to become an international force by influencing ethical relations among nations. As Trudeau put it: "What I dare to believe is that men and women everywhere will come to understand that no individual, no government, no nation is capable of living in isolation, or of pursuing policies inconsistent with the interests – both present and future – of others. That self-respect is not self-perpetuating but depends for its existence on access to social justice. That each of us must do all in our power to extend to all persons an equal measure of human dignity – to ensure through our efforts that hope and faith in the future are not reserved for a minority of the world's population, but are available to all."[24]

In terms of motility, Canada's best role internationally was no longer presented as one of seeking dominance over rivals, but rather of acting as a mediator that brings rival factions together to ensure the international brotherhood of all states and humans. To this end, Canada would offer itself up as the body, in keeping with the rationalism best captured by *A Just Society*, that could be sacrificed for the good of humanity. This paradigm and consciousness is best epitomized in the universal picture of Canada as the peacekeeper, as the international Boy Scout, and as the reliable and honest broker in such international forums as the United Nations and the Organization of American States.

In this regard, Canada rejected all the promises from its leading elites and intellectuals going back to the beginning of modernity, that, materially, it would become the leading light in the Americas, if not the entire world. Its leadership would instead be in the realm of ideas and morality. In the 1960s, Canada positioned itself as a "middle power" that did not have the purity or Whiteness of might or entitlement, but whose strength came from its creolization and hybridization, in its ability to understand and mediate among nations and states fixated with their self-determination of unchangeable Whiteness and between those who, at different times, were positioned as unchangeably White and superior and those countries that were positioned as among the changeable in their Blackness and powerlessness. Canada's claim to an unchangeable nature would be its commitment to reason and rationalism.

Perhaps, the most significant acknowledgement that Canada is not White and no longer aims to become teleologically a White man's country was in the official acknowledgement that the country is a multicultural liberal democracy. This pronouncement resulted from Canada's development as an unhappy consciousness and the efforts of the elites to resolve this dilemma by resorting to a new form of Whiteness in the form of a universal commitment to rationalism. Again as Trudeau put it:

Every single person in Canada is now a member of a minority group. Linguistically our origins are one-third English, one-third French, and one-third neither. We have no alternative but to be tolerant of one another's differences. Beyond the threshold of tolerance, however, we must have countless opportunities to benefit from the richness and variety of a Canadian life which is the result of this broad mix. The fabric of Canadian society is as resilient as it is colourful. It is a multicultural society; it offers to every Canadian the opportunity to fulfil his or her own cultural instincts and to share those from other sources. This mosaic pattern, and the moderation which it includes and encourages, makes Canada a very special place.[25]

This is a type of rationalism that is akin to what Aristotle suggested, when he postulated that the unchangeable in a nation has to be the commitment of the people within its borders to maintaining that nation. In other words, a nation or state does not exist unless so willed by the people. Yet, contradictorily, the state continues on a daily basis much as does the river that in the universal, as Aristotle maintains, remains unchangeable over the ages. The "river" as a concept is unchanged, even though on a daily basis it is changing – every drop of water is different from those that went before and different from those to come. Importantly, Trudeau again indicated that the ethnic or linguistic identity of Canadian occurs after immigrants have already entered the state and have become Canadian. This means that the identity Canadian becomes a second identity after the primary universal identity of being a member of the human race, and that ethnic, national, and linguistic identification falls into a lower category behind these two primary ones.

This is a significant demarcation, for under Trudeau's scheme ethnicity is not a primordial characteristic, and at best can only be accidental and contingent. Ethnicity, in the Canadian sense, is thus an attempt to maintain a prior cultural and constructed identity along with a primary one that is Canadian. It is a limiting factor – not a category of freedom. Conceptually, ethnicity is the finite component in the infinity that is Canada and the infinity that is Canadian. More than that, as a subset within the wider infinites, ethnicity can only be a minimum and can never be the maximum of what it means to be fully Canadian. This is a point that is often lost on those who argue that multiculturalism creates ghettoes and leads to the fracturing of Canadian unity.[26] Such arguments do not recognize that ethnicity is the idealized and cultural Whiteness that dialectically must be transcended and sublated in the idealized Blackness that is Canada and Canadian.

At the same time, however, Trudeau was also fighting for a Whiteness that was neo-mythically rational. This Whiteness was humanity as a universal abstraction, but as an essence that could only be "constructed" in and through the legitimization of the state while at the same time, as Trudeau argued, the state was to be opposed as an unnecessary preservation of Whiteness and a lack of liberty. In this respect, Trudeau fought against the rigidity of idealized Whiteness and in favour of the Blackness that produces creativity. Yet at the same time, Trudeau also fought against a tendency that he discerned in Canadians towards decentralization or centrifugalism, a Blackness that tended towards fragmentation into ethnic homelands that Trudeau called cultural nations and which was occurring at a time when he felt the universe was moving towards a unity that was best epitomized by globalism. In a Hegelian way, Trudeau saw freedom leading to reconciliation in a greater universal that incorporates differences within its body. In his words:

It is unlikely that any *nation*-state – or for that matter any multi*national* state – however strong, could realize a complete and perfect society; economic, military, and cultural interdependence is a *sine qua non* for states of the twentieth century, to the extent that none is really self-sufficient. Treaties, trade alliances, common markets, free-trade areas, cultural and scientific agreements, all these are as indispensable for the world's states as is interchange between citizens within them; and just as each citizen must recognize the submission of his own sovereignty to the laws of the state – by which, for example, he must fulfil the contract he makes – so the states will know no real peace and prosperity until they accept the submission of their relations with each other to a higher order. In truth, the very concept of sovereignty must be surmounted, and those who proclaim it for the *nation* of French Canada are not only reactionary, they are preposterous.[27]

## WHITENESS: THE MYTHOLOGY
## OF REBIRTH

Under Trudeau's leadership, Canada made the biggest steps towards coming to terms with its Blackness. This was achieved through his rethinking of what was good and meaningful in life for Canada and Canadians. Trudeau broke with history and advanced new notions of Canada and Canadians: specifically, what is known about them with certainty, what they are capable of becoming, what makes them happy, and which tasks they are most useful for.[28] These new notions resulted in a different consciousness that took Canada away from the historical presentations of the country and Canadians as White ontologically, epistemologically, existentially, and in their ethical relations.

According to *A Just Society*, ontologically, a Canadian was not necessarily European, and Canada was no longer presented as a European country heading teleologically towards an end of history that was preordained as good for Europe and Europeans. Epistemologically, Canada and Canadians did not have a discernible essence, natural virtue, or purity: they were not always good, but were constantly confronting the angst of death and the darkness of known limits that is common to all human knowledge and experience. Canadians were not by essence, or through a cosmological will, super-humans that were almost godlike in their existence. This means that they were White in status only constructively because they were presented by themselves in their exclusive group as superior to the rest of humanity, but that superiority occurred only in a place called Canada. In that exclusive space that is the Canadian nation-state, they were constructed as having rights and privileges ahead of all other humanity – rights and privileges of Canadian citizenship exercised through a Canadian sovereignty that was limited to the space they inhabited and over which they took dominion.

Rather, they were commonly human – as fragile and miserable as the rest of humanity struggling for freedom, liberty, and choices against an endless number of potential tyrannies. The commonality reflected the recognition that Canadians were drawn from – not separated from as was originally presented – humanity itself, with all its diverse languages, cultures, religions, and colours of skin, among other qualities. It is only once in Canada that these members of humanity become created as Canadians. Before then, they are part of the undifferentiated aboriginals to Canada in their primordialism. To this end, existentially, Canada was not yet the Promised Land, for it was beset on all sides by the threatening darkness of fragmentation, the tyranny of totalitarian rule, and the physical ethno-racial death of personal dreams. However, it could still aspire neo-mythically to become the Promised Land by nurturing hope and by striving to become a just society. Every day, Canada would be a practical act of re-creation – a compromise between occupying the limits of the ethno-racial register, while at the same time slipping into the neo-mythic future of rebirth and hope.

Trudeau's aim was to break Canada and the identity Canadian out of the finite limits that always promised a physical death akin to perceived White-ness changing to idealized Blackness – ultimately through fragmentation of the state into separate unities – and to recognize Canada and its citizens as infinites, with potentials and probabilities that were limitless. Canada would be recognized as a conceptual barbarian that is a composite: a unity with many different parts, with, in the Hegelian sense, the official recogni-tion of different *darknesses* that come together – not to occlude the light – but to synchronize it into a single beam that is miraculously pure White light. Canada would stop searching for an essence or Whiteness that imposes unchangeable limits on the way the country and its citizens can be manifested. Multiculturalism, based on an abstract universalism, would be the new ideology that captures this infinitude that is Canada and its citi-zens, for multiculturalism is the privileging of re-creation, with emphasis placed on the "multi" in terms of the plentitude of forms and spirit that are available to Canada and Canadians. And at the same time, Canada would still remain a modern state, thereby claiming a filiality to the good of West-ern culture that is the legacy of modernity; but at the same time, because it had overturned and overthrown so many of the "essential" teachings of modernity on identity and culture, Canada would be revolutionary. It would be the first post-modern state – in our categories it would try to be Black and White simultaneously, and from this mixing it would end up with a Black identity and existing in Blackness. Among other things, multi-culturalism and its dream of a just society would be a search in Blackness by a Black subject for freedom.

Sociologically, culturally, and politically, Canada would thus stop trying to produce a society with a single essence: conceptually, multiculturalism would be a composite and would be multidimensional so as to fully capture all the freedoms dialectically bound in the infinity that is multiculturalism. And as a self-conscious ego, Canada would recognize that it is phenomeno-logically Black and was a hybrid or composite in structure. Officially, then, with *A Just Society* Canada was recognizing itself as creolized Black, as just about every aspect of Canadian life belied the notion of purity or a White essence and pointed instead to hybridity. In so doing, it was challenging and subverting modernity's very notion of itself and of identity.

Having recognized itself as Black in this contingent moment, the next step was to make the moment necessarily and unchangeably part of the Canadian quest and even the raison d'être for the country's existence. This came about when the official narrative of Canada was rewritten to make a significant correction: Canada was not originally intended by modernity to be a White man's country – for, with the benefit of hindsight, such a claim could be understood as having been a misrecognition that was born of a false consciousness that was itself a product of the ideals of the founding people. Rather, Canada is, and was always intended to be, a liberal democracy that is officially multicultural. At the new moment of creation that was the 1960s onward, the option of becoming a White man's country was thus rejected.

To this end, Canada now seeks to manifest itself contingently and necessarily as a just society based on the idealized Blackness of abstract constitutional rights and freedoms, and not the purity and essence of a specific ethnicity or somatic colour. In this way, Canada would be reconciled in full knowledge of itself and by others as an infinity, consisting of both the ethno-racial and neo-mythic registers. Such is the universal identity Canadian, which must always be determined according to both registers; otherwise something meaningful would always be left out of the Canadian identity. But a Canadian is also a particular, and as such is finite – but with the finitude incorporated conceptually in the infinitude. This finitude and particularism is an issue of subjective choice, letting the self-consciousness determine itself solely according to either register, but always having the choice of negating this determination that must always be changeable. Such is the case of the ethnic identity that many Canadians have as part of their search for ethno-racial authenticity.

The new end of history, when the dialectics of history and freedom are permanently at rest, would be when, in this new narrative, Canada becomes a just society. This would not be a static utopian moment, but one that was dynamic, constantly changing, and where everything is always new. This would be when Canada is idealistically White by recognizing that it has a Black body, based on the presence within its body of somatic Blackness and cultural Blackness, but no longer status Blackness, because such inequalities would have been eradicated.

Therefore, the task for Canada, on its way neo-mythically to genuine multiculturalism, is to eliminate status Blackness, as defined ethno-racially, from its ethical considerations, for the nation has already recognized idealistic, cultural, and somatic Blackness as Canadian. To the extent that somatic Blackness still amounts to status Blackness, the Canadian multicultural ideal, remains blemished and this blemish is one of the reasons that Canada has not yet become a fully just society in intent and practice and that it has not yet achieved the idealized Whiteness of genuine multiculturalism. That somatic Blackness will one day no longer equate to status Blackness, but instead may change to status Whiteness, is the promise of multiculturalism for all those constructed as ethnically and racially Black in Canada.

There thus still exists in Canada an alienation of intention and outcomes, of subjectivity matching objectivity epistemologically, of perception submitting to reason, as the country is not yet in a position where its ideals are translated faithfully into what is called reality in a common sense way. The result is that the Canadian consciousness we started out with, the one phenomenologically situated outside of its body and examining itself according to its own laws of reason, would rationally have to think that its body is Black, even at a time when by perception it thought is was most White. And since this consciousness had said that it could only be happy if it was White, and that it was only when situated in society as White that its motility could be ideally situated, this self-examining being would be unhappy by its own standards. Rational knowledge or cognition would tell it that in all categories – even including the somatic with the growing number of non-White citizens – the consciousness was Black and all that it has been producing so far is still the muddled uncertainty of Blackness with its instability and continuous changes. This being the case, then, Canada as a multicultural state is a Hegelian unhappy consciousness: its best intentions have not produced exactly what was intended; rather there are times when intentions have produced the dialectical opposite of what was intended, as if they have put the wrong emphasis on the finite combinations in the infinite concept, as if the outcome could only ever be that which negates the positive desires.

Existentially, Trudeau captured the human condition and the phenomenological unhappy consciousness that Canada is: "In historical terms we are on the way to becoming one of the freest, one of the most prosperous democracies in the world. We are the inheritors of two of the main languages and cultures of Western civilization. We've built a tremendous country politically and we've expanded it geographically. We've brought in some of the most progressive social and political systems in the world. We're a plural society. But look around. Talk to the people. Read the media. Listen to the grumblings. Canadians aren't happy with their fate. And this, in spite of the success of our country."[29]

With luck, good will, and a commitment to reason, however, and the yearning for enlightenment as well, Canada could become a paradise that, through its internal ethical relations, could show the rest of the world how humanity can live in peace and harmony. This is the hope for Canada that Trudeau understood multiculturalism to be offering. The highest aim for Canada, internationally, would be to become a good role model; internally, this goal would be to become a reconciled body where the wishes of individuals and of the state are in harmony and are governed by immutable rules of abstract reason:

The die is cast in Canada: there are two main ethnic and linguistic groups; each is too strong and too deeply rooted in the past, too firmly bound by a mother-culture, to be able to engulf the other. But if the two will collaborate at the hub of a truly pluralistic state, Canada could become the envied seat of a form of federation that belongs to tomorrow's world. Better than the American melting-pot, Canada could offer an example to all those new Asian and African states who must discover how to govern their polyethnic populations with proper regard for justice and liberty. What better reason for cold-shouldering the lure of annexation to the United States? Canadian federalism is an experiment of major proportions; it could become a brilliant prototype for the moulding of tomorrow's civilization.[30]

To this end, Trudeau envisioned a Canada that is idealistically White because of its commitment to an ethical purity that privileges individuality and the state as the changing unchangeable. These are principles that Trudeau viewed as going to the heart of liberalism and democracy: the ideals which he believed that Canada, as a free country, must aspire to.

## DUELING CONCEPTS OF MULTICULTURALISM: EXISTENTIAL BLACKNESS

But there is another sense in which official multiculturalism is Blackness. It is so existentially – living in a kind of false consciousness. This is where this existence is situated in the deficit between the actual sociological lived experiences of being Canadian and the ideal. This is what I have called the dream deficit – the failure of all Canadians to enjoy the justice that is imagined in what I also called genuine multiculturalism. This is an indication of the distance still to be travelled to attain universally the ideal Whiteness Trudeau and creators of this new Canada had envisioned.[31] For there exists in a practical way a version of multiculturalism that really differs from Trudeau's. This version is a holdover from the previously but now discredited mythology of biculturalism as the mythology that best explains ideals for justice in Canada. This thinking and hope for state formation is still at the centre of the politically lived experience in Canada. Many in the mainstream of the elites and governments would prefer an ethno-racial Whiteness determined by somatic and cultural characteristics. This is a purported Whiteness made up ontologically of those Canadians who are of ancient lineage and come historically from the largest ethnic populations. This would be the dominant cultures of the anglophones and francophones coming together in an ethno-racial ideal called biculturalism – a twosome acting as one, where both groups and cultures would be recognized as solely "authentically" Canadian.

In this mythology, these manifestations of the pure Canadian are called the two founding peoples of Canada. This alternate ideal of multiculturalism is just another form of pluralism, so similar to what is practiced in Europe and elsewhere, and where there is a privileged position for the historically determined "founding" or "original" peoples that were the original creators of the country. In the alternate mythology, this French-English

core would then be surrounded by the polyglot of somatic and cultural
Blackness, with both the core and the periphery dedicated, in a hub-and-
spoke arrangement analogous to a wheel, to an idealized Whiteness which
accepts the creativity of idealized Blackness and which continues to spurn
the idealized Blackness of the United States. This manifestation falls way
short of the ideals of egalitarianism and equality that are the cosmopolitanism of Trudeau's multiculturalism. For another model, Trudeau turned
to the neo-mythic register, where all Canadians in the abstract were idealistically White. They were all free and abstract individuals, interchangeably
bundles of liberal rights and freedoms. They would be unchangeable in
their neo-mythic diversity and in their site of unity, as a Canadian body that
is highly diversified but with no inequalities based on differences and hierarchies among different types, forms, or sorts of Canadians. These two
models fighting for dominance and hegemony within the single consciousness that is today's Canadian multiculturalism give this moment its creativity and newness. It is what accounts for the constant lurching between
idealistic hope and despair for the future of the country as the Black
Canadian consciousness struggles within itself over the correct ethical path
that will take it to idealistic Whiteness.

This result is existential Blackness – a hybridity or creolizations where, in a
lordship and bondage relationship, daily living is marked by compromise,
and even unhappiness as no side is winning absolutely. Indeed, epistemologically and ontologically, in practical terms, or in what Trudeau calls *realpolitik*, where wishes and desires clash with the hard pragmatism of reality,
Canada and Canadians might not always be officially bilingual with English
and French as the two dominant languages. Neither would it be somatically
and culturally White or European, its traditional but discredited neo-mythic
aspiration. Indeed, Trudeau spurned the very idea of Canada having a firm
and fixed "national" culture, even if in seeming contradiction he argued that
governments must defend a Canadian culture – with paradoxically English
and French as the unchangeable hub – to protect the interests of a specific
and sovereign group of people against what was perceived as the more rav-
enous American culture. In raising a conformist American culture as the
bogeyman, Trudeau continued the tradition of showing the same disdain and
distrust of those earlier Canadian leaders who readily accepted that Canada
and the United States were, from the beginning of modernity, locked in a
struggle for material as well as intellectual dominance.

Yet, contradictorily, even as he resisted the changes that he did not like,
Trudeau was also the agent of change advocating still deeper changes as he
openly courted American finances to develop Canada. Paradoxically, he
also spoke existentially and ethically of a Canada that is a multicultural
and just society, but with a fully changeable hub. The spokes would be
changeable and the hub of the wheel as well. Ontologically, the material of

Canada, the form it takes, the culture that is produced, and the honouring of specific cultures – all resulting from the choices of daily living in a free world – would change from time to time. The main determinant would not be a claim grounded in the Platonic sense in history, ancestry, or filial relationships, but in the relative strength of the individuals forming different groups within a society that was constantly being renegotiated, reformulated, and reborn. As Trudeau explained in an Aristotelian sense, it is possible, if enough citizens so wish, that Canada's official languages could change while Canada as a country or unitary consciousness remains unchangeable: "Historical origins are less important than people generally think, the proof being that neither Inuit nor Indian dialects have any kind of privileged position. On the other hand, if there were six million people in Canada whose mother tongue was Ukrainian, it is likely that this language would establish itself as forcefully as French. In terms of *realpolitik*, French and English are equally Canada because each of these linguistic groups has the power to break the country."[32]

The same thing was true of somatic features in Canada. They, too, could be Black, as Trudeau explained in an argument that seemingly contradicted the idea that an enlightened Canada could have a core of English and French working in harmony. In this argument, he challenged the long established ontological notions of the existence of "old stock" peoples of ancient lineage in Quebec, in the specific, and Canada, in general. In the latter case, Trudeau, in arguing for the rights of the living over the dead in terms of cultural recognition, asked: "Can Haitian Quebeckers, for instance, protect certain aspects of their own culture by claiming protection as part of the French-speaking collectivity? ... Can neo-Canadian Quebeckers of whatever origins choose to renounce their heritage and origins so as to share with 'old stock' Quebeckers the protection sought by the French-speaking collectivity? Or are we dealing with a frankly racist notion that makes second-and third-class citizens of everyone but 'old stock' Quebeckers?"[33]

Indeed, it is tempting to argue that in asking these questions, and by making specific references to Ukrainians and Haitians, Trudeau was consciously making a point ontologically, epistemologically, and existentially about Blackness. Trudeau, as a student of philosophy and modernity, had to be mindful that *old stock* Canadians of both French and English lineages, as discussed earlier, have long held the Ukraine to be part of the Black world. Also, Trudeau would have been aware of the impact of the Haitian Revolution on modernity and the importance of this revolution in terms of nationalism and national identity in the modern state. He would have been conscious of how the dominant Canadian elites, along with their South African counterparts, had long presented Haiti as the dystopia that awaited them if they did not entrench laws privileging somatic and cultural Whiteness in the homelands they were creating.[34]

But in making references to Ukrainians and Haitians, Trudeau appeared to be making a bigger point about the ontology and epistemology of Canada and Canadians. This is the position that specific identities are created and constructed within a state after individuals have agreed to create the state. In the Hegelian sense, epistemology comes before ontology, existentialism, and moral choices in ethical relations. Issues of nationalism and other forms of cultural identity are not primordial for Trudeau. Only the generality of human nature and the moral agency of individuals are primordial and predate the state.

To this end, Trudeau argued that there is neither an essence nor permanent goodness or evil to Canadians. Therefore, in the dialectical Manichean world in which modernity tried to categorize good and evil for nation-state formation, Canadians are *essentially* Black ontologically: Canada is always trying to produce a pure, uniform, and singular ethno-racial determination out of its heteronomy, diversity, and differences. A Canadian is always what is being created and what will fully appear on the scene in the next moment. In this regard, a Canadian is dependent on a messianic arrival – that new moment of creation when the true identity is fixed permanently and when a saviour confirms an existence of hope over despair. Forms of Whiteness can only occur after a separation from the rest of humanity not physically, as was once claimed, but through the adoption of good intentions by those in a cosmopolitan universe who believe in the given cause. This separation occurs in the state but, importantly, only after individuals in their non-essence have agreed to confer on one another a common Whiteness that they themselves have constructed, and after they have agreed on the idealized Whiteness of culture and civilization to which they aspire. But, alas, even then, the result can only be another expression of Blackness. For such seems to be the eternal story of all humanity. As we have noted, Blackness is a composite and therefore cannot have an essence. A multicultural Canada that is idealistically White would be a cosmopolitan composite. Therefore, ontologically, again, Canada can have no essence. A country with parts of it still thinking it is essentially White and others using the same agreed upon rules asserting its Blackness is most likely a very conflicted consciousness, one where it is never fully happy with itself or with what it is trying to achieve. Such, then, is the story of multicultural Canada as a unity idealized in modernity but in practice united only in so far as it is an unhappy consciousness.

## CANADA'S AFFECTIVITY AND MOTILITY

Trudeau presented the answer to Canada's unhappy consciousness as reason, a commitment to the universal rationalism of the law, and a desire for order, stability, and predictability to daily life that was matched by an unceasing yearning by individuals to be free of all non-consensual constraints and restrictions. In effect, Trudeau was arguing for a lordship and bondage relationship with reason as lord and dominant to intuitive and sensory perception. In this way, what individuals feel about themselves and what their senses tell them about others would not be as important as how all individuals, as constructed abstract archetypes, are recognized. "The Canadian nation must be founded upon reason," Trudeau said. "If it isn't reasonable, it shouldn't exist. But if it is reasonable, it can take a variety of positive, even emotional, measures to defend itself, so long as they don't degenerate into an ethnically based or culturally specific nationalism. That's why, to avoid confusion, I like to distinguish such positive, pragmatic, nation-building devices as patriotism."[35]

This is how, idealistically, Canada would become epistemologically White. This is how Canadians would know the history of who is truly Canadian; how, for example, through the same citizenship immigrants and native born can be changed into the same kind of being; how they can equally share the same mythology about arriving together in a Canada that is a just society. Reason would be the sovereign or the mediator that tames the darkness present in the primordial beings that enter the state. Reason would discern which changes to accept and which to spurn. Reason would impose limits on desire and consent without favouring one over the other. But, rationally, these had to be limits that were clear and known in advance of any action and which would be unchangeable whatever the circumstances. Reason, therefore, would identify a new ontology for Canada, and it would be an ontology suggesting that Canada was Black epistemologically, existentially, and in its ethical relations. Reason would be a new Whiteness in the Canadian setting to replace the old ontological Whiteness that presented Canada as White somatically, culturally, idealistically, and in status.

In Trudeau's view, the old collective imagery of Whiteness had resulted in ontological racism in Canada's domestic and international affairs. The new ontology would lead to a replacement of the old with new ethical relations that produce different existences within Canada and abroad. Trudeau's new Whiteness de-emphasized the body, specifically its colour, as the leading attribute of humanity. Sensory perception, therefore, was relatively unimportant to a reasoned existence. This is so because, in Trudeau's eyes, the body is changeable, as it has no essence.

Rather than trying to build a society that is founded on concepts of *quantity*, the governments that I had the honour of leading tried to make more and more of their decisions based on *quality*. We didn't reject the material values, the civilization of the "more" that brought Canada to a very advanced degree of progress and gave Canadians one of the very highest standards of living in the world. But we were -

saying that now, having reached the point where there are enough goods and enough technological skills, we should be able to help the less fortunate and trade off some of our material aims and goals for more spiritual, more qualitative values.[36]

His goal was to deal with the unchangeable, to discern and apply rational truths and principles, in a Kantian manner, where the general will is always good and pure, and the sovereign is a Reason that transcends the emotions and weaknesses of the corporeal. Trudeau's analysis thus suggests that it is the mind, its development, and the mind's commitment to specific goals and ideals that matter most. In the mind, reason can play the unchangeable role of an "essence," developed through construction and deliberation, thereby giving to the dualism that is humanity the unchangeability that it did not receive from Nature. This new approach that divorces the body from the mind rejects as false and evil the historical somatic racism of Canada, for racism was specific to the body and by Trudeau's time had long been discredited as a basis for an unchanging essence.[37] Instead, the aim is to create a new country based on individuality, equality, and fraternity – with all three contributing to a new reality or phenomenon that, as a new ethical relation and existentialism in Canada, is officially named multiculturalism. Indeed, it is in the mind that all ethno-racial contradictions can be reconciled. This is where a people's essence can be established even if it does not exist socially. And it is for this reason that Trudeau and others like him privileged meaning from the neo-mythic register over that from the ethno-racial in searching for an answer to Canada's condition as an unhappy consciousness. In his mind, Canada and Canadians would be what they imagine themselves to be.

Yet, as this chapter shows, Trudeau's commitment to reason appears to work only in the abstraction and not in the concreteness of real life. A problem for Trudeau and Canada is how to reconcile specific behaviours and wishes with rational ideals. Contradictions occur because a country is not only an ideal, as captured abstractly on the neo-mythic register; it must be body as well as mind – it must have an ethno-racial component, and neither register universally and unchangingly dominating the other. The two parts of this dualism are not always easily reconciled, and the body cannot be divorced without difficulty from the mind; in his scheme of things, Trudeau willingly sacrificed the body to the wishes of the mind.

Trudeau would discover this in the world of *realpolitik* when he tried to implement his ideals and achieved only limited success. This occurred either because others blocked his way politically in a dialectical struggle involving a split sovereignty at the federal and provincial levels in Canadian federation, or because his solutions only succeeded in raising other seemingly irreconcilable differences and contradictions within the idealized solutions themselves. The world of *realpoltik* is where the externalities of the ethno-racial register dominate.

By privileging reason, Trudeau was still searching for an answer within the neo-mythic register, where a clear choice is made between that register and the ethno-racial. Yet, at times, he argued that the ethno-racial register had to be accepted. This was why Canadians were free to privilege their ethnicity – to ask for recognition not according to what they are imagined to be, but based on what they determine themselves ethno-racially to be at any given moment. The concern here was how to limit this determination to one that is bodily and physical, and not to an alternative meaning that involves making neo-mythic valuations based on ideals of good and evil. In terms of coming up with a single identity, Trudeau's vision still resulted in an unhappy consciousness. Much of the unhappiness is over the question of who authentically is a Canadian and whether or not the Canadian identity should become hyphenated, with an ethnicity or region before the hyphen.

Many of the contradictions resulted from the way in which Trudeau attempted to implement a plan that would recognize Canada as idealistically Black. Trudeau's reliance on the reason of laws and regulations would effectively recognize individuals only as universals. This was the way to treat everyone equally. Neo-mythically, nobody would have a prior history of having been differentiated based on outer characteristics and through a hierarchical ranking of forms and types, which gives her or him a preference or an inequality. Every individual would instead continue to live in a mythological unchanging present, the same time and place created by the mythological gods and founding fathers of the country. This would be a time before the start of a history of determinations as recorded on the ethno-racial register, or before the beginning of the movements of errantry on the neo-mythic, movements that inevitably add up to failure in history, but are the epitome of hope for the future. Everyone would have an equal say in the formation and government of civil society, and every individual would begin the march towards an agreed to ending on the same footing.

In this regard, Trudeau pointed to the laws his government passed in order to privilege the individual over the state, or the state over tendencies for fragmentation into what he discerned as calcified and static cultural groups of nationalism – into static utopias that were from his moral perspective dystopias. These laws would seek to represent the neo-mythic as the ethno-racial, but with the clear understanding that because they were born of reason the laws were filially of a higher order than the forms that they took. The intentions for goodness and good faith would be a more fitting discernment of the ethical relations in the system than what forms appeared within this system at any given moment. These formal expressions of reason included new laws about immigration, a declaration of the official languages, and a Charter of Rights and Freedoms that is entrenched in the Canadian Constitution. The aim was to free Canada from the crassness of materialism and power politics so that Canada would be governed by ideals and not according to the physical power of individuals or groups. This would be the new Kuhnian paradigm that governs how Canada conducts itself as an organic unity.[38]

However, these laws are not intended to be constitutive, but regulative. They have no body and can only achieve the high goals to which they aspire by working through individuals, particular bodies, and groups within the society. In Trudeau's thinking, the rational truth of these laws could be asserted without their realization in every corporeal form, collectively or individually. However, the reality of recognizing that the mind needs a body would produce new contradictions, for these truths and laws are abstract and could not easily be embodied, even as the reality of politics would claim by privileging an anglo-franco mainstream in a manner that Trudeau did not originally intend. Contradictions arose when the reality did not conform to the ideals of *A Just Society*. One of the freedoms that is the eternal quest conceptually for universals, such as what is imagined as the ideal Canadian, is for citizens to share a common social equality. At the same time, these citizens as specific individuals or minority groups can be recognized and determined as particulars within this larger universal. As individuals or minorities, for example, they can demand to be recognized according to how they express themselves ethno-culturally. They will be as free and equal as any other Canadian, and they will be as different from some groups of Canadians as they wish – all at the same time. Only as individual citizens will they have the right to decide at any given moment which characteristic to privilege. In addition, their Canadian identity as universal will always be unchangeable – this is part of their liberal right: effectively, they can never lose this Canadianness for the state and other Canadians would always recognize them as Canadian. This is so even if when the individuals and minority groups are choosing to be identified only by their ethno-cultural designation – for this could only be a secondary choice and not one that could ever negate the universal characteristic. This freedom of choice, to determine who they want to be identified as at any given moment – as a universal or as representing a specific culture not common to all Canadians – is the ideal Canadian existence and new ontology. This is a freedom that always seems elusive in multicultural Canada.

### BLACKNESS TO WHITENESS: RATIONAL IMMIGRATION

Immigration, which has always been necessary for the physical and bodily survival of the country, resulted since the 1960s in fundamental changes to

Canada's demography through the presence of peoples from different cultural and linguistic backgrounds and from all parts of the globe. On first look, this appears idealistically to be exactly what *A Just Society* anticipated. But on closer examination, it becomes apparent that there is alienation in the body politic. Claiming to be choosing the brightest and best immigrants according to an objective code, Canada was taking in new citizens from more regions of the globe and more cultural and linguistic communities than previously. Its population thus appeared more diverse and fragmented and quite unlike the unity that reason promised.

In addition, as an existing consciousness, Canada was placing the newcomers according to their perceived economic utility and functionalism in Canadian society. The position of the immigrant was based on perception of the immigrant's affectivity and motility solely from the perspective of the Canadian state – a state that, in practice, started from the position that those who were already its citizens possessed higher claims and entitlements than those who were not yet its citizens. This was particularly the case ethno-racially at the provincial level in Canada, as the Canadian provinces and territories were and remain responsible for the settlement of immigrants, a process through which the provinces must mediate directly the dialectical tensions between those that have prior claims and rights and those who are demanding these rights and recognition. In this approach, and from the provincial perspective or gaze, the citizens were already unchangeable and the immigrants, even though chosen for their seeming universal Whiteness, were deemed to be among the changeable once they arrived in Canada.

These immigrants, selected at the federal level because they were judged to be as good idealistically as any Canadian, were now positioned within the Canadian society as functionally inferior and lower in status. The newcomers did not undergo the kind of mythological creation or rebirth that would transform them into the full Whiteness of being Canadian. Although a rebirth had taken place, it was a hybrid of bits of idealized Whiteness that made them Canadian in an idealistically Black body. As a result, today, as in the past, they continue to struggle to attain the universal acceptance of full citizenship. They become unhappy and alienated because they do not feel they are free to become what they hope for themselves. Canada is unhappy because the immigrants believe Canada is hypocritical and playing according to the old rules instead of the seemingly more enlightened laws and regulations of *A Just Society.*

There are two main causes for this unhappiness. First, in accordance with an old model that idealized Whiteness as somatically and culturally European, the immigrants enter a society that has been constructed historically to favour anglophones and francophones as the main constitutive components of the elites and governing mainstream. This is the hub and spoke model that Trudeau seemed to have envisaged as possible, which he said was forced on him by the dialectics of power, but which was not the model he preferred. His preference was for a more egalitarian and inclusive version in which power was distributed among individuals universalized as citizens, rather than shared among specific ethno-racial groups. Second, the newcomers find themselves pitted in a war with multiple dimensions for recognition on the ethno-racial register. One of the dimensions comes from having to claim a cultural ethnicity or an aboriginal idealized Blackness to receive full recognition by the state.

Contradictions also arise over the way individuals are treated in Canadian society, for every individual does not have equal access to the good life, and, in some cases, is not always treated equally before the law. A specific example of this inequality is the treatment of members of an ethnicity called Black, in particular the somatically Black males. The result is the opposite of what Trudeau anticipated: each Other was to be treated in a relationship with any other Canadian self as free and equal, but the material reality defies the new law of reason and continues to privilege somatic Whiteness. In this respect, even though it aspires to an idealized Whiteness of equality and equity as just for all, Canada is still ethically Black because of the resulting unhappy consciousness.

The resulting unhappiness is shared equally by Canada and the immigrants who feel they are fully Canadian. There is also another factor contributing to it. Trudeau's idealism presents a picture of universalism and egalitarianism in the areas where he had full influence: this was at the federal level, domestically, and in international relations. This too contributed to Canada's unhappy consciousness, for it is the image of Canada encouraged by Trudeau that the immigrant brings to Canada, and the immigrant later realizes that this image is not the full picture.

Trudeau's ideals are less apparent in those areas where the federal government has joint jurisdiction with the provinces and territories or where it has no control at all, as in the settlement of immigrants, the assessment of their credentials, and the regulating of human rights. Trudeau as much as recognized this dilemma of jurisdictions as being essential to Canada, and as resulting from "creative tensions" where the federal government is always aiming at a higher level of becoming, while the provinces are concerned with the status quo and preserving the given order. This tension goes back to the founding notion that Canada consisted of provinces that were essentially ethnic homelands. Trudeau explained the idealized ethical relation that flowed out of this argument: "I never objected to that tension. I did object when a premier tried to get more power for his province in order to help a particular ethnic group. The duty of a premier is to fight for the good of all the people in that province, not just one ethnic group, even if it happens to be the majority."[39]

As a legacy of *A Just Society*, from the 1960s onwards Canada has come to terms with Blackness fully in its idealized, cultural, and status forms. This was particularly true in the nation's universal and international relations, where Canada even appeared to be coming to terms fully with somatic Blackness in advocating equality between all races of the world. However, in domestic ethical relations, Canada today continues to be divided in a bodily sense over who among the Canadian citizenry and residents are essentially and unchangeably White and by analogy good. These are the citizens that have entitlement to full membership in the mainstream – the national leisure class and power elites. This group is separate and different from those perceived as culturally, socially, and idealistically Black and changeable, those who functionally should be excluded from positions of privilege and power. Canadians that are somatically Black, particularly the males, best exemplify the latter group. They are not yet brought through the neo-mythic transformation into Whiteness that is offered to all who belong mythologically in the sacred place and time called Canada, and who can thereby claim full citizenship as a right of belonging. In all his actions, the somatically Black male is still determined primarily on the outer and assimilative ethno-racial register, where he tends to show up stereotypically as essentially a form or type of a group or class of people, rather than as an individual and different being who contingently happens to be human.

The contradictions inherent in *A Just Society* and its legacy are best illustrated in Canada through an existentialist examination of this male group constructed as a homogeneous and unchangeable Black ethnicity in a multicultural society. Here, the contradictions show up, as Fanon says, in the rigid determination of a specific group of people.[40] These individuals lose a vital aspect of their full humanity: the ability to make choices about themselves, to achieve the goals of these choices, and to be recognized by others as having that right and ability to change. Those determined as somatically Black males do not have the right or ability to choose their own death and to seek a rebirth in the form of their choosing. They have no influence over their affectivity and motility. This is an existence not only without the human feature of choice, but without the faith, hope, and love that are central to the mythologies on which the modern Western state is based.

These contradictions exist not only in Canada perceived as a unity but also within the ethnicity of Blackness itself. Contradictorily, while Canada appears to be asserting internationally that there is no essence of humanity, in its internal ethical relations, it argues for a specific essence based solely on somatic characteristics. The contradictions show up in Canada in the lack of social mobility for somatic Blacks, which amounts to a failure in the test of individualism in a liberal and democratic state.

BLACKNESS: A LEGACY THAT THINKS WHITENESS

Trudeau did not reconcile all the contradictions captured in *A Just Society*. As Canada's prime minister from 1984 to 1993 and a Great Man of his time as produced by the Canadian consciousness, Brian Mulroney appeared as the heir to Trudeau's legacy. Mindful of his desire for a distinctive legacy of his own, Mulroney seemed to be taking Canada further along the road to Blackness. But in doing so he seemed to be coming to terms with some of the glaring contradictions inherited from Trudeau's legacy. Mulroney would carry the sacrifice of the body to a higher level, to the point of signing a free trade agreement with the United States, thereby linking Canada materially to the bigger economic giant. He would also bring Canadian foreign policy in line with that of the United States. In both cases, he would be going further than Trudeau. A notable exception was Mulroney's opposition to apartheid in South Africa, and against which he fought in open disagreement with Canada's major trade and military allies, the United States and Britain. For Mulroney, such actions were in keeping with the established notion that the Canadian body is perishable and can be sacrificed for the benefit of the unchangeable. While implementing his policies, Mulroney would argue that the mind of Canada – the spirit that was contained in Canadian culture and sovereignty – remained untouched, unsullied, and unchanged even if the Canadian body was not.

To this end, Mulroney would argue that the true expression of Canada, which he saw ethno-racially as being its culture, remained unchangeable.[41] This, too, was the thinking behind Mulroney's attempts to "bring Quebec into the Constitution" by officially recognizing the distinctiveness of the French-speaking province. Once again, Mulroney was arguing that the inner core of Canada that made it a manageable confederation was unchangeable even if the bodily expression – how the provinces relate to one another – changed.

The contradictions of this dialectic showed up when Trudeau argued that what Mulroney took for the changeable in Canada was, in fact, the unchangeable. Mulroney's argument was that the good that was Canada could be maintained ethno-racially in a confederation in which the specific physical manifestation did not matter. Therefore, he was willing to accept, for example, an asymmetric union, where all centres of power and differences were not equal.

In a dispute over what place and position an entity called Quebec should have in Canada, Trudeau on the other hand argued for the neo-mythic good to take a form where unity was made up of equals and there was symmetry among parts. The difference was over the determination of Canada as a unity on the ethno-racial register – whether Quebec was distinctively French and the rest of Canada, English, or, as Trudeau offered, both Canada and Quebec should be viewed as no more English nor French than the other. This was an argument which started with a fleeting recognition of what is the good for Canada and for Quebec as entities. A second quarrel was over what form on the ethno-racial register this expression of the Quebec/Canadian good should take, such as the shape and determination of agencies and institutions, and what common rights individuals determined only as Canadians should have in all parts of Canada.

For these reasons, Trudeau bitterly fought Mulroney over his attempts to change the Constitution and to rearrange the symmetry of provinces in Confederation. Theirs was an argument between and within registers, over different forms of constructions and which was deemed to be essentially Canada and Canadian. To this day these contradictions play themselves out in different ways depending on whether Canada presents itself as a universal that is unchangeably Black, with no essence, or as a particular that consists of separate notions of the unchangeable and changeable battling each other within the same state to be determined as White.[42]

I shall now look at the implications of Canada's recognition of its Blackness as a multicultural society and some of the main contradictions that arose dialectically from this recognition.

# 15

# Promises of Multiculturalism

## BLACKNESS IN MULTICULTURALISM

In this chapter, I explore some of the contradictions in multiculturalism as the lived reality of a new form of idealized Whiteness in Canada that is based on the acceptance of idealized Blackness as the country's official good. This is an idealization based on the recognition that, in the least, Canada is neo-mythically and ethno-racially Black because of the lack of purity that is now the state of Canadian culture. Officially, Canadian culture is fully recognized as a composite produced by a population that reflects the diversity or idealized Blackness of the world in terms of skin colours, cultures, and social statutes.

If there is an essence to being Canadian, it is one that is paradoxically constructed: an idealized category consisting of a finite number of fundamental rights that are constitutional. In this regard, a major transformation has taken place in the imaginary of what Canada is, what Canadian culture is, and who is a Canadian citizen – a transformation that, in keeping with the mythology that underlies the Canadian imagination, has resulted in turning what was formerly Black and Blackness into idealized White and Whiteness. This is a transformation away from a Canadianness founded solely on tradition – cosmological or otherwise – as a state that has already been towards a tradition where Canadianness is always in a process of becoming.

In this chapter, I will look at the limits of finite multiculturalism in the one-sided way it is practised and discuss how Canada still remains an unhappy consciousness, as it still has not made the final transformation to reconciliation and the purity of being a singular unity. This is in spite of the collective best intentions to be tolerant, accommodating, and accepting of all groups and ethnicities within a new definition of the ideal life and of freedom in Canada.

Some of this unhappiness stems from the way that some agencies of government, which are the unchangeable of the country, react to some specific groups that are still considered to be among the changeable in Canada. This is an ethical relationship that is based on the ideology on which Canada has been built so far, a way of thinking that, as part of the commonly perceived Western civilization, Canada cannot fully, or easily, eschew. This is an appeal to a patterned way of finding meaning in the world that is well-entrenched for determining what is unchangeably Black and White, what is good and evil, and which of the two can be changed or excluded. Here, we will analyse the contradictions that arise in an ethical relationship over the need to recognize a specific group of people as Black in a way that would allow them fuller entry into the social consciousness. Often, it is not easy conferring this recognition on a group that, at best, has only an imputed unchangeableness.

To this end, I am arguing that the racial attitudes that are inherent in this unhappiness are embedded dialectically in the concept of Canada and that race and racialism are, indeed, rational and intentional norms in Canadian society.[1] Therefore, I am more inclined to side with theorists like Charles Mills, who presents racism in Western civilization as emanating from a racial contract, although I argue the agreement is, indeed, a covenant – but accepting his position that any such arrangement by those with the power speaks to a thoughtfulness, deliberation, and importantly, intentions to create and maintain a specific ethical order.[2] This means that even if racism is manifested on the ethno-racial register, its validation comes through the neo-mythic register, and for this reason, as an action of subjectivity and agency, it is rational. It is deemed to be neo-mythically good by those deemed to be lords of the universe they inhabit.

Goldberg similarly argues that racism is a rational outcome of the prevailing ideology, especially that of nation-state formation, and is a means "not only to rationalize already established social relations but to order them."[3] Indeed, this is a rationalism, that, as we saw earlier, subjects perception to proof, but which, paradoxically, holds up as the ideal and good arguments by which perception must be judged, what perception has already established under a different guise. In this way, instead of perception submitting idealistically to a higher form of knowing that is reason, it is the sovereign reason that is forced to conform to or choose as ideal one of the many options earlier provided by perception. In a practical sense, therefore, no decision can be taken outside of the consciousness that produced it, as reason is unable to escape from the consciousness in which it must judge, in the same way that Hegel suggests no person can jump over his shadow.

This is very different from the argument that comes under the guise of tolerance and suggests that racism is emotional and irrational, and comes from ignorance, and can be eradicated by making people more enlightened through anti-racism education. Indeed, at the same time, this irrationalism is presented as received education, as something that is taught to children, or something that is deeply held in perception – all arguments which unintentionally support the case that racism is intentionally structural. The implication of an ingrained rational approach to racism is that meaningful change would have to come out of the dialectic – out of the system that produces meaning in our cultures – rather than by trying to change the meaning without really affecting the structure.

In this respect, as an element in Black existentialism, racism can only be eradicated through a new creation, or rather by moving to a new stage of its *becoming,* of letting the racism that is an institutional and systemic way of thinking die as an idealized Blackness to be resurrected as something ethically new and idealistically White. Like other concepts we have encountered, race and racism, too, must be viewed as concepts that are in transition and movement, where a one-sided understanding is always in the process of moving over to another one-sided understanding that is its other. Each movement along this scale of being is another determination of the being that is race and racism. To this end, there must be a pre-creation willingness for change: for it is the intention that is the White hope on which to create and build in a time that is racialized and Black. Therefore, in an ethical sense, the individual must have a good intention not to be racial, and this requires something much stronger than formal education to negate and even refute the old Black perception of race and racism. The intention to change must exist prior to the actual construction or transfiguration.

I will show, however, that the unhappiness also stems from another source – one that is traditionally ignored in the literature. In this respect, I will argue (1) that the unhappiness flows out of the intentions of all concerned to do good, to be all-inclusive of all groups in Canada; and (2) that the proposed outcome of achieving a life of happiness and contentment has not been realized, especially by some of the people on whose behalf the new policies were implemented and who, with the best of intentions, had advocated for them. Ironically, some of the people that are now the most unhappy because of the perceived restrictions of multiculturalism had campaigned to be recognized as a specific and distinct group in Canada. So here we are dealing with the catch of living a Black existentialism, of intending good but ending up with unintended outcomes.

One of these groups is constructed ethno-racially in modern day Canada as ethnically Black. It is a group that stands out from all others in Canada primarily because somatic characteristics are what is necessary and essential to this group. This chapter will look at what could account for this contradiction at the heart of Canada's unhappy consciousness: where a policy that was courted by a specific group as a guarantor of liberal rights, recognition, and standing in the state is now imagined by some members of the same group as leaving them less than free, as leaving them trapped within an ethnicity that is imposed on them for their own protection. In contradiction, at the same time that all Canadians are perceived neo-mythically as essentially a composite idealized group with no specific natural essence, a group of Canadians, Blacks, are perceived as having a prior essence – one that is primordial, necessary, and unchangeable even if Blacks were to be transformed into the full abstractness of being universal Canadians who are socially constructed in the social order in which they now claim membership. In this regard, ironically, primordiality does and does not matter at the same time.

In their view, opposed to such positioning and placement, this imprisonment in a racialized grouping where their humanity is limited exclusively to determinations on the ethno-racial register denies them the creative Blackness that is usually reserved for those who have the right to make an assessment of who or what they are at a particular moment, to determine what they want to become at a later point, and, just as importantly, to actively undertake the changes necessary to fulfilling the dream and to achieving the desired transformation. In this regard, members of this group are denied the hope of self-transformation that is social mobility, which would allow them to become White idealistically and in status. Dialectically, they are denied the existentialism of infinite multiculturalism, a multiculturalism that reconciles both registers of meaning. Dialectically, with this finite construction, they are trapped in despondency and unhappiness as opposed to perceiving themselves as being free in the hope and promise of multiculturalism.

This racialized Blackness, in the guise of an ethnicity, merely offers individuals recognition as liberal individuals that are equal to all others, while doing nothing to allow them to pragmatically exercise this recognition as an act of *becoming* or as simply amounting to having a distinct history. Both sides of the unhappy consciousness had presented the act of simply recognizing this group as having pride of place in Canada as being central to the development of anti-racist policies and liberal procedures. These innovations were intended to correct historic exclusions of Black-skinned people from full participation in and acceptance into Canadian society.

Yet, there remained and remains unhappiness on both sides. In the collective, the unhappiness is expressed in the feelings of those who think that Canada's international image as a tolerant and non-racist society is unfairly tarnished by a group that was intended to be one of the main beneficiaries. The raising of grievances is seen as an attack on Canada's liberalism and as placing Canada in a position where its well-intentioned liberal policies appear to be bankrupt and liberalism a bad word.[4] On the other side, there is the belief that placing them in an ethnicity deprives individuals of upward social mobility, as is the case for those constructed as Black, whose skin colour is the main determinant of their identity and their social and ethical relations with other Canadians and the state.[5] An indication of this imprisonment is the continued failure by individuals constructed as Black to make meaningful gains into the Canadian mainstream. This is especially the case in terms of an inability over time by Canadian Blacks to improve their economic lot. Evidence of this is seen in an analysis of the income levels of Blacks in Canadian society, where the tendency for Blacks is to settle at the bottom of the economic pile.[6]

This is historically the seemingly unchangeable position of somatic Blacks, whether they are Canadian born and trained, or immigrants that have been selected because of their high levels of social capital and a perceived ability to adapt easily and successfully to Canadian values.[7] Any social mobility that somatic Blacks may have, as individuals and as groups, tends to be downward, which contrasts with other ethnic groups that have over time made their way up the vertical mosaic of Canadian stratification toward the Whiteness of acceptance and personal fulfillment at the top. Liberal recognition does not easily translate into individual advancement; rather, it tends to lead to grievances of feeling unappreciated, restrained, and dissatisfied with one's motility and affectivity.[8] Neither side in the Canadian debate on race relations, for example, is happy despite the best efforts and intentions of both sides.

This chapter will show that this unhappiness has it genesis equally in the assumptions that both sides have made about what is good for them in the universal and the particular. Ironically, these are assumptions and intentions that were intended to fuel hope. To this end, multicultural Canada is unhappy because it cannot have its cake and eat it too: it cannot be finite and infinite at the same time; it cannot see itself as holding on to a consciousness that is the culmination of specific choices and narratives, while it at the same time rejects these choices and narratives as flawed and too exclusionary. Unhappily, there cannot be a break in the narrative while it is at the same time being held to. Before continuing along this path, let us now get an explanation of what multiculturalism is as a phenomenon.

## PHENOMENOLOGY OF MULTICULTURALISM

The universal vacuity of indeterminacy is idealistic Blackness. In terms of desire, it is also Black and Blackness culturally, in status and, possibly, semiotically. This universal is also Black and Blackness ontologically, as well as epistemologically – in terms of knowing the absolute – and finally ethically, in so far as what kind of society, social hierarchy, stratification, and positioning should be allowed as good. Out of this universalism burst forth attempts at particularisms. These are the many forms of determination, the many types of finite formations, that Black and Blackness can take. They may mutate further and, as Hegel would say, add colour to the Blackness of this universality. This is multiculturalism.

Therefore, contrary to common sense, phenomenologically, multiculturalism is the "degradation" of a pure Blackness and not, as it is usually presented, of Whiteness. Phenomenologically, multiculturalism is merely another attempt collectively at Whiteness, but an attempt that like all others before it will end in failure. Multiculturalism is Blackness in all its cosmopolitanism still trying to become White, but having to go through the many colours of the rainbow – and then more – to arrive at this Whiteness. Since none of these colours is ever White, by definition they must rest somewhere on the sliding scale between the binaries of Black and White, and must be some form of Black since White can only occupy an absolute position on this scale.

Yet on another scale, multiculturalism is "the becoming" – the process we are all going through as humans, and apparently will always be going through, in our elusive quest for idealized freedom and the Whiteness of a "pure" and unchanging identity. So that, at any moment, we are recognizing in our multiculturalism the Blackness of our bodies, cultures, aspirations, and material world. We are caught in the existentialist Blackness – the despair of realizing we are still an other to our idealized being – and the conflicting hope that some day yet we will arrive in a place and time when we are Black no more.

Historically, this has been the story of Canada, as it recognized that it was acting out of perception in claiming it was a White man's country ethnically and that its conduct in terms of race and ethnic relations was good ethically and morally. This is the recognition that Canadians are in a false awareness when they postulate, as has been the case, that Canadian Whiteness has been watered down through the Blackening of multiculturalism. Indeed, the early notions of a White man's country and now of multiculturalism are of the same series of determinations and creation – they are attempts at different times, and in light of different circumstances and material experiences, to produce a state that is other than the one in which we have always found ourselves as Canadians. Multiculturalism, neo-mythically and ethno-racially, is the recognition of otherness in ourselves and the acknowledged realization that our concept of Whiteness must, by definition, always be changing the closer we appear to be to the end of the journey that is the quest for an exclusively free identity. Alternatively, it is the recognition that, as we look back from our new vantage points in this journey, what we thought initially to be Black is a lot richer, fuller, more colourful, and more human than we thought. Indeed, the actual Black and Blackness was much closer to the actual White and Whiteness than we realized and we are now forced to recognize this. Finally, multiculturalism is the recognition that the very concepts of what we thought were Black, White, and Canadian changed during the examination, and that armed with this new knowledge, now even we who are conducting the examination have changed and moved on from being the people we were at the beginning of this journey. Indeed, what we might discover is that the one thing in our concepts that was unchangeable all along was Blackness – for White and Whiteness would have to be changeable for either to be produced out of a universe that is eternally Black. Therefore, most of our perception of equating good on the neo-mythic register to the unchangeable position on the ethno-racial register should have meant equating good to Blackness and Black and not to the false consciousness of equating it to Whiteness. The alternative would be to acknowledge, as is the case, that it is only possible to equate positions between the two registers by force – to socially construct the relationships and then to enforce them: so that we can arbitrarily equate good on the neo-mythic register to Whiteness on the ethno-racial and then socially try to make it happen. This is one way we can rationalize the equating of Blackness and Black with evil and for the presence of racism as a cancer in social consciousness.

Finding ourselves in such positions of false consciousness in terms of knowledge and of conflating unequal positions on the two registers to produce a social unity has always been part of the struggle by the ideal that is Canada to become actual, real, and rational. And it all starts with the recognition that multiculturalism is another place of Blackness, and not some determination of Whiteness – since by definition White can only be pure, of one determination or form, and unchangeable. For a state to be White, it would have to inhabit an exclusive universe. There could be no relationship with others – not even a lordship and bondage arrangement with White and Whiteness racialized as superior. White and Whiteness require for their existence and then perseverance an absolute rendering from all others. Such an absolute has never been achieved in history anywhere. Black is the colour of humanity in all its diversity and differences, with Blackness the single existence of this humanity in all its universality. Multiculturalism shows, phenomenologically, that as concepts Black/Blackness and White/ Whiteness are only one-sided views of a single concept, and that a fully understood concept must include them both. The unity that is the social order and the resulting consciousness cannot be explaining fully by dwelling only on the quest for freedom and the hope of bringing Whiteness out of Blackness. Neither can it be explained fully by spotlighting what is the "natural" existence – for to be human is to be creative, and to be creative means that humans are always thinking and rethinking how they can change the existing order and how they can perfect through change themselves and what is around them. To be human is to be creative and to be creating.

Multiculturalism seeks to harness this creativity and to guide the creation towards a specific perfection – a time when there could be a social order that is not based on a lordship and bondage relationship. This is why it presents Canada to us as a work in progress, as creation not yet completed and as a body or consciousness that is changeable. To this end, then, multiculturalism is based on achieving an imaginary unity – it is idealism in all its Whiteness. For in this way of thinking, because it must eventually be a social construction, one that privileges a decided ethical way of existence, idealized Whiteness must be seen as nothing more than a product of idealized Blackness – and, as modernity has falsely taught us, rationally Blackness can only produce Blackness, for Whiteness is perceptually unchangeable and always prior to Blackness. When it negates this initial perception and comes into fuller knowledge or cognition, the self-examining consciousness must recognize Blackness as the unchangeable and White/Whiteness as only the unfulfilled wish – and therefore only a hope – to be other than Black. Multiculturalism is this consciousness coming into fuller knowledge and then trying to act rationally.

Most important, in practice in the material world of the idealistic Blackness struggling with Whiteness, or of *realpolitik* as Trudeau called it, multiculturalism is the question of how to behave and treat others when we recognize that we cohabit a single system that whether determined ethno-racially or neo-mythically is Black, fragmented, diversified, and alienating with no clear path into the future – and in this diversity and among these differences it is the question of what values, judgments, and arrangements we should make through negotiations between the two registers about the present and, possibly, the future.

## BLACKNESS AND THE WHITE IMAGES OF MULTICULTURALISM

Since the 1960s, Canada has developed its image of being the first post-modern nation that is based on an official integrationist policy of multiculturalism.[9] This is the image of Canada as a tolerant, inclusive, and pluralistic society, where differences are celebrated, individual rights are protected, and the state refrains from efforts that might appear culturally assimilationist or hegemonic. This is the mythology of there being a good life that is shared by everyone deemed good enough to be a member of this society, a good life that is supposedly indicative of free choices by individuals living according to their individualistic pasts based on origins in times and spaces other than Canada. This is a new mythology that defines idealized Whiteness in Canada with fairness and justice, and is the framework for a country that is a multicultural liberal democracy.

Idealized Blackness, in this setting, is to treat members of the Canadian family intolerantly. It is to deny them their liberal rights as individuals, to refuse to recognize their group identities, or to put limits on group cultures, and to deny immigrants from around the world easier entry into Canadian society. Once in Canada, they can exercise the full liberal freedom to advance according to their wishes and abilities, as long as they demonstrate the good will of living according to accepted societal norms. Idealized Whiteness also amounts to excluding any specific group from the construction of the majority or the mainstream that supposedly makes the decisions on the governance of the country democratically and contributes fully to the determination of Canada and Canadians in the future.

In contrast, idealized Whiteness requires that all Canadians, whether as individuals or through the group identity of their choice, have full entitlement to all the rights and privileges guaranteed by the state to its citizens. Indeed, the highest achievement of a Canadian is to be recognized as someone possessing, at a minimum, all the abstract rights offered by the Canadian state – someone who has been reduced to an abstraction and on whom recognition is offered in an abstraction instead of specifically according to some contingent identity such as ethnicity, race, gender, sexuality, or the colour of skin. In this thinking, the unchangeable in Canadians is their abstract rights, which are necessary for their new ontology and which produce an ideal existentialism for them. As the *Canadian Citizenship Act* states, "A citizen, whether or not born in Canada, is entitled to all rights, powers and privileges and is subject to all obligations, duties and liabilities to which a person who is a citizen ... is entitled or subject and has a like status to that of such a person."[10]

In this mythology, the original good expressed through a desire to make Canada an idealized White country remains unchangeable. The change that has occurred is in the redefinition or restatement of what ethno-racially constitutes Canada's original good. According to this reasoning, the United States and Europe might be multicultural, but not officially so, and Canada's uniqueness in this regard is an indication of its greater tolerance.[11] Based on the redefined good in terms of its ethno-racial manifestations in Canada, the United States remains idealistically Black, as Black as it was when compared to Canada, and as Black as Canada was White, back in 1783.

Typical of this argument expressing a new manifestation of the neo-mythic good of happiness and belonging for all is the following by Jeffrey Reitz in *The Warmth of Welcome*: "Race is a less traditional issue in Canada than in the United States, and Canada's highly touted policy of multiculturalism has been adapted in an attempt to meet the equity issues raised by the so-called visible minorities (a Canadian term referring to the perception of distinctive physical features of the new racial groups."[12] Reitz takes

a positive view of Canada as enlightened by suggesting that most traditional indicators of ethnic or racial discrimination, such as anti-Semitic and
racist name-calling, show "a trend over time towards greater tolerance."[13]
He says there are also greater levels of acceptance, recognition, and equality for all groups within the Canadian family or mosaic.

Yet, as Reitz notes, there are contradictions and tensions in a policy of
multiculturalism that is still "far from the universally accepted" policy it
was expected to be when it was first formulated as a way to settle differences within a population of racial equals that was overwhelmingly
European, and mainly English and French.[14] This is where the definition of
the common good is determined exclusively on the ethno-racial register,
according to the violence of a forced conflation of the neo-mythic good
with somatic and cultural Whiteness. Indeed, invoking the notion of tolerance is usually a code for suggesting that racism is not as virile and open as
in the United States in its epistemological and ethical Blackness, and that
Canada is more accepting of racial and ethnic minorities. This is the image
that is captured in the egalitarian norms of *A Just Society,* the official ideology since the 1960s, where racism and ethnic discrimination are administratively things of the past.[15] Will Kymlicka's view is typical: "Canadians
have managed to build a prosperous, tolerant, peaceful, free and democratic society in what is one of the most ethno-culturally diverse countries
in the world. We have become so accustomed to diversity that we often fail
to notice how exceptional Canada is in this regard. Consider immigration.
We debate the best overall level of immigration, and the criteria that should
be used in selecting immigrants (age, language, skills, family reunification,
refugee status, etc.). But almost everyone accepts that we should continue
seeking immigrants, and that immigration is an important part of our
development as a country."[16]

Indeed, Kymlicka and other representatives of the dominant narrative
argue that multiculturalism as practised in Canada is a success story and
one that is emulated internationally.[17] For this to be true, such a development would arise only if there was a common meaning flowing unforced
from the two registers, with the registers breaking out of the lordship and
bondage relationship that often makes us privilege the ethno-racial emphasis on the somatic and cultural as the authentic way of knowing the good.
Kymlicka strongly disputes the argument by some that multiculturalism is
leading to the creation of ethnic ghettoes, to the fracturing of Canadian
identity, and to greater incidences of separation within the Canadian state.
Rather, Kymlicka argues, multiculturalism is a potent lever for the state in
its effort to integrate ethnic and racial minorities and immigrants. And it is
a mechanism that works splendidly. "On every indicator of integration,
then, Canada, with its multiculturalism policy, fares better than the United
States, with its repudiation of (officially recognized) multiculturalism. We

would find the same story if we compared Canada with other immigrant countries that have rejected multiculturalism in favour of an exclusive emphasis on common identities – such as France. Canada does better than these other countries not only in actual rates of integration, but also in the day-to-day experience of ethnic relations."[18]

Yet, as Kymlicka notes, there is a significant body of opinion within Canada itself that argues that Canadian multiculturalism is a failure. Indeed, Kymlicka maintains that most of the debate about multiculturalism is in keeping with a misguided and misplaced discussion on separation and nation-state building for national minorities within Canada, an argument that I would say flows out of the discussion on the struggle between the entrenched French and English interests for dominance. Conceptually, Kymlicka sees only the positives of a finite multiculturalism. For him, the negatives that adumbrate are conceptually not part of multiculturalism as now the new good. Another feature of the disagreement is existentialist, and is captured in the notion that governments in liberal states should not be involved in culture, just as they ought not to be involved in religion.

Kymlicka observes that conceptually there is no validity to this argument for, the world over, all states are involved in the production of a societal culture. I take this to mean that these states can be identified as different based on different societal cultures that are all determined within the same ethno-racial register. In this regard, Kymlicka is acknowledging that the historic intention of all modernist states is to transform a group of people that were initially culturally Black into a unified polis that is culturally White. This would amount, mythologically, to raising them idealistically to a level of civilization most appropriate for the preservation of the people and the state. This intent is captured existentially in what he calls societal cultures – a distinct way arising out of a social consciousness of doing things and producing a specific, particularist, and common meaning of life. This ethno-racially derived societal culture is based intentionally on transforming a people into cultural or idealized Whiteness, or to preserving them as such if they have already reached this moment of enlightenment. Thus, their Whiteness is a contextualized cultural, idealistic, and status Blackness that has been transformed by the circumstances. Kymlicka explains: "I use the term 'societal culture' to emphasize that it involves a common language and social institutions, rather than common religious beliefs, family customs, or personal lifestyles ... Thus a societal culture is a territorially concentrated culture centred on a shared language that is used in a wide range of societal institutions, including schools, media, law, the economy, and government. Participation in such a culture provides access to meaningful ways of life across the full range of human activities – social, educational, religious, recreational, economic – encompassing both public and private spheres."[19]

Kymlicka claims that one of the main reasons for this awareness is that many of the commentators on multiculturalism are misinformed about the intent, purpose, and assumptions of the policy. Second, many Canadians do not know the intended and practical limits of multiculturalism – in other words, Kymlicka is arguing that the opponents are not mindful of the mythological meanings. In his view, then, Canadians are not of a single consciousness on the finiteness of multiculturalism; they cannot even decide what the salient, necessary, and essential characteristics of multiculturalism are. By this reasoning, Canadians are quite Black existentially and ontologically, and are quite an unhappy consciousness because of their split desires. Even if he does not say so directly, Kymlicka is arguing that there is a profound metaphysical disagreement among Canadians on what the virtues and teleological aims of multiculturalism are. He further notes that even many of the defenders of Canadian multiculturalism are guilty in this respect:

Part of the problem may be that Canadians have no clear sense of the limits of multiculturalism. They are not sure that certain "non-negotiable" principles or institutions will be protected and upheld, even if they conflict with the desires or traditions of some immigrant groups. Canadians are not averse to multiculturalism within limits, but they want to know that those limits exist. They value diversity, but they also want to know that this diversity will be expressed within the context of common Canadian institutions, and that it doesn't entail acceptance of ethnic separation. Similarly, Canadians are generally tolerant, but they also believe that some practices, such as clitoridectomy, are intolerable, and they want to know that they won't be asked to "tolerate" the violation of basic human rights.[20]

## RATIONALIZING THE BLACKNESS STILL IN MULTICULTURALISM

So who is right: the critics like myself who argue that multiculturalism has failed to produce (or as I claim, prevented from producing) what Trudeau envisioned as part of the ideals of *A Just Society*, or the supporters like Kymlicka who suggest that multiculturalism has more than delivered within the practical and pragmatic limits in which the policy was established and implemented? Perhaps, contradictorily, both schools of thought are right – with each school drawing on different finite constructions that are part of the same infinite that is multiculturalism.

The answer depends on what each critic takes away from Trudeau's dream, from multiculturalism as the infinity that a Hegelian conception insists we view it as, an infinity in which negative and positive components struggle to establish finite limits as a common lived experience. This is a struggle for the dominance of the one-sided view, a battle that is so well described by Charles Taylor as a purported master-slave narrative in

*Politics of Recognition.*[21] The difference is that what one school treats as essential and necessary the other sees as accidental and contingent. Is multi-culturalism intended to produce a Canada with a core or mainstream of somatic and cultural Whiteness made up of the French and English ethnicities that have power and the longest lineage in Canada, and surrounded by a periphery of somatic and cultural Blackness made up of newer immigrants who are treated with tolerance and dignity as humans but racially are deemed not to have the same claims and entitlements as the established Canadians – the hub and spoke model of multiculturalism that Trudeau appears to have offered? If this were the case, then unchangeably Canada would be somatically White, with this Whiteness having an essence that is culturally and socially English and French.

Or is the goal of multiculturalism idealized Blackness where there is no essential or natural core and periphery, where idealistically all ethnicities are equal, where race genuinely does not matter, and where Canadians are idealistically Black in their common humanity? In this case, Canada would genuinely have no essence; the hub of which Trudeau spoke would be re-constructible, changeable, and indeterminate, as in the night when all cows are Black. It would be truly free, in that determinations of status, culture, and identity would always be fluid and contingent, changing from moment to moment, with any essence there is coming to the fore in the actions of individuals who are moral agents in ethical relations. In this case, power would be based on contingent factors: such as those who are dominant having the ability to gain or cling to power. Power and influence would not flow naturally from some source other than what has been constructed as a composite general will.

Does the answer to these questions depend on the *realpolitik* of living in changing times in Western civilization in late modernity with its baggage of race, inequalities, and tyrannies along with the successes of liberty and freedom? Or does the answer rest in the recognition that the dialectic of freedom aspires in Western thought to the rationalist transcendentalist world of idealized Whiteness, a world to which Trudeau and Canada consciously aimed but have yet to attain?

The implicit contradictions in these questions have to do with the legacy of *A Just Society*, Trudeau, and the dialectic of freedom in Canada that has as its source an embedded position in the aims, goals, and consciousness of the dominant Western thought. Canada appears to have come to terms with idealized, cultural, and status Blackness. Somatic Blackness provides a new round of contradictions in the Canadian body politic and shows that the final idealized transformation into a singular imagined unity has not yet occurred in Canada.

In trying to answer these questions and to rationalize the explanations, most critics are simply trying to impose limits on multiculturalism. In so doing, we are setting both the minimum and maximum boundaries of the concept. Some theorists see only the negative components of the concept. Rinaldo Walcott and Himani Bannerji, for example, see multiculturalism as an attempt to erase from the national narrative all that is not somatically and culturally White, while Neil Bissoondath argues that multiculturalism produces idealized Blackness that is chaos and fragmentation with no clear sense of a common unity, history, or culture.[22] Others like Kymlicka accentuate the positive. One side's necessary finite attribute for multiculturalism becomes the other side's contingent attribute in this debate.[23]

I want to suggest that neither side is right nor wrong. It is just that neither, on its own, provides a full picture of the infinity of multiculturalism – multiculturalism as it moves towards genuine multiculturalism or its absolute. Second, both betray a different level of understanding: Bissoondath follows his common sense way of reflecting on the world to a logical conclusion that Hegel would call analytic cognition, and which leaves him with seemingly unanswerable contradictions thrown up by the competing registers of meaning; Kymlicka offers synthetic cognition, a seemingly higher level of thinking that emphasizes recognition but also a possible resolution of the contradictions produced in analytical thinking. Kymlicka's is where forms are seen as related to each other and there is a need for the imposition of laws and propositions based on a categorical understanding. It is a reflection of the inner as outer, but as C.L.R. James suggests, "Synthetic Cognition always has large areas of the Object outside its fundamental categories, areas of which its categories can make no sense."[24]

However, what James just described is an understanding for the benefit of the subject's perspective and to confirm its initial way of knowing. It is not one that fully explains the object, which was the original aim of our journey for understanding. It is not dialectical and it does not produce the highest dialectical knowledge that is a priori and synthetic, a knowledge that is the conception or notion as both universal and particular – that for which we were searching from the beginning. With this phenomenology of Blackness and multiculturalism, we are aiming for dialectic cognition or the "cognition of creative cognition" that results in knowing the absolute idea as far possible. This is the full knowledge of universals and notions.[25]

On its own, none of the finite notions offered by analytic and synthetic cognition fully embodies the fullness and completeness that is the despair and, of equal importance, the hope that are equally inherent and necessary to infinite multiculturalism. That there are deep-seated disagreements over the meaning and intentions of multiculturalism can be traced phenomenologically back to the desire to impose finite limits on the concept, and on the assumptions that support the need and desire for these finite boundaries. Existential issues of multiculturalism, of the kinds of ethical relations that are at stake, flow out of the assumptions on which the finite construction is based. Once again, we can test the viability of the suggested limits by search-ing for what we can call the essence or, indeed, natural combinations of char-acteristics that are necessary for explaining multiculturalism. These assumptions, I will argue, are based on the ideology that underpins the mas-ter narrative that accounts epistemologically for Canada as a consciousness that knows from where it has come and where it is going.

## LIMITS OF MULTICULTURAL BLACKNESS: THE SOMATIC

There is one limit that, in general, goes unnoticed in most discussions on multiculturalism. This is the practical side of the notion that a Black ethnic-ity exists naturally ethno-racially in Canada on the same footing as other ethnicities, such as Italian-Canadian, Scottish-Canadian, Aboriginal, or French-Canadian. Indeed, even the federal government and its various departments, including the Department of Multiculturalism in the Depart-ment of Heritage, have identified Black as an ethnic identity. The need to give Canadians an ethnicity, as Trudeau suggests, has created classification problems for Statistics Canada about how to deal with some groups, espe-cially those who, historically, have been identified by racial characteristics, such as somatic features, rather than by other forms of ethnicity.

Statistics Canada, as the official collector and sorter of data based on Canadian categories of compilation, notes "the concept of ethnicity is somewhat multidimensional as it included aspects such as race, origin or ancestry, identity, language and religion."[26] Right away, if it is multidimen-sional, the concept, in terms of an essence, must be seen phenomeno-logically as having several layers of darknesses and of being the type of conceptual barbarism associated with composites. Statistics Canada says:

Identity has a certain appeal because it attempts to measure how people perceive themselves rather than their ancestors. Nevertheless, it retains certain dimensions of not only origin but race as well. In addition, it may include aspects of citizenship. A typical question might be, with which ethnic group do you identify? Some respon-dents may associate the question with citizenship and report Canadian. Others may associate it with origin and report Italian. Others might see it as involving both citi-zenship and origin and report Italian-Canadian. Others might see racial dimensions and report black or black-Canadian. Furthermore, in some contexts, ethnicity might be implied but the reference is actually language. For example, there are fre-quent references to French Canadians and English Canadians which are not on the basis of ethnicity per se but on the basis of the language spoken.[27]

Applying this explanation for category determination in multicultural Canada, it is apparent that Black is different from other ethnic categories, in that it is viewed more as a racial labelling that is also unintentionally evaluative than are any of the other multidimensional aspects of identity that are included under ethnicity. This point is further emphasized when Statistics Canada gives a detailed definition of the races in Canada, in effect offering the full spectrum of the official ethno-racial register. These include the *Aboriginal* (Inuit, Métis, North American Indian), *Arab/West Asian* (e.g., Armenian, Egyptian, Iranian, Lebanese, Moroccan), *Black* (e.g., African, Haitian, Jamaican, Somali), *Chinese, Filipino, Japanese, Korean, Latin American, South Asian, South East Asian*, and *White* (Caucasian).

Once again, phenomenologically, on closer examination the identity Black stands out as a finite category, and it is most ambiguous and equivocal in meaning, for this category refuses to remain stable. Technically, members of all groups, except possibly White or Caucasian, can at different moments be classified ethno-racially as Black. This is the determination of the being – placing her or him at a beginning in history that is a determination out of the indeterminacy that is universal humanity. Even here, we start with a contradiction: for if the being is already determined, then it cannot also be indeterminate. The being would have to be already mediated, which means that Black and Blackness could not come to us fully as unconstructed givens and in their sensuous immediacy of thought. For example, Egyptians and Moroccans can be included in the African component of Black. Children born to Filipinos, Japanese, and Koreans in Jamaica can be classified as Black when they arrive in Canada, if place of birth is the main determinant of race. In addition, the millions of people of African ancestry living in Brazil and Costa Rica can be classified as Black as well as Latin American. The same goes for South Asians and the descendents of South East Asians living in Black countries like Jamaica, Trinidad, and Guyana. Therefore, even on the ethno-racial register, and even when common sense as perception expects there to be, there are no clear limits and boundaries – no categories based on clear and fixed essences.

Second, all the other categories are associated with geographic or linguistic communities which means that it is possible for people of African ancestry to be integrated into these communities by living in the region or by speaking the language. In this regard, Black and White are indeterminate and equivocal. Black and White are somatic identities, unlike the others categories.[28] As a finite group, there is no clear essence – no movement or transition within the category – or naturally essential combination that by law makes it Black. In practice, Black and Blackness, therefore, is an infinity ontologically and epistemologically, even if it is approached as a finite concept. In the end, Blackness is reduced perceptually and non-cognitively to the colour of the skin, back to what we started out with and took as the given, and which we wanted to test before accepting. In effect, phenomenologically we are trapped perhaps in the most perverse of one-sided thinking.

What is merely one of many contingents in the concept Blackness is presented as the unchangeable and necessary. All else, particularly the immanent transitions and movements, that makes up the infinity of Black and Blackness is lost in this finite group, thereby existentially and ethically negating the hope and intentions of idealistic multiculturalism.[29]

In devising the policy of multiculturalism, Canada intended to shift away from static racial determinants to more fluid ethical ones – from a determination of Blackness purely as ethno-racial to the neo-mythical. However, where Canada can be faulted is that in so doing it replaced the old racial category of Black, which was based on racial characterization and even stereotyping with its empty content, with a presumed Black ethnicity without fully pulling off a transformation in attitudes to or treatment of those categorized officially as Blacks and Blackness. On the scale of being, Blacks are still seen cognitively through the lenses of the old perception. They have not moved towards their other that is part of the full conception of, at least, Black, Canadian, and citizen as absolutes rather than finite groups. Canada retained the historical common sense approach for determining who is Black, a way of knowing that supposedly served it so well in modernity. It did not create a mythically pure White body as intended, but for citizens made only partial Whiteness as perceptually the main ingredient for accepted recognition of citizenship in a body that is still ethically Black idealistically from the way somatic and cultural Blacks are excluded from the social imagination of who is truly Canadian. This common sense approach was less useful for other groups, for the other ethnicities could claim the nature of their being based on essences that are not readily determined by looks and perception alone. In a post-modern moment, Black retained a determination that is fully modern, even if it is one that is grounded also in a pre-modern ideology, a strain of which was crystallized in the modern state as a site of racial exclusion.

Evidence of this is that, as Trudeau illustrates, all other recognized ethnicities in Canada were determined as a constructed "essence" based on the conferring of an identity after the formation of the state to which the individuals were supposedly native. Ontologically, theirs was a finite constructed around some essence that was culturally determined in a particular way. In a broader sense, this finite categorization is one that can later be subsumed back into the larger infinity that is, paradoxically in our case, Blackness and Whiteness. Therefore Chinese, Filipino, and Korean identities or ethnicities arise after the formation of these states. Even before coming to Canada, immigrants from these countries have been determined ethno-racially. They have already left the Blackness of indeterminacy and entered a history that socialized them, gave them a culture, a particular way of knowing, and a perceived good that is based on a national or group way of understanding the world. The challenge for them in Canada is one of positioning, whether they are superior, inferior, or equal – whether they are White or Black culturally and/or in status. However, they are identities that in a wider scheme of things can be Black or White, even somatically if the primary determination is culture or geography.

Black, as an ethnicity in Canada, is not immanent to a specific state ethno-racially, to a specific region, language, or culture. It is as universal and primordial as the Caucasian denominator in a common sense way. Black speaks to an ontology that says that if there is an essence or unchange-ableness of Blackness it predates any civil society as recognized in a first negation of indeterminateness on the ethno-racial scale – unlike any Chinese, Arab, Latin American, Korean, or other national essence – and speaks to an ontology that situates the Black body in a state of nature or perma-nent indeterminacy even when it has entered into civil society. There has been no prior determination; rather there is only an ahistorical changeless-ness. Blackness is presented in multicultural Canada as an indeterminate infinity, which can take any form socially and ethically in a later nation-state determination. In this way, once again, Black can be transitioned into Chinese, Filipino, Korean or any national construction, if the essence is not somatic.

On the other hand, ethically, Black is supposed to be a designation of a culture or ethnicity on the same level neo-mythically as all other such par-ticular groupings in a Canadian universal. In this seeming determination, the ethical rather than ontological question is how to evaluate objectively the culture and way of life peculiar to this particular group in the new Can-ada – whether it should be Black or White culturally and in status. Here, then, arises a very clear contradiction of being Black and Canadian. As Hegel says: "If being had a determinateness, then it would not be the abso-lute beginning at all; it would then depend on an other and would not be immediate, would not be the beginning. But if it is indeterminate and hence a genuine beginning, then, too, it has nothing with which it could bridge the between itself and an other; it is at the same time the end."[30]

This is the contradiction of the category Black: it is supposedly a begin-ning and an ending, but in practice is more likely to be used as a beginning – where there is the vacuity of the night when all cows are black, instead of speaking of a mixed determination of light and darkness. This is the ideal illumination, at least for me, where as Hegel says Black and Blackness are seen "only (as) darkened light and illuminated darkness which have within themselves the moment of difference and are, therefore, *determinate* being."[31]

Even the way Black as an ethnicity is supposedly determined ethno-racially does not allow the concept to become a particular on this register. It remains defiantly a universal that subsumes all other particulars. Which means that Trudeau's argument that every Canadian has a linguistic or cultural identity to go along with his or her Canadian identity does not hold true for those constructed as Black. Here, we are reminded of John Burbidge's ideas on how different categories of knowing can be translated into rational thought, into action based on reflection – of how eventually specific categories are deemed to be accidental and contingent, while at least one is deemed to be essential, necessary, and unchangeable.[32] However, Black-Canadian is made up of two supposedly unchangeable essences, contradictorily, with neither of them contingent and accidental, and both instead necessary and essential. Ethically, reason has to choose one as more important than the other. Indeed, this is a case where the contradictions are seemingly reconciled only in the mind. But at what cost, especially when the price is also the imagined equality of every citizen in the state? This imagining of an essential Blackness even in the presence of a plenitude of previous social constructions of those now totalized as Black creates, as Sartre and others have pointed out, an ontological and epistemological absurdity – a composite with a single essence: where the thinking does not match the object that is thought about.

Rather, all previous and linguistic characteristics as thought are negated and subsumed into an amorphous and equivocal Blackness on arrival in Canada. This would be the same if all the many dark-skinned soccer players that are representing European national teams in the World Cup were to immigrate to Canada. On arrival, they would lose their Polish, English, or French ethnicity and would be expected to claim a Black ethnicity as part of a fraternal sense of belonging with other dark-skinned people from various parts of the world, and with whom they may have little in common, culturally or linguistically. In other words, epistemologically, it is and always is skin colour that determines whether the body has any specific culture and, ultimately, whether it is good or evil. And skin colour is immune to visible change through social construction.

In this respect, the equivocation of Blackness points to the contradictions inherent in the ideology and legacy of *A Just Society* and in its policy for achieving justice, multiculturalism. What is not known cognitively about the members of this group is privileged as important and necessary, once an essence of them, contradictorily, is assumed. This is an argument that seems to turn idealized multiculturalism on its head. In practice, it is saying that ontology precedes epistemology, a theoretical argument that was debunked as part of Canada's decision to become officially multicultural. This is just one of the ways where, to recall Grossman from chapter seven, phenomenologically and existentially, we are living in an unreal world of accidents and contingencies. The result is what may appear to be neither what we want nor what truly exists.

In terms of ethical relations, the rhetoric of multiculturalism presents such a favourable view of Canada as a land of idyllic Whiteness, based on the intention to achieve this status. As a concept, the favourable rhetoric accepts as common knowledge the existence already of the positive elements in the infinity that is multiculturalism. For example, in announcing Canada's official multiculturalism policy, Prime Minister Trudeau gave the following as the (positive) goals of the policy:

A policy of multiculturalism within a bilingual framework commends itself to the government as the most suitable means of assuring the cultural freedom of Canadians. Such a policy should help break down discriminatory attitudes and cultural jealousies. National unity, if it is to mean anything in the deeply personal sense, must be founded on confidence in one's own individual identity; out of this can grow respect for that of others and a willingness to share ideas, attitudes and assumptions. A vigorous policy of multiculturalism will help create this initial confidence. It can form the base of a society which is based on fair play for all. The government will support and encourage the various cultures and ethnic groups that give structure and vitality to our society. They will be encouraged to share their cultural expression and values with other Canadians and so contribute to a richer life for us all.[33]

In Trudeau's view, multiculturalism limited only by bilingualism would be good for the country, for different ethnic groups, and for individuals seeking self-actualization. Alluding specifically to social mobility for individuals, he says, "the individual's freedom would be hampered if he were locked for life within a particular cultural compartment by the accident of birth or language."[34] This, then, was for Trudeau the essence of the negative components that are included in the concept that is multiculturalism. Therefore, by his very reasoning, individual social mobility is intentionally a major test of the effectiveness of multiculturalism. It is the point of negation between the positive and negative elements in the concept. Social mobility is the test that official multiculturalism is purportedly really an infinity, even if limited by bilingualism, or the official language in which it exists and is recognized. To this end, Trudeau suggests that, translated into existentialism and ethical relations, multiculturalism is "basically the conscious support of individual freedom of choice. We are free to be ourselves. But this cannot be left to chance. It must be fostered and pursued actively. If freedom of choice is in danger for some ethnic groups, it is in danger for all. It is the policy of this government to eliminate any such danger and to 'safeguard' this freedom."[35] With this statement, Trudeau has finally set both positive and negative goals for multiculturalism as an all-inclusive concept. Trudeau has included in his social construction the notion of what is morally good and evil, and what is idealistically Black and White.

Already, there seems to be an inherent contradiction conceptually in Trudeau's pronouncement on the freedom of the individual and the freedoms

380 Canadian Blackness and Identity

of the ethnic group. This is a contradiction that Trudeau exemplified in his cultural Blackness, in proudly claiming to be of French-Canadian ethnicity but also arguing for the purity of the individualism that always seeks to escape from the confinement of a predetermined group formation. Trudeau reconciled his personal conflict – and that of Canada's – by appealing to reason and not to the emotion of common sense or a societal capital, by appealing to a higher meaning that comes through a determination that is not usually easily understandable through the senses or perception. His Canadian Whiteness came through a double determinacy.

### MULTICULTURALISM: RECOGNIZING INDIVIDUAL OR COLLECTIVE SELVES

If there were to be a clash between the two types of freedom – between the individual's determination of itself and the determination ascribed to it as part of a purported ethnicity – which would be privileged? This would become more than an academic question, for, as I argue in this book, the struggle for individual social mobility for individuals constructed as Black is a primary test of Canadian multiculturalism.[36] It is the major flaw in Canada's multiculturalism narrative. This is so because in constructing an ethnic group called Black, ethically multicultural Canada also assigned that group a specific ranking in society: the bottom of the social and economic hierarchy. This point is demonstrated by the failure of Canada to undertake any remedial work, such as affirmative action in the United States, that would allow for the improved social conditions for those who have been historically disadvantaged. There was never any collective atonement and righting of past wrongs to eliminate the legacy of exclusions or inferiority for marginalized groups now brought conceptually into the mainstream.[37]

Second, if individuals are to be free, how can a Black individual, still claiming her or his assumed ethnicity as a primary identity, escape from the social ranking of the group? With his idealistic view of striving for "freedom," Trudeau announced specific steps that the government would take to promote multiculturalism and which emphasized group norms:

First, resources permitting, the government will seek to assist all Canadian cultural groups that have demonstrated a desire and effort to continue to develop a capacity to grow and contribute to Canada, and a clear need for assistance, the small and weak groups no less than the strong and highly organized. Second, the government will assist members of all cultural groups to overcome cultural barriers to full participation in Canadian society. Third, the government will promote creative encounters and interchange among all Canadian cultural groups in the interest of national unity. Fourth, the government will continue to assist immigrants to acquire at least one of Canada's official languages in order to become full participants in Canadian society.[38]

Additionally, the *Canadian Multiculturalism Act* of 1985 makes similar claims in its preamble about the freedoms, egalitarianism, and anti-racist norms of Canada. It starts by recognizing a number of features that are fundamental to Canada:

- every individual in Canada is equal before the law;
- the *Canadian Citizenship Act* provides that all Canadians, whether by birth or by choice, enjoy equal status, are entitled to the same rights, powers and privileges and are subject to the same obligations, duties and liabilities;
- the *Canadian Human Rights Act* provides equality of opportunity for all individuals, to make them aware of their duties and obligations as members of society, and in order to secure that opportunity, establishes the Canadian Human Rights Commission to redress any proscribed discrimination, including discrimination on the basis of race, national or ethnic origin or colour;
- Canada is a party to the *International Convention on the Elimination of All Forms of Racial Discrimination*, which Convention recognizes that all human beings are equal before the law and are entitled to equal protection of the law against any discrimination and against any incitement to discrimination, and to the *International Covenant on Civil and Political Rights*, which Covenant provides that persons belonging to ethnic, religious or linguistic minorities shall not be denied the right to enjoy their own culture, to profess and practise their own religion or to use their own language.

The policy of the government, according to the *Multiculturalism Act*, is to:

(a) recognize and promote the understanding that multiculturalism reflects the cultural and racial diversity of Canadian society and acknowledges the freedom of all members of Canadian society to preserve, enhance and share their cultural heritage;

(b) recognize and promote the understanding that multiculturalism is a fundamental characteristic of the Canadian heritage and identity and that it provides an invaluable resource in the shaping of Canada's future;

(c) promote the full and equitable participation of individuals and communities of all origins in the continuing evolution and shaping of all aspects of Canadian society and assist them in the elimination of any barrier to that participation;

(d) recognize the existence of communities whose members share a common origin and their historic contribution to Canadian society, and enhance their development;

(e) ensure that all individuals receive equal treatment and equal protection under the law, while respecting and valuing their diversity;

(f) encourage and assist the social, cultural, economic and political institutions of Canada to be both respectful and inclusive of Canada's multicultural (identities);

(g) promote the understanding and creativity that arise from the interaction between individuals and communities of different origins;

(h) foster the recognition and appreciation of the diverse cultures of Canadian society and promote the reflection and the evolving expressions of those cultures;

(i) preserve and enhance the use of languages other than English and French, while strengthening the status and use of the official languages of Canada; and

(j) advance multiculturalism throughout Canada in harmony with the national commitment to the official languages of Canada.[39]

In addition to dealing with the ethno-racial, a primary intention of this policy is as much enlightenment on the neo-mythic scale, where the goal is to change perception by formal and informal education. Anti-racism education would become a major plank in the efforts to inculcate a more accepting attitude towards diversity and difference, especially towards those officially declared to be visible minorities. But the practice of multiculturalism in Canada tells a different story from the rhetoric as it applies to racialized Blacks categorized as an ethnicity. A more contentious argument is that, despite the claims in the *Multiculturalism Act* and policy, Canada effectively places immigrants and "visible minorities" in a hierarchy of ethnicities and racialized groups based on group, and not individual, concerns. This is a placement that is based on the mythology that some immigrants and cultures are limited in their good and cultural suitability for Canada and should, therefore, be positioned on the periphery of the society.

It is as a result of this contradiction between ways of knowing within the same intended system that official Canada struggles so hard to transform different ethnic groups from mainly the Caribbean and Africa – along with other somatic Blacks from other parts of the world – into a single ethnicity called Black. In this case, Blackness is determined solely by appearance or somatic features, as, ironically, even somatic Whites can be culturally Black. Indeed, even in a multicultural moment, Trudeau's claim that individual freedoms would be hampered for those "locked for life within a particular cultural compartment by the accident of birth" appears still to apply to a specific group of Canadians – those whose "accident of birth" is the colour of their skin or the region of the world that is considered to be their primordial home. Yet, implicit in the generally-accepted concept of ethnicity is the notion of a primordial sacred place and time that produces a living culture or social capital that is inseparable from the people the culture produces and who in turn produce the culture.[40]

By the way they are positioned collectively in Canada, members of this *ethnicity* are supposed to share a common status and culture and possibly believe in the same ideals. In the prevailing mythology, regardless of where they originate from in the world, constructed Blacks share the same ontology, existence, and epistemology – all of them examples of categories of being human that fall outside the prevailing Canadian common sense explanations of what is good and appropriate for the country. Therefore, Blacks are treated differently from most other groups, a treatment that in effect denies them social justice and the opportunities to share in the common national aspiration to a White idealism.[41] They are positioned at the bottom of the social hierarchy by most measurements. And in this categorization, Blacks live in a diaspora that does not have a centre in a specific culture, space, and time with its own sacred history and culture; rather, theirs is global and universal.

This is a diaspora whose referent is a universal concept called Africa, whose existence did not come into being by the intervention of African gods or their superhuman beings bringing into existence a superior people called Black or African. Rather, according to the prevailing ideology and mythologically, they were created in the cosmos whose good depended on Africans and Blacks living in chaos and bondage so that others may live in freedom. The construction of a Canadian ethnicity of Blackness is not primordial. It is synchronous and within a White Canadian space and time that was already in existence.

This approach of manufacturing a Black ethnicity is yet another attempt by Canada to force conformity of the lived experience into a pre-creationist model of the good, one that says that it is best for Canada to *appear* as a tolerant society based on the equality of ethnicities. This was effectively a retreat from the hope and full implications in a practical sense of the idealized Blackness that is multiculturalism. In other words, appearance and not action is what matters most. It is also another attempt by Canada to shift to a mode of semblance when faced with the fear of the unknown: the prevailing good on which the society was based had reached its limits and Canada was facing an unwelcome transformation. The need for immigrants to build the country continued unabated, and even accelerated, although Canada reduced the flow significantly after the 1970s oil shocks to the economy. However, even then, supplies of immigrants from traditional source countries declined precipitously, while those from non-preferred countries became the main sources for new Canadians.[42]

So, Canada shifted from nation-building based explicitly on race to one officially based on abstract human rights and an objective points systems for choosing immigrants, while keeping the social structures, the agencies, and the social ordering of a nation-state founded on a racist ideology. Part of the reason for this was Canada's decision to shift emphasis from choosing new immigrants based on selecting applicants with family members already in Canada, in what is known as family class immigrants, to those who are financially well off and have the skills of the highly trained, especially those in high technology. This, along with the placement of most immigration officers in Western Europe and Asia, led to a situation where the supply of immigrants still seemed to be racist in orientation as the emphasis appeared to be placed on the highly skilled and the highly educated, who were mainly from developed countries. As the structures and functionalism remained in place, the only thing that changed, effectively, was the appearance of Canada trying to be fair in keeping with its multicultural rhetoric. Tolerance became a catchword for the management of relations between groups, a concept that is easily violated by individuals seeking to escape the placement and restrictions of their group by aspiring to what might be considered the entitlement of other groups.

Even on the issue of the recognition of ethnicity, the modern myth of Canada being a fount of tolerance is still questionable. Immigration, for example, was never as willingly accepted by mainstream Canadians, for Canada has always followed a very selective immigration policy and still continues this approach. Indeed, Kymlicka expounds against the intolerance in Canadian nation-building policies that were predicated on "Anglo-conformity" prior to the 1960s in a bid to force all newcomers into becoming ideal Canadians, that is, White and English.[43] The period of Anglo-conformity coincided with efforts by official Canada to get immigrants mainly from Britain, or from expatriate British living elsewhere in the world; and even to force a significant French minority to reject its culture and assimilate into English norms.[44]

Kymlicka's suggestion of a drastic change since the 1960s is contestable, especially by those who argue that there is no real qualitative change in the way that Canada looks for ideal immigrants and then tries to position them in Canadian society.[45] All decisions start from a notion of what is good for the country and the existing order, whether the new arrival is good enough to fit in so as to leave the structures of the country and notions of entitlement unchanged.[46] This is primarily a problem in the province of Quebec,[47] where immigrants are selected ideally for their ability to maintain the "French-factor" in Canada, thereby creating tensions between the old establishment and its support of the existing order and newer arrivals who might have different motives.[48] These positions of the fixity and unchangeability of Canada in its old manifestation were, indeed, the very opposite of the hope that led to Trudeau's multiculturalism. Indeed, such finiteness and unchangeableness were considered, philosophically and sociologically, the very epitome of slavery. Simply, however, they were social death. And in reverting to the old measurements, Canada was pragmatically turning its back on the infinite hope inherent in genuine multiculturalism.

Indeed, Canada was returning idealistically to an immediate past even if the demographics of who is a Canadian were already changing irrevocably.[49] At a minimum, this is an argument of superior and inferior claims: of an idealized good and evil, an argument that, from its inception, was always central to the discourse on Canadian citizenship and identity. The battle is between the idealism of good and evil, with the good defined as the struggle to keep Canada White, first somatically and in terms of group status, but then also culturally in terms of reason and order. This results in the need through institutional practices to protect and maintain the established good in its purest form. Idealistically, this Whiteness has always been in competition with a need for the country to dilute its commitment to purity. Canada has always had to accept growing numbers of immigrants from parts of the world that have traditionally been defined as Black, somatically, and by status. While needed in growing numbers for the country to continue to prosper, these outsiders disrupt the existing order by making claims of their own to a space and time that originally was not intended for them. The outsiders would not only create problems for the Canadian elites by not readily accepting lower social positions, but also by aspiring to be among the aristocracy of the land – in other words, they tested Canada's commitment to its own multiculturalism. Administratively, this was a continuous struggle within the White homeland over how much Blackness should be allowed in, and at what price in terms of social disruption and even subversion of the extant order. As the Law Union of Ontario suggests in *The Immigrant's Handbook*: "From our earliest history, our constant need for more and more strong arms and sturdy backs forced us to look beyond our borders. Immigration provided our only hope for economic and political growth. As we formulated the policies which would regulate the flow of immigration, we used extreme caution, ensuring always that our laws would protect our privileged life style. We bolstered our peace of mind by fostering a deceptive ideal of equality among men and women, many of whom had little hope of ever sharing it."[50]

Indeed, the Law Union recalls the backdrop against which this debate on immigration was taking place as late as the 1980s: "[opponents of immigration contend] we are destroying the good British stock on which the country was founded. They claim we are inviting racial tension by allowing within our peaceful borders too many foreigners with their varying skin colours and accents. Until quite recently, even our trade unions shrugged nervously when it was suggested that more immigrants meant less work for native-born Canadians."[51]

Even at the beginning of the twenty-first century, there is still a hardcore 30 percent of the Canadian population, according to a poll by Ekos Research Associates and *The Toronto Star*, who believe "there are too many immigrants and visible minorities in Canada."[52] This sizeable nucleus remains even in the face of a very selective immigration process, which selects the peoples of the world based on an established notion of the good: those who are the "brightest and best," in official parlance, who will be accepted into Canada.[53] It is a mainstream thinking which still believes that those constructed as Black, based primarily on somatic but also cultural characteristics associated with the geography of their homelands, should live a Black experience on arrival in Canada. This is an experience based on accepting a lower and inferior class status – an experience that is qualitatively lower in status than that offered to citizens and nationals deemed by Canadian agencies and institutions to have more of an entitlement to, and who are more representative of, the good in Canada. With these competing aims, Canada as an imagined unity remains torn and an unhappy consciousness: instead of idyllic Whiteness and happiness, it is still wracked with the idyllic Blackness of disagreements, disunity, and a diversity of aims and goals.

## MULTICULTURALISM AS THE BEST OF INTENTIONS

The unhappiness over the positioning of a group called Blacks in Canadian society seems ironic. From the inception of what would become Canada, a group of people that calls itself Black, based on a presumed common African lineage and Black skins, has been advocating for recognition in the Canadian polity. This has been the case since the first Blacks that arrived as United Empire Loyalists in 1783 attempted to create a "White man's" country that was philosophically different from the idealized Blackness that had produced the United States of America. But as succeeding writers have shown, the struggle for recognition was mainly as a group – as those who had the common trait of being excluded from the society because they were not considered to be authentically free and Canadian.[54]

When in the 1960s Canada was reformulating itself in terms of how it was recognizing itself, a group called Blacks was among those advocating for a collective recognition based on core values and existences that are peculiar to this group.[55] Indeed, as George Elliott Clarke notes in the introduction to his anthology *Eyeing the North Star*, the struggle for recognition by other groups that saw themselves as separate ethnicities had by then caught up to the erstwhile battle for inclusion by those called Black in Canada.[56] In this case, the raison d'être of multiculturalism was to provide them with a mechanism to fight exclusion based on perceived racial inferiority, a perceived affectivity and motility that would require them to be accepting of such marginalization, and to allow them to agitate for physical inclusion in the Canadian state through an immigration policy that actively recruited people that were deemed to be somatically and culturally Black.[57]

The intention was for this group to find protection and refuge within a state that was being determined along group identities and to be considered contingently equal to all other groups. They wanted to be known, just like any other group of human beings, simply as citizens. Achieving similar goals was one of the aims of official multiculturalism: to fully recognize groups of people as they wished to be recognized. The peculiar and particular forms that Canadians took were no longer important – since a Canadian was universally defined in an abstract way as a possessor of rights. Recognition would be based on how individual Canadians, in their many contingent forms, chose to identify their unchangeableness. Only the individual would decide what meaning to confer on her or his contingent manifestation that occurred after the requested social rebirth as citizens. In this regard, Blackness was intended to solve primarily an issue of racial categorization, not one of ethnicity – a point most noted since many of those described as Black often present themselves as otherwise: English, Jamaican, Nigerian, Somali, American, and so on, based on their last socialization, their unique nationalities and cultures before becoming Canadian. This was a problem that dealt ultimately with the question of whether some groups are inferior and should have no real standing in society. Recognition of a group of Blacks was intended to bring equality of citizenship to individuals who share a common existence of exclusion based on a perceived inherent inferiority encoded in the colour of their skin.

Recognition as a group, like any other, offered them the very fundamental minimums of what it takes ontologically, epistemologically, and ethically to become Canadian. Grouping these individuals as Black was intended primarily as a strategic alliance, as a way of homogenizing them into an ethnic purity that is essentially Black. In this case, members of the group were not fully accepting of a second determination, which would transform their previous Whiteness gained as elites in other cultures into a Whiteness that was an essence of Blackness. Black, then, was primarily an ethical determination for these individuals, and that was the primary basis on which they sought recognition. It was also a reflection of their inferior status – and their questionable affectivity and motility – in Canada. Multiculturalism was supposed to solve this problem.

Another goal of multiculturalism, as Trudeau explained it, is to offer members of specific ethnic groups the right to be non-conformist, to put on or throw off the group identity – thereby treating the identity as contingent and not necessary to their being – whenever it pleases them. This is an aim that Kymlicka thinks is a crowning glory of Canadian multiculturalism as an expression of liberalism. For this is where the door is open for the individual to be truly free and creative in how he or she self-determines.[58] Liberation was also to be achieved by any individual Canadian rejecting her or his particularist identity, such as in claiming an ethnicity, race, or gender, and choosing to be recognized simply as an abstract universal – a Canadian citizen. Freedom, then, becomes a matter of choice – to be recognized based (1) solely on knowledge meaningful only on the ethno-racial register, (2) on knowledge meaningful only on the neo-mythic register, or (3) in a case of what I have been calling having the cake and eating it too, to be recognized simultaneously according to knowledge meaningful on both registers. This is an argument for the ultimate freedom of self-identity and self-affirmation specific to a context or regardless of the situation. Indeed, in the Canadian setting it is often argued that an individual can go through life without having to deal with or to be determined by her or his ethnic identity. In this regard, the individual has ultimate choice: the freedom of self-determination, of deciding when or if she/he wishes to be a hyphenated Canadian, such as an Italian-Canadian or a Black-Canadian. To this end, Canada has imaginatively solved the classic philosophical dilemma of how to reconcile the epistemic dualism of subjects and objects, or how to have resolution where the individuals are seen and known by the public exactly the way the individuals want to be seen and known. They would be totally free in the Hegelian sense, where Spirit as a Subject knows and recognizes itself unchangeably as a contingent and contextualized Object that may or may not be different from the Subject.

This ideal appears impractical for one specific group in Canada: ethnically constructed Blacks. Few individuals in this group have the choice that allows them to be accepted and fully recognized as unchangeably unhyphenated Canadians. In a world that has returned in all practical sense to upholding racialized knowledge, such status is not usually conferred on them as objects: what is seen and conferred is always different from what they as subjects intended. As theorists like Appiah and others show, even in the most liberal of democracies with the best intentions for colour blindness, in a racialized world, a somatically Black person is also presented as ontologically and epistemologically Black. "Collective identities differ, of course, in lots of ways; the body is central to race, gender, and sexuality but not so central to class and ethnicity." Going further, Appiah explains, "racial ascription is more socially salient: unless you are morphologically atypical for your racial group, strangers, friends, officials are always aware of its public and private context, always notice it, almost never let it slip from view."[59]

This is so because the colour of the skin is not ethnically derived but is used epistemology by others to determine an individual. Secondly, the meaning that is intended from this knowledge is moral and ethical: it is intended to be used racially. Therefore, the somatically Black person cannot escape the objective determination that is projected on her or him. Skin colour in this sense is not the same as an ethnicity evident in speech pattern and accent, that can be changed or even covered up. Skin colour is revealed every time, and usually, phenomenologically, as the very first thing. This is fixity as an object from which somatic Blacks cannot escape and which results in the unhappiness that crops up so often in Canadian society over such issues as Black racial profiling and the optics of the absented presence of Blacks in Canadian power circles – for the colour of the skin has a specific meaning on its own that might be different from what the Subject and the Other intended.

In this way, a "Black Canadian" is always already supposedly essentialized universally in two ways, as the unchangeable in the Canadian society that produces her or him, and as the unchangeable Black that speaks to a primordial nature. In the case of a composite with two unchangeables, which unchangeable is contingent and which necessary, which becomes dominant and which inferior? Primarily because of a history that has always positioned somatic Blacks as contingent to the Canadian nation-state, with multiculturalism in a practical sense simply reformulating historic identities, the Blackness can easily be perceived as the universal or unchangeableness of the individual – making her or him contingent to the state in keeping with historical perceptions. So that the abstract rights inherent to universal Canadianness would be the perishable, accidental, and unreal component of the somatically Black Canadian citizen. As is the case with composites of two or more essences and unchangeable natures, there is no final essence – unless a totally new one metamorphoses or a radical change occurs. When this metamorphosis does not take place in social construction, we can end up with the unhappiness where Black Canadians claim they are idealistically fully Canadian citizens but, in a practical sense, as demonstrated by their positioning in society, they are excluded from areas of full citizenship in keeping with the historical norms.

The unhappiness is an inescapability that results existentially in somatically Black Canadians of several generations being asked repeatedly by well-intentioned Canadians of more recent vintage and transformation where they are from. The inescapable implication is that because of the colour of the skin the Canadian of several generations was born elsewhere or is the descendant of people who were born elsewhere and who might not have become Canadian. This means that the Black-skinned person is still perceived as changeable, including possibly and ultimately into becoming Canadian. Such observations are the subject of a burgeoning literature on the inevitability and the unchangeability in the African or Black Canadian experience if being the perennial outsider, of being homeless, and of not belonging in the dominant Canadian imagination of who and what is Canadian.[60]

This unhappiness over recognition stems from the role Blackness has played historically in determining conceptually who is Canadian. Blackness, like Whiteness, was always intended as an analogy: the colour of the skin was supposed to convey perceptively in a very common sense way particular insights about the individual. Blacks find it difficult to escape this epistemological history in which their treatment is based phenomenologically on perception rather that the Whiteness of cognition or knowledge. To this end, it is nearly impossible for a somatic Black not to be seen, in a common sense way, primarily as somatically Black and secondarily as Canadian. Indeed, in a supposedly common sense way, it is even more challenging to get to the stage where somatic Blacks are seen and accepted as fully White in terms of determinations based on the cultural, social, and idealized norms of Whiteness in Canadian society.

Effective multicultural citizenship in Canada is predicated on individuals attaining the second level of determination, that of phenomenological cognition and not perception, where their Whiteness has little to do with what the senses tell. Multicultural citizenship, as Trudeau argues, has to be based on reason and rationalism that transcend the mere sensory given in analytical thinking. In this common sense way, on entering a room, it is usually very difficult for anyone to be mistaken about when he or she is dealing with a racialized Black, even if the individual sees her- or himself differently as an ethnically constructed Black. The ambiguity and equivocation invariably lead to an ethical relation that produces an unhappy consciousness, as perceptually the Black individual cannot freely move on to the second level of determination that is demanded by multiculturalism, even when the relation is intended by the participants as being good for all.

And that is the rub with Blackness in multiculturalism – how can a subject that sees herself as having one identity set herself apart from another identity that is imposed on her identity based on her looks? Worse still is when there is no upward social mobility for the individual, when she or he ends up being trapped in her or his skin despite what were Trudeau's best intentions. The main problem is that from all sides multiculturalism was seen as a panacea, but on closer examination it turns out not to have been one. Maybe we should be discussing why there was even the need for such categorization – and if we do we will see it is part of a long history of trying to really know who is good and evil, who should belong within the nation-state, what roles are best suited for specific groups, and what kind of treatment and behaviour would make them happy. Indeed, the way to hell is paved with good intentions. Similarly, the way to multiculturalism as an unhappy consciousness, at times a living hell of seemingly incurable frustrations, is also paved by good intentions. In the end, the questions still remain: Who is ontologically and epistemologically Black? and Is Black primarily a racial and ethnic category? – for ideologically Blackness is the status of exclusion and denial, and seldom of inclusion except in a pejorative sense.

This chapter took a closer look at the ideology and the legacy of *A Just Society* and analysed many of the dialectical contradictions that bedevil it. The chapter argues that the contradictions were inherent in the process and that the mastermind of *A Just Society*, Pierre Elliott Trudeau, was the epitome of the contradictions that he tried to master. However, the result of the struggle was that Canada recognized that it is Black idealistically, culturally, and in status. But, there remains also a greater reluctance to come to terms with the somatic features of the Blackness that is present in the Canadian state. Part of this stems from the argument that Blackness is a racial categorization and that Canada has moved on from racial to ethnic determinations, resulting in a policy of multiculturalism at home and abroad as a search for social justice. The problem is that within this multiculturalism that is based on the recognition of ethnicities, Blackness, while presented as an ethnicity, has always been associated epistemologically with notions of good and evil and how these characteristics can be inscribed symbolically on humans.

At the same time, Canada is a product of modernity and Western civilization with all the attendant ideologies, mythologies, and philosophies that are based on knowing and discerning good and evil and ranking them racially. This racialization is based on providing, in an unthinking or common sense way, answers to two specific questions that are a holdover from the historical development of meaning in Western culture. One is the premodern question of what race of being is the Other, that of human or gods. The second, based on its modernist credentials, is how to determine on sight which groups in all humanity are superior, more advanced, and closer in orientation to the race of gods, and which are inferior and primitive, and furthest away from godlike status.

To this end, this chapter argues that one of the limits of multiculturalism is racial – it has not answered the question of how Canada should deal with citizens whose secondary identities are primarily racial and not ethnic. But in fairness to the good intentions of the framers of multiculturalism and its supporters, it is necessary to take them at their word that Black is intended to be just an ethnicity in Canada. This would remove any suggestion of ill will and deceit that might stem from the suggestion that multiculturalism's supporters intended to treat Blacks as racially constructed while using the language of ethnicity that is appropriate for multiculturalism as a new way of thinking.

In the next chapter, I shall discuss more fully the contradictions that are inherent in the classification of Black as an ethnic category. Statistics Canada and other government agencies say that Black as an ethnicity, because of its equivocal nature, ultimately depends on self-identification. This implies that as rational beings, epistemologically, Black people are cognitively White: they must know who they are and what the unchangeable Blackness in them is. Who then is unchangeably and truly Black, and is this Blackness ethnic or racial? I shall trace the dialectics of the phenomenology of Blackness and how this search ends in failure because there is no essence, ethnically or racially, of Blackness.

Then, I will argue that even if an ethnic category called Black is accepted, as Canada purports and constructs it within a world where everyone has an ethnic identity and is treated equally, then the experiences of those constructed as Black bring into disrepute the White ideal of *A Just Society* and its commitment to egalitarianism and equality. I will be arguing that Blackness as an ethnicity in Canada, while appearing universally in a common sense way to be a meaningful expression, fails phenomenologically under closer scrutiny the test that allows it to be accepted nominally as a given. In the case of Blackness in Canada, this is particularly true of the existential reality, for even those who are supposed to be recognized universally as Black cannot agree among themselves, as a particular entity, on what is unchangeably Black about them and their presumed group.

# 16

# Blackness

## *Essences, Mythologies, and Positioning*

This chapter looks at the question of who is authentically Black in a multicultural setting from the particular gaze of purported Black Canadians. In the prevailing Canadian mythology, only presumed Black people, through a process of self-identification that is the quintessence of a liberal democracy, know that they are Black. Phenomenologically, this approach is the ultimate in privileging intuitive perception over sensory perception and even reason, for who can persuade a somatic Black who believes she or he has undergone the rigours of the miraculous double negation of citizenship that she or he is not genuinely White? So it is also with the children of supposedly mixed parents – what is to stop them from identifying with one and not the other parent? How can any individual be convinced that her or his Blackness is not racial – including class as a form of racialization, with its notions of inferior and superior finite groups – and not ethnicity as simply a non-pejorative and non-evaluative identity of a specific group? Or this self-identification might very well lead to the opposite conclusion, where the individual knows with absolute certainty that her or his Blackness is race or ethnicity – or as the infinite that it is, that her or his Blackness is both and importantly much more.

Appealing objectively to sensory perception – which, ironically in multicultural Canada, is how Blacks are objectively recognized and, ultimately, are expected to acclaim themselves as subjects and citizens – would be for nought. Similarly, reason would be forced to conform to intuitive perception rather than hold it in bondage. Only by the negation of intuition would reason be elevated. In all cases, what we have as an answer to who is Black is neither the reason nor cognition for which we initially started our search. The Canadian consciousness that imagined itself as Black will still be no farther ahead in knowing itself. Yet self-identity seems to be the most practical or common sense approach to dealing with these contradictions of knowing and power – of attaining perception, affectivity, and motility in an idealized ethical relation where all subjects of the state are, paradoxically, both lords and bondsmen in separate determinations over themselves and within the state. They are free as individuals and they are free to form groups of their choice: to perform as individuals and groups that may limit their choices.

For existentially and ontologically, only infinities that are truly free can limit themselves to any specific manifestation in any space and time. According to the rationalist expectations of Western thought, only sovereigns should impose on themselves ethical rules and moral imperatives that are norms of behaviour. And epistemologically, only through self-determination can an infinite that is a self-conscious ego choose the method, form, and identity that genuinely manifest itself in a manner where the outer is reconciled with the inner, where it is known with certainty that the subjective is the same as the objective and where the set in any finite order is conceptually the same, or at a minimum the essential and necessary elements, in the infinity. In this respect, and in keeping with the notion that it takes one to know one, only by being Black could a self-conscious ego, which is the Canada of our discourse, know what is authentically Black.

But this is limited knowledge. Self-identification as self-determination is an epistemological argument that does not provide a full phenomenological explanation of Blackness for it does not account fully for the ontology and peculiar existentialism of those presented as Black. In the form epistemologically of intuitive perception masquerading as deliberative reason that is also pure cognition, self-identification provides one-sided knowledge and a perspective that assumes only the subject knows itself and that, to the outsider, epistemologically the body would always be cognitively Black. In addition, the explanation fails, epistemologically, for it does not provide answers, with certainty and predictability, on who is Black. It also does not offer much that is useful in terms of motility and affectivity about those recognized as Black or about what kinds of ethical relations they should have with fellow Blacks and with Whites, those humans that are the Others of Blacks. These are things that we set out to know objectively; so that we could have clear and absolute knowledge about objective Blackness, so that we could then pursue sound ethical relations based on reason and cognition. We must know what the thing means and genuinely symbolizes when it appears to us as Black and Blackness without having to rely on the thing to first identify itself. We should also be aware of the power in the politics of naming, equally for those who as subjects call themselves Black and those who are objectified as Black.

Self-identification of Blackness might work for the subject, but such an epistemology would leave it as an unknowable object for other subjects, leaving our phenomenological search at the point where we started – not knowing with certainty what is objective Blackness, what makes Blacks happy, and for what roles, stations, and statuses in society, as objects, they are most useful. If, as we have been arguing, our search is intended to allow the self-conscious ego to recognize the thing that is its body, but this body appears to the ego as other and Black, then the self-conscious ego will never have an epistemology of itself that it can trust. Phenomenologically, the self-consciousness would not be able to fully recognize itself because of this otherness, thereby putting it in a contradictory position of genuinely knowing itself as a subject and then not knowing objectively with any real certainty the self that it thinks is its other. Yet, what this self-consciousness calls its body, whether black or White, good or evil, is important to the role that it would expect this body to perform. Such is the problem of defining Blackness in multicultural Canada – of a subject that is the individual Blacks knowing who they genuinely are, of the subject that is the self-consciousness that is Canada not knowing with certainty the meaning of parts of its body politic that are recognized as Black.

This chapter, then, begins the examination in greater detail of the dialectical search for an essence of Blackness – an examination that will continue into the following chapter. Indeed, in both chapters I argue that this search for its essence by a purportedly Black consciousness also does not produce cognition and unassailable knowledge or reason but, ultimately, falls back on unenlightened perception. This, too, is an indication of how some people that are constructed socially as Black have accepted the finite limitations that have been imposed on them. As an example, we need only look at those Blacks who employ the term "nigger," or as commonly used "niggerz," ostensibly for empowerment, yet are unable to shed, no matter how hard they try, the pejorative connotations of the word.[1]

Self-identification as Black is based not so much on cognition, but on affectivity and intuitive perception in terms of how individuals *feel* about themselves personally or collectively. Phenomenologically, this is not cognition or reason. It also depends on the kind of motility that individuals counting themselves as Black are willing to accept for themselves. This raises the question of whether self-identifying Blacks can ever on their own volition enter into an uncontested lordship and bondage relationship that is necessary for civil society, especially if they were to forever remain unknowable to the other participants in this social arrangement. Contradictorily, individuals who feel that they are either optimally utilized or underutilized in society still have the choice of calling themselves Black, but only if they are somatically Black or of African heritage. Or, for the same motility reasons, they may claim that they are not. To this end, even Blacks, who are presumed to be idealistically White epistemologically, can end up appearing cognitively Black, unable to discern among themselves who is genuinely and authentically Black ethnically.

The reason for this uncertainty and confusion is that the label Black is equivocal, due to its long history in the dominant thought of Western civilization in which it developed different meanings depending on the circumstances. However, based on the mythologies and philosophies on which the modern state in Western civilization rests, Black, epistemologically, was associated by analogy with evil, and Whiteness with good. Black was also intended to be a symbol of those who are inferior, whether this inferiority is based on biology or culture.[2] I will show how the equivocation occurs through a dialectical search within Blackness for an essence of who is truly Black. This will be a discussion of the ontology of Blackness in Canada and whether, epistemologically, this phenomenon was recognized, historically, as race or ethnicity. The argument will show that there is no unchangeable identity or experience within the ethnic category called Black Canadian.

The difference shows up within Blackness along such lines as nationalism, place of birth, level of education, and importantly, in the level of integration in Canadian society. I will examine prevailing Canadian mythologies to show that while historically these mythologies have been presented as a search for Whiteness, they were really an attempt to erase Blackness, primarily somatic Blackness, from the national discourse. Somatic Blackness in particular and the culture of those so constructed as a group have always been a part of the national Canadian discourse through an absented presence that fell short of full recognition in the perceived Canadian finitude. Black and Blackness have been positioned as the Other to the Canadian self in the dominant narrative. Noteworthy, in this respect, is the emerging evidence of a marked difference in achievement, education, earning power, and acceptance in the wider society between Black females and Black males.

Finally, I will argue that official Blackness, even if granted as a constructed category, and even factoring in the higher levels of financial success for Black females, fails the tests of fairness and equality in the universals of ethnicity and families as promised in a liberal democracy that is multicultural. I will be examining the existence of those members of the Canadian societies homogenized as ethnically Black and whether they share as fully in the good life as promised for all ethnicities regardless of colour, creed, or race by the ideology of *A Just Society*.

## BLACKNESS: SELF-IDENTIFICATION AND PERCEPTION

Two seemingly conflicting perspectives arise from a reasoning based on self-identification in multiculturalism. First, in the universal, Canada constructs an ethnic group called Black as a necessary category for good governance. This finite classification of Black is required for taxonomy purposes such as the provision of government services and for a specific group of people to receive recognition from authorities. The question is how authorities decide in a way that is unquestionable. In this case, Canadian authorities, when forced to discern – for everyone is expected to have an ethnicity in Canada – equate Black with dark skins or ultimately an African lineage.[3] Second, within that finite category as a particular, there is debate over a ranking of who is most Black or most Black Canadian, thereby creating a hierarchy of rights, claims, and entitlements that flow internally from this categorization. Once again, the pivotal question is who is essentially Black in this presumed Black ethnicity.[4] In the latter case, the argument goes beyond a common shade of skin or African lineage to include questions of culture and levels of enlightenment and advancement – in effect, an argument on who, within this so-called Black ethnicity, is idealistically, culturally, and by status White in a Black culture.[5]

This is the dialectic of who is Black, producing a crisis in existentialism for Blackness, a sociological and cultural disagreement as described in Rinaldo Walcott's *Black Like Who? Writing Black Canada,* and a misunderstanding in Black epistemology and ontology, as discussed in George Elliott Clarke's *Treason of the Black Intellectuals.*[6] It also shows up in a debate over whether it is possible, or even ethically appropriate, for people with African heritage who misnominally categorize themselves as mixed race rather than mixed ethnicity because they share the lineage of another ethnicity to be included as Black.[7]

Even though there is much confusion over the exactness of meaning, this debate is crucial for those who want to take for themselves or give to others intellectual agency as local subjects, people, that is, who feel they can be empowered with a politicized understanding of "to be Black" and "becoming Black." This is more than debating what is objective Black and Blackness and rendering a label knowable for some and unknowable for other subjects. Indeed, it might be more than providing a full phenomenological explanation of Black and Blackness. Such a debate might be important for explaining the many performances and rhetorics of Black and Blackness as self and as imposed in a supposedly multicultural space that comes with its own history, hopes, and finite limits – where performing Blackness and being Black can be both empowering and disempowering in the same discourse.[8]

While this debate rages within the self-identified Black community, in the wider Canadian society it has been an ongoing discussion since the beginning of modernity. This has been an argument over what terms and circumstances must exist for somatic Blacks to become fully Canadian,[9] and about their acquisition of Canadian experience, and their incorporation into the mainstream.[10] This is also a question about status and class, and about culture as well – of how a free individual can escape the bondage of biology for the freedom of self-actualization as she or he sees fit or according to the standards of social mobility that are universal to the wider society in which that individual is embedded.

In all cases, the arguments are based on knowledge of a presumed essence of unchangeable Blackness of which the individual is an embodiment or the epitome. For public policy purposes, the government needs an essence around which to gather a disparate group of people from the various parts of the world so that the members can receive group recognition in equality with all other cultural groups. The members of this Black cultural group want to know why, as Walcott explores, they are included or excluded in that group and not in another. As Clarke argues, they also become involved in an argument internal to that *ethnicity* over who ultimately has the right to speak for and to represent their presumed ethnic group.[11]

To this end, Blackness in multicultural Canada becomes a site of confusion, even for those who by the same rational standard are perceived to be Black. This, too, is a result of the contradictions that arise from the dialectics in Canadian history that produced the prevailing finite multiculturalism, which in turn has resulted in additional contradictions in the resulting Canadian social order. While the government claims that, like any other ethnicity, Black is based on self-identification, this is what the government would prefer. In practice, these discussions start from the presumption that everyone in Canada has an ethnicity that is non-negotiable and fixed. One feature of this ethnicity is that it is ascribed, so that individuals, as objects, have no choice over the ethnicity that subjects recognize them as belonging to: the so-called Blacks find themselves already placed and positioned in a lordship and bondage relation that ascribed an identity and culture to them. In this relationship, because they are objectified, they are once again the bondsmen, while those who have the authority to fix Blacks in place are the lords. The most those identified as Black can do is demand a specific form of recognition, but as objects they have no powers of coercion.[12] This lordship is the position taken primarily by those government departments entrusted to assist with the integration of Canadians based on the respect of different cultures.[13] Blacks are ethnically Black when the agencies say so.

Part of the confusion arises from the thinking behind the offer of multiculturalism as a new social order, primarily from the misunderstanding emanating from two conflicting views. On the one hand, knowledge is viewed as the preserve of an enlightened educated group that provides leadership to the country, and on the other hand, it is viewed as residing in each and every individual, for only individuals know themselves and what is good for them. This contradiction results from efforts by the father of *A Just Society* and Canada's multicultural orientation, former prime minister Pierre Elliott Trudeau, to reconcile the dialectic tensions within society that at the same time tend towards expressing freedom in the form of a collective or state and, contrarily, in the form of personalism and individuality. In the first case, Trudeau argued for enlightened leadership by a strong government led by educated parliamentarians, and secondly for a core or mainstream consisting of the French and English ethnicities. In the second case, he offered as the solution to the same problem enlightened citizens fully dressed in their individuality, sovereign with their full knowledge of themselves, and freed of the constraints of ethnicities and nationalist cultures. All are necessary, Trudeau argued, for a just society that is normatively a liberal democracy and multicultural in form or expression.

A second explanation for the contradictions is that the discussion over who is Black is not about ethnicity, but also about race and even class. A clear distinction needs to be made between ethnicity, race, and class as concepts within Blackness. These distinctions compare to our categories that are usually associated with cultural, somatic, and status Blackness respectively. This is an explanation that sees the dialectic tensions in Canada evolving through a discourse on which groups of people are racially superior and inferior. Such a result stems from Canada's lineage as a child of modernity and as a product of the dominant thought in Western civilization. This is a debate on which groups should be incorporated and recognized in the state that was intended to be a White homeland and which groups of people should be excluded or held only on the periphery of the society. This argument suggests that, systemically, Canada's institutions are still based on the models that were intended to produce a somatically White country.

Even though the Canadian ideals have changed, as evidenced by the official recognition of the Blackness of multiculturalism and the egalitarianism objectives of *A Just Society*, the institutions and agencies that help maintain what Kymlicka calls a societal culture have not kept in step with the changes. There is still a systemic lag in the Canadian social order that is best exemplified by the social position of the peoples of many different and diverse ethnicities that are homogenized within Canada into a cultural unit called Black. As Hegel would argue, dialectically nothing dies in a concept: old ideas and paradigms of meaning are simply sublimated, which leaves them underneath the surface but still ever present in the determination of what is and what is not the perception. Even if negated, they still remain as forces for good or evil.

This argument says that Black ethnicity in Canada is not constructed, or explained ontologically, according to the same rules as all other ethnicities. For example, Black is the only ethnicity where the essential characteristic is based, epistemologically, on such semiotics as the colour of skin or on a universal heritage like Africa, a place that itself is multiethnic in the extreme, but often reduced homogeneously to somatic Blackness. These are not symbols that are commonly constructed in a culture, such as language, religion, or nationalism. Rather, they are signifiers that cosmologically indicate the intent and desires of persons that would create a specific kind of culture in civil society. These symbols supposedly testify to a specific way of life or culture that is Blackness, and is produced by Blacks, who are known ontologically primarily by the colour of their skin.

Therefore, the being that is somatically Black and the actions of evil, which are epistemologically in opposition to the order and goodness of Whiteness, are brought together through the conflation of the two registers of knowing. Somatic Black and cultural Blackness are conflated, in keeping with Goldberg's argument that ethnicity is really about culture, and race about descent.[14] To this end, the presumed essence of Blackness that forms the Canadian category of ethnic Blackness is not perceived to have been constructed in a civil society, as it is not based strictly on lineage, nationalism, religion, language or geography, as is the case for other cultural groups. In effect, Black is not a composite from a specific group of people having no prior essence, but is a reflection of a specific *kind* or as Locke would say *quality* of people, those who are judged and known according to a perceived primordial nature based on their individuality and which predates their entry into any state.

In this regard, a Black ethnicity in Canada does not presuppose a different Whiteness in this group, unlike for other ethnicities, like the Italian, German, Polish, Filipino, and Chinese that were constructed as second determinations of Whiteness within a previous state that has already been separated from the rest of humanity. Black is the state of humanity before the separation into, for example, Jamaican, Somali, English, French, Ghanaian, and Chinese – where the primary determinants are the colour of the skin and African lineage. In the Hegelian sense, Blackness, as an ethnicity, does not presuppose a second negation based on values into the Whiteness of citizenry of a civil society. It is still the pre-determined and the pre-conscious state that occurs in the night when all cows are Black.

Therefore, as a finite taxonomy, Black Canadian and its presumed culture of Blackness require those so determined to ethnically give up their idealized, cultural, and status Whiteness, or an already extant second level of determination, and to return ontologically and epistemologically to a prior position in their prehistory. This is a return to when they were merely presumed essences, when they were essentially good or, in the modernist thought, evil, unconflicted, superstitious, and backward. In this way, they are fully determined as having previously existed only in a state of nature and as essentially never having been cultured and nurtured by any civil society. For regardless of where they received their primary socialization, they are still considered to be socially and phenomenologically undifferentiated in their essences and primordialism. This is not the return promised by multiculturalism: for this is a return to perceived and self-recognized

Blackness that is idealized Blackness and not the idealized Whiteness to which a self-conscious human aspires.

Under this argument, Black is an indicator of those who are Black in status – a class of people perceived, and even constructed by a ruling elite, to be inferior to the perceivers – and of a group whose motility is alleged to be optimally suited to being the workers and producers for those most apt for leisure, ruling, and thinking. This group's affectivity would thus come from its members settling for less of an entitlement to the good life than those of the class that is White in status. Historically, in the Canadian context, the group that is Black in status also has a core membership of individuals whose skin is Black or whose lineage can be traced by those in power to Africa. This group of individuals is constituted as socially Black regardless of what parts of the world the individual members were native to and of the Whiteness of their statuses in their native cultures and ethnicities. So, is there an essence of Blackness that this Black consciousness can find by examining itself?

### HISTORICAL BLACKNESS: DIALECTICAL MANIFESTATIONS

In a discussion on the relevance of marking February as Black history month in Canada, writer André Alexis notes that the celebrations have very little to do with things that are both ontologically Canadian and Black.[15] The heroes celebrated, and the honouring of great events and achievements of Blacks, are from other countries and times. The only commonality is the skin colour of the celebrated and the celebrants. "African Heritage ought not to become nostalgia for a place one has never been, a place always brighter, lovelier and more wonderful for being elsewhere."[16] Alexis argues that Black Canada's celebration should be about people and achievements that are peculiarly Canadian – the history of Blacks in Canada.

On closer examination, Alexis's ideal appears impractical and contextually ungrounded. As I shall show, Alexis and others are treating Blackness as ethnicity rather than as the racial construct that is most often intended. Race is demonstrated through the way some groups are positioned as being of lower status within society and how the motility value for members of these groups is calculated as being lower than that of the elites of society. In this regard, Alexis is presenting Black as a peculiar Canadian ethnicity, seeking to establish an organic and even primordial relationship with Canada. Yet, the status that somatic and cultural Blacks holds in Canadian society is racially motivated and springs from the functionalist notions that in society some groups are naturally superior and inferior to others. This distinction is important for understanding the construction and existence of Blackness in Canada, and how and when the two aspects are different.

An appreciation of the difference could help explain where and how Blacks are situated in a multicultural society that is based on ethnicity. Race cuts across ethnicity, as somatic and cultural Blacks from around the world know in their lived experiences, but ethnicity does not necessarily specify a race.

Indeed, it is worth restating that race implies notions of inferiority and superiority, good and evil, whereas ethnicity suggests natural group formation.[17] This distinction has always provided a problem for Canada: its French population has at times been referred to as a race with the full implication of a hierarchy of superior and inferior positioning, in comparison with an Other that determines the Blackness of status and cultures.[18] However, within Quebec, the French have been constructed as a specific ethnic group with its own homeland and claims to sovereignty and nationalism. In both cases, either as a race or ethnicity, the French and Québécois identities are constructed. This is equally a problem within the Black community, particularly for those who do not see all members of the community as ethnically equal.

There is another problem for Blackness in a multicultural setting: historically, in the official myth of the country, there has been an absence of recognition by both Blacks and White elites of somatic and cultural Blackness as being important to the national character and history – even in its idealized form – so that those looking to celebrate Blackness within Canadian spaces have to import and even reconstruct it. Such imported heroes and representatives are of different ethnicities – such as a Marcus Garvey of Jamaica or a Nelson Mandela of South Africa – which are then reconstructed racially as good and evil.

In this case, the celebration of heroic somatic and cultural Blacks – such as those who pioneered blood transfusion or developed the elevator – is not intended to show that a specific group of people has mastered technology and produced a unique culture. Rather, the testament is that these pioneers show that somatic and cultural Blacks, in general, are as good as any other eclectic group of people, regardless of their ethnicity. This is an argument of essence, of showing that somatic Blacks are ontologically human even before they enter civil society.

Blacks, then, have a right and entitlement to be slotted in among humanity in general. Their achievements are intended to show that, equally, people with Black skin, just like those of any other classification, can function effectively and can receive their affectivity and motility within civil society in general. This is seldom an argument about how individuals, who are deemed to be Black, assisted with the development of a specific culture, or nationalism, or ethnicity. It is usually an argument about how members of a specific group triumphed over an evil, such as slavery, segregation, genocide, and other forms of discrimination based on ideals of good and evil, which from the perspective of those constructed as Black are the results of a Hobbesian state of natural existence.

These are narratives that are seldom relevant to the recognition of somatic Blacks as a separate ontological group in Canada. This is what makes the celebration of Black history incongruous in the Canadian setting, as every ethnicity has produced its share of good and evil. These historic developments and achievements by somatic Blacks helped or hindered humanity in general, as well as the ethnic clan, nation, or group to which the developers belonged. Ethnicity is nativism; Blackness, as race, is not. There is a problem when race and ethnicity are conflated into Blackness, especially when somatic features become the symbol for both, and there is a return to indeterminacy between the two concepts.

Black history, in terms of recognition and subjectivity, can only be celebrated as a subversion of the official Canadian history, for in the Hegelian sense of history this is not a narrative of a people that arrive in enlightenment, in their full freedom of knowing themselves and their capabilities, thinking about what they want to become, and achieving a record of freely trying to self-actualize what they think of themselves, but are unable to self-actualize. Black history is effectively, phenomenologically, the other in the body behaving as if it is an independent self-consciousness reflecting on itself and its otherness, which in this case would be the universal Canadian society of which it is a member or on all the rest of the universal, from which it is perceptually separate and distinct.[19]

To imagine this would be to assume that the Other in Canadian society is really the Subject, that it is the universal instead of being a particular in the Hegelian phenomenological sense. Such would be an absurd reading of what is taken to be the reality of the phenomenon that is Canada that includes Black parts and a phenomenon that is Blackness itself and is categorically distinct from a universal Canada.

There is no Black history in Canada. Blacks, officially, may have a presence, but not a history, as it can be argued that Blacks are still not fully incorporated in the Canadian consciousness, so that their consciousness and that of the rest of Canadians are not the same.[20] Sociologically, as a racialized group, they have not, as an action of volition, entered into a lordship and bondage relation where they can be the lords to their bondsmanship. As they are traditionally positioned, they are bondsmen, but never lords, so that without the ability to freely exercise their intention to be party to this arrangement they are denied the double negation that is necessary for full history-making citizens.

Plato, for example, makes this point about the beginning of time for a living organization. It begins only with the organization's creation out of already existing matter, when the created is separated and made distinct from a previous time – the time of its maker. "Time, then, came to be together with the heavens so that just as they were begotten together, they might also be undone together, should there ever be an undoing of them." This suggests that time, and the start of history, begins only with the coming into consciousness, into being in the lordship and bondage of the state.

Becoming in the intended image of the creator is time and history as "that which is always changeless and motionless cannot become either older or younger in the course of time – it neither ever became so, nor is it now such that it has become so, nor will it ever be so in the future."[21] For Blacks, even as an ethnic group, to have a distinct history would be to presume a choice that would have involved their national development as distinct and separate from Canada. This is the kind of separateness that is envisioned by separatists in Quebec who anticipate a separate and distinct national narrative for a country or nation called Quebec. If there is a Black "history," it has to be a particular in a universal and infinite Canadian history.

Similarly, Sartre would argue that racially in the dominant Western ontology, the Black person like "the Jew is not yet *historical,* and yet he is the most ancient of peoples, or nearly so. That is what gives him the air of being perpetually aged and yet always young: he has wisdom and no history."[22] Modernity transformed groups constructed as Black into non-age beings, since they are not yet born into the "White" state, leaving them with no sense of history and lasting cultural achievements. In this respect, modernity goes against the grain of what Plato suggests in the *Timaeus* when Solon visited the Egyptian sages. Then, Plato had offered an argument for self-knowledge as the key for those seeking to come into history – into control over the time and space they inhabit and over which they claim sway. Merleau-Ponty and Fanon made similar arguments centuries later in explaining how individuals and groups can become over-determined and held in a past that is a suffocating present. Then, this would be an existence with no hope for change in the future.[23]

History, in all cases, is self-determination by the fully self-conscious, and the ability to become, or to be, created. It is the realization of hope and the negation of hope's dialectical other, despair and despondency. Thus, there can be no Black history for there is no genuine Black ethnicity in Canada; and there is no history as Black is a racialized category, and this assumes that as inferiors the members of this group are not yet at the step of history, the self-consciousness that would allow them to see themselves as an ethnicity whose cultural and idealistic Whiteness makes them different from the rest of humanity.

Indeed, Blacks in Canada only started to have the making of official recognition as a full particular in the Canadian body politic in the 1960s, with the development of three events of note, not in Canada but, in the rest of the Americas:

- The civil rights movement in the United States of America, which attempted to bring African-Americans fully into the mainstream. In this case, the recognition that was earned by somatic and cultural Blacks in the United States was partially conferred on Blacks in Canada. George Elliott Clarke argues, for example, that in Halifax "as a child, I became African American ... I was, irredeemably, African American ... I was not alone."[24] This was in keeping with the notion that Canadian Blacks were generally viewed as outsiders in Canada as a particular or finite concept. They were situated as either transnationals or members of an African-American diaspora centred in the United States. Theirs was a universal or infinite identity, paradoxically, within a particular nationalistic one.
- The granting of political independence to mainly somatically Black nations of the Caribbean and Africa. This, too, conferred recognition on Canadian Blacks, but in the sense that they were still members of a diaspora – this time a somatically Black diaspora that had developed in the British Empire and then the British Commonwealth, of which Canada was an "elder sister." Political independence for these Black colonies also coincided with a change in Canada's immigration policy, an alteration that allowed into Canada larger numbers of somatic and cultural Blacks, mainly from the Caribbean, and then after the 1980s mainly from the Horn of Africa. In these emerging conditions, when they arrived in Canada, would the Blacks retain a universal identity that situated them as still embedded in the primordialism that predates the state itself or would they acquire the fullness of the particular that is Canada and Canadian?
- The arrival in major Canadian cities of large numbers of somatically Black Caribbean peoples, most of them steeped in distinct national fervours that resulted from the civil rights and independence struggles. The presence of the Caribbean Blacks and the agitation in the urban centres gave Canadian-born Blacks the numbers that allowed Blacks what little critical mass they now have in Canadian society, raising them to just under 2 percent of the population. Ironically, many of the Caribbean arrivals thought themselves to be White idealistically, culturally, and in status – a way of thinking that ultimately drove a wedge between them and the somatic Blacks that they found already in Canada.[25]

Therefore, when celebrating Black myths and achievements, Canadian Blacks tend to look to diasporic developments for their inspiration. Their heroes are the same as those that triumphed in other lands, possibly the homelands that Blacks are encouraged to identify with under the prevailing official policy of multiculturalism. And this will continue until they become fully part of the Canadian finite consciousness, where they can imagine attaining their hopes and dreams as part of the dialectic of existence. This is the promise of multiculturalism for them: hope and a particular history.

FROM ETHNICITY TO RACE: CANADIAN CONTEXT

The celebration of Blackness in Canada is intended, then, to subvert the
natural order of a nation-state that asserts ethnicity as essential to understanding this social order and those who belong within it. Traditionally, the
movement in group and nation construction seems to go from a starting
position of recognition, which is race, and which tends to be an issue at the
individual level. Then this movement evolves into different forms of human
collectives that, as Aristotle and modernist theorists suggest, ends in the
highest form that is the state. Blackness, in its practice and as a Modernist
construct, is a movement in the opposite direction: conceptually it is the
going assimilatively from ethnicities to a single race.

All ethnic groups that are branded Black are treated as if race matters
most in how they are perceived, rather than the culture and history that has
long been associated with ethnicity and nationalism. This, too, has been a
feature of the dialectic of freedom and recognition in the West. Indeed, race
is an asymmetrical relationship between ethnicities, a relationship that is
not the same within an ethnicity for there are no racialized categorizations
within the same group. When there are differences that mimic race in the
group, they are categorized as issues of class. Race is the relationship
between finite groups that are ethnicities. The infinity Blackness, however,
captures both the race issues between different groups and the class relationships within the various groups.

An example of this is the various ethnic groups from West-Central Africa
that lost their distinctive ethnic identities when they arrived in the Americas
as slaves. Their identities were reduced to that of being Black, as a racialized relation they shared as a group, regardless of any other distinctive ethnic characteristics. This is a process that still continues today in Canada,
where Ethiopians and Somalis, who do not see themselves as Black in their
native countries, are objectified as Black and ethnicized as part of a homogeneous group called *Blacks* in Canada. A good illustration of this is to
look at the homogenization that transformed slaves from the area that is
generally called Nigeria today. First, they were supposedly members of
tribes and nations, then they were transformed into a singular Yoruba
ethnicity, an identity that, according to historians Biodun Adediran and
Robin Law, was meaningless before the nineteenth century.[26]

Even then, according to Law, the identity was used to rub out the ethnic
identities of various subgroups in the area from which the slaves came.
Afterwards, their ethnicity was further negated and they were identified
simply as Black. This was quite different from the process that happened to
Western Europeans, the other major partners in the making of the Black
Atlantic, when they arrived in the Americas. In most cases, Europeans were
free to maintain their ethnicity, no matter their numbers or the relatively

small size of the European nation-state from which they claimed a primordialism, or to give up their ethnicities and submerge into the racial category
of White – as they pleased.

Such was the case because the Europeans were constructed individually
as liberal or moral agents, and the countries from which they came were
presumed to be liberal democracies. Many European groups, primarily
those with an advantage of dominance to be gained from such actions,
fought to maintain their ethnicity and nationality. However, there are
some, such as the Germans and Scandinavians, who willingly gave up most
of their obvious "ethnic" appearance and became assimilated into the more
privileged racial position of being White and ethnicized as anglophone.
This racialized relationship was between them as a group and others in
groups, not so much within their common ethnicities.

Adediran shows that the area called Yorubaland covers an extensive area
of southwestern Nigeria, and southern parts of Benin Republic and Central
Togo. Further, it encompasses many geographic, linguistic, and cultural differences. This means the region is ethnically diversified with different customs and cultures. Historically, one of the differences was that in times of
war people that lived in the same region would enslave one another based
on ethnic differences, resulting in a racial relationship between the masters
and the slaves, both of different ethnicities and, importantly, where both
masters and slaves were somatically Black. This was particularly the case
with each group in the area "trying to assert its political supremacy; consequently, each took pride in its own identity."[27]

Adediran notes that "similarly, there were regional variations in religious
worship" and different forms of political organization, with the highest
form, that of the sovereign state, headed by an *oba* (king) with symbols
that included exclusive uses of crowns. Political life was different among
the groups. Women participated and played dominant roles in some, while
in others the women were excluded. Different geographic variations and
historical experiences shaped life in the various groups. "Thus," Adediran
states, "the Oyo in the fairly open savannah region succeeded in establishing a large political State in contrast to the over sixteen independent states
that existed in the rugged area of the Ekiti."[28]

Slavery, and the colonial trade between Europe, Africa, and the Americas,
led to the homogenization, or creolizing, of the Yoruba culture. Adediran
traces this to the symbolic use of the terms *Nago* and *Lucamee* or *Lucumi*
in the Americas to identify and to commodify multi-ethnic slaves that were
no longer differentiated according to ethnicity. "But during the 19th century
Yoruba civil wars, the consciousness of belonging to different sub-groups
was given a practical demonstration, it was during this time for instance
that the Yoruba began to enslave each other. With the imposition of European Colonial rule, this consciousness was further intensified as a result of

conflicting claims by various sub-groups for political and social privileges in the colonial order. Then, everybody suddenly became aware of the differences that existed between one sub-group and others, a phenomenon which found a parallel development in Yoruba historiography."[29] The commodities that were to be slaves in the Americas were transformed in a mass of humanity called Nago, Lucamee, or Lucumi depending on the spelling and ultimately negro, niggers, coons, Blacks, and a variety of other names that suggest the slaves and their descendents were less than fully human and were just a commodity that is chattel or the property of others who are fully human.

Law states, "Europeans, for their part, regularly distinguished different ethnicities among the slaves they purchased, and American markets developed preferences for slaves of particular ethnic origins." This was the case, as Law shows, of the plantation owners in Barbados, who complained racially in 1686, to the Royal African Company in West Africa, that it had delivered "the worst of Negroes" by offering slaves of a different ethnicity, a supposedly inferior temperament, than from the more acceptable Gold Coast Negroes that had been promised them. The Yoruba identity was developed to facilitate the slave trade, especially the terms *Lucumi* and *Nago* that predated the Yoruba identity. As Law explains:

The term "Nago" is best-known as a term for Yoruba-speakers in Brazil, especially through their involvement in the Bahia slave uprising of 1835, which drew its support predominantly from the Nago. As in Cuba, the predominant elements in the Afro-Brazilian religion, called *candomble*, are clearly Yoruba in origin. The term "Nago" was also used in the French colony of Saint-Domingue (modern Haiti). Although the "voodoo" religion of Haiti is mainly derived from that of the Aja-Ewe peoples, it also incorporates a distinct Nago "nation" of deities. The term is also attested in British West Indian colonies, and in Louisiana in the 1770s/1780s.[30]

Law argues that when used in Africa, Lucumi and Nago had distinct meanings that were different from their usage in the Americas. Lucumi referred primarily to Southern Yorubaland, which exported slaves and other commodities through the Lagos lagoon. Nago applied to western Yorubaland, which supplied slaves mainly through Dahomey. "The substitution of 'Nago' for 'Lucumi' in diasporic usage in the eighteenth century thus seems to have reflected shifts in trading patterns, more specifically, a shift in the principal source of supply of Yoruba slaves to the coast – away from southern and towards western Yorubaland." Subsequently, all the slaves from the area would be identified as Yoruba with no regard paid to their distinct ethnicity. Later, this appellation would give way, too, to simply Black as an identity. This would be a creolized composite identity based on only an imputed ethnicity or racial essence. Black would not only be the new identity of all slaves from the numerous ethnic groups in Central Africa, but it would also be the common identity of those from the Gold Coast and from Sudan and Angola. By then, in the new homes of the slaves in the Americas, ethnicity had been transformed into race.

Creole or hybridized identities would be imposed on this cultural Blackness, especially after slavery ended, and again when Caribbean islands became fully independent, with each identity reflecting the local environment from which it sprang. However, these would be identities of choice in a lordship and bondage relationship, a sign of different cultures and ethnicities within somatic Blackness. They would be treated with little regard in power relations where Blacks were the Other, where Black was a symbol of inferiority regardless of the culture of the somatic Black. Even within these variations in the African slave population in the Americas, ethnicities and nationalities were treated as superficial. In power relations, the essence was identified simply as Blackness, with all Others creolized and assimilated into this singular identity while maintaining ethnicities of choice.

The significance in the Caribbean context was that a shift in power also went with a shift in the construction of the mainstream. A mainstream consisting of what previously were Others, which started out as a group of people with no power or social mobility, reversed the situation in a double negation and through power acquired social mobility. It also opened doors to those who had previously positioned themselves as separate and apart in Whiteness to become part of a mainstream that had switched through a construction around the primacy of Blackness as representing all that is not the purity and the essence of idealized Whiteness.

This common identity and classification for all peoples with an African ancestry created problems that were accentuated by a Canadian policy that called for the recognition of ethnic groups. In this case, the common identification given to those Canadians with such a history was just described as Black. A major question was whether there is an essence or primordialism to being Black, a commonality that is at the root of what is called the Black community in Canada. Is there an essence to a culture of Blackness that is similar to the essence found in such communities that claim to be Irish, Greek, German, or Italian? Is there a common factor or identification? Otherwise, how is it possible for those deemed to be Black, but sharing no real common traits other than the colour of their skin, to compete in a system that is based on the recognition of and on privileging the essences of specific ethnic groups, and then on the ranking of these essences?

That so many of the somatically Black immigrants, and those already living in Canada, came from different countries with their own symbols of nationalism suggests that the members of the so-called Black community are very ethnically distinct and diverse. In their previous homelands, a first stage of homogenization or creolization had already taken place and pro-

duced distinct ethnicities. When in 1962 Jamaica, for example, became the
first English-speaking Caribbean island to gain political independence, it
took as its national motto the homogenizing and creolized *Out of Many
One People*. Similarly, the prime minister of Trinidad and Tobago, Dr Eric
Williams, in taking his twin-island state into independence later in 1962
enjoined them to create a new nationality and nationalism that was a Trinidad and Tobago ethnicity. In an oft repeated phrase, Williams, in referring
to the African and Indian ancestry of the majority of the population,
remarked that just as an independent Trinidad and Tobago no longer had
a Mother England, the people should no longer have a Mother Africa
nor Mother India. They were to recognize a composite "ethnicity" and
"essence" that were distinctly Trinidadian and Tabagonian. At the same
time, Jamaica and Trinidad and Tobago were helping to assert a wider
identity that was also Caribbean, and later Latin American.

This integrationist/assimilationist model, as attempted by Caribbean
nations in the post-colonial period, was different from the model followed
in many post-colonial African nation-states, several of which were intent
on making an appeal to a primordiality as the basis of the new states. Notable examples are a post-independence Uganda that expelled thousands of
citizens that were of Indian descent; Burundi, where a minority elite slaughtered large numbers of the racially inferior majority; and Rwanda, when it
was governed by a Hutu elite that committed genocide on the Tutsi minority. On the other hand, the decision by the African National Congress in
South Africa to reject insular Bantu lands based on supposed ethnic differences and to fight for an assimilation model of nation-state formation that
would include all "ethnic" and "racial" groups as equals in the state was a
model that was similar to the Caribbean one.

## RECOGNIZING CANADIAN BLACKS:
## AUTHENTICITY AND BELONGING

This, then, raises a problem, for Blacks in Canada rarely see themselves as
an essentialized group with a specific culture and its own boundaries.
Rather, by definition, there can be no natural boundaries to Blackness in
Canada. Blacks tend to see themselves as different groups that are affiliated
in one common bond, not because of an ethnicity or national origin, but
because of race: the second class status that they experience as a collective
within Canada. Race signifies them as outsiders, and is the one thing they
have in common.

This argument of belonging as entitlement pervades African diasporic
discourse, especially in North America, where the dispute is more openly
hostile between Caribbean-born Blacks and their children, on one hand,
and Blacks that have lived on the continent for several generations, on the

other. In Canada, this is an argument that has been captured succinctly in the writings of the poet and academic George Elliott Clarke, who argues strongly for the recognition of specific finite ethnicities in Canadian Blackness.[31] According to Clarke, not only should these ethnicities be recognized, they should, he seems to imply, be ranked and valorized, for all Black ethnicities are not equal, either within Blackness or within the wider Canadian or North American setting.

In the Canadian setting, Clarke argues for primacy for what he calls the *Africadian,* a term he coined for the somatic Blacks in Canada of long standing, who, in three centuries, have built communities, sometimes almost in segregation from the wider Canadian society, as in Nova Scotia.[32] According to Clarke, *Africadians* – as opposed to newer arrivals, notably from the Caribbean – should have ascendancy when speaking about the Black experience in Canada. By implication, this group would probably assimilate similar Black groups of long standing in Ontario and Western Canada.[33]

This difference was based on their previous socialization and acculturation, and their perceived misperceptions about Canada and its social and political institutions and cultural agencies. It also sprung from the feeling of the newer arrivals that they were coming from a culture that had recognized them as somatically Black but idealistically, culturally, and socially as White. It was a status that they wanted to maintain in Canada. Long-standing Blacks in Canada had never lived idealized Whiteness, because they were in a society that refused them the double negation that would miraculously transfigure them into the idealistic Whiteness of intuitive perception and reason. This distinction in lived experiences still hangs over the descendants of Caribbean somatic Blacks in Atlantic Canada's Black community, where there are those who traditionally view them as idealized White and those who view them as idealized Black, both in their ethically constructed Black country and in the wider universal Canada.

But such an arrangement for clear distinctions within the group called ethnic Blacks still runs up against the question of boundaries and the concomitant notion of cultural entitlement in a multicultural setting. This can be seen most clearly in the disputes over perceptions and ways of life that would develop between Blacks from three main regions: the Caribbean, continental Africa, and Canadian born Blacks, some of whom in the latter group can trace their ancestry back to the United Empire Loyalists and to the Caribbean but who seem to be placed by their "indigenes" in the "Caribbean" category, and are therefore not indigenous, and some of whom are placed in the Caribbean category by other non-Black Canadians, primarily by White Canadians that make up the mainstream. This issue is of crucial importance, apparently, to Canadian-born Blacks, especially those arguing for a right of entitlement – based on notions of belonging that privileged longevity – that is superior to that of newcomers.

This is a right that is calculated on length of stay in the country, and by subscribing to the perception that newcomers have not experienced nor contributed to the social capital that is now due to Blacks. It is what Sartre calls the acquisition of the "true value" and genuineness that is associated only with those considered the natural preserves, only with those who are considered to be inclusive of the group in the nation and nation-building:

In a bourgeois society it is the constant movement of people, the collective currents, the styles, the customs, all these things, that in effect create *values*. The values of poems, of furniture, of houses, of landscapes derive in large part from the sponta-neous condensations that fall on these objects like a light dew; they are strictly national and result from the normal functioning of a traditionalist and historical society. To be a Frenchman is not merely to have been born in France, to vote and pay taxes; it is above all to have the use and the sense of these values. And when a man shares in their creation, he is in some degree reassured about himself; he has a justification for existence through a sort of adhesion to the whole society.[34]

In this case, which is similar to the argument raised by Robertson Davies, the essence of Canadianness can be recognized only through longevity, and this is true of Blacks whether they become "White" in the Davies under-standing or, in the imagination of Clarke and others, they are foreign-born Blacks becoming Canadian.[35] The argument that Caribbean Blacks, in par-ticular, do not understand Canadian cultural institutions is no different from that offered by George Grant to show a distinction between the cul-tures of Americans and Canadians which bases the distinction on a natural affinity: on sharing this common culture that is best epitomized by the way they react to specific institutions and agencies in their cultures.[36] Indeed, this is the very expression of cultural Whiteness that is equated with civili-zation, an order that Fanon wrote about when he referred to the distinc-tions Blacks impose on people of the same group, distinctions based largely on how White and official one group of Blacks has become through its association with and exposure to edification. As Fanon states in *Black Skin, White Masks*: "I have known – and unfortunately I still know – people born in Dahomey or the Congo who pretend to be natives of the Antilles; I have known, and I still know, Antilles Negroes who are annoyed when they are suspected of being Senegalese. This is because the Antilles Negro is more 'civilized' than the African, that is, he is closer to the white man; and this difference prevails not only in back streets and on boulevards but also in public service and the army."[37]

In his case, Grant saw a peculiar culture being developed on the north-ernmost part of North America, one that was quite distinct, and, when val-orized, better than what was produced farther south.[38] Clarke suggests that the same is true for the distinctions in Blackness constructed on the north-ernmost tip of North America when compared with Blackness from the islands off the southern tip of the continent.[39]

Most of the issues raised in this chapter can be accounted for in the way Blackness became a form of assimilation, one that was imposed at times, and one that was accepted and encouraged by those that would be called Blacks. Somatic Blacks in Canada, as is generally true in most of the Americas, have been forced during and since slavery to give up most of their ethnic diversity and become assimilated into a normative Black nation, one that has been on the periphery of the main (White) power centres in the Americas. This means that while most new arrivals to Canada could choose a model that was exclusionary, integrationist, or assimilationist, somatic Blacks have had to fit into the dominant society as an already assimilated group and not as individuals to be integrated.

The lordship and bondage relationship that they entered was via a double or second negation between English and French groups that each had its own and unique lordship and bondage relationship. Their ethical relation was between ethnicities forming a state, and not between individuals seeking to set up a primary and single state. They entered the Canadian state, already having been determined by the universality, something that Canada asks all its bondsmen to give up in return for a particular identity that is Canadian.

Blackness is an assimilationist project that began with the arrival of the first Africans in the hemisphere – the arrival of millions of people from several different ethnic backgrounds and what would eventually be termed nationalisms in west-central Africa – who became simply creolized Black labourers in the Americas. This was a motility based on the assumed inferiority of a class of people from many ethnicities but sharing two things, primarily: a common colour of skin and a heritage from Africa. In assimilating all somatic Blacks into a finite group, the effect was to place limits and boundaries on them, thereby denying them all the infinite attributes, characteristics, and aspirations of humanity. These are limits that some somatic Blacks will eventually internalize and even perform as their essence, race, and ethnicity.

# 17

# Neo-Mythic Multiculturalism

## Blackness in Canada's Mythology

In its mythology, Canada is a Promised Land primarily for groups constructed as Black, specifically by those whose Blackness is an indication of how they have been constructed as Africans. In a famous Massey Lecture broadcast on the Canadian Broadcasting Corporation Radio in 1964, Black civil rights advocate Reverend Martin Luther King Jr praised Canada as having a special place in the mythology of somatic and cultural Blacks, as a place of refuge. He mentioned that Canada was described in Negro spirituals as A Placed Called Heaven where escaping slaves found refuge via the Underground Railroad.[1] In this mythology, any escape from slavery was into freedom and out of a wilderness. Enslaved Africans and their descendants viewed slavery as the "wilderness through which and out of which, a good Providence has already led us."[2]

Booker T. Washington, who was born in slavery, recalls in his memoirs *Up From Slavery* the way that this particular mythology influenced the lives of the slaves on the eve of Emancipation in the United States: "Most of the verses of the plantation songs had some reference to freedom. True, they had sung those same verses before, but they had been careful to explain the 'freedom' in these songs referred to the next world, and had no connection with life in this world. Now they gradually threw off the mask; and were not afraid to let it be known that the 'freedom' in their songs meant freedom of the body in this world."[3] Since, the worst was supposedly behind them, Blacks, as a group consolidated mainly by the experiences and institution of slavery, could have "faith in the future of [their] race," a faith and hope that, even for Washington, remained largely in the transcendent.

In the official Canadian mythology, Canada is invariably presented by the dominant culture as a wilderness of existential Blackness, lawlessness, and chaos, or a garrison against the barbarians, as a place to which specially elected people, largely without choice, had withdrawn in a respite of law and order until circumstances changed and they could escape.[4] In this dominant mythology, Canada is not a site of freedom, but of an eternal struggle between the forces of good and evil, of enlightenment and darkness. It is a site of inclusion and not of exclusion. It is a cosmopolitanism that as Kojève says was given to Western thought by Alexander the Great and by the Pauline Christian doctrine – a temporary home at best, one that could only be measured in this life by alienation, human trials, fragmentation, and a yearning for better times. In this mythology, Canada was always part of the journey, not so much the terminus as was suggested by somatic and cultural Blacks who presented Canada in their mythology as the *end* of an underground railroad, or the place to which the travellers from around the world would find a final home. Indeed, Canada in the mythology of the somatically and culturally Black was the place to which the enslaved arrived already transformed in the crossing to a *freeman,* the other being that was ontologically and existentially a bondsman – for Canada was where they fully become human, and as British subjects and then Canadian citizens, lords of the piece.[5] This transfiguration from existential evil to good supposedly took place after a physical and symbolic crossing over of the rivers or sea – whether symbolically Jordan River, the Red Sea; whether the Ohio River or any of the North American Great Lakes – that flow through life, or are symbolically life itself.

As Rick Helmes-Hayes and James Curtis note in *The Vertical Mosaic Revisited,* over time nine central images of Canadian society have been identified in contemporary sociology.[6] They create a prevailing mythology that, from different perspectives, points to Canada and Canadian life as alienated and removed from Europe, from a real and sacred time and space that is authentic. They list the images of Canada as:

*A vertical mosaic:* In Canada, ethnicity and social class have been historically tied together, with the founding anglophone group holding the positions of greatest attainment and power.

*A class society:* Class is the primary fact of one's life; affecting everything from self-perception to education, life chances, and work experiences in Canada. The class structure and class relations have been and continue to be primary determinants of economic, political, and social change.

*Accommodating elites:* Canada's economic, governmental, bureaucratic, ideological, and labour elites maintain contact and pursue their own competing interests by means of accommodation and compromise.

*Two solitudes/deux nations:* Canada is a society of two quite different cultures, with different ways of thinking and living that have little contact with each other.

*A British fragment:* English-speaking Canada's institutional structure and culture (values) reflect a British heritage, making Canadians more traditionalist, law-abiding, and so on than Americans.

*A closed frontier:* Canada's geography has allowed social control to remain firmly in the hands of powerful central interests exploiting the country's staple products.

*A metropolis and hinterland/Canada is a colony:* Canadian regions, cities, and towns are tied to one another, and to the outside world, through a chain of dominance based on capital and, often, related to the exploitation of staples.

*A fragile federation:* Canada's national culture and identity are not robust, its regions are weakly tied together in a confederation, but Canadians' sentiments, cultures, and allegiances are local, not national.

*A double ghetto:* Canadian society has a sexist institutional structure and culture so that women are disadvantaged in both domestic and paid labour. At home they do the bulk of domestic labour, and in the paid labour force they are concentrated in lower status, lower paying jobs.[7]

Through different gazes that are mythologically associated with the somatic Blacks and Whites, we see the infinity of human existence: of the hope of a finite Canadian group called Blacks and of the despair and despondency of those called White. Both groups started out as changeable Canadian in the form of an Other – of technically and ontologically belonging elsewhere – and were hoping to become unchangeable Canadian. Multiculturalism would try to capture the full gamut of human existence and then, as a social goal, to privilege and accentuate officially the component best exemplified by somatic Blacks in their collective mythology. But in creating a syncretic and hybridized way of rationalizing who or what is Canada and Canadian, the emerging new mythology would contain the two components emphasized by somatic and cultural Blacks and Whites. On the one hand, there were the hope and expectation of a transformation from evil to good, from existentialist and idealistic Blackness to its opposite Whiteness, from a bondsman's position to that of lord. On the other extreme was the rationalization of Canada as a cold, deserted place and as a site of despair over the potential for continued human survival; of the physical difficulties of making the land habitable, and of always living the life of a bondsman. In this case, the lord took many ethno-racial forms: as Nature; as a benevolent Mother Country across the Atlantic; as having an elephantine neighbour to the south with notions of its own manifest destiny that included eventually swallowing up Canada. Or the bondage came in the form of the fear that Canada, as supposedly naturally a White man's country, might eventually be overwhelmed by the ideological and existential Blackness that was natural to the Americas. This supposed lawlessness and chaos, regression and social degeneracy were best exemplified by the Haitian existence following the Haitian Revolution of 1804.[8] As I have been arguing, the new mythology that currently seeks to rationalize the Canadian experience as multiculturalism is an exercise in creolism – syncretism of the best and the worst of two mythologies to form a single hybrid.

However, in this mythology, especially in its literary imaginings and in its political rhetoric, Canada is presented as a modernist state based on knowledge and as the embodiment of a natural spirit that arose out of the land, the wind, and nature in general. This is captured in the works of such Canadian luminaries as Robertson Davies, Margaret Atwood, and Stephen Leacock in their arguments that have been privileged collectively as the dominant or mainstream view on who can become Canadian, and what is the essence of such Canadianness.[9]

Invariably, it is an identity and an essence based on the control and domestication of a base Nature, an idealized and cultural Blackness according to our categories. Lionel Stevenson, in the 1924 publication *Manifesto for a National Literature*, sets the tone for this hegemonic view which persists even in a moment of official multiculturalism by describing ontologically a creolized and hybridized Canada – as existentially and epistemologically cultural Blackness. He wrote:

In Canada the primordial forces are still dominant. So Canadian art is almost entirely directed to landscape, Canadian poetry to the presentation of nature. But there are deeper implications than that. The distinctive type of landscape painting which has established itself in this country is anything but the photographic type; it is essentially interpretative. And Canadian poetry is equally concerned with the apocalyptic. The poetic mind, placed in the midst of natural grandeur, can scarcely avoid mysticism. It is not the sectarian mysticism of the Old World, steeped in religion and philosophy, but an instinctive pantheism, recognizing a spiritual meaning in nature and its identity with the soul of man.[10]

Stephen Leacock, after whom a major literary prize on Canadian humour is awarded annually, wrote *Sunshine Sketches of a Little Town*, which has been presented as the quintessential Canadian novel for generations. The novel's first sentences place Canada within the dominant Western tradition of knowledge, but with a people battling against the wilds and pending chaos. But in the beginning and ending of this mythology –as the beginning of this book suggests – Canada is most easily recognizable as a place in the imagination. "I don't know whether you know Mariposa. If not, it is of no consequence, for if you know Canada at all, you are probably well acquainted with a dozen towns just like it."[11] This was a Canada that was physically and existentially at battle with the wilds of nature in terms of geography and, in terms of human nature, particularly with the cultural and to a lesser extent the somatic and cultural Blackness of the United States of America. But, in the mind, Leacock suggests Canada is a "real" or pragmatic country, a survivor despite the folly of its human inhabitants living effectively at their wits and at the mercy of greater gods. This was a country imaginatively in a lordship and bondage relationship and having its own past, present and, potentially, future.

Indeed, Blacks in the Americas, as a constructed group, subscribe strongly to this modern Western mythology that is based on knowledge – but often in Canada they do not get the justice that is promised by the myth as an act of escaping. Social mobility, according to the prevailing mythology, is based on how much the subject knows. This explains the high premiums that Blacks, especially since the ending of slavery in the Americas, have placed on formal education – a premium that, ironically, appears to become diminished for some Blacks by the death of hope for them in terms of upward social mobility in Canada. This is the same mythology that encourages, for example, governments in the Caribbean to invest heavily in education in the hope of producing modern subjects that can immigrate to other countries, and based on knowing, find positions in the new state. It is a hope that within a generation seems to burn out, as the experience of modern somatically Black immigrants to Canada shows.

Even after the 1960s, when Canada began to construct its own national organic narrative through government support for the arts, Canada was presented, dialectically, either as a part of another people's culture and history, or as a community of diasporic people trying to live together and struggling to build a unified nation.[12] As Daymond and Monkman argue, the whole cultural system in North America is "not, as in older civilizations, the product of many centuries during which the natural influences of the country have moulded the soul of the people."[13] In a discussion that pointedly erases the First Nations people from the Canadian national imaginary, they suggest that generations have not lived on the land and grown out of it. They argue that the taming of nature is still relatively new, a point that is often presented, in the Canadian imaginary, to make Canadian culture even chronologically more recent than that of the United States of America. Within the body that is Western civilization, this would mean that Canada is culturally Black in terms of its youthfulness and seeming unenlightenment from experience, even Blacker than the United States which was for a long time the *bête noire* in the northern part of North America from a Canadian perspective. Lionel Stevenson's argument about the formation of a national spirit in Canada suggests this youthful Blackness:

In this country [Canada], the civilization is not thus indigenous; it is a perfected mechanism evolved under very different conditions and introduced ready made. It has gradually become modified to some extent by the inherent character of the continent, but the change has been delayed and disrupted by constant transfusion of people from varied races, each with a different mental background, as well as by unbroken intercourse with the Mother Country. In The United States, the outcome is a situation still anomalous enough; Canada, a newer country with more scattered population, has had even less chance of developing a homogeneous outlook.[14]

If Canada is presented as newer, it is because for centuries Canadian elites have fought to remain tied to a mother country, England, and to perfecting cultural agencies created in a European theatre that might not have been suited to the Americas. This was so unlike in the United States, where the revolutionary fervour of the late eighteenth century onward called for a clear break with Europe as a cultural mother, or in the Caribbean where many agencies and institutions were openly creolized and syncretized. Structurally, Canada had tried to remain loyal to a perceived European cosmological good; even if similar attempts at hybridity were operating within the Canadian body politic, they went unrecognized by the elites for as long as possible.[15]

Yet, while arguing for the newness of Canada and for its diverse sources of peoples and cultures, the notion would, contradictorily, develop from early on that there is a soul, distinct, singular, and unified, in Canada that is as homogeneous in nature as is that of its modernist twin the United States. This contradiction in the Canadian imaginary – as being too young to have a fully formed culture but of being old enough to have a very distinct cultural character – is noted as recently as 1938 by Frederick Philip Grove, when in response to the argument that there is no clearly, discernable Canadian culture, he stated that if one listened carefully to the average Toronto businessman one would hear him blindly swearing, "There can be no country to equal Canada in cultural opportunities – Canada being, thank the Lord, still largely 'a white man's country.'"[16] As we have seen, intellectuals like Deacon and many eminent Canadian politicians shared this same view.

That there is a Canadian soul or essence and that it is White was emphasized by Robertson Davies, the internationally revered icon of Canadian literature and culture. It is noteworthy that he made the following point at a time when the Canadian population was undergoing fundamental change in its makeup because of increased immigration from non-traditional sources. In the Neil Gunn Lecture in Edinburgh, Scotland, in 1988, Davies looked at the ways Canada has been presented in the imagination of Canadians and visitors alike. The lecture was given the seemingly provocative title "Literature in a Country without Mythology." Obviously ignoring the mythology of non-European groups about Canada, Davies said:

Canada has a mythology, but it is only now, after about four hundred years of history, forced to decide what it is going to do about it. The pressure comes from outside. Canada was for long a British colony, never the favourite colony because it is a land that has never appealed powerfully to the European imagination. The French have never thought of it. The early explorer Jacques Cartier wrote quite seriously that it was "the land God gave to Cain." Voltaire called it a few acres of snow. Napoleon, when he was reduced to giving advice from his seclusion on St. Helen, said that England would be better off without it. British administrators who were sent there tended to regard it as a place of exile. Things have not got better. It is asserted that our name comes from the remark of a Spanish explorer, "Acanada" – nothing there. Kingsley Amis nominates *Canadian Wit and Humour* as one of the world's shortest books.[17]

Davies did not pick up on the assertion about the original and natural owners of Canada that was advanced "quite seriously" by Jacques Cartier, the famed French explorer who arrived in Atlantic Canada in 1534 and led the opening charge for European colonization on the northern part of the continent. Cartier was one of the first Europeans to encounter Canada in what Europeans considered to be a state of nature or in the possession of its authentic and primordial owners.[18] In the Hebraic sense, Cartier saw what would become Canada as the land that still had to be brought under cultivation and civilization – into a place fit for the habitation of both a Christian God and humans, as becoming a sacred time and sacred place of mythical enchantment. In the Greek mythology, it was the part of nature that as Plato would suggest could not be associated with a god or demiurge that was completely good by nature – instead, in this thinking, this land was part of the Nature that started out as not good at all, not already in the likeness of a good god, and would have to be converted mythologically by goodness.

Perhaps, Davies averted his eyes to Cartier's claim that Canada was the land given to Cain, because Davies, in a lecture on mythology, was mindful that in the Hebraic tradition to which Cartier referred the cosmological and natural owner of Canada, Cain, is acknowledged as somatically, culturally, and idealistically Black, and because of these characteristics was deemed to be deserving of a lower Black status among humans. Cain being the quintessential existential Black man in Hebraic tradition, this would explain why a land "discovered" in its primordial Blackness and indeterminateness would be considered to be the land that God gave to Cain. Second, Davies ignored three other markers that made Canada mythologically Black: (1) Canada had asserted that European and Europe were idealized Whiteness, that to which it aspired from a position of darkness; (2) as a self-conscious ego, it had recognized, phenomenologically, that it had never attained that authentic Europeanness, that it had never escaped cultural and somatic

Blackness; (3) in terms of gaining international respect, as the quote Davies took from Amis suggests, Canada was still Black in status – still considered perceptually to be culturally and existentially inferior to other more privileged and elite countries.

These points were confirmed, as Davies's own argument showed, by those who represent European thought in his imagination – Cartier, Voltaire, Napoleon, and Amis – and amount to a European self-consciousness looking at itself. Those enlightened and cognizant Europeans, who saw themselves as idealistically, culturally, and socially White, did not recognize Canada as part of their White body, not even as a foreign member of the European body. More than that, they saw Canada and Canadians as a Black object outside of their body.

Davies's argument was the very opposite, for it asserted powerfully that what would become the modernist Canada was mythologically a White man's, or European, country. In this pre-history, as discerned by Davies, the land that would become Canada was by nature culturally a Black amorphous mass in need of enlightenment and civilization, which, according to Davies's narrative, started only when a hardy group of Europeans brought a history, culture, and sacred time to the land by carving out of the Blackness a White civil society.

Such thoughts on the struggle between idealized Whiteness and Blackness are usually expressed as the search for the soul or essence of Canada, in the Platonic sense and are an acknowledgment that the real thing, the essence or soul, could be different from the corporeal manifestation of an embodiment. Davies explains it this way: "The land and the climate are all-pervasive, and we know that the *blackest or most turbaned* newcomer to our country will have descendants who will, within three generations, be Canadian in spirit."[19]

Four points are worth making: First, Davies takes it as a practical phenomenological possibility for people that are officially Black existentially and even ontologically to become Canadian, or in our analysis be created into idealistic Canadian Whiteness. Second, his image of the most extreme non-Canadian is somatically and culturally Black or turbaned, putting Blackness at the natural extreme of and inferior to Whiteness and Canadian, and locating somatic Blacks and the turbaned newcomer within the wider Blackness that is the chaotic and uncivil state of nature from which a Canadian must be manufactured and fashioned. Alternately, and paradoxically, he could be suggesting prophetically that ultimately Canada is destined to become somatically, culturally, and socially Black, but this would not be in keeping with the tone and spirit of his address.

Davies makes allowances for the entry of Blackness into the Whiteness of the state by suggesting that only time, as measured in generations, can bring about a meaningful and authentic transfiguration or recreation that is the kind of second negation that is necessary for full White citizenship; and until time has run its course, in other words, the Others in Canadian society, who have merely been transfigured by the first negation out of their complete Blackness, will naturally be excluded from the mainstream imaginary of the country. In this respect, a second negation is not automatic and a time of two or three generations is the minimum limit or requirement for the transfiguration to occur.

Third, Davies suggests that what is Canadian comes out of a culture that has already escaped from the Blackness of the wilderness that is both encircling and inside the sacred place; that Canadians are shaped by their culture, rather than that people living in Canada shape the country's culture and history.

Finally, and fourthly, in suggesting that it takes generations for the idealistically Blackest and most turbaned to become Canadian in spirit, Davies presents a Canadian myth that is in stark contrast with the American Dream myth which suggests a social rebirth for newcomers within a single lifetime, indeed a transfiguration that occurs physically with the taking of an oath. This suggests that, unlike what is experienced by somatically White immigrants, there will always be alienation for somatic and even cultural Blacks in a Canadian space. This rationalization would help explain why some groups, such as somatic and cultural Blacks, would hold inferior statuses in Canadian society and why, by and large, they would be excluded from the prevailing Canadian imaginary. For as Davies suggests, it would take generations of creation for ontological or somatic Blacks and the turbaned to acquire the Canadian spirit and to be accepted fully as Canadian.

Indeed, it was not coincidental that Davies used the example of a Black person to illustrate his point on how to make the idealized Whiteness of citizenship out of the uncivilized. It is also instructive that Davies goes a step further in suggesting that merely attaining citizenship does not make a newcomer an equal partner in Canada, for putting on the outward trappings of citizenship does not add them to the soul of the country. This is a point that he says is fundamentally at odds with the founding principles of an assimilationist United States of America. As Davies suggests in another lecture to an American audience on what constitutes the Canadian spirit, the Canadian method is the exact opposite of what obtains in the United States of America and the national mindset that it creates:

Our history is not like yours, for you were born of revolution, and our roots are deep in dogged loyalty. The people who first settled our country were not like your Pilgrims, or the handful of aristocrats who settled in Virginia and thereabout. The stories of most of our earliest settlers were sad ones, and not the least unhappy was the tale of those supporters of the British cause who, at the time of your Revolution, were compelled to go north and begin life afresh. Many of my own forebears were of that group ... There is an element of loss and betrayal in our history which even yet tends to make us an introverted people, with the particular kind of inner strength that introversion implies. No, we are not like you, though if you come to our country on a visit you may not be strongly aware of having left the United States. But stay with us for a year, and the difference will be amply apparent. We do not wear our hearts on our sleeves.[20]

Davies's images of Canada, as stoic and indeterminate, is of a culture and history that are, therefore, cosmological. Phenomenologically, however, these are actually the characteristics of a Black body stoically thinking it is White while everything about it is hidden and will only be revealed in the fullness of time. It is also the picture of a culture and history that has not changed since 1783, despite fundamental changes in the ethnicities of the population. And it is a view that is based on a mythology of Whiteness as Eurocentrism. This explanation ignores the presence and contributions of First Nations peoples, former African slaves, and other non-European immigrants who have been struggling in all the Americas – and most specifically, North America – to carve civil societies out of nature. This view of Canada and Canadian identity – although expressed more openly a generation ago – has not been eradicated in multicultural Canada. This view persists and is the core of much of the discussion that multicultural Canada has a mainstream bicultural as well as bilingual core of English and French Whiteness. And this analysis is in keeping, despite official protestation to the contrary, with the view held by the elites and mainstream that Canada, at heart, is still European and a White man's country, a country where Whites are the only genuine Canadians.

This is a determination that does not stand up to reason – as indicated by the flaws in Davies's own argument – or by cognition through what sense certainty shows as the diversified demographic composition of the country. Such is the idealized and cognitive Blackness of a false consciousness. This is a reversal of the method for attaining certainty, for intuitively all that is sought is to validate and uphold a specific moral and ethical relationship that is in place. There is no desire to challenge it.

Sartre makes the point that those who are constructed as the Other and deemed not to share the innate national character and values seldom acquire them to become "genuine" citizens. In his example of how the French national character is constructed and valued, Sartre could just as easily have been thinking of the same kinds of perceptions that would later inform Davies's notions of who is a Canadian and how Canadianness can be attained within a specific social ordering:

He [the Other] can, indeed, acquire all the goods he wants, lands and castles if he has the witherwithal; but at the very moment when he becomes a legal proprietor, the property undergoes a subtle change in meaning and value. Only a Frenchman, the son of a Frenchman, son or grandson of a peasant, is capable of possessing it. To own a hut in a village, it is not enough to have bought it with hard cash. One must know all the neighbors, their parents and grandparents, the surrounding farms, the beeches and oaks of the forest; one must know how to work, fish, hunt; one must have made notches in the trees in childhood and have found them enlarged in ripe old age.[21]

Thus, as Davies suggests, time, tradition, and belonging are what make up citizenship. This norm for approaching citizenship, culture, and history, Davies says, captures a fundamental difference between Canada and the United States. Davies was exemplifying a strain of thought that remains sublated in Canadian thought but is not far from the surface even in a multicultural Canada that has supposedly erased such thoughts and narratives of Canadian history. This is a type of thinking that shows up in the words of many Canadian intellectuals, from Thomas D'Arcy McGee, Thomas Chandler Haliburton, and such twentieth-century nationalists as George Grant, Davies, and Northrop Frye. Frye in particular made a similar assessment of the Canadian identity and psyche, especially of the *official* or dominant view of Canadians' construction of their identity in opposition to Americanism in the wake of a type of globalism that is an attempt, as Frye sees it, by the United States of America to homogenize the cultures of the world.[22]

From its neo-mythic inception, both following the refugee trek north in 1783 and again in the 1867 Confederation, Canada was an exercise in semblance, so unlike its neighbour to the south. Canada's history is a reversal of what happened in the United States, "an indication that the two halves of upper North America were to have different directions and destinies."[23] As Frye claims, "Much of English Canada was settled by disaffected Tories from America, and there was a strong reaction against the Whig spirit that won the American Revolution, with its liberal mercantile values, its confidence in laissez-faire, its equating of freedom with national independence."[24]

Frye speaks to the question of semblance in the Canadian national psyche, a consciousness which, he notes, is different from that born in a culture that is based on revolution, with its "self-evident" principles and written constitutions.[25] He suggests that the result is a prudish Canadian mentality that is less flexible and accepting of differences than in the United States: "This deductive pattern [of wiping out ethnic and cultural differences through assimilation] has no counterpart in Canada, where nothing has ever been self-evident. Canadians usually try to resolve social tensions and conflicts by some form of compromise that keeps the interest of both parties in view, in the conservative spirit of Edmund Burke [with its reliance on customs and traditions]. The result is that the country seems to an outsider, and often to insiders as well, to be perpetually coming apart at the seams, with nothing to sustain it but a hope that some ad hoc settlement will keep it together until the next crisis."[26] What Frye is explaining is what we have been calling the ethno-racial Blackness that is death – reaching an ontological limit of being that for progress results in a plunge into the Blackness of nothingness or absolute otherness, in a time and place that is unknown.

To extend Frye's analysis, Canada lives daily with the possibility of an untimely death, with the prospect of a catastrophic and apocalyptic return of chaos that is so much part of a continuing struggle with nature. This demise could happen either through the downfall of the raison d'être for its existence as a nation – as a White outpost for British conservatism – with the downfall occurring through the arrival of those who might not share this idealism or by a splitting apart because of alienation in some part of the country, such as Quebec, Atlantic Canada, or Western Canada, which might lead to secession and the physical death of the federation. Canada's aim always seemed to be to stave off idealized or physical death, and in doing so has been managing the creativity and transformations that result from the transcending of limits and boundaries. Canada does not have a fully incorporated myth that accentuates rebirth in the dialectics of existence; rather, national death is often described in the most morbid terms. This is particularly true when the issue of Quebec separation arises.

The spectre of Canadians taking a leap into an abyss, into a financial unknown with cataclysmic results permeates the debate. Death is the ultimate and the absolute. It is despair and despondency in this way of thinking. To this end, the language of federalists when raising the prospect of Quebec's separation usually speaks of a "jump into the unknown," a "leap into an abyss," or the courting of darkness, chaos, and destruction.[27] Indeed, this is an image that is tantamount to perishing in the extreme in the Aristotelian and Derridian sense. In this consciousness, there is no belief in rebirth, no Socratic leap of faith into the transcendent. There is no hope and enthusiasm. There is no anticipation of a social rebirth as that imagined historically by somatic and cultural Blacks – of the ending of one history and the beginning of a new one that would be happier and hopefully everlasting. There is no expectation for the overcoming of the nihilism of the existential Blackness of life. The ultimate task for any Canadian under this dominant myth is to avoid national death, even if this means being fixed into a position that stifles natural change, a status that is a living death.

But the reality of Canadian life is different from this idealization. The story of Canada's pragmatic survival seems not to support much of the despair in the dominant myth. Death and renewal are, indeed, central to Canada, but it is a renewal that often challenges the idealized Whiteness and attempts to preserve Canada as a homeland for somatic and cultural Whites or Europeans. A different reading from that presented by many Canadian nationalists would produce a different picture of Canadian identity and the forces that created it, often in opposition to what has been presented in the prevailing mythology. This contrary view suggests that Canadian Confederation in 1867 was formed under the spectre of death in the fear of an expected annexation of the separate colonies, one by one, by the United States of America. This contrary view claims that Canada is constantly a creation, a process, which means, by extension, that it is a continuous death as well.

This is why in the 1960s Canada was among the first states to give up the notion of becoming a strong modern state based on the concept of a unified people with a unified future. In an example where hope triumphs over despair in the dialectics of existence, Canada recognized that there is the possibility of many futures, all of them probable, even if the ruling elites have their own ideas of what the appropriate future for the country is. Therein holds the liberating magic and enticement of the Canadian experience: the notion of choices that are basic to humanity, that are infinite Blackness, the negotiations of conflicts that arise from constructed boundaries and limits. This is the realization of the possibility of any number of futures – not a specific one. This is the site for the struggle in multiculturalism in Canada: if the elite and the powerful would fully accept Blackness and allow the prevailing social orders to lose their legitimacy.

The Canadian social, political, economic, and cultural institutions and agencies have not willingly accepted these notions of death and rebirth because they were set up, as Davies and others suggest, for a specific end: to create a country, people, and identity that was White somatically, culturally, idealistically, and in status when compared to other countries, especially the United States of America. This is why setting multiculturalism as its ideal – as a universal goal that aims for a just society in a liberal democratic framework but leaves the particular outcomes indeterminate as exercises in freedom and choice – was so revolutionary for Canada. For in so doing, Canada exhibited a boldness of idealism that was not usually part of its character, a boldness, judging by some of the subsequent retreating in idealism, that might have been no more than a carnivalesque moment, or one of mere contingency.

This is unlike the United States, which has always dealt firmly with questions of its own death when they arose, by resolving them definitively, either through social integration by advocating assimilation and meritocracy as viable goals, or by the strengthening of the union at the expense of the individual states and regions. Indeed, while there is no doubt that there are significant differences, existentially, between racialized Whites and Blacks in the United States, and the way the country appears to be dealing intellectually and conceptually with this issue, at different points in its history, particularly the Civil War and the Civil Rights eras, the United States has been forced to re-examine what is its good, and in those two cases, to refute and reverse the prevailing order. These were recognitions of a problem resulting from different conceptions of good and evil. In both eras, mental and physical deaths were real, with long-lasting effects on the psyche and national consciousness.

Such is the legacy of that country's revolutionary beginning, when there was a fight to the painful end and one side won and the other was vanquished. Indeed, what contributed partly to that country's exuberance at the beginning of the second millennium was that Americans had no fear of national death. As Fukuyama suggests, Americans believe they have already witnessed the working out of history and it has ended with the triumph of this American state, a nation, according to the prevailing myths and prophesies, that should reign for a long time unless it becomes corrupted and socially diseased.[28]

Importantly, any perceived threat to the American nation is imagined as coming from outside – as in the case of international terrorism at the beginning of the twenty-first century – and not primarily from within the nation-state. A succeeding number of US presidents have declared in countless State of the Union addresses to the American Congress that the state of the union is strong and united in purpose and intent from within. As former US president Bill Clinton said in the first State of the Union message for the millennium, the twenty-first century belongs to Americans, in the same way that they had claimed the twentieth century. American elites can see only a continuous and long life for their nation, reflected in dominance at the international level and prosperity and social unity at the domestic level.

In contrast, as Frye puts it, the preoccupation in Canada is with history in the sense of venerating old institutions and ways, with preserving fully intact what the institutions have produced, and with dissecting how the country has managed to survive so far and if it can survive a bit longer. Frye says this is the necessary characteristic of Canada. Such is traditionally the fear of a cosmology: the end is always at hand in the darkness that is encroaching. In the Hegelian sense, Canada is more concerned with the uplifting, preserving, and carrying forward of specific cultural artefacts and their positioning in society than with constantly re-evaluating and making decisions anew about what to uphold, preserve, and carry forward – about, just as importantly, what is worthy of being discarded. Official Canada, then, is trapped in memory and traditions, in what Nietzsche and Thomas Paine call the dead hand of history, where possibilities that are the future have already been selected and all that is left to be done is for history and culture to work themselves out according to a specific destiny.[29] According to this thinking, any moment from then on could only result in despair.

This approach of privileging the historic as opposed to the present and the future, Frye suggests, is captured best in the Quebec motto *Je me souviens* (I remember). Compared to Americans, Canadians have less of a sense of their nation as emerging from history or shaping its own destiny, far less still the sense of it having the audacity to shape the future of others. Indeed, history and the cosmological good idealistically that have to be always unchanging – unlike in the US when they changed during different internal wars and civil rights uprisings – still shape the dominant view of Canada and Canadians. Frye observes: "The fact that a revolution is based on the success of violence is doubtlessly connected with much of the lawlessness in American history: the lynching, the labour violence, the anarchy at the frontier as it proceeded through an increasingly wild West. Canada was controlled first by the British military occupation, after which a military police force (the Mounties) moved into the northwest to keep order there. As a result violence in Canada has tended to be mainly repressive, or 'law-and-order,' violence."[30] In this view, as Frye is suggesting, Canada, then, has to be a seamless good – one that is as pure, singular, eternal, and as White as it was at the beginning of Canadian history – when, indeed, in a practical sense, Canada is in reality ontologically and existentially a hybrid or a composite, as we have been discussing. In their social construction, Canadian culture and identity are creole and syncretic, and therefore neo-mythically Black instead of the neo-mythic Whiteness that is the false consciousness of the dominant view, including that of the likes of Leacock, Davies, and others.

This part of the prevailing mythology, unlike the American Dream, offers newcomers little hope that a rebirth will bring them untried possibilities. Instead, it suggests to newcomers that they should take a step back diachronically and become part of a historical struggle that was before their time and outside their history. This is a myth that takes Others back from initial consciousness, or keeps them fixed in sensory perception, instead of bringing them into being, instead of helping them to become what they wish – instead of holding out to them the possibility of creating a new and different history from that which they entered, a history as equal partners with fellow subjects with the common identity Canadian. It is a mythology that, however, little reflects the intentions and goals of the majority of people in multicultural Canada. The contradictions and tensions arise when the people in their diversity, as the material available for the making of a country, its culture, and history, are forced to conform to discredited myths – all of which serve to create an imaginary of exclusivity for a special elect with full rights of entitlement and belonging and the power to confer or not rights and privileges on others who in the Blackness of nature do not fit dated, idealized norms of citizenry.

If Frye is right in his argument of what, based on their actions, is the presumed *essence* of Canadians, history lessons do not present multiculturalism as more than a contingent moment in Canada. It is for this reason that those still looking for justice in Canada need to seize the phenomenon of multiculturalism and examine it for the hope it flashed in all its White brightness in what, like the Greek myth of Phaeton, might be a fleeting moment, but one with lasting and even earth-shaking implications. We shall now look at the consequence of the promise of being fully included in society that multiculturalism represents for Canadians determined to be Black ethnically and racially.

# 18

# Blackness: Social and Political
# in Canada

## BLACKNESS: CLASS AND PROFESSIONALISM

From the foregoing analysis, it becomes clear that phenomenologically there is no essence of Blackness that can be discovered, ontologically and epistemologically, either within the wider Canadian society or within the more narrowly defined Black community. Assuming, however, for argument's sake, the common sense acceptance that there is such a thing as a Black ethnicity, this chapter now discusses the existentialism and ethical relations enjoyed by those who are perceived to be Black in Canada mainly because of their somatic features. The still ongoing placement of a particular group called Canadian Blacks at the bottom of the social, economic, and political pecking order in society raises issues of social justice and the question of whether Canada as a multicultural site is still committed to issues of social justice.

Engin Isin argues in *Who Is the New Citizen: Class, Territory and Identity* that the developments of citizenship and democracy happened in the breach rather than as a continuous narrative. Traditionally, gains were made through class conflict, primarily when a new class emerged to challenge and even force concessions out of the ruling elites. According to Isin, this is not only true in the European narrative but for other cultures and people.[1]

Isin contends that in liberal democracies, such as Canada, a new elitist class has emerged. Its members are the professionals that now run knowledge-based societies either as the administrators, manipulators, or experts. These are the current lords of society. This means, Isin argues, that all the classical class analyses, primarily those with a Marxist grounding and with emphasis on civic virtue, have to be re-evaluated because this new class does not fit the old moulds. Indeed, it is because society tries to treat this group as just any other working class that the professionals are deceptively so powerful. This is so primarily because they are members of an elitist group that is not constrained by nationality, nation-states, or any of the generally expected restraints of citizenship. As Isin says: "The new class is neither based on the ownership of landed property as was the aristocracy nor is it based on the ownership of industrial capital as was the modern bourgeoisie. The new class is based on ownership of knowledge and its accumulation as cultural capital."[2] Among the occupations listed in this group are those in engineering, politics, research, medicine, law, journalism, planning, advising, policy setting, consulting, writing, management, administration, adjudication, negotiation, advertising, inspection, investigation, and caring. These are professionals working for a salary, yet their pay cannot be measured in the terms used for wage earners. Unlike the traditional worker, they own and hold the social capital, thereby deciding the values and norms of the society. These professionals can be found at universities, conferences, and symposia talking about subjects that seem only to matter to them and which only they understand. Indeed, this group has become so narrow and inbred that it is virtually impossible for anyone who does not have university training to gain entry, for this is how social capital is acquired. To break into this market, whose primary clients are members of the same class, the new member must find a niche in the same knowledge-based industry.

For Isin, the professional ideal that aims to accumulate social capital has replaced the entrepreneurial ideal that had fuelled earlier advancements in liberal democracies. Like other ruling classes, the professionals are hegemonic and achieve this in their case by controlling the circulation and dissemination of ideas and ideals. They are adept at seizing power without appearing to be in control, mainly by getting politicians and the social elites to buy into their agenda. For after all, they are the pollsters and the advisors on whom governments rise and fall – and they speak a language laced with the latest technological phrases that only they fully understand. This group is in total control of the agenda of any state. Isin explains further: "Another means through which the new class members exercise power is to persuade the citizenry to speak on its behalf. In other words, professional guardians persuade citizens to appoint them on their behalf as delegates. Many members become professional advocates of causes where citizens almost religiously follow. There is a new form of priesthood where salvation is promised in this world."[3]

One result of this development is that the idea of citizenship, with its primary goal of equality among all who belong to the state, becomes even more abstract. Citizens who are not members of this professional group find that their social world is becoming less accessible and meaningful to them. They are the new socially Black and the social bondsmen to the new status White lords. The old focus of citizenship – conditions of the political (rights and obligations), territorial (urban, national, global), and moral (virtue and values) – become blurred, vague, and questionable.

Isin's analysis raises interesting questions about the social mobility of Blacks and visible minorities who receive citizenship in a state like Canada: Do they have unimpeded entry into this aristocratic class of professionals to thereby become part of a national and international elite? Can they change their bondsmanship into an unchangeable lordship? Isin notes that since 1945 there has been a major increase in membership in this professional class: "The American professional sector, for example, made up just 4 per cent of the labour force in 1900. But this sector reached 9 per cent in 1950 and more than 20 per cent by 1988. A similar rise was also noted in England ... In Canada, while the professional sector made up about 22 per cent of the labour force in 1975, it reached 33 per cent in 1994. More importantly, since 1975 the professional occupations have been alone in showing a consistent upward trend."[4]

The implications of this development are quite dire for somatic Blacks unless there is a radical change for them. Very few somatic Blacks have made it into this professional class, which means that Blacks, as a group, will continue to be shut out of power and influence. It also means that somatic Blacks will continue to be part of the unskilled world that is now undesirable and is Black in status, being a world for the immigrant and passive citizens only. Recent research supports Isin's analysis. A recent study by the Canadian Bar Association found "racial minorities" – a group that includes mainly First Nations people, Asians, and Blacks – are locked out of the legal profession and the judiciary: "In Canada, today, there are still so few people from racialized communities in law faculties, in law firms, in courthouses and in government."[5]

The report found that visible minorities face major obstacles at every turn in trying to get into the legal profession. They do not make it easily into law school, they do not go on to do graduate work, and they have difficulty getting articling positions. When they do article, they seldom get called back for jobs, and if they are hired they seldom move on to become senior partners, judges, or university lecturers. According to the report, minority lawyers do not feel accepted even in the Canadian Bar Association.

Similarly, a study by Frances Henry and Carol Tator in *Racist Discourse in Canada's English Print Media* finds that in the journalism profession, primarily the print media, there is a virtual absence of somatic Blacks and other minorities as "reflected by the absence from on-air roles such as anchors, reporters, experts, or actors and the lack of representation at all levels of staffing operations, production, and decision-making positions in communications. Their limited participation is considered the result of both overt bias and systemic discrimination."[6] The authors point to a study that showed that out of 1,731 full-time newsroom employees in Ontario in 1986 only 30 were people of colour, people with a disability, or Aboriginal peoples, and the situation has not changed much since then. "One of the primary factors in this invisibility is cultural racism and the belief in the conception of the 'rightness of (somatic) Whiteness.' Whiteness is considered the universal (hidden) norm and allows one to think and to speak as if Whiteness described and defined the world."[7]

Indeed, the implication from Isin's analysis is that the situation will get worse for somatic Blacks and, if we learn from recent history, for society in general. This would not be a realization of the hope for inclusion and other forms of social mobility that so many somatic Blacks envisaged in a multi-cultural Canada that is a liberal democracy. Indeed, it would be the exact opposite of hope – despair and despondency.

I shall now analyse how members of the group constructed as Black despite their many different ethnicities view their existence in Canada and whether they see Black as more a sign of status, and therefore a marker of race, than of ethnicity. I shall then look more closely at the reality of living for a specific group of somatic Blacks, those who immigrated to Canada from the Caribbean, where in status and culture they identified themselves as White. This will be done by looking at the dialectic tensions that arose when the immigrants were slotted into positions in the Canadian state. The dialectic tensions arose when the immigrants believed that for optimum motility and affectivity they should have been positioned as socially White whereas, based on the Canadian epistemology of Blackness, they were placed in lower positions and according to traditional perceptions about what can be known about the human body that is somatically Black and about the cultures of people from somatically Black areas of the globe. In the following section, I will examine whether Canada lives up to its claim of fairness and equality in the way it treats all ethnicities.

## BLACKS IN CANADIAN SOCIETY: EXISTENTIALISM

In the spring of 1999, Canada's largest and most liberal of newspapers began running a series of articles that examined the achievements of multi-cultural Canada in the past century and how the country was likely to fare in the new century as a liberal democracy that was multicultural. The year-long series was a study of Greater Toronto's growing ethnic and cultural mix. In general, these articles highlighted how Canada has changed demo-graphically, but perhaps just as importantly, they also illustrated how power and influence remained unchanged in the hands of the same groups over the century. In effect, they were an indication of how far Canadians have come towards the recognition of somatic and cultural Blackness in the national body politic, but they were also an indictment of how far they have fallen short of the goal of egalitarianism, multiculturalism, and colour-blindness that was first raised to the level of a national dream some forty years earlier. Some of the stories looked specifically at discrimination and the fate of minorities in Canada's largest city, Toronto. A poll conducted by the Goldfarb Consultants, the basis for these stories, found:

- that while few Torontonians (29 per cent) have personally experienced discrimination, the figures are much higher for specific ethnic and visible minority groups that were surveyed: Chinese (37 per cent), Filipinos (40 per cent), and Hispanics (37 per cent), and *more than double for Blacks (62 per cent).*[8]
- that discrimination is manifested primarily in finding work, lower wages, and being passed over for raises or promotions. While 11 per cent of Torontonians cite finding a job as their most pressing problem, the numbers are more than double for Blacks (27 per cent), west Asians/Arabs (24 per cent), and South Asians (23 per cent).[9]
- that the situation was just as bleak for Blacks when it comes to enjoying the good life in Toronto. Most studies show that almost two-thirds of Canadian Blacks live in the greater Toronto area, with smaller numbers in Halifax, Montreal, Edmonton, Winnipeg, and Windsor, Ontario. How well they fared in Toronto, where some 65 per cent of Canadian Blacks live, is an indication of how Blacks are treated nationally. According to the same Goldfarb poll, half the Black community – constitutive for the poll of somatic Blacks of many ethnicities – is very uncomfortable with the level of violence and drug use in schools, with the incidence of both being higher for Blacks than for any other ethnic group.
- that Blacks also expressed the most dissatisfaction with life in Toronto among the groups surveyed in the poll, although overall, 80 per cent are at least somewhat satisfied with life in Toronto, a measurement of satisfaction that was lower than for other presumed ethnic groups. "Blacks feel they're treated unfairly by the police, courts and the media and that other Torontonians don't understand them. Thirty-eight per cent feel Toronto has become worse in the past two years and 31 per cent say it will get worse in the next two." In general, while two-thirds of Torontonians think politicians represent Toronto's diversity at least somewhat well, 38 per cent of Blacks, as opposed to 33 per cent in the general population, think politicians do not represent them well at all. They also feel that negative stereotyping and jobs are big problems and 28 per cent feel they are not at all or only a little accepted. "Blacks in each and every category, more than anyone else, feel discriminated against."[10]

This research coincided with findings of the Commission on Systemic Racism in the Ontario Criminal Justice System that the "provincial incarceration rate for Black adult males in Ontario was five times that for white adult males, proportionate to their representation in the population."[11] As legal scholar Clayton Mosher explains:

The report found that Black males were significantly more likely than Whites or Chinese to be stopped by the police and that a disturbingly high percentage of Blacks perceived that judges treat Blacks worse than they do Whites. In a study comparing the criminal justice system's processing of 821 Black and 832 White adult male offenders charged with various crimes, the commission found that Blacks were less likely than Whites to be released by police before trial, and were more likely to be refused bail, even when other legally relevant factors such as prior record and seriousness of offence were controlled for. In the same sample of offenders, 49 per cent of Blacks convicted of possession of drugs, compared with 18 per cent of White offenders, were incarcerated. As the commission report noted, these findings "indicate that some Black convicted men were sentenced to prison when White convicted men with the same personal and case characteristics were not sentenced to prison."[12]

As Mosher further notes, similar trends and attitudes towards Blacks were discernable across the country and represent a picture where historically Blacks have not been treated fairly by the legal and judicial system in the Canada.

Exclusion and marginalization by the state are not supposed to be part of the new Canada – the multicultural Canada, where opportunities are open to all, where groups are recognized as equal, where the elevation of culture and community symbols are privileged, where governments use civil society to underpin policies aimed at strengthening the welfare state and egalitarianism.

In keeping with this analysis is the emerging body of work on somatic and cultural Blacks in the educational system across Canada, but particularly in areas of high Black concentration such as Toronto, Montreal, and Halifax. George Stefa Dei has quantified and analysed the high "drop-out" rates for Blacks in the school system and has suggested that in some areas, like Toronto, the remedy might be to introduce Black Focus schools, where Black students would be treated sensitively as minorities in Canada. While it is not appropriate to enter a fuller discussion on Black focus schools here, the wider point that Dei and others are making is that some somatically and culturally Black students feel they are forced to perform a type of Blackness in the schools that results in missed opportunities normatively and in failure by the wider societal standards.[13]

## WEST INDIAN IMMIGRANTS:
## DOWNWARD SOCIAL MOBILITY

Jorge Duany describes the types and quality of immigrants that left the Caribbean for North America since the Second World War. He suggests that the immigrants are motivated and looking for a better standard of living. He assumes them to be the type of people who would see politics as a way to improve their lot. "The constant movement of people from one Caribbean territory suggests that they are not pushed and pulled passively by economic forces but rather that they are actively pursuing and creating new opportunities for social mobility through migration."[14]

Duany suggests that Caribbean immigrants tend to be young people from largely urban centres in their home countries and well educated. They are mainly somatically Black. "A sizeable minority of Caribbean migrants have a college education. Hence, Caribbean migration is strongly elective of the middle and higher educational levels of the population."[15]

In addition, Duany argues that Caribbean immigrants do not fit the stereotypes of unskilled country bumpkins for "as many as four thousand Caribbean professionals, such as doctors, engineers, teachers and nurses form part of the annual 'brain drain' from the region." By our categories, then, these immigrants are White idealistically, culturally, and in status. Arriving in North America, Caribbean immigrants suffer what Duany calls a downward occupational mobility, as they end up almost invariably on the lower rungs of the receiving economies. This means that on arrival they undergo a transfiguration that changes their "primordial" nature: however, this time the change is dystopically from idealized, cultural, and status Whiteness to the opposite categories in Blackness. Only their somatic categorizations remain unchanged, yet, ironically, skin colour becomes their primary identity marker and that on which ethical decisions will be made in regard to their motility and affectivity, and on whether they should be included or excluded from society.[16]

Contrary to the hope inherent in multiculturalism, somatic Blackness, and as we discussed earlier, a corresponding Black ethnicity, are still equated automatically with status Blackness and its lack of social mobility and social justice; and contrary to the promise of life and rebirth promised by multiculturalism, these Canadians who were narrowly defined in a finite way as Black found themselves denied the full expanse of the infinite virtues, aspirations, abilities, and potentials of all humanity. In the new classification, which was a return to a pre-multicultural sensibility, their finite Blackness associated them with racialized inferiority and denied them the creativity, genius, and freedoms of their Blackness in humanity. Indeed, with this classification they found that, contrary to the promise of multiculturalism, their contingent nature was assumed to be their Canadianness and what was universal and necessary about them was their Blackness – in effect a reversal of what obtains for other ethnicized Canadians, where their ethnicity is the contingent component.

Looking at Caribbean immigration to Canada in general, but specifically to Toronto, Henry points out that the dominant groups in Canada had set up obstacles to a successful integration of Caribbean migrants into the society by denying them equal access to goods and resources. "Thus, people of Caribbean origin face employment, housing, and other forms of racial discrimination."[17] It is possible to draw a profile of the Black community, as did researchers at the McGill Consortium for Ethnicity and Strategic Social Planning in a study called *Diversity, Mobility and Change – The Dynamics of Black Communities in Canada.*[18] The researchers found that the Canadian Black population is mainly immigrant, with 70 per cent of the immigrants coming from the Caribbean. They also found that, contrary to popular opinion, somatic Blacks, especially the immigrants, were better educated than members of the wider society.

But it is a community with severe problems that require political attention. Single parenthood is twice as high in the community as in the wider society; about 31.5 per cent of the somatic Black population lives in poverty compared with 15.7 per cent for the wider population; somatic Blacks have substantially lower incomes; they are less likely to be self-employed or supported by investments; and they are less likely to hold senior management positions. In the workplace, they are more concentrated in manufacturing, technical, and in recreational and service sectors. The men work largely in factories and the women in better-paying jobs in the tourism and medical service sectors, for example as nurses and care givers. The picture is of a community that is excluded from the political and economic spheres of the country, and is a picture that is not faithful to the positivity of inclusiveness that is conceptualized in multiculturalism.

## SOCIAL AND POLITICAL IMPLICATIONS

John Porter challenged the notion that the "caste-like status" in which some groups found themselves in Canada had anything to do with their recent arrival in the country. While immigrants tended to take the low-paying jobs on arrival, entering society primarily as socially determined bondsmen, "over time the position of entrance status may be improved or it may be a permanent caste-like status ... Most of Canada's minority groups have at some time had this entrance status. Some, but not all, have moved out of it."[19]

Canada's immigration policy and its methods of social incorporation were developed to prevent social mobility. Immigrants were chosen because they fitted a specific stereotype for doing a specific job, but such choice was based on group characteristics rather than individual desires. Porter quotes

Clifford Sifton, the architect of Canada's immigration policy at the beginning of the twentieth century: "When I speak of quality, I have in mind
something that is quite different from what is in the mind of the average
writer or speaker upon the question of immigration. I think a stalwart peasant in a sheep-skin coat, born on the soil, whose forefathers had been farmers for generations, with a stout wife and half-a-dozen children, is good
quality."[20] This is the same perception of the usefulness of specific groups
for inferior positions in Canada that saw the entry of Chinese into Canada,
primarily to build the transcontinental railway. In any case, it was only
once it was recognized that without the help of the Chinese the project
would be postponed indefinitely that the Chinese were permitted to enter
Canada.

Not until 1962 were coloured people from Commonwealth countries looked upon
as possible immigrants, except for a small number who were allowed in – without
families, or in the appropriate sex ratio to form families – to work as domestic servants, an entrance status previously held by lower class British and eastern European females. Many of these non-British immigrants went into low status
occupations because there was a fairly high rate of illiteracy among them, and a few
of them spoke the charter group languages of English or French. This cultural barrier at the time of entry hardened into a set of historical relations tending to perpetuate entrance status.[21]

Porter did not make the point then, possibly because he was unaware, but
many of the Caribbean women who came to Canada in the 1960s as nan-
nies were "overqualified" for any entry-level jobs. Many of them were
highly educated, spoke English, and were simply using the only means possible to get into the country. One notable example is Jean Augustine, who
arrived from Grenada, where she was a schoolteacher, to work as a nanny.
Unsuited for the job, because she was operating at a class much lower than
what she had worked at in her native land, Augustine soon left the employment, completed graduate school, became one of the first Black principals
in Toronto, and in 2000 was elected for her third consecutive term as a
member of Parliament, where she has at different times been parliamentary
assistant to the prime minister and head of the women's caucus for the ruling Liberal party. In 2002, Augustine became the first self-identifying
somatically Black woman to be made a member of the Privy Council when
she was made a junior minister with responsibility for multiculturalism.
However, her achievements were exceptional and many talented somatically Black women have been unable to escape their initial placement in
Canadian society.[22]

Porter also broke ranks with the Canadian elites when he suggested that
the melting-pot model of social integration practised in the United States

was more equitable and just than the Canadian mosaic of communities, on which multiculturalism was based. "It might be said that the idea of an ethnic mosaic, as opposed to the idea of the melting pot, impedes the processes of social mobility. The difference in ideas is one of the principal distinguishing features of United States and Canadian society at the level of social psychology as well as that of social structure."[23] It is worth noting that even in choosing the title of his work, Porter was responding to an earlier study, John Murray Gibbon's *Canadian Mosaic: The Making of a Northern Nation*. This work depicted Canada as a place where thirty "races" of Europe, each with its own distinct history, culture, and language, were living in peace. In language that is mindful of our earlier epigraph by Hegel on light, composites, and darknesses, Gibbon wrote: "The Canadian people today presents itself as a decorated surface, bright with the inlays of separate coloured pieces, not painted in colours blended with brush on palette. The original background in which the inlays are set is still visible, but these inlays cover more space than that background, and so the ensemble may truly be called a mosaic."[24]

The Gibbon study noted that its publication coincided with a debate on the future of Canada, a debate with two characteristics. As Gibbon stated, one side of the discussion was suggesting that Canada should fuse these races into a single Canadian race that was "being superimposed on the original Indian races." The side proposing assimilation said that Canada should meld these groups into a common nationality. "Others believe in trying to preserve for the future Canadian race the most worthwhile qualities and traditions that each racial group brought with it."[25] To this end, Gibbon's book was to be an inventory of the customs and traditions of the European races in Canada.

A second reason for the book was that Canada was looking to increase its number of immigrants, partly to offset "the drain of population into the United States." The book would serve as a guide to the main features of the immigrants. Canadians could decide, based on the evidence of the performance of earlier groups, what kind of welcome they should give to the new immigrants and how they should expect them to behave. The book was to be part of the Canadian epistemology on the ontology of the stranger, traces of which can still be found in the current immigration policy. For example, Gibbon argued that "the character" of any people should be examined for a true assessment of the members of the ethnicity. With this knowledge, it becomes easier to understand the social qualities of this people "since human beings are so much the creation of their environment ... We should consider first the physical background, the kind of country in which that people lives – whether forested or open country, whether mountainous or level, whether any or much of it is lake or river country, whether it lends itself to grain or fruit farming, so that it can grow sufficient food, whether it is served by roads, waterways or railways providing easy communications between its different areas."[26]

It was also necessary to make a predetermination of the races and groups based on the social and political conditions in which they lived. This would assist in understanding and positioning them correctly in Canada. As Gibbon advised:

We should ask ourselves – how did the people get there? – are their neighbours friendly? – have they been troubled much by wars with other peoples or by civil wars? – what are their religious beliefs – are they a home-loving people, or are they restless and inclined to be on the move? – are the women expected to do hard manual labour? – do they have large families? – what sort of schools do they have? – are they music lovers? – what are their sports? – do they like to work together, or are they inclined to act and get things for themselves? – are they the kind of people who do just what they are told? – or do they like to criticise and think the world should be reformed?[27]

But in searching through the genesis and essence of the ethnicity, Canadians would be looking also for a trace of something else. The hope would be to find the individual who is the embodiment of these national and racial characteristics, for in the end these questions can only be asked concretely of an individual, not of a nation. The individual can only be assessed and placed in a racial manner – on the basis of a criterion which states whether the individual is as good as or better than the next person from his or her group, or even from the wider society.[28] It is worth noting that in this concept of a mosaic, culture and group is everything. In terms of integration, individuality counted for very little.

Reitz and others argue that the situation in modern Canada might not be the same as what Porter found in the 1960s: "Subsequent researchers have criticized Porter's analysis but focused almost entirely on the mobility of minority-group immigrants after they arrive. This research essentially has disproved the hypothesis of lower mobility rates for non-Wasp immigrants. There are no greater barriers to minority group mobility in Canada for those of European origins, at least by comparison to the majority population or to British-origin immigrants. This part of the strategy to maintain a 'vertical mosaic' seems to have failed."[29] Reitz might be too quick to come to this conclusion, however, for the connection between somatic Blackness and status Blackness subverts the modern myth of a Canada without a hierarchy of ethnicities and reaffirms the validity of Porter's assessment. The treatment of somatic Blacks in Canada reinforces the notion of a racial divide. While some European immigrants once classified as Black can cross over this divide and become White, it is a divide, as Simmons and others have shown, that is too wide and too deep for somatic Blacks, whether they be immigrants or native born.

Reitz's analysis, ironically, points to this conclusion. For example, in comparing the placement of somatically Black immigrants in the United States and Canada, Reitz notes that somatically Black immigrants start at a higher earning level in Canada than do their counterparts who went to the United States. Reitz takes the average salary of the White male as the norm in Canada and the United States. How and if the norm is attained becomes the measurement for social mobility and justice. His study finds that in the US somatically Black immigrant men receive 54 per cent of the wages of the top White males; in Canada they receive 70 per cent. The same is true generally for somatically Black women, whose entry-level earnings are also higher in Canada. Reitz places their average earnings at 46 per cent of the male earnings in Canada and 39 per cent in the United States. As Reitz explains: "As with White immigrants, the explanation for this difference is the higher relative position of women in general in Canada; the position of Black immigrant women relative to mainstream women is the same in both countries. What this means for Black immigrant women in Canada is that their actual entry level is approximately equal to the entry for *White* immigrant women in the United States."[30]

A study by Carl James, Dwaine Plaza, and Clifford Jansen, as presented in a paper titled *Issues of Race in Employment: Experiences of Caribbean Women in Toronto*, examined employment participation rates among immigrants from the Caribbean living in Toronto to find out if there were earning differences between males and females. In findings similar to those of Reitz, they found that, "whether born in the Caribbean or having immigrated at a young age, men and women of the Caribbean origin all seemed to be at a disadvantage in the world of work, even if they had completed some or most of their primary, secondary, or post-secondary education in Canada. Our research compares unemployment rates, proportions in full and part-time work, proportions in managerial/professional occupations (including management/administration, natural and social sciences, teaching, medicine and artistic) and their wages incomes in 1990."[31] Two points flow from this study. First, the researchers found that unemployment rates for Caribbean-born women were higher than for Caribbean-born males and for the general Toronto population. The rates were 23 per cent and 11 per cent for Caribbean females and males, respectively, compared with rates of 7 and 6 per cent for the wider population. Foreign-trained Caribbean men earned more and had higher levels of employment. However, Caribbean-educated females had higher proportions of managerial and professional jobs than their male counterparts. Second, they indicate that Black women were more likely to work in jobs related to their education:

Our survey data shows that among all respondents who were in jobs, most were in clerical – with a more or less equal number of men and women (22 percent). Those in professional occupations were teachers, mainly high school (16 percent), social work (15 per cent), and medical, mainly nurses (seven per cent). Fifteen per cent were managers, and eight per cent were skilled and unskilled workers. Those in sales, services, and government administration accounted for six, five, and five per cent, respectively. Just over half were working in a field related to their work, but this was more likely the case for Black women (56 percent) compared to Black men (45 percent).[32]

The researchers found that while somatically Black immigrant women might be perceived as being "triply minoritized" in that they are female, somatically Black, and immigrant, they have nonetheless been able to use the resources and skills that are available to them to "effectively navigate the opportunity structures."[33] And they have been able to make their gains while more often performing as single parents relative to the rest of the Toronto population. This study indicates that 8 per cent of the Caribbean population were female single parents compared to 3 per cent for the rest of the city, and that 15 per cent of the Caribbean population were children living in female single parent homes, compared with 5 per cent for the city in general. I shall return to this point in my penultimate chapter.

### MOTILITY AND AFFECTIVITY: SOCIAL MOBILITY AND EDUCATION

As Reitz notes in the above section, lower entry levels are generally true for all immigrants in the United States, and interprets this as being part of a rite of passage as the immigrant acquires social capital and learns how to master the competitive risk of operating in the society. Reitz also argues that the lower status for immigrants in general in the US results from the level of education being generally higher there compared to Canada, so that only the most highly educated immigrants could expect to enter the society with an elite status. Another significant reason for the higher entry level in Canada is that Canada is more selective in choosing immigrants, as it puts greater emphasis on education, skills, and general ability to fit into the Canadian economy than does the United States, where the emphasis is on family reunion. In addition, even though there has been some change in perception of late, traditionally the Canadian educational system was considered to be inferior to that of the United States and some parts of Western Europe.

Thus, being better-educated in general and relative also to Canadians, immigrants arriving in Canada now come with higher levels of social capital and therefore enter the workforce at higher levels than in the United

States. To stop here would be to draw an incomplete picture, however, for there is also the problem of what happens after they have been placed in Canadian society. In addition, educational levels have been rising in Canada over the past thirty years so that even the best educated immigrants from around the world are now finding themselves in entry-level positions that are lower than those for immigrants in general a generation ago. For somatic Blacks, however, there are also other extenuating circumstances. As earlier analysis in this chapter shows, systemic barriers and racism enter into play and, in the case of the somatically Black male and the somatically Black family, there is a downward social mobility towards the "natural" level for Blacks that has been established over generations. In the end, the immigrant somatic Black and the native-born somatic Black end up in the same position – at the bottom of the social order.[34] Levels of education as an indication of social capital, or of currency in Kymlicka's societal culture, do not seem to make a difference in Canada for somatic Blacks. The result in general is status Blackness.

An examination of what happens in the United States paints a different picture. Julius Williams Wilson suggests that race as an issue has become less significant for the social mobility of Blacks in the US. Unlike in Canada, there is a strong and vibrant somatically Black middle class in the United States. Those that remain in lower status positions are those Blacks who are primarily the victims of economic decline generally, such as when specific industries die or when business moves out of urban areas. Such events do not specifically affect the rise of the Black middle and upper classes.[35]

Writing in *The Truly Disadvantaged*, Wilson notes that an underclass among Blacks was created in the United States beginning in the 1940s, and that this process coincided with the escape of some upwardly mobile and educated somatic Blacks into the American middle class because of civil rights gains.[36] But there was also a rise of single-parent families among Blacks, primarily because of the failure of significant numbers of somatically Black males to be fully incorporated into the mainstream, primarily in the workforce. The lack of jobs destroyed the social standing of the males in their families and wider communities, and accounts in part for socially deviant behaviour among somatically Black males and the development of the typical female-led Black family.

This is the same kind of deviant behaviour that at the beginning of this new millennium in multicultural Canada is a growing concern in Toronto's somatically Black community and to a lesser extent in Montreal. This concern has produced heated debate in the somatically Black press – some of which has also spilled over into the mainstream press – over the increasing levels of "Black-on-Black" violence that by one account resulted in the death of 100 youths in five years, the failure of somatic Blacks to co-operate with the police investigating these murders, and the general feeling of malaise and exclusion among somatically Black youth.[37] A statement in one of the community newspapers addressed this issue: "We need to end the marginalization and hopelessness among our youth. We need a plan of action from all levels of government and other sectors of society for jobs, skills training, youth programming, affordable housing, community services and income support. We need to restore hope through action now."[38] Wilson comments specifically on the impact of joblessness: "The weight of the evidence on the relationship between the employment status of men, and family life and married life suggests that the increasing rate of joblessness among Black men merits serious consideration as a major underlying factor in the rise of Black single mothers and female-headed households. Moreover, when the factor of joblessness is combined with high Black-male mortality and incarceration rates, the proportion of Black men in stable economic situations is even lower than that conveyed in the current unemployment and labor-force figures."[39]

It is possible to see a parallel between the development of an underclass among somatic Blacks in the United States and concerns that such a class has been developing in Canada. Indeed, a strong claim can be made that Canada's immigration policy since the 1960s and the different ways that somatically Black males and females were incorporated into Canadian society resulted in the development of female-led families similar to those in the United States. We have already seen that somatically Black females earn more than their male counterparts and that overall the somatically Black family does not do as well as mainstream families or as well as families in other visible minority or immigrant groups. Part of the result has been that somatically Black females earn more than males; thereby creating new tensions in somatically Black families; and males also find it harder to fit into Canadian society.

When they examined Caribbean migration to Canada between 1967 and 1987, Simmons and Turner noticed this trend towards the social advancement of the somatically Black females compared to their male counterparts. This immigration was female-led both in numbers and in terms of which of the sexes was more welcome in Canada and received better entry-level placement in the society:

Our findings indicate that Caribbean women have a fundamental leadership role in the Canadian case. Based on several studies of recent non-European origin immigrants in Canada, we also anticipated that prejudice and economic disadvantage would be important features of Caribbean immigrant experience. These expectations were born out. In addition, the findings reinforce existing studies on differences between male and female Caribbean immigrants in economic achievement. The greater relative success of Caribbean women immigrants is the result of an intersection between migrant culture, Canadian policy and labour force opportunity in Canada.[40]

Canadian policy towards immigration from the Caribbean was initially based on a demand for cheap female labour.[41] The women came primarily as caregivers and to work in the service sectors. Most of them were young and unmarried, which, as Simmons and Turner argue, was the policy's intention. Ultimately, the partners of the women began arriving in Canada and eventually the policy was changed so that more Caribbean males were allowed into Canada. Children began to join their mothers as well. These developments resulted in females taking on the leadership roles in somatically Black families: they earned more and they sponsored spouses and children. There being more women than men, many women also had difficulty finding suitable male partners of marriageable status who were somatically Black. The somatically Black men that arrived tended to be married or to get married soon after arrival, but "social and economic conditions in Canada were generally less hospitable to Caribbean men and family gender roles disputes in the new context did not help [create overall happiness in Canada]."[42]

In a later study, Simmons and Plaza found that inequalities between somatically Black males and females eventually became more ingrained and institutionalized, especially in how the two groups attained social capital in Canada that would allow them to fit in better. The researchers found that the women tended to be better educated. While "young Black women have a profile of educational achievement somewhat lower than that of other ethnic groups," their level was still higher than that of somatically Black males.[43] As Simmons and Plaza argue, these factors have a clear bearing on how somatically Black males and females are positioned in Canadian society.

Blacks aged twenty to twenty-four in Toronto are quite diverse in terms of their educational attainment. First of all, sex differences in HLS [Highest Level of Schooling] are very large. While roughly two thirds of young Black women have gone beyond secondary schooling, only half of young Black men have done so. Black women who go beyond secondary schooling are roughly divided between those who do technical studies (32 percent) and those who do university studies (31 percent). In contrast, Black men who proceed beyond secondary studies are more likely to pursue technical studies (28 percent) than university studies (20 percent). Technical studies cover various practical fields in office work, repairs, construction and manufacturing.[44]

Simmons and Plaza note generally, as others have found in terms of long-term income prospects, that somatically Black children born of immigrants "are still not going to university in proportions equal to the average in the host society."[45] They also suggest that somatic Blacks with higher education might eventually find themselves in a higher class than those with less education, but this prediction which would be consistent with Wilson's findings in the United States has not yet shown up in further studies. It would seem, then, that race is not as insignificant in Canada as Wilson suggests it is in the United States. Indeed, Porter's conclusion that some immigrants remain held in a caste-like placement is still highly valid for somatic Blacks in Canada. Moreover, it can be argued that through its immigration policy Canada added numbers to a somatically Black underclass that historically was always present in Canada, and socially Black. In this respect, Canada constructed an ethnic group based on racial characteristics.

This chapter began in an attempt to examine the question of who is Black in Canada and whether Blackness is a genuine ethnicity or effectively a racial categorization masquerading as ethnicity. The argument revolved around what can be known and made out of somatic Blackness. Is it an indication of an unchangeable essence, or are the somatic features merely part of the outer husk that is the changeable body in the Trudeau worldview of multiculturalism? From the analysis in the chapter, it is apparent that Canada has not yet fully come to terms as promised in multiculturalism with one key form of idealistic Blackness – the somatic. In the next chapter, I will now show why this is.

# 19

# New Ideals of Canadian Blackness

TOWARDS A NEW CONSCIOUSNESS

In this chapter, I make a fuller examination of Canadian identity and question whether, even in this post-modern moment, official Canada is still wedded to a modernist notion of the Canadian good that is based on original racial categories associated with the ethno-racial register or if Canada has instead opened itself to the positive promises that are conceptually inherent in full multiculturalism. I argue, ethically, not only for recognition of other goods, but for a reversal and return, diachronically, to a moment of creation as is suggested neo-mythically to be necessary for converting multicultural from a contingent to a necessary moment in the Canadian narrative. This is necessary: for not only must there be a synchronous change in course, but, as in any good Greek or Shakespearean tragedy, there should be public refutation of past actions and there ought to be a publicly stated attempt to make amends. The change cannot be surreptitious nor muted if it is to be affective and effective. There must be a return diachronously to a moment of pre-creation, where the old good is overthrown, and another of the possibilities for good is selected and tried.

Rational thought would suggest that the new choice for Canada's good must take into account the experiences of the past if the same old changes and ensuing drama are not to be repeated. They must therefore flow out of what is already known to be contained dialectically in the infinity. But at the same time, idealistically, the new beginning must be fashioned out of the dust and material that is the changeable body of history – out of the finite options that are already available and known. The new good would thus be the breath or the unchangeable spirit that inhabits this body. I will make this argument in terms of Canada's growing demand for immigrants.

Immigrants have become the Hegelian mediator in the Canadian dialectic. They are in one form the unchangeable, in another the changeable, and in a third a combination of both that is a new form. Immigrants are the material that will produce the Canadian bodies. I will look at how immigration is forcing Canada to re-evaluate what is the Canadian good and who is, and who can become, a Canadian. The immigrant, to become fully Canadian, will have to undergo the transformation or death from changeable to unchangeable, this being the second negation that makes him or her fully a citizen. Similarly, the Canadian spirit must become changeable to inhabit the body of the new kind of immigrant. And the immigrant, as a representative of the old history, must be transformed into the new being that is fully the Canadian of the future.

To this end, and by looking into the dialectics of the mythologies that produced it as a social consciousness, Canada has to come to terms with a mental death of the finite concepts which have been used historically to portray it if there is be a hope for a rebirth into something better. This is the death of the immigrant, for she or he now willingly accepts a transformation from the old finite self into a new person: into the infinite as a Canadian that is a full moral and democratic agent with choices, possibilities, and freedoms; it is the mental death of the state, which must change as ideals change. Finally, I will argue, in this chapter, that Canada has to reopen its debate on race and ethnicity so as to deal effectively with the systemic racism that is the source of the difference between Canadian political rhetoric about a just society and Canada's actual practices that still leave groups of people – of so many different ethnicities – out of the mainstream because of the colour of their skin.

## BLACKNESS AS WHITENESS: MULTICULTURALISM AND CREATION

In these early years of a new millennium, Canada appears once again to be at a turning point, to be stressing finite limits where it has to make choices, some of which might require Canada to return, mythologically and intellectually, to its pre-creation moment, when a decision was made on what kind of country should be created and for whose benefit and entitlements. As Will Kymlicka asserts, "it would seem that we are at a pivotal point in the history of race relations in Canada."[1] This is crucial as race has always been important to the construction of the imagination of Canadians and to who is a Canadian, even if, with time, particularly from the 1960s onwards, it became politically opportunistic to mask issues of race with those of ethnicity. The issue of race is never far from the Canadian consciousness, for it can never be fully negated. There is always more than a trace that is left phenomenologically in the movement from one understanding of consciousness to another. Race is always already part of the national discourse. It seems also impossible, and one may wonder if it is even desirable, to escape the ethno-racial register of knowing in order to be embedded fully and exclusively in the neo-mythic register, to arrive as a self-consciousness at a point, indeed, where race does not matter and there is a new spirit of modernity.[2]

In the young age of this new millennium, the dialectic of freedom that is human history appears once again to be applying pressure on what has become the old system that is the West in general and Canada in particular. Building to a head, the pressure has to be dissipated or the system could collapse under the weight of growing inequalities. The old way has run up against its limits and boundaries, which is part of the continuing dialectical process that has produced a history of ever deeper meanings of freedom. The growing inequalities can no longer be easily explained away as unintended results while the system produces its idealized good. And in Canada, what in a Hegelian analysis would be seen as contradictions in a Canadian moment of unhappy consciousness can only be seen as absurdities in this modern time of enlightenment and rationalism.

The problem is that the system, based on the materials that it is using, seems destined to produce mainly inequalities even though it is part of a dialectic that has already supposedly passed through the unhappy consciousness of *A Just Society* and emerged into the enlightenment and reason of multiculturalism. It can do no better because of the way it was set up to function. Race remains a significant part of daily life for a growing segment of the Canadian citizenry even though, normatively, and based on its rhetoric of multiculturalism, Canada is committed to eradicating inequalities, and race is supposed to have been eliminated from the national consciousness. This is a case where reason itself – what is produced by the system as a single, pure, and intended good – is subject to a lordship and bondage relationship. Reason contains conceptually a racist desire and an anti-racist one struggling for dominance – to become the dominant way of determining the "actual" lived experiences in the ethical relationship that is now called multiculturalism. It is for this reason that I think it is a mistake to treat racism as if it were an aberration or as something that can be corrected or eradicated through dealing with seemingly isolated cases. Representing the old way of perceiving the good, racism is deeply systemic and psychological and is born out of the perceived quest for freedom. That this particular quest might now seem to be misguided and antisocial is only because we have changed our evaluations and rationalizations – but everyone might not be of the same mind to accept the new over the old.

In a multicultural country that is a liberal democracy, rational individuals have the freedom to assert an ethnicity of choice or to reject it when appropriate, while remaining unchangeably Canadian. But for many members of the Canadian family, their ethnicity of choice is not recognized and instead must be homogenized into an unchangeable ethnicity that is Black, or, as Hegel says, into the equivalent of the night of indistinguishables in which all cows are Black. Just as important, this is an unchangeableness that becomes a prison of full determination from which the individual cannot easily escape through an act of free choice. The agent remains bound even if it is part of a mature dialectic of freedom. Such are the absurdities still possible from this rationalist system.

These irrationalities are reflected, dialectically, in three specific areas – two being universal in nature and one domestic – that are likely to change Canada significantly. They are, first, the increasing need for Canada to renew and even augment its population base through levels of immigration that have not been needed since the second decade of the twentieth century, when Canada received 400,000 immigrants in 1913; second, the impact of globalization and the development of transnational citizenship that challenges old notions of citizenship, belonging, and entitlement in a modern state; and last, internally, the continuing struggle between those holding on to old dreams of carving up Canada into homelands for either of two European groups that traditionally were the heroes and villains in the symbolic Greek tragedy that is Canadian history. This is a tragedy in which political and social death always appears as lamentable.

The seemingly unchangeable issue is still one that is based on somatic characteristics: what is to be done with Canadians that are somatically Black, a group that historically has been the unchangeable Other and the marginalized and, at times, excluded in Canada? As Kymlicka sees it, Canada has two choices: It can institute "meaningful reforms" that redefine the Canadian good and unchangeable within the existing limits and allow people constructed as Black to overcome racial barriers and follow the historical pattern of immigrant incorporation into the society over time.[3] Or, it can continue on the same course, dialectically, between established notions of what is changeless and what can be changed so that "the drift towards the sort of oppositional subculture found amongst some African-Americans could snowball."[4] This drifting unintentionally into confrontation and a further aggravation of the Canadian unhappy consciousness, Kymlicka fears, could stem from the calcifying of the disadvantaged into caste-like social positions or from increasing social conflict between members of disadvantaged groups seeking social mobility as an escape into privileged positions from which they appear to be excluded in Canada's agencies and institutions.

Meaningful reforms on their own, despite the prescience in Kymlicka's warning, might not be enough, if they amount merely to a re-arrangement almost exclusively on the ethno-racial register of a finite order within the framework of liberalism. The very limits and boundaries might have to be re-established. The finite must pass into the infinite. What might be required to stop the drift into oppositional subcultures *and* to break down racial barriers based on somatic, cultural, and idealistic values is a fundamental restructuring of the Canadian nation-state, something that mainstream Canadians have so far been reluctant to consider. Such a radical choice can only be exercised diachronously, for it goes to the heart of what Canada is: it involves who the country should be constructed of; who should have the rights and benefits of full citizenship; and whether Canada should accept, in principle, the ideals of merit and equality of opportunity for social and distributive justice.[5]

This is not a synchronous decision that simply calls for a moment's pause to reflect on how well the existing good compares to an idealized good and what tinkering might be necessary to ensure the expected outcome. Rather, the very outcome has to be up for discussion, which means the discussion must take place before the re-creation starts. There must be an opportunity not only for recognition, but for refutation and reversal. In the Hebraic tradition, this is a moment of reflection that ensues after the command to "Let us make man." It is the key ontological and existential decision of in *whose* likeness and, ontologically, with what somatic and phenotypic features (hu)man is to be created. It is only after that decision that another can be made about the moral codes and ethical relations that will govern the created humans.[6] Only by addressing these questions – and by deciding who should be entitled to become a Canadian and whether all Canadians should be genuinely equal – will Canada get out of the political morass of the ambiguities, for example, in its immigration policy.

The Canadian identity that emerges from this new ethical determination would be based on recognizing that the existing system has reached its limits and boundaries and needs to be transformed, in this case, radically. The old system must be transformed back into the material that is the dust from which it came and the dust from which new bodies can be moulded and new and different spirits placed in them. Again, this is why racism and structural inequalities are not unintended consequences in the liberal democratic state that is multicultural Canada, and the system appears incapable of eradicating these inequalities according to its own devices. Racism and its attendant social, political, cultural, and economic inequalities are both contingent and necessary for the proper functioning of Canadian society as intended and established. Canada's social system appears incapable or unwilling to speedily offer social mobility as a form of social justice for individuals in some "ethnic" groups.

At the same time, there is no mechanism or method that would allow individuals to escape from the prison of ethnicity, because the idea of Canada starts with the notion of groups of peoples operating according to different social cultures that somehow collectively produce a national consciousness. Those without a societal consciousness –that is, those lacking a group identity ascribed by the wider society – must be given one for the system to function; otherwise they would be left out, and the system would be inefficient. Neither can they, as individuals, engage the system without first being sponsored and legitimated by an ethnic group, for traditionally rights and entitlements have flowed from the notion that Canada consists of a number of ethnic "homelands" or communities, whether these homelands are socially constructed as actual lived experiences or are still solely in the imagination.

The Canadian system is still intent on producing the good for which it was originally established: to deliver entitlements and benefits of belonging to a mainstream group that is idealistically, somatically, and culturally White, and whose members enjoy the fruits of living in their homeland. This cosmological good applies to two main ethno-racial groups. The first is immigrants from specific parts of the world – and having economic and professional standing – that are traditionally constructed in Canadian immigration as somatically and/or culturally Black. They arrive in the country and are remoulded as Black in status and by their positioning are unable to fully enjoy the entitlements reserved for the neo-mythic Whites separated into deserving such status by their Canadian citizenship. The second group is made up of somatic and cultural Blacks who are unable or even incapable of washing themselves White in Canada's prevailing secular ideology. In this way, we have the construction of Blackness, which includes characteristics based on the somatic, the cultural, and status.

Currently, a Black ethnicity is necessary to account for the treatment of a group of people, most of whom freely immigrated to Canada as individuals, and who were chosen through a universal and clear points system that "cherry picks" the world's brightest and best with no regard, theoretically, for ethnicity, nationality, or race. Coming from different ethnicities and nationalities, these individuals find themselves homogenized under a Black ethnicity. This is the only way the state can recognize them, the only way these immigrants can make a primary claim for entitlement. Once placed in that *ethnicity*, there is no escape for the individual: there is equality of opportunity and little recognition of individual merit for members of some groups. There is no choice of entry or exit for the individual into this ethnicity. But as Kymlicka argues, this is contrary to liberal values, especially those at the heart of what he calls multicultural liberalism, and in which category he places Canada. He explains what should instead obtain:

We can specify a number of constraints that must be respected on a distinctly liberal conception of multiculturalism: membership of these groups must not be imposed by the state, but rather be a matter of self-identity; individual members must be free to question and reject any inherited or previously adopted identity, if they so choose, and have an effective right of exit from any identity group; these groups must not violate the basic civil or political rights of their members; and multicultural accommodations must seek to reduce inequalities in power between groups, rather than allowing one group to exercise dominance over other groups.[7]

Measured against this definition, life for the somatically and culturally Black is disruptive of the prevailing image of Canada as being normatively and practically a liberal, multicultural nation-state, for it shows that the constructed image is alienated from the reality of living in Canada, and that this difference is what gives Canada "authenticity." As stated earlier, this authenticity has to be first imagined as desirable; then Canadians would act towards one another as if this authenticity does exist. In daily living, often, those who are constructed as ethnically Black are not imagined in common sense thinking as sharing this Canadian authenticity. Therefore, the unhappy consciousness is prolonged – those who think they know who or what is authentic Canadian cannot understand why those who are deemed not to be Canadian would want to be recognized as authentic Canadian; outsiders like somatic and cultural Blacks who claim Canadian citizenship and all its rights and privileges might continue to fight to be included in the imaginary of who or what is Canadian. In the social construction that is daily living, they would want to be treated as if they are fully Canadian. The problem that leaves these two positions unreconciled is structural and stems from Canada applying criteria it had developed for racial consideration – for deciding who is good and evil, superior and inferior, and what groups can be made out of these binaries – and that are based, one-sidedly, on the ethno-racial register and are used to construct a specific ethnic group. In this way, racial characteristics are deemed to be ethnic characteristics for one group, making that constructed group, in its very construction, different from all other ethnic groups. In its construction, that group is discriminated against, leaving it, mythologically, with a lesser birthright than the group recognized as its non-identity, and as White.

In this respect, Canada is neither genuinely liberal nor democratic, as is attested to by the limits placed on the social mobility, recognition, and self-actualization of some individuals in contrast to the privileging of ethnic collective norms; and it is not genuinely multicultural or cosmopolitan,[8] as seen by its need, in the first place, to construct an artificial ethnicity of Blackness to give the appearance of inclusion and universal justice and to hold its constituent members in a particularistic caste. Rather, as Hollinger implies, Canada's multiculturalism appears to be in the throes of existing in a tension between enforced ethnicity, which he calls cultural pluralism, and cosmopolitan ethnicity, with the cosmopolitan, in the long term, appearing ambiguous, impermanent, and equivocal. This is an ethnicity that is constantly being constructed within a particular context, in specific moments, and according to specific needs and the materials that are available. Hollinger describes the struggle and its combatants:

Multiculturalism is rent by an increasingly acute but rarely acknowledged tension between cosmopolitan and pluralist programs for the defense of cultural diversity. Pluralism respects inherited boundaries and locates individuals within one or another of a series of ethno-racial groups to be protected and preserved. Cosmopolitanism is more wary of traditional enclosures and favours voluntary affiliations. Cosmopolitanism promotes multiple identities, emphasizes the dynamic and changing character of many groups, and is responsive to the potential for creating new combinations. Pluralism sees in cosmopolitanism a threat to identity, while cosmopolitanism sees in pluralism a provincial unwillingness to engage the complex dilemmas and opportunities actually presented by contemporary life.[9]

Based on what we have been discussing, cosmopolitanism is idealistic Blackness while cultural pluralism is idealized Whiteness – and both are dialectical parts of the infinite that is freedom. This means that cosmopolitanism, too, suffers from all the contradictions and tensions of an ideal. Such Whiteness might have been appropriate for a given moment, might even have been a form of Blackness for challenging previously held notions that an efficient and effective society cannot be pluralistic, but the dialectic of freedom seems to have moved beyond that moment. Cultural pluralism had metamorphosed, had become transfixed and transfigured into a Whiteness of fixity, prescribed formulas, and immutability. It had become cosmological, had been given mythologically to Canadians by thoughtful and super intellectual representatives of two founding peoples as a fully formed system with a clear beginning and ending.

Cultural pluralism might have been an appropriate solution for a struggle that started over the rights and entitlements of members of the "family," metaphorically and mythologically between brothers who might be considered to have devolved autonomously into different branches or were living independently in different houses, but still shared the same bloodlines and strove for the same idealized ending. In this regard, this was tantamount cosmologically to a struggle in Greek mythology between the gods for individual dominance in clearly defined areas, a struggle for recognition of their godliness and godhead, but a struggle taking place in the already accepted consciousness that the combatants, as a group, were separate from and racially superior to all other groups in humanity.

In this case, it was a struggle for recognition between the English and the French in Canada, for the respecting of clear boundaries and limits so that each group could maintain and preserve its culture and perspectives, a struggle to decide which of these two groups should have, in the Hebraic tradition, dominance over all that God had given them. This was a struggle for power among the groups that saw themselves as elites, with each group identifying itself as the most aristocratic in the Canadian cosmos. But as soon as these two groups appeared headed for a rapprochement taking form as biculturalism, the consciousness broke down into greater demands by excluded groups, even within the already recognized homelands, for recognition and inclusion. The emerging consciousness became one of recognized ethnic groups existing in a culturally plural multiculturalism that emphasized liberal group rights and entitlements.

However, the dialectic has continued, as a traditional group of individuals, lacking a unified ethnicity or wanting to escape such an ethnicity, are now demanding full recognition and inclusion without first having to construct, or be constructed, in an ethnicity.[10] It appears unlikely that Canada can contain these tensions within traditional ethnic arrangements. Black, as a group, is not just a constructed ethnicity; it is in fact a consciousness of many ethnicities, and that creates a problem in the mix that makes Blackness, in its equivocation, the force in the dialectic. In an age when globalism is now within the nation-state, and is not a feature from without as was previously thought, it thus appears that Canada is being pushed further into idealized Blackness, into cosmopolitan multiculturalism.

As Hegel suggests in *Phenomenology of Spirit,* such are the contradictions and conflicts that arise in an Enlightenment consciousness that has to deal with the reality of faith in the actual world. This faith is pure insight that is devoid of content, but the real world demands more than faith for existence, for when challenged by the material, insight vanishes. It demands more than good intentions. In this sense, mind and body appear to be out of step with each other. Insight is confused, lashes out at its detractors, and ultimately flees to the safety of its rationalist world of perfection, Whiteness, and pure intentions. As Hegel suggests, such a consciousness is more than a little confused when examining itself:

It entangles itself in this contradiction through engaging in dispute, and imagines that what it is attacking is something other than itself. It only *imagines* this, for its essence as absolute negativity implies that it contains that otherness within itself. The absolute Notion is the category; in that Notion, knowing and the *object* known are the same. Consequently, what pure insight pronounces to be its other, what it asserts to be an error or a lie, can be nothing else but its own self; it can condemn only what it is itself. What is not rational has no *truth,* or, what is not grasped conceptually is *not.* When, therefore, Reason speaks of something *other* than itself, it speaks in fact only of itself; so doing, it does not go outside of itself. This struggle with its antithesis, therefore, also has the significance of being the *actualization* of insight.[11]

Hegel explains what could easily be the phenomenology of what happened as Canada tried to move from the alienation of an unhappy consciousness to a presumed tranquil consciousness of enlightenment and reason in multiculturalism but has ended up instead as an alienated and

even confused consciousness. In Canada's case, the effort has led to one
school, consisting of Kymlicka and others, defending the success of multiculturalism based on its purity and good intentions.[12] The competing school,
made up of Bissoondath and other critics of multiculturalism, has been
debating what are the true intention, purpose, and limits of the policy and
the moral and ethical implications of the guiding principle for individuals
and the state.[13] Each school has its own purity of insight; each sees the other
as its Other and tries to negate it. Rather than tranquility, there is an internal war based on the interpretation of an ideal. The different conceptions
of what ought to be the "reality" of living multiculturally remain at war,
even in the use of the language that explains the ideals that fire both sides.
In this regard, Hegel observes the limitations:

We have already mentioned the tranquil consciousness that stands opposed to this
turmoil which, having once settled down starts up all over again; it constitutes the
side of pure insight and intentions. This tranquil consciousness, however, as we saw,
has no *special insight* into the world of culture; this latter has itself rather the most
painful feelings and the truest insight about itself: the feeling that all its defences
have broken down, that every part of its being has been tortured on the rack and
every bone broken; it is the language of this feeling and the brilliant talk which pronounces judgement on every aspect of its condition. Here, therefore, pure insight
can have no activity and content of its own and thus can only behave as the formal
and faithful *apprehension* of its own brilliant insight into the world and of its own
peculiar language.[14]

In going forward, the dialectic appears to be pushing Canada backwards,
diachronously, to the beginning of modernity itself and its peculiar limits and
boundaries, to a moment where, as Stephen Toulmin argues in *Cosmopolis:
The Hidden Agenda of Modernity*, Western civilization had to make a decision based on an array of possible choices.[15] The finite limits have to be
revalidated or changed for higher and wider limits and boundaries to contain
the dialectics that are straining the old finitude. Each choice would produce a
specific path out of the incipiency of Blackness and the chaos of contending
options and rivalries, a path intended usually towards an idealized good of
Whiteness. To get from cultural pluralism to cosmopolitan multiculturalism
would be to envisage, and even actively court, the death of the old and historical system and the acceptance of a radical new beginning over again. This
is a prospect that Canada, with, as Frye and others argue, its reliance on
group norms and collective memories, as treasured typically in such mottoes
as *Je me souviens,* appears unwilling to countenance.

If the latter is the case, and if Canada is to remain committed to an ideology of transcendental rationalism, a *nouveau Trudeauism*,[16] this development points to the need for a re-mining of the existing mythology to

harness the dialectics within to bring new meaning to what it means to be a Canadian, and to accept neo-mythically the role that death and rebirth play inspirationally in this process of becoming. But as we have seen, the ideal of Trudeau-like multiculturalism has resulted in absurdities in a moment of seeming enlightenment. Rationally, this seems to suggest that the option of cosmopolitan multiculturalism as an ideal might produce the same results. This would amount to no more than shifting from one perspective to another within the same framework, limits, and boundaries – to going from a particular view to a universal one but of the same picture. As Hegel suggests, this would be tantamount to looking forward to a solution to occur out of the blue, "on 'one fine morning' whose noon is bloodless if the infection has penetrated to every organ of spiritual life. Memory alone then still preserves the dead form of the Spirit's previous shape as a vanished history, vanished one knows not how. And the new serpent of wisdom raised on high for adoration has in this way painlessly cast merely a withered skin."[17] New ethical meaning is not emerging "bloodless" – at least not in the intellectual sphere as the struggle continues over whether genuine multiculturalism is cosmopolitan racelessness, egalitarianism and radical democracy, or merely another restrictive form of pluralism with built-in and unchanging social hierarchies. Only the raceless version is likely to produce the *nouveau Trudeauism*. For genuine multiculturalism to emerge from this struggle, not only must the dominant gaze change, but the picture too, especially in the way it is imagined and rationalized.

An alternative to the unhappiness emerging from the dominant view and approach to multiculturalism is to look within the dynamics of the process itself and pick the threads that offer the most promise for building a new tapestry both out of and around them.[18] Refashioning this tapestry might require cutting a Gordian knot or two that have left us so badly entangled – where the very act of cutting might produce intended results. The entire process would be aimed at producing the liberty that is similar to the death and "new beginning" Trudeau associated with the constitutional entrenchment of the Canadian Charter of Rights and Freedoms. As he said, the entrenchment was "to strengthen the country's unity by basing the sovereignty of the Canadian people on a set of values common to all, and in particular on the notion of equality among all Canadians."[19] This is tantamount, mythologically, to returning to the very dust that was at the beginning and determining whether the body should exhaust all the material that is available or whether some particles should be deemed inferior or superior and accordingly excluded or included in the body. The materials in this imaginary are the immigrants in their many hues, shades, and shapes. They will produce ethno-racially the new Canada – the hope and rebirth that are already present conceptually in the dialectics of freedom as genuine multiculturalism.

## A NEW CANADA THROUGH IMMIGRATION

The new millennium begins with the Canadian government beating the drum in the hope of awakening Canadians and the specially identified would-be-immigrant worldwide to the growing need for immigrants. Speaking at the recent Metropolis Conference in Vancouver, the then immigration minister, Elinor Caplan, noted that in the same way that Canada must compete to buy and sell goods and services in a global market it must also compete for ideal immigrants in a global setting. Elsewhere, she noted that Canada, with a declining birth rate and an aging population, needs to drastically increase its immigration intake. The existing Canadian system seems to be in its death throes because of a basic flaw, the inability to reproduce and maintain itself. Canada's population, and therefore its culture, is not fully self-perpetuating. The cosmos created in a specific time and space faces collapse into the idealized Blackness of the unknown, not through the encroachment of evil from the outside, but from Canada's own inability to fully sustain itself. As Caplan explained: "If the projections are correct, and if immigration is the only policy lever pulled, maintaining a constant ratio of retired to working people would require annual immigration levels of at least 430,000 (over the next 20 years). I say 'at least' because this figure is ... of these arrivals to be of working age, which of course, is extremely unlikely owing to family sponsorships and so forth. I can't help noticing that this figure of 430,000 exceeds the Government's long run target of annual levels of 1 per cent of the population. Indeed, it is nearly two and a half times the number of immigrants Canada accepted last year."[20]

Adding to the challenge of increasing its immigration numbers to levels that are greater than the historical trends is that Canada is also looking for a specific type of immigrant. These are the people that Caplan and others referred to in the abstract sense so common to multiculturalism as "the brightest and the best" from around the world, immigrants that are idealistically White. For this reason, Canada cherry picks its immigrants, choosing an individual foremost according to his or her ability to fit into the existing Canada, rather than by class, such as family, or by occupation and skills. Ideally, in the particular, this is a highly educated, business oriented individual, someone that, as Alan Simmons argues, comes into the country without much cost to Canada, who has paid his or her way in the world, and who is willing to import high levels of social capital into the country.[21] Canada is not simply looking for immigrants as raw material, for it does not just want bodies; they must already have been formed and shaped into a specific mould to be eligible for consideration.

This ideal immigrant is in high demand elsewhere, particularly in the United States, but also in member countries of the European Union. This is part of the rub for Canada: many of the European countries – such as Italy,

Greece, Portugal, and Ireland, which for generations had helped populate Canada – are now themselves competing against Canada for highly skilled labour.[22] International immigration, as part of a single global market, has now entered the phase where, as in the prevailing capitalist/market economy mythology, the immigrant is king or queen in the market place and, just like the proverbial customer, will spend his or her social capital on products that give the highest level of utility and enjoyment.

The abstract international immigrant insists that utility be a freedom of choice that translates into social mobility within the adopted country and, often, the freedom to live in transnational spaces in the new country. As a transnational, the immigrant can live in her or his place of birth and any number of countries, claiming to give allegiance to each without feeling too conflicted patriotically. This gives a new meaning to Benedict Anderson's notion of an imagined community, as the transnational can occupy different moments and different patriotisms and levels of belonging.[23] In the international market for immigrants, the choice is with the ideal candidates, not with the countries trying to entice them. This means that the new designer immigrant might be free of the constraints of citizenship, for such an immigrant can choose among countries, opting for the one where he or she will feel most accepted, and where the options for social mobility are perceived as being the best.

The result of this development is the difficulty, in the pragmatic and practical sense, that Canada is having in trying to reach its annual targets for these "ideal" immigrants. Translating the necessary abstract ideals into contingent bodies, and in large enough numbers to meet the Canadian demand, is difficult. This is another case of where the finite and infinite become a battle of limits. The dialectic of freedom has recognized new freedoms for the professional class of which Engin Isin writes, a group that is in high demand internationally and which freely flits from country to country following the best deal.[24] In this regard, conceptually, members of these groups may not shift loyalty from one country to another, but may instead retain loyalty to a country of birth, or to a specific place that is the main and spiritual residence, while splitting their commitment to the countries in which they do business. The practical implication for rights of entitlement is severe: for this professional class demands rights as the entry price for participating in a specific country, but at the same time its members are not providing a concomitant pledge of loyalty as has been the tradition for linking individuals and countries in a bond or contract.[25] It is not easy to imagine that "the brightest and best" immigrants would be willing to give up everything else and commit themselves fully to a Canada that, as an unchangeable, imposes limits on them. In addition, these immigrants do not always see themselves as changeable, yet Canada tends to view them as material that is willing to be changed into the unchangeableness that is

Canada and Canadian. There is an initial difference in perception, assumptions, and even intentions on both sides. Joaquín Arango, in *Immigration in Europe: Between Integration and Exclusion,* observes: "Certainly, not all migrants want to adopt the nationality of the host country, either for sentimental reasons – many would like to have dual citizenship, but few countries allow it – or for practical consideration, that is, because it is doubtful that it implies a major change. In fact, nationality does not seem to be a decisive factor in gaining access to basic services."[26] This is a trend that is developing internationally, especially among the designer immigrants Canada wants, and one which Canadian policy-makers are now coming to terms with. There is thus a growing demand, as Soysal argues, particularly in Europe but it is growing in developed countries also, for a split between rights of entitlement that are held according to citizenship and nationality, respectively.[27] If this trend persists, there will be less emphasis on the national identity and more on citizenship rights that are acquired by legal consideration in a social contract entered into freely by consenting members. Cosmological rights to entitlement and status, over the newcomers and those that were previously excluded at birth or status within the society, are likely to fall in this continuation of the dialectic struggle for freedom.[28] Canada's competitors for the idealized immigrants are already moving to allow the newcomers to have the same rights, privileges, and expectations as the native born. Upward social mobility will not be restricted based on place of birth and family lineage.

There is a second issue that flows out of this change at the international level in the immigrant's status. Canada needs not only skilled workers but also the traditional unskilled labourers that have always done the work that upwardly mobile Canadians have always rejected. This is the work that has been described as triple D: Dangerous, Difficult, and Dirty. Traditionally, Canada has turned to countries that were considered less developed to fill these slots. This has accounted for the importation of domestic workers from the Caribbean and the Philippines, for example, and in the arrival of thousands of seasonal agricultural workers from the Caribbean and Mexico annually.[29] There is every indication that for the next while Canada will continue to need unskilled labour simply as a result of a growing economy. The question, like that for the highly-skilled, is where these workers will come from. Most likely, Canada's future immigrants will come from countries that were traditionally constructed as Black culturally, somatically, and idealistically, in the Canadian imagination, and the implication, as we saw earlier, is a deeper Blackening and creolization of the complexion of Canada and Canadians.[30]

This change in the area of immigration reflects a changing paradigm for Canadian citizenship and nation-building. The natures, types, and sources of immigrants have changed fundamentally since Canada last had to make major changes to its immigration policy – and notions of national identity – in the 1960s. Another significant change is that Canada is now, as the federal government suggests, competing for the choice immigrants. It has to make its best offer, fully realizing that the subject in this piece, the immigrant, has choices. Canada is hoping that its national narrative, based on a mythology of tolerance, acceptance, and cultural plurality will entice the best prospects. Canada has not yet accepted the paradigmatic change by incorporating a new paradigm in its dominant ideology: there has been no real shift and no attempts at reversal.

Instead, Canada continues to make an offer to its potentially new citizens based on an old paradigm or mythology with its finite limits and boundaries. Such an offer was captured in the "vision" enunciated by former prime minister Jean Chrétien at the beginning of the new millennium of the country Canada could become with the help of immigrants. In his dream, "Canada, is the place to be in the 21st Century, the place where people will want to come and stay, and learn, to pursue opportunities, to raise children, to enjoy natural beauty, to open new frontiers, to set the standard for the world of a high quality of life, a Canada that is a leader and an example to the world."[31] This is a vision in which Canada is a benevolent Subject, and which presents Canada as an idealized homeland that is the natural aspiration for people around the world sill trapped in their darkness. This thinking still sees Canada as apart and different from the rest of the world. In an address to a Metropolis Conference in Washington at the end of 1999, Elinor Caplan further explained the vision of a Canada in which immigrants will play a crucial role: "Our vision is of a diverse and cohesive society. A global society that is home to all the world's cultures. A multicultural society. A society that serves as an example to the world of how different peoples can live, learn and work together successfully, in a climate of acceptance, respect and understanding."[32]

The ideal of Canada as a multicultural, liberal democracy was based partly on an immigration policy that suggested that Canada should peg its number of annual immigrants at 1 per cent of the population. This means that the break in the 1960s was not as clear and as clean as it was touted to be. The ideal of what is Canadian and who should become Canadian was still based on the retention of an old colonial policy of a manageable flow of immigrants that was carefully limited to allow for the creation of a specific type of country and culture.[33] Australia, for example, had adopted the same 1–per cent threshold for the absorption of newcomers so as not to disrupt the existing way of life. Jock Collins and Frances Henry note that Canada and Australia, as British dominions that were White homelands, had developed the same approach to immigration and that both countries changed immigration policies reluctantly: "By 1947, 90 percent of Australians were of British origin, with another 8.4 per cent of European origin.

The Labor Government's First Minister for Immigration, Arthur Calwell, launched the largest immigration program in Australian history. Post-war immigration was to add 1 per cent to Australian population growth per year under the slogan 'Populate or Perish!'. Calwell gave assurances that a white Australia would not be under challenge, since nine out of every ten migrants would come from Britain."[34]

If the Canadian government has to increase immigration beyond the annual 1–per cent threshold, to maybe even 3 per cent, in order to meet expected demands for labour and citizenship, this would be to a level that was always viewed as dangerous for the country and its existing culture and social order. In addition, Canadian officials are aware that in the international, globalized market for immigrants, Canada is now perceived differently by the much sought after immigrants. For many of them, Canada does not offer the hope that would encourage them to throw off their old nationality and to become a Canadian. Here, we might be reminded of what we earlier quoted Kuhn and Hegel as suggesting: that sometimes paradigmatic changes and new consciousnesses require revolutionary changes, for the old way does not die easily.

In *The Illusion of Difference*, sociologists Reitz and Breton argue that there is no significant difference between the economic and social incorporation of immigrants in Canada and the United States.[35] This argument undermines a long-held notion which is part of the prevailing perception in Canada. This is the notion that Canadian life shields immigrants from the rough and tumble of competitive life in the United States, and helps them adjust to a new environment in a less stressful way by allowing them to remain in communities of people of their own cultures. Indeed, the authors argue that the United States – a country with a very clear assimilationist myth – appears to be more multicultural and diverse than Canada.

Reitz and Breton give a specific reason for this: the different immigration policies in the two countries.[36] Canada tries to control its immigration intake and strives for a more idealized and perfect immigrant. It places less emphasis on the family class immigrant, mainly because there is no control over the "quality" of this category of immigrant. Indeed, family class members tend to be less educated than the business and independent immigrants, those Simmons calls designer immigrants, who can fit easily into Canadian society and who arrive relatively cost-free to Canada. This is a highly trained citizen-in-the-making that has been educated and nurtured by another country, with Canada going throughout the world and picking what its immigration ministers have continuously called, the "brightest and the best." As a result, Canada has, generally, a better-educated immigrant population than the Canadian population in general. But in de-emphasizing the family, Canada is also denying itself the creativity and benefits that are randomly present in the group – in all those who might have no greater ideal than to live in a country like Canada and to loyally help with the building of an ideal country, primarily by making it a home for their children.

The United States, on the other hand, puts less emphasis on selecting immigrants that are good for its economy, and focuses instead on those who want to become citizens and be a part of the population. The United States thus separates its population requirements from its immediate needs for specific workers or professionals, which makes it easier to meet its population demands. This does not mean, however, that it therefore fails to attract the brightest and best from around the world. The latter is achieved through the awarding of "green" cards to "exceptional aliens." This policy allows employers and others with specific manpower needs to sponsor immigrants to the country and to fast-track these applications. Under this policy, the United States successfully attracts such groups as doctors, nurses, and teachers from less developed countries, and even from Canada, primarily those immigrants who first attempt to settle in Canada and then make a second migratory move to the United States.

But there is another important feature to American immigration. It is its emphasis on family reunion, which means that it starts out by attracting people who do not have to scale high education hurdles to get in, but people who are following a human quest of wanting, along with their family, to belong. Once in the United States, these generally less educated immigrants have to rely on their ambitions and their merit to get ahead. They must be willing to be assimilated into a society where, theoretically, they have as much right to jobs, prestige, and status as do the people already living there. The American Dream mythology tells them that they can become the best American. This dream tells them that the entry of every new immigrant into the society changes the dynamic of the game and in the process changes the players too. Each entry is a essentially a risk then: both for the individual and the members of the adopting society.

This is not the case in Canada, where each entrant is positioned in the society – in veritable Platonic and Aristotelian notions – and the incorporation of this newcomer must be as free of economic costs and other forms of disruption as possible. This is an incorporation that is based on the self-sufficiency of the society and involves asking the newcomer to be virtuous by accepting a station in life based on how well he or she can assist the existing society, a status that is assigned to him or her by the wider society. There is no displacement of the long established order; new members of the society are selected like winemakers and shoemakers in the Platonic just society: because of their specific skills, how much their skills are in demand by the society, and the expectations that those skills will be used for the benefit of the nation and not necessarily for that of the individual. Much of the risk attendant to immigration is controlled in the Canadian policy.

The results of these two policies, according to Reitz and Breton, as marked, specifically, by Canada's failure to get as many designer immigrants as it wishes, show the impossibility of designing a perfect immigration policy, and of getting the desired outcomes. Life, in its Blackness, is too random for an imposed order. Contrary to expectations, the United States, without directly striving for this outcome, gets better-educated immigrants than Canada. Indeed, the US has its pick of immigrants over all other countries – including Britain, Germany, and Canada, which have been more selective – as the United States is the main choice for most immigrants around the world. On the other hand, Canada, with its more selective process, is unable to find all the "ideal" immigrants that it needs and to even keep at home those that did come to Canada as a first choice, but only to cross over to the United States. And when it does find them, Canada's success in incorporating the immigrants into its economy is no different than that of the United States – unless they are somatically Black, in which case the experience of incorporation is unique to Canada.[37] Only now is Canada beginning to take seriously this leakage of immigrants to the United States as part of the brain drain from Canada.

The question then becomes, in a world of infinite choices, Why would immigrants choose Canada, as opposed to the United States, or other countries that might give them greater hope? This becomes a bigger issue when it is made clear that the old mythology of Canada, as a place of greater tolerance and less racism than the United States, becomes undermined. As Reitz and Breton state:

Our findings about employment discrimination against racial minorities do not support the view that there is less racial discrimination in Canada than is in the United States ... The general cultural differences between Canada and the United States imply differences of tone in ethnic and race relations in the two countries. The Canadian style is more low-key than the American; moreover, Canadians have a conscious tradition of "tolerance" that Americans do not have. In terms of their effects on the experiences of minority groups, however, these differences are more apparent than real. Some have argued that the Canadian style serves to camouflage underlying racial animosities. We have no data that directly supports this argument, but we can say that the cultural differences between the two countries have not produced less pressure towards conformity in Canada, or less propensity to discriminate in employment or housing.[38]

In terms of attracting ideal immigrants, it appears that the old mythology that Canada offers is no longer an attractive incentive for people who know better, who have improved living standards at home, or who are in demand in other countries that offer them different prospects. And in a strange way, this is perhaps the most recent verdict on the outcome of the congenital battle over choices of lifestyle and culture that go back to the beginning of modernity, to the formation of two separate, distinct, and rival nations out of what were the British North American colonies. Even in the eyes of prospective immigrants, Canada appears to have lost the battle for dominance. Therefore, if only for the reason that Canada must remain unchangeable, but also for purposes of continuous renewal within this unchanging form, Canada needs a new mythology in which death, transformation to dying, and then rebirth into a new being do not appear as prominently.

Otherwise, if Canada is to be faithful to its ideal and rational – according to the reasons and expectations that we have now argued to be the ideals of Western culture – then, in this particular, Canada will have to allow for an easier passage of immigrants in their primordial Blackness into the ethical Whiteness that Western ideology says is possible. Currently, the Canadian mainstream appears unwilling to accept such an "easy" passage or transformation for immigrants as either rational or consistent with the Canadian good. But the dominant mainstream cannot have this issue determined according to two separate and distinct sets of rules – otherwise, as we have argued, it would be angling for the creation of another and different lordship and bondage relationship within the lordship and bondage struggle that already exists in the form of Canada, itself, as a social consciousness.

For to follow such an approach would not only deepen the malaise and existential Blackness of the current unhappy consciousness, but, in terms of rationality, would be gesturing towards the creation of a social absurdity – a kind of apartheid by separating native-born and somatically White Canadians from Canadians who are foreign-born and usually non-White somatically. Such a consciousness and social structure would be an absurdity since Canada has already rationalized the unchangeable good of citizenship as being equality among all who qualify. This is a good, conceptualized as citizenship, that is already imagined to be consistent with the diversity and differences immanent to ethno-racial determinations. Neo-mythically, the good establishes that rationally and physically there should be no setting apart within Canada of Canadians into social hierarchies based on superiority or inferiority. To pick up on what Frye was saying earlier, in the end mythology and ideology are not about proving truths, per se: rather they are what determine truth. They give us the notions or forms we regard as eternal and unchanging "truths." We either accept them or we do not. And if we accept the "truth" of the mythology as rational, we stop contesting the rationality itself. We so order our lives so as to live the "truths." Ideologically, the "truths" become second nature to us – they become the mythological skeleton in our consciousness. Canada can be adjudged as rational and consistent only through the application of the rules that Canadians say should be the test for rationality and consistency. Canada, then, must appear as White as it has established as its ideal of Whiteness. Failing to meet its own rational standards or eternal truths would leave the Canadian consciousness still wallowing in, at least, ethical Blackness. Frustrated, it will remain unhappy and not knowing quite what to do with itself and how best to make itself happy.

## NEW CANADA: NO RACE, NO ETHNICITY, NO HOMELANDS

In his book *Culture, Citizenship and Community,* Joseph H. Carens makes the case for the recognition of specific inherent group rights that flow out of ethnicity and nationalism.[39] This is particularly the case when he discusses legislation by the province of Quebec, which – in a Rousseauian way of using a constructed goodwill to force people to be free – is an attempt to make immigrants and non–French speaking minorities free by forcing them to become culturally and linguistically French.[40] Building on a politics of identity from Taylor as it pertains to Quebec,[41] Carens's position is quite clear: "I contend that Quebec's language policies and its official expectations of immigrants are morally defensible from the perspective of justice as evenhandedness because these are the sorts of demands that go hand in hand with a commitment to provide immigrants and their children with equal opportunity in Quebec and with the other rights and freedoms that a liberal democratic political community should provide to its members."[42]

To back this argument, Carens must make some assumptions that, on close reading, are inherently anti-democratic and illiberal in terms of the individual will: there is no choice for newcomers or, just as importantly, for their children that are born in the new country. The immigrant comes into a country already framed by boundaries that are non-negotiable, and which even current citizens are not allowed to change as these limits must be preserved at all cost as the best of the goods that are available. Carens's assumptions contest the claim that Canada is a liberal democracy that is multicultural. They also subvert the notion that Canada as a nation is more concerned with the future and the choices that are available to make such a future, than with maintaining the structures of the past. The children of immigrants, for example, do not come endowed with the rights of all other French-speaking Canadians born in the province of Quebec. They are forced to assimilate into the French culture: they do not have the freedom to become what they want and they do not help shape their new society according to their imagination. Place of birth has no real meaning or cultural significance for the children of immigrants born in Canada. Neither do their dreams.

Of principal importance in this dialectic is the cosmological good expressed as the society that has been handed to them. It comes first. These newcomers are thus bound to abide by rules and expectations that were created before their arrival and which they are not expected to challenge, far less change. If there is a notion of rebirth in this arrangement, it is for the newcomer to die as a cultural being formed and conditioned in another time and space, and to be changed into a being that is shaped and conditioned by others whose dreams and concerns are presumed to be different and alien. This is a resurrection into a kind of slavery, as there is a lack of choice and social determination. If there is a future, it is not one to be shaped by the newcomers: their task is simply to help in the realization of an ideal that was lifted up prior to their arriving in the country. If there is a hope, it must be, in keeping with the nihilistic advice of the mythical Greek Silinus, that their dreams and aspirations should die as a quickly as possible so that they can conform to the boundaries that they find.

The immigrant's status is therefore one of existential and status Blackness, an existence of over-determination lacking in ambiguity and meaningful choice. The belief that anyone would be willing to undergo such changes, only to endure such restrictions, can only be based on the notion that newcomers remain eternally grateful for the opportunity to become Canadian. The limits they that are offered must be seen as infinite compared to what they could otherwise have. The gift of becoming Canadian, in itself, is worth the restrictions. The belief is based on the notion that immigrants do not have finite choices that exhaust those offered by Canada, and that it presumes that they are entering into a moral contract with their new country at a severe disadvantage. Never is it considered that Canada might, indeed, be offering the multi-talented and in-demand immigrants reduced options. Indeed, Carens makes this point explicit: "Most immigrants are not able to pick and choose among alternative host societies. They must chose between moving to the one that has admitted them and staying at home. That is still a choice, of course, but it is misleading to construct it as an entirely free choice. It is no doubt true, given the conditions in the world today, that most immigrants would readily agree to Quebec's requirements. But many would undoubtedly agree to much harsher terms, even perhaps indentured servitude. No one today would defend that sort of contract."[43]

Carens's argument is not based on a "given the conditions in the world today," for he is still operating on the assumption that the mass of humanity has an equal chance of gaining entry into Canada, and Quebec.[44] The reality is that this is not so: Canada has a very selective and restrictive immigration policy. Second, his argument presupposes that immigrants fortunate enough to be selected by Canada do not have the opportunity to "pick and choose among alternative host societies." That, again, is an erroneous assumption. The idealized immigrants that Canada is after *do* have choices and often exercise them to the detriment of Canada. The contract negotiations between Canada and its idealized immigrants are much more an exercise among equals than Carens and others recognize, so much so that often the courted immigrants walk away from Canada when the terms are not to their liking. This is the crux of the problem Canada faces: it needs large numbers of idealized immigrants but, at the same time, has a larger than needed supply of people from around the world who do not have choices. Canada's choice is to have people with choices; but such people only accept Canada when they feel they have full freedom to exercise their choices, to, for example, achieve full self-actualization as moral, democratic agents within Canada. So the immigrant of choice for Canada must have choices *within* Canada and cannot be limited and positioned in an alienated space reserved for Canadian Others. As the federal Immigration and Citizenship minister put it at the end of the millennium: "Among the highly skilled – the group from which Canada is seeking to attract more immigrants – it is becoming more and more difficult to encourage a sustained commitment to country. As international markets become more fluid, we will need to look at non-traditional ways to bind newcomers more closely to their communities and to Canada. We need to do this by creating the kind of society that people will *want* to live in – in other words, offering them unparalleled quality of life. Otherwise, social cohesion will suffer."[45] Canada's desire is to select idealized Whites as immigrants – those who meet abstract universal notions of goodness – but this is also matched by a desire and practice, based on the history of how the immigrants are inserted socially in society, to convert these immigrants into status Blacks when they arrive in the country.[46]

Undoubtedly, the conditions would have to appear to offer social mobility to the highly-prized immigrants. Unfortunately, the debate in Canada takes place within a framework or paradigm that suggests that Canada has all the power and can confer life or death on those milling outside the gates for entry. In practice, Canada has little interest in the throngs of barbarians, and, instead, is actively scouring the world for the few hundred thousand people who, in their elitism, have the choice of going to any of the immigration receiving countries or of staying at home. As the dialectic of nation-state formation works itself out, Canada's need for people might force it to again abandon its ideals and, as it did in the 1960s, condescend to accept more of the barbarians, which it would then try to "civilize" or educate within a Canadian civil society. The alternative is to abandon its ideals of Canada as a privileged White space where specific groups have an earned entitlement and privilege that even the "brightest and best" from around the world who are not somatically White will be willing to accept as the price of gaining entry into this sacred space. Either way, Canada experiences a clash of ideals.

For Carens, Quebec, as an analogy of the Canadian society, is a fully formed linguistic society, a specific homeland carved out cosmologically over the centuries for a French-speaking ethnic group that is mainly White and European. Nativism, based ontologically and epistemologically on the French language, has priority over acquired citizenship, including the right to decide the future of the society and to demand that others of lesser vintage conform to a privileged view and position. For him the immigrant enters a state and culture that is already fully formed, based on an ethnic nationalism, with its privileged notions of good and evil and of race and ethnicity. This is not a state with a conflicted notion of the good, for the good is already decided and established by those that have gone before and by those who can claim a direct lineage. All others must conform, or be forced to conform. This is the price for entry into the society. People enter the state not as individuals, with conflicting notions of the good, but as members of ethnic groups. Development of the state is predicated on the idealism of the past, not on the speculative history that is available and possible in the potential that is people, who with their dreams, hopes, and fears shape a nation-state by negating limits one after the other, with each one resulting in a transcendental leap of faith into the unknown. Will Kymlicka, in *Politics in the Vernacular,* is one of the few to challenge Carens and others on the privileging of a previous good at the expense of the future. Kymlicka notes:

Many citizens are still confused about the limits of multiculturalism. Indeed, many feel unable to even raise the issue in public forums, for fear of being labelled racist or prejudiced. People want to know that there are certain fundamental requirements of being a citizen, including respect for human rights and democratic values, yet debate on this issue has been suppressed by political elites, who suggest that anyone who criticizes multiculturalism is prejudiced. This attempt to stifle the debate over the limits of multiculturalism is counter-productive. It does not promote understanding or acceptance of the policy, but simply leads to resentment against it.[47]

The problem is not so much with multiculturalism, or Quebec, per se, but rather with an approach that reduces nation-state building and maintenance to a formula and to a method that has already been ordained as good and most appropriate. The problem is when the limits on citizenship are seen as permanent and non-negotiable; it is when human rights and democratic values are seen as the preserve of specific groups, as entitlements, and to others merely as privileges; it is when the structures and forms are deemed to be more important than the content or aims. The limits become prisons rather than temporary barriers that can be transcended. The problem is the long-held tradition that immigrants, and their children, should be willing to accept as permanent their entry-level status in the society and in deference to those, as Porter calls them, with Charter membership and a sense of a higher claim and entitlement.[48] The resistance and resentment is against a society where one group has found the way and believes that it deserves to keep going in its separateness after a specific way that results in a distinct culture and distinct path to a Garden of Eden. This curtails the rights of some individuals, particularly the rights of those constructed as Others to a peculiar kind of Canadian, which in the first instance is called French Canadian, but ultimately is a form of Whiteness.

Indeed, Carens's argument begins from a space which suggests that not only do immigrants have little choice over which country to move to, but that immigrants are hoping in all cases to preserve the cultures that they are leaving behind. This is also the argument advanced by Kymlicka.[49] In discussions by both Carens and Kymlicka, the assumption is made that, individually, immigrants are not willingly choosing cultural death. This is at the heart of Kymlicka's argument about "societal cultures," which sees immigrants arriving in a new country and hoping to form, establish, and preserve their old culture, often in opposition to the prevailing. They arrive and form societies of their own and from there demand specific group rights.

Often, then, there are tensions between the dominant and minority cultures, from two unchangeables struggling for dominance in the same unity, and liberal theorists must find a way to reconcile these differences. Yet, Kymlicka argues that most members of the new immigrant societies are liberal in orientation and that often their demands, such as for religious tolerance, are easily accommodated in liberalism.[50] This suggests that the immigrants do not come as an unchangeable finite, but rather see themselves as infinite: intentionally, they want to incorporate their old contingent selves into a bigger and wider infinite that is Canada. This is the wonderful promise of multiculturalism: the assumption that finite death is to exercise a transcendent hope of rebirth into a wider infinity with so many more potentialities. To perceive it as a death of conformity to narrowly defined limits is to betray the hope of multiculturalism.

But even Kymlicka's assessment of a societal culture that should be retained indicates a flaw in the approach to immigration, settlement, and cultural rights. It assumes that the society, community, or ethnicity precedes the individual, and it assumes that what is true primarily for refugees, those who are fleeing death, is also true of all other immigrants. Indeed, most voluntary immigrants know that they are undertaking an act of death, for they are leaving, like Oedipus Rex, their old society in the hope of redemption in a new one: in no way do they really expect to become dominant in their new society unless they are claiming the society through some extant primordial right. They will begin life anew as children, often blinded to the cultural and social mores, but with a strong and firm belief in their individuality and its ability to survive fundamental change. Immigrants know they must change, adapt, and transform themselves. Indeed, often they leave their homeland for the very chance at rebirth into an unknown, into a new society that offers them most hope. Otherwise, if the immigrants really wanted to remain in a closed and fully formed culture and society, they would not voluntarily leave their native countries. It is for the excitement, the randomness, and the unpredictability of being born again that they leave. A meaningful choice for immigration is therefore death and rebirth, rather than to be held fixed in an entry position.

Such thinking is not captured in Canadian attitudes, for the dominant view is that immigrant groups have to be protected from an expected death, and that they must be maintained in groups that make life as close as possible to that from which they left. Perhaps this is a throwback to dominant Canadian mythologies in which the country was always presented as a place of refuge for specific groups, and a reflection of the Canada created out of a group of refugees fleeing the American Revolution. In this mindset, people coming to Canada are always running from something more onerous and frightful than that which they are moving towards. Canada, in this reasoning, provides a refuge for the fortunate and preserves them from that from what they have fled. As is usually the case, immigrants, once they have decided to leave, have already mentally transformed themselves into new beings, and Canada becomes simply the site for their re-birth. The dominant question in the Canadian dialectic of freedom has been how to hold on to the finite boundaries and limits: whether the goal was to keep out the randomness of life that was assumed to be epitomized by Blackness in the western hemisphere,[51] or within Canada itself, to preserve a French culture perceived as idealized Whiteness in an environment of idealized Blackness, a dominant English culture, that is, as seen through the eyes of some Québécois.[52]

Once again, the creation in Canada of an ethnic group called Black challenges this notion, for most immigrants that are somatically and culturally Black come to Canada already knowing it is "a White man's" country, but hope they can be reborn in Canada as idealistically White. And many of them come looking not for their "societal cultures" to mediate for them in a battle with a dominant and hostile mainstream, but with the wish that they will be adopted into the mainstream. On the ethno-racial and neo-mythic registers, they see themselves as candidates that are good enough for assimilation into the Canadian mainstream. For this they choose death willingly and individually. For them the colour of the skin is imaginatively changeable, so that on the neo-ethical they can be differentiated otherwise than by skin colour. Indeed, many of them hope that their virtues – their willingness to work hard, their adaptability, and their creativity and social capital – will be the sacrifice accepted by the lords of the land and that they will be accepted under a covenant that respects the differences that they feel are more important in them.

That they are often denied this rebirth or full integration and acceptance as Canadians is a question of racism and not of societal and ethnical cultural preservation. Their bodies, and not their works and thoughts, are chosen as their essences. They are determined in every way on the ethnoracial register. Rather than resisting assimilation, they find that they as objects are not offered assimilation, but are set apart and placed on the periphery to the mainstream of the system as mere bondsmen instead of lords.

In the end, Blacks, regardless of which official language they speak or culture they live in, find themselves in an unintended struggle between two dominant groups, the anglophones and francophone in Canada, neither of which is willing to accept the death of a way of life or of their dominant positions. Consequently, the assumption that Blacks are a separate group, with common concerns and intentions, is merely a projection by the dominant groups of their fear of death on those who have already accepted, and even wished, for a speedy transformation into a transcendent that they think is achievable.

According to the prevailing argument, a very specific way of life, then, is privileged over the intentions, dreams, and hopes of those doing the living. There is a manifest destiny presented teleologically as the retention at any cost of a specific aspect of a culture, such as its language or way of behaviour. The outcome is too highly determined. This is a case, as Nietzsche suggests in *On the Advantage and Disadvantage of History for Life,* of the heavy hand of history rising up to be a dead hand on the hopes and aspirations of the individual constructed as other, Black, and immigrant.[53] So justice for immigrants and non-francophones comes in the form of being assimilated into a way of life, without being offered the attendant hope of rebirth into something of their own likeness or making. The state does not promise, as in *Antigone,* rewards for dying on behalf of the universal culture, for, in fact, the universal culture is that of a particular group. There is no will to power granted to the person that must risk death. Rather, there is the fixed expectation of inauthenticity, of having to negate the old self only to become someone else, of accepting a life of mimicry, of pretending to be gods and White, while knowing inherently that this is a case of a daily playing out of one's life as a forced assimilation without meaningful benefits. It is living where any disobedience or rebellion against authority is seen as a fall in the mythological Garden of Eden. Carens's argument has primordial roots in Enlightenment thinking, especially in the view of Kant.

## KANTIAN MULTICULTURALISM AND FREEDOM

Justice, Kant suggests, starts with the individual's freedom to try to become whatever that individual – if genuinely released from a self-imposed tutelage

– wants to become, to choose how he or she should be recognized in the state, and not be subjected to what the state dictates. Moreover, Kant argues that competition and struggle must return to societies that are naturally constructed: "The highest purpose of Nature, which is the development of all the capacities which can be achieved by mankind, is attainable only in society, and more specifically in the society with the greatest freedom. Such a society is one in which there is mutual opposition among the members, together with the most exact definition of freedom and fixing of its limits so that it may be consistent with the freedom of others."[54]

Nature imposes desires that compel humans to seek freedom, and to compete in this freedom. In botany, this is when the best comes out, not only for the individual plants, but for the garden or forest. Here, then, is an argument for meritocracy within a social order that, like that of Hobbes,[55] is conflicted. As Kant sees it: "It is just the same with trees in a forest: each needs the others, since each in seeking to take the air and sunlight from others must strive upward, and thereby each realizes a beautiful, straight stature, while those that live in isolated freedom put out branches at random and grow stunted, crooked, and twisted. All culture, art which adorns mankind, and the finest social order are fruits of unsociableness, which forces itself to discipline itself and so, by a contrived art, to develop the natural seeds to perfection."[56]

Kant argues that humans enter society for two main reasons: (1) because they want to become more than mere men and women, in keeping, I would suggest, with the Aristotelian notion of human-gods; and (2) because they need a master to reward and even punish, essentially to ensure their freedom by making sure others do not transgress them. The role of the master, akin to the function of Hobbes's Sovereign, is to uphold points in a commonly agreed to contract to ensure justice. For Kant, "the highest master should be just in himself, and yet a man. This task is therefore the hardest of all; indeed, its complete solution is impossible, for from such crooked wood as man is made of, nothing perfectly straight can be built."[57]

Reason, spawned of a collective memory, would not only be the master keeping humans in check, but, aesthetically, would be a measurement of the alienation that is human experience, the gap between the dream of permanent or perpetual peace and carefree behaviour, and the daily hardships of human existence. It would be a semblance at best. And because reason comes out of a collective memory humans would be the natural masters of themselves.

It is for the reasons given above that nature made it natural for humans to live in a society, one formed from and endowed with a specific, common memory. This is the most important point of creation, where humans moved from being the savage and uncultured to becoming the civilized and cultured. But the competition did not end there. It was now manifested on two fronts. There was the inter-societal competition to become the "strongest and straightest" trees in the forest that was society, and there was intra-societal warfare between different groups and cultures for dominance. This dominance was manifest in control over the land, as in Kant's example of the struggle between agriculturist and nomadic tribes. Their ways of life were in conflict, with the agriculturists needing to parcel off land to cultivate crops, and the nomads needing the land for their animals to graze – and the result that the nomads' animals often grazed on the agriculturists' cultivation.

Both groups felt their god gave the land to them; each side rejoiced in its freedom to do as it pleased. Both saw the other as an interloper. The result was war and the dominance of the agriculturist. The result was that humans had to turn their back on the goodness and peace they naturally wanted for themselves by choosing war. This, too, resulted in a positive action: the dominance of a specific people with a specific culture. But humans are rational, and reason is a reminder of what is missing from their lives: the peace and tranquility of the state of nature, of the womb. So, eventually, reason, as Kant explains, teaches humans that different ways of life can exist, in full freedom, as long as the different parties enter into a contract that respects the autonomy of the individual states: "Nature forces them to make at first inadequate and tentative attempts; finally, after devastation, revolution, and even complete exhaustion, she brings them to that which reason could have told them at the beginning and with far less sad experience, to wit, to step from the lawless condition of savages into a league of nations. In a league of nations, even the smallest state could expect security and justice, not from its own power and by its own decrees, but only from this great league of nations. From a united power acting according to decisions reached under the laws of their united will."[58]

This, for Kant, is the dialectic of the nation-states of human civilization: it is the story that starts with the privileging of individual freedoms but results in the competition of cultures and nations with one idealistic ending: a universal of different nations and different cultures, a universe of particulars that can eventually be ranked. Humans can live in constant warfare by struggling for dominance through the triumph of a single state or way of life. Or, relying on reason, humans can see the futility and destruction of such wars, and come to an understanding that allows for multiple nations with multiple cultures in one universe.

This raises the question of multiculturalism, or the issue of a state like the province of Quebec forcing the production of a unitary culture. Is it feasible to have more than one culture in a single state and for that state to be natural? Kant says no, judging from his story about the war between the nomads and the agriculturists, in which one had to dominate to form the state and the operative way of life. Yet, might not a social contract allow for multiculturalism that does not privilege a specific unitary identity within a single state? Kant again says no, for the contracts are between individuals to form a single state, a state that then gives the individuals a culture by stopping them from warring with one another even if they continue to compete within boundaries set by the general will. The second contract is between fully formed independent states, with fully formed cultures. In both cases, there is a specific master-and-slave configuration. Indeed, in the proposed contract for states in *Perpetual Peace* – a concept that John Rawls borrows for his *Theory of Justice*, in which the social contract is negotiated from behind a veil of ignorance[59] – Kant rules out remnants or residues of any other culture within the existing states. The first clause in that ideal constitution proposes that there should be no matter reserved in the state that could precipitate a future war, which means that the dominated must give up its right to recognition as a separate and distinct entity. The slave must be recognized in relation to her or his position, but also that of the master. Differences have to be totalized. This point is strongly implied in the second clause, which says that no independent state can come under the domination of another: "A state is not, like the ground which it occupies, a piece of property. It is a society of men whom no one else has any right to command or to dispose except the state itself. It is a trunk with its own roots. But to incorporate it into another state, like a graft, is to destroy its existence as a moral person, reducing it to a thing; such incorporation thus contradicts the idea of the original contract without which no right over a people can be conceived."[60]

On this score, no hybrid culture would work, yet there could be a diaspora. In the latter case, a Kantian analysis would allow for the argument that Canada, even separated physically from England, is a continuation of a dominant English culture and history. While Kant suggests that there is a primordial element to nation-states, he seems equally to be arguing that such primordialism is not necessary or even important, especially for the dominated or minority in a culture. Primordialism, a form of naturalism, seems to matter only for the fittest and strongest, for those physically capable of defending it and then imposing their ways. The defeated and the minorities must be willing to settle for the state that is constructed for them. They cannot then be fully free. Here Kant is suggesting that culture is the natural development of the human race, depending on the local conditions and the level of development.

A state for Kant is not the ground but the expressed will of the people, a culture that has jelled and homogenized its members. Multiculturalism, with its concentration on the recognition of even competing cultures as equal, would smell of an unfinished project, where the first stages of the dialectic have not worked themselves out. The Kantian model of social integration is idealistic assimilation, based on the dominance of the stronger over the weaker. A Kantian model, therefore, would create a multicultural state in which peoples and groups are free but within their little world, whereas in the wider society the dominant, like the largest and strongest tree, would hold sway over all others. This is a model that offers little scope for social justice for the weak and those, based on strength and power, unfortunate enough to be located on the periphery of society. In this regard, the Kantian transcendental model fails to provide social justice and to allow social mobility as a necessary test of freedom.

Carens seems to be following the Kantian argument and to be valorizing a fully formed culture over a culture in formation. His argument is based on the power of the dominant and its ability and willingness to be ruthless or benevolent with the perceived less fortunate. As Homi Bhabha suggests, it is an argument that is based on the possibility of a singular, totalizing narrative that itself is based on conformity and conferral for the history of people.[61] This is a history with clearly defined limits and boundaries that have been developed in the past and cannot be disrupted. These are narratives, as Bhabha says, that "never pose the awkward question of the disjunctive representation of the social, in the double-time of the nation."[62] Immigrants in Quebec would be held in tutelage for the good of the society – thereby underlining an inherent contradiction in the democratic ideals of Kant and others over how individuals can claim their freedom but be in tutelage to a greater good.

Therefore, the role of the state is never neutral in this discussion. As a neo-Hegelian reading of *Antigone* implies, the state also faces the challenge of deciding on and producing the context and conditions of individual social justice, a social justice that, I would argue, is best tested by the freedoms and choices inherent in individual social mobility. It is a freedom where the state risks death, where it philosophically accepts the inevitably of death, while at the same time understanding that to do nothing is like accepting a perpetual death by accepting the prevailing conditions. This is the freedom to be Black. There is the need for a new spirit, one that, for the first time, genuinely commits to the mythology based on individualism and equality of opportunity, so that those who make individual decisions to die for the state can expect individual rewards in an afterlife, a life when all old things are made new again. So drastic would be this change in spirit and attitude, so dramatic the paradigmatic shift and reversal that the result would be akin to adopting a new mythological beginning.

Hegel recommends, in *Phenomenology of Spirit,* that possible solutions to the contradictions produced by the dialectic of freedom can lie within the dialectic and the contradictions themselves. The solution is to find what lessons of history are appropriate for making rational choices about the future. He explains how moral and ethical relations are reconciled in the real world: "What virtue learns from experience can only be this, that its

End is already attained in principle, that happiness is found directly in the action itself, that action is the good."[63] This suggests that, in the existence that is the tragedy of life, the resolution to contradictory or absurd problems of moral and ethical relations can be found within the tragedy itself. They will not be found through an appeal for a divine-like intervention from a source outside the tragedy, an intervention whose plausibility is on the grounds of faith only.

This solution must flow from actions that, equally, are the idealistic wishes of a Trudeau and his followers for a just and fair world or from those detractors who maintain that the ideal world does not exist. Neither position should be an end in itself, as each is subject to its own dialectical contradictions and absurdities. Rather, the reality and truth is what occurs to achieve the idealism of the two conflicting schools, and how these actions stand up to the prevailing ethical and moral consciousness. This is good advice for the play in progress that is Canadian multiculturalism. This would be an idealistic reconciliation; for multiculturalism as reified Blackness is a dynamic utopia in which the order is welcomed disorder, flux and eternal creation.

In the next and final chapter, I shall explore the possibility that the seed for a reconciliation of Canadian Blackness already exists within the Canadian soil. It is incarnate in the somatically Black female, who, traditionally in the mythology of the Black Atlantic, has been the mediator between somatic Whiteness and Blackness. In her dealings with somatic Whiteness, she has been at times the unchangeable good that nurtures the next generation – somatically Black and White – in the form of the mammy figure. Yet, she has been at time the temptress, defiler, and creative genius, the embodiment of the evil that is the Eve-like figure that passionately sacrifices her body to negate seeming limits and boundaries in order to produce the hybridity that is idealized Blackness.

From the somatic Black perspective, she has been the unchangeable that has embodied the faith and hope of better times, the mother who, in a hostile environment, maintains and nurtures the Black family, many times on her own as the sole parent. She, too, has been the changeable in the Black family, the one out of whose body the family comes physically and who is constantly sacrificing this body, keeping her ego in check, for the good of the family, and by extension that of the state in which she lives. In terms of offering hope, the Black woman is the Antigone of Canadian multiculturalism. She is the mediator offering to society in general and also to somatic Blacks as a distinct socially constructed group the option of recognizing that limits should be placed on what are deemed to be socially changeless.

# Black Canada – Reconciliation?

## THE SOMATICALLY BLACK FEMALE: HOPE AND DIVINITY

The middle of the twentieth century was one of the bleakest for Canada. This was when the dialectical forces of the nation-state appeared most unreconciled, with the country seemingly destined to be fractured into two distinct and separate bodies. For the dominant elites of the day, this change in the prevailing mythology would have been perceived ethically as death. This would have been the unwanted and unnatural change that occurs when goodness turns into Blackness. In 1963, Canadians turned to a Royal Commission to avoid falling into the abyss that appeared to be awaiting them. The Royal Commission on Bilingualism and Biculturalism was intended to steer Canadians clear of this gulf of despairs. It was a search for enlightenment and, ultimately, for ethical Whiteness by putting off an unintended death.

This commission was a Hegelian phenomenological inquiry. It was akin to a self-conscious Canadian ego, as embodied in the commissioner and staff examining the Canadian body as if it were an object – as if clinically the examined were separate and distinct from the examiners and the examining process. Analogously, this was the case of a Canadian subject, from a position of epistemic distance, reflecting on itself as an object and trying to determine why it was unhappy. It needed to know why it felt so alienated between so many different and diverse parts and why there was no coherence between its goals and intentions. At the same time, it had to show a way ahead into this epistemological Blackness out of which it must carve a future, one in which there is still the hope of making Canada a land of ethical Whiteness.

This was a case of the subject itself acknowledging its epistemological and ontological Blackness. It did not know everything it needed to know about itself, including who was a true and unchangeable Canadian. It did not know if the Canada that existed was perpetual and everlasting, or whether in the fulfilment of history in the future it would become a Canada that was anglophone, a separate Canada that was francophone, or some combination of both. In turn, this lack of cognition spawned an ethical Blackness because the subject did not know how to act and which actions would be deemed morally right or wrong by the members making up the collective body. It did not know what the ideal tasks and actions were for a Canadian and, ultimately, what would transform those who claim to be Canadian into citizens about whom there could be no doubt in regard to their essence of Canadianness, and about what would make them happy.

In this final chapter, I argue that many of the lessons learned by examining the dialectic of freedom in the 1960s can point Canada today towards a fuller, even if grantedly more idealistic, reconciliation. Such an idealistic approach might yet get the society out of the unhappy consciousness that is its current state of existence. The forces within the dialectic of freedom created the unhappiness at a contingent moment in Canadian history. They also created other choices as a legacy of that consciousness. In this plenitude of hope and despair, one of the choices is for the full and complete acceptance and recognition of somatic Blackness as indispensable to full citizenship in multicultural Canada.

This is the point, phenomenologically, where the consciousness that is Canada recognizes, in its latest and fullest knowledge, that it is not White as it had thought. Rather, the consciousness is Black ontologically, epistemologically, existentially, and ethically since every Canadian is not happy with her or his lot in life. In addition, this consciousness realizes that it is Black idealistically, culturally, in status, and also somatically because of a growing dependence on non-Europeans for its continued existence. At this point in time, the only Whiteness this consciousness can rationally aspire to is an ethical one – a new humanism, of sorts, but one in which it would gain idealistic Whiteness through its acts of freedom: in the way that out of a good will it treats all members of its society as equals and according to its norms of justice. Put another way, rationally, to become White in any form, this Black consciousness must not rely on nature or ontology but rather on a social construct, on its imagination to create norms of Whiteness. Which means that this Whiteness would first have meaning on the neo-mythic register where the concepts for a social order would be based on values that are internal to the consciousness.

The challenge will then be, in an ethno-racial sense, for this consciousness to complete this phenomenology by determining what way is socially correct and appropriate – the White way – to integrate those who have always been falsely positioned as outsiders to this presumed Whiteness and were Black and the Blackness in this body. Therefore, a key test of this ethical Whiteness will be how somatic Blacks can become happy and feel useful in this new consciousness that is multicultural Canada. But at the same time, this happiness and usefulness must occur within norms that have been agreed upon by all other groups – including the agreement of somatic Blacks themselves – that are manifested on the ethno-racial scale of Canadian humanism. Contrary to the old mythological narrative of Canada having no foundation in revolution, the 1960s was as revolutionary a moment in Canada and Western thought as the contemporaneous Civil Rights Movement was in the United States. Official multiculturalism and the search for *A Just Society* collectively was a refutation of the old order and, in the spirit of *novus ordo seculorum* (new order of the ages) usually associated with American and French Revolutions, was revolutionary for Canada.[1]

I want to explore this option as an intended good. In this way, the idealistic Blackness of multiculturalism will be transformed into a necessary and indispensable feature of the Canadian narrative. This would be achieved through the shedding of the accidental characteristics of multiculturalism, which give it its unhappy countenance. The solution would be a way of narrowing the choices within the infinities of freedom and Blackness that produced Canada as an embodied manifestation of a will to freedom. Its method would be to mine or excavate the prevailing mythologies that inform the current rational, idealistic ideology that produced Canada sociologically and anthropologically. These methods of gaining knowledge of the world would be dissected to disclose the consistent and unchangeable features in the mythologies and philosophies.

One of these features is the unchangeableness of the somatically Black female, who has traditionally been the symbol of hope in Western mythology.[2] We can undertake this examination today from a position of fuller and more complete knowledge that is based on cognition, and in our recognition that a significant part of the struggle over time has been to reduce infinities such as Canada, freedom, and Blackness to finites, but in such a way that conceptually we do not lose what is most necessary and essential to these infinities. One example of some of the ethical gains that have been made, and which as a trend could hold a ray hope that could very well burst into the full ethical White light as genuinely multicultural Canada, is what has happened in recent times to the somatically Black female in Canada.

In examining the somatically Black female as constituted ethno-racially in Canada, it is important to search also for the neo-mythic changeableness in her unchangeability, for what will present her as a useful case study of bondsmanship becoming lordship by choice and of remaining in bondsmanship when so desired. In effect, we will be looking at what it is about the somatically Black female in her Canadian creation that is idealistically Black and idealistically White at the same time. We will be looking at the somatically Black female as so symbolic of how the double negation of idealized Blackness can become idealized Whiteness. This double negation is the fulfilment of mythological and philosophical hope for humanity.

## MINING THE DIALECTICS
## OF MYTHOLOGY

The Royal Commission on Bilingualism and Biculturalism was the forerunner to Trudeau's reformulation, idealistically, of what Canada is and who Canadians are – it would lead to its dialectical opposite: hope that is multiculturalism.[3] The commission paved the way for some of the main features forming the ideological package that was *A Just Society*. These elements would include, specifically, the recommendation for Canada to officially become a bilingual but multicultural country. This commission, indirectly, would lead to Canada's recognition of its Blackness idealistically, culturally, somatically, and in status, especially in terms of its relations with the United States and many other more fully developed countries.

The Royal Commission had looked to the future in terms of who a Canadian *ought* to be by status and in terms of affectivity and motility. This was a creationist gaze, an attempt to figure out what could be made out of the physical materials that were available. It began its quest with an epistemological review of who was ontologically Canadian, noting that Canadian citizens saw themselves pragmatically as more than mere descendents of European stocks in France and England, as more than this somatic and cultural Whiteness as an untested perception had resolutely maintained for so long. The commission also looked at the existential behaviour of Canadian citizens: how they live, under what conditions of freedom or slavery they existed; what kind of ethical relationships they had with one another and with the rest of world; whether or not they were happy in that contingent moment because they were free of alienation and could fully self-actualize however they chose; and whether they were approaching the future with despair or hope.

To do this, the commission re-examined the makeup of the country's population and the impact that immigrants, as the perceived changeable in this drama, were having on the country. The commission looked specifically at the motility and the affectivity of Canadians, not only in an idealized setting that stretches into the future, but in the here and now that is their daily affairs. This motility and affectivity were based on perceptions about different ethnic and linguistic groups and what kinds of ethical relations and forms of happiness and agreed upon usefulness they should experience within the country. The commission examined the ease and speed with which groups that entered Canadian society Black in status achieved the Whiteness of acceptance and full citizenship, which it measured in terms of graduating to what it called "high status" professions and occupations:

Some immigrants have been recruited and admitted to Canada for specific, and usually lower-level occupations. The occupations that new arrivals enter, but later try to avoid, are generally those which require little or no skill, have low wage levels, and make few linguistic demands (for example, certain jobs in construction, mining, logging, the needle trades, the restaurant industry and domestic service). If an ethnic-origin category has a considerable foreign-born component, it will tend to be overrepresented in the occupations associated with entrance status. The high representation of Italian men among labourers in construction, of Italian, Portuguese, and Greek women in the needle trades, and of Italian, Portuguese, and Negro women in domestic services are all examples of entrance status.[4]

The commission noted that some immigrants did attain high statuses by occupying skilled occupations and later professions, such as in the medical and scientific fields, drafting, architecture, and electronics. Such a movement in status frees these immigrants from the contingent identities, positions, and status with which they entered Canadian society, allowing them to become part of the unchangeableness that is necessary for the survival of Canadian society and for Canadians, as both individuals and groups, to find self-determined happiness. However, when this transition happened, the commission noted that the immigrants got these jobs and positions only when native-born Canadians had avoided the occupations, were unable to get the training to fill them, or had immigrated to the United States after receiving training.

On the question of what factors enabled some groups to rise faster and further in the economy than others, the commission stated: "it seems likely that cultural characteristics have a considerable influence on the diversity in the economic status among different groups. Ethnic identity often affects behaviour and values that influence occupational choices, work habits, and spending, saving and investment practices."[5] The commissioners were silent on the question of individual social mobility; however, it was well acknowledged that the individuals were representative of the group and had no personal claims such as individual values or characteristics that made them distinct in the group. Citizens, potential citizens, and residents, especially those without a long lineage in Canada, were determined socially and positioned in the prevailing ethical relations by group traits.

Several decades later, and in the early years of a new millennium, a reading of the commission's report finds that one group that was mentioned among the changeable immigrant groups stands out, ontologically, as an unchangeable in a society that has changed significantly since the report was first issued. And this is more than passing strange: for there have been changes in the Canadian society since the 1960s. Even the expected motility value of the immigrant has changed from low-skilled to the "brightest and best" that are the most highly trained and elite of the world's population. Yet, contradictorily, this group that was so identified by the commissioners, and which at first look also appears epistemologically and ontologically to be unchangeable, is also changeable. It has had to be over the ages so that it could adapt and survive. By constructed ethnicity and racialization, this group is Black. Mythologically and perceptually, within this unchangeable concept is what appears, ironically, as another unchangeable: the female. So, phenomenologically, what have we here?

While, as Kymlicka and Hawkins have shown, such ethnic groups as Italians, Portuguese, and Greeks have been transformed into the unchangeable Whiteness that is represented by the Canadian mainstream,[6] the Black woman, as the perceived conventional Black, has not. Stereotypically, as part of a universal that is an ethnicity, in perception she has remained unchangeable. This is not an unusual approach to the somatically Black woman in what we may call Western philosophy. In the universal, she has been traditionally the unchangeable but also the misrepresented and unrecognized. This is the case in the quote above from the commissioners. But even in this reference the commissioners were misrecognizing the somatically Black female both cognitively and in terms of her affectivity and motility. While they were recognizing the presence of the Black female as Negro and domestic, they were failing to capture the being that she was in her fullness or infinity.

While many of the groups – even other domestic workers such as Italians and Portuguese – mentioned by the commission were immigrants, the typical Canadian somatically Black woman of the 1960s was mostly likely born in Canada and had a lineage that could be traced back to the formation of Canada and the founding United Empire Loyalists.[7] Indeed, as the report stated only a few pages later, possibilities for immigration by "Asians and Negroes have been restricted, in fact sometimes excluded."[8] At the time of the report, it was unlikely that the typical somatically Black woman would have been an immigrant. Yet, contradictorily in this version of the Canadian narrative, the Black woman is presented as an immigrant who must be willing to accept "entrance status" in Canada. Rather, it would not have been a stretch under the conditions that existed at the time of the commission to position the Black female, historically, as representing one of the founding peoples of Canada: "I am a fifth-generation Canadian whose ancestors came here from the United States during the fugitive slave era, as abolitionists and free Blacks trying to escape racial oppression in their homeland. Yet, routinely, I am asked, 'Where are you from?' or 'What nationality are you?' as if to be Black, you have to come from somewhere else."[9] Making this point is Adrienne Shadd, a direct descendent of Mary Ann Shadd, a woman who is associated in Canadian mythology with a different image of Canada. This is the image of a country where ontological somatic Blacks and Whites live in harmony and where, existentially, somatic Blacks can be free to determine who they want to become.

As I will show in this chapter, the realities of the Shadd women 150 years apart speak not only of the changing identity of Canadians but of the changing motility and affectivity associated with somatic Blacks in a Canadian space. The positioning of the somatically Black female within an unchangeable Blackness that is immigrant and socially inferior masks a dialectical struggle over time within Canadian society, and within the ethnic group constructed as Black, over what is by nature changeable and unchangeable in these ethical orders. It is a dialectic of freedom that, conceptually, alternates over time between hope and despair. In this dialectic, the somatically Black female is traditionally identified with divinity and hope.

## MANIFESTATIONS OF THE BLACK FEMALE

The quote above of Adrienne Shadd is from a study which shows that the somatically Black female is traditionally presented as an outsider and holder of an inferior position. In the Canadian context, she represents the agent through which, in the Hegelian sense, divine and human law interacted in ethical orders.[10] Perceptually, the somatically Black female was presented as the image of the Black body, somatically, culturally, idealistically, and in status. Even though she was an inseparable part of the Canadian body, she was misrecognized as always contingent, foreign, and Black in a White space. In the ensuing years as perception changed to historic developments, there would be a notable change in what is perceived as the changeable and unchangeable in Canadian society. On their way to attaining greater happiness and effectiveness in society through social mobility, members of genuine immigrant groups would bypass the group that in the eyes of the commissioners was represented by the somatically Black female and would thereby avoid her inferior positioning. In any discussion on ethnicities, the somatically Black female and her family remain positioned as newcomers with no claim to a prior history in Canada. Let's now look at some distinct manifestations associated perceptually with the Black female.

In the first respect, as a universal, this group has remained unchangeably Black in perception, and not only in skin colour, but also in terms of the idealized, culture, and status. However, contrary to this perception and at the level of the particular, there have been dynamics at work within this Black group. They resulted in a change in status along gender lines. The somatically Black female would become more sociologically, economically, and politically adaptable in the civil society, even to the point of attaining higher earnings than the White female. The somatically Black male, in contrast, became the embodiment of social Blackness. As a group, the somatically Black males would be ranked among the lowest in the country. However, in the prevailing thinking, these changes in status for the somatically Black female have not been fully recognized. There is still the notion of a universalized Blackness based strictly on somatic features, a contrived essence that in the public sphere often negates gender differences within the socially constructed Black ethnicity.

Second, the nature of the work associated with the motility and affectivity of the somatically Black woman is important in this dialectical struggle over what is changeable and unchangeable, an observation that can be discerned from the commissioners' report. Over the centuries, somatic Blacks in Canada had been restricted mainly to working as domestic workers, or in domestic service type jobs.[11] Theirs was the lot to service a leisure class, the socially Black or menial producers catering for the status Whites or elites. This, too, is the unchangeable in the constructed experience of ethnic Blacks. The somatically Black female has for the most part been the nurturer of her family and of the wider society where she has played, and continues to play, the role of nanny, health care provider, or worker in the service sector.[12]

None of these jobs is perceived socially as elitist. When Canada could not find enough domestic workers in the 1960s, it turned to the Caribbean, relying on somatic Blacks to continue a function that was associated, historically and unchangeably, with somatic Blacks in Canada.[13] In this respect, and contrary to what the commission report suggested, ethnic or linguistic groups could not move up freely in a hierarchy of skilled jobs and professions, a movement that leads to self-actualization in terms of happiness and a feeling of acceptance.

The specific job of domestic servant was reserved, not for an ethnicity or linguistic group, but rather for a racialized faction of society, one that in terms of its perceived motility was deemed best suited for inferior jobs. These jobs do not command the higher social statuses that many somatically White Canadian females were demanding as they entered the unchangeable that is the Trudeau-imagined mainstream, with anglophone and francophone ethnicities at the core surrounded by other accepted ethnic groups. That this racialization was associated with somatic Blackness was demonstrated in Canada's decision to recruit somatically Black Caribbean women solely for these jobs.

While somatic Whites such as the Italians and Portuguese were selected for some domestic work, this selection was not considered to be their finite motility and affectivity.[14] In this regard, the somatically Black female, as identified by the commission, subverted the notion that immigrants were chosen because of ethnic and linguistic backgrounds and that they could reasonable expect to escape from such initial positioning. The somatically Black females that would be chosen to come to major Canadian cities from the 1960s onwards would come from many different ethnicities and nationalities – including Canadian – and speak many different languages. This was so even though the majority spoke English and French.

Third, trains and domestic service are associated with pleasant thoughts in Canadian mythology about somatic Blackness and Blacks. The notion of trains is captured in the Underground Railroad, the name given to the network that allowed Africans to escape from slavery in the United States into freedom in Canada. This is part of the national narrative that Canadians are proud of. It shows them as different from the United States and as a place where liberty existed regardless of the colour of one's skin. This is part of a mythology that was shared equally by somatically White and Black Canadians, the latter group consisting of many of the slaves who used the Underground Railroad to escape slavery beyond the reaches of the *Fugitive Slave Act* in the United States.[15] It is an image of a heavenly existence for somatic Blacks and Whites alike, one that was drawn upon by the American-born Mary Ann Shadd, who published in 1852 *A Plea for Emigration*, a book in which she presented Canada as the natural place for somatic Blacks to find liberty and the freedom to excel and to self-actualize.[16] Canada was an attractive place for those who found life unbearable in the United States. Having immigrated to Canada herself, Shadd became a leading spokesperson for immigration to Canada:

In Canada, as in other recently settled countries, there is much to do, and comparatively few for the work. The numerous towns and villages springing up, and the great demand for timber and agricultural products, make labour of every kind plentiful. All trades that are practised in the United States are there patronized by whomsoever carries on: no man's complexion affecting his business. If a coloured man understands his business, he receives the public patronage the same as the white man. He is not obliged to work a little better, and at a lower rate. There is no degraded class to identify him with, therefore every man's work stands or falls according to merit, not as is his colour. Builders and other tradesmen of different complexions work together on the same building and in the same shop, with perfect harmony, and often the proprietor of an establishment is coloured, and the majority or all of the men employed are white. Businesses that in older communities have ceased to remunerate, yield a large percentage to the money invested.[17]

In Shadd's words there is much that resonates with today's idealistic discussion of multiculturalism and the assessment of Canada as a place of potential harmony where somatic Blacks would be fully integrated and attain their expected motility and affectivity.

Two metaphors are central to this discussion: one is the term "underground," which suggests that the system was in epistemological Blackness, for nothing about it was then fully revealed and much still awaits enlightenment. There is the mythology in Canada, for those who arrived by night via the Underground Railroad did not find Canada as accepting of them as the legends would suggest.[18] Mary Ann Shadd, like many of the former slaves and free Blacks, would later see Canada as inhospitable to her aims and ambitions, and eventually return to the United States, leaving behind a rich legacy that included the achievement of becoming the country's first female publisher.[19]

The other metaphor is of the somatically Black female as leader: one of the figures associated with the success of the Underground Railroad is a Black woman, in the person and leadership of Sojourner Truth. Shadd joins Truth among the earliest somatically Black leaders in Canada. These are metaphors that are worth mining or uncovering, phenomenologically, for the truths about the changeable and unchangeable that make up the experience of the somatically and culturally Black in Canada. They may also hold the truth to Canada coming to terms fully, or doing so more quickly, with the somatic Black as the Other that is also the Self in the Canadian body politic.

Fourth, in the commission's eyes, it was a woman, working as a domestic, that in terms of affectivity and motility, represented the Negro or somatically Black group. This, too, is in keeping with Canadian mythology. Over the centuries, the somatically Black female, as the unchangeable, has been the representative of the constructed ethnicity called Black. The Black community, a constructed ethnicity based primarily on somatic Blackness, has traditionally been matrifocal in a wider society that is patriarchal. The Black family has never been transfigured and recreated to look, in the main, like the typical Canadian family.[20] This is a reality that remains unchangeable to this day as demonstrated by the number of female-headed families in the Canadian Black community and the primary role that the somatically Black female plays as a nurturer in her family. Leadership in the Canadian Black community is overwhelmingly female. An example of this leadership in Canada is in the area of immigration: Canadian immigration from somatically Black countries has been traditionally female led, contrary to the models for Britain and the United States where the male preceded the female. This is particularly true of immigration from the Caribbean.

But the somatically Black female has resisted being determined as unchangeable. In recent times, she continues to march slowly towards her own attainment of freedom and to determine herself, her family, and her community. The somatically Black female has over the years transformed herself into a higher income earner in Canada, attaining a position that is higher than her male counterpart and White females, but still lower than that of the dominant White male.

James, Plaza, and Jansen have shown the adaptability of the somatically Black female in terms of learning how to survive by using her skills to their most effective ends.[21] The somatically Black female also continues, compared to her male counterpart, to make strides, academically and professionally, as demonstrated in the research by Simmons and Plaza, Simmons and Turner, and others.[22] This is particularly true, phenomenologically, of the somatically Black female in Canada who traces her culture and lineage to the Caribbean, but who in her transformation as a Canadian Black has been able to choose what from the Caribbean should pragmatically remain unchangeable in her new identity and culture and what should be discarded as part of a refashioned, hybridized cultural existence.

In this respect, the somatically Black female appears over time to be happier and better positioned in Canadian society than she once was, and than the somatically Black male. By pointing to her, Canadian society can indicate how it is making efforts to fully incorporate somatic Blackness into the Canadian ideal. But the more she is accepted and feels accepted, the more the somatically Black male appears alienated. Reconciliation, in this dialectic of Blackness, appears centred on the somatically Black female as both unchangeable and changeable, and as the mediator; the somatically Black male might be more successful by changing to become like, or even mimicking, the somatically Black female while holding onto what is innately and socially unchangeable; Canadian society should aspire to bring the somatically Black male fully into society in much the same way that the somatically Black female appears to be progressing; the somatically Black female must seek her own actualization and happiness that might be independent of the somatically Black male and of the wishes of a patriarchal society.

By way of raising issues that result from the dialectics of Canadian history and which are sited in the somatically Black female, this chapter argues that the somatically Black female plays a significant role in Canadian mythology, and that she holds out hope for a reconciliation over somatic Blackness within Canada. This could be the final step to Canadians coming to terms fully with Blackness in its four forms: the idealized, cultural, somatic, and status. A full explanation of this potential for reconciliation is beyond the scope of this book. This chapter seeks merely to highlight tensions and contradictions that arise dialectically out of the phenomenon that is the somatically Black female and to raise potential areas of continued research that might hold promise for a full reconciliation of Blackness in Canada.

This will be achieved by looking, specifically, at how the somatically Black female from the Caribbean has adapted to Canadian multiculturalism and fashioned for herself a place in the Just Society. A question that might be of concern in this discussion, for example, might be whether it was easier in terms of lessening social equalities for Canada to incorporate the Black female into society because the Caribbean female was chosen for a specific role and function in society – unlike the somatically Black male, who came as a companion to the female and secondarily as part of a universally accepted group without a defined function within the idealized civil society. Just as important, on the surface, the somatically Black female has accepted this incorporation and positioning as a first step towards advancement and as necessary for maintaining body and soul and the survival of the somatically Black family. The positioning of somatically Black males has been more problematic.[23]

In raising these sociological issues, I offer an analysis that argues philosophically that the somatically Black female is the divinity within the family and the wider society. I present the Black female as the mediator that holds the potential for helping Canada to escape from an unhappy consciousness that results from the ethical relations between a changeable group constructed ethnically as Black and the unchangeable that is Canada itself.

## SOMATICALLY BLACK FEMALE: THE MEDIATOR OF UNHAPPINESS

From the Canadian perspective, the unhappiness is reflected in the socially constructed deviant behaviour by some somatically Black males, who appear impervious to attempts by Canadian society to socialize them.[24] Unlike the somatically Black female, the somatically Black male is not perceived in the prevailing Canadian consciousness as having changeable qualities. I will present the somatically Black female of Caribbean socialization and creolized culture as representing the attainment of the idealized good that is associated with the unchangeable that is Canada, but who is changeable because she is also an immigrant, or presented as immigrant, and as female in a wider society that is patriarchal in its ordering.[25]

Socially, she is changeable. As perceptually the strong spirit in the family, the somatically Black female, as a universal, ensures the survival of this basic unit of society, a unit that she maintains in many cases without the presence of the father. She nurtures the male partner in her family and supports him in his struggles with the forces of nature that he encounters in the wider civil society. The somatically Black female sacrifices her body when necessary and also, when appropriate, remains strong and committed to her ideals. "Although (somatically) Black women are significantly more likely to head single parent families than Canadian women in general, Black women still have higher employment rates than Canadian women in general. Similar trends with regard to public assistance rates can be observed. Notwithstanding the higher percentage of single parents in the Black population, Black women are less likely to be dependent on government transfer payments for their support than Canadian women in general (13.5% of Black women; 15.2% for all Canadian women.)"[26]

In her culture, the difference between body and mind depends on the context, but, universally, she is committed to the survival of the family and not necessarily the wider society. Mythologically, in the Hegelian analysis, the Black woman is the Antigone of Greek tragedy and the Eve of Hebraic tradition – the epitome of idealized, cultural, and status Blackness. In *Phenomenology of Spirit*, Hegel argues that the state or government that is constructed out of individuals and by the family represents the ethical order at any given time. It acts according to human law. Yet, contradictorily, in dialectical opposition to this order, and also as an expression of Spirit, is the family, which is governed by divine law. Within the family, the male is the preferred conduit through which the human and divine laws, as separate ethical orders, interact. This suggests that in this ethical world of clearly defined roles and order, the public sphere of civil society can be presented as the primary site for patriarchy, and the private sphere, as represented by the hearth and home, for matriarchy.

Ultimately, the male sibling must leave the home and go out into the real world to make a living and to attach himself to another family. In this sense, the man appears in this ethical order to fulfil the role of a permanent immigrant of sorts, or indeed of even a refuge, who must leave his old home to find a new life elsewhere and who must find refugee from an unloving world in the home with the female at its heart. Here, the males are the changeable in a society of families, and females represent the unchangeable – the blood that flows within families and, hence, within societies. From this analysis, I postulate that in many respects the somatically Black family in Canada follows the Hegelian explanation of an ethical order in which the female governs and controls the home and where the position of the male is largely superfluous. His main task within the divine order is to help women to procreate. In doing this, he effectively ensures the continuation of a family that, in terms of being an unchangeable across generations, is more the lineage of the wife/woman than of the male. The procreation of the family and its nurturing are the duties of the female. In Hegel's ethical order, the somatically Black male is to find meaning mostly in the wider civil society, but this is an order that in practice will deny him recognition and meaning in life, and, ultimately, could destroy him.

The somatically Black female is thus the one keeper of the culture and gods of her particular family. It is her duty to produce the next generation, something that she does intuitively. She is the embodiment of divine law that is expressed through the family, an unchangeable in the form of divinity that she will pass on through her female offspring. This she will do by bringing a recognized man into her family as a husband. With him, she will make the children that will be the changeable in the unchangeable that is the family and which exists across generations even though the individual members die. In this regard, mythologically, the somatically Black female is the quintessential Eve of the Hebraic tradition – the one who impresses upon the male the need to reproduce and, in the process, makes him confront the possibility of his own death and the need for him to beget bodies as replacements.

At the same time, she is the temptress Eve of Christian tradition, the one that is capable of using her body to tempt and defile the male and thereby undermine the purity and even the nativity of the idyllic society. This is the woman as outsider in a rational world but who comes into the body politic with the role of defiling it – a role that was traditionally associated with the somatically Black female who was determined by dominant White males in Western civilization and its mythologies to be a sexual predator, through her cunning and sexuality capable of undermining society by casting a sexual spell on White males. The result is death of the society through defilement and impurity at the hands of the temptress.

Usually, this death occurs, and primarily for the male members, in the ethical order of human law, where the males must go out to achieve self-actualization, pleasure, and recognition. This is where the male finds the new family within which he gets the children to perpetuate himself across generations, but where he is likely to be confronted by a Nature that is constantly trying to kill him. In this regard, the male goes forth from the shelter of the family and its divine law, like a Biblical Adam, whose consciousness is only about his individuality, until he is brought into another family by a female for the primary purposes of procreation and to help with the preservation of what is accepted as the female's family.

However, the relationship between the male and female is ultimately determined by "testing, not the laws, but what is done,"[27] which for the female is the preservation of her family. This certainty in the law and regulations for the woman is unlike what happens to the somatically Black male, who has no idea of how to concretely achieve his happiness, which must be attained, idealistically, in the wider universal that is the nation. If the woman sacrifices herself, it is not usually for the wider community. As in the case of the Greek tragedy *Antigone*, the somatically Black female's sacrifice is for the good of the family and its preservation. When the male sacrifices himself, it is usually, like a soldier, for the wider society and not primarily for the family. Seldom does he sacrifice himself in the other ethical order that is the divine, or family. In this way, the male is unchangeable or concerned primarily with human law.

The somatically Black female, however, is adaptable, and to make this point I shall look, specifically, at one group of somatically Black women: those that were initially socialized in the Caribbean and have had to make a distinction in their native land between status Blackness and Whiteness. These are adaptation skills that helped this group of somatically Black females when they immigrated to Canada and established families while trying to integrate into an alienating society. Somatically Black Caribbean males, who were not socialized to have these differentiating skills, perform much worse than the more adaptable somatically Black females. It is a difference that could lead to a fuller understanding of the social differences, along the lines of gender, among somatic Blacks in terms of performance, achievements, and family relations.

It is necessary to be cautious, however, in raising these issues, for there is the danger of appearing to overly romanticize the position of the somatically Black female as fully actualized and fulfilled within Canada and to present her as always sacrificing herself selflessly. The intention is not this, but simply to examine her universal status and attitudes for what can be learned. Second, neither is the analysis intended to "blame the victim" by disparaging somatically Black males; rather, the intention is to examine the dialectical contradictions that arise from the socialization of these males in the home and the expectations they have for themselves and the treatment they expect in the wider ethical order, which expectation could leave them conflicted and unhappy when "reality" proves different from the expected.

As with a Hegelian analysis, it should be taken for granted that even within the reconciliation that is presented as the somatically Black female, dialectical tensions and contradictions are already at work. In a second and later look, these tensions are likely to negate, in the particular, what can be discerned in a first step as the universal. Here, critics might say that we are merely scavenging through the rubble of history at the feet of this unhappy consciousness that thought it was White but now knows it is Black – a scavenging that we hope will produce some nuggets of the good, a few uncut gems on which we can speculatively base any hope for the future. This is not intended to produce a false consciousness by presenting the world as it is not – rather it is a conscious and rational attempt to ignore the obvious evil and to claim refuge in what good there might be.

As an additional caution, there is the likelihood of appearing to dehistoricize the discussion on the somatically Black female by appearing to de-emphasize the agencies and institutions that helped to create the somatically Black Canadian male and female. This, too, is not the aim. To this end, and having discussed somatic Blackness as a particular in a specific context, I shall then reinsert the issues I raise on the Black female, and her potential mediating role, into the wider discussion of Canadian Blackness.

### BLACK FEMALE: CHANGEABLE AND UNCHANGEABLE

In the 1960s, Canada turned to the English-speaking Caribbean to recruit domestic workers to replace the women who were finding employment in the workforce and thus leaving the nation's homes.[28] In doing this, Canada departed from the model that had been developed in the United States and Britain that relied on male-led immigration from this region. For decades, the United States, and later Britain, had recruited low-skilled workers from the Caribbean, with the majority of these immigrants being somatically Black males.

British migration started with the arrival in the Caribbean of the ship *Windrush*, which has gone into history, and British and Caribbean folklore, as providing a modern time and date for beginning the official transformation of England into an uncontested Black country.[29] In 1948, the ship went to islands in the then-British Caribbean as part of a labour recruitment drive for the metropolitan country. Elaine Arnold presents the motives for the ensuing migration to Britain: "Unemployed West Indians responded to the recruitment drive for labor in what was considered the 'mother country.' Some were ex-servicemen (from the Second World War) who found that on return from the war, the economic conditions, especially in Jamaica, had so deteriorated that it was impossible to find any form of employment; there seemed no alternative but to return to Britain. Others regarded migration to Britain for a period of time as an opportunity to improve their education and economic status."[30]

An important feature of this migration was that it was male-led, in keeping with the tradition in the English-speaking Caribbean of exporting excess male labour, either permanently or temporarily, to such places as Panama, Cuba, and the United States, and as seafarers also. Arnold states: "From the beginning of West Indian migration, there was a high proportion of women among the immigrants, but the pattern that finally emerged showed that men migrated first to secure employment and housing before their partners followed. The latter arrived with one or more children. Most children, however, were left with grandmothers, aunts, and other adults within the extended family. It was estimated that during the peak period of immigration, 1953 to 1956, 162,000 individuals came to Britain of whom 52% were men, 40% were women, and 8% children."[31]

As the authors of the book *Windrush* show, life changed markedly for the immigrants, and importantly, for the receiving society, with the arrival of the somatically Black female in large numbers in Britain. Until then, the males were sojourners of a sort, with their familial ties "back home." They were useful to their new society only for the low-skilled jobs that they filled. Their primary usefulness was to their Caribbean society, where, idealistically detached from their surroundings and clothed in their rational Whiteness from another world, they would remit money in keeping with their traditional role of economic provider. Most immigrants had expected that they would stay abroad for a short while, make some money or acquire an education or profession, and return home as soon as possible to cement their positions as idealistically and socially White. In general, they appeared happy with their positioning as socially Black in the receiving country. With the arrival of the women to join their mates, and with the ensuing creation, or reuniting, of families, Caribbean Blacks began demanding inclusion in the society: the motility and affectivity changed and became centred in the land in which they lived rather than in the places from which they had come.

It was the females who called for a social rebirth. The immigrants started to make demands for better housing and for better education and working conditions. They wanted an improved quality of life and full recognition for their worth to the society. They wanted to be recognized not as foreigners and visitors but as full citizens. They demanded to be recognized and treated fully as White in all respects. They demanded to be recreated in the image of the state and at the same time demanded the right to make the state in their image as immigrants and citizens. As Phillips and Phillips explain, in Britain the arrival of the female in larger numbers after 1960 caused a major shift in migrant lifestyles: "The new influx [of women] made a fundamental alteration to the tone of life for the majority of immigrants. For one thing it sharpened the pressure to own property, and the Caribbean migrants began moving out of the centres where they had originally settled. Few migrants qualified for council housing and private ownership became the overwhelming pattern. The immediate result was to privilege the habits and institutions which would help in this process."[32]

The Caribbean female that is somatically Black was acting according to her first forms of socialization, as shown by her actions in the Caribbean, in the United States, and wherever else she had gone to join her partner. Baptiste, Hardy, and Lewis show in their research in *Clinical Practice with Caribbean Immigrant Families in the United States* that the immigrant pattern followed the tradition male-first model and had the same results. "For example, a spouse (often the male) may emigrate and later be joined by the other spouse and children, if any, and often relatives of one or both spouses."[33] This was the case at the height of Caribbean migration to the United States from 1948 to 1978, but this pattern was also part of the long-term immigrant trend from the early nineteenth century. The transformation from the Blackness of the immigrant to Whiteness of citizens occurred through the female – the female often leading the quest for the Whiteness of a new determinacy of citizenship and belonging and for the family to put down new roots in a new place. The males tended to remain focused on back home, especially when the female and the rest of the family had remained there.

Indeed, African-American literature is replete with the image of the strong West Indian female who, as a specially created somatic Black, demanded changes and acceptance in the receiving society. This image is consistent with the two contrasting views of the female in this literature. One image is of the somatically Black female as the voice of reason that encourages her mate to fight for such ideals as liberty and freedom in the wider society, and to even sacrifice himself for the idealistic good of the wider society. The other image is of the female who sacrifices the male, and not for ideals, but exclusively for material gain that will advance her family. The latter is the image of the woman who joins with the forces of nature in the wider society to destroy her mate.[34]

In his seminal work *Invisible Man,* noted African-American author Ralph Ellison gives the role of inciting African-Americans to physical struggle for their freedom, not to African-Americans themselves as a separate ethnicity or even to men in general, but to the West Indian woman as typical of a specially created somatically Black female.[35] This is so even though, in a book that chronicled fictionally the drive for freedom and recognition in African-America, he found a pivotal role for a Marcus Garvey-like inciter in Ras the Exhorter.[36]

Ras the Exhorter aside, in *Invisible Man* it is the West Indian woman that becomes the voice of the Hebraic and vengeful God issuing commands and commandments to the African-Americans so that they may rise up and not only claim their heritage and rights, but punish those who have offended them, and through a new covenant create an existence pleasing to their God and themselves. The pivotal incitement occurs after an old somatically Black woman strikes a White policeman, representing officialdom and the prevailing order and good, who was trying to remove her from her home, the site of divinity and, dialectically, a different ethical order: "'The brute stuck that gentle woman, poor thing!' the West Indian woman chanted. 'Black men, did you see such a brute? Is he a gentleman, I ask you? Give it back to him, black man. Repay the brute a thousandfold! Give it back to him unto the third and fourth generations. Strike him, our fine black men. Protect your black woman! Repay the arrogant creature to the third and fourth generations.'"[37]

In keeping with Greek tradition, the men then went into battle for the honour of their women, to protect the hearth and their cultural gods, to liberate their Helen of Troy. Later, as she looked on the disarray that resulted from rioting, the woman joined with others of her gender and declared that, in the Hebraic sense again, the world that resulted from her command was good. This was the rioting that foreshadowed what occurred in the 1960s over issues like housing and which would become so central to the US civil rights freedom struggle. Here again, Ellison gives the identity of this somatically Black or African god that is mindful of the past, present, and future occurring in the same moment to a West Indian woman. He writes:

"I feel so good," a woman said. "I feel so *good!*"
"Black men, I'm proud of you," the West Indian woman shrilled.
"Proud!"[38]

Ellison allows the West Indian to echo the Christian affirmation by the Hebraic God, who, looking at the handiwork of his son, the mediator, Jesus, proudly proclaimed, "I am well pleased." If, in a Hegelian sense, Ellison is claiming that the nameless invisible man of his story is indeed human Spirit as it moves through the Americas, then in this case it reacts to the commands of the somatically Black woman, specifically in the strong West Indian woman, who gives the creation a morality.

The role of the West Indian woman is also fictionalized in another seminal work in African-American literature, Paule Marshall's *Brown Girl, Brown Stone*, which looked at the material-acquiring tendency of the West Indian female.[39] Here, she is not only the god who thinks, but one who acts, builds, acquires, and destroys unintentionally. Again, as we discussed earlier, mythologically, this is the god whose actions invariably produce what is different from what was imagined, so that creation is never complete, as perfection is always, at least, one round of construction and manifestation away. This is the frustrated god that has to look to the next generation to complete its task, and to correct all flaws and aberrations that were unintentionally produced through detours to the intended ending of history. This tendency of existing in an imperfect world placed the somatically Black female in a dialectical relationship with a rational Adam-like husband, who aspired to dreams about perfection, who was even willing to minimize the existing imperfections and their effects, but who did little to achieve the preferred ending or to change the circumstances that were in the way of his self-actualization. But this doggedness of intent by the female is a kind of attitude that, at times, has been presented in some quarters as detrimental to the liberation of the somatically Black male in both the family and wider society. This was a concern that was addressed, and refuted from the 1960s onwards, by such noted writers as Toni Morrison and Alice Walker.[40] They presented an alternative route to upliftment and freedom for somatic Blacks and African-Americans from a female perspective.[41] In all cases, the images of the strong somatically Black female as God and even temptress persist.

By following a female-led model of immigration, Canada truncated the traditional process and, in so doing, provided the somatically Black female with the stage on which to seek excellence without first having it prepared by the somatically Black male. Canada, in a sense, liberated the somatically Black female as the creative force. Canada collapsed the separate divine and secular laws of the ethical order into one category of Blackness, the Black female, even if they remained apart for the Black male. In this way, the somatically Black female became the lead actor in the tragedy that is hers, her family's, and that of her adopted country. Like Ellison's somatically Black woman, she gives commands and approval, but is reliant on someone else's actions. Like Marshall's tragic figure, she not only dreams to satisfy the needs of the mind, but schemes and acquires to make happy the bodily passions. To pull this off, the somatically Black female fell back on the mythologies and metaphors that had helped shape her in her homeland. The adaptation was to the setting and time.

## "HOW DID SHE COME SO?": ADJUSTING TO PATRIARCHY

The attitudes to social integration exhibited by the somatically Black female were created in the Caribbean, a place where she was forced to develop her skills as a mediator. Her motility also was discerned, ultimately, as Edith Clarke suggests in her pivotal work *My Mother Who Fathered Me*, in an environment where the somatically Black female is often forced to perform the traditional roles of both genders.[42] Her happiness comes from being able to be leader and follower at the same time, and from negotiating these contradictions often at the expense of her body. Hyacinth Evans and Rose Davies describe the gender roles in the Caribbean this way:

The family household is an important context for gender role socialization. The evidence suggests that in two-parent families in the Caribbean, the man and woman are expected to perform different roles. The male role is conceived as primarily an economic one. The woman, on the other hand, cares for the children and the home, and her role is that of a nurturer, even though she may also be a significant provider in the home. Men traditionally do not perform household tasks, which are relegated to the female helpers or female members of the household. Since observational learning is important in gender role learning, boys and girls learn about gender differentiation from the roles their parents assume in the home and in the society at large.[43]

This kind of socialization or social creation occurs across classes, with the result that the Caribbean males are "pampered and catered to" because of the gender inequality. The value of the male is primarily economic and the family's utility is to prepare him for this struggle in the wider society: in the home, idealistically, he does not have to struggle also. This is the case even in status White upper-class homes, where neither boys nor girls are expected to do household chores on a regular basis. Nonetheless, the female child is still expected to learn the rudiments of household management while the male learns how to be waited on.[44] However, there is a cost to the males from this pampering and a benefit to the females. I raise the argument that the costs and benefits from this socialization provide a possible explanation for the differences in achievements and attitudes between somatically Black Caribbean males and females and their offspring in Canada. Evans and Davies explain:

Despite any feelings about unfairness that they may have, girls who carry out these household tasks on a daily basis learn more things that boys do not – a sense of responsibility, discipline, a sense of the process getting done. Such qualities make girls more disposed to adjusting to the institutional requirements, such as those of the school. Because there are fewer opportunities for boys to learn these skills and dispositions, differential socialization may have implications for learning and per-formance in school, on the job, and in various societal roles. The concern is that boys are brought up to regard themselves as superior to girls, but girls are provided the experiences that make them in the long run more competent and more able to cope with the demands of life.[45]

Using statistics for Jamaica, Evans and Davies note that the results of this socialization are apparent in the way females outnumber males in high schools, in females having a two-to-one entrance ratio at the University of the West Indies, and in female literacy rates that are ten percentage points higher than for males. Another result is the absence of fathers in homes, so that the female provides the love and stability to the children while the male meets a responsibility that is defined primarily as economic. This trend is replicated in Canada, but with one significant difference: in Canada the Black male has lost the status Whiteness he had in the Caribbean.

In her article *Class, Race, and Gender Issues in Child Rearing in the Caribbean,* Elsa A. Leo-Rhynie explains that there are three major catego-ries of marital relationships in the Caribbean.[46] First is the visiting male, where the man and woman share a sexual relationship, but they are not legally united or do not share a common residence. Second is the common-law relationship, where the man and the woman are not legally united, but share a sexual union and a common residence. Third is where the man and the woman are legally married and share the same residence. In terms of child bearing, some 50 per cent of Caribbean women start having children while they are adolescents. "Only about 25% of children in the Caribbean are born into a married union; the others are born and reared in a family situation in which there is no resident male, and/or where the persons in residence may not be actual relatives."[47]

In the Caribbean, females head more than 30 per cent of households. Typically, young mothers are in visiting unions, which are the least stable, and the mother may later move on to another relation with someone who is not the child's father. This creates the contradiction where the female pro-vides the leadership in the home in all areas but the economic, a situation that exists even in the traditional nuclear family, but with the woman still playing a subordinate role to the male.[48]

Like other immigrants, those from the Caribbean travel with their cul-tures and try to re-establish them in the new land, especially as culture applies to such institutions as the family. Canada's adoption of a female-led migration of somatic Blacks undermined the intended effects and social ordering of the Caribbean patterns of socialization. First, it freed the female economically. She was, and is, the one that makes more money in the fam-ily. Second, in a way reminiscent of Wilson's description of how the United States constructed an underclass, somatically Black males in Canada felt further disempowered by their inability to find satisfactory employment.[49] This development effectively negated the notion that the male's responsibility is primarily economic. Indeed, it reversed the traditional male and female roles by making the male economically dependent on the female. The result is that the somatically Black male in Canada finds himself in an alien land, and without adequate socialization for a successful adaptation. With, idealistically, his sole area of responsibility taken away, his motility was questionable, as was his contribution to the affectivity of the family. Having lost his economic role in the family, all that remains is his most basic procreative function.

Mythologically, the somatically Black male is like a Biblical Adam. He thinks he is the centre of the universe. When confronted by what he sees as the negating forces of nature, he returns into himself stoically and withers psychologically. In this case, the Black males appear more likely to become the activists and the intellectuals, primarily those who continue to criticize the society at the expense of their personal material gains, and who are forever reminding Canada of its failure to live up to its professed ideals which it has offered up as universals.

Alternately, they become sceptics, those who become disruptive in the Canadian system because they no longer believe in the purity of the Canadian ideals. This is demonstrated by the number of males who have dropped out of society, noticeably in education, who do not fully participate in the agencies and institutions of official Canadian culture, and who are involved in judicial and penal systems.[50] The somatically Black male from the Caribbean finds that, in Canada, he is not socially White. The somatically Black male thus gives the appearance of being unable to cope effectively with the unexpected circumstances.

The somatically Black male, true to his training and socialization, imagines that he is recreating the world from back home, but with one significant part missing. What is missing is his traditional role, for in the creation of roles in the wider society he has no control and, indeed, no say. Without a role, he cannot improvise, for he has not been trained to do so as instinctively as the somatically Black female; he cannot function adequately in a family and wider society that is constructed according to cultural norms that do not privilege him as White in status. Rather than finding freedom in Canada as imagined from a special kind of socialization before immigration or in families still structured as they were outside Canada, the somatically Black male feels imprisoned and fully determined as unessential to both the family *and* society.

The experience of the somatically Black female from the Caribbean is different, though she, too, finds existence in Canada and the Caribbean not as idealistic as she would have wished. She at least has been trained to adapt, even when she was middle or upper class in her homeland and was idealistically and culturally White. She has learned to use what materials are available to create an existence. Her socialization tells her that despite this Whiteness, her virtue even in the Caribbean is, as Hegel suggests, impure, as she has been trained to be Black in status and to be idealistically impure in the expectation of the world, for she has been socialized to expect that the world could turn cold on her and she would have to react by fending for herself in the wider society while maintaining her main responsibilities in the family. She does not expect to make the world beyond her family, which she produces out of her body, but only to react to what she finds. The result is that when she arrives in Canada, freed of the economic constraints of back home, she does not have to rely on an inherited Canadian mythology of Frye or Davies in which nature threatens humans. She already knows that, and she knows that nature in particular would always be a threat to her.

She instead experiences herself as seeking full actualization and individuation within universal nature, for she, too, is nature in the particular – for even instinctively she knows she is in a lordship and bondage relationship within nature in general. That she is not recognized as White in status does not throw her off for long, for she had been prepared for this eventuality and for the misrecognition. The somatically Black female does not rely on a scientific diagnosis of what the objective world demands as being "realistic," for she sees the Other not as a projection of herself but as an independent other who can and should be cherished for its own sake. This is true whether that other is a spouse, her fatherless child, the children in the homes where she works, the patients in the hospital, the boss in the office, fellow ministers of government, or the Blackness that lives in her body and which she has been socialized to be aware of constantly. The somatically Black female performs in the circumstances in which she finds herself and, in so doing, she remains true to herself as the bondsman does in its relationship with a lord, even to the point of acquiring the consciousness of the lord, and in all these things she becomes a being that as an embodiment of Nature and the times brings out the ethical truth of the spirit of what Canada is at any given time. Meanwhile, in the home, the private space away from the lord, she nurtures and keeps alive the creole culture that is best epitomized by her adaptability. She is constantly the creative force, always extending boundaries and shaping new orders out of the old.

However, as the somatically Black male fails to make progress in the new environment, how happy can she be? Does she sacrifice her personal affectivity for a motility that at least guarantees survival moment to moment, and as such becomes a bridge between the somatically Black make and the wider Canadian society, or between the consciousness that is her culture and home and the universal consciousness that is the state? These are some of the implications that need a fuller examination, especially those that look at the somatically Black female in the particular. However, if as Hegel suggests, the keeper of home and the gods of culture is divinity, then the Black female is divine.[51]

And within this divinity rests an infinite hope and the White light that is the promise of multiculturalism. This is a promise based on the main threads of the dominant view in the perceived Western civilization, namely, that in an ideal and just society it is possible to turn somatic and status Blackness into idealized Whiteness. This is the promise for a group of people in multicultural Canada clinging to the hope that somatic Blackness is not necessarily and unchangeably social or status Blackness. By looking within this dialectic, we can identify some of the forces that, within the same unity, produce despair or its opposite, hope. To this end, the hope of the Black female, and the way that she embodies the dreams of life, justice, and fulfilment in society, might hold the key to how somatic Blacks are integrated in society and to how society as a universal becomes reconciled fully with the Blackness, and the attendant promises of full inclusion, that is now the hue, creativity, and hope of multicultural Canada. In her creation, the somatically Black female epitomizes the reification of multiculturalism as idealized Blackness and Blackness as the seeming unchangeable in multiculturalism.

In this respect, she offers Canada the hope for an ethical relation that brings together the best of what is meaningful from the ethno-racial and neo-mythic registers, and in an order that does not have to be completely transcendental to produce happiness and a fully understood licensed freedom.

## ASSESSING THE PHENOMENOLOGICAL SEARCH

In this light then, our Canadian consciousness has arrived phenomenologically at a moment of fuller knowledge of itself within a social order that is Western culture. It now knows rationally what to make of its past, how it is positioned at this moment in history, and what some of the bright lights are that will beckon it towards the future. This consciousness now knows how to combine these three phases into a new narrative – one that presents Canada and Canadians in all shapes, forms, and manifestations as always intended to achieve goodness – and how this consciousness might still be able to meet this goal. Indeed, the consciousness has a better idea of what this consciousness truly is, what makes it happy and unhappy as aspects of its affectivity, and what, in terms of its motility, the consciousness and others alike may think is the best use that can be made of the consciousness's ontological and anthropological Black body. This new knowledge from a social phenomenology like what we have just completed leaves the consciousness aware that it is still Black idealistically, culturally, in status, and somatically because of the growing presence of somatic Blacks in its population. Particularly, it is even ethically Black, or neo-mythically *baaad* even in the jargon of today's somatically Black ghettoes, hoods, projects, and jungles: for the consciousness has been unjust even by standards of its own reasonableness, in the way that it treats some part of its body politic, of its own Self. Indeed, citizenship does not equate universally into an abstract equality for all Canadians – but rather there is the unhappiness of some citizens enjoying fewer benefits than others. Therefore, this consciousness has not created a lived experience of idealized Whiteness, so that its existence is still Blackness – heck, the consciousness still does not even know what *is* the essence of Canada and Canadian; (it knows some of the things this purported essence is *not*, including those that it has found out not to be the essence as it had once thought). Yet, in this epistemological Blackness, this Self has to continue acting conceptually and imaginatively as if such an essence does exist. This means on just about every account, attempts at creating Whiteness, and treating this creation as if Whiteness is a natural position and hence unchangeable, have been a failure. The promise by modernity to the West of unchangeable certainty, surety, and predictability from systematically knowing the Self either as an individual or a collective union has turned out to be false.

But, idealistically, as an exercise in errantry, what the consciousness has produced through this self-examination is not knowledge that should lead to despair – it is an awareness of the characteristics, values, and virtues of the human materials that the consciousness has to deal with if it truly wants to convert its lived Blackness into an ethical and idealized Whiteness. Indeed, this is the idealistic sentiment captured in the words of the former Canadian prime minister Pierre Elliott Trudeau and his dream of making Canada genuinely a just society – a Black world where all humanity in all its Blackness can live together as equals, where none of us would be a bondsman to the lords among us. "To seek to create the just society," Trudeau says, "must be amongst the highest of those human purposes."[52] But in a summation of what has been the outcome of the eternal quest by humanity for freedom so far, Trudeau warns that more of the same failures should be anticipated. Still, he suggests, there could be a difference in the face of such errors. There should be hope. "Because we are mortal and imperfect, it is a task we will never finish; no government or society ever will. But from our honest and ceaseless effort, we will draw strength and inspiration, we will discover new and better values, we will achieve an unprecedented level of human consciousness. On the never-ending road to perfect justice we will, in other words, succeed in creating the most humane and compassionate society possible."[53] Indeed, in its eternal Blackness, humanity must strive for that Whiteness of a new humanism, even though it will fail – for from its failings humanity will gain knowledge, and who knows perhaps become lucky enough to find itself living in a world just like what it has imagined. In a specific way, through its imagining, and then through the creation of social norms, the Canadian consciousness has the power to imagine what could be *genuine multiculturalism* – a radical form of democracy, marked by egalitarianism and inclusiveness for members in the idealized social order. This is the hope to found a single ethical relationship that as a creation is currently only a work in progress. Such a creation will always be coloured and influenced by the Blackness of creativity, the carnivalesque and what is generally accepted as *jouissance*. And with good will as the main plank of this social order, the Canadian consciousness can proceed to attempt to complete the creation of its world in its own idealistic and perfected likeness – a world of idealistic Whiteness where equally, without contradictions, every human being in the social order would be as free as any lord can imagine for herself or himself.

# Notes

## PROLOGUE

1 Hegel's *Encylopedia* ii:320, as quoted in M.J. Inwood, *Hegel* (London: Routledge, 1998), 69.

2 W.E.B. Du Bois, "The Conservation of Races," in *Identities: Race, Class, Gender and Nationality*, ed. Linda Martin Alcoff and Eduardo Mendieta (Oxford: Blackwell, 2003), 46.

3 Himani Bannerji, *The Dark Side of the Nation: Essays on Multiculturalism, Nationalism and Gender* (Toronto: Canadian Scholars' Press, 2000); Neil Bissoondath, *Selling Illusion: The Cult of Multiculturalism in Canada* (Toronto: Penguin, 1994); Wsevolod W. Isajiw, *Multiculturalism in North America and Europe: Comparative Perspectives on Interethnic Relations and Social Incorporation* (Toronto: Canadian Scholars' Press, 1997); Will Kymlicka, *Multicultural Citizenship: Liberal Theory of Minority Rights* (Oxford: Clarendon Press, 1995); ibid., *Politics in the Vernacular: Nationalism, Multiculturalism, and Citizenship* (Oxford: Oxford UP, 2000); Alvin J. Schmidt, *The Menace of Multiculturalism: Trojan Horse of America* (Westport, Conn.: Praeger Publishers, 1997); Jon Stratton and Ien Ang, "Multicultural Imagined Communities: Cultural Difference and National Identity in the USA and Australia," in *Multicultural States: Rethinking Difference and Identity*, ed. David Bennet (London: Routledge, 1998); Charles Taylor, "The Politics of Recognition," in *Multiculturalism: Examining the Politics of Recognition*, ed. Amy Gutmann (Princeton: Princeton UP, 1994)); Cecil Foster, *Where Race Does Not Matter: The New Spirit of Modernity* (Toronto: Penguin, 2005).

4 Here we are reminded of the metaphor of a journey that is used by Robert Solomon to explain the Hegelian quest for knowledge and the "method" that is involved in this acquisition. "It [the process] has its definitive movements, even improvements, but it is the journey, not the final destination, that gives us our appreciation of humanity, its unity and differences." Robert C. Solomon, *In the*

*Spirit of Hegel: A Study of G.W.F. Hegel's Phenomenology of Spirit* (New York: Oxford UP, 1983), 26.

5 Édouard Glissant, *Poetics of Relation*, trans. Betsy Wing (Ann Arbor: University of Michigan Press., 2000); ibid., *Caribbean Discoures: Selected Essays* (Charlotteville, N.C.: University Press of Virginia, 1989); Edward Kamau Brathwaite, *Contradictionary Omens: Cultural Diversity and Integration in the Caribbean* (Kingston, Jamaica: Savacou Publications, 1974); ibid., "Nation Language," in *The Post-Colonial Studies Reader*, ed. Bill Ashcroft, Gareth Griffiths, and Helen Tiffin (London: Routledge, 1995); Aimé Césaire, *Discourse on Colonialism* (New York: Monthly Review, 1972); Aimé Césaire, *A Tempest*, trans. Richard Miller (New York: UBU Repertory Theater, 1992).

6 Martin Heidegger, *The Question of Being* (New York: NCUP, 1956); Stuart Hall, "Subjects in History: Making Diasporic Identities," in *The House That Race Built: Black Americans, U.S. Terrain* (New York: Pantheon Books, 1997); ibid., "Cultural Identity and Diaspora," in *Identity: Community, Culture, Difference*, ed. Jonathan Rutherford (London: Lawrence and Wishart, 1990).

7 Philip Fisher, *Hard Facts: Setting and Form in the American Novel* (New York: Oxford UP, 1985), 3–4.

8 Emmanuel Levinas, *Otherwise Than Being: Or beyond Essence* (Pittsburgh: Duquesne UP, 1998).

9 Karl Marx, "On the Jewish Question," in *Identities: Race, Class, Gender, and Nationality*, ed. Linda Martin Alcoff and Eduardo Mendieta (Oxford: Blackwell, 2003), 27.

10 Ibid., 28.

11 Immanuel Kant, *Critique of Practical Reason*, trans. Lewis White Beck (Indianapolis: Bobbs-Merrill Company, 1956), 61. Kant further developed this point when he said on the next page: "But good or evil always indicates a relation to the will so far as it is determined by the law of reason to make something its object, for the will is never determined directly by the object and our conception of it; rather, the will is a faculty which can make an object real. Thus good or evil are properly referred to actions and not to the sensory state of the person. If something is to be, or is held to be, absolutely good or evil in all respects and without qualification, it could be a thing but only the manner of acting, i.e., it could be only the maxim of the will, and consequently the acting person himself as a good or evil man."

12 Fisher, *Hard Facts*, 4.

13 Ibid., 4–5.

14 C.L.R. James, *Notes on Dialectics: Hegel, Marx, Lenin* (London: Allison and Busby, 1980), 9.

15 Ibid., 10. Similarly, we may think of what the French critic and theorist Maurice Blanchot had to say of this dialectical search that, as he says, really has no last question: "Where we finish, we begin. Where we begin, we do not truly begin unless the beginning is once again at the term of everything, that is, unless the

beginning is the result – the product – of the movement of the whole. This is its demand for circularity. Being unfolds as a movement turning in a circle; and this movement goes from the most interior to the most exterior, from the underdeveloped interiority to the exteriorization that alienates it, and from this alienation that exteriorizes up to an accomplished and reinteriorized plenitude. A movement without end and yet always already completed. History is the infinite accomplishment of this movement that is always already realized." Maurice Blanchot, *The Infinite Conversation*, trans. Susan Hanson (Minneapolis: University of Minnesota Press, 1993) 15.

16 James, *Notes on Dialectics*, 10.

17 David Kolb, *The Critique of Pure Modernity: Hegel, Heidegger, and After* (Chicago: University of Chicago Press, 1986), 45.

18 Ibid.

19 John Russon, *Reading Hegel's Phenomenology* (Bloomington and Indianapolis: Indiana UP, 2004), 39–55.

20 James, *Notes on Dialectics*, 90–1.

21 Jean-Luc Nancy. *Hegel: The Restlessness of the Negative*, trans. Jason Smith and Steven Miller (Minneapolis: University of Minnesota Press, 2002).

22 Solomon, *In the Spirit of Hegel*, 20. As Solomon emphasizes: "Freedom, for Hegel, has to do with identification – how one sees oneself (as citizen, as rebel, as stoic, as master, as slave), it is not the political question of societal restraints and duties" (21).

23 Stuart Hall, *Representation: Cultural Representations and Signifying Practices* (London: Sage, 1997), 9.

24 Immanuel Kant, *Critique of Practical Reason*, trans. with intro. Lewis White Beck (Indianapolis: Bobbs-Merrill Company, 1956), 111–12.

25 Parvis Emad, *Heidegger and the Phenomenology of Values: His Critique of Intentionality* (Glen Ellyn: Torey Press, 1981) 88. Indeed, Emad argues that this will to power is cosmological, as "the essence of things are unfulfilled and yet somehow identifiable," and as "where neither will is without power nor power is extraneous to the will." In this regard, "Nietzsche essentially conceives power as preservation *and* enhancement of power since the idea of becoming requires that any stabilization of power be surpassed" (85–6).

26 Martin Heidegger, *Being and Time*, trans. John Macquarrie and Edward Robinson (Oxford: Blackwell, 2000).

27 Although not specifically in terms in identifiable categories of Blackness and whiteness, there is much in the mythology that is Canadian immigrant literature over the transformation that occurs within Canada to make somatic Blacks, who are culturally and idealistically white in the native countries, also culturally and idealistically Black in Canada. This is a strong narrative in the fiction work of Caribbean-born Canadians, for example, as well as in the writings of Asians and aboriginal Canadians. For a good discussion of how this transformation takes place in the writings of Austin Clarke, the foremost somatically Black/Caribbean

writer in Canada—but again without the recognition of the categories of Blackness – see *Clarke versus Clarke: Tory Elitism in Austin Clarke's Short fiction*, in George Elliott Clarke, *Odysseys Home: Mapping African-Canadian Literature* (Toronto: University of Toronto Press, 2002), 238–53.

28 Stuart Hall, "Cultural Identity and Diaspora," *Identity: Community, Culture, Difference*, Jonathan Rutherford (London: Lawrence and Wishart, 1990).

29 Said, *Orientalism*, 15.

30 Foster, *A Place Called Heaven*; ibid., *Island Wings* (Toronto: HarperCollins, 1998).

31 Hall, "Cultural Identity and Diaspora."

32 bell hooks, "Representing Whiteness in Black Imagination," in *Displacing Whiteness: Essays in Social and Cultural Criticism*, ed. Ruth Frankenberg (Durham: Duke UP, 1997).

33 Henry, *Caliban's Reason*.

34 Derek Walcott, *Omeros* (New York: Farrar, Straus and Giroux, 1990); V.S. Naipaul, *India: A Million Mutinies Now* (Minerva: London, 1991); ibid., *The Loss of El Dorado* (Middlesex, England: Penguin, 1969).

35 Henry, *Caliban's Reason*, 11.

36 Ibid, 59.

37 Ibid, 13.

38 Ibid.

39 Indeed, a check of the three main library systems in Ontario under the category of Blackness in Canada showed the following: in the library at York University, for example, I found 20 titles under the category of Canadian Black. Most of them were a repeat of the same titles several times. Second, this is not a rigorous classification, but one that includes a very loose understanding of what is Black in Canada. Curiously, there are no separate titles classified as Blackness. Also it is not clear what qualifies as Black Canadian. One example is George Elliott Clarke's *Odysseys Home: Mapping African-Canadian* Literature (Toronto: University of Toronto Press, 2002), which includes a compilation of all know text by Black Canadians. But as Clarke argues in the book, there is no clear definition of Canadian Black and neither is all the text listed on Blackness. In the library system that supports the universities of Guelph, Laurier, and Waterloo, there are no books classified under Canadian Blacks, although there are some individual titles that speak to different categorizations of Canada and Black. In the University of Toronto library system, there are 158 listings under Black Canada, but this is an eclectic collection from newspaper articles, music on LPs and CDs, books and magazines. However, this is not to argue that there is not an abundance of published material on race in Canada. However, as this book argues, race is not synonymous for Black or Blackness.

40 See, for example, an excellent collection of essays on this issue in George Yancy, ed. *What White Looks Like: African-American Philosophers on the Whiteness Question* (New York: Routledge, 2004).

41 Ibid.

42 Hall, "Cultural Identity and Diaspora," pp. 222–37.
43 Immanuel Kant, *Critique of Pure Reason*, intro. A.D. Lindsay, trans. J.M.D. Meiklejohn (London: Everyman's Library, 1934).

## CHAPTER ONE

1 Henry Louis Gates Jr and William L. Andrews, eds, *Pioneers of the Black Atlantic: Five Slave Narratives from the Enlightenment, 1772–1815* (Washington, D.C.: Civitas, 1998).
2 David Wilkins, for example, speaks of this contradiction in a universal sense when he notes the ambiguity that now surrounds discussions of colour and race. This ambiguity flows out of the well-known statement by W.E.B. Du Bois that "the problem of the twentieth century is the problem of the color-line." W.E.B. Du Bois, *The Souls of Black Folk* (New York: Modern Library Edition, 1996), ix. Speaking specifically of the United States, Wilkins notes:

   Not only are we as a nation destined to fail to solve the problem of the color-line in [the twentieth] century, but we are in danger of losing our ability even to talk about the subject intelligently. For, too often, speakers on both sides of the contemporary debate about race acknowledge only half of America's complex racial legacy. Those who oppose taking race into account, for example, when awarding benefits or designing educational curricula, point to the fact that our political institutions rest on principles of individual freedom and equality that expressly deny the moral or political significance of ascriptive characteristics such as race ... Supporters of affirmative action or multiculturalism, on the other hand, cite the fact that Americans – frequently acting in the name of individual freedoms and equity ... restricted legal naturalization to "white" persons. For these advocates, "color blindness" in our political and moral discourse has been little more than a smoke screen for the pervasive "color consciousness" (and, more specifically, white supremacy) that has been a dominant feature of the American saga. (David B. Wilkins, "Introduction: The Context of Race," in *Color Conscious: The Political Morality of Race*, K. Anthony Appiah and Amy Gutmann [Princeton: Princeton UP, 1996], 3–4).

   In this case, if we are to read America in the truly hemispheric sense, what Wilkins says about a specific particular called the United States would be true for the entire region, and especially in the case of the subject of this study, Canada. This is partly why I am arguing, somewhat in agreement with Wilkins, that a fuller discussion of Blackness as part of the colour-line discourse in, as Wilkins says, an era of multiculturalism, affirmative action, welfare reform, and crime must be about more than race. For a fuller reflection of the implications for ethical relations, a discussion on Blackness must break free historically of the racialized limits that tend to produce a one-sidedness or exclusionary view based strictly on perceptions and the somatic.
3 Du Bois, *The Souls of Black Folk*.

4 Ibid., *The Philadelphia Negro: A Social Study* (New York: Benjamin Bloom, 1967).

5 Robin W. Winks, *The Blacks in Canada: A History* (Montreal and Kingston: McGill-Queen's UP, 1971).

6 Ibid., *Canadian-West Indian Union: A Forty-Year Minuet* (Toronto: Oxford UP, 1968).

7 Paul E. Lovejoy, *Transformations in Slavery: A History of Slavery in Africa* (Cambridge: Cambridge UP, 2000); ibid., *Identity in the Shadow of Slavery* (London: Continuum, 2000).

8 Here I should make clear the difference between "Black" and "Blackness." Sometimes these are the same, and there might be times when a slippage in terms is justified, but in many instances they are not the same and should not be conflated. By Black, generally, I mean a state of being, whether real or perceived, that has its own consciousness. Blackness, on the other hand, is generally a consciousness that is the product of being Black; it is an attitude and an approach to life, for example. However, all people who are Black, especially those who are Black semantically and somatically, might not necessarily have a Black consciousness that makes what they do or produce an exercise in Blackness. They might, in fact, be part of Whiteness, especially those who aspire to overcome what is generally termed the human condition in which they find themselves. Similarly, at the purely somatic level, it is quite possible for some "White" people to indulge in Blackness – say for example those liberals who struggle to change dominant views and norms – and it is possible for some somatic Blacks – one can think for example of a Black-skinned judge in the service of conservative causes – who might be steeped in and be a practitioner of Whiteness.

9 Susan Neiman, *Evil in Modern Thought: An Alternative History of Philosophy* (Princeton: Princeton UP, 2004), 12.

10 Charles Taylor, *Sources of the Self: The Making of the Modern Identity* (Cambridge: Harvard UP, 1989), 3.

11 Fredric Jameson, *The Cultural Turn: Selected Writings on the Postmodern, 1983–1998*, (London: Verso, 1998), 3.

12 Ibid., 5–6.

13 Ibid., 6. Similarly we are reminded by Stuart Hall of the death of the essential Black subject, thereby signalling a further rupture in modernist thought about the wholesomeness and non-alienability of the individual. Stuart Hall, "Subjects in History: Making Diasporic Identities," chap. in *The House That Race Built: Black Americans, U.S. Terrain* (New York: Pantheon Books, 1997).

14 Julia Kristeva, *Black Sun: Depression and Melancholia*, trans. Leon S. Roudiez (New York: Columbia UP, 1989).

15 Joseph I Godfrey. *A Philosophy of Human Hope* (Dordrecht: Martinus Nijhoff Publishers, 1987).

16 Throughout this book, I refer to Western civilization or Western thought to indicate a specific and dominant consciousness that has developed over time. This is a

specific way of perceiving meaning in the world and of achieving meaning from
what would otherwise appear as random contingent acts. Clarence J. Munford, in
writing about civilizational historicism, says that, as explained by history,

This doctrine conceives of civilization as a rhythmically patterned social organism evolving through historical time, born of specific circumstances. Such an
array consists of differentiated socio-economic formations that sometimes take
the form of nation-states, without, however, any racial, social-class, cultural, or
any other superficial unity being required. Ultimately the whole rests on a
determinative bedrock of language and kinship, family and marital bonds. To
apply a metaphor, a civilization is like a vast living entity, with distinctive
organs whose unified interaction contributes to the dynamic function and mat-
uration of the whole over time. It can be likened to an organism whose hor-
mone secretes a vast array of social phenomena – philosophy, religion, social
psychology, collective mentality, mass attitudes, prejudices, purpose and value,
ethics, art, and aesthetics. (Clarence J. Munford, *Race and Civilization: Rebirth
of Black Centrality* [Trenton, N.J.: African World Press, 2001], 21–2).

What I want to take from Munford is the notion that civilization is evolutionary
and all embracing, and that it behaves like an organism that shapes and reshapes
itself over time. At the same time, it has a foundation, something which, I argue,
we can try to know and understand through phenomenology. Munford speaks
about, and here I am not persuaded by his essentialist argument, of three world
civilizations – Africoid, Caucasoid, Mongoloid – each with its own phenotypes,
somatic appearances, and proto-cultural senses, which set the stage for a struggle
for dominance that resulted in the current racialized European and White superiority in the world. I am interested in what is a syncretic organism, one that comes
out of the interaction of any finite number of cultures or civilizations, as Munford
calls them, and which is best described as a Hegelian consciousness that emerges
out of a dialectics of its own conception.

Writing in *Hegel's Phenomenology: The Sociality of Reason,* Terry Pinkard
compares the social consciousness that is the Hegelian state to what he calls a
*social space,* a site where humans, as products of their peculiar history and its
contingent choices, act out a culture that is the carrying forward of the past into
the future. In this space, the actors are performing scripts handed down to them
and which they must project into the future. Even if they try to personalize their
acts, this can only be done with reference to what they already know – the cultural capital that has been handed down to them along with the script itself.
Therefore whatever they do is contingent on what went before, what has constructed them as individual actors, and what materials they do or do not possess
at a specific moment. Pinkard says:

A distinguishing feature of a particular "social space" is the set of what counts
within that "social space" as the basis "ground-rules" for agents to justify their
beliefs and to guide their actions. The structure of authoritative reasons within
each "social space" thereby naturally appears to each agent to constitute not

just the way that he and others contingently happen to reason but the way in which people in general *should* reason. That is, those sets of authoritative reasons appear as both certain and as structuring what is to count as truth, and as necessary, as something that is not optional for the kinds of agents they are. When a set of such reasons and the accounts given of them undermine themselves, they of course lose that appearance of necessity and they lose their link to truth for those agents. (Terry Pinkard, *Hegel's Phenomenology: The Sociality of Reason* [Cambridge: Cambridge UP, 1994], 8.)
However, in presenting the dominant view as a consciousness, the point must be made that there is nothing inevitable about its development. Western civilization is the result of a series of actions resulting from a specific series of acts, all intended to bring meaning to life. However, some of the outcomes in this consciousness might have been unintended – such as much of what has occurred in the area of racial profiling of specific groups that were originally deemed inferior but who have now been elevated to statuses of equality. Indeed, as many thinkers have lamented, Western civilization is the story of only the dominant strain in human thought, one that has traditionally been backed up by force of compulsion and conformity – points that are so well made by members of the Frankfurt school in their criticism of reason and by others in their criticism of modernity. A good discussion of the choosing of a particular path can be found in Stephen Toulmin's *Cosmopolis: The Hidden Agenda of Modernity* (Chicago: University of Chicago Press, 1992) and in Robert Young's *White Mythologies: Writing History and the West* (London: Routledge, 1999). To this end, the point is made clear, in keeping with the notions of freedoms and choice in this book, that Western civilization is the privileging of one master narrative. What this book argues is that multiculturalism in Canada, in a post-modern moment, challenges this master narrative and has returned to examine the plenitudes of narratives that are available for an alternate explanation for the beginning of history, the ordering of society, and how we should arrive at the purported and desired end of history.

17  It is in this sense, as a struggle between good and evil forces for world dominance, that several critics have been assessing the continued unfolding of world history. See Samuel P. Huntington, *The Clash of Civilizations and the Remaking of World Order* (New York: Simon and Schuster, 1996).

18  Edward W. Said, *Orientalism* (New York: Vintage Books, 1979), 5. Further, we may consider Said's argument about the social construction of the West or Western civilization and East and Eastern civilization as academic and research terms with widely accepted common sense meaning: "The Orient is an integral part of European *material* civilization and culture. Orientalism expresses and represents that part culturally and even ideologically as a mode of discourse with supporting institutions, vocabulary, scholarship, imagery, doctrines." Said adds that "Orientalism, is a style of thought based upon an ontological and epistemological distinction made between "the Orient" and (most of the time) "the Occident" (1). Thus a very large mass of writers, among whom are poets, novelists, philosophers,

political theorists, economists, and imperial administrators, have accepted the basic distinction between East and West as the starting point for elaborate theories, epics, novels, social descriptions, and political accounts concerning the Orient, its people, customs, "mind," destiny, and so on (ibid., 2–3).

19 University of Michigan Documents Center, "America's War against Terrorism: World Trade Center/Pentagon Terrorism and the Aftermath," <http://www.lib.umich.edu/govdocs/usterror.html>, 21 March 2004.

20 Kristeva notes that death is at the heart of understanding change and continuity in the Christian-dominated West. This death is most meaningful when played out along what we are calling the neo-mythic register. "A true initiation is thus elaborated, at the very heart of Christian thought, which takes up again the deep intrapsychic meaning of initiatory rites that are anterior or alien to its domain, and gives them new meaning. Here as elsewhere, *death* – that of the old body making room for the new, death to oneself for the sake of glory, death of the old man for the sake of the spiritual body – lies at the center of experience. But, if there be a Christian initiation, it belongs first and entirely within the imaginary realm." Kristeva, *Black Sun,* 134.

21 Strictly speaking, in the Kantian sense "a priori" means that which is a universal condition of any kind of knowing rather than of the order of appearance of a broad generalization that is immune to refutation. In this text, when I use the term "a priori" I will be using it in a less rigorous sense, such as in the taking of fundamental assumptions that prohibit falsification.

22 Michael Walzer, *On Toleration* (New Haven: Yale UP, 1997), xii.

23 C.L.R. James, *Notes on Dialectics: Hegel, Marx, Lenin* (London: Allison and Busby, 1980) and Ralph Ellison, *Invisible Man* (New York: Vintage International, 1995).

24 Jacques Derrida, *On Cosmopolitanism and Forgiveness* (London: Routledge, 2001); Édouard Glissant, *Poetics of Relation,* trans. Betsy Wing (Ann Arbor: University of Michigan Press, 2000).

25 Eze begins his enquiry this way: "How would an African or a black person anywhere think about the world – the global modern world which thinks of 'blacks' as a race – beyond the idea of race but without denying the fact that racial identities and racism are important aspects of the modern experience? In what ways could one transcend the race-conscious traditions of both modern European and African thought which sustain ideologies of race and racism while recognizing that there are in these intellectual traditions powerful tools against racialism and racism?" Emmanuel Chukwudi Eze, *Achieving Our Humanity: The Idea of the Postracial Future* (New York: Routledge, 2001), ix.

26 Thomas C. Holt, *The Problem of Race in the Twenty-First Century* (Cambridge: Harvard UP, 2000), 4.

27 Ibid., 4. It is also worth pointing out that physical lynching has never been of the same importance in Canada, which, as Frye suggests, was founded on respect for law, order, and good government. However, "electronic" lynching, through

negative stereotypes in the media and elsewhere, and economic and social lynching are undoubtedly hemispheric phenomena, with Canada fully part of this social consciousness. For a fuller discussion of Blackness and the media, see Frances Henry and Carol Tator, *Racist Discourse in Canada's English Print Media* (Toronto: The Canadian Race Relations Foundation, March 2000).

28 Holt, *The Problem of Race in the Twenty-First Century*, 5.

29 Lucius T. Outlaw Jr, *On Race and Philosophy* (London: Routledge, 1996), 2.

30 Ibid.

31 Pierre Elliott Trudeau, *Multiculturalism: Government Response to Volume 4 of the Report of the Royal Commission on Bilingualism and Biculturalism*, Hansard, House of Commons (8 October 1971), <http://www.Canadahistory.com/sections/documents/trudeau_-_on_multiculturalism.htm>, 22 May 2004.

32 Outlaw, *On Race and Philosophy*, 2.

33 This is similar to what Appiah calls that act of racialism, which for me is the limiting in a negative way to finite qualities of Black and Blackness. This is the idea that "we could divide human beings into a small number of groups, called 'races,' in such a way that the members of these groups shared certain fundamental, heritable, physical, moral, intellectual, and cultural characteristics with one another that they did not share with members of any other race." K. Anthony Appiah and Amy Gutmann, *Color Conscious: The Political Morality of Race* (Princeton: Princeton UP, 1996), 54.

34 One problem, as Wilkins suggests, is that trying to place limits on what is meant in the discourse on race or colour-blindness always leaves something important out of the discussion. This is the case, for example, among those who argue that the discussion should be idealistic, about issues of inclusiveness, fairness, and justice, and those who want to contest what should be included in the finite description of what it is to be Black and what it has meant historically to be Black. For Wilkins "the two spheres cannot be entirely separated. In a society committed to individual liberty and mutual respect, we depend upon our democratic institutions to foster a social world in which free and equal citizens can enjoy the fruits of our rich cultural heritage. One cannot advocate color consciousness (or color blindness, for that matter) in public policy without examining how this choice is likely to affect this ultimate goal – just as it would be equally wrong to form judgements about culture and identity that ignore the political consequences of these important choices." Wilkins, "Introduction," 15. Here the argument is for a holistic and even transcendentalist approach to colour, in this case who and what is Black and Blackness. This is a knowledge that, I argue, can only be ascertained by knowing how Black and Blackness are contextualized or socially constructed analogously in a specific moment, only by knowing what are the several perceived finite categories in this infinity, how they were constructed and for what purposes. Indeed, I contend that one of the major intentions of multiculturalism is not to strive so much for a "colour-blindness" – where the emphasis is placed on the ocular perception, on knowledge gained primarily through seeing – but more for the

harmony, melody, rhythm, and unity "heard" in music. Multiculturalism, existentially and ontologically, is the call of a Black voice to Black subjects, who respond to this interpolation as socially constructed Whites, responding and reacting in the Whiteness of their citizenship. Indeed, multiculturalism is analogous to the call-and-response that is associated with ethnicized Black and African music and the rapture and rupture associated with modern subjectivity, as discussed, for example, in John Mowitt's *Percussion: Drumming, Beating, Striking* (Durham: Duke UP, 2002), 43–66.

35 Stuart Hall, "Subjects in History: Making Diasporic Identities."

36 Charles Taylor, "The Politics of Recognition," in *Multiculturalism: Examining the Politics of Recognition*, ed. Amy Gutmann (Princeton: Princeton UP, 1994), 38. Emphasis added.

37 Taylor, "The Politics of Recognition," 38.

38 Frantz Fanon, *Black Skin, White Masks* (New York: Grove Press, 1967).

39 Howard Adelman, "Of Human Bondage: Labour, Bondage, and Freedom in the Phenomenology," in *Hegel's Social and Political Thought: The Philosophy of Objective Spirit*, Donald Philllip Verene (New Jersey: Humanities Press, 1980); M.J. Inwood, *Hegel* (London: Routledge, 1998); Northrop Frye, *The Bush Garden: Essays on the Canadian Imagination* (Toronto: House of Anansi Press, 1971); ibid., *The Eternal Act of Creation: Essays, 1979–1900* (Bloomington: Indiana UP, 1993); Jeffrey M. Perl, *The Tradition of Return: The Implicit History of Modern Literature* (Princeton: Princeton UP, 1984).

40 Edward Kamau Brathwaite, *Contradictionary Omens: Cultural Diversity and Integration in the Caribbean* (Kingston, Jamaica: Savacou Publications, 1974); Édouard Glissant, "Creolization in the Making of the Americas," in *Race, Discourse, and the Origin of the Americas: A New World View*, Vera Lawrence Hyatt and Rex Nettleford (Washington: Smithsonian Institution Press, 1995).

41 Paul Gilroy, *The Black Atlantic: Modernity and Double Consciousness* (Cambridge: Harvard UP, 1993); Gates Jr and Andrews *Pioneers of the Black Atlantic*; Vincent Carretta and Philip Gould, *Genius in Bondage: Literature of the Early Black Atlantic* (Lexington, Ky: University Press of Kentucky, 2001); Adam Potkay and Sandra Burr, *Black Atlantic Writers of the Eighteenth Century: Living the New Exodus in England and the Americas* (New York: St Martin's Press, 1995).

42 David Eltis, *The Rise of African Slavery in the Americas* (Cambridge: Cambridge UP, 2000); ibid., *Economic Growth and the Ending of the Transatlantic Slave Trade* (New York: Oxford UP, 1987); ibid., "The Volume and Structure of the Transatlantic Slave Trade: A Reassessment," paper presented at Enslaving Connections: Africa and Brazil During the Era of the Slave Trade, an international conference co-sponsored by the Department of History and the Nigerian Hinterland Project (Toronto, York University, 12–15 October 2000); Lawrence W. Levine, *Black Culture and Black Consciousness: Afro-American Folk Thought from Slavery to Freedom* (Oxford: Oxford UP, 1977); Paul E. Lovejoy, *Identity in the Shadow of Slavery* (London: Continuum, 2000); ibid., *Transformations in*

Slavery: A History of Slavery in Africa (Cambridge: Cambridge UP, 2000); Barbara L. Solow, *Slavery and the Rise of the Atlantic System* (New York: Cambridge UP, 1991); Vann C. Woodward, *American Counterpoint: Slavery and Racism in the North/South Dialogue* (Oxford: Oxford UP, 1983); Hugh Thomas, *The Slave Trade: The History of the Atlantic Slave Trade 1440–1870* (London: Picador, 1997); John Thornton, *Africa and Africans in the Making of the Atlantic World, 1400–1680* (Cambridge: Cambridge UP, 1995).

43 David Carney, *Soul of Darkness: Introduction to African Metaphysics, Philosophy and Religion* (New York: Adastra, 1991).

44 Northrop Frye, *The Eternal Act of Creation: Essays, 1979–1900* (Bloomington: Indiana UP, 1993).

45 Charles Taylor presents two models that help us understand modernity and differences. The first is what he calls a "cultural theory of modernity," which argues that what has developed in the modern West is a new culture. This is a model that accounts for diversity and differences: "The contemporary Atlantic world is seen as a culture (or a group of closely related cultures) among others, with its own specific understandings, for example, of person, nature, the good, to be contrasted to all others, including its own predecessor civilization (with which it obviously has a lot in common)." Charles Taylor, "Modernity and Difference," in *Without Guarantees: In Honour of Stuart Hall*, ed. Paul Gilroy, Lawrence Grossberg, and Angela McRobbie (London: Verso, 2000), 365.

The second model for Taylor is what he called the "acultural," which presents transformations as culture-neutral: "By this I mean an operation that is not defined in terms of the specific culture it carries us from and to, but rather is seen as of a type that any traditional culture could undergo" (365). This is a model that homogenizes and imposes hegemony so as to sublate, if not wipe out, differences and diversity within the culture.

> An example of an acultural type ... would be one that conceives of modernity as the growth of reason, defined in various ways: for example, as the growth of scientific consciousness, or the development of a secular outlook, or the rise of instrumental rationality, or an ever-clearer distinction between fact-finding and evaluation. Or else modernity might be accounted for in terms of social as well as intellectual changes: the transformations, including the intellectuals ones, are seen as coming about as a result of increased mobility, concentration of populations, industrialization, or the like. In theses cases, modernity is conceived as a set of transformations which any and every culture goes through – and which all will probably be forced to undergo. (Taylor, "Modernity and Difference," 365)

The danger of this two-model approach is to determine where one stops off and the other takes over in taking us to a better understanding. Indeed, there are times when the two models seem to be dialectically at odds, yet useful as an explanation of the phenomenon at hand. This book, using Taylor archetypes, would probably tend towards the acultural theory model as an ideal for modernity, while suggesting that the cultural theory model has some relevance in explaining the dynamics and dialectics that produce modernity and are still pushing it on. In the end, in keeping with the approach of this book, I am inclined towards a hybridity or syncretism of the two models.

### CHAPTER TWO

1 John Mowitt provides an interesting example in his book *Percussion: Drumming, Beating, Striking* of how, in our music, existential and even somatic Blackness was first presented as evil, but then accepted in the dominant culture and re-presented as Whiteness. Speaking of Fanon's notion of *lactification*, Mowitt notes: "the desire for whiteness fostered among non-whites within colonial regimes, is invoked here to rename the oft-repeated notion that rock-and-roll began as a black music, but, with the appearance of Elvis Presley (among others), quickly became a white music. The transformation was oddly consummated, according to some, by the 'British Invasion' of the 1960s when musicians deeply influenced by African Americans played back to Americans a music then heard as European, if not exactly white." John Mowitt, *Percussion: Drumming, Beating, Striking* (Durham: Duke UP, 2002) 8. This is a case of a Blackness that was presented as having been changed and purified into an acceptable goodness that is White. Indeed, phenomenologically, what is presented as White was really an unchangeable Blackness, which means in the larger scheme of things that at least in rock-and-roll music Blackness is the unchangeable and Whiteness is changeable. A further example of this is captured again by Mowitt is his notion of how what was once one-sided Black in terms of the prevailing morality is now accepted as White and therefore considered acceptable. The example he cites is that of Elvis "The Pelvis" Presley, whose gyrations on television the first time he appeared were considered as too vulgar. As a result, the television audience saw him only from the waist up. "The flight, perhaps consummately figured in the 'black out' (a graphic censorship technique common in print advertising) that protected predominantly White eyes from Elvis 'The Pelvis.'"

2 In this regard, one cannot ignore the perennial debate over the suitability, and even appropriateness or political correctness, of using Hegel as an entry for discussion on such topics. Indeed, this is particularly present in much of the discussion from Karl Popper and others who argue that Hegelianism leads to totalitarianism and hegemony, especially of European over African, Third World, or Black thought. Such is not my reading of Hegel. For one, I do not accept that Hegel's methodology is a totalizing one: rather, I view it as showing how particulars can be contained in universals in a tension-filled relationship. Indeed, as I suggest in this book, my reading of Hegel is that he privileges Black and Blackness as vital and necessary forces, as, in fact, the spirit of humanity. But for a fuller debunking of the critics of Hegel on this issue, the reader should consult the excellent introduction by Stuart Barnett in the collection of essays that he edited *Hegel*

*after Derrida* (London: Routledge, 1998), 1–37. In this introduction, Barnett effectively argues that it is virtually impossible to have a modern discussion about such things as identity, culture, citizenship, and modernity and to understand the positions of the leading thinkers without reference to Hegel. Indeed, Barnett argues that just about every major modern theorist is in conversation with Hegel. Even those who have tried to refute Hegel have found themselves using methods pioneered by Hegel:

> Wherever the emphasis lies, then, the current critical temper seems caught in a Hegelian labyrinth. It is a Hegelianism, moreover, that need never mention the name Hegel. As Paul de Man remind us: "Few thinkers have so many disciples who have never read a word of their master's writing."
>
> It is thus not too far-fetched to suggest that one could easily recast the story of post-war French philosophy (and recent American literary theory and criticism) as the story of Hegelianism by other means. Although one cannot make an argument such as the one just outlined in anything but a Hegelian manner, it is necessary to put it forth because we will inhabit a Hegelianism of sorts. To truly think the end of Hegel it would be necessary to remain Hegelian to a degree. Most of the confident attempts to transcend Hegelianism have been, in point of fact, brilliant continuation of Hegelianism. As a result, speculative thought remains for the most part unchallenged. To truly confront Hegel, therefore, it will be necessary to account for our failure to transcend Hegel. It will be necessary to inhabit Hegel, our Hegel. (25–6)

This is an argument that holds true for much of the discussion that is of central importance to us in this book: that concerning Blackness and Canadian multiculturalism. I shall return to this point in chapters 19 and 20.

## CHAPTER THREE

1 John Locke, "An Essay Concerning Human Understanding," *The Empiricists: Locke, Berkeley, Hume,* (New York: Anchor Books, 1974), 95.

2 G.W.F. Hegel, *Hegel's Science of Logic,* trans. A.V. Miller, ed. H.D. Lewis (New York: Humanity Books, 1969) 73–4.

3 David Kolb, *The Critique of Pure Modernity: Hegel, Heidegger, and After* (Chicago: University of Chicago Press, 1986), 50.

4 This notion of a "world history" to explain a system or consciousness is taken from Hegel. As Harry Brod states: "For Hegel, however, the concept of world history arises out of the meaning of events as they are organized in a coherent narrative rather than as they are arranged in a bare succession. Some events are quite definitely more world-historically significant than others, and some do not properly enter into the scope of world history at all." Harry Brod, *Hegel's Philosophy of Politics: Idealism, Identity and Modernity* (Boulder, Colo.: Westview Press, 1992), 13.

5 As Russon states: "Absolute reading thus occurs when my social substance reads itself through me, and when this act of self-reading/writing reads/writes an

inscribed prescription to have so pre-in-scribed. Absolute knowing is the recognition that I can read only the autobiography that I have always been writing, or again, I can write only the autobiography I have always already been reading." John Russon, *Reading Hegel's Phenomenology* (Bloomington: Indiana UP, 2004), 80.

6 As Parvis Emad notes: "Through his idea of a 'will to power' Nietzsche denies things a permanent, unchangeable essence because such would be contradictory to the basic trait of becoming. Nietzsche uses the composite expression 'will to power' to conceive the essence of things as unfulfilled and yet somehow identifiable." Parvis Emad, *Heidegger and the Phenomenology of Values: His Critique of Intentionality* (Glen Ellyn: Torey Press, 1981) 85. Phenomenologically, then, will to power starts out being Black and remains Black throughout all its striving and becoming, hoping that at the end of its quest – or history – it will be a being that is White.

7 Cornel West, *Race Matters* (New York: Vintage Books, 1993), 5. Indeed, West is worth quoting in full on this issue of limits and how they inhibit understanding and choices of public policy. Although his example deals specifically with the United States of America, what West says is generally true of the western hemisphere, or of most of what we now called the Black Atlantic. "Our truncated public discussions of race suppress the best of who or what we are as a people because they fail to confront the complexity of the issue in a candid and critical manner ... The liberal notion that more government programs can solve racial problems is simplistic – precisely because it focuses *solely* on the economic dimension. And the conservative idea that what is needed is a change in moral behaviour of poor black urban dwellers (especially poor black men, who, they say, should stay married, support their children, and stop committing so much crime) highlights immoral actions while ignoring public responsibility for the immoral circumstances that haunt our fellow citizens" (4–5).

My aim is to try to grasp this inclusiveness and comprehensiveness that has troubled West and others, but to argue that such goals cannot be achieved through a discussion *solely* of race. Race, itself, is conceptually an attempt to create a finite category out of Blackness, so that it becomes almost impossible, as West's example suggests, to meaningfully discuss issues of economic and social morality in the same breath. They are constructed according to the meaning of the two different registers. However, such a discussion can take place within Blackness as an infinite category, where some features and characteristics can be made into a secondary finite set that is race, or economics and/or morality for that matter. Second, the kind of critical analysis for which West is aiming can be achieved through a foundational analysis that takes us back to the earliest construction of the notions we are discussing. This is why it is meaningful to start with specifying categories of Blackness. This is why there is so much to be gained through a phenomenology of Blackness. Doing so allows us to start our discussion with a clear understanding of the assumptions and intentions that undergird the frameworks of meaning in our daily lives and how we make choices. And that is why such an analysis unfolds on at least two different tracks, with two different terminals, at least.

8 Here we may want to consider the thinking of Sartre on this matter. Sartre argues that the essence of anything is its appearances or manifestations and that these appearances are what the object is to a subject, with no hidden qualities, a view that is in opposition to the Hegelian one adopted in this book, which holds that objects first appear as dualisms and that their essence is discerned through action. But that difference aside, it is worth considering what Sartre has to say about finite and infinite categories, and how he presents the object in a Hegelian sense as a concept that is an infinity:

Does this mean that by reducing the existent to its manifestations we have succeeded in overcoming all dualism? It seems rather that we have converted them all into a new dualism: that of finite and infinite. Yet the existent in fact cannot be reduced to a *finite* series of manifestations since each one of them is a relation to a subject constantly changing. Although the *object* may disclose itself only through a single *Abschattung* [appearance in profile], the sole fact of there being a subject implies the possibilities of multiplying the points of view on that *Abschattung*. This suffices to multiply to infinity the *Abschattung* under consideration. Furthermore if the series of appearances were finite, that would mean that the first appearances do not have the possibility of *reappearing*, which is absurd, or that they can be all given at once, which is still more absurd. Let us understand indeed that our theory of the phenomenon has replaced the *reality* of the thing by the *objectivity* of the phenomenon and that it has based this on an appeal to infinity. (Jean-Paul Sartre, *Being and Nothingness: An Essay on Phenomenological Ontology*, trans. with introduction by Hazel E. Barnes [London: Methuen, 1957], 5.)

9 Michael Ignatieff, *Blood and Belonging: Journey into the New Nationalism* (Toronto: Penguin, 1993), 5.

10 Jeffrey M. Perl, *The Tradition of Return: The Implicit History of Modern Literature* (Princeton: Princeton UP, 1984).

11 Mircea Eliade, *Myth and Reality* (London: George Allen and Unwin, 1964); Northrop Frye, *Myth and Metaphor: Selected Essays 1974–1988*, ed. Robert D. Denham (Charlottesville: Virginia UP, 1990).

12 Emmanuel Chukwudi Eze, *Achieving Our Humanity: The Idea of the Postracial Future* (New York: Routledge, 2001), xiii.

13 Here we are reminded of the similar experiences described by Edward Bruner for African-American tourists "returning" diasporically to Ghana only to discover that the locals do not consider them as "Black" but as "White." The Ghanaian term for these "visitors" is *obruni*, which translates as "White man" but also as a foreigner that could just as well be European, Asian, or American. The difference is that the Ghanaian sees the Black-skinned tourists not as "brothers" and "sisters" who were removed from them in time and space by transatlantic slavery, but as foreigners enjoying the "Whiteness" of a better standard of living, and enough

wealth to make visits to places like Ghana. They are seen as coming from parts of the world where the inhabitants are White idealistically and in terms of culture and status, because they are better served by technology and all the modernist trappings associated progressively with development and even enlightenment. Edward Bruner, "Tourism in Ghana: The Representation of Slavery and the Return of the Black Diaspora," *American Anthropologist* 98, no. 2 (1996). I thank my graduate student Stacy Milford for drawing this to my attention.

14 M.I. Ebbutt, *Hero-Myths and Legends of the British Race* (Colchester, England: The Cambridge Society Ltd., n.d.), 70.

15 Ibid., 73.

16 Alfred Nutt, *Studies on the Legend of the Holy Grail: With Especial Reference to the Hypothesis of Its Celtic Origin* (New York: Cooper Square Publishers, 1965), 19.

17 Ibid., 64a.

18 John Burbidge has drawn to my attention the importance of this double transformation for an understanding of Hegel's *Logic*, which is intended by the philosopher to be a mapping of the mind of God. John W. Burbidge, *Hegel on Logic and Religion: The Reasonableness of Christianity* (Albany: State University of New York Press, 1992). Indeed, as Burbidge suggests, Hegel added paragraph 241 to the *Encyclopedia* and in later revisions of *Larger Logic* to emphasize this point about the double negation, or what Burbidge calls the double transition. Similarly, the double transformation also shows up in Hegel's *Phenomenology of Spirit* as reconciliation for the unhappy consciousness in human civilization, the point at which the Christian church and state become models for modern ethical living.

19 Nutt, *Studies on the Legend of the Holy Grail*, 64b.

20 Ibid., 220–7.

21 V.S. Naipaul, *Literary Occasions: Essays* (New York: Alfred A. Knopf, 2003) 9.

22 Édouard Glissant, *Poetics of Relation*, trans. Betsy Wing (Ann Arbor: University of Michigan Press, 2000), 71–2.

23 J.S. Woodsworth, *Strangers within Our Gates: Or Coming Canadians* (Toronto: F.C. Stephenson, 1909).

24 In this discussion of the *act* of transformation, we are reminded of the statement by Hegel to describe *Being*. He was responding to what he called the empty tautology of *ex nihilo nihil fit* (nothing comes out of nothing), the description of Being that was such a powerful concept in early Western thought. But as Hegel said, the aphorism speaks of a proposition that is in opposition, not to separate and distinct states that are individually *being* and *nothing*, but against the "transitioning" of one state to the other. The proposal stands in contradistinction to becoming, a point between the static bookend positions of being and nothing. "Later, especially Christian, metaphysics whilst rejecting the proposition that out of nothing comes nothing, asserted a transition from nothing into being; although it understood this proposition synthetically or merely imaginatively, yet even in the most imperfect union there is contained a point in which being and nothing coincide and their distinguishedness vanishes." Hegel, *Hegel's Science of Logic*, 84.

If we replace the words "being" and "nothing" with "good" and "evil," we will get the same result conceptually – where, in all humans, as not just static but living and changing beings, there is some good and some evil, and that each point is one of transition from some portion of good to some portion of evil or vice versa. However, because we tend to view these movements as one-sided, we hope for a movement from evil to good, from life to death, as in our consciousness these are what we privilege as goods in themselves, and for us, these goods are unchangeable in our thinking.

25 Ralph Ellison, *Invisible Man* (New York: Vintage International, 1995).

26 Bruner, "Tourism in Ghana."

27 Maurice Merleau-Ponty, *The Primacy of Perception and Other Essays*, ed. James M. Edie (n.p.: Northwestern UP, 1964).

28 Locke, for example, argues that this lack of essence or real knowledge of concepts in the real world presents an additional problem: how do we know what is justice or a correct and appropriate ethical relation in a society made up of supposedly conceptual beings? "If moral knowledge be placed in the contemplation of our own moral ideas, and those, as other modes, be our own making, What strange notions will there be of justice and temperance? What confusion of virtues and vices, if every one may make what ideas of them he pleases." Locke, "An Essay Concerning Human Understanding," 95.

29 The following is a list of some of the published works on Blacks in Canada. They are notable for starting from the assumption that Black is somatic or cultural – in that it is either a symbol of African and Caribbean cultures, or refers to peoples with a lineage to Africa. Indeed, in some cases Black and African are used interchangeably, sometimes even as dialectical opposites, and in the case of immigration they seem to suggest a category of Blackness that is based on status: Clarke George Elliott, ed., *Eyeing the North Star: Directions in African-Canadian Literature* (Toronto: McClelland and Stewart, 1997); ibid., ed., *Fire on the Water: An Anthology of Black Nova Scotian Writing*, vol. 1, *Early and Modern Writers 1785–1935* (Lawrencetown Beach, N.S.: Pottersfield Press, 1991); ibid., vol. 2, *Writers of the Renaissance* (Lawrencetown Beach, N.S.: Pottersfield Press, 1992); ibid., "Contesting a Model Blackness: A Meditation on African-Canadian African Americanism, or the Structures of African Canadianite," *Essays on Canadian Writing No.63* (Toronto: ECW Press, Spring 1998); ibid., *Odysseys Home: Mapping African-Canadian Literature* (Toronto: University of Toronto Press, 2002); Rinaldo Walcott, ed., *Rude: Contemporary Black Canadian Cultural Criticism* (Toronto: Insomniac Press, 2000); Cecil Foster, *A Place Called Heaven: The Meaning of Being Black In Canada* (Toronto: HarperCollins, 1996); Carl E. James, *Making It: Black Youth, Racism and Career Aspirations in a Big City* (Oakville: Mosaic Press, 1990); ibid., "Up to No Good: Black on the Streets and Encountering Police," in *Racism and Social Inequality in Canada: Concepts, Controversies and Strategies of Resistance*, Vic Satzewich (Toronto: Thompson Educational Publishing, 1998); Althea Prince, *Being Black: Essays* (Toronto:

Insomniac Press, 2000); Sheldon Eric Alister Taylor, "Darkening the Complexion of Canadian Society: Black Activism, Policy-Making and Black Immigration from the Caribbean to Canada, 1940s–1960s," Ph.D. thesis (University of Toronto, 1994); James W. St. G. Walker, *The Black Loyalists: The Search for a Promised Land in Nova Scotia and Sierra Leone 1783–1870* (Toronto: University of Toronto Press, 1992); Robin W. Winks, *The Blacks in Canada: A History* (Montreal and Kingston: McGill-Queen's UP, 1971); Agnes Calliste, "Canada's Immigration Policy and Domestic Blacks from the Caribbean: The Second Domestic Scheme," in *The Social Basis of Law*, 2d ed., edited by Elizabeth Cormack and Stephen Brickley (Halifax: Garamond Press, 1991); Frances Henry, *The Caribbean Diaspora in Toronto: Learning to Live with Racism* (Toronto: University of Toronto Press, 1994).

30 For a fuller discussion of race and modernity as this pertains to equating the somatic almost exclusively with Blackness, see Oliver C. Cox, *Race: A Study in Social Dynamics*, preface by Cornell West, introduction by Adolphi Reed Jr (New York: Monthly Review Press, 2000); David Theo Goldberg, *Racist Culture: Philosophy and the Politics of Meaning* (Oxford: Blackwell, 1993); Paul Gilroy, *Against Race: Imagining Political Culture beyond the Color Line* (Cambridge: Harvard UP, 2000); Henry Louis Gates Jr, *"Race," Writing and Difference* (Chicago: University of Chicago Press, 1986).

31 Thomas Axworthy and Pierre Elliott Trudeau, eds, *Towards a Just Society: The Trudeau Years* (Toronto: Viking, 1990); Will Kymlicka, *Multicultural Citizenship: Liberal Theory of Minority Rights* (Oxford: Clarendon Press, 1995); Jon Stratton and Ien Ang, "Multicultural Imagined Communities: Cultural Difference and National Identity in the USA and Australia," *Multicultural States: Rethinking Difference and Identity*, David Bennet (London: Routledge, 1998).

32 Derek Hum and Wayne Simpson, "Wage Opportunities for Visible Minorities in Canada," *The Income and Labour Dynamics Working Paper Series*, catalogue No. 98-17, November 1998; James L. Torczyner, *Diversity, Mobility and Change – The Dynamics of Black Communities in Canada*. (Montreal: McGill Consortium for Ethnicity and Strategic Social Planning, 1997).

## CHAPTER FOUR

1 Marcus Garvey, "The Negro's Greatest Enemy," *African American Political Thought, 1890–1930*, ed. Carl D. Wintz, (Washington: M.E. Sharpe, 1996), 172.

2 Lawrence Hill, *Black Berry, Sweet Juice: On Being Black and White in Canada* (Toronto: Harper Flamingo Canada, 2001).

3 Toni Morrison, *Playing in the Dark: Whiteness and Literary Imagination* (Cambridge: Harvard UP, 1990).

4 K. Anthony Appiah and Amy Gutmann, *Color Conscious: The Political Morality of Race* (Princeton: Princeton UP, 1996), 97.

5 Constance Backhouse, *Colour-Coded: A Legal History of Racism in Canada, 1900-1950* (Toronto: University of Toronto Press, 1999), 1.

6 Ibid.
7 That there should be such a change yet remains but an ideal, as shown by a series of articles in mainstream North American media. One example of this was a recent article published under the headline "The New Science of Race" in the Toronto *Globe and Mail* newspaper on June 18, 2005, page F1. Written by Carolyn Abraham, the medical reporter for the newspaper, the article suggested there is renewed thinking that there is a genetic link to race in such things as why Jews of European descent have won 27 per cent of Nobel Prizes given to Americans.

   In another story a week later, under the headline "Molecular Eyewitness: DNA Gets a Human Face," *Globe and Mail*, 25 June 2005, A6, Abraham continues in the same vein: "Now, teams are planning for gene types to help explain why West Africa produces the fastest runners in the world. A university of Toronto researcher is hunting the gene types that account for skin colours." This is despite the fact that in recent times, as measured by how quickly they cover 100 metres and 200 metres, most of the acclaimed fastest runners in the world have come from the Americas, including Canada. However, that most of them are somatically Black might explain why they were misrecognized as West African.
8 A subsequent chief of police for the Toronto force later conceded there was racial profiling in the force, mainly against somatic Blacks, and promised to stamp out this evil.
9 Elizabeth Meehan, "Citizenship and Identity," in *Fundamentals in British Politics*, ed. Ian Holliday, Andrew Gamble, and Geraint Parry (New York: St Martin's Press, 1999), 241.
10 Mason Stokes, *The Color of Sex: Whiteness, Heterosexuality, and the Fiction of White Supremacy* (Durham: Duke UP, 2001).
11 David Malouf, *Johnno: A Novel* (St Lucia, Queensland: University of Queensland Press, 1975); ibid., *Remembering Babylon* (New York: Pantheon Books, 1993).
12 Okot p'Bitek, *Song of Lawino; and, Song of Ocol*, African Writers Series (London: Heinemann, 1984).
13 N.E. Cameron, *The Evolution of the Negro: In Two Volumes*, vol. 1, *Which Deals with the Civilization of the Africans before and during the Time of Their Involuntary Voyage to the Americas* (Georgetown, Demerara: The Argosy Company, 1929; Negro Universities Press, 1970).
14 Christie Blatchford, "Cone of Silence Spreading: Murder Witness Not Responding to Pleas from Police," *National Post* (Toronto), 13 November 2002.
15 Ibid.
16 Ibid.
17 David Wootton, ed., *Divine Right and Democracy* (London: Penguin, 1986), 97.
18 Ibid., 94.
19 Indeed, Blackness was associated with anti-order in the Christian mythology. An example is the definition of Satanism as "the worship of Satan, possibly a survival of heathen fertility cults. In the twelfth century it gained strength through a secret

rebellion against the Church. At its center is the Black Mass, a parody of the Christian Mass, with a nude women on the altar, with the Host sometimes being the ashes and blood of murdered children. It was revived during the reign of Louis XIV in France and again in the 1890s, when it attracted some literary attention. Interest in witchcraft and Satanism, or at least their literary expression, seems to be increasing." William Harmon and C. Hugh Holman, *A Handbook to Literature*, 5th ed. (Upper Saddle River, N.J.: Prentice Hall, 2000), 460. Indeed, this point is alluded to by Hazel Barnes in the translator's introduction to Sartre's *Being and Nothingness* in a discussion on guilt as a false denial of a person's free subjectivity: "The reverse situation occurs when one without rejecting God's existence tries to make him an absolute object by performing black masses, desecrating the Host, desiring evil for evil's sake, etc. (In this last instance, however, it must be noted that this is to desire evil only in accordance with the conventional definition of it.)" Hazel E. Barnes, translator's introduction to Jean-Paul Sartre, *Being and Nothingness: An Essay on Phenomenological Ontology*, trans. with introduction by Hazel E. Barnes (London: Methuen, 1957), xxxix. The point to be made is that this category of Blackness is an attempt to escape construction and imprisonment in an imposed definition, including that of the presumed creator of those defiantly performing these masses – and to be free of the guilt that comes from such licentiousness and limits on freedom of determination.

20 Wootton, *Divine Right and Democracy*, 94.

21 E.P. Thompson, *Whigs and Hunters: The Origin of the Black Act* (London: Penguin, 1975), 22.

22 OBJ Border Morris, "OBJ Border Morris History," *The Welsh Border Morris Tradition*, <http://www.obj.org.uk> 14 May 2006.

23 Peter Mark, *Africans in European Eyes: The Portrayal of Black Africans in Fourteenth and Fifteenth Century Europe* (Syracuse, New York: Maxwell School of Citizenship and Public Affairs, Syracuse University, 1974), 13.

24 Emmanuel Chukwudi Eze, *Race and the Enlightenment: A Reader* (Cambridge, Mass.: Blackwell, 1977); Julie K Ward and Tommy L. Lott, eds, *Philosophers on Race: Critical Essays* (London: Blackwell, 2002).

25 G.W.F. Hegel, *Phenomenology of Spirit*, trans. A.V. Miller (Oxford: Oxford UP, 1977).

26 Martin Heidegger, *Being and Time*, trans. John Macquarrie and Edward Robinson (Oxford: Blackwell, 2000), 127.

### CHAPTER FIVE

1 Northrop Frye, *Mythologizing Canada: Essays on the Canadian Literary Imagination*, ed. Branko Gorjup (Ottawa: Legas, 1997), 74.

2 More than a generation after Frye, political scientist Philip Resnick turns to the same mythology, and presumed categories of Blackness and Whiteness, to explain Canadian identity and the country's presumed future. Even in an age of official

multiculturalism, Resnick sees Canada as somatically, culturally, and idealistically White, even if it is still Black in status to the idealistically Black United States and to the European Union, which is White somatically, culturally, idealistically, and in status. This supposedly makes Canada ontologically and existentially White, even if epistemologically Canadians are still Black in a false consciousness that causes them not to fully appreciate their European past and future. Only when they become fully aware of their White body will they also enter a time of ethical Whiteness. Resnick concludes his book: "What began as an offshoot of European colonization has come to resemble, at the start of the twenty-first century, the continent from which the overwhelming majority of its people – of French, British, and of diverse cultural origins – originally derive. Canadians are more European in their reflexes, their behaviour, and ultimately their destiny as citizens of a sovereign North American state than they have been prepared to acknowledge. Perhaps Canada is ultimately a Euro-American state, situated on the doorstep of the most unabashedly American of New World states, a state that would fit remarkably well into the European Union, were it located on the European continent, but which finds itself instead on the North American. And our fate as Canadians may well lie in bridging the divide between the geographical, physical, and economic North Americanness that we share with the United States and the more existential features of our identity that we share with the continent of Europe." Philip Resnick, *The European Roots of Canadian Identity* (Peterborough, Ont.: Broadsview Press, 2005), 96–7. From this analysis, it is hard to discern what are the unchangeable in such concepts as Canada, Europe, the United States – for as consciousnesses they have all changed over time (even Canada which once denied people perceived as Black Europeans inclusion in Canadian Whiteness). Can a Canada that is as creolized as what Resnick described speak only of its European roots, ignore the scorching of those supposed roots in the 1960s, and the planting of additional roots from all over the world since the 1960s? Can a Canada that is so creolized be really presented exclusively in its Whiteness as European? I think not.

3 Here it is useful to indicate the distinction I will be making between culture and civilization. As Appiah suggests, civilization presumes there is a coherence and that all cultural acts are universally part of the civilization. "The second, connected, difference between culture and civilization is that the latter takes values to be central to the enterprise, in two ways. First, civilization is centrally defined by the moral and aesthetic values: and the coherence of a civilization is primarily, the coherence of those values with each other and then, of the group's behaviour and institutions with its values. Second, civilizations are essentially to be evaluated: they can be better and worse, richer and poorer, more or less interesting." K. Anthony Appiah and Amy Gutmann, *Color Conscious: The Political Morality of Race* (Princeton: Princeton UP, 1996), 84. Put another way, and in keeping with the language of this book, civilization is the consciousness of a people or state based on an accepted ideology; culture is the acting out of this consciousness. This

is important to bear in mind when thinking of the cultural categories of Blackness and Whiteness.

4 Will Kymlicka, Politics in the Vernacular: Nationalism, Multiculturalism, and Citizenship (Oxford: Oxford UP, 2000), 189.

5 Will Kymlicka, Finding Our Way: Rethinking Ethnocultural Relations in Canada (Toronto: Oxford UP, 1998), 80.

6 Kymlicka, *Finding Our Way*, 81.

7 Similar points are raised in the United States, for example, over the differentiation between those classified as African-American and such groups as the Hispanic, Chinese, Vietnamese, Chicano, and so on. Are they separate and different from Black Americans, and should they not get the same affirmative action entitlements as African-Americans? Wilkins asks, "As America becomes an increasingly multiracial society, one can legitimately ask whether it is possible to discuss responding to injustice against blacks without considering the impact that race conscious public policies will have on other racial minorities. To cite only one prominent example, the recent controversy involving a challenge by some Asian-Americans to a desegregation order that allocates by race places in a prestigious California high school dramatically underscores the additional complexity in the moral argument for race consciousness that is introduced once one moves away from a world in which there is only black and white." David B. Wilkins, "Introduction: The Context of Race" in *Color Conscious: The Political Morality of Race*, K. Anthony Appiah and Amy Gutmann (Princeton: Princeton UP, 1996), 28. Indeed, Wilkins raises a good argument against limiting Blackness solely to race, and in this case to a somatic category or finite group, instead of seeing Blackness as an infinity, and race as simply a moral and ethical attribute. As an infinity, ontological Blackness would include all those other minorities that have been socially constructed as other than White in society, those who have been racialized as inferior idealistically, culturally, and in status. We must bear in mind that ideationally in the Black and White world with which Kymlicka and Wilkins are grappling, White has always been pure and unchangeable, whereas Blackness has always been the catch-all category for those who are not White. Therefore Hispanics, Vietnamese, and so on may be Black in status, culture, and idealistically, even if they are not Black somatically. Importantly, while they are Black they are still not African-American, for African-American is a finite ethno-racial determination within the Black infinity. They could be constructed as possessing a finite bundle of traits and attributes that do not include non African-Americans who are otherwise Black.

8 Kymlicka, *Finding Our Way*, 82.

9 Kymlicka, *Politics in the Vernacular*, 190.

10 Claude Lévi-Strauss, *Structural Anthropology* (New York: Basic Books, 1963).

11 Immanuel Kant, *Critique of Practical Reason*, translated and with an introduction by Lewis White Beck (Indianapolis: Bobbs-Merrill Company, 1956), 107.

12 Stuart Hall, *Representation: Cultural Representations and Signifying Practices* (London: Sage, 1997).

13 Aristotle, "Categoriae (Categories)," in *The Basic Works of Aristotle,* ed. Richard MacKeon, (New York: Modern Library, 2001), 1.

14 Immanuel Kant, *Critique of Pure Reason,* trans. Vasilis Politis, (London: J.M. Dent, 1934; 2004), 84. In this regard, Kant notes the recognition of the need for categories of understanding: "[It] was a design worthy of an acute thinker like Aristotle, to search for these fundamental concepts" (86).

15 Thomas C. Holt, *The Problem of Race in the Twenty-First Century* (Cambridge: Harvard UP, 2000), 13. For a discussion of this issue in the Canadian context, see Lawrence Hill, *Black Berry, Sweet Juice: On Being Black and White in Canada* (Toronto: Harper Flamingo Canada, 2001).

16 Holt, *The Problem of Race,* 13.

17 Ibid. 16.

18 This is certainly the case in much of the debate on Blackness in Canada. For example, the following is the description provided by the social scientist Joseph Mensah in his book *Black Canadians*:

> Prior to the 1960s, non-Whites, notably Chinese, East Indians, and Blacks, were brought to Canada mainly to perform the hard, dirty, hazardous, and low-paying jobs (e.g., coal mining, railroad construction, and farm cleaning) that White Canadians generally did not want to perform. Most of these immigrants worked as indentured labourers, enduring race-related abuses and harassment at the hands of White Canadian employers. Indeed, Black and Aboriginal people were subjected even to slavery. Indeed, Canada was built on the backs of ethno-racial minorities, most of whom "were welcomed when they came to perform hard and dirty work, [but] were often rejected when those duties were completed, or when economic recessions occurred and it appeared they were taking jobs away from White Canadians. Joseph Mensah, *Black Canadians: History, Experiences, Social Conditions* (Halifax: Fernwood Publishing, 2002), 1.

Mensah conflates idealistic, somatic, cultural, and status Blackness and Whiteness. For example, it is notable that the Canadian universe or system starts out as being divided into Whites and non-Whites, who by extension must be Black if they are not White, since White is the site of purity. But this non-White group includes the Chinese, East Indians, and even "Blacks" – people constructed in distinct groups because of somatic features and by cultural, national, and regional traits. Later, immigrants are presented as socially Black, as being placed at inferior levels in society; they are idealistically Black in the way they are denied the same recognition and rights as (somatic, cultural, status, and idealistic) White non-immigrants who are Canadians. Finally, Black and Aboriginal peoples are determined by their cultures and the kind of existence historically typical for them in Canada.

19 Charles W. Mills, *The Racial Contract* (Ithaca: Cornell UP, 1997), 1–2.

20 Ibid., 4.

21 Holt, *The Problem of Race,* 18.

22 Northrop Frye, *Mythologizing Canada: Essays on the Canadian Literary Imagination*, ed. Branko Gorjup (Ottawa: Legas, 1997); ibid., *The Bush Garden: Essays on the Canadian Imagination* (Toronto: House of Anansi Press, 1971).

23 Terry Eagleton, *The Idea of Culture* (Oxford: Blackwell, 2000).

24 As Kant noted:

On the other hand, the categories of the understanding do not represent the conditions under which objects are given to us in intuition; objects can consequently appear to us without necessarily connecting themselves with these, and consequently without any necessity binding on the understanding to contain *a priori* the conditions of these objects. Thus we find ourselves involved in a difficulty which did not present itself in the sphere of sensibility, that is to say, we cannot discover *how the subjective conditions of thought can have objective validity,* in other words, can become conditions of the possibility of all knowledge of objects; for appearances may certainly be given us in intuition without any help from the functions of understand. (Italics in original), Kant, *Critique of Pure Reason*, ed. Politis, 94.

25 Here we are reminded of the reconciliation of perspectives that ideology produces for the religious and scientific branches of Western thought. As Paul Ricoeur says, for example:

Need we say that Marx's attention to the totality of appropriation is reminiscent of religious thinking? I do not want to emphasize this aspect, because it would offer too easy a way for theologians to deal with Marx, as if he set forth a laicization of religious thought. We must accept Marx precisely in his attempt to speak in new terms of what he calls emancipation. I have already quoted the expression, "the resurrection of nature"; surely embedded here is a reminiscence of the Christian theology of Easter. Redemption, as Jürgen Moltmann has suggested, is the Easter of humanity. We must not make a mixture of Marxism and Christianity but perhaps think with both in a creative way. Just as Heidegger observes that poetry and philosophy sit on two different peaks and do not see the same thing, we should say the same about Marxism and Christianity. Paul Ricoeur, *Lectures on Ideology and Utopia* (New York: Columbia UP, 1986), 63.

26 In this respect, we may take into account the dominant interpretation of sin and of death in the Adam and Eve story in the Bible. In both instances, responsibility for sin and death is placed on a desire that is sexual, or on disobedience, the two sides of the same coin. The subversive tradition says that the sin is Adam's failure to recognize and take responsibility for his body and for being embodied. Thinking that he was made in the *image* of God, Adam believed and acted as if he was a God without an image or form, that is, as if he was an abstraction. This is the Black understanding of the myth and puts the sins on the back of Whiteness, that is, on abstraction, dis-embodiment, rational thought, and the denial of death. Instead, the Black God, death, says to humans that they shall surely die, and says this not as a threat, as if they were already blessed with eternal life, but because,

given that they are embodied and Black, they face the inevitability of death. In this light, the ethical correlations are made clear. I am particularly grateful to Howard Adelman for this explanation.

27 Charles Taylor refers to a double determinacy, without calling it such, in his explanation of the genealogy of multiculturalism as a politics of recognition in Western thought. Placing his argument in terms of a dialectical struggle for recognition based either on privileges or dignity already taking place in a nation-state coming out of feudal Europe into modernity, Taylor says:

> We can distinguish two changes that together have made the modern preoccupation with identity and recognition inevitable. The first is the collapse of social hierarchies, which used to be the basis for honor. I am using *honor* in the ancien régime sense in which it is intrinsically linked to inequalities. For some to have honor in this sense, it is essential that not everyone have it. This is the sense in which Montesquieu uses it in his description of monarchy. Honor is intrinsically a matter of "préférences." It is also the sense in which we use the term when we speak of honoring someone by giving her some public award, for example, the Order of Canada. Clearly, this award would be without worth if tomorrow we decided to give it to every adult Canadian. Charles Taylor, "The Politics of Recognition," in Amy Gutmann, ed., *Multiculturalism: Examining the Politics of Recognition* (Princeton: Princeton UP, 1994), 26–7.

Here Taylor is describing three things of importance to our discussion. One, that what I define as idealistic Blackness is the original starting position where everyone is equal in their inequality outside the state; two, that those who are plucked out of this primordial Blackness are transformed into an idealistic and ethical Whiteness of citizenship in the state; three, that all citizens are not equal, for there is a further determination that produces a hierarchy of those who are fully White – those that are honoured. This is the double determinacy that produces social Whiteness for the elite and social Blackness for the non-elite even in an idealistic White nation-state. This is so because by modernity's definition there can be only one unchangeable Whiteness, which means there can be no hierarchies in Whiteness. This means that the non-elites are socially or status Black.

One other thing that Taylor is describing is how, in effect, multiculturalism, with its privileging of an inherent neo-mythic dignity in all humans over an ascriptive honour system for a select few, is a determination of Blackness, for it tries to get rid of the hierarchy that produces an elite Whiteness. Effectively, because the previous elites and the non-elites are now equal this can only happen in Blackness – since there can be no differentiation in Whiteness. In this Blackness, there is no further determination within the idealistically White state of who is authentically White. Alternatively, those who have traditionally positioned themselves as White must, for them to be made equal to everyone else, have their preferences, privileges, and higher statuses taken away as they are brought back into a lower status – into what is now presented as idealistic Whiteness but which for them is idealistic Blackness.

28 Technically, First Nations people are nor entering or re-entering Canada, but rather their own nations. The practical side is that these nations are supposedly within the borders of the Canadian nation-state, which means that, ironically, First Nations people must first enter Canada to get to their respective nations.

29 Immigration and Refugee Protection Act, 2001, C.27. Department of Justice Canada.

30 We will bear this double determinacy in mind when we discuss in chapter 9 the Aristotelian approach to the creation of Whiteness, where pure White is placed at the top of a hierarchy and the lower levels are occupied by different mixtures of Black and White, the whole on a sliding scale to Blackest Black at the bottom.

31 Canadian Charter of Rights and Freedoms and Canadian Constitution Act, 1982 (79), <http://laws.justice.gc.ca/en/charter/#egalite>.

32 Ibid.

33 Derek Heater, *What Is Citizenship?* (Cambridge: Polity Press, 1999), 80–114.

34 Lewis R Gordon, "Sartrean Bad Faith and Antiblack Racism," in *Philosophers on Race: Critical Essays*, ed. Julie K. Ward and Tommy L. Lott (Oxford: Blackwell, 2002).

35 John Burbidge, *Being and Will: An Essay in Philosophical Theology* (New York: Paulist Press, 1977), 52.

36 Pierre Vallières, *White Niggers of America*, trans. Joan Pinkham (Toronto: McClelland and Stewart, 1971).

37 Noel Ignatiev, *How the Irish Became White* (New York: Routledge, 1995).

38 Kymlicka, *Politics in the Vernacular*, 179.

39 Édouard Glissant, *Poetics of Relation*, trans. Betsy Wing (Ann Arbor: University of Michigan Press, 2000).

40 Arthur O. Lovejoy, *The Great Chain of Being: A Study of the History of an Idea* (Cambridge: Harvard UP, 1971).

41 Northrop Frye, *The Eternal Act of Creation: Essays, 1979–1900* (Bloomington: Indiana UP, 1993).

42 Plato, *Phaedrus*, trans. W.C. Helmbold and W.G. Rabinowitz (Indianapolis: Bobbs-Merrill Company, 1956); Immanuel Kant, *Foundations of the Metaphysics of Morals*, trans. Lewis White Beck (Indianapolis: Bobbs-Merrill Company, 1959); Immanuel Kant, *On History*, ed. Lewis White Beck, trans. Beck, Robert E. Anchor, and Emil L. Fackenheim (Indianapolis: Bobbs-Merrill Company, 1963).

43 Roger Scruton, Peter Singer, Christopher Janaway, and Michael Tanner, *German Philosophers: Kant, Hegel, Schopenhauer, Nietzsche* (Oxford: Oxford UP, 1997), 88.

44 Kant, *Foundations of the Metaphysics of Morals*.

45 Immanuel Kant, "This Fellow Was Quite Black: A Clear Proof That What He Said Was Stupid," in *Race and the Enlightenment: A Reader* ed. Emmanuel Chukwudi Eze (Cambridge, Mass.: Blackwell, 1977); Georg Wilhelm Friedrich Hegel, "Race, History, and Imperialism," in *Race and the Enlightenment: A Reader*; Scruton et al., *German Philosophers*.

46 Richard Taylor, *Good and Evil* (New York: Prometheus Books, 2000).

47 David Carney, *Soul of Darkness: Introduction to African Metaphysics, Philosophy and Religion* (New York: Adastra, 1991); John Thornton, *Africa and Africans in the Making of the Atlantic World, 1400–1680* (Cambridge: Cambridge UP, 1995); Paget Henry, *Caliban's Reason: Introducing Afro-Caribbean Philosophy* (New York: Routledge, 2000).

CHAPTER SIX

1 Terry Eagleton, ed., *Ideology* (London: Longman, 1994), 1.
2 Ibid., 15.
3 Northrop Frye, *Myth and Metaphor: Selected Essays 1974–1988*, ed. Robert D. Denham (Charlotteville: University Press of Virginia, 1990).
4 Michel Foucault, *The Archaeology of Knowledge and The Discourse on Language* (New York: Pantheon Books, 1972).
5 Charles Taylor, *Sources of the Self: The Making of the Modern Identity* (Cambridge: Harvard UP, 1989) 25–52.
6 Frye, *Myth and Metaphor*, 88.
7 Stephen Toulmin, *Cosmopolis: The Hidden Agenda of Modernity* (Chicago: University of Chicago Press, 1992).
8 Frye, *Myth and Metaphor*, p.5.
9 A.C. Erwing, *Idealism: A Critical Survey*, 3d ed. (London: Methuen, 1961).
10 Frye, *Myth and Metaphor*, 7.
11 Ibid.
12 Ibid.
13 Mircea Eliade, *Myth and Reality* (London: George Allen and Unwin, 1964).
14 Ibid., 18.
15 Frye, *Myth and Metaphor*, 88. Epistemologically, here we are reminded of the earlier statement by John Locke that from an empiricist standpoint what an individual perceives internally as ideas that become concrete objects are made up of two different qualities. The first is a primary quality, which is in effect the essence of the thing perceived, and which is inseparable from the thing no matter what form the object takes. "Take a grain of wheat, divide it into two parts; each part has still solidity, extension, figure, and mobility: divide it again, and it retains still the same qualities; and so divide it on, till the parts become insensible; they must retain still each of them all those qualities." These qualities from Locke's perspective are what are necessary. The secondary qualities, "are nothing in the objects themselves but powers to produce various sensations in us by their primary qualities, i.e. by the bulk, figure, texture, and motion of their insensible parts, as colours, sounds, taste, &c." The second group are contingent to the concept. In terms, then, of an individual knowing with some degree of certainty, primary qualities are more important than the secondary ones. John Locke, "An Essay Concerning Human Understanding," *The Empiricists: Locke, Berkeley, Hume*, (New York: Anchor Books, 1974), 24–5.

16 Mircea Eliade, *The Sacred and the Profane: The Nature of Religion*, trans. Williard R. Trask (New York: Harper and Row, 1961), 45.

17 Frye, Ibid., 88.

18 Ibid., 21.

19 Ibid., 88.

20 Ibid.

21 Ibid., 22.

22 Ibid.

23 Ibid., 22–3.

24 Ibid., 87. In chapter 19, we shall use Frye's analysis to explain how Blackness was developed as status in the creation of Canadian culture – especially in politics, economics, and the arts – a culture that was developed for a society that is based on a functionalist ideology that depends on categories of high and low cultures and reserves different roles for specific categories of people in the production of this culture. In officially becoming multicultural, instead of sticking to its models of Anglo-conformity and Franco-conformity, Canada was switching to an anthropocentric worldview from an existing ethnocentric one. However, Canada did not make a corresponding switch in emphasis from secondary to primary concerns.

25 Ibid., 14.

26 Thomas S. Kuhn, *The Structure of Scientific Revolutions*, 2d ed. (Chicago: University of Chicago Press, 1970).

27 For a fuller discussion, see Paul Ricoeur, *Lectures on Ideology and Utopia* (New York: Columbia UP, 1986), and his discussion on the ideological break that is located in Marxian thought as an alternate way of explaining developments in ideology.

28 A.C. Erwing, *Idealism: A Critical Survey*, 3rd ed. (London: Methuen, 1961).

29 Emmanuel Chukwudi Eze, *Race and the Enlightenment: A Reader* (Cambridge, Mass.: Blackwell, 1977); Charles W. Mills, *The Racial Contract* (Ithaca: Cornell UP, 1997).

30 Roger Scruton, Peter Singer, Christopher Janaway, and Michael Tanner, *German Philosophers: Kant, Hegel, Schopenhauer, Nietzsche* (Oxford: Oxford UP, 1997).

31 Emmanuel Levinas, *Totality and Infinity: An Essay on Exteriority* (Pittsburgh: Duquesne UP, 1961).

32 David Carney, *Soul of Darkness: Introduction to African Metaphysics, Philosophy and Religion* (New York: Adastra, 1991); Paget Henry, *Caliban's Reason: Introducing Afro-Caribbean Philosophy* (New York: Routledge, 2000).

33 Errol E Harris, *The Problem of Evil* (Milwaukee: Marquette UP, 1977).

34 Cecil Foster, *Where Race Does Not Matter: The New Spirit of Modernity* (Toronto: Penguin, 2005).

35 K. Anthony Appiah and Amy Gutmann, *Colour Conscious: The Political Morality of Race* (Princeton: Princeton UP, 1996), 56.

36 Maurice Merleau-Ponty, *Phenomenology of Perception*, trans. Colin Smith (London: Routledge and Kegan Paul, 2000).

37 Here, too, we are reminded of John Locke's claim regarding epistemology: that in the absence of full demonstrated proof, which is a higher level of intuitive knowledge than is reason, that in this epistemological void of knowing, all we are left with is faith or opinion:

> These two, viz. intuition and demonstration, are the degrees of our *knowledge;* whatever comes short of one of these, with what assurance so ever embraced, is but *faith* or *opinion*, but not knowledge, at least in all general truth. There is, indeed, another perception of the mind, employed about *the particular existence of finite beings without us*, which, going beyond bare probability, and yet not reaching perfectly to either of the foregoing degrees of certainty, passes under the name of *knowledge*. There can be nothing more certain than that the idea we receive from an external object is in our minds: this is intuitive knowledge. Locke, "An Essay Concerning Human Understanding," 81.

In this epistemological Black hole, we are plunged into the dialectic of hope that conceptually is inclusive of its finite other, despair.

38 Alvin Plantinga, *The Ontological Argument: From Anselm to Contemporary Philosophers* (New York: Anchor Books, 1965); E.L Mascall, *Existence and Analogy* (n.p.: Anchor Books, 1967); Humphrey Palmer, *Analogy: a Study of Qualification and Argument on Theology* (London: Macmillan, 1973); Kenneth Surin, *The Turning of Darkness and Light: Essays in Philosophical and Systematic Theology* (Cambridge: Cambridge UP, 1989).

39 Humphrey Palmer, *Analogy: A Study of Qualification and Argument on Theology* (London: Macmillan, 1973).

40 Martin Heidegger, *Being and Time*, trans. John Macquarrie and Edward Robinson (Oxford: Blackwell, 2000).

41 Palmer, *Analogy*, 59–60.

42 Ibid.; Terence Hawkes, *Structuralism and Semiotics* (Berkeley: University of California Press, 1977); Roland Barthes, *Mythologies*, selected and translated by Annette Lavers (London: Jonathan Cape, 1972).

43 Umberto Eco, *A Theory of Semiotics* (Bloomington: Indiana UP, 1976), 7.

44 Charles Taylor, "The Politics of Recognition," in *Multiculturalism: Examining the Politics of Recognition*, ed. Amy Gutmann (Princeton: Princeton UP, 1994).

45 David Wootton, ed., *Divine Right and Democracy* (London: Penguin, 1986); Marc Egnal, *A Mighty Empire: The Origins of American Revolution* (Ithaca: Cornell UP, 1988); Bernard Bailyn, *The Ideological Origins of the American Revolution: Enlarged Edition* (Cambridge: Harvard UP, 1992).

46 Jean-Paul Sartre, *Being and Nothingness: An Essay on Phenomenological Ontology*, trans. with introduction by Hazel E. Barnes (London: Methuen, 1957).

47 Northrop Frye, *Reflections on the Canadian Literary Imagination* (Rome: Bulzoni Editore, 1991); ibid., *The Educated Imagination* (Montreal: CBC Enterprises, 1991); ibid., *Mythologizing Canada: Essays on the Canadian Literary Imagination*, ed. Branko Gorjup (Ottawa: Legas, 1997).

48 Frye, *Mythologizing Canada*.

49 Jeffrey G. Reitz and Raymond Breton, *The Illusion of Difference: Realities of Ethnicity in Canada and the United States* (Ottawa: C.D. Howe Institute, 1994); Jeffrey G. Reitz, *Warmth of the Welcome: The Social Causes of Economic Success for Immigrants in Different Nations and Cities* (Boulder, Colo.: Westview Press, 1998).

50 Reitz, *Warmth of the Welcome*; Reitz and Breton, *The Illusion of Difference*.

51 Daiva Stasiulis, "Participation by Immigrants, Ethnocultural/Visible Minorities in the Canadian Political Process" paper presented in Montreal at Second National Metropolis Conference, 23–25 November 1997).

52 Paul Barry Clarke, *Deep Citizenship* (London: Pluto Press, 1996).

53 David Cesarani and Mary Fulbrook, eds, *Citizenship, Nationality and Migration in Europe* (London: Routledge, 1996).

54 Kymlicka, *Multicultural Citizenship: Liberal Theory of Minority Rights* (Oxford: Clarendon Press, 1995); ibid., *Finding Our Way: Rethinking Ethnocultural Relations in Canada* (Toronto: Oxford UP, 1998); ibid., *Politics in the Vernacular: Nationalism, Multiculturalism, and Citizenship* (Oxford: Oxford UP, 2000; Frances Henry, *The Caribbean Diaspora in Toronto: Learning to Live with Racism* (Toronto: University of Toronto Press, 1994); Frances Henry, Carol Tator, Winston Mattis, and Tim Rees, *The Colour of Democracy: Racism in Canadian Society* (Toronto: Harcourt Brace, 1995) ; Peter S. Li, *Race and Ethnic Relations in Canada* (Toronto: Oxford UP, 1990); Joseph H. Carens, *Culture, Citizenship, and Community: A Contextual Exploration of Justice as Evenhandedness* (Oxford: Oxford UP, 2000); Carl E. James, *Making It: Black Youth, Racism and Career Aspirations in a Big City* (Oakville: Mosaic Press, 1990); Carl E. James, "Getting There and Staying There: Blacks' Employment Experience," in *Transitions: Schooling and Employment in Canada*, Paul Anisef and Paul Axelrod (Thompson Educational Publishing, 1993); Carl E. James, "Up to No Good: Black on the Streets and Encountering Police," in *Racism and Social Inequality in Canada: Concepts, Controversies and Strategies of Resistance*, Vic Satzewich (Toronto: Thompson Educational Publishing, 1998); Carl E. James, Dwaine Plaza, and Clifford Jansen, "Issues of Race in Employment: Experiences of Caribbean Women in Toronto," *Canadian Woman Studies* 19, no. 3 (1998); Rinaldo Walcott, *Black Like Who? Writing Black Canada* (Toronto: Insomniac Press, 1997).

55 Kymlicka, *Multicultural Citizenship*; ibid., *Finding Our Way*; ibid., *Politics in the Vernacular*; Henry et al., *The Colour of Democracy*; Frances Henry and Carol Tator, *Racist Discourse in Canada's English Print Media* (Toronto: The Canadian Race Relations Foundation, March 2000); Li, *Race and Ethnic Relations in Canada*; Carens, *Culture, Citizenship, and Community*; Alan Simmons, "Canadian Immigration Policy: An Analysis of Imagined Futures," paper prepared for the Symposium on Immigration and Integration (Winnipeg: Department of Sociology, University of Manitoba, 25–27 October 1996); ibid., "Racism and Immigration Policy," in *Racism and Social Inequality in Canada: Concepts, Controversies and*

*Strategies of Resistance*, Vic Satzewich (Toronto: Thompson Educational Publishing, 1998); Anthony H. Richmond and Warren E. Kalbach, *Factors in the Adjustment of Immigrants and Their Descendants* (Ottawa, Minister of Supply and Services, Canada, 1980); Reitz and Breton, *The Illusion of Difference*; J.L. Granatstein, *Nation: Canada Since Confederation* (Toronto: McGraw-Hill Ryerson, 1990); ibid., *Who Killed Canadian History?* (Toronto: HarperCollins Publishers, 1998); ibid. *How Britain's Weakness Forced Canada into the Arms of the United States* (Toronto: University of Toronto Press, 1989); Desmond Morton, *A Short History of Canada* (Toronto: McClelland and Stewart, 1997); W.L. Morton, *The Canadian Identity* (Toronto: University of Toronto Press, 1961); Rinaldo Walcott, *Black Like Who? Writing Black Canada*, 2d rev. ed. (Toronto: Insomniac Press, 2003).

56 Sources as in n55.

57 Kymlicka, *Multicultural Citizenship*; ibid., *Finding Our Way*; ibid., *Politics in the Vernacular*; Henry et al., *The Colour of Democracy*; Henry and Tator, *Racist Discourse in Canada's English Print Media*; Li, *Race and Ethnic Relations in Canada*; Carens, *Culture, Citizenship, and Community*; Simmons, "Canadian Immigration Policy"; ibid., "Racism and Immigration Policy"; H. Anthony Richmond and Warren E. Kalbach, *Factors in the Adjustment of Immigrants and Their Descendants* (Ottawa: Minister of Supply and Services, Canada, 1980); Reitz and Breton, *The Illusion of Difference*; Granatstein, *Nation: Canada Since Confederation*; ibid., *Who Killed Canadian History?*; ibid., *How Britain's Weakness Forced Canada*; Desmond Morton, *A Short History of Canada*; W.L. Morton, *The Canadian Identity*; Walcott, *Black Like Who?*; James, *Making It*; ibid., "Getting There and Staying There"; ibid., "Up to No Good."

58 Emmanuel Levinas, *Otherwise Than Being: Or Beyond Essence* (Pittsburgh: Duquesne UP, 1998).

59 Mircea Eliade, *The Sacred and the Profane: The Nature of Religion*, trans. Williard R. Trask (New York: Harper and Row, 1961); Northrop Frye, *Myth and Reality*; ibid., *The Eternal Act of Creation: Essays, 1979–1900* (Bloomington: Indiana UP, 1993).

60 Friedrich Nietzsche, *On the Advantage and Disadvantage of History for Life*, trans. with introduction by Peter Preuss (Indianapolis: Hackett Publishing, 1980); ibid., *Beyond Good and Evil: Prelude to a Philosophy of the Future*, trans. with introduction and commentary by R.J. Hollingdale (Middlesex, England: Penguin, 1984).

CHAPTER SEVEN

1 G.W.F Hegel, *Hegel's Philosophy of Right*, as quoted by Walter Kaufmann, *From Shakespeare to Existentialism: Studies in Poetry, Religion, and Philosophy* (Boston: Beacon Press, 1959), 101.

2 Agnes Calliste and George J. Sefa Dei, *Anti-Racist Feminism: Critical Race and Gender Studies* (Halifax: Fernwood Publishing, 2000); Elizabeth Comack,

*Locating Law: Race, Class, Gender Connections* (Halifax: Fernwood Publishing, 1999); Oliver C. Cox, *Race: A Study in Social Dynamics*, prefaced by Cornell West, introduction by Adolphi Reed Jr (New York: Monthly Review Press, 2000); Carl M. Degler, *Neither Black Nor White: Slavery and Race Relations in Brazil and the United States* (New York: Macmillan, 1971); Leo Driedger and Shiva S. Hall, eds, *Race and Racism: Canada's Challenge* (Montreal and Kingston: McGill-Queen's UP, 2000); Ivan Hannaford, *Race: The History of an Idea in the West* (Washington: The Woodrow Wilson Center Press, 1996); Frances Henry, Winston Mattis, Carol Tator, and Tim Rees, *The Colour of Democracy: Racism in Canadian Society* (Toronto: Harcourt Brace, 1995); Thomas C. Holt, *The Problem of Race in the Twenty-First Century* (Cambridge: Harvard UP, 2000); Lisa Marie Jakubowski, "'Managing' Canadian Immigration: Racism, Ethnic Selectivity, and the Law," in *Locating Law: Race, Class, Gender Connections*, ed. Elizabeth Cormack (Halifax: Fernwood Publishing, 1999); Carl E. James, *Seeing Ourselves: Exploring Race, Ethnicity and Culture*, 3d ed. (Toronto: Thompson Educational Publishing, 2003); Peter S. Li, *Race and Ethnic Relations in Canada* (Toronto: Oxford UP, 1990); Martin Loney, *The Pursuit of Division: Race, Gender, and Preferential Hiring in Canada* (Montreal and Kingston: McGill-Queen's UP, 1998); Angus McLaren, *Our Own Master Race: Eugenics in Canada, 1885-1945* (Toronto: McClelland and Stewart, 1990); Clarence J. Munford, *Race and Civilization: Rebirth of Black Centrality* (Trenton, N.J.: African World Press, 2001); John Thornton, *Race, Discourse, and the Origin of the Americas: A New World View*, ed. Vera Lawrence Hyatt and Rex Nettleford (Washington: Smithsonian Institution P., 1995); Frances Henry and Carol Tator, *Racist Discourse in Canada's English Print Media* (Toronto: Canadian Race Relations Foundation, March 2000); Julie K Ward and Tommy L. Lott, eds, *Philosophers on Race: Critical Essays* (London: Blackwell, 2002); Cornel West, *Race Matters* (New York: Vintage Books, 1993); William Julius Wilson, *The Declining Significance of Race: Blacks and Changing American Institutions* (Chicago: University of Chicago Press, 1978).

3 As Appiah notes, in the case of racial classification the characteristics in the finite group account for what every member of the group shares in common. Together, they determine "what we call the *essence* of that race; they were characteristics that were necessary and sufficient, taken together, for someone to be a normal member of the race." K. Anthony Appiah and Amy Gutmann, *Colour Conscious: The Political Morality of Race* (Princeton: Princeton UP, 1996), 55. Appiah's depiction here is of Truth appearing in the form of perception as a correspondence between the essential characteristics of a thing as it appears and the characteristics of the same item as a universal class.

4 Thomas S. Kuhn, *The Structure of Scientific Revolutions*, Second (Chicago: University of Chicago Press, 1970).

5 In the introduction to a collection of essays on the influence of Hegel on both modern and postmodern philosophy, editor Stuart Barnett says this of the connection between Hegel and Kuhn:

Kuhn did a thoroughly Hegelian examination of that supposedly most empirical branch of knowledge, science. It was the merit of Kuhn, then, to drive the point home for many philosophers of science and analytic philosophers that no field of knowledge is immune from the vicissitudes and transformations of history. In fact, Kuhn argued, all knowledge is riddled through with historicity ... The truth of reason, such as it is, reveals itself in the course of history as a series of crises and self-negations. This thoroughly Hegelian reading of that field of knowledge felt to be most securely anchored in the empirical began to open up analytic philosophy to questions of history and culture. Stuart Barnett, *Hegel after Derrida* (London: Routledge, 1998), 10.
In making this point, Barnett was illustrating how Kuhn's work, which was Hegelian in nature, influenced such philosophers as Paul Feyerabend and Richard Rorty, and how these analytic thinkers used Hegelian methods to explain the world. Barnett states: "What particularly interests Feyerabend is the notion that each form of reason will necessarily produce contradictions within its own system that inevitably lead to its dissolution. In this he subscribes to the Hegelian notion that the truth of reason lies not in any particular moment but in its self-contradictory historical unfolding. Like Hegel, Feyerabend embraces that anarchic and pitiless core at the heart of dialectics that lays waste to all systems of thought." Of Rorty, Barnett says that he "embraced a Hegelian solution to the paradoxes of the analytic tradition. Like few others, Rorty understands that Hegel is the architect of postmodernism ... Rorty focuses on those moments in a culture where contradiction comes to the fore – when a culture becomes aware of the contingency of its own vocabulary. This then is what throws that culture into a spasm of self-doubt and inaugurates a renewed self-description. It takes only a single shift in vocabulary to see this pragmatist version of an ironist culture as what Hegel discussed as the historical evolution of spirit." Barnett, *Hegel after Derrida*, 10–11. The implications are severe for those offering a single and unchanging common sense meaning for any concept.

6 G.W.F. Hegel, *Lectures on the Philosophy of History*, trans. J. Sibree (London: George Bell and Sons, 1878); ibid., *Phenomenology of Spirit*, trans. A.V. Miller (Oxford: Oxford UP, 1977).

7 Paul Weiss, *Beyond All Appearances* (Carbondale and Edwardsville, IL: Southern Illinois UP, 1974), 21.

8 Martin Heidegger, *The Basic Problems of Phenomenology* (Bloomington: Indiana UP, 1982; Vittorio Klostermann, 1975), 1.

9 Dyer George, "The Theology of Death," in *Death and Hope*, ed. Harry J. Cargas and Ann White (New York: Corpus Books, 1970), 35.

10 Reinhardt Grossmann, *Phenomenology and Existentialism: An Introduction* (London: Routledge and Kegan Paul, 1984), 4–5.

11 As Zaner notes in Richard M. Zaner, *The Way of Phenomenology: Criticism as a Philosophical Discipline* (New York: Pegasus, 1970): "Criticism is not a whim of the philosopher, but has its ground in that pervasive philosophical, indeed human,

activity called claiming. In fact, it is not excessive to suggest a more general thesis: not only epistemic claims, but every claim – whether axiological, ethical, meta-physical, religious – necessarily invites philosophical criticism" (79). This is what Zaner calls the *Descartes invitation to evidence*, the search for "that kind of 'true and evident cognition' which is alone capable of investigating and discovering the 'first causes' or the 'principles' of all things" (84). This is a rigorous and critical search for evidence that is foundational; a going back to the beginning to under-stand genuine knowledge, when that which is given is not accepted as being with-out immediacy.

12 René Descartes, *Discourse on Method and Meditations* (Indianapolis: Bobbs-Merrill Company, 1960).

13 Here we are reminded by Descartes's scientific method of subjecting his writing to critical analysis before publication. In this way, his claims were tested dialecti-cally, thereby helping him think that he was arriving at a higher and more com-prehensive truth claim. But even then, Descartes knew that an essential doubt remained so that he was not in absolute knowledge. See Zaner, *The Way of Phe-nomenology*, 79–124.

14 Grossmann, *Phenomenology and Existentialism*, 139.

15 Maurice Merleau-Ponty, *Phenomenology of Perception*, trans. Colin Smith (Lon-don: Routledge and Kegan Paul, 2000).

16 Grossmann, *Phenomenology and Existentialism*, 146.

17 David Wilkins makes a somewhat similar point on contextualization as a way of trying to balance moral claims that arise from the dualism that is race: is the phe-nomenon historically and culturally constructed, or is it ideational? "Often this will involve deciding how to balance three distinct kinds of moral claims. The first ... stems from the fact that in our nonideal society, race matters in ways that plau-sibly affect moral decision-making. The second results from the fact that those who decide how they will take race into account frequently occupy social roles – lawyers, public servants, university officials – that also constrain moral deci-sion-making. Finally ... we are more than the sum total of our racial and role obligations ... Once again, deciding how to balance these claims in any particular case requires that we pay attention to context." David B. Wilkins, "Introduction: The Context of Race," in *Color Conscious: The Political Morality of Race*, K. Anthony Appiah and Amy Gutmann, (Princeton: Princeton UP, 1996), 19–20.

18 Here again, Sartre reminds us of a similar claim: "The new opposition, the 'finite and the infinite,' or better, 'the infinite in the finite,' replaces the dualism of being and appearance. What appears in fact is only an aspect of the object, and the object is altogether *in* that aspect and altogether outside of it. It is altogether *within*, in that it manifests itself *in* that aspect; it shows itself as the structure of the appearance, which is at the same time the principle of the series. It is alto-gether outside, for the series itself will never appear nor can it appear. Thus the outside is opposed in a new way to the inside, and the being-which-does-not-appear, to the appearance." Jean-Paul Sartre, *Being and Nothingness: An Essay*

*on Phenomenological Ontology*, trans. with introduction by Hazel E. Barnes (London: Methuen, 1957), 7.

19 As Dyer explains, "What constitutes existence or personal being is a particular complex temporal nexus in which the three dimensions of the past, present, and future are brought into a unity ... In an existence that is fulfilling its potentialities, the three dimensions are held together in a unity and balance. The authentic present does not shut out the past or the future, but, open to them both, it forges them into a unity. Authentic selfhood, therefore, implies a unified existence in which potentialities are actualized in an orderly manner and without loose ends." Dyer, "The Theology of Death," 37–8.

20 M.J. Inwood, *Hegel* (London: Routledge, 1998), xxiv.

21 Hegel, *Lectures on the Philosophy of History*, 18.

22 Ibid., 20–1.

23 Ibid., 20.

24 Ibid.

25 Ibid., 18.

26 Ibid.

CHAPTER EIGHT

1 Michel Foucault, *The Archaeology of Knowledge and The Discourse on* Language (New York: Pantheon Books, 1972); Homi K. Bhabha, *Narration and Nation* (London: Routledge, 1999).

2 Bhabha, *Narration and Nation*, 311.

3 G.W.F. Hegel, *Lectures on the Philosophy of History*, trans. J. Sibree (London: George Bell and Sons, 1878), 5–6.

4 Ibid., *Phenomenology of Spirit*, trans. A.V. Miller, (Oxford: Oxford UP, 1977), 2.

5 Hegel, *Lectures on the Philosophy of History*, 6.

6 Ibid., 8.

7 Ibid.

8 Emmanuel Levinas, *Totality and Infinity: An Essay on Exteriority* (Pittsburgh: Duquesne UP, 1961).

9 Hegel, *Lectures on the Philosophy of History*, 6.

10 Ibid., 27.

11 Alexandre Kojève, *Introduction to the Reading of Hegel: Lectures on the Phenomenology of Spirit*, ed. Allan Bloom (Ithaca: Cornell UP, 1969).

12 Charles Taylor, "The Politics of Recognition," in *Multiculturalism: Examining the Politics of Recognition,* ed. Amy Gutmann, Amy (Princeton: Princeton UP, 1994).

13 Howard Adelman, "Of Human Bondage: Labour, Bondage, and Freedom in the Phenomenology," in *Hegel's Social and Political Thought: The Philosophy of Objective Spirit*, ed. Donald Phillip Verene (Atlantic Highlands, N.J.: Humanities Press, 1980).

14 Daniel Elazar, *Covenant and Civil Society: the Constitutional Matrix of Modern Democracy* (New Brunswick, N.J.: Transaction Publishers, 1998).

15 Hegel, *Lectures on the Philosophy of History*, 27.

16 Homi K. Bhabha, *The Location of Culture* (London: Routledge, 1994).

17 Hegel, *Phenomenology of Spirit*, 113.

18 Ibid., 121.

19 Pierre Elliott Trudeau, *The Essential Trudeau*, ed. Ron Graham (Toronto: McClelland and Stewart, 1998), 80.

20 Hegel, *Phenomenology of Spirit*, 123.

21 Ibid., 126.

22 Trudeau, *The Essential Trudeau*, 4–5.

23 Hegel, *Phenomenology of Spirit*, 278.

24 Ibid., 279.

25 Roberston Davies, *The Merry Heart: Selections 1980–1995* (Toronto: Penguin, 1996); Daiva Stasiulis, "Participation by Immigrants, Ethnocultural/Visible Minorities in the Canadian Political Process," paper presented in Montreal at the Second National Metropolis Conference, 23–25 November, 1997).

26 Hegel, *Phenomenology of Spirit*, 110–11.

27 Hegel, *Lectures on the Philosophy of History*, 27.

28 Ibid., 30.

29 Ibid.

30 Ibid., 28.

31 Ibid., 6.

32 Ibid., 9.

33 Ibid., 21.

34 Ibid., 22.

35 Ibid., 32.

36 Ibid.

37 Ibid., 23.

38 Ibid., 24.

39 Immanuel Kant, *Foundations of the Metaphysics of Morals*, ed. Lewis White Beck (Indianapolis: Bobbs-Merrill Company, 1959).

40 Hegel, *Lectures on the Philosophy of History*, 24–5.

41 William Shakespeare, *Midsummer Night's Dream*, 5.1.170–1.

42 Hegel, *Phenomenology of Spirit*, 446nn1–6.

43 Martin Heidegger, *The Question of Being* (New York: Twayne Publishing, 1958), 69. It should be noted that *Phenomenology of Spirit* was often translated as *Phenomenology of Mind* in English.

44 Hegel's *Encyclopedia*, II.320, as quoted in M.J. Inwood, *Hegel* (London: Routledge, 1998), 69.

45 Ibid.

46 Hegel, *Phenomenology of Spirit*, 237.

47 Paul Franco, *Hegel's Philosophy of Freedom* (New Haven: Yale UP, 1999), 98.

48 Antonio Gramsci, *Selections from the Prison Notebooks of Antonio Gramsci*, trans. Quintin Hoare and Geoffrey Norwell Smith (New York: International Press, 1997).

49 Margaret Masterman, "The Nature of a Paradigm," in *Criticism and the Growth of Knowledge*, ed. Imre Lakatos and Alan Musgrave (London: Cambridge UP, 1974).

50 Ibid., 59.

51 Ibid., 65.

52 Ibid., 66.

53 Terry Eagleton, *Ideology* (London: Longman, 1994).

54 Northrop Frye, *Myth and Metaphor: Selected Essays 1974–1988*, ed. Robert D. Denham (Charlottesville: University Press of Virginia, 1990).

55 Mircea Eliade, *The Sacred and the Profane: The Nature of Religion*, trans. Willard R. Trask (New York: Harper and Row, 1961); ibid., *Myth and Reality* (London: George Allen and Unwin, 1964); ibid., *Rites and Symbols of Initiation: The Mysteries of Birth and Rebirth*, trans. William R. Trask (New York: Harper Torchbooks, 1965).

56 Masterman, "Nature of a Paradigm," 69.

57 George Psathas, *Phenomenological Sociology: Issues and Applications* (New York: John Wiley and Sons, 1973), 19.

59 Thomas S. Kuhn, *The Structure of Scientific Revolutions* (Chicago: University of Chicago Press, 1970), 6.

59 Ibid., 11.

60 Homi K. Bhabha, *The Location of Culture* (London: Routledge, 1994).

61 Hegel, *Phenomenology of Spirit*.

62 Bernard Bailyn, *The Ideological Origins of the American Revolution*, enlarged ed. (Cambridge: Harvard UP, 1992).

63 T.W. Adorno, *Negative Dialectic*, trans. E.B. Ashton (New York: Seabury Press, 1973); Max Horkheimer and T.W. Adorno, *Dialectic of Enlightenment*, trans. John Cumming (New York: Continuum, 1982); Max Horkheimer, *Eclipse of Reason* (New York: Seabury Press, c1974).

64 Will Kymlicka, *Finding Our Way: Rethinking Ethnocultural Relations in Canada* (Toronto: Oxford UP, 1998).

65 Martin Loney, *The Pursuit of Division: Race, Gender, and Preferential Hiring in Canada* (Montreal and Kingston: McGill-Queen's UP, 1998); Diane Francis, "Why Size Doesn't Matter: We Don't Need More Immigrants to Support Us As We Get Older," *National Post* (Toronto), 28 September 2002; Daniel Stoffman, *Who Gets In? What's Wrong with Canada's Immigration Program – and How to Fix It* (Toronto: Macfarlane Walter and Ross, 2002).

## CHAPTER NINE

1 Plato, "Laws," *The Collected Dialogues of Plato Including the Letters*, ed. Edith Hamilton and Huntington Cairns, Bollingen Series 71, (Princeton: Princeton UP,

1980) XII:956A. However, it is worth noting that Plato is not contrasting White with Black, per se, but with coloured decorations. The gods do no like that which is sacrificed to them to be unnaturally coloured through dyes. White is a sign of purity and naturalness.

2　Aristotle, *The Nicomachean Ethics* (Hertfordshire: Wordsworth Editions, 1996) 1096B.22.

3　Robert Jewett and John Shelton Lawrence, *Captain America and the Crusade against Evil: The Dilemma of Zealous Nationalism* (Grand Rapids, Mich.: William B. Eerdmans Publishing, 2003).

4　Jean-Paul Sartre, *Being and Nothingness: An Essay on Phenomenological Ontology*, trans. with introduction by Hazel E. Barnes (London: Methuen, 1957).

5　Plato, *Phaedrus*, ed. W.C. Helmbold and W.G. Rabinowitz (Indianapolis: Bobbs-Merrill Co., 1956) 2481E.

6　In *Racist Culture: Philosophy and the Politics of Meaning*, Goldberg argues that race is a feature of modernity and that it is wrong to attribute such thinking to the Greeks, or to anyone for that matter before the arrival of modernity. His argument is that race is essentially a modernist construct. "Not only did the Greeks have no concept of racial identification, strictly speaking they had no conception of race. There is considerable evidence of ethnocentric and xenophobic discrimination in Greek texts, of claims to *cultural* superiority, yet little evidence that these claimed inequalities were generally considered to be biologically determined. In the absence of both the term and the conception, the social sense of self and other can hardly be said to be racially conceived nor the social formation to be one properly considered racist." David Theo Goldberg, *Racist Culture: Philosophy and the Politics of Meaning* (Oxford: Blackwell, 1993), 21.

　　Goldberg is not being dialectical; otherwise he would see the categorical contradictions in his argument. He is also not allowing for changes within the concept race, including those that may have predated modernity. Indeed, because the word "race" came into a common sense meaning in the fifteenth century, as he claims, does not mean that dialectically it did not exist within the infinite term. Indeed, Goldberg seems to suggest as much when he states: "I do not mean to deny that discriminatory exclusions were both common and commonly rationalized in various ways in Greek and medieval society, only that these exclusions and their various rationalizations did not assume racialized form." And as we see, he has already noted that there were notions in Greek thought about cultural superiority. Here Goldberg seemed overly concerned with finite terms and definitions in a specific moment, rather than with what they mean in a historical sense. He is also too keen to reduce race to the somatic, ignoring the cultural component, or what is now known conceptually as new racism.

　　If he is right, then, the easiest way to eradicate racism today would be to redefine or re-limit the concept in order to, at some future point, remove references to today's inequalities. Of course, as Sartre suggests, such thinking would be absurd. Similarly, as Jeffrey Perl argues in *The Tradition of Return*, there is always the danger for historians and social scientists thinking that any period, such as modernity, has finite boundaries in time and that there is no antecedent. Jeffrey M. Perl, *The Tradition of Return: The Implicit History of Modern Literature* (Princeton: Princeton UP, 1984).Perl argues that the story of humanity is one of constantly looking to return to an earlier period, and this was also true of the modernists who saw their period as an attempt to return to the halcyon days of Greek antiquity. And in trying to fashion a society to suit their conception of the past, they incorporated and extended many of the concepts and ideals from antiquity. One of these was the concept of separation based on notions of inferiority that came to be systematized in modernity as race. But even so, this raises the question, again, of what a concept is and whether it is ever fully developed. This, as Inwood said, is what Hegel tried to capture in his definition of a concept as an infinite that also incorporates its negative or what is not fully expressed, so that it could be argued that even if the Greeks were not thinking of race in the modernist sense, dialectically they still had a concept of race, even if they did not express it precisely as modernity did.

And, indeed, there is even some suggestion that the Greeks did capture the concept in a way very similar to that of modernity. Rachana Kamtekar argues specifically on this point: "The condition for using and making sense of the concept of race is not a specific scientific theory or investigative context, but rather, the rough idea that people who are related by birth resemble one another. This notion is clearly available to the ancients in general and to Plato in particular ... Plato's ways of classifying people, [allows for] treating his term 'genos' as a rough equivalent to our 'race,' but remaining sensitive to differences between the two concepts." Rachana Kamtekar, "Distinction without Difference? Race and Genos in Plato," in *Philosophers on Race: Critical Essays*, ed. Julie K Ward and Tommy L. Lott (London: Blackwell, 2002), 1–13.

Indeed, Holt makes a significant point of the dialectics that are at work historically in our understanding of race. "Part of the solution," he argues, "is to adopt a conception of historical transformation, in which we recognize that a new historical construct is never entirely new and the old is never entirely supplanted by the new. Rather the new is grafted onto the old. Thus racism, too, is never entirely new. Shards and fragments of its past incarnations are embedded in the new. Or, if we switch metaphors to an archaeological image, the new is sedimented onto the old, which occasionally seeps or bursts through. Our problem then, is to figure out how this happens and to take its measure." Thomas C. Holt, *The Problem of Race in the Twenty-First Century* (Cambridge: Harvard UP, 2000), 20.

One further point is worth making: it is for this reason that we are doing a phenomenology of Blackness – not race – for there can be no denying that the early Greeks had clear and categorical conceptions of Blackness, even if these categories contain what scholars like Goldberg may question as racial overtones. And, as we said, a study of Blackness is more than a study of race.

7 Plato, *Phaedrus* 252D.

8 Ibid., 251E.
9 Cynthia Farrar, *The Origins of Democratic Thinking: The Invention of Politics in Classical Athens* (New York: Cambridge UP, 1988), 11–12.
10 Ivan Hannaford, *Race: The History of an Idea in the West* (Washington: The Woodrow Wilson Center Press, 1996), 18. Emphasis added.
11 Plato, *The Republic*, trans. Desmond Lee (London: Penguin, 1987), III:2.379C.
12 Ibid., III:2.380C.
13 Farrar, *Origins of Democratic Thinking*, 1–14.
14 Plato, "Philebus," *The Collected Dialogues of Plato Including the Letters*, 12E.

CHAPTER TEN

1 Typical was the State of the Union address by US President George W. Bush on 31 January 2006. Invoking this mythology about the American destiny, he said:
In this decisive year, you and I will make choices that determine both the future and the character of our country. We will choose to act confidently in pursuing the enemies of freedom – or retreat from our duties in the hope of an easier life. We will choose to build our prosperity by leading the world economy – or shut ourselves off from trade and opportunity. In a complex and challenging time, the road of isolationism and protectionism may seem broad and inviting – yet it ends in danger and decline. The only way to protect our people, the only way to secure the peace, the only way to control our destiny is by our leadership – so the United States of America will continue to lead.
Abroad, our nation is committed to an historic, long-term goal – we seek the end of tyranny in our world. Some dismiss that goal as misguided idealism. In reality, the future security of America depends on it. On September the 11th, 2001, we found that problems originating in a failed and oppressive state 7,000 miles away could bring murder and destruction to our country. Dictatorships shelter terrorists, and feed resentment and radicalism, and seek weapons of mass destruction. Democracies replace resentment with hope, respect the rights of their citizens and their neighbors, and join the fight against terror. Every step toward freedom in the world makes our country safer – so we will act boldly in freedom's cause.
Far from being a hopeless dream, the advance of freedom is the great story of our time. In 1945, there were about two dozen lonely democracies in the world. Today, there are 122. And we're writing a new chapter in the story of self-government – with women lining up to vote in Afghanistan, and millions of Iraqis marking their liberty with purple ink, and men and women from Lebanon to Egypt debating the rights of individuals and the necessity of freedom. At the start of 2006, more than half the people of our world live in democratic nations. And we do not forget the other half – in places like Syria and Burma, Zimbabwe, North Korea, and Iran – because the demands of justice, and the peace of this world, require their freedom, as well.

<http://www.whitehouse.gov/news/releases/2006/01/20060131-10.html> 17 May 2006

2 Willie Nelson, "The Promised Land," *Willie Nelson: 16 Biggest Hits*, lyrics and music by D.L. Jones (November 1985).

3 Nelson, "The Promised Land."

4 Aimé Césaire, *Discourse on Colonialism* (New York: Monthly Review Press, 1972); Max Horkheimer, *Eclipse of Reason* (New York: Seabury Press, c1974); Max Horkheimer and T.W. Adorno, *Dialectic of Enlightenment*, trans. John Cumming (New York: Continuum, 1982).

5 Frantz Fanon, *Black Skin, White Masks* (New York: Grove Press, 1967).

6 Nas, featuring Quan, "Just a Moment," *Street's Disciple*, lyrics by Nas (November 2004).

7 Ibid.

8 Juergen Habermas, "Faith and Knowledge: An Opening Speech by Juergen Habermas Accepting the Peace Prize of the German Publishers and Booksellers Association," *Sueddeutsche Zeitung*, 15 October 2001, English, <http://www.sueddeutsche.de/aktuell/sz/artikel86740.php>.

9 Charles Taylor, *Hegel* (New York: Cambridge UP, 1995), 9.

10 Thomas Bulfinch, *The Golden Age of Myth and Legend: The Classical Mythology of the Ancient World* (London: Wordsworth Editions, 1993).

11 Thomas Holt reminds us of the special place of lightning as idealistic Whiteness in the mythology of the United States, a mythology that has historically associated thunderbolts and lightning with idealistic, cultural, and somatic Whiteness. As Holt shows, 1915 was a historically important year in the battle between Whiteness and Blackness for it was in that year that the somatically Black boxer Jack Johnson was defeated by the new "White Hope," Jess Willard, and that D.W. Griffith's racist movie *Birth of a Nation*, based on Thomas Dixon's racist novel *The Clansman*, opened to rave reviews by somatic Whites and protest by somatic Blacks: "[President] Woodrow Wilson's famous response upon screening the film in the White House was: 'It was like writing history with lightning.' In ways Wilson himself could not have imagined, his analogy speaks powerfully to what was indeed at stake, focusing attention on this medium's new power – one that, like lightning, can illuminate *and* do great harm. Lightning, an elemental, primitive force, is also associated with the modern – as in electricity, where it is tamed and harnessed to domestic ends." Thomas C. Holt, *The Problem of Race in the Twenty-First Century* (Cambridge: Harvard UP, 2000), 80–1.

12 Bulfinch, *The Golden Age of Myth and Legend*, 64.

13 Ibid.

14 Plato, *Phaedrus*, translated with introduction by W.C. Helmbold and W.G. Rabinowitz (Indianapolis: Bobbs-Merrill Co., 1956).

15 Bulfinch, *The Golden Age of Myth and Legend*, 337.

16 Nas, featuring Millennium Thug, "My Country," *Stillmatic*, lyrics by Nas (December 2001).

17 Mircea Eliade, *The Sacred and the Profane: The Nature of Religion*, trans. Willard R. Trask (New York: Harper and Row, 1961); ibid., *Myth and Reality* (London: George Allen and Unwin, 1964); Mircea Eliade, *Rites and Symbols of Initiation: The Mysteries of Birth and Rebirth*, trans. William R. Trask (New York: Harper Torchbooks, 1965); Northrop Frye, *The Eternal Act of Creation: Essays, 1979–1900* (Bloomington: Indiana UP, 1993).

18 David Carney, *Soul of Darkness: Introduction to African Metaphysics, Philosophy and Religion* (New York: Adastra, 1991).

19 Eliade, *The Sacred and the Profane*.

20 Saint Augustine, *Confessions*, The Fathers of the Church series, trans. Vernon. J. Bourke (Washington, D.C.: The Catholic University of America Press, 1953); ibid., *Concerning The City of God against the Pagans*, trans. Henry Bettenson with introduction by David Knowles (Middlesex, England: Penguin, 1972).

21 Alicia Keys, featuring Nas and Rakim, "Streets of New York (New York, New York)," *The Diary of Alicia Keys*, lyrics by Alicia Keys, featuring Nas and Rakim (December 2003).

22 In Jewish homiletics, the dominant interpretation is that the Tower of Babel symbolizes the efforts by humans to unite together in one place and with one language so as to seek a universal order. This is the counterpoint to the divine commandment that humans should disperse over the face of the earth and populate it with as many peoples and as many languages as possible.

23 Part of the irony here is that the hijackers, even as non-Christians, might very well see a parallel between the destruction of the towers and the venerable example of Jesus in the temple chasing out the money changers. I thank professor Nigel Thomas for pointing this out to me.

24 Taylor, *Hegel*.

25 Eliade, *The Sacred and the Profane*, 47–8.

26 Ibid.

27 William Julius Wilson, *The Declining Significance of Race: Blacks and Changing American Institutions* (Chicago: University of Chicago Press, 1978); Wahneema Lubiano, ed., *The House That Race Built: Black Americans, U.S. Terrain* (New York: Pantheon Books, 1997).

28 G.W.F. Hegel, *Phenomenology of Spirit*, trans. A.V. Miller (Oxford: Oxford UP, 1977), 9.

29 CNN.com/U.S., "September 11: Chronology of Terror," CNN.com, 1 January 2002, English, <http://www.cnn.com/2001/US/09/11/chronology.attack>; CNN, "In-Depth Special," *September 11: A Memorial*, CNN.com, 1 January 2001, English, <http://www.cnn.com/SPECIALS/2001/memorial>.

30 Virgil, *The Aeneid*, trans. John Jackson (Hertfordshire: Wordsworth Editions, 1995).

31 In the museum that carries his name, a mosaic in one room shows a somatically Black looking Virgil sitting between the muses of history and of tragedy. See <http://www.tourismtunisia.com/culture/bardo.html/> (5 August 2003). I would

like to thank my friends Orville Folkes and Alka for pointing this out to me, and providing picture and all in support of their discovery. Obviously, Virgil's complexion is another sign that for someone like Emperor Augustus, looking to write himself and his people into history officially, skin colour did not have any moral significance – at least not for a storyteller.

32 Jeffrey M. Perl, *The Tradition of Return: The Implicit History of Modern Literature* (Princeton: Princeton UP, 1984).

33 Virgil, *The Aeneid*, 68.

34 Ibid., 69.

35 Indeed, many pre-modern and modern writers that helped shape nationalist views in Western thought – Dante, Chaucer, Spenser, Milton, Tennyson, Shakespeare – owe much in their craft to Virgil and *The Aeneid*. See <http://www.crystalinks.com/virgil.html> (5 August 2003).

36 Virgil, *The Aeneid*, 19–20.

37 Ibid., 21.

38 Ibid., 12.

39 Gerald Heard, *The Ascent of Humanity: An Essay on The Evolution of Civilization from Group Consciousness through Individuality to Super-Consciousness* (London: Jonathan Cape, 1929), 69–70.

40 Virgil, *The Aeneid*, 250.

41 Arthur L. Little Jr, *Shakespeare Jungle Fever: National-Imperial Re-Vision of Race, Rape, and Sacrifice* (Stanford: Stanford UP, 2000).

42 William Shakespeare, *The Tempest*, ed. Stanley Wells, Oxford World's Classics (Oxford: Oxford UP, 1987); ibid., *The Tragedy of Othello The Moor of Venice* (New York: First Signet Classic Printing, 1998); ibid., *Anthony and Cleopatra*, The Pelican Shakespeare, ed. A.R. Braunmuller (New York: Penguin, 1999); ibid., *Titus Andronicus*, The Pelican Shakespeare, ed. Russ McDonald (New York: Penguin, 2000).

43 Christopher Marlowe, *Dido, Queen of Carthage* in *Christopher Marlowe. The Complete Plays* (London: J.M. Publishing Group, 1999).

44 Little Jr, *Shakespeare Jungle Fever*, 68.

45 G.W.F. Hegel, *Lectures on the Philosophy of History*, trans. J. Sibree (London: George Bell and Sons, 1878), 10.

46 Ibid., 11.

47 Paget Henry, *Caliban's Reason: Introducing Afro-Caribbean Philosophy* (New York: Routledge, 2000), 25.

48 Eliade, *The Sacred and the Profane*, 50.

49 Habermas, "Faith and Knowledge."

50 Thomas Jefferson, *Writings* (New York: Literary Classics of the US, 1984), 264.

51 K. Anthony Appiah and Amy Gutmann, *Colour Conscious: The Political Morality of Race* (Princeton: Princeton UP, 1996), 46.

52 Ruth Frankenberg looks at this matter with a different gaze when she, as Appiah puts it, "records the anxiety of many white people who do not see themselves as

white "ethnics" and worry, therefore, that they have no culture." Appiah, *Colour Conscious*, 89. This is because they reject the culture ascribed to them as White and they are more fulfilled in a culture that is "ethnically" not theirs. In this case, these women are culturally, and even idealistically and socially, Black, even if they are White somatically – proving once again that the somatic is only a very limited category of knowing Blackness. See Ruth Frankenberg, *White Women, Race Matters: The Social Construction of Whiteness* (Minneapolis: University of Minnesota Press, 1993).

53 As it turned out, despite the images presented in the media, the Canadian military fighting international terrorism was not homogeneously White somatically. When Canada mourned the death of four soldiers bombed by US warplanes in a friendly-fire attack in Afghanistan in 2002, one of the soldiers was somatically Black. Indeed, by most standards Alwyn Dwyer might have been considered Black culturally and socially: he was born in Jamaica and, as immigrants, his family had endured the social inferiority that led him to joining the military as a way of achieving social mobility. When he received a state funeral, he had been transformed into the full idealistic Whiteness of complete acceptance as a Canadian citizenship and as a hero honoured for dying to protect and preserve the idealistic Whiteness or good of Canada. Conceptually, Canada was much more of an infinity than what the media had portrayed.

54 Herodotus, "*Histories*," trans. George Rawlinson (Hertfordshire: Wordsworth Editions, 1996), II:11.

55 Ibid., II:50–1.

56 Ibid., II:104.

57 Bulfinch, *The Golden Age of Myth and Legend*, 47.

58 Ibid., 50–1.

59 Ibid., 52.

60 Ibid., 53.

61 Aristotle, *Politics*, trans. C.D.C. Reeve (Indianapolis: Hackett Publishing, 1998), II:11.1272B.26–33.

62 Frederick J.E. Woodbridge, *The Son Of Apollo: Themes of Plato* (Boston: Houghton Mifflin, 1929), 1–6.

63 Woodbridge, *The Son Of Apollo*.

64 Walter R. Agard, *What Democracy Meant to the Greeks* (Chapel Hill: University of North Carolina Press, 1942), 45–6.

65 Plato, *Timaeus*, trans. Donald J. Zeyl (Indianapolis: Hackett Publishing, 2000), 22B.

66 Ibid., 22E.

67 Ibid., 23C.

68 Ibid.

69 Ibid., 23D.

70 Plato, "Philebus," *The Collected Dialogues of Plato Including the Letters*, ed. Edith Hamilton and Huntington Cairns, Bollingen Series 71 (Princeton: Princeton UP, 1980), 18B.

71 Plato, *Phaedrus*, 253D.
72 Ibid., 254E.
73 Ibid., 253D.
74 Ibid., 238E.
75 Ibid., 254A.
76 Ibid., 246E.
77 Ibid., 247B.
78 Ibid., 254E.
79 Plato, "Philebus," 26B.
80 Plato, *Phaedrus*, 256E.
81 Ibid., 247E.

### CHAPTER ELEVEN

1 Aristotle, *Politics*, trans. C.D.C. Reeve (Indianapolis: Hackett Publishing Company, 1998) VII:15.1334A.11–20.
2 Ibid., I:1252A.1–5.
3 Ibid., I:2.1253A.4–5.
4 In *Philosophers on Race,* Julie Ward looks at the racial implications of the term "barbarian" in early Greek philosophy, especially as found in Aristotle. She makes a clear case that even if some may consider the use of the term "race" anachronistic if applied to antiquity Greece that there are clear categorical differences of what I call Whiteness and Blackness in Greek thought. "It is undeniable that ancient Greek social and political institutions are non-egalitarian, based on acceptance of 'natural' differences among humans, as is reflected in their thinking about slaves and women." This, I argue, equates to notions of idealized and social Whiteness and Blackness. "Yet the presence of inequality in their institutions and practices does not appear to be linked one to one to their concern about racial differences. One obvious counter-example to the proposed correlation would be Greek citizen women: these women could be the same race as citizen men, but would be considered in Athens as elsewhere to be the social, political, and intellectual inferiors to men." This is a discussion on status Blackness, based on inferior positioning in society. The women would have undergone a first determination that separates them from all other barbarians into White Greek citizens. They would not, however, undergo the second determination that would transform them into the White elites and superiors of their society. Ward also suggests there was what I call cultural Whiteness and Blackness as "nonetheless, it might be supposed that Greek male citizens also found non-Greek men their inferiors for racial reason." In addition, there was also what is generally acknowledged to be somatic Blackness and Whiteness, but this proves more problematic especially when coupled with a wish to impose a singular and unchanging meaning on somatic and phenotypic features. "First, the ambiguous meanings connected to color-terms give scant indication of a linkage between skin color or

other morphological traits, and moral or intellectual differences. Greek writers and philosophers use the term ... *leukos* ('light', 'pale') and ... *melas* ('dark') to describe the persons and things, but the meanings vary ... Plato employs *leukos* in the *Republic* in an ironic reference to those who, though praised by lovers, nonetheless are lacking in masculine qualities (*Republic*, 474e); thus, the terms 'pale' and 'pale-skinned' may signify weakness, perhaps 'effeminacy' of character. In similar fashion, Aristotle employs terms for being pale-skinned or dark-skinned in reference to women in his biological work, claiming light-skinned women are typically feminine, and dark-skinned women, more masculine by nature ... Finally, in Metaphysics, VII.4, Aristotle employs the term *leukos* in a discussion about essences and accidental compounds." Julie K Ward and Tommy L. Lott, eds, *Philosophers on Race: Critical Essays* (London: Blackwell, 2002), 15–16. What I am illustrating here is that in Greek thought there are supposed categories of knowing, including those based on the somatic. These categories were intended to explain human nature and to help ascertain moral qualities of good and evil for ethical relations, to discern who should be included and excluded in society, and what positions different categories of people should hold in society. Ward's research shows how equivocal the categories and meanings were. However, these categories and thoughts crystallized around the concept of the barbarian, the ultimate embodiment of Blackness, as those who were not Greek even in a first determination of cultural and idealistic Whiteness. Indeed, Ward suggests that Aristotle gives "two additional theories that provide suggestive bases for our investigation, first, a climate theory of national or racial differences, and second, a theory of natural slavery." These, I argue, are separate theories on cultural and idealized Whiteness and Blackness. Ward's problem is that she feels incapable of providing conclusive evidence of a direct link in Greek thought between Whiteness and Blackness as moral signifiers based on skin colour. "Nonetheless, one does find an overriding concern by the Greeks to differentiate themselves culturally, and perhaps ethnically, from various non-Greek nations, especially the Persians after the Persian wars." Ward, *Philosophers on Race*, 15. For the Greeks, Blackness was more than skin colour, which as a single category may or may not have any moral significance. Finally, a return to our original epigraph from Hegel. Here we see the significance of his equating Blackness with the darknesses that are conceptual barbarism and a composite – Blackness that is existentially and ontologically derived. Here we can trace a link back from this Enlightenment era to the ancient Greeks, particularly to Aristotle's discussion on essences and compositions.

5 Aristotle, *Politics* I:2.1253B.29–36.
6 Aristotle, *The Metaphysics*, trans. Hugh Lawson-Tancred (London: Penguin, 1998), 983.15.
7 Ibid., 981.20.
8 Ibid., 982.10–15.
9 Aristotle, *Politics* VII:10.1330A.25–8.
10 Ibid., I:1252A.6–16.

11 Ibid., I:1253B.3–14.

12 Ibid., I:3.1253B.19.

13 Plato, *The Republic*, trans. Desmond Lee (London: Penguin, 1987), II:2.369B.

14 Ibid., II:2.370A.

15 Ibid., II:2.374C. Emphasis added.

16 Ibid., IX:8.552A.

17 Aristotle, *Politics* I:10.1258A.10–18.

18 Plato, *Republic* IX:8.555B–C.

19 Ibid., VII:5488B–E.

20 Ibid., VII:6.484B.

21 Aristotle, *Politics* III:8.1279B.36–1280A.6.

22 Ibid., II:2.1261A.15–20.

23 Ibid., II:3.1261B.33–4.

24 Ibid., II:1263B.1–25.

25 Ibid., II:1263B.29–40.

26 Edith Hall, *Inventing the Barbarian: Greek Self-Definition through Tragedy* (Oxford: Clarendon Press, 1989); Perikles Georges, *Barbarian Asia and the Greek Experience: From the Archaic Period to the Age of Xenophon* (Baltimore: John Hopkins UP, 1994).

27 Homer, *The Odyssey of Homer*, trans. Richmond Lattimore (New York: Harper and Row, 1967).

28 Homer, *The Iliad of Homer*, trans. Ennis Rees (New York: Oxford UP, 1991).

29 Plato, "Laws," *The Collected Dialogues of Plato Including the Letters*, ed. Edith Hamilton and Huntington Cairns, Bollingen Series 71, (Princeton: Princeton UP, 1980), VIII:843A.

30 Ibid.

31 Ibid., XII:949D.

32 Ibid., VII:850A.

33 Philip Brook Manville, *The Origins of Citizenship in Ancient Athens* (Princeton: Princeton UP, 1990), 5–6.

34 Ibid., 7–8.

35 Ibid., 9–14.

36 Plato, *Laws* XII:950B.

37 Ibid., VIII:840D–841C.

38 Aristotle, *Politics* III.2.1275B.16–20.

39 Ibid., III:3.1275B.22–33.

40 Ibid., III:1276A.33–1276B.13.

41 Ibid., III.5.1278A.26–33.

42 Ibid., III.6.1278A.34–9.

43 Sophocles, *The Oedipus Trilogy: King Oedipus; Oedipus at Colonus; Antigone*, ed. Stephen Spender (New York: Random House, 1985).

44 Aristotle, *The Nicomachean Ethics* (Hertfordshire: Wordsworth Editions, 1996), I:10.7.

45 Ibid., I:12.2–5.
46 Ibid., I:12.7–8.

## CHAPTER TWELVE

1 Rev. 3:4–5. Thompson Chain-Reference Bible New International Version.
2 Jacques Derrida, *Writing and Difference*, trans. Alan Bass (Chicago: University of Chicago Press, 1978), 86.
3 Jean-Paul Sartre, *What Is Literature? and Other Essays* (Cambridge: Harvard UP, 1988), 292.
4 David Carney, *Soul of Darkness: Introduction to African Metaphysics, Philosophy and Religion* (New York: Adastra, 1991).
5 Irving M. Zeitlin, *Ancient Judaism: Biblical Criticism from Max Weber to the Present* (Cambridge: Polity Press, 1984), 20.
6 Ibid., 27.
7 Orlando Patterson, *Slavery and Social Death: A Comparative Study* (Cambridge: Harvard UP, 1982).
8 Alexandre Kojève, "Tyranny and Wisdom," in *On Tyranny*, revised and enlarged by Leo Strauss (Ithaca: Cornell UP, 1975), 181.
9 Ibid., 181–2.
10 Ibid., 183.
11 Ibid.
12 I want to thank one of my outside reviewers for making this point in the evaluation of this book in manuscript form.
13 C.L.R. James, *Notes on Dialectics: Hegel, Marx, Lenin* (London: Allison and Busby, 1980).
14 W.E.B. Du Bois, *The Souls of Black Folk* (New York: Modern Library Edition, 1996); James A. Snead, "Repetition as a Figure of Black Culture," in *the Jazz Cadence of American Culture*, ed. Robert G. O'Meally (New York: Columbia UP, 1998); Paul Gilroy, *The Black Atlantic: Modernity and Double Consciousness* (Cambridge: Harvard UP, 1993); Paul Gilroy, *Against Race: Imagining Political Culture beyond the Color Line* (Cambridge: Harvard UP, 2000).
15 Judith Butler, *Undoing Gender* (New York: Routledge, 2004).
16 Aimé Césaire, *A Tempest*, trans. Richard Miller (New York: UBU Repertory Theater, 1992).
17 Carney, *Soul of Darkness*.
18 Césaire, *A Tempest*, 48.
19 Henry Louis Gates Jr, *The Signifying Monkey: A Theory of African-American Literary Criticism* (New York: Oxford UP, 1988), 6.
20 K. Anthony Appiah and Amy Gutmann, *Colour Conscious: The Political Morality of Race* (Princeton: Princeton UP, 1996), 101.
21 Carney, *Soul of Darkness*, 15.
22 Ibid., 16.

23 Ibid., 36.

24 However, in reflecting on what Carney is saying, we may consider what Karl Rahner says about death and how a catholic view like his might draw us closer to associating similar thoughts from the Greek and African philosophies in Christianity.

If one thinks that death is the end of everything, because man's time does not really go on, because what once began must sometime end, because finally time spinning itself out into infinity, the empty endless pursuit of the new that annuls the old, is really impossible and would be worse than hell: then one is the victim of the conceptual framework of our empirical time just as much as if one considered that the soul 'went on.' In reality, it is *in* time, as its own mature fruit, that 'eternity' comes about. It does not come 'after' the time we experienced, in order to prolong time: it eliminates time by being released from the time that was for a while so that the definitive could come about in freedom. (Karl Rahner, "The Life of the Dead," in *Death and Hope*, ed. Harry J. Cargas and Ann White [New York: Corpus Books, 1970], 51.)

Indeed, Rahner goes further: "There is no place in Catholic Christianity for intercourse with the dead as individuals, such as spiritualism aims at – not because the dead do not exist, not because they are really separated from us, not because their fidelity and love, made perfect before God, do not watch over us, not as if their existence were not truly embedded by death above all in the silent, secret ground of our own existence. But we are yet creatures *in time*. And … if the reality of the living dead as individuals were to be transposed into our concrete world, they could only appear as *we* are, not as *they* are" (57). There seems to be much commonality of thought with the African explanation, as suggested by Carney, for why we do not sense the spirits around us and why the departed ultimately appear to recede from participation in our time, even to the point of avoiding our attempts to contact them in a finite and limited bodily sense.

25 Carney, *Soul of Darkness*, 36.

26 Grasped as thus distinguished, each moment is in the *distinguishedness* as a unity with the *other*. Becoming therefore contains being and nothing as two such unities, *each* of which is itself a unity of being and nothing; the one is being as immediate and in relation to nothing, and the other is nothing as immediate and in relation to being; the determinations are of unequal values in these unities. G.W.F. Hegel, *Hegel's Science of Logic*, trans. A.V. Miller, ed. H.D. Lewis (New York: Humanity Books, 1969), 105.

27 Carney, *Soul of Darkness*, 17.

28 Ibid., 20.

29 Ibid., 28.

30 Mircea Eliade, *The Sacred and the Profane: The Nature of Religion*, trans. Willard R. Trask (New York: Harper and Row, 1961).

31 Eliade, *The Sacred and the Profane*, 224–5.

32 Saint Augustine, *Confessions*, The Fathers of the Church series, trans. Vernon. J. Bourke (Washington, D.C.: The Catholic University of America Press, 1953), 1.5.5.

33 Warren Thomas Smith, *Augustine: His Life and Thought* (Atlanta: John Knox, 1980), 9.
34 Carol Harrison, *Augustine: Christian Truth and Fractured Humanity* (Oxford: Oxford UP, 2000).
35 Ibid., 5.
36 Alvin Plantinga, *The Ontological Argument: From Anselm to Contemporary Philosophers* (New York: Anchor Books, 1965); Kenneth Surin, *The Turning of Darkness and Light: Essays in Philosophical and Systematic Theology* (Cambridge: Cambridge UP, 1989).
37 It might be useful to remember the limits that Kant places on epistemology, which in turns informs our ethical relations. "The whole interest of reason, speculatively as well as practical, is centered in the three following questions:

    1 WHAT CAN I KNOW?

    2 WHAT OUGHT I TO DO?

    3 WHAT MAY I HOPE?"

    Immanuel Kant, *Critique of Pure Reason*, intro. A.D. Lindsay, trans. J.M.D. Meiklejohn (London: Everyman's Library, 1934), 457.
38 Jacques Derrida, *Writing and Difference*, trans. Alan Bass (Chicago: University of Chicago Press, 1978).
39 One of the contradictions of thought is who or what is really Black and White in the immediate post-creation moment. If the creator is White, at least in thought, an objective judge looking on at the process can rationally be expected to assume that, analogically, what the White creator produces will be White. But there is also the possibility that a conflicted being that is both good and evil might also produce a state that is evil. If the creator is White and finds itself in bondage to the new social order, is the creator still White or is the social order Black? Seen from the perspective of the social order, then, the creation is White and the creator, contradictorily, Black; from the perspective of the creator, since it is White, the social order of its own creation would have to be Black – so the creator has failed to produce the good of its imagination, and the process of creation which is to produce good and perfection could not yet be completed. But the social order might have a different belief: in its freedom it might think that creation is complete and that further tampering would destroy perfection. Hence the creator will be locked in a lordship-bondage struggle with its creation: each will be trying to change the other into its likeness, into its notion of its own Whiteness. Each will think that the other is trying to impose Blackness on it.
40 Arthur S. Peake, *A Commentary on the Bible* (London: T.C. & E.C. Jack, 1920), 141.
41 Frank M. Snowden Jr, *Before Color Prejudice: The Ancient View of Blacks* (Cambridge: Harvard UP, 1983), 44.
42 Ibid.
43 Ibid.
44 Ibid., 46.

45 Lev. 13:3–4. New Revised Standard Version
46 James Walvin, *The Black Presence: A Documentary History of the Negro in England, 1555–1860* (New York: Schocken Books, 1972), 36–7.
47 G.K. Hunter, *Othello and Colour Prejudice* (London: Oxford UP, 1967),148.
48 Ibid., 152.
49 Elliot H. Tokson, *The Popular Image of the Black Man in English Drama, 1550–1688* (Boston: G.K. Hall, 1982).
50 Ibid., 10.
51 Hunter, *Othello and Colour Prejudice*, 142.
52 Frantz Fanon, *Black Skin, White Masks* (New York: Grove Press, 1967), 189.

## CHAPTER THIRTEEN

1 Orlando Patterson, *Freedom*, vol. 1, *Freedom in The Making of Western Culture* (n.p.: Basic Books, 1991).
2 Ibid., *Slavery and Social Death: A Comparative Study* (Cambridge: Harvard UP, 1982).
3 Thomas Hobbes, *Leviathan* (Oxford: Oxford UP, 1996); John Locke, *Two Treatises of Government*, ed. Peter Laslett (Cambridge: Cambridge UP, 1998); Jean-Jacques Rousseau, *The Social Contract and Other Later Political Writings*, ed. and trans. Victor Gourevitch (Cambridge: Cambridge UP, 1997); Thomas Paine, *Rights of Man, Common Sense and Other Political Writings* (Oxford: Oxford UP, 1995).
4 In the Hebraic tradition, slavery per se is not presented as unnatural. As epitomized by the story of Hebraic bondage and escape from Egypt, the central point was that Egyptian slavery was ethically evil for the following reasons: (1) according to the traditions of the day, the Jews were not conquered in battle; they had not entered into a covenant whereby they had agreed to have their lives spared by further agreeing to live as "otherwise dead" or slaves; (2) the Jews were not treated properly according to even the Egyptian ethical codes as impossible tasks were demanded of them and they were treated cruelly; (3) the Jews were left without hope that they would have self-determinacy and that life would get better for them in Egypt.
5 Derek Heater, *What Is Citizenship?* (Cambridge: Polity Press, 1999).
6 Francis Fukuyama, *The End of History and the Last Man* (New York: Avon Books, 1998). It is worth noting that according to this categorization of the differences in the world, there was supposedly a Third World as well. This was made up of the societies not yet even close to freedom. The inhabitants were still in bondage to some human or Natural tyrant lording over them. One example of this lordship was their bondsman colonial relationship with a metropolitan centre. Another more pervasive explanation of this lower status was that the inhabitants of this order had not yet been liberated through the mastery of science, technology, knowledge, and good government. They had not yet reached the point of

having some control over their destinies, where their communities were effectively self-sufficient in terms of meeting their daily requirements for living. As such, they were not, therefore, their own lords in control of their own fates. Another way of looking at the lordship and bondage relations is what is called the North-South poles of the world – where the supposedly advanced, developed, and prosperous countries (those of the First and Second World) were largely in the northern hemisphere, and the undeveloped, supposedly backward, and poor countries were in the southern hemisphere. We still see much of this thinking in discourses on international development.

7 Mircea Eliade, *Rites and Symbols of Initiation: The Mysteries of Birth and Rebirth*, trans. Willard R. Trask (New York: Harper Torchbooks, 1965).

8 Ibid., 128–9.

9 Ibid., 128.

10 Ibid., 131–2.

11 Friedrich Nietzsche, *The Birth of Tragedy and The Case of Wagner*, trans. Walter Kaufmann (New York: Vintage Books, 1967), 65.

12 Saint Augustine, *Concerning the City of God against the Pagans*, trans. Henry Bettenson, (Middlesex, England: Penguin, 1972), 511.

13 Saint Augustine, *Confessions*, The Fathers of the Church series, trans. Vernon. J. Bourke (Washington, D.C.: The Catholic University of America Press, 1953); ibid., *Concerning The City of God against the Pagans*.

14 Robert Gibbs, *Correlations in Rosenzweig and Levinas* (Princeton: Princeton UP, 1992).

15 Ibid., 45.

16 David Carney, *Soul of Darkness: Introduction to African Metaphysics, Philosophy and Religion* (New York: Adastra, 1991).

17 Hobbes, *Leviathan*.

18 Locke, *Two Treatises of Government*.

19 Rousseau, *The Social Contract and Other Later Political Writings*.

20 Howard Adelman, "Of Human Bondage: Labour, Bondage, and Freedom in the Phenomenology," in *Hegel's Social and Political Thought: The Philosophy of Objective Spirit*, ed. Donald Phillip Verene (New Jersey: Humanities Press, 1980).

21 Alexandre Kojève, *Introduction to the Reading of Hegel: Lectures on the Phenomenology of Spirit*, ed. Allan Bloom (Ithaca: Cornell UP, 1969).

22 Gibbs, *Correlations in Rosenzweig and Levinas*, 36.

23 James A. Snead, "Repetition as a Figure of Black Culture," in *The Jazz Cadence of American Culture*, ed. Robert O'Meally (New York: Columbia UP, 1998).

24 Gibbs, *Correlations in Rosenzweig and Levinas*, 37.

25 Plato, *Timaeus*, trans. Donald J. Zeyl (Indianapolis: Hackett Publishing, 2000); Saint Augustine, *Confessions*; ibid., *Concerning the City of God against the Pagans*; René Descartes, *Discourse on Method and Meditations* (Indianapolis:

Bobbs-Merrill Company, 1960); Immanuel Kant, *Foundations of the Metaphysics of Morals*, ed. Lewis White Beck (Indianapolis: Bobbs-Merrill Company, 1959).

26 David White, *Myth and Metaphysics in Plato's Phaedo* (Selinsgrove, Pa.: Susquehana UP, 1989), 38.

27 Ibid.

28 Ibid.

29 Karl Jaspers, *Way to Wisdom: An Introduction to Philosophy* (New Haven: Yale UP, 1954); Karl Jaspers, *Tragedy Is Not Enough* (n.p.: Archon Books, 1969).

30 White, *Myth and Metaphysics in Plato's Phaedo*, 44.

31 Ibid., 53.

32 Plato, *Symposium and the Death of Socrates* (Hertfordshire: Wordsworth Editions, 1997); Aristotle, *The Nicomachean Ethics* (Hertfordshire: Wordsworth Editions, 1996); Jacques Derrida, "Specters of Marx: The State of the Debt, the Work of Mourning, and the New International," trans. Peggy Kamuf (New York: Routledge, 1994); Jaspers, *Way To Wisdom*.

33 Robert Borden, *Robert Laird Borden: His Memoirs* (Toronto: Macmillan, 1938), xii.

34 Homer, *The Iliad of Homer*, trans. Ennis Rees (New York: Oxford UP, 1991), 235.

35 Hannah Arendt, *The Portable Hannah Arendt*, ed. Peter Baehr (New York: Penguin, 2000).

36 For a fuller debate on current Canadian attitudes to immigration see Diane Francis, *Immigration: The Economic Case* (Toronto: Key Porter Books, 2002); Informetrica Limited, "Canada's Recent Immigrants: A Comparative Portrait Based on the 1996 Census," in *Recent Immigrants in Metropolitan Areas* (Ottawa: Citizenship and Immigration Canada, January 2001); Valerie Knowles, *Strangers at Our Gates: Canadian Immigration and Immigration Policy, 1540–1997* (Toronto: Dundurn Press, 1997); Jeffrey G. Reitz, *Warmth of the Welcome: The Social Causes of Economic Success for Immigrants in Different Nations and Cities* (Boulder, Co.: Westview Press, 1998); ibid., "Immigrant Skill Utilization in the Canadian Labour Market: Implications of Human Capital Research," (Toronto: Center for Industrial Relations and Department of Sociology, University of Toronto, October 2001); Anthony Richmond, H. and Warren E. Kalbach, *Factors in the Adjustment of Immigrants and Their Descendants* (Ottawa: Minister of Supply and Services, Canada, 1980); Daniel Stoffman, *Who Gets In? What's Wrong with Canada's Immigration Program – and How to Fix It* (Toronto: Macfarlane Walter and Ross, 2002); Martin Collacott, *Canada's Immigration Policy: The Need for Major Reform*, Public Policy Sources No. 64, A Fraser Institute Occasional Paper (Vancouver: The Fraser Institute, 2002).

37 Orlando Patterson, *Freedom in The Making of Western Culture*.

38 Ibid., xvi.

39 Patterson, *Slavery and Social Death*, xiii.

40 Frantz Fanon, *Black Skin, White Masks* (New York: Grove Press, 1967), 224–5.

## CHAPTER FOURTEEN

1 Trudeau spent a brief period in 1979 to 1980 out of office, when he was leader of the opposition and Joe Clark was the prime minister.

2 Here we are reminded of the argument by Holt that racism, which I argue is a subset of Blackness, is essentially a child of modernity as part of what he called the pre-Ford regime in the *longue-durée* of history. One of the major ties between racism and Blackness is African chattel slavery. Another is the development of the modern state as a site of purity – of blood, race, religion, and so forth. "Race is linked to modernity first in the fact that racializing institutions – like the slave plantation – are thoroughly modern in form and function; in the fact that racial thought shares with other modern forms of knowledge a 'disenchantment' of the world; and finally, in the fact that modernity produces social and psychic conditions for which racial knowledge appears to offer a solution." Thomas C. Holt, *The Problem of Race in the Twenty-First Century* (Cambridge: Harvard UP, 2000), 29.

The pre-Fordist era was intended to keep groups of people separated and fixed physically in place, geographically, nationally, and socially. Next, was what Holt called the Fordist regime that spans the period from the early twentieth century to the 1970s. This was a time when emphasis was placed on greater consumption by the working class and the need for higher production – with the power of the state used primarily to unlock specific racialized groups in their places as part of the effort to create a greater mass-production, mass-consumption society. One of the main features of this period was mass migration and the hiring of somatically Black people in industries and in urban centres. This migration meant that for the first time in history the world's Black population – from Cape Town to Detroit, from Sao Paulo to Dakar – would be predominantly urban rather than predominantly rural (71). This led to a breaking down of society along the pre-Fordist lines of purity that were established at the beginning of modernity. The third period, in which he places modernity, is the post-Fordist, that "began in the 1970s and stretches into an indeterminate future" (23). This is a period marked by "the creation of global relations of labor and consumption [that] is to some extent constitutive of the advent of modernity ... In some ways, the changes set in motion in the late twentieth century can be thought of as the further unfolding of that trend; the old is not entirely effaced, the new never entirely new" (98). Multiculturalism would appear on the scene historically when the Fordist period was giving away internationally to a post-Fordian time that Holt argues was a return to pre-modernist conceptions of race, identity, and nationalism. Using this analysis, we can see how multiculturalism is a return to idealized Blackness of pre-modernity – with one major difference: the greater knowledge that had been gained from passing through the pre-modern and modernist periods, including in the latter the pre-Fordist, Fordist, and post-Fordist periods. Significantly, Holt notes that there was a radical change in the post-Fordist era in Blackness – in how race positions people based on somatic, social, cultural, and idealized characteristics. Indeed, in the post-Fordian period, status Whiteness and Blackness are the pre-eminent social categories. "Unlike in the early twentieth century, however, race no longer follows a colour line. The racialized other may well be white and hail from the Caucasus. Nevertheless, as ostensibly indigenous citizens of the G-7 nations watch their birthrate decline, the need for immigrant labor grows and, with it, a collective anxiety about national *and racial* integrity" (100).

3 Pierre Elliott Trudeau, *The Essential Trudeau*, ed. Ron Graham (Toronto: McClelland and Stewart, 1998), 18–19.

4 Ibid., 182. Emphasis added. Similarly, Trudeau noted: "Canadians continue to cherish the value system which has made them among the most fortunate of all the world's peoples. A system which embraces human relationships – tolerance, friendship, love, laughter, privacy; a system which pays heed to the beauty of our country and seeks to preserve the balance of nature; a system which accepts the inevitability of change but which at least consciously encourages only those changes which respect, rather than exploit, the human spirit; a system, in short, which regards individuals as the ultimate beneficiaries" (179).

5 Trudeau, *The Essential Trudeau*.

6 Thomas Axworthy and Pierre Elliott Trudeau, eds, *Towards a Just Society: The Trudeau Years* (Toronto: Viking, 1990), x–xi.

7 Trudeau, *The Essential Trudeau*, 1.

8 Ibid., 52.

9 Ibid., 3.

10 Ibid., 5.

11 Ibid., 53.

12 Ibid., 147–57.

13 Ibid., 5–6.

14 Ibid., 176.

15 Ibid., 100.

16 Ibid., 73–4.

17 Ibid., 45.

18 Ibid., 65.

19 Trudeau saw Canada firmly entrenched within "Western-type democracies with free markets," striving to preserve the egalitarianism of collectivism. Happily, he suggests, this dialectic of freedom would take Canada into paradise. "So there is hope that we will continue to live in a pluralistic world for a while yet. And we will continue to struggle with problems raised by Plato, Aristotle, by Rousseau and Locke. How can individuals remain free, yet be restrained by the state? How can the exercise of liberty lead to a society of equals?" Trudeau, *The Essential Trudeau*, 42.

20 Robin W. Winks, *Canadian-West Indian Union: A Forty-Year Minuet* (Toronto: Oxford UP, 1968); ibid., *The Blacks in Canada: A History* (Montreal and Kingston: McGill-Queen's UP, 1971); James W. St. G. Walker, *The Black*

*Loyalists: The Search for a Promised Land in Nova Scotia and Sierra Leone 1783–1870* (Toronto: University of Toronto Press, 1992).

21 Trudeau, *The Essential Trudeau,* 21.

22 Will Kymlicka, *Finding Our Way: Rethinking Ethnocultural Relations in Canada* (Toronto: Oxford UP, 1998).

23 Axworthy, *Towards a Just Society,* 24.

24 Ibid., 29.

25 Trudeau, *The Essential Trudeau,* 146.

26 Neil Bissoondath, *Selling Illusion: The Cult of Multiculturalism in Canada* (Toronto: Penguin, 1994); Alvin J. Schmidt, *The Menace of Multiculturalism: Trojan Horse of America* (Westport, Conn.: Praeger Publishers, 1997); David A. Hollinger, *Postethnic America: Beyond Multiculturalism* (New York: HarperCollins, 1995).

27 Trudeau, *The Essential Trudeau,* 113.

28 William Arthur Deacon, *My Vision of Canada* (Toronto: Ontario Publishing Company, 1933); Vincent Massey, *The Making of a Nation* (Boston: Houghton Mifflin, 1928); W. L. Morton, *The Canadian Identity* (Toronto: University of Toronto Press, 1961); John W. Dafoe, *Canada: An American Nation* (New York: Columbia UP, 1935); J.L. Granatstein, *Nation: Canada Since Confederation* (Toronto: McGraw-Hill Ryerson, 1990); George Grant, *Lament for a Nation: The Defeat of Canadian Nationalism* (Toronto: Macmillan, 1978); Maclean's Hunter Publishing Limited, *Canada in the Fifties: From the Archives of Maclean's* (Toronto: Viking, 1999); Donald F. Warner, *The Idea of Continental Union: Agitation for the Annexation of Canada to the United States 1849–1893* (n.p.: University of Kentucky Press, 1960).

29 Trudeau, *The Essential Trudeau,* 177.

30 Ibid., 181–2.

31 Cecil Foster, *A Place Called Heaven: The Meaning of Being Black in Canada* (Toronto: HarperCollins, 1996) and *Where Race Does Not Matter: The New Spirit of Modernity* (Toronto: Penguin, 2005). Readers might also see how I presented this deficit in fiction, particularly in the two novels *Sleep On, Beloved* (Toronto: Random House, 1995) and *Slammin' Tar: A Novel* (Toronto: Random House, 1998).

32 Trudeau, *The Essential Trudeau,* 143.

33 Ibid., 86.

34 Foster, *Where Race Does Not Matter.*

35 Ibid., 124. Trudeau is borrowing from Lord Acton's hatred and distrust of all forms of nationalism expressed in Lord Acton, *Essays on Freedom and Power* (Glencoe, Ill.: Free Press, 1948).

36 Trudeau, *The Essential Trudeau,* 16. Emphasis added.

37 Andre Siegfried, *The Race Question in Canada* (Toronto: McClellan and Stewart, 1968); Collette Guillaumin, *Racism, Sexism, Power and Ideology* (London: Routledge, 1995); Michel Wieviorka, *The Arena of Racism,* trans. Chris Turner (London: Sage, 1995); Peter S. Li, *Race and Ethnic Relations in Canada* (Toronto:

Oxford UP, 1990); Angus McLaren, *Our Own Master Race: Eugenics in Canada,
1885–1945* (Toronto: McClelland and Stewart, 1990); Ivan Hannaford, *Race:
The History of an Idea in the West* (Washington: The Woodrow Wilson Center
Press, 1996); Constance Backhouse, *Colour-Coded: A Legal History of Racism in
Canada, 1900–1950* (Toronto: University of Toronto Press, 1999).

38 It is worth pointing out the sequence of events making Canada officially multicultural and then how Canadians went about creating this ideal. Contrary to claims
made by such theorists as Michael Ignatieff, and a position now argued with
much vehemence in mainstream politics and the media, multiculturalism was not
intended as a way to prove the effectiveness of the Canadian Charter of Rights
and Freedoms. Put another way, Canada did not first determine it would be a liberal democracy and that multiculturalism would be the best expression of this liberalism. For a good example of this argument, see Michael Ignatieff, *The Rights
Revolution* (Toronto: Anansi, 2000), in which he argues that multiculturalism
was, indeed, a result of this revolutionary change towards liberal rights in the
West. This is a case where the cause and the effect are placed on their heads and
where the dialectics of history and the consciousness that is Canada are
misrecognized. Canada decided first to adopt multiculturalism as official policy in
1971. This was an immediate jettisoning by Canada of the twin ideals that it was
a White man's country and that it was a bicultural state. Canada chose a bilin-
gual-multiculturalism ideal to replace them. It was not until 1977 that Canada
received its *Human Rights Act* and it was not until 1982 that Canada repatriated
its Constitution from the United Kingdom and entrenched in it an amending formula to allow future changes to the Constitution. Canadians also entrenched in
the name of good governance – and not as a means of identifying who they are
ontologically – a Charter of Rights and Freedoms in the Constitution, which was
effectively the agreed-upon narrative that tells how Canada is to become a multicultural space and how it was to start acting as if it was already fully multicultural. This Charter spells out the rights enjoyed by all citizens living in a country
already determined, ontologically and epistemologically, to be a multicultural
Canada, a country that is a liberal democracy ethically and existentially. As is
usually the case, the epistemological trumps all other ways of knowing, and this is
the case in the practical sense of Canada. In Canada, the rights revolution had to
be a path chosen to help Canadians realize the ideal they had set for themselves –
that of a just society. This was not the case where the rights revolution determined
that Canada should become multicultural as a just society. Indeed, the presence of
such things as a notwithstanding clause that overrides Charter rights and Canada's continued commitment to a common good over, as Trudeau calls it, neo-lib-
eral greed – higher taxation, government paid healthcare, communal pension
plans – might very well provide an argument that the full extent of this rights revolution is only now changing Canada from the communitarian society it was until
very recently. But throughout these changes, Canada, according to its new ontology, was already officially multicultural.

39 Trudeau, *The Essential Trudeau*, 169.
40 Frantz Fanon, *Black Skin, White Masks* (New York: Grove Press, 1967).
41 Ibid., 158–67.
42 See Foster, *Where Race Does Not Matter*, for a fuller discussion on Mulroney's role in the fight for the international recognition of Blackness, particularly the equality of somatic Blacks, as typified in his leading the international struggle to destroy the apartheid regime and ideology in South Africa – an ideology and system that Canada had spent much of the first half of the last century trying to make a success. In both that work and *In a Place Called Heaven*, I also discussed specific steps by Mulroney to further integrate somatic Blacks into the mainstream of Canadian society.

## CHAPTER FIFTEEN

1 Leo Driedger and Shiva S. Hall, eds, *Race and Racism: Canada's Challenge* (Montreal and Kingston: McGill-Queen's UP, 2000); Will Kymlicka, *Multicultural Citizenship: Liberal Theory of Minority Rights* (Oxford: Clarendon Press, 1995); Neil Bissoondath, *Selling Illusion: The Cult of Multiculturalism in Canada* (Toronto: Penguin, 1994); Strategic Policy, Planning and Research, "The Economic Performance of Immigrants: Education Perspective," IMDB *Profile* Series (Ottawa: Citizenship and Immigration Canada, 2000).
2 Charles W. Mills, *The Racial Contract* (Ithaca: Cornell UP, 1997).
3 David Theo Goldberg, *Racist Culture: Philosophy and the Politics of Meaning* (Oxford: Blackwell, 1993), 45.
4 Althea Prince, *Being Black: Essays* (Toronto: Insomniac Press, 2000); Martin Loney, *The Pursuit of Division: Race, Gender, and Preferential Hiring in Canada* (Montreal and Kingston: McGill-Queen's UP, 1998); Martin Collacott, *Canada's Immigration Policy: The Need for Major Reform*, Public Policy Sources No. 64, A Fraser Institute Occasional Paper (Vancouver: The Fraser Institute, 2002); Driedger and Hall, *Race and Racism*; Kenneth McRoberts, *Misconceiving Canada: The Struggle for National Unity* (Toronto: Oxford UP, 1997); J.L. Granatstein, *Who Killed Canadian History?* (Toronto: HarperCollins, 1998).
5 Carl E. James, "Getting There and Staying There: Blacks' Employment Experience," in *Transitions: Schooling and Employment in Canada*, ed. Paul Anisef and Paul Axelrod (Toronto: Thompson Educational Press, 1993); Stanley A. Barrett, *Is God a Racist? The Right Wing in Canada* (Toronto: University of Toronto Press, 1989); Frances Henry and Carol Tator, *Racist Discourse in Canada's English Print Media* (Toronto: The Canadian Race relations Foundation, March 2000); James L. Torczyner, *Diversity, Mobility and Change: The Dynamics of Black Communities in Canada.* (Montreal: McGill Consortium for Ethnicity and Strategic Social Planning, 1997).
6 Derek Hum and Wayne Simpson, "Wage Opportunities for Visible Minorities in Canada," *The Income and Labour Dynamics Working Paper Series*, catalogue

No. 98-17, (November 1998); Torczyner, *Diversity, Mobility and Change*; Cecil Foster, *A Place Called Heaven: The Meaning of Being Black in Canada* (Toronto: HarperCollins Publishers, 1996).

7 Derek Hum and Wayne Simpson, "Wage Opportunities for Visible Minorities in Canada," *The Income and Labour Dynamics Working Paper Series*, catalogue No. 98-17, November 1998; Alan B. Simmons and Dwaine E. Plaza, "Breaking through the Glass Ceiling: The Pursuit of University Training among African-Caribbean Migrants and Their Children in Toronto," *Canadian Ethnic Studies* 30, no. 3 (1998): Frances Henry, *The Caribbean Diaspora in Toronto: Learning to Live with Racism* (Toronto: University of Toronto Press, 1994).

8 Ironically, in much of the discussion, several liberal theorists have interrogated the notion of adopting a colour blind approach to social justice. Amy Gutmann, for example, asks whether it is possible within the existing culture to arrive at an idealistic point of colour blindness. Indeed, she argues, as do Canadian theorists like Kymlicka, Carens, and Jacobs, for fairness based on the equality of abstract individuals who are all citizens. "But the color blind response to injustice in our society is doubly mistaken. Color blindness is not a fundamental principle of justice. Nor is it the strongest interpretation of such a principle for our society. Fairness is a fundamental principle of justice and ... it is a principle that does not always call for color blindness, at least not with regard to employment, university admissions, or electoral redistricting in our nonideal society. To respond to racial injustice with a color conscious principle or policy is therefore not to commit any wrong at all, provided the principle or policy is consistent with fair." K. Anthony Appiah and Amy Gutmann, *Colour Conscious: The Political Morality of Race* (Princeton: Princeton UP, 1996), 109. Indeed, I want to extend Gutmann's thoughts on fairness further by arguing that the fairness she is advocating is idealized Whiteness. So, justice should not be colour blind: it should be a kind of idealized Whiteness, the type of which Fanon spoke, for example. This is the fairness that is assumed when we plunge the goddess of justice into visual Blackness by blindfolding her. Yet, in so doing, we still give some people that appear before her a decided edge in communicating with her and influencing her. Perhaps, in a modern world of recognized gender differences and varying forms of ableism, we need to plunge the goddess further into darkness by, at a minimum, closing off her ears and mouth as well. This might be done to correct for the dominant dispositions in our culture, so that, in our ideal fairness, even the justice dispensed by the spoken word or evidence heard verbally would not disadvantage those who might not be equally able. The problem is that we tend to fall back in our discussion on justice to a racialized category of Blackness that reduces everything to a finite somatic category. This limits the discussion: indeed, even disabling those constructed as Black purely by somatic features. This is a position that, in a way, is no different from how in the past society reduced and disabled many citizens because they did not conform to some finite notion of what is normal and good. Here, I am thinking of the infinite "deaf" and "dumb," who were historically denied their infinite

humanity and idealized Whiteness. The main point I am making here is that idealistically justice in a multicultural world has to be idealistically White, which means it cannot be colour blind – it has to be the colour of an idealistic Whiteness which results in, among other things, the double negation of somatic and status Blackness that are the main planks of racism and a lack of social justice. Idealized White justice would be the aim for all those people that society has identified in such legislation as the *Bill of Rights* and *Charter of Rights and Freedoms* as idealistically White, as fully citizens, despite a range of finite identities that in the past were equated with a combination of somatic, status, and cultural Blackness. In this regard, my argument is that politicians like Trudeau, in reaching for a just society based on abstract constitutional rights that were the minimum on which citizenship is constructed, were not hoping for colour blindness in Canadian ethical relations. Instead, they were hoping that every Canadian would be recognized as idealistically White, and infinitely human and just.

9 Jon Stratton and Ien Ang, "Multicultural Imagined Communities: Cultural Difference and National Identity in the USA and Australia," in *Multicultural States: Rethinking Difference and Identity*, David Bennet (London: Routledge, 1998). The policy of official multiculturalism was announced in 1971.

10 *Citizenship Act*, R.S.C. 1985, chapter C-29.

11 Nathan Glazer, *We Are All Multiculturalist Now* (Cambridge: Harvard UP, 1997); Bissoondath, *Selling Illusion*; Michael Ignatieff, *Blood & Belonging: Journey Into The New Nationalism* (Toronto: Penguin, 1993); Alvin J. Schmidt, *The Menace of Multiculturalism: Trojan Horse of America* (Westport, Conn.: Praeger Publishers, 1997); Pico Iyer, *The Global Soul: Jet Lag, Shopping Malls, and the Search for Home* (New York: Vintage Books, 2000).

12 Jeffrey G. Reitz, *Warmth of the Welcome: The Social Causes of Economic Success for Immigrants in Different Nations and Cities* (Boulder, Co.: Westview Press, 1998), 4.

13 Ibid., 38.

14 Ibid., 4.

15 Thomas Axworthy and Pierre Elliott Trudeau, eds, *Towards a Just Society: The Trudeau Years* (Toronto: Viking, 1990); Pierre Elliott Trudeau, *The Essential Trudeau*, ed. Ron Graham (Toronto: McClelland and Stewart, 1998).

16 Will Kymlicka, *Finding Our Way: Rethinking Ethnocultural Relations in Canada* (Toronto: Oxford UP, 1998), 1.

17 Will Kymlicka and Magdalena Opalski, *Can Liberal Pluralismus Be Exported?: Western Political Theory and Ethnic Relations in Eastern Europe* (Oxford: Oxford UP, 2001).

18 Kymlicka, *Finding Our Way*, 21.

19 Ibid., 27.

20 Ibid., 23.

21 Charles Taylor, "The Politics of Recognition," in *Multiculturalism: Examining the Politics of Recognition*, ed. Amy Gutmann (Princeton: Princeton UP, 1994)

22 Rinaldo Walcott, *Black Like Who? Writing Black Canada* (Toronto: Insomniac Press, 1997); Himani Bannerji, *The Dark Side of the Nation: Essays on Multiculturalism, Nationalism and* Gender (Toronto: Canadian Scholars' Press, 2000); Bissoondath, *Selling Illusion*.

23 Augie Fleras and Jean Leonard Elliott present a detailed discussion on what is involved in conceptualizing multiculturalism: "There is almost no limit to the definitions. Multiculturalism can be everything, or nothing; it can empower and enable, or it can disable and disempower; it can describe a state of society, or it can describe what society must not be allowed to become; it can enlighten people, or it can conceal the truth from them; it can reassure them, or it can instill fear in them. Further complicating the cultural landscape are the different perceptions people hold regarding what multiculturalism is *supposed* to do, what it is *really* doing, what it can do, what people *think* it is doing, and what people think it *should* do. Finally, multiculturalism can focus on social equality (for individuals), cultural identity (for groups), or broader national interests. And all of the above overlap and intersect." Augie Fleras and Jean Leonard Elliott, *Engaging Diversity: Multiculturalism in Canada*, 2d ed. (Toronto: Nelson Thomson Learning, 2002), 14. Unfortunately, Fleras and Elliott decry the "ambiguity," "uncertainty," and "ambivalence of feeling" in multiculturalism and treat the concept as an obstacle to a clearer understanding of what is necessary for meaningful relations between the groups and individuals living in an officially multicultural country like Canada. In this regard, the authors fall back on a modernist need for a single concrete definition of multiculturalism, a move that would rob the concept of its full potential and fix its meaning. To achieve this would mean reducing multiculturalism from an infinity to a mere subject of characteristics and meanings. Much would be lost in the name of precision and in making the concept unchangeable in meaning. In the end, Fleras and Elliot note that a single meaning would not suffice. "Most people use the term multiculturalism in all circumstances, if only because it is the easiest one to reach for, after decades of familiarity" (17). I argue that they use the term multiculturalism because the concept captures both their hopes and fears alike, and that it gives them the freedom they need to change and reshape identities, expectations, cultures, and other lived experiences through a process of becoming and by choosing different identities for different contexts and circumstances.

24 C.L.R. James, *Notes on Dialectics: Hegel, Marx, Lenin* (London: Allison and Busby, 1980), 160.

25 As James explains: "Analytic cognition has identity for the kind of determination it recognizes as its own. It is concerned only with what simply *is*. Synthetic Cognition tries to form a Notion of the object. That is, it tries to grasp the numerous different thought determinations into which thought can divide the object, and tries to see them in their unity. For this reason it can be seen that Synthetic Cognition has as its goal, its objective. That is necessity, but necessity in general. That is to say, it is aware of the fact that by the thought determination you can

see that the object is moving inevitably in a certain direction, must move that way" (158).

26 <http://www.statcan.ca/english/concepts/definitions/ethnicity.htm> 16 June 2002

27 Ibid.

28 <http://www.statcan.ca/english/concepts/definitions/ethnicity01.htm> 16 June 2002

29 Accepting this reduction to the somatic, as several self-identifying Blacks have done, is to imprison Blacks and Blackness within a discourse on multiculturalism to racism and the struggle for inclusion. This has been the case with much of the discussion on race. See, for example, David Theo Goldberg, *Racist Culture: Philosophy and the Politics of* Meaning (Oxford: Blackwell, 1993); Julie K Ward and Tommy L. Lott, eds, *Philosophers on Race: Critical* Essays (London: Blackwell, 2002); Charles W. Mills, *The Racial* Contract (Ithaca: Cornell UP, 1997); K. Anthony Appiah and Amy Gutmann, *Colour Conscious: The Political Morality of Race* (Princeton: Princeton UP, 1996); Oliver C. Cox, *Race: A Study in Social Dynamics*, preface by Cornell West and introduction by Adolphi Reed Jr (New York: Monthly Review Press, 2000); Carl M. Degler, *Neither Black Nor White: Slavery and Race Relations in Brazil and the United* States (New York: Macmillan, 1971); Henry Louis Gates Jr, *"Race,"* in *Writing and Difference* (Chicago: University of Chicago Press, 1986); Paul Gilroy, *Against Race: Imagining Political Culture Beyond the Color Line* (Cambridge: Harvard UP, 2000); Stuart Hall, "Subjects in History: Making Diasporic Identities," in *The House That Race Built: Black Americans, U.S. Terrain*, ed. Wahneema Lubiano (New York: Pantheon Books, 1997); Ivan Hannaford, *Race: The History of an Idea in the* West (Washington: The Woodrow Wilson Center Press, 1996); Arthur L Little Jr, *Shakespeare Jungle Fever: National-Imperial Re-Vision of Race, Rape, and Sacrifice* (Stanford: Stanford UP, 2000); John Rex and David Mason, *Theories of Race and Ethnic Relations* (Cambridge: Cambridge UP, 1986); Gerhard Schutte, *What Racist Believe: Race Relations in South Africa and the United* States (Thousand Oaks: Sage, 1995); Cornel West, *Keeping Faith: Philosophy and Race in* America (New York: Routledge, 1993).

Race, indeed, is a very important factor in modern life. However, I want to offer an argument that takes race as a given, and one that is morally wrong, but an argument that instead of explaining racism and its effects tries to subvert the intentions and assumptions of racialism. For me, such subversion – cultural and idealistic Blackness if you will – is the hope that is offered by multiculturalism, for it attempts to liberate Blackness from merely a racial discourse, from merely the somatic, and places it at the heart of positive nation-state formation. Multiculturalism looks at Blackness in its totality, so that somatic racism is only a contingent part of the infinite bundle that is Black and Blackness. That racism still remains a moral and ethical problem in this utopian world is what I call the challenge for genuine multiculturalism, of how we can discursively get to the point where idealistically somatic Blackness does not translate automatically into a status Blackness that relegates individuals to being second or third class citizens. In this book, I have used the concept of the return or the Hegelian cycle in history, philosophy, and sociology. See Jeffrey M. Perl, *The Tradition of Return: The Implicit History of Modern Literature* (Princeton: Princeton UP, 1984); M.J. Inwood, *Hegel* (London: Routledge, 1998); Northrop Frye, *The Eternal Act of Creation: Essays, 1979–1900* (Bloomington: Indiana UP, 1993).

In this regard, I am indeed arguing for a discursive return to a pre-modern time when in the mythologies and philosophies of the ancients – the Greeks, Hebrews, Africans, and early Christians that provide the ideological underpinning for our modern societies – Blackness of skin had no special status or moral value. That does not mean that Black skin did not have meaning. When it did, however, the meaning was contingent and often covered a very wide range, while at the same time rarely meaning moral or ethical superiority or inferiority. In this sense, multiculturalism in Canada, as a post-modern moment, aims to return modernism to its primordial Blackness. This was the original time, when all was freedom and there was plenitude of choices and no single privileged narrative of what is good and evil. This was before, in the Hegelian sense, evil entered the world through the intention and attempts to separate humanity determinately into Whites and Blacks, good and evil, and, ultimately, racialized superiors and inferiors. This is the legacy of modernism, an era that intentionally shares the same horrors as African slavery, Aboriginal genocide, and the Holocaust, among other evils, as a legacy of presumed Whiteness and goodness. See Jacques Derrida, *Writing and Difference*, trans. Alan Bass (Chicago: University of Chicago Press, 1978); Max Horkheimer and T.W. Adorno, *Dialectic of Enlightenment*, trans. John Cumming (New York: Continuum, 1982); Max Horkheimer, *Eclipse of Reason* (New York: Seabury Press, 1974); Emmanuel Levinas, *Basic Philosophical Writings* (Bloomington: Indiana UP, 1996). Since that entry of evil at that moment of creation, we have been striving – in what is our quest and hope – to return to the initial good, freedom, and wholesomeness that lies in the infinity of Blackness from which all humanity has been alienated. Multiculturalism is idealistically a return to a long distant past, to a time long hoped for again.

30 G.W.F. Hegel, *Hegel's Science of Logic*, trans. A.V. Miller, ed. H.D. Lewis (New York: Humanity Books, 1969), 94.

31 Ibid., 93.

32 John Burbidge, *Being and Will: An Essay in Philosophical Theology* (New York: Paulist Press, 1977) 40–61.

33 *House of Commons Debates* (8 October 1971).

34 Ibid.

35 Ibid.

36 K. Anthony Appiah raises several questions of interest around this point in terms of identity formations. Identity becomes even more complicated when the individual is viewed as a wider infinity than the finite identity – and one that is group-based at that, or constructed for the individual. K. Anthony Appiah, "Identity,

Authenticity, Survival: Multicultural Societies and Social Reproduction," in *Multi-culturalism: Examining the Politics of Recognition*, ed. Amy Gutmann (Princeton: Princeton UP, 1994). Indeed, Appiah raises the troubling questions of, in such a situation, how one is to deal with such other identity characteristic as gender, sexuality, class, and so on, and in a way that still conforms to the liberal charac-terization that the lordship and bondage struggle at the heart of multiculturalism is based an a fight for recognition. If this is true, the questions arise: recognition of what, and is this recognition won for all times? Similarly, if the liberal ideal is for the individual to "know thyself" and then to demand recognition based on this knowledge, what is there to be known in the specific – except that the individ-ual is ephemeral, perhaps, unknowable as a constant throughout the changes of time? Therefore, how can recognition be worthwhile, except in a very limited and specific moment? Recognition, against all the best of intentions, would still lead into an unhappy consciousness – of which the only escape is idealistically and tragically a death that kills off the old unknowable self. As with tragedy, out of this death would emerge the hoped-for rebirth of a new idealized self: a self that is socially constructed in the moment and according to specific characteristics and values privileged by the new lord that is the state or the culture in which the individual is embedded and also fully reconciled. This single and idealized identity in such a universe is citizenship. This is what every member has in common and it is the highest identity. The problem for members of a so-called Black ethnicity is that no matter how many times they die neo-mythically, they are reborn Black in status and idealization – they are not transformed fully into the Whiteness of citi-zenship; they are deemed to be truly citizens of Blackness and having a presence in Canada but not really belonging as such. Try as they may, Blacks cannot be transfigured in the social imaginary as authentically Canadian and with that achieve status Whiteness – for they are repeatedly (re)categorized with each social rebirth as Black somatically, culturally, idealistically and, importantly, in status.

37  Canada does have a limited form of employment equity in the Federal Civil Ser-vice but nothing along the scale of affirmative action in the United States. Indeed, it can be argued that authorities that have the most sovereign power – the prov-inces – for righting this historic legacy have refrained from such action. Labour and employment standards, education, and immigration settlement, for example, are the responsibility of the provinces in Canada. One controversial case was the effort by the socialist New Democratic Party government of Ontario to institu-tionalize a form of affirmative action called employment equity in the 1990s. This was a very controversial move that led to what came to be known as a main-stream backlash against immigrants and minority groups who were intended to be the beneficiaries of the policy. Ultimately, the Conservative Party of Ontario killed the policy as its first act when it won a populist election campaign based on the motif of introducing a common sense revolution to the province, a campaign that at its heart was a virulent opposition to employment equity that was

presented pejoratively as an enforced quota system. Cecil Foster, *A Place Called Heaven: The Meaning of Being Black In Canada* (Toronto: HarperCollins, 1996); Martin Loney, *The Pursuit of Division: Race, Gender, and Preferential Hiring in Canada* (Montreal and Kingston: McGill-Queen's UP, 1998); Hellen J. Beck, Jeffrey G. Reitz, and Nan Weiner, "Addressing Systemic Racial Discrimination in Employment: The Health Canada Case and Implications for Legislative Change," *Canadian Public Policy* 28, no. 3 (2002). However, one of the things worthy of consideration is how, by not going the route of an official affirmative action program, Canada has tried to achieved universal social justice without appearing to compound previous and historic mistakes and wrongs by creating new ones. While I do not accept the argument that affirmative action is a form of reverse discrimination, as even suggested by somatically Black conservatives like Sowell and Steele, I think that Canada does provide a chance to examine how redress can be achieved without a proactive affirmative program. Shelby Steele, *The Content of Our Character: A New Vision of Race in America* (New York: Harper Perennial, 1991); ibid., *A Dream Deferred: The Second Betrayal of Black Freedom in America* (New York: HarperCollins, 1998); Cornel West, *Keeping Faith: Philosophy and Race in America* (New York: Routledge, 1993); ibid., *Race Matters* (New York: Vintage Books, 1993). The evidence, I would suggest, is that aiming idealistically for redress on its own does not enhance distributive justice for those that have been wronged historically. The continued racialized and political and economic inferiority of somatic Blacks and First Nations Peoples in Canada provide the best testament of the need for government, or collective, intervention.

38 *House of Commons Debates* (8 October 1971).

39 *Canadian Multiculturalism Act*, R.S.C. 1985 (4th Supp.), c. 24.

40 Ernest Gellner, "Adam's Navel: Primordialists Versus Modernists," in *People Nation & State: The Meaning of Ethnicity & Nationalism* (London: I.B. Tauris Publishers, 1999); Anthony D. Smith, *Theories of Nationalism* (London: Gerald Duckworth and Company, 1983); Anthony D. Smith, "The Nation: Real or Imagined?" in *People Nation & State: The Meaning of Ethnicity & Nationalism* (London: I.B. Tauris Publishers, 1999).

41 Constance Backhouse, *Colour-Coded: A Legal History of Racism in Canada, 1900–1950* (Toronto: University of Toronto Press, 1999); Agnes Calliste, "Canada's Immigration Policy and Domestic Blacks from the Caribbean: The Second Domestic Scheme," in *The Social Basis of Law*, 2d ed., ed. Elizabeth Cormack and Stephen Brickley (Halifax: Garamond Press, 1991); Canadian Bar Association, "Working Group on Racial Equality in the Legal Profession," (Ottawa: Canadian Bar Association, 1999); George Elliott Clarke, ed., *Fire on the Water: An Anthology of Black Nova Scotian Writing*, volume 2, *Writers of the Renaissance* (Lawrencetown Beach, N.S.: Pottersfield Press, 1992); George Elliott Clarke, "Contesting a Model Blackness: A Meditation on African-Canadian African Americanism, or the Structures of African Canadianite," in *Essays on Canadian Writing*, No. 63 (Toronto: ECW Press, Spring 1998); Tania Das Gupta,

*Racism and Paid Work* (Toronto: Garamond Press, 1996); Carl E. James, *Making It: Black Youth, Racism and Career Aspirations in a Big City* (Oakville, Ont.: Mosaic Press, 1990); ibid., "Getting There and Staying There"; ibid., "Up to No Good: Black on the Streets and Encountering Police," in *Racism & Social Inequality in Canada: Concepts, Controversies & Strategies of Resistance*, ed. Vic Satzewich (Toronto: Thompson Educational Publishing, 1998); Carl James, Dwaine Plaza, and Clifford Jansen, "Issues of Race in Employment: Experiences of Caribbean Women in Toronto," *Canadian Woman Studies* 19, no. 3 (1998); Frances Henry, *The Caribbean Diaspora in Toronto: Learning to Live with Racism* (Toronto: University of Toronto Press, 1994).

42 Freda Hawkins, *Canada and Immigration: Public Policy and Public Concern* (Montreal and Kingston: McGill-Queen's UP, 1972); Lisa Marie Jakubowski, "'Managing' Canadian Immigration: Racism, Ethnic Selectivity, and the Law," in *Locating Law: Race, Class, Gender Connections*, ed. Elizabeth Cormack (Halifax: Fernwood Publishing, 1999).

43 Will Kymlicka, *Multicultural Citizenship: Liberal Theory of Minority Rights* (Oxford: Clarendon Press, 1995).

44 John Porter, *The Vertical Mosaic: An Analysis of Social Class and Power in Canada* (Toronto: University of Toronto Press, 1985); Pierre Vallières, *White Niggers of America*, trans. Joan Pinkham (Toronto: McClelland and Stewart, 1971).

45 Calliste, "Canada's Immigration Policy and Domestic Blacks"; Alan Simmons, "Canadian Immigration Policy: An Analysis of Imagined Futures," paper prepared for the Symposium on Immigration and Integration, 25–27 October 1996 (Winnipeg: Department of Sociology, University of Manitoba); Alan Simmons, "Racism and Immigration Policy," in *Racism & Social Inequality in Canada: Concepts, Controversies & Strategies of Resistance*, ed. Vic Satzewich (Toronto: Thompson Educational Publishing, 1998); Sedef Arat-Koc, "Good Enough to Work But Not Good Enough to Stay: Foreign Domestic Workers and the Law," in *Locating Law: Race, Class, Gender Connections*, ed. Elizabeth Cormack (Halifax: Fernwood Publishing, 1999).

46 Elinor Caplan, "Trends in Global Migration Forum," notes for an address by the Honourable Elinor Caplan, minister of Citizenship and Immigration, to the Maytree Foundation. <http://www.cic.ca/english/press/speech/maytree-e.html> 7 September 2001

47 Joseph H. Carens, *Culture, Citizenship, and Community: A Contextual Exploration of Justice as Evenhandedness* (Oxford: Oxford UP, 2000); Will Kymlicka, *Politics in the Vernacular: Nationalism, Multiculturalism, and Citizenship* (Oxford: Oxford UP, 2000).

48 Carens, *Culture, Citizenship, and Community*; Kymlicka, *Politics in the Vernacular*.

49 Informetrica Limited, "Canada's Recent Immigrants: A Comparative Portrait Based on the 1996 Census," in *Recent Immigrants in Metropolitan Areas* (Ottawa: Citizenship and Immigration Canada, January 2001); Daiva Stasiulis,

"Participation by Immigrants, Ethnocultural/Visible Minorities in the Canadian Political Process," (Montreal: Second National Metropolis Conference, November 1997); Strategic Policy, Planning and Research, "The Economic Performance of Immigrants: Education Perspective," in IMDB Profile Series (Ottawa: Citizenship and Immigration Canada, 2000); ibid., "Towards a More Balanced Geographical Distribution of Immigration," Special Study: Strategic Research and Review (Ottawa: Citizenship and Immigration Canada, May 2001).

50 Law Union of Ontario, The Immigrant's Handbook: A Critical Guide (Montreal: Black Rose, 1981) 12.

51 Ibid., 11.

52 Ekos Research, June 2000.

53 Caplan, "Trends in Global Migration Forum."

54 Robin W. Winks, Canadian-West Indian Union: A Forty-Year Minuet (Toronto: Oxford UP, 1968); ibid., The Blacks in Canada: A History (Montreal and Kingston: McGill-Queen's UP, 1971); George Elliott Clarke, ed., Fire on the Water: An Anthology of Black Nova Scotian Writing, volume 1, Early and Modern Writers 1785–1935 (Lawrencetown Beach, N.S.: Pottersfield Press, 1991); ibid., volume 2, Writers of the Renaissance (Lawrencetown Beach, N.S.: Pottersfield Press, 1992); James W. St. G. Walker, The Black Loyalists: The Search for a Promised land in Nova Scotia and Sierra Leone 1783–1870 (Toronto: University of Toronto Press, 1992); David V.J. Bell, "Nation and Non-Nation: A New Analysis of the Loyalists and the American Revolution," Ph.D. thesis (Cambridge: Harvard University, 1969); J.S. Woodsworth, Strangers within Our Gates: Or Coming Canadians (Toronto: F.C. Stephenson, 1909).

55 Winks, The Blacks in Canada.

56 George Elliott Clarke, ed., Eyeing the North Star: Directions in African-Canadian Literature (Toronto: McClelland and Stewart, 1997).

57 Stanley G. Grizzle, My Name's Not George: The Story of the Brotherhood of Sleeping Car Porters in Canada (Toronto: Umbrella Press, 1998); Bromley L. Armstrong, Bromley – Tireless Champion for Just Causes: Memoirs of Bromley L. Armstrong, written with Sheldon Taylor (Pickering, Ont.: Vitabu Publications, 2000); Journey to Justice, prod. Karen King-Chigbo, dir. Roger McTair (Montreal: National Film Board of Canada, 2000) video cassette: focusing on the 1930s to 1950s, this film documents the struggle of six people living in Canada who refused to accept inequality and took racism to court; Sheldon Taylor, "Many Rivers to Cross: The African-Canadian Experience," National tour 1992–1994, circulated in co-operation with the Canadian Museum of Civilization, Sheldon Taylor, curator (Toronto: Multicultural History Society of Ontario, 1992); ibid., "Darkening the Complexion of Canadian Society: Black Activism, Policy-Making and Black Immigration from the Caribbean to Canada, 1940s–1960s," Ph.D. thesis (Toronto: University of Toronto, 1994).

58 Will Kymlicka, Politics in the Vernacular.

59 Appiah, Colour Conscious, 80–1.

60 Prince, *Being Black*; Carle E James and Adrienne Shadd, eds, *Talking about Identity: Encounters in Race, Ethnicity, and Language* (Toronto: Between the Lines, 2001); Lawrence Hill, *Black Berry, Sweet Juice: On Being Black and White in Canada* (Toronto: Harper Flamingo Canada, 2001); Foster, *A Place Called Heaven.*

### CHAPTER SIXTEEN

1 I would like to thank Nigel Thomas, author and professor of English, Laval University for this point. This is another indication of how difficult it is perceptually to see Blackness as more than skin colour or race. It is part of the metaphors of everyday life. Even when we try to subvert this connection, we run the risk of upholding it, as the concept and the links shift in meaning.

2 Hannah Arendt, *The Origins of Totalitarianism* (Cleveland: World Publishing, 1958); Robert North, *Teilhard and the Creation of the Soul* (Milwaukee: Bruce Publishing, 1967); Oliver C. Cox, *Race: A Study in Social Dynamics*, preface by Cornell West, introduction by Adolphi Reed Jr (New York: Monthly Review Press, 2000); Emmanuel Chukwudi Eze, *Race and the Enlightenment: A Reader* (Cambridge, Mass.: Blackwell, 1977); John Thornton, *Race, Discourse, and the Origin of the Americas: A New World View*, ed. Vera Lawrence Hyatt and Rex Nettleford (Washington: Smithsonian Institution Press, 1995); Collette Guillaumin, *Racism, Sexism, Power and Ideology* (London: Routledge, 1995); Michel Wieviorka, *The Arena of Racism*, trans. Chris Turner (London: Sage, 1995); Wahneema Lubiano, ed., *The House That Race Built: Black Americans, U.S. Terrain* (New York: Pantheon Books, 1997); Paul Gilroy, *Against Race: Imagining Political Culture beyond the Color Line* (Cambridge: Harvard UP, 2000).

3 This definition sets Canada at ontological variance with Britain and the United States in defining who or what is Black. In Britain, Black is primarily status: a collection of all non-mainstream groups and individuals who position themselves against the perceived Whiteness and privilege of the English and the British. In the Black group, for example, are many of the immigrants from former British colonies, people who felt positioned as outsiders in Britain. Phenotypically and somatically, this group could include people from Africa, South Asia, the Caribbean, and the "Whites" of Ireland. As Stuart Hall notes: "In the 1970s, the signifier 'black' was adopted as a political category of struggle, both by Afro-Caribbean migrants and by migrants from Asia. People who manifestly were not, in any significant ways in which the term 'race' had ever been used, the same race, called themselves by the racial signifier ... Since they were manifestly not white, they were black. They call themselves black. They organized under that *political* roof ... [But] people now call themselves not only Asians, but Indians, Bangladeshis, Pakistanis, and indeed, South Indians. Things have moved to a new ethnicized politics of difference. And that has presented certain profound difficulties of

Note to page 397

political organization when the signifier 'black' disappears." Stuart Hall, "Subjects in History: Making Diasporic Identities," in *The House That Race Built: Black Americans, U.S. Terrain, e Wahneema Lubianod* (New York: Pantheon Books, 1997), 295. In the United States, Black is much more of a racial label. The preferred name for Americans whose ancestry is African is African-American. Hispanic, Puerto Rican, and other "black" countries and identities are not included in African-American. As Carole Boyce Davies remarks: "It is significant that in the United States, the term 'Black' does not include other 'Third World' peoples (Asians, Arabs, Latino/as) as it does in the United Kingdom. For the United States, the historical convergence between 'race' and 'nationality' has kept separate, for the most part, all the possibilities of organizing around related agendas and has operated in terms of polarization of various races. It has also either sublimated racial differences or reified them in essential ways. Interrogating 'African-American' as a defined terminology first mandates moving beyond the limited definition of what is American. In this way, 'African-American' could correctly refer to the African peoples of the Americas: North America, the Caribbean and South America." Carole Boyce Davies, *Black Women, Writing and Identity: Migration of the Subject* (London: Routledge, 1994), 34. One of the most perverse and essentialist definitions of "Black," but one that has some legitimacy in Black communities in the United States and Canada, is offered by Debra J. Dickerson: "*blacks* are those Americans descended from Africans who were brought here voluntarily as slaves. This definition would include free blacks, even those who owned slaves. Immigrants of African descent, even if descended from South American or Caribbean slaves, are not included in this definition." Debra J. Dickerson, *The End of Blackness: Returning the Souls of Black Folk to Their Rightful Owners* (New York: Pantheon Books, 2004), 259. For a Canadian version of this definition, see note 35 below.

4  In a discussion on who is authentically Black, Cornel West makes clear that there is no essence or authenticity of Blackness: "First, blackness has no meaning outside of a system of race-conscious people and practices." Cornel West, *Race Matters* (New York: Vintage Books, 1993), 39. I would put the argument differently by stating that it is race that has no meaning outside of a discussion on Blackness. Blackness is the infinite; race the finite in it. This is in keeping with my argument that the epistemology of Blackness preceded the ontology and existentialism of Blackness, of which race is only one ontological manifestation, or one finite subset. The subset can only provide partial meaning. Indeed, West seems to be arguing as much in the same breath: "After centuries of racist degradation, exploitation, and oppression in America, being black means being minimally subject to white supremacist abuse and being part of a rich culture and community that has struggled against such abuse. All people with black skin and African phenotype are subject to potential white supremacist abuse." West, *Race Matters*, 39. By his reasoning, then, racialization follows from a presumed meaning of inferiority and superiority. This flows from the wider notion, which came to a head in

modernity, that it is possible to divide people into separate, distinct, and authentic groups, and, secondly, to impose values on these groupings by placing them in binaries. Indeed, only a page earlier West had argued for "dismantling each pillar systematically" of the framework of racial reasoning as a way of producing meaning in the world. "The fundamental aim of this undermining and dismantling is *to replace racial reasoning with moral reasoning,* to understand the black freedom struggle not as an affair of skin pigmentation and racial phenotype but rather as a matter of *ethical principles* and wise politics" (38, italics added). Moral reasoning and ethical principles can flow out of the epistemology and existentialism for which West yearns, but which must be based on antecedent knowledge of good and evil, or what is Black and White. The problem occurs when evil is ultimately reduced, as West recognizes, solely to the Black skins and African phenotypes as markers of Black status or racialized inferiority and as representative of the total attributes of any group in humanity. The solution, then, is to transcend the finite limits of race while remaining within the infinity of Blackness, where, based on additional information, different moral and ethical decisions can be made.

5 This is the situation in a practical sense that Goldberg was dealing with in a conceptual manner when he wondered that if he were to suggest that the concept "*race* is a fluid, transforming, historically specific concept parasitic on theoretic and social discourses for the meaning it assumes at any historical moment ... how can I continue to insist that racism and premodern forms of ethnocentrism differ." David Theo Goldberg, *Racist Culture: Philosophy and the Politics of Meaning* (Oxford: Blackwell, 1993), 74. Indeed, this seems to be a problem of dialectical limits in concepts, which Goldberg comes to explain partially through boundary construction as well as the content imagined within the concepts: "Ethnicity, then, tends to emphasize a rhetoric of cultural content, whereas race tends to resort to a rhetoric of descent. Nevertheless, these are rhetorical tendencies, not fixed conceptualizations. Like race, ethnicity may be cast and managed as much in terms of inherent as deeply historical identities, either of which may be claimed as the basis of sedimented and immutable differences. And again, like race, ethnicity may serve to veil domination and exclusion via population disaggregation" (76). In providing only a partial answer, Goldberg is searching for explanations within fixed definitions for the conceptually unfixed, and seems to be arguing both ways at the same time, as if to suggest that race is only an issue of inferiority for somatic Blacks. His problem is that, invariably, he is trying to reduce race to the fixed somatic Black category. For in reducing the difference to primarily one of rhetoric, his explanation works discursively just as well when race and ethnicity are substituted for each other, so that there is really no difference in the concepts as he explains them. The problem for Goldberg, and which is obvious in multiculturalism, is that in the "real" world a concept like Black can be racial or ethnical without having an intentionally negative or inferior overtone. Further, Black and Blackness will take different meanings depending on the subjective and objective position. Thus, there are times when for a subject the positive notion of ethnicity

might coincide with that of race; while at other times it might not, especially
when race and ethnicity – whether individually or collectively – are used to signify
inferiority. In the case where race and ethnicity are the same, we may have what
Goldberg calls "ethnorace." When they are not, we may have separate categories.
This, I am suggesting, is the challenge of multiculturalism: discerning when Black
is positive and inclusive in an ethno-racial way, when it is negatively or positively
ethnicity, and when it is negatively or positively racial. A further problem for
Black, in this regard, is the epistemological baggage that it carries – where perceptually Black is racially reduced to somatic Blackness and status Blackness. However, as intended by multicultural Canada, ethnic Blackness might intentionally be
idealized, cultural, and status Whiteness – as for example is the case in Haiti and
other countries that have traditionally positioned themselves as having an idealized White citizenry that manifests itself mainly in somatic Black bodies.

6  Rinaldo Walcott, *Black Like Who? Writing Black Canada* (Toronto: Insomniac
Press, 1997); George Elliott Clarke, "Treason of the Black Intellectuals?" English,
McGill University <www.arts.mcgill.ca/programs/misc/ clarke.htm> 7 July 2002.
See also George Elliott Clarke, *Odysseys Home: Mapping African-Canadian Lit-
erature* (Toronto: University of Toronto Press, 2002).

7  Lawrence Hill, *Black Berry, Sweet Juice: On Being Black and White in Canada*
(Toronto: Harper Flamingo Canada, 2001); David A. Hollinger, *Postethnic America: Beyond Multiculturalism* (New York: HarperCollins, 1995).

8  I wish to thank one of my external reviewers for emphasizing this point.

9  William Arthur Deacon, *My Vision of Canada* (Toronto: Ontario Publishing
Company, 1933); Robin W. Winks, *The Blacks in Canada: A History* (Montreal
and Kingston: McGill-Queen's UP, 1971); David V. J Bell, "Nation and Non-
Nation: A New Analysis of the Loyalists and the American Revolution," Ph.D.
thesis (Cambridge: Harvard University, 1969); James W. St. G. Walker, *The Black
Loyalists: The Search for a Promised Land in Nova Scotia and Sierra Leone
1783–1870* (Toronto: University of Toronto Press, 1992); Robertson Davies, *The
Merry Heart: Selections 1980–1995* (Toronto: Penguin, 1996); ibid., *Happy
Alchemy: Writings on the Theatre and Other Lively Arts* (Toronto: McClellan
and Stewart, 1997).

10  Davies, *The Merry Heart*; John Porter, *The Vertical Mosaic: An Analysis of Social
Class and Power in Canada* (Toronto: University of Toronto Press, 1985); Jeffrey
G. Reitz and Raymond Breton, *The Illusion of Difference: Realities of Ethnicity in
Canada and the United States* (Ottawa: C.D. Howe Institute, 1994); Jeffrey G.
Reitz, *Warmth of the Welcome: The Social Causes of Economic Success for Immi-
grants in Different Nations and Cities* (Boulder, Co.: Westview Press, 1998).

11  Part of the problem is clearly an ontological misunderstanding of who or what is
Black or even African-Canadian. This is made clear in Clarke's rather confusing
and incoherent ontological explanation of Canadian Blacks and African-Canadians, which identities he uses interchangeably at times. In *Odysseys Home*, Clarke
makes the startling statement that "I argue that African-Canadian culture and

literature have domesticated – nationalized – their influences enough to create an aboriginal *blackness*, even if this mode of being remains difficult to define or categorize." Clarke, *Odysseys Home*, 13. Difficult, indeed, if not impossible without a clear answer to the questions: *aboriginal* to what? Is it possible to construct an "aboriginal" status or nature within the state? Clarke's argument is that essence is based on skin colour and a lineage that is traced to Africa – the primary rationale on which he proceeded to compile a separate chapter, "Select Bibliography of Literature by African-Canadian Authors," in his book. Lacking in this bibliography is a clear and inviolate definition of African-Canadian that does not go beyond skin colour and a perceived or imputed African ancestry.

Clarke's problem becomes even more palpable as he argues that his essays in the book "assume a modicum of *essentialism*, so that I am enabled – empowered – to discuss 'Africadian' and 'African-Canadian' literature with a fair (or black?) conviction that 'Africadians' and 'African-Canadians' have *some* corporeal, 'real' existence. For, if these people do not have some coherency in the world, this book is so much nothing" (15). Here again, Clarke appears confused ontologically, even to the point of unintentionally destroying the very thesis of the book. Corporality does not require an essence. Indeed, philosophically, one of the longest arguments has been whether bodies require an essence as a necessary condition for existence. The answer appears to be clearly no, and that is the position taken ontologically in this book. The question was never whether or not the body existed, but rather what it is phenomenologically: How can we know it authentically, in a way that the common sense meaning is consistent with the way the body actually is? How can the dualism be known in exactly the same way whether defining the subject or object? This is why we conduct a phenomenological search for what is essential or natural about the body, rather that presume that there is an essence. So, indeed, an Africadian or African-Canadian body can exist without an essence per se. Second, there has always also been the question of whether a composite or hybrid has an essence – part of the barbarism of composition of which Hegel spoke. Clarke does not hide his understanding about the compositeness, the constructiveness, and the hybridization of his African-Canadian group: "To speak about an 'African-Canadian' literature, then, I must be 'essentialist' enough to believe that an entity describable as 'African-Canadian' exists ... In fact, I hold that African Canada is a conglomeration of many cultures, a spectrum of ethnicities. That perception colours the essays gathered here. For instance, the old, indigenous, African-Canadian communities ... of Black Nova Scotian literature. The 'New Canadian' black communities, mainly of Caribbean origin ... Finally, the import of African American literature for African-Canadian literature" Clarke, *Odysseys Home*, 14–15. So an aboriginal or indigenous Black essence is made up of essences that have already been creolized and hybridized separately in the anglophone Caribbean, francophone Caribbean, Nova Scotia, and elsewhere in Canada and the United States of America – all sites of essences that have been blended further into a new or *aboriginal* Canadian essence.

Later, seemingly drowning in his confusion, with "aboriginal" meaning primordial and newly constructed at the same time, Clarke argues that

nevertheless, *blackness* remains an absolutely relative epistemology. The 'Canadian species' is not identical to the 'American,' and neither is the same as the 'Caribbean.' The structural conditions of each 'region' of blackness impinge upon its theorization and definition. Thus, some African Canadians call themselves *Black* to signal their affiliation with some larger *African* universe; but others call themselves *African,* choosing to accent their ancestral heritage. Some add the adjective *Canadian,* to express a Canadian identity modified by 'blackness.' Others identify with an ex-colonial heritage – either 'British' or 'Français.' Still others ask to be classed solely as *Canadian.* The oft-cited 'lack of unity' among African Canadians is, then, the result of the instability of *black*-as-signifier *chez nous.* Here the diversity of black communities proves that 'black' is essentially a politically and *culturally constructed* category, which cannot be grounded in a set of fixed transcultural or transcendental racial categories and which therefore has no guarantees in Nature. (16)

If this is so, how then can there be an aboriginal, nationalistic, or constructed essence of Blackness as Clarke claims? Clarke seems intent to argue against himself – a job that he does quite successfully by his use of italics above – to show the difficulty of trying to reduce to finite statuses concepts that are themselves infinites. How much more difficult is it to make a finite category out of all the contested infinities?

Clarke recognizes the problem is his search for even a "modicum" of Black essence: "Given that *blackness* is so undefined and indefinable, one potential objection to my essays is that they group human beings on the specious – and spurious – grounds of shared 'race,' a matter of chance apportioning of pigmentation and melanin" (16). So true.

12 Charles Taylor, "The Politics of Recognition," in *Multiculturalism: Examining the Politics of Recognition,* ed., Amy Gutmann, (Princeton: Princeton UP, 1994).

13 Will Kymlicka, *Finding Our Way: Rethinking Ethnocultural Relations in Canada* (Toronto: Oxford UP, 1998).

14 See note 2 above.

15 André Alexis, "Borrowed Blackness (Black Canadians Have Yet to Elaborate a Culture Strong Enough to Help Evaluate the Foreignness of Foreign Ideas)," *This Magazine* (Toronto), May 1995.

16 Ibid., 14–21.

17 Ernest Gellner, "Adam's Navel: Primordialists Versus Modernists," *People Nation and State: The Meaning of Ethnicity and Nationalism* (London: I.B. Tauris Publishers, 1999); Anthony D. Smith, *Theories of Nationalism* (London: Gerald Duckworth and Company, 1983); ibid., "The Nation: Real or Imagined?," in *People Nation and State*; John Rex and David Mason, *Theories of Race and Ethnic Relations* (Cambridge: Cambridge UP, 1986).

18 Pierre Vallières, *White Niggers of America*, trans. Joan Pinkham (Toronto: McClelland and Stewart, 1971).

19 In this regard, attention should be drawn to those who use "Black history" month to focus on African-Canadian or Black Canadian heroes and their achievements and to link their achievements and celebration to the broader realm of Canadian and world history.

20 For a fuller discussion on the contradictions of celebrating Black History Month in Canada, see Cecil Foster, "Black History and Culture in Canada: A Celebration of Essence or Presence," in *Canadian Cultural Poesis: Essays on Canadian Culture*, ed. Garry Sherbert, Annie Gérin, and Seila Petty (Waterloo, Ont.: Wilfrid Laurier UP, 2006).

21 Plato, *Timaeus*, trans. Donald J. Zeyl (Indianapolis: Hackett Publishing, 2000), 24.

22 Jean-Paul Sartre, *Anti-Semite and Jew* (New York: Schocken Books, 1965), 84.

23 Plato, *Timaeus*; Maurice Merleau-Ponty, *Phenomenology of Perception*, trans. Colin Smith (London: Routledge and Kegan Paul, 2000); Frantz Fanon, *Black Skin, White Masks* (New York: Grove Press, 1967).

24 Clarke George Elliott, ed., *Eyeing the North Star: Directions in African-Canadian Literature* (Toronto: McClelland and Stewart, 1997), xi.

25 Winks, *The Blacks in Canada*.

26 Biodun Adediran, "Yoruba Ethnic Groups or a Yoruba Ethnic Group? A Review of the Problem of Ethnic Identification," *Africa: Revista do Centro de Estudos Africanos da USP* 7 (1984); Robin Law, "Ethnicity and the Slave Trade: 'Lucumi' and 'Nago' as Ethnonyms in West Africa," *History in Africa* 24 (1997).

27 Adediran, "Yoruba Ethnic Groups or a Yoruba Ethnic Group?"

28 Ibid.

29 Ibid.

30 Law, "Ethnicity and the Slave Trade."

31 Clarke, *Eyeing the North Star*; ibid., "Contesting a Model Blackness: A Meditation on African-Canadian African Americanism, or the Structures of African Canadianite," *Essays on Canadian Writing* 63 (Spring 1998).

32 Clarke makes his distinction as follows:

I term Black Nova Scotia *Africadia* and its people and cultural works *Africadian*. A fusion of *Africa* and *cadie*, the Mi'kmaq term for 'abounding in' (and the probable cognate of the French toponym *Acadie* [Acadia], *Africadia(n)* serves to stress the long history of Africans in Maritime Canada. *Black Nova Scotian, Afro-Nova Scotian, 'Scotian,* and *African-Nova Scotian* are popular terms denoting the Africadian populace. While these labels have their merits and their defenders, I think they obscure the long residency of Africans in Nova Scotia, the first of whom, Matthieu da Costa, settled at Port-Royal, Acadie, with Samuel de Champlain in 1605. (Clarke, *Odysseys Home*, 18n3)

33 Clarke makes the distinction among Canadians of African descent this way: "I use four terms to refer to persons of African descent," which means that ultimately

Blackness is reduced to African lineage, which might exclude pigmentation and
obvious melanin characteristics. As he states:

New World Africans ... refers to all persons of African descent in the Americas.
African Canadian covers all Canadians of Negro/African heritage, whether they
arrive here from the United States, the Caribbean, South America, Europe or
Africa itself; the term also applies to all those born in Canada. African Americans applies to those black [emphasis added here] people whose homeland is
the United States; likewise, African (or Afro-) Caribbean denotes those whose
homelands are in the Caribbean archipelago. Finally, I use black as a generic
term distinguishing peoples and cultures of African descent from those of either
Asian or European descent. (Clarke, Odysseys Home, 18n3)

Clarke's definitions are problematic in the extreme, especially when such words and
phrases as "black as a generic term" and "homelands" are used along with the
notions that there are distinguishing people and cultures from Africa, Asia, and
Europe. Obvious questions arise: who are the authentic and essential peoples and
cultures of Africa, Asia, and Europe and what becomes of them when they meet in a
place like the Americas? Second, to assume the privileging of one of these finite
groups within finite Blackness, as Clarke does with his constructed "Africadians,"
can be seen as inter-Blackness racism, rather than as being a class issue, because of
the ontological and epistemological boundaries he builds around each group.

Still later, Clarke seems to be re-evaluating his definition and thinking about
Canadian Blacks and their supposed authenticity. This seems to be the case when
he picked up his poet's pen and wrote: "True: I am African-Canadian. My roots
go back two centuries in Nova Scotia; and, before that, to the U.S. So I am African-American, proudly, but my 'belonging' carries an asterisk, one shaped like a –
ragged – maple leaf." George Elliott Clarke, Black (Vancouver: Raincoast Books,
2006), 6. Ah, the sweet Blackness of poetry that solves all contradictions.

34 Sartre, Anti-Semite and Jew, 80.

35 Davies, The Merry Heart; ibid., Happy Alchemy.

36 George Grant, Technology and Empire: Perspectives on North America (Toronto:
House of Anansi Press, 1969); George Grant, Lament for a Nation: The Defeat of
Canadian Nationalism (Toronto: Macmillan, 1978).

37 Fanon, Black Skin, White Masks, 26.

38 Grant, Technology and Empire; ibid., Lament for a Nation.

39 Clarke, Eyeing the North Star; ibid., "Contesting a Model Blackness." Indeed,
Clarke often draws heavily on Grant's analysis to explain Blackness, Africadians,
and Black or African nationalism in Canada. He particularly points out that
Grant, who he had studied and liked at university, had warned of the dangers to
Canadian nationalism of the liberal democratic policies introduced by Trudeau as
part of multiculturalism in A Just Society. In the essay "Toward a Conservative
Modernity: Cultural Nationalism in Contemporary Acadian and Africadian
Poetry," Clarke claims: "The critique of modernity offered by conservative Cana-
dian philosopher George Grant (1918–88) must be considered by those who

would conserve a national or regional poetic. If modernity (read by Grant as the cosmopolitan liberalism of international capitalism) dissolves nationalism and regional cultures, then the embracing of modern/post-modern poetics by poets who issue from such cultures is imperilled. Significantly, the poets of Acadie and of Nova Scotia's Black Loyalist and Black Refugee-settled communities – an ethnocultural archipelago I term Africadia – confront modernity without even a buffer of a state to call their own" Clarke, *Odysseys Home*, 150. The kind of nationalism that Grant proposes in order to preserve Canada from external forces would also work at a different level for Africanadians in Clarke's imagination. It would protect their particular and homegrown culture, like a group religion, from those who are more universal in orientation, style, and thought. It could provide the buffer between the desired particulars and the rejected universalism in Blackness that Clarke borrows from Grant. Indeed, in an essay titled "Treason of the Black Intellectuals," Clarke accuses a number of mainly Caribbean-born Black immigrants of betraying Canadian nationalism as suggested by Grant, and, Clarke claims, Trudeau also. Clarke states that the immigrants support a rapacious universalism best epitomized by the capitalist culture of the United States. Contradictorily, Clarke accuses the Black intellectuals, even though (or because) they have become Canadian citizens, of treason for peddling "received ideas of blackness, despite the call for universalism (and Pan-Canadianism) that emanate from other [foreign and immigrant] quarters of the political and cultural 'strivers'" (197).

## CHAPTER SEVENTEEN

1 Cecil Foster, *A Place Called Heaven: The Meaning of Being Black In Canada* (Toronto: HarperCollins, 1996).
2 Booker T. Washington, "Up from Slavery," *Three Negro Classics* (New York: Avon Books, 1965), 37.
3 Ibid., 39.
4 Northrop Frye, *Mythologizing Canada: Essays on the Canadian Literary Imagination*, ed. Branko Gorjup (Ottawa: Legas, 1997); Rick Helmes-Hayes and James Curtis, "Introduction," *The Vertical Mosaic Revisited*, ed. Rick Helmes-Hayes and James Curtis (Toronto: University of Toronto Press, 1998).
5 Simon Schama, *Rough Crossings: Britain, the Slaves and the American Revolution* (Toronto: Viking, 2005); Cassandra Pybus, *Epic Journeys of Freedom: Runaway Slaves of the American Revolution and their Global Quest for Liberty* (Boston: Becon Press, 2006).
6 Ibid.
7 Ibid., 11–12.
8 Cecil Foster, *Where Race Does Not Matter: The New Spirit of Modernity* (Toronto: Penguin, 2005).
9 Robertson Davies, *The Merry Heart: Selections 1980–1995* (Toronto: Penguin, 1996); ibid., *Happy Alchem: Writings on the Theatre and Other Lively Arts*

(Toronto: McClellan and Stewart, 1997); Margaret Atwood, *Survival: A Thematic Guide to Canadian Literature* (Toronto: House of Anansi Press, 1972); Stephen Leacock, *Sunshine Sketches of a Little Town* (1912; Toronto: McClelland and Stewart, 1989); Philip Resnick, *The European Roots of Canadian Identity* (Peterborough, Ont.: Broadsview Press, 2005).

10 Douglas M. Daymond and Leslie G Monkman, *Towards a Canadian Literature: Essays, Editorials and Manifestoes*, vol. 1, *1752–1940* (Ottawa: Tecumseh Press, 1984), 207.

11 Leacock, *Sunshine Sketches of a Little Town*, 13.

12 Paul Litt, *The Muses, The Masses and the Massey Commission* (Toronto: University of Toronto Press, 1992); Northrop Frye, *Culture and the National Will: The Convocation Address to Carleton University*, 17 May, 1957 (Carlton U./Institute of Canadian Studies: Ottawa, 1957).

13 Daymond and Monkman, *Towards a Canadian Literature*, 204.

14 Ibid.

15 As Philip Resnick, for example, re-presents this narrative within official multiculturalism: "It is a well-known feature of Canadian history that this country, unlike the United States, was not born of revolution. Instead of the *novus ordo seculorum* (the new order of the ages) that the American founding fathers set out to create after the success of the thirteen colonies in the revolutionary wars, Canada's founding fathers were satisfied with achieving Dominion status within the British Empire with a constitution modelled on that of Great Britain. French Canadians, for their part, the failed rebellion of 1837–38 aside, had imbibed little of the revolutionary spirit from either France or the United States, and were to pursue a decidedly counter-revolutionary course with a strong dose of traditional Catholic doctrine to guide them. If France had betrayed its mission as eldest daughter of the Church in the aftermath of 1789, Quebec, down until the Quiet Revolution of the early 1960s, would not." Philip Resnick, *The European Roots of Canadian Identity* (Peterborough, Ont.: Broadsview Press, 2005), 21.

16 Ibid., 263.

17 Davies, *The Merry Heart*, 44–5.

18 More specifically, this is what the French explorer Jacques Cartier wrote about sighting Canada: "If the land was as good as the harbors there are, it would be an advantage; but it should not be named the New Land, but [a land of] stones and rocks frightful and ill shaped, for in all the said north coast I did not see a cart-load of earth, though I landed in many places. Except at Blanc Sablon there is nothing but moss and small stunted woods; in short, I deem rather than otherwise, that it is the land that God gave to Cain." James Phinney Baxter, *A Memoir of Jacques Cartier: His Voyages to the St. Lawrence* (New York: Dodd, Mead and Company, 1906), 86. Brackets in original.

19 Ibid., 179–80. Emphasis added.

20 Ibid., 180.

21 Jean-Paul Sartre, *Anti-Semite and Jew* (New York: Schocken Books, 1965), 83.

22 Frye, *Mythologizing Canada*.

23 Northrop Frye, *The Eternal Act of Creation: Essays, 1979–1900* (Bloomington: Indiana UP, 1993), 42.

24 Ibid., 142.

25 This point was illustrated in the bitter fight by Trudeau to give Canadians a written constitution that included a written Charter of Rights and Fundamental Freedoms. To achieve this, Trudeau had to fight all the way through First Ministers conferences with the premiers, the parliament of Canada, and in the Supreme Court, where he settled finally for a partial victory that captures the spirit of Frye's description of the psyche of Canada. The court ruled that Trudeau could act independently at the federal level and repatriate the Canadian Constitution from England so as to make it a genuine Canadian constitution that was not subject to outside interpretations for validity. However, the court also ruled that Trudeau should be mindful of Canada's existing traditions of co-operation with the provinces. Another was the long held belief that written constitutions and bills of rights were too American and republican, and that ultimately they would lead to judge-made rules and thereby limit the sovereignty of parliament – a development that was also presented as too imported from the United States for it to become Canadian. Pierre Elliott Trudeau, *The Essential Trudeau*, ed. Ron Graham (Toronto: McClelland and Stewart, 1998).

26 Frye, *The Eternal Act of Creation*, 142–3.

27 Hugh R. Innis, *Bilingualism and Biculturalism: An Abridged Version of the Royal Commission Report* (Toronto: McClelland and Stewart, 1973).

28 Francis Fukuyama, *The End of History and the Last Man* (New York: Avon Books, 1998). Importantly, any perceived threat to the American nation is imagined as coming from outside – as in the case of international terrorism at the beginning of the twenty-first century – and not primarily from within the nation-state. A succeeding number of US presidents have declared in countless state-of-the-union addresses to the American Congress that the state of the union is strong and united in purpose and intent from within.

29 Friedrich Nietzsche, *On the Advantage and Disadvantage of History for Life*, trans. with introduction by Peter Preuss (Indianapolis: Hackett Publishing, 1980); Thomas Paine, *Rights of Man, Common Sense and Other Political Writings* (Oxford: Oxford UP, 1995).

30 Frye, *The Eternal Act of Creation*, 143.

## CHAPTER EIGHTEEN

1 Engin F. Isin, *Who Is the New Citizen? Class, Territory, Identity* (Toronto: York University, 1995).

2 Ibid., 5.

3 Ibid., 10.

4 Ibid., 3.

5 Canadian Bar Association, "Working Group on Racial Equality in the Legal Profession" (Ottawa, Canadian Bar Association, 1999).

6 Frances Henry and Carol Tator, *Racist Discourse in Canada's English Print Media* (Toronto: The Canadian Race Relations Foundation, March 2000).

7 Ibid.

8 "The City That Works Could Be Even Better," *Toronto Star*, 1 May 1999.

9 Ibid.

10 "Opportunity Knocks. But Not for All," *Toronto Star*, 2 May 1999. For those who like to compare race and racism in Canada and United States to find out if there is "really" a difference, a comparative study of the existentialism of somatic Blacks in the United States is worth considering. The following are some of the results from a survey conducted by the *Washington Post*, the Henry J. Kaiser Family Foundation, and Harvard University in early 2006. The survey "aimed to capture the experiences and perceptions of black men at a time marked by increasing debate about how to build on their achievements and address the failures that endure decades after the civil rights movement." Some of the findings are:

• Six in 10 black men said their collective problems owe more to what they have failed to do themselves rather than "what white people have done to blacks." At the same time, half reported they have been treated unfairly by the police, and a clear majority said the economic system is stacked against them.

• More than half said they place a high value on marriage – compared with 39 percent of black women – six in 10 said they strongly value having children. Yet at least 38 percent of all black fathers in the survey are not living with at least one of their young children, and a third of all never-married black men have a child. Six in 10 said that black men disrespect black women.

• Three in four said they value being successful in a career, more than either white men or black women. Yet majorities also said that black men put too little emphasis on education and too much emphasis on sports and sex.

• Eight in 10 said they are satisfied with their lives, and six in 10 reported that it is a "good time" to be a black man in the United States. But six in 10 also reported they often are the targets of racial slights or insults, two-thirds said they believe the courts are more likely to convict black men than whites, and a quarter reported they have been physically threatened or attacked because they are black.

• Black men said they strongly believe in the American Dream – nine in 10 black men would tell their sons they can become anything they want to in life. But this vision of the future is laden with cautions and caveats: Two-thirds also would warn their sons that they have to be better and work harder than whites for equal rewards.

Steven A. Holmes and Richard Morin. "Black Men Torn between Promise and Doubt: Poll Respondents Relay Optimism, Disappointment in Themselves," *The Washington Post* on-line, <http://www.msnbc.msn.com/ id13123005/from/ET/print1/displaymode/1098/> 3 June 2006. These points will be of interest when we discuss in chapter 20 possibilities for harvesting more of the optimism and less of the disappointment for somatic Blacks in multicultural Canada.

11 Clayton James Mosher, *Discrimination and Denial: Systemic Racism in Ontario's Legal and Criminal Justice System, 1892–1961* (Toronto: University of Toronto Press, 1998), 4.

12 Mosher, *Discrimination and Denial*, 25–6.

13 George J. Sefa Dei, Elizabeth McIsaac, Josephine Mazzuca, and Jasmin Zine, *Reconstructing "Drop-Out": A Critical Ethnography of the Dynamics of Black Students' Disengagement from School* (Toronto: University of Toronto Press, 1997).

14 Jorge Duany, "The Recent Cuban Exodus in Comparative Caribbean Perspective," *Cuba and the Caribbean: Regional Issues and Trends in the Post-Cold War Era*, Joseph Tulchin, Andres Serbin, and Rafael Hernandez (Washington: SR Books, 1997).

15 Ibid.

16 Derek Hum and Wayne Simpson, "Wage Opportunities for Visible Minorities in Canada," *The Income and Labour Dynamics Working Paper Series*, catalogue No. 98-17, November 1998; James L. Torczyner, *Diversity, Mobility and Change – The Dynamics of Black Communities in Canada* (Montreal: McGill Consortium for Ethnicity and Strategic Social Planning, 1997); Alan B. Simmons and Dwaine E. Plaza, "Breaking through the Glass Ceiling: The Pursuit of University Training among African-Caribbean Migrants and Their Children in Toronto," *Canadian Ethnic Studies* 30, no. 3 (1998).

17 Frances Henry, *The Caribbean Diaspora in Toronto: Learning to Live with Racism* (Toronto: University of Toronto Press, 1994), 15.

18 Torczyner, *Diversity, Mobility and Change*.

19 John Porter, The Vertical Mosaic: An Analysis of Social Class and Power in Canada (Toronto: University of Toronto Press, 1985), 64.

20 Ibid., 66.

21 Ibid.

22 Cecil Foster, *A Place Called Heaven: The Meaning of Being Black In Canada* (Toronto: HarperCollins, 1996).

23 Porter, *The Vertical Mosaic*, 70.

24 John Murray Gibbon, *Canadian Mosaic: The Making of a Northern Nation* (Toronto: McClelland and Stewart, 1938), viii.

25 Ibid., vii.

26 Ibid.

27 Ibid.

28 Ibid., viii.

29 Jeffrey G. Reitz, *Warmth of the Welcome: The Social Causes of Economic Success for Immigrants in Different Nations and Cities* (Boulder, Co.: Westview Press, 1998), 30.

30 Jeffrey G. Reitz and Raymond Breton, *The Illusion of Difference: Realities of Ethnicity in Canada and the United States* (Ottawa: C.D. Howe Institute, 1994), 51.

31 Carl James, Dwaine Plaza, and Clifford Jansen, "Issues of Race in Employment: Experiences of Caribbean Women in Toronto," *Canadian Woman Studies* 19, no. 3 (1998).

32 Ibid.

33 Ibid.

34 Hum and Simpson, "Wage Opportunities for Visible Minorities in Canada"; Simmons and Plaza, "Breaking through the Glass Ceiling"; James, Plaza, and Jansen, "Issues of Race in Employment"; Dwaine Plaza, "The Strategies and Strategizing of University Educated Black Caribbean-Born Men in Toronto: A Study of Occupation and Income Achievements," Ph.D. thesis (Toronto: York University, 1996); Henry, *The Caribbean Diaspora in Toronto*; Anthony H. Richmond and Warren E. Kalbach, *Factors in the Adjustment of Immigrants and Their Descendants* (Ottawa: Minister of Supply and Services, Canada, 1980).

35 For a fuller discussion, see William Julius Wilson, *The Declining Significance of Race: Blacks and Changing American Institutions* (Chicago: University of Chicago Press, 1978); ibid., *The Truly Disadvantaged: The Inner City, the Underclass, and Public Policy* (Chicago: University of Chicago Press, 1987); and ibid., Power, Racism, and Privilege (New York: Macmillan, 1973).

36 Wilson, *The Truly Disadvantaged*.

37 Lennox Farrell, "Dead Black Men Talking," *Pride Newspaper* (Toronto), 23–29 August 2001; Raynier Maharaj, "Turning Racism Around," *The Caribbean Camera* (Toronto), 23 August 2001; Herman Silochan, "Operation TRIGGER," *The Caribbean Camera* (Toronto), 23 August 2001; Errol Townshend, "Don't Blame Killings on Poverty," *Share Newspaper* (Toronto), 23 August 2001.

38 Black Action Defence Committee et al, "End The Shootings Stop the Killings: Break The Silence Violence Affects All of Us," *Pride Newspaper* (Toronto), 19–23 August 2001.

39 Wilson, *The Truly Disadvantaged*, 83–4.

40 Alan B. Simmons and Jean E. Turner, "Caribbean Immigration to Canada, 1967–1987," CERLAC, York University (Toronto), 18 February 1991.

41 Agnes Calliste, "Canada's Immigration Policy and Domestic Blacks from the Caribbean: The Second Domestic Scheme," *The Social Basis of Law*, 2d ed., ed. Elizabeth Cormack and Stephen Brickley (Halifax: Garamond Press, 1991); Simmons and Turner, "Caribbean Immigration to Canada"; Alan Simmons, "Canadian Immigration Policy: An Analysis of Imagined Futures" (paper prepared for the Symposium on Immigration and Integration, Winnipeg, University of Manitoba, Department of Sociology, 25–27 October 1996); Alan Simmons, "Racism and Immigration Policy," in *Racism and Social Inequality in Canada: Concepts, Controversies and Strategies of Resistance*, ed. Vic Satzewich (Toronto: Thompson Educational Publishing, 1998); Sedef Arat-Koc, "Good Enough to Work but Not Good Enough to Stay: Foreign Domestic Workers and the Law," in

*Locating Law: Race, Class, Gender Connections*, Elizabeth Comack (Halifax: Fernwood Publishing, 1999).

42 Simmons, "Caribbean Immigration to Canada."
43 Simmons and Plaza, "Breaking through the Glass Ceiling."
44 Ibid.
45 Ibid.

## CHAPTER NINETEEN

1 Will Kymlicka, *Politics in the Vernacular: Nationalism, Multiculturalism, and Citizenship* (Oxford: Oxford UP, 2000), 192.
2 Cecil Foster, *Where Race Does Not Matter: The New Spirit of Modernity* (Toronto: Penguin, 2005).
3 Kymlicka, *Politics in the Vernacular*.
4 Ibid., 192.
5 Lesley Jacobs, chaps 2–5 in *Pursuing Equality: The Theory and Practice of Egalitarian Justice* (unpublished, March 1999).
6 Emmanuel Levinas, *Totality and Infinity: An Essay on Exteriority* (Pittsburgh: Duquesne UP, 1961); ibid., *Otherwise Than Being: Or Beyond Essence* (Pittsburgh: Duquesne UP, 1998); ibid., *Basic Philosophical Writings* (Bloomington: Indiana UP, 1996).
7 Kymlicka, *Politics in the Vernacular*, 42.
8 David A. Hollinger, *Postethnic America: Beyond Multiculturalism* (New York: HarperCollins, 1995).
9 Ibid., 3–4.
10 Neil Bissoondath, *Selling Illusion: The Cult of Multiculturalism in Canada* (Toronto: Penguin, 1994); J.L. Granatstein, *Who Killed Canadian History?* (Toronto: HarperCollins, 1998).
11 G.W.F. Hegel, *Phenomenology of Spirit*, trans. A.V. Miller (Oxford: Oxford UP, 1977), 333.
12 Will Kymlicka, *Finding Our Way: Rethinking Ethnocultural Relations in Canada* (Toronto: Oxford UP, 1998).
13 Bissoondath, *Selling Illusions*.
14 Hegel, Phenomenology of Spirit, 328.
15 Stephen Toulmin, *Cosmopolis: The Hidden Agenda of Modernity* (Chicago: University of Chicago Press, 1992).
16 An argument might be made that even the decision that Canada subscribes to a transcendentalist ideology should be debated in this pre-creationist moment, but that position is too radical even for me, as it would assume wiping out some 3,000 years of history. That seems impractical, if not impossible, for the very discussion on choices is already taking place within a structure contingent on transcendentalist rationalism.
17 Hegel, *Phenomenology of Spirit*, 332.

18 As Trudeau had envisioned, "Canada has often been called a mosaic, but I prefer the image of a tapestry, with its many threads and colours, it beautiful shapes, its intricate subtlety. If you go behind a tapestry, all you see is a mass of complicated knots. We have tied ourselves in knots, you might say. Too many Canadians only look at the tapestry of Canada that way. But if they would see it as others do, they would see what a beautiful, harmonious thing it really is." Pierre Elliott Trudeau, *The Essential Trudeau*, ed. Ron Graham (Toronto: McClelland and Stewart, 1998), 177.

19 Ibid., 79.

20 Elinor Caplan, "Trends in Global Migration Forum," notes for an address by the Honourable Elinor Caplan, minister of Citizenship and Immigration, to the Maytree Foundation, Citizenship and Immigration Canada, <http://www.cic.ca/english/press/speech/maytree-e.html>, 7 September 2001.

21 Alan Simmons, "Canadian Immigration Policy: An Analysis of Imagined Futures," paper prepared for the Symposium on Immigration and Integration, Winnipeg, University of Manitoba, Department of Sociology, 25–27 October 1996.

22 Joaquin Arango, "Immigration in Europe: Between Integration and Exclusion," *Metropolis International Workshop Proceedings, Lisbon, September 28–29, 1998* (Lisbon), Luso-American Development Foundation (1999).

23 Benedict Anderson, *Imagined Communities* (London: Verso, 1991).

24 Engin F. Isin, Cities without Citizens: The Modernity of the City as Corporation (Montreal: Black Rose, 1992); Engin F. Isin, Who Is the New Citizen? Class, Territory, Identity (Toronto: York University, 1995).

25 David Cesarani and Mary Fulbrook, eds, *Citizenship, Nationality and Migration in Europe* (London: Routledge, 1996).

26 Arango, "Immigration in Europe," 249.

27 Yasemin Nuhoglu Soysal, "Changing Citizenship in Europe: Remarks on Postnational Membership in the Nationalism State," *Citizenship, Nationality and Migration in Europe*, David Cesarani and Mary Fulbrook (London: Routledge, 1996); Yasemin Soysal, "Identity, Rights and Claims-Making: Changing Dynamics of Citizenship in Postwar Europe," *Metropolis International Workshop Proceedings, Lisbon, September 28–29, 1998* (Lisbon), Luso-American Development Foundation (1999).

28 Soysal, "Changing Citizenship in Europe"; ibid., "Identity, Rights and Claims-Making"; Arango, "Immigration in Europe."

29 Sedef Arat-Koc, "Good Enough to Work but Not Good Enough to Stay: Foreign Domestic Workers and the Law," in *Locating Law: Race, Class, Gender Connections*, Elizabeth Comack (Halifax: Fernwood Publishing, 1999); Agnes Calliste, "Canada's Immigration Policy and Domestic Blacks from the Caribbean: The Second Domestic Scheme," *The Social Basis of Law*, 2d ed., ed. Elizabeth Cormack and Stephen Brickley (Halifax: Garamond Press, 1991); Frances Henry, *The Caribbean Diaspora in Toronto: Learning to Live with Racism* (Toronto: University of Toronto Press, 1994); Alan B. Simmons and Dwaine Plaza, "Breaking

through the Glass Ceiling: The Pursuit of University Training among Afro-Caribbean Migrants and Their Children in Toronto," *Canadian Ethnic Studies* 30, no. 3 (1998); Alan B. Simmons and Jean E. Turner, "Caribbean Immigration to Canada, 1967–1987," *CERLAC*, York University (Toronto), 18 February 1991.

30 Citizenship and Immigration Canada, "Planning Now for Canada's Future: Introducing a Multi-Year Planning Process and the Immigration Plan for 2001 and 2002," (Ottawa: Citizenship and Immigration Canada, 2001).

31 Caplan, "Trends in Global Migration Forum."

32 Elinor Caplan, "Building Community in Multi-Ethnic Societies," address by the Honourable Elinor Caplan, minister of Citizenship and Immigration, to the Metropolis Conference Plenary, Washington, DC, 10 December 1999, Immigration and Citizenship Canada, <http://www.cic.gc.ca/english/press/speech/met-e.html<2/1/2002> 2002.

33 Hugh R. Innis, *Bilingualism and Biculturalism: An Abridged Version of the Royal Commission Report* (Toronto: McClelland and Stewart, 1973).

34 Jack Collins and Frances Henry, "Racism, Ethnicity and Immigration," *Immigration and Refugee Policy: Australia and Canada Compared*, vol. 2, Howard Adelman, Allan Borowski, Meyer Burstein, and Lois Foster (Toronto: University of Toronto Press, 1994), 525.

35 Jeffrey G. Reitz and Raymond Breton, *The Illusion of Difference: Realities of Ethnicity in Canada and the United States* (Ottawa: C.D. Howe Institute, 1994).

36 Ibid.

37 Ibid.

38 Ibid., 132–3.

39 Joseph H. Carens, *Culture, Citizenship, and Community: A Contextual Exploration of Justice as Evenhandedness* (Oxford: Oxford UP, 2000).

40 Jean-Jacques Rousseau, *The Social Contract and Other Later Political Writings*, trans. and ed. Victor Gourevitch (Cambridge: Cambridge UP, 1997).

41 Charles Taylor, "The Politics of Recognition," in *Multiculturalism*, Amy Gutmann (Princeton: Princeton UP, 1994).

42 Carens, *Culture, Citizenship, and Community*, 18.

43 Ibid., 119.

44 Ibid.

45 Caplan, "Building Community in Multi-Ethnic Societies."

46 Agnes Calliste, "Canada's Immigration Policy"; Citizenship and Immigration Canada, "Planning Now for Canada's Future"; Martin Collacott, *Canada's Immigration Policy: The Need for Major Reform*, Public Policy Sources No. 64, a Fraser Institute occasional paper, Kristin MaCahon (Vancouver: The Fraser Institute, 2002); Lisa Marie Jakubowski, "'Managing' Canadian Immigration: Racism, Ethnic Selectivity, and the Law," in *Locating Law: Race, Class, Gender Connections*, ed. Elizabeth Cormack (Halifax: Fernwood Publishing, 1999); Shirley Seward and Marc Tremblay, *Immigrants in the Canadian Labour Force: Their Role in Structural Change* (Ottawa: The Institute for Research and Public Policy, 1989);

Strategic Policy, Planning and Research, "The Economic Performance of Immigrants: Education Perspective," IMDB Profile Series (Ottawa, Citizenship and Immigration Canada, 2000).

47 Kymlicka, *Politics in the Vernacular*, 175.

48 John Porter, *The Vertical Mosaic: An Analysis of Social Class and Power in Canada* (Toronto: University of Toronto Press, 1985).

49 Kymlicka, *Politics in the Vernacular*.

50 Ibid.

51 Donald F. Warner, *The Idea of Continental Union: Agitation for the Annexation of Canada to the United States 1849–1893* (n.p.: University of Kentucky Press, 1960); Robin W. Winks, *The Blacks in Canada: A History* (Montreal and Kingston: McGill-Queen's UP, 1971); John W. Dafoe, *Canada: An American Nation* (New York: Columbia UP, 1935); William Arthur Deacon, *My Vision of Canada* (Toronto: Ontario Publishing Company, 1933); Constance Backhouse, *Colour-Coded: A Legal History of Racism in Canada, 1900–1950* (Toronto: University of Toronto Press, 1999); Stanley A. Barrett, *Is God a Racist? The Right Wing in Canada* (Toronto: University of Toronto Press, 1989).

52 Pierre Vallières, *White Niggers of America*, trans. Joan Pinkham (Toronto: McClelland and Stewart, 1971); J.L. Granatstein, *Nation: Canada Since Confederation* (Toronto: McGraw-Hill Ryerson, 1990); Hugh MacLennan, *Two Solitudes* (Toronto: Macmillan, 1945).

53 Friedrich Nietzsche, *On the Advantage and Disadvantage of History for Life*, trans. with introduction by Peter Preuss (Indianapolis: Hackett Publishing, 1980).

54 Immanuel Kant, *On History*, ed. Lewis White Beck, trans. Beck, Robert E. Anchor, and Emil L. Fackenheim (Indianapolis: Bobbs-Merrill Company, 1963), 17.

55 Thomas Hobbes, *Leviathan* (Oxford: Oxford UP, 1996).

56 Kant, *On History*, 17.

57 Ibid., 19.

58 Ibid.

59 John Rawls, *A Theory of Justice* (Cambridge: Harvard UP, 1971).

60 Kant, *On History*, 86.

61 Homi K. Bhabha, *Narration and Nation* (London: Routledge, 1999); ibid., *The Location of Culture* (London: Routledge, 1994).

62 Bhabha, *Narration and Nation*, 294.

63 Hegel, *Phenomenology of Spirit*, 21.

## CHAPTER TWENTY

1 Taking this idea of a new revolutionary order for new revolutionary times, I argue that Canadian multiculturalism borrows heavily from the American and French Revolutions but that it is really the fulfilment of the spirit of freedom that was best expressed and idealized in the Haitian Revolution. Indeed, contrary to those who look ethno-racially to Europe for the roots of Canada, I look to the Haitian

Revolution and its ideal of radical democracy and racelessness as providing the neo-mythic spirit of official multiculturalism – a radicalism that Canadians have not yet fully harvested. Cecil Foster, *Where Race Does Not Matter: The New Spirit of Modernity* (Toronto: Penguin, 2005).

2 In this discussion, I want to look within the infinite concept that is the Black female to the positive traits that have been associated with this group of Canadians. I want to go beyond the dehumanized and stereotypical traits and characteristics that dialectically have been used to define and limit the Black female. In doing this, I am going even beyond the limits that some "African-Canadian Feminists" have accepted as necessary, and as the starting definition, for the Black female and her role in Canadian society. For example, Erica Lawson presents the Black female in her essay *Images in Black: Black Women, Media and the Mythology of an Orderly Society*, this way:

> Black women are marked as racial outsiders in neo-colonial societies. Their bodies are associated with degeneracy and promiscuity in ways that support systems of oppression. Negative representations of these racialized bodies are perpetuated in the media, which play a role in Black women's subordination. The media stigmatize Black women as "mammies," "whores," "hoochie mamas" and "welfare queens" who exploit the state's "generosity." These constructed images and accompanying discourses have political, social and economic currency that justifies the exploitation of Black women's labour and sexuality. Moreover, sexualized and servile images of Black women are widely disseminated in popular culture. (Njoki Nathani Wane, Katerina Deliovsky, and Erica Lawson, eds, *Back to the Drawing Board: African-Canadian Feminisms* [Toronto: Sumach Press, 2002], 199)

True. But this is only *part*, and the dehumanized and unfree, of the mythological representation of the Black female. Our task is to go beyond this limited definition and to capture what is usually left out in this stereotypic construction so that we can claim more of the totality of the Black female as an infinite, fully human, and striving for freedom and hope.

3 Hugh R. Innis, *Bilingualism and Biculturalism: An Abridged Version of the Royal Commission Report* (Toronto: McClelland and Stewart, 1973).

4 Ibid., 140.

5 Ibid., 140–1.

6 Will Kymlicka, *Politics in the Vernacular: Nationalism, Multiculturalism, and Citizenship* (Oxford: Oxford UP, 2000); Freda Hawkins, *Canada and Immigration: Public Policy and Public Concern* (Montreal and Kingston: McGill-Queen's UP, 1972).

7 Robin W. Winks, *The Blacks in Canada: A History* (Montreal and Kingston: McGill-Queen's UP, 1971); James W. St. G. Walker, *The Black Loyalists: The Search for a Promised Land in Nova Scotia and Sierra Leone 1783–1870* (Toronto: University of Toronto Press, 1992).

8 Innis, *Bilingualism and Biculturalism*, 142.

9 Carle E James and Adrienne Shadd, eds, *Talking about Identity: Encounters in Race, Ethnicity, and Language* (Toronto: Between the Lines, 2001), 12.

10 There is much discussion over the positioning of women in the Hegelian system, particularly on whether Hegel allows for a role for women in the public sphere of civil society. Alison Leigh Brown, for example, questions the absence in Hegel of women as full participant in the public sphere as Hegel was writing at "not a time when women were silent about their exclusion." Alison Leigh Brown, *On Hegel* (Belmont, Calif.: Wadsworth/Thomson Learning, 2001), 71. Similarly, Luce Irigaray has similar problems with Hegel on the question of equality for women in civil society. However, I am suggesting that there is provision within the Hegelian system that allows us to "reach back" from one era to an earlier one, and that it can provide us with an analysis that goes beyond simply making women the equal of men. In this case, they may even be recognized as socially superior and more knowledgeable. Indeed, Brown, herself, offers a similar argument as an explanation (perhaps exculpation?) for the Hegelian method:

Hegel does not pay attention to the importance of women coming to know themselves as women occurring all around him during the time he was writing. (If he does he does not find it of systemic importance.) He excludes from the movement to absolute spirit at the point where the family dissolves itself to move into civil society. He suffers a second blind spot when he then fails to realize that even though there is henceforth silence about sexual division, every other institution is dependent on the material reality of the women left behind. This criticism is important because it does not deviate from Hegel's terms nor methodology. What we leave behind stays with us in the next stage in some other form. (76–7)

In a practical sense, what I am offering here also allows for an entry of somatic Blacks – and their full incorporation – into a wider civil society. This is a historical society in which, conceptually, somatic Blacks were presented as the other for somatic Whites. This resulted from an ideology spawned by patriarchy where, for both the somatically White and Black males, their maleness was perceptually the important point of differentiation and the site of struggles for dominance and acceptance. But even here, conceptually, the actors are presented as finite representatives of humanity – where there is an absence, that of the female, within the acknowledged absence of somatic Blackness. The somatic Black female is captured in the Hegelian system, as the other to both the somatically Black and White male, but also as the Black spirit that makes forays among them in the finite positions, barricades, and limits, of recognizing her limits based on the given context, of always having to transcend those limits while appearing to live within them, and as always operating from a higher and more advanced level of knowledge. In the end, in the Hegelian sense, she is not the forgotten woman sitting at home waiting for the male to return all battered and bruised from daily warring in society. Instead, she is often the one that returns not only to the family from civil society, but is also the family itself when the somatically Black male is absent. She is the spirit of mediation and, ultimately, of reconciliation in the public sphere, the private sphere, and the world that she inhabits between both spheres. Truly, then, the somatically Black female, the epitome of a double negation, is at the same time contingent and necessary for understanding full multiculturalism.

11 The male counterpart to the domestic servant was, traditionally, the railway porter. For generations, this job was seen as the ultimate in attainment and achievements for somatic Blacks in Canada, as discussed in Stanley G. Grizzle, *My Name's Not George: The Story of the Brotherhood of Sleeping Car Porters in Canada* (Toronto: Umbrella Press, 1998), and Cecil Foster, *A Place Called Heaven: The Meaning of Being Black in Canada* (Toronto: HarperCollins, 1996).

12 Aloma Mary Mendoza, "An Exploratory Study on the Socioeconomic, Cultural and Sociopsychological Experiences of Caribbean-Born Women in Ontario, Canada," Ph.D. thesis (Toronto: York University, 1990); Carl James, Dwaine Plaza, and Clifford Jansen, "Issues of Race in Employment: Experiences of Caribbean Women in Toronto," *Canadian Woman Studies* 19, no. 3 (1998).

13 Mendoza, "An Exploratory Study"; Agnes Calliste, "Canada's Immigration Policy and Domestic Blacks from the Caribbean: The Second Domestic Scheme," in *The Social Basis of Law*, 2d ed., ed. Elizabeth Cormack and Stephen Brickley (Halifax: Garamond Press, 1991); Alan B. Simmons and Jean E. Turner, "Caribbean Immigration to Canada, 1967–1987," CERLAC, York University (Toronto) 18 February 1991; Frances Henry, *The Caribbean Diaspora in Toronto: Learning to Live with Racism* (Toronto: University of Toronto Press, 1994).

14 Sheldon Taylor, "Darkening the Complexion of Canadian Society: Black Activism, Policy-Making and Black Immigration from the Caribbean to Canada, 1940s–1960s," Ph.D. thesis (Toronto: University of Toronto, 1994); Taylor, "Many Rivers to Cross: The African-Canadian Experience," National tour 1992–1994, circulated in cooperation with the Canadian Museum of Civilization, art exhibition (Toronto: Multicultural History Society of Ontario, 1992); Agnes Calliste, "Canada's Immigration Policy and Domestic Blacks from the Caribbean: The Second Domestic Scheme," *The Social Basis of Law*, 2d ed., ed. Elizabeth Cormack and Stephen Brickley (Halifax: Garamond Press, 1991).

15 In a bit of inter-diasporic rivalry, Toni Morrison claims that the somatically Black Canadians were the Blacks who "thought" they were free in comparison to those in the United States whom the Canadian Blacks felt they had left behind in slavery or some other form of bondage. Toni Morrison, *Sula* (New York: New American Library, 1982).

16 Mary A. Shadd, *A Plea for Emigration: Or, Notes of Canada West*, edited, annotated, and with an introduction by Richard Almonte (Toronto: Mercury Press, 1998).

17 Shadd, A Plea for Emigration, 59.

18 Alan G. Green, "A Comparison of Canadian and U.S. Immigration Policy in the Twentieth Century," in *Diminishing Returns: The Economics of Canada's Recent Immigration Policy*, Don Devoretz (Toronto: C.D. Howe Institute, 1995).

19 Shadd, *A Plea for Emigration.*
20 This point is reinforced in a study by the McGill Consortium of Ethnicity and Strategic Social Planning in an evaluation of the Canadian 1991 Census. This study works on the assumption, as stipulated in the *Canadian Multiculturalism Act* and by Statistics Canada, that there is an ethnicity in Canada called Black and is made up of several different communities. It profiles this Black family:
    Living arrangements are much more diverse in the Black communities than they are in the total population. In both the Black and total populations, Census family living arrangements are the predominant household expression. Census families include husbands and wives, persons living in common-law relationships, single parents and the children who grow up in these different types of households. Eighty percent (80%) of all Black persons and 84% of the total population lived in Census families in 1991.
    Notwithstanding, the structure of Census families is much more varied in the Black population. In the overall population, more than 4 out of 10 persons of all ages (42.4%) were married at the time of the 1991 Census. In the Black population the proportion was less that 3 out of 10 (28.6%). Twice as many persons in the Black communities as in the total population were single parents in 1991 (8.1% of the Black population; 3.6% in the total population. While rates of single parent families were much higher in the Black communities, the percentage of persons in the Black communities who were living in common law relationships in 1991 was much lower than in the total population. Census findings are that 5.4% of the total population and 3.3% of the Black population had common-law partners in 1991 ... A higher percentage of persons within the Black communities was likely to live with relatives outside the immediate family. Of the Black population, 6.9% lived with their extended families; of the total population, 3.2%. (James L. Torczyner, "Diversity, Mobility and Change: The Dynamics of Black Communities in Canada," in *Canadian Black Communities Demographics Project Preliminary Findings*, McGill Consortium for Ethnicity and Strategic Social Planning [Montreal: MCESSP/McGill School of Social Work, February 1997], 27–8)
21 James, Plaza, and Jansen, "Issues of Race in Employment."
22 Alan B. Simmons and Dwaine Plaza, "Breaking through the Glass Ceiling: The Pursuit of University Training among Afro-Caribbean Migrants and Their Children in Toronto," *Canadian Ethnic Studies* 30, no. 3 (1998); Alan B. Simmons and Jean E. Turner, "Caribbean Immigration to Canada."
23 This is not to say that there were not women from other ethnic groups, such as Nordic immigrants, who came to Canada under similar circumstances. The difference between them and the somatically Black female is that these somatically and culturally White women quickly assimilated into the mainstream. They transfigured quickly and easily into the dominant anglophone and francophone communities.
24 Frances Henry, *The Caribbean Diaspora in Toronto*; Foster, *A Place Called Heaven*; Lennox Farrell, "Dead Black Men Talking," *Pride Newspaper* (Toronto),

23–29 August 2001; Errol Townshend, "Don't Blame Killings on Poverty," *Share Newspaper* (Toronto), 23 August 2001; Raynier Maharaj, "Turning Racism Around," *The Caribbean Camera* (Toronto), 23 August 2001.

25 James, "Issues of Race in Employment."

26 Torczyner, "Diversity, Mobility, and Change," 35.

27 G.W.F. Hegel, *Phenomenology of Spirit*, trans. A.V. Miller (Oxford: Oxford UP, 1977), 277.

28 Alan Simmons, "Canadian Immigration Policy: An Analysis of Imagined Futures," paper prepared for the Symposium on Immigration and Integration," Winnipeg, University of Manitoba, Department of Sociology, 25–27 October 1996; Alan Simmons, "Racism and Immigration Policy," in *Racism and Social Inequality in Canada: Concepts, Controversies and Strategies of Resistance*, Vic Stazewich (Toronto: Thompson Educational Publishing, 1998).

29 Mike Phillips and Trevor Phillips, *Windrush: The Irresistible Rise of Multi-Racial Britain* (London: HarperCollins, 1998).

30 Elaine Arnold, "Issues of Reunification of Migrant West Indian Children in the United Kingdom," in *Caribbean Families: Diversity among Ethnic Groups,* ed. Jaipaul Roopnarine and Janet Brown (Greenwich, Conn.: Ablex Publishing, 1997), 244.

31 Ibid., 245.

32 Phillips and Phillips, *Windrush*, 201.

33 David A. Baptiste Jr, Kenneth V. Hardy, and Laurie Lewis, "Clinical Practice with Caribbean Immigrant Families in the United States: The Intersection of Emigration, Immigration, Culture, and Race," in *Caribbean Families: Diversity among Ethnic Groups*, ed. Jaipaul Roopnarine and Janet Brown (Greenwich, Conn.: Ablex Publishing, 1997), 277.

34 Madhu Dubey, *Black Women Novelists and the Nationalist Aesthetic* (Bloomington: Indiana UP, 1994).

35 Here we should point out that Ellison is not reducing all the experiences of somatically Black females to that of the West Indian women. Instead, I would argue that he is using the West Indian female to illustrate a wider point about social construction and the types of characters than can be created out of a specific social, political, and historical development.

36 Ralph Ellison, *Invisible Man* (New York: Vintage International, 1995), 391.

37 Ibid., 281.

38 Ibid.

39 Paule Marshall, *Brown Girl, Brown Stone* (New York: Random House, 1959).

40 Toni Morrison, *Sula* (New York: New American Library, 1982); ibid., *Playing in the Dark: Whiteness and Literary Imagination* (Cambridge: Harvard UP, 1990); Alice Walker, *The Color Purple* (New York: Harcourt Brace Jovanovich, 1992); ibid., *By the Light of my Father's Smile: A Novel* (New York: Random House, 1998).

41 Dubey, *Black Women Novelists*.

42 Edith Clarke, *My Mother Who Fathered Me: A Study of the Family in Three Selected Communities in Jamaica* (London: George Allen and Unwin, 1957).

43 Hyacinth Evans and Rose Davies, "Overview of Issues in Childhood Socialization in the Caribbean," in *Caribbean Families: Diversity among Ethnic Groups*, ed. Jaipaul Roopnarine and Janet Brown (Greenwich, Conn.: Ablex Publishing, 1997).

44 Elsa A. Leo-Rhymie, "Class, Race, and Gender Issues in Child Rearing in the Caribbean," in *Caribbean Families: Diversity among Ethnic Groups*, Jaipaul Roopnarine and Janet Brown (Greenwich, Conn.: Ablex Publishing, 1997).

45 Evans and Davies, "Overview of Issues in Childhood Socialization."

46 Leo-Rhymie, "Class, Race, and Gender Issues in Child Rearing."

47 Ibid.

48 Ibid.

49 William Julius Wilson, The Truly Disadvantaged: The Inner City, the Underclass, and Public Policy (Chicago: University of Chicago Press, 1987).

50 Foster, *A Place Called Heaven*; Rinaldo Walcott, ed., *Rude: Contemporary Black Canadian Cultural Criticism* (Toronto: Insomniac Press, 2000); ibid., *Black Like Who? Writing Black Canada* (Toronto: Insomniac Press, 1997).

51 Hegel, *Phenomenology of Spirit.*

52 Pierre Elliott Trudeau, *The Essential Trudeau*, ed. Ron Graham (Toronto: McClelland and Stewart, 1998), 19.

53 Ibid., 20.

# Index